1987-88

EVANGELICAL

Sunday School Lesson

COMMENTARY

THIRTY-SIXTH ANNUAL VOLUME

Based on the

Evangelical Bible Lesson Series

Editorial Staff

James E. Humbertson—EDITORIAL DIRECTOR

O. W. Polen—EDITOR IN CHIEF

Floyd D. Carey—GENERAL DIRECTOR OF PUBLICATIONS

James E. Humbertson—ADMINISTRATIVE EDITOR,
CHURCH SCHOOL LITERATURE

Lesson Exposition Writers

A. D. Beacham, Jr.   Oliver McMahan

Eugene C. Christenbury   Homer G. Rhea, Jr.

Published by

PATHWAY PRESS   **Cleveland, Tennessee**

Lesson treatments in the *Evangelical Sunday School Lesson Commentary* for 1987-88 are based upon the outlines of the Evangelical Bible Lesson Series prepared by the Evangelical Curriculum Commission (formerly the Curriculum Commission of the National Sunday School Association).

Copyright 1987

PATHWAY PRESS, Cleveland, Tennessee

ISBN: 0-87148-315-7

Printed in the United States of America

TABLE OF CONTENTS

SPRING QUARTER LESSONS

SUMMER QUARTER LESSONS

INTRODUCING THE 1987-88 COMMENTARY

The *Evangelical Sunday School Lesson Commentary* contains in a single volume a full study of the Sunday school lessons for the months beginning with September, 1987, and running through August, 1988. The twelve months of lessons draw from both the Old Testament and New Testament in an effort to provide balance and establish relationship between these distinct but inspired writings. The lessons in this 1987-88 volume are drawn from the third year of a seven-year cycle, which will be completed in August, 1992. (The cycle is printed in full on page 14 of this volume.)

The lessons for the *Evangelical Commentary* are based on the Evangelical Bible Lesson Series Outlines, prepared by the Evangelical Curriculum Commission. (The Evangelical Curriculum Commission is a member of the National Association of Evangelicals.) The lessons in this volume are drawn from the Old and New Testament and taken together with the other annual volumes of lessons in the cycle, they provide a valuable commentary on a wide range of biblical subjects.

The 1987-88 commentary is the work of a team of Christian scholars and writers who have developed the volume under the supervision of Pathway Press. All the major writers, introduced on the following pages, represent a team of ministers committed to a strictly evangelical interpretation of the Scriptures. The guiding theological principles of this commentary are expressed in the following statement of faith:

1. WE BELIEVE the Bible to be the inspired, the only infallible, authoritative Word of God.

2. WE BELIEVE that there is one God, eternally existing in three persons: Father, Son, and Holy Spirit.

3. WE BELIEVE in the deity of our Lord Jesus Christ, in His virgin birth, in His sinless life, in His miracles, in His vicarious and atoning death through His shed blood, in His bodily resurrection, in His ascension to the right hand of the Father, and in His personal return in power and glory.

4. WE BELIEVE that for the salvation of lost and sinful men, personal reception of the Lord Jesus Christ and regeneration by the Holy Spirit are absolutely essential.

5. WE BELIEVE in the present ministry of the Holy Spirit by whose cleansing and indwelling the Christian is enabled to live a godly life.

6. WE BELIEVE in the personal return of the Lord Jesus Christ.

7. WE BELIEVE in the resurrection of both the saved and the lost—they that are saved, unto the resurrection of life; and they that are lost, unto the resurrection of damnation.

8. WE BELIEVE in the spiritual unity of believers in our Lord Jesus Christ.

USING THE 1987-88 COMMENTARY

The *Evangelical Sunday School Lesson Commentary* for 1987-88 is presented to the reader with the hope that it will become his weekly companion through the months ahead.

The fall quarter 1987 continues the seven-year cycle of lessons which will be completed with the summer quarter 1992. The twenty-eight quarters of studies will draw from both the Old and New Testaments. Also a number of studies will be topical in nature as attention is focused on contemporary issues. A complete listing of the topics that will be included in the seven-year cycle, is printed on page 14 of this volume.

Quarterly topics for the 1987-88 volume are as follows:

Fall quarter—"God Leads His People." These are lessons taken from the book of Exodus, Numbers, Deuteronomy, and Psalms.

Winter quarter—"Teachings of Christ." These lessons are taken from the New Testament books of Matthew and Mark.

Spring quarter—"The Pauline Epistles." This series of lessons are taken from the New Testament books of Ephesians, Philippians, Colossians, and 1 Thessalonians.

Summer quarter—"The Christian in Today's World." As the theme title suggests, the lessons for this quarter deal with a wide range of subjects relative to the Christian of today.

The lesson sequence used in this volume is prepared by the Evangelical Curriculum Commission. (The Evangelical Curriculum Commission is a member of the National Association of Evangelicals.)

The specific material used in developing each lesson is written and edited under the guidance of the editorial staff of Pathway Press.

STUDY TEXT: At the opening of each week's lesson, you will see printed the Study Text. These references point out passages of Scripture that are directly related to the lesson, and it is advisable for you to read each one carefully before beginning the lesson study.

TIME and PLACE: A time and place is given for each lesson. Where there is a wide range of opinions regarding the exact time or place, the printed New Testament works of Merrill C. Tenney and Old Testament works of Samuel J. Schultz are used to provide the information.

PRINTED TEXT and CENTRAL TRUTH: The printed text is the body of Scripture designated each week for verse-by-verse study in the classroom. Drawing on the Study Text the teacher delves into this printed text, expounding its content to the students. Although the printed text contains different insights for each teacher, the central truth states the single unifying principle that the expositors attempted to clarify in each lesson.

DICTIONARY: A dictionary, which attempts to bring pronunciation and clarification to difficult words or phrases, is included with most lessons. Pronunciations are based on the phonetic system used by Field

Enterprises Educational Corporation of Chicago and New York in *The World Book Encyclopedia.* Definitions are generally based on *The Pictorial Bible Dictionary,* published by Zondervan Publishing Company, Grand Rapids, Michigan.

EXPOSITION and LESSON OUTLINE: The heart of this commentary —and probably the heart of the teacher's instruction each week—is the exposition of the printed text. This exposition material is preceded by a lesson outline, which indicates how the material is to be divided for study. These lesson outlines are not exhaustive, but provide a skeleton for the teacher to amplify upon and to build around.

REVIEW and DISCUSSION QUESTIONS: Immediately following the expository material in each lesson are five review questions. These questions are designed as discussion starters, along with the discussion questions appearing throughout the expository material. The review questions also serve to restate the major bits of information in the text and may be supplemented by questions of your own drawn from the expository material.

GOLDEN TEXT HOMILY: The golden text homily for each week is a brief reflection on that single verse. As the word *homily* implies, it is a

discourse or sermon on a particular point. The homily may often be used effectively to give the lesson a life-related slant.

SENTENCE SERMONS: Two or more sentence sermons—popular and pithy single-line thoughts on the central truth of the lesson—are included each week.

EVANGELISTIC APPLICATION: The evangelistic application relates the general theme of the week's lesson to the ongoing task of evangelism. The theme of the lesson (but not necessarily of the lesson text) is used to make this application. At times the emphasis of the section bears on direct evangelism of class members who may not be Christians; at other times the emphasis bears upon exhorting the class members to become more involved in evangelizing others.

ILLUMINATING THE LESSON: In this section, illustrative material is provided for the teacher to use to support the lesson at whatever point seems most appropriate.

DAILY DEVOTIONAL GUIDE: The daily devotional guides are included for the teacher to use in his own devotions throughout the week, as well as to share with members of his class.

EXPOSITION WRITERS

Writers for the expository materials for the 1987-88 volume are as follows:

The lesson expositions for the fall quarter (September, October, November) were prepared by the Reverend A. D. Beacham, Jr. (M.Div., Th.M., D.Min.), a former faculty member of Emmanuel College, who is currently

pastor of the prestigious Pentecostal Holiness Church of Franklin Springs, Georgia.

The Reverend Dr. Beacham is a graduate of Emmanuel College, University of Georgia, and Union Theological Seminary in Virginia. He holds three graduate degrees including the Master of Divinity, Master of Theology, and Doctor of Ministry, all from Union Theological Seminary.

Dr. Beacham is an ordained minister of the Pentecostal Holiness Church, and is a chaplain with the rank of Captain in the U. S. Army Reserve.

Lesson expositions for the winter quarter (December, January, February) were written by the Reverends Homer G. Rhea and James E. Humbertson.

The Reverend Mr. Rhea is pastor of the Church of God in Charleston, Mississippi. He formerly served as editorial administrative assistant at the Church of God Publishing House, Cleveland, Tennessee; and in conjunction with the Editor in Chief, prepared the *Church of God Evangel,* the official journal of the denomination. Reverend Rhea was reared and educated in Mississippi, where he served in the pastoral ministry for over fifteen years. He is an ordained minister in the Church of God and has held positions as district overseer and member of the Mississippi State Council and the State Youth and Christian Education Board.

The Reverend Mr. Rhea is author of the Instructor's Manual to the Church Training Course *Highlights of Hebrew History* by Charles Conn; and *A New Creation: A Study of Salvation* for the Christian Faith Series of the International Correspondence Program.

The Reverend James E. Humbertson, (M.R.E., D.Min., Litt.D.) is administrative editor of Church School Literature at the Church of God Publishing House, Cleveland, Tennessee.

The Reverend Dr. Humbertson holds an undergraduate degree in biblical education, and two graduate degrees, including a Master of Religious Education and a Doctor of Ministry in the field of Christian education. Dr. Humbertson has also received an honorary Doctorate of Literature.

Dr. Humbertson's experience includes years of service as a seminary and college professor, college administrator, a chairman of boards of Christian education, and a lecturer at writers' and educational seminars.

The Reverend Dr. Humbertson has written many articles and book chapters published in Pathway Press magazines and workers' training courses. He has also written three courses including "The History and Philosophy of Christian Education" for Lee College where he taught resident courses in Christian education from 1972-78.

Lesson expositions for the spring quarter (March, April, May) were written by the Reverend Oliver McMahan (B.A., M.Div., D.Min.).

The Reverend Dr. McMahan is former dean of students/associate professor at Northwest Bible College, Minot, North Dakota. Presently, he is professor of religion at Jimmy Swaggart Bible College, Baton Rouge, Louisiana. He is a graduate of West Coast Bible College and of Brite Divinity School, at Texas Christian University.

An ordained minister in the Church of God, Dr. McMahan has served his denomination as pastor, educator, and personal counselor. From 1976-81 he served as minister of youth and outreach at the Oak Cliff Church of God in Dallas, Texas.

Lesson expositions for the summer quarter (June, July, August) were written by the Reverend Eugene C. Christenbury (B.A., M.A., Ed.D.), who is associate professor of education, Lee College, Cleveland, Tennessee.

The Reverend Dr. Christenbury earned his Bachelor of Arts and Master of Arts degrees at George Peabody College for Teachers and his Doctorate of Education from the University of Tennessee. An ordained minister in the Church of God, Dr. Christenbury is a popular speaker both on campus, and in the broader church community.

GOLDEN TEXT HOMILY WRITERS

French L. Arrington, Ph.D.
Professor of New Testament Greek and Exegesis
Church of God School of Theology
Cleveland, Tennessee

Terry A. Beaver
Pastor, Church of God
West City, Illinois

Richard Y. Bershon
Chief, Chaplain Service
VA Medical Center
Tomah, Wisconsin

Daniel L. Black, Th.D.
Editor, Adult Sunday School Literature
Pathway Press
Cleveland, Tennessee

Ralph Brewer
Pastor, Church of God
Cramerton, North Carolina

Noel Brooks, D.D. (Retired)
Writer, *Adult Sunday School Teacher* Quarterly
International Pentecostal Holiness Church
Oklahoma City, Oklahoma

Karl L. Bunkley, (Retired)
Former General Sunday School President
International Pentecostal Holiness Church
Oklahoma City, Oklahoma

James R. Burroughs
Chaplain (Major) U. S. Army
Fort Jackson, South Carolina

Edward Call
Librarian
West Coast Christian College
Fresno, California

Hector A. Chiesa
Chaplain
Woodbourne Correctional Facility
Woodbourne, New York

Eugene C. Christenbury, Ed.D.
Associate Professor
Lee College, Cleveland, Tennessee

Percy Dennis
Chaplain
Draper Correctional Center
Elmore, Alabama

Ralph S. Douglas
Chaplain, (LT) 1st Marine Division
Camp Pendleton, California

James L. Durel
Chaplain, Director of Prison Ministry
Chicago, Illinois

Calvin L. Eastham
Chaplain (LT) U.S. Army
Fort Hood, Texas

Kenneth K. Foreman, D.Min.
Director of Christian Education
Messenger Publishing House
Joplin, Missouri

Chancel E. French
Associate Pastor
North Cleveland Church of God
Cleveland, Tennessee

Thomas Griffith, Jr., D.Min.
Pastor, Church of God
Salinas, California

Marcus V. Hand
Editor, Lighted Pathway
Church of God Publishing House
Cleveland, Tennessee

Joel Harris
Registrar and Coordinator of Public Relations
Church of God School of Theology
Cleveland, Tennessee

William M. Henry, Jr.
Instructor, Missions and
New Testament Greek
West Coast Bible College
Fresno, California

James E. Humbertson, D.Min.
Editorial Director, *Evangelical Commentary*
Pathway Press
Cleveland, Tennessee

Leroy Imperio, Th.D. (Retired)
Former Pastor
Elkins, West Virginia

W. E. Johnson (Retired)
Former Executive Secretary
Church of God World Missions
Cleveland, Tennessee

Raymond Lankford
Chaplain, Mississippi
Department of Corrections
Parchman, Mississippi

David L. Lemons, D.D.
Faculty Member
Church of God School of Theology
Cleveland, Tennessee

Kenneth R. Looney
Director of Evangelism and Home Missions
Eastern North Carolina

F. J. May
Associate Professor
Church of God School of Theology
Cleveland, Tennessee

Robert D. McCall
Youth Missions Coordinator
Youth and Christian Education
General Offices
Cleveland, Tennessee

Aaron Mize
Chaplain
Mississippi Department of Corrections
Parchman, Mississippi

Levy E. Moore
Chaplain, Emmanuel College
Franklin Springs, Georgia

Christopher C. Moree
Editor of Missions Publications
Missions Department
General Offices
Cleveland, Tennessee

Ronald M. Padgett
Director Chaplaincy Services
Mississippi Department of Corrections
Parchman, Mississippi

Luther E. Painter, D.Min. (Retired)
Former Assistant Professor of Religion
Lee College
Cleveland, Tennessee

O. W. Polen, D.D.
Editor in Chief
Church of God Publishing House
Cleveland, Tennessee

Wayne S. Proctor
Pastor, Church of God
Lexington, Kentucky

Jerry Puckett
Plant Superintendent
Church of God Publishing House
Cleveland, Tennessee

Gene Robinson
Pastor, Church of God
Chicago, Illinois

Philip Siggelkow
Church Planter
British Columbia, Canada

David E. Simpson
Chaplain, Scott County Counseling
and Mental Health Center
Scottsburg, Indiana

Henry J. Smith, D.Min.
Director of Academic Advising
Lee College
Cleveland, Tennessee

Marion H. Starr
Pastor, Church of God
Portland, Oregon

Joe Stephens
Pastor, Church of God
Stockton, California

Robert B. Thomas, D.Litt.
Pastor, Church of God
Bloomington, Minnesota

Fred Whisman
Cost Analyst
Church of God Publishing House
Cleveland, Tennessee

Eugene Wigelsworth
Coordinator of Student Services
Church of God School of Theology
Cleveland, Tennessee

Florie Brown Wigelsworth, M.Div.
Cleveland, Tennessee

Charles G. Wiley
Pastor, Church of God
Pine Bluff, Arkansas

Jimmy D. Wood
Associate Pastor, Church of God
Martinsville, Virginia

Sabord Woods, Ph.D.
Professor of English
Lee College
Cleveland, Tennessee

SCRIPTURE TEXTS USED IN LESSON EXPOSITION

Exodus	15:1-21	September 6	Luke	10:25-37	July 17
	22-25	September 13		24:46-49	August 7
	16:1-21		John	1:40-42	August 7
	31-35			3:14-21	October 25
	19:3-14	September 20		14:27	August 28
	20:18-20			16:32, 33	June 5
	32:1-14	September 27	Acts	1:6-8	August 7
	30-34			2:14-47	May 22
	35:4, 5,	October 4		8:26-40	August 7
	10, 21			10:1-4	June 12
	29-35		Romans	3:23	August 7
	36:1			4:13	July 24
	40:34-38			19-21	
Numbers	13:17-33	October 11		6:20-23	August 7
	14:6-24	October 18		8:5-8	July 3
	30, 31			12:1, 2	
	38			13:1-10	July 10
	21:4-9	October 25		14:1-12	August 14
	27:12-23	November 1		13-23	August 21
	35:9-28	November 8		15:1, 2	July 17
Deuteron-			1 Corin-		
omy	4:31-40	November 15	thians	2:9-16	July 3
	7:6-11			8:4-13	August 21
	11:8-32	November 22		9:24-27	
	31:11-13	June 12		10:23-33	July 17
Joshua	24:14, 15	June 12		12:4-31	July 31
Psalm	46:1-11	August 28	2 Corin-		
	78:5-8	November 29	thians	5:18-20	June 5
	56, 72		Galatians	6:9, 10	July 17
	91:1-11	August 28	Ephesians	1:3-23	March 6
	9-12	June 12		2:1-22	March 13
Proverbs	3:32, 33	June 12		3:1-21	March 20
Isaiah	26:3, 4	August 28		4:1-7	March 27
	53:6	August 7		11-32	
	58:6, 7	July 17		5:1-33	April 10
Matthew	1:1-25	December 20		6:11-13	June 19
	5:1-16	December 13	Philip-		
	17-48	December 27	pians	2:1-16	April 17
	6:1-18	January 3		14-16	July 10
	6:19-34	January 10		3:7-16	April 24
	7:13-29	January 17		20, 21	
	10:16-22	June 26		4:4-9	
	24-42	January 24		6, 7	July 24
	13:18-30	January 31		12, 13	June 5
	37-43		Colossians	1:9-29	May 1
	16:13-27	February 7		2:1-23	May 8
	21:21, 22	July 24		3:1-17	May 15
	24:32-51	February 14		3:22-25	July 10
	25:14-36	February 21		4:1	
	28:16-20	February 28	1 Thessa-		
Mark	1:14, 15	December 6	lonians	4:1-7	August 14
	21-39			4:13-18	May 29
	16:1-14	April 3		5:1-10	
	14-20	February 28	1 Timothy	1:3-11	July 24
				4:1, 2	June 19

	8, 12	July 24	1 Peter	1:3-9	June 19
	5:17, 18	July 31		1:13-16	August 14
	6:11-16	August 21		2:13-17	July 10
				21-24	June 5
2 Timothy	3:1-8	June 19		5:8, 9	June 19
	14, 15	June 12	2 Peter	1:5-8	July 24
	4:3, 4	July 3		3:1-4	July 3
Hebrews	11:32-40	June 26	Jude	24, 25	June 19
	12:1, 2	June 5	Revelation	1:17, 18	April 3
	13:17	July 31		2:26-28	June 26
				21:1-7	

SCRIPTURE TEXTS USED IN GOLDEN TEXT HOMILIES

Book	Ref	Date	Book	Ref	Date
Exodus	15:2	September 6	Acts	1:8	February 28
	32:29	September 27		2:39	May 22
Numbers	14:18	October 18	Romans	8:6	July 3
Deuteron-				13:8	July 10
omy	4:39	November 15	1 Corin-		
	11:8	November 22	thians	12:27	July 31
Joshua	24:15	June 12		15:20	April 3
2 Chroni-			2 Corin-		
cles	29:11	October 4	thians	5:20	June 5
Psalm	31:3	November 29	Galatians	6:10	July 17
	46:1	November 8	Ephesians	1:3	March 6
	91:1	August 28		1:7	May 8
	103:2	September 13		2:8	March 13
Isaiah	53:6	August 7		3:21	March 20
Matthew	1:23	December 20		5:1	April 10
	5:6	December 13		6:13	June 19
	5:44	December 27	Philip-		
	6:1	January 3	pians	3:14	April 24
	6:26	January 10	Colossians	1:10	May 1
	7:21	January 17		3:1	May 15
	10:39	January 24	1 Timothy	4:12	July 24
	13:23	January 31	Titus	2:13	May 29
	16:16	February 7	Hebrews	11:6	October 11
	24:42	February 14	1 Peter	1:16	August 14
	25:23	February 21		2:21	April 17
Mark	1:17	December 6		4:19	June 26
John	3:14, 15	October 25		5:2	November 1
	4:24	September 20	2 Peter	3:18	March 27
			1 John	2:15	August 21

ACKNOWLEDGMENTS

Many books, magazines, and newspapers have been used in the research that has gone into this 1987-88 *Evangelical Commentary*. A few of the major books that have been used are listed below.

Bibles

King James Version, Oxford University Press, Oxford, England
New American Standard Bible, A. J. Holman Co., Publishers, New York, New York
New English Bible (NEB), Oxford University Press, Oxford, England
New International Version (NIV), Zondervan Publishing House, Grand Rapids, Michigan
The Berkeley Version, Zondervan Publishing House, Grand Rapids, Michigan

Commentaries

Clarke's Commentary, Abingdon-Cokesbury, Nashville, Tennessee
Commentaries on the Old Testament (Keil & Delitzsch), Eerdmans Publishing Co., Grand Rapids, Michigan
Ellicott's Bible Commentary, Zondervan Publishing House, Grand Rapids, Michigan
Expositions of Holy Scriptures (Alexander MacLaren), Eerdmans Publishing Co., Grand Rapids, Michigan
The Broadman Bible Commentary, Volumes 10 and 11, Broadman Press, Nashville, Tennessee
The Interpreter's Bible, Abingdon Press, New York, New York
The Letters to the Corinthians, William Barclay, Westminster Press, Philadelphia, Pennsylvania
The Pulpit Commentary, Eerdmans Publishing Co., Grand Rapids, Michigan
The Wesleyan Commentary, Eerdmans Publishing Co., Grand Rapids, Michigan
The Expositor's Greek Testament, Eerdmans Publishing Co., Grand Rapids, Michigan

Illustrations

Dictionary of Illustrations for Pulpit and Platform, Moody Press, Chicago, Illinois
I Quote, George W. Stewart Publishers, Inc., New York, New York
3,000 Illustrations for Christian Service, Eerdmans Publishing Co., Grand Rapids, Michigan
Knight's Master Book of New Illustrations, Eerdmans Publishing Co., Grand Rapids, Michigan
Notes and Quotes, The Warner Press, Anderson, Indiana
The Pointed Pen, Pathway Press, Cleveland, Tennessee
The Speaker's Sourcebook, Zondervan Publishing House, Grand Rapids, Michigan
1,000 New Illustrations, Al Bryant, Zondervan Publishing Co., Grand Rapids, Michigan
The Encyclopedia of Religious Quotations, Fleming H. Revell Co., Old Tappan, New Jersey

General Reference Books

Harper's Bible Dictionary, Harper and Brothers Publishers, New York, New York
The International Standard Bible Encyclopedia, Eerdmans Publishing Co., Grand Rapids, Michigan
The Interpreter's Dictionary of the Bible, Abingdon Press, Nashville, Tennessee
The World Book Encyclopedia, Field Enterprises Education Corp., Chicago, Illinois
Pictoria Dictionary of the Bible, Zondervan Publishing House, Grand Rapids, Michigan
Word Pictures in the New Testament (Robertson), Broadman Press, Nashville, Tennessee

EVANGELICAL BIBLE LESSON SERIES (1985-92)

FALL QUARTER (September, October, November)	WINTER QUARTER (December, January, February)	SPRING QUARTER (March, April, May)	SUMMER QUARTER (June, July, August)
1985 TRUTHS FROM GENESIS (Genesis 1-24)	1985-86 BOOK OF HEBREWS	1986 THE PATRIARCHS (Genesis 25-50)	1986 THE BIBLE AND CRITICAL ISSUES
1986 THE BOOK ISAIAH	1986-87 PEOPLE WHO MET THE MASTER	1987 THE LIFE AND TEACHINGS OF MOSES	1987 THE HOLY SPIRIT IN ACTION
1987 GOD LEADS HIS PEOPLE	1987-88 THE TEACHINGS OF CHRIST (Matthew-Mark)	1988 OTHER PAULINE EPISTLES (not covered elsewhere)	1988 THE CHRISTIAN IN TODAY'S WORLD
1988 MEETING THE NEEDS OF HUMANITY (Gospel of Luke)	1988-89 THE CHURCH IN ACTION (The Book of Acts)	1989 EARLY DAYS IN CANAAN (Joshua, Judges, Ruth)	1989 THE FAMILY (In Biblical Perspective)
1989 ROMANS AND GALATIANS	1989-90 BIBLICAL EVANGELISM	1990 GENERAL EPISTLES (1 and 2 Peter, James, Jude, 1, 2, 3 John)	1990 LEARNING FROM PSALMS AND PROVERBS
1990 THE GOSPEL ACCORDING TO JOHN	1990-91 GREAT PEOPLE OF THE BIBLE	1991 LEARNING FROM THE OLD TESTAMENT KINGS	1991 UNDERSTANDING THE SPIRITUAL REALM (God, Angels, Man, Satan)
1991 THE MAJOR DOCTRINES OF THE BIBLE	1991-92 THE PROPHETS AND THEIR MESSAGE	1992 1 AND 2 CORINTHIANS	1992 PROPHECY AND THE END TIMES (Daniel and Revelation)

INTRODUCTION
TO FALL
QUARTER

The lessons for the fall quarter (September, October, November) are presented under the theme "God Leads His People." This is a series of lessons from the books of Exodus, Numbers, and Deuteronomy. One final study is taken from Psalm 78, as the Psalmist reflects upon God's faithful guidance to all who obey Him in righteousness.

This quarter of lessons might also be thought of as studies in the life of Moses. But Moses—towering personality that he was—was only God's instrument in the unfolding of a miracle plan that brought deliverance to the people of Israel from their bondage in Egypt to the Promised Land.

Although the series of lessons encompasses a great period of time, it also focuses on great feats accomplished at the hand of God. Three major factors are evident in the studies: (1) the unfolding of God's plan of deliverance; (2) the providential power of God to confront any obstacle; and (3) God's use of human personalities to accomplish His ends.

GOD LEADS
HIS PEOPLE

THE GREAT SEA
(Mediterranean)

Sidon

Tyre

Dan

Hazor

Accho

Sea of
Cinnereth
Galilee

Mt. Carmel

C A N A A N

GILEAD

Jordan River

Jabbok River

Joppa

Jericho

A M M O N

Jerusalem

Gilgal

Hebron

Gaza

Dead
or
Salt
Sea

Mt. Nebo
(Pisgah)

Arnon River

Beer-sheba

Hormah

N E G E V
(The South)

M O A B

Zoar

Brook Zered

Brook of Egypt

Wilderness of Zin

Rameses
(Zoan)

Baal Zephon (?)

Wilderness of Shur

Mt. Hor (?)

Obath

Punon

G O S H E N

Lake
Ballah

Kadesh-barnea

E D O M

Pithom

Succoth

Lake
Timsah

(Egyptian Influence)

Etham(?)

Bitter
Lakes

Jebel Nebi Harun
(Mt. Hor?)

On

E G Y P T

Marah

Ezion-geber
Elath

Gulf of Suez

Elim

SINAI

M I D I A N

Wilderness of Sin

PENINSULA

Dophkah

Hazeroth

Gulf of Akabah

Rephidim

Mt. Sinai
(Horeb)

D E S E R T

RED SEA

God Delivers His People

Study Text: Exodus 14:13 through 15:21

Supplemental References: Psalms 59:1-17; 106:7-12; Colossians 1:9-14; Revelation 5:1-13

Time: Scholars differ on the date of the Exodus, but the date of 1450-1442 B.C. seems most acceptable.

Place: At the edge of the Red Sea after crossing it on dry ground by a miracle of God.

Golden Text: "The Lord is my strength and song, and he is become my salvation" (Exodus 15:2).

Central Truth: God's redemptive love provides deliverance from the bondage of sin.

Evangelistic Emphasis: God's redemptive love provides deliverance from the bondage of sin.

Printed Text

Exodus 15:1. Then sang Moses and the children of Israel this song unto the Lord, and spake, saying, I will sing unto the Lord, for he hath triumphed gloriously: the horse and his rider hath he thrown into the sea.

2. The Lord is my strength and song, and he is become my salvation: he is my God, and I will prepare him an habitation; my father's God, and I will exalt him.

3. The Lord is a man of war: the Lord is his name.

4. Pharaoh's chariots and his host hath he cast into the sea: his chosen captains also are drowned in the Red sea.

5. The depths have covered them: they sank into the bottom as a stone.

6. Thy right hand, O Lord, is become glorious in power: thy right hand, O Lord, hath dashed in pieces the enemy.

7. And in the greatness of thine excellency thou hast overthrown them that rose up against thee: thou sentest forth thy wrath, which consumed them as stubble.

13. Thou in thy mercy hast led forth the people which thou hast redeemed: thou hast guided them in thy strength unto thy holy habitation.

14. The people shall hear, and be afraid: sorrow shall take hold on the inhabitants of Palestina.

15. Then the dukes of Edom shall be amazed; the mighty men of Moab, trembling shall take hold upon them; all the inhabitants of Canaan shall melt away.

16. Fear and dread shall fall upon them; by the greatness of thine arm they shall be as still as a stone; till thy people pass over, O Lord, till the people pass over, which thou hast purchased.

17. Thou shalt bring them in, and plant them in the mountain of thine inheritance, in the place, O Lord, which thou hast made for thee to dwell in, in the Sanctuary, O Lord, which thy hands have established.

18. The Lord shall reign for ever and ever.

19. For the horse of Pharaoh went in with his chariots and with his horsemen into the sea, and the Lord brought again the waters of the sea upon them; but the children of Israel went on dry land in the midst of the sea.

20. And Miriam the prophetess, the sister of Aaron, took a timbrel in her hand; and all the women went out after her with timbrels and with dances.

21. And Miriam answered them, Sing ye to the Lord, for he hath triumphed gloriously; the horse and his rider hath he thrown into the sea.

LESSON OUTLINE

I. GOD'S MIGHTY POWER
  A. Song of Joy
  B. Great Victory
II. GOD'S PEOPLE REDEEMED
  A. A Place for God's People
  B. Fear Among the Nations
III. SONG OF VICTORY
  A. Deliverance Remembered
  B. Celebrating Our Redemption

LESSON EXPOSITION

INTRODUCTION

This quarter complements Spring Quarter, 1987. The theme of Spring Quarter was *The Life and Teachings of Moses.* Basically the same block of material is covered in both quarters. The Spring Quarter focused specifically on events in the life of the great leader of the Jews, Moses. Our Fall Quarter study will also be in the same books of the Old Testament known as the *Pentateuch* (Exodus-Deuteronomy; note that Genesis does not contain information on Moses and there are Psalms that speak specifically of events described in the Pentateuch).

The teacher will find it a useful study avenue to read again the lessons from the Spring 1987. The teacher will also find it valuable to read Exodus through Deuteronomy before the quarter begins.

Recorded in these books are not mere history. What is recorded is the mighty act of salvation of Israel from Egyptian bondage that prefigures the mighty act of salvation in Christ Jesus. Also recorded is the story of God's leadership of His people, the obedience and disobedience of that people, and God's continued covenant love that remains to this day toward

I. GOD'S MIGHTY POWER (Exodus 15:1-10)

Exodus 14:31 records: "Israel saw that great work which the Lord did upon the

Egyptians: and the people feared the Lord, and believed the Lord, and his servant Moses." From this introductory verse, we learn four significant things. First, it was the Lord who worked salvation for Israel. Israel was privileged to "see" what He did; but she did not participate in this liberation in any way other than acting in response to His actions. Second, the mighty act of God in destroying the Egyptians (symbols of oppression and sin) brought genuine fear of the Lord into the hearts of the Israelites. Third, the people "believed" the Lord who had rescued them. This implies that belief in the Lord was weak; this quarter will show just how limited that belief was. Yet, it still remains a fact that the mighty act of deliverance at the Red Sea became the basis for Israel's active faith. Fourth, the people entered into a special relationship with the Lord's servant, Moses.

It is the mighty deliverance at the Red Sea that forms the background for the study this week. This entire lesson deals with themes of His mighty deliverance that are expressed in two songs of praise: Moses' (vv. 1-18) and Miriam's (v. 21). It will aid understanding of these verses to see them as Hebrew poetry. (A version of the Bible that prints these verses as poetry will assist your insights into the material.)

A. Song of Joy (vv. 1-3)

1. Then sang Moses and the children of Israel this song unto the Lord, and spake, saying, I will sing unto the Lord, he hath triumphed gloriously: the horse and his rider hath he thrown into the sea.

Singing songs of praise is characteristic of worship of the living God. The Hebrew hymnal, the Psalms, contain numerous references to singing praises to God. Here is a brief look at several of these and the themes they reveal: (Psalm 89:1) "I will sing of the mercies of the

Lord for ever"; (Psalm 92:1-4) "It is a good thing to give thanks unto the Lord, and to sing praises unto thy name, O most High: To shew forth thy lovingkindness in the morning, and thy faithfulness every night, Upon an instrument of ten strings, and upon the psaltery; upon the harp with a solemn sound. For thou, O Lord, hast made me glad through thy work: I will triumph in the works of thy hands." Other references to singing include: Psalms 95:1, 2; 96:1, 2; 98:1, 4, 5; 100:1; 101:1; 147:7; and 149:1. In the New Testament we find these references to singing also: Ephesians 5:19; Colossians 3:16; Revelation 4:8, 10; and 5:9.

It is important to note that salvation springs forth from the inner man in the shouts of newness and joy. This is far more than an emotional experience; it is the song of life that springs from a transformed heart. It is a song born from thanksgiving and humble gratitude. It is a song filled with thanksgiving for God's marvelous acts of deliverance.

It is important to note that Moses is not mentioned in the song itself. He is mentioned at the introduction (v. 1) as are the children of Israel. The song is directed exclusively to the Lord. It should also be noted the singing always has an objective reason for praising God. In this instance, it is because He has triumphed gloriously. We learn immediately from the end of the verse that this glorious triumph took place at the crossing of the Red Sea. It is a victory over nature (the sea was divided at God's command) and a victory over evil men (the pursuing Egyptians). The "horse and his rider" refers to the chariots of the pursuing Egyptian army (Exodus 14:23-26).

It should be noted this hymn of praise is given immediately after the victory (Old Testament scholars have shown the antiquity of these verses). There is a need for immediate gratitude on our part for the acts of deliverance God brings our way. Such gratitude not only benefits us spiritually, but it is also an appropriate witness to the world of our faith in Christ.

2. The Lord is my strength and song, and he is become my salvation: he is my God, and I will prepare him an habitation; my father's God, and I will exalt him.

3. The Lord is a man of war: the Lord is his name.

Both Isaiah 12:2 and Psalm 118:14 contain references from verse 2. If portions of this entire hymn sound like a psalm it is because many of the phrases and themes are found in the Psalms. It means that for Israel's later understanding of God's presence she often referred to this hymn of praise sung at the time of deliverance.

Several elements of verse 2 need further comment. First, note that "my father's God" is now "my God." That means the God of Abraham, Isaac, and Jacob, is still acknowledged. It means the covenant promises made to the patriarchs have been forgotten by neither man nor God. It affirmed that God is indeed the same yesterday, today, and forever.

Second, salvation results in a life of praise (that is the meaning of the phrase "prepare him a habitation." The passage in Ephesians 1:3-14 shows what it is to be a people of praise. Verse 12 in particular shows "that we should be to the praise of his glory." Markus Barth, in *Ephesians* (Anchor Bible, Vol. 1), shows this means we are to literally, "become a praise of God's glory." He further comments, "This people was destined not only to give praise, but 'to be a praise' . . . He who *is* a praise is characterized by more than just occasional outbursts of enthusiasm or by martyrdom once bravely endured. His total existence in good and evil days, from the cradle to the grave, his strength and his weakness are included." This means that for the people of God praise is not something limited to specified worship services; praise is an attitude of life that is constantly aware of God's presence.

The reference to the Lord as "a man of war" indicates the "power" of the Lord. It should also be noted it becomes the model for understanding spiritual warfare. While there were obvious physical dimensions in the deliverance from Egypt, it was primarily a spiritual battle between God and His servants (Moses, Aaron) and Satan and his servant (Pharaoh). That God is a God of war means He actively participates in that battle on the side of righteousness. Several key New Testament passages speak of this warfare and show God's presence through the Holy Spirit in this matter. The first, and probably most well-known, is Ephesians 6:10-18. Note that verse 11 reveals "the whole armour of God, that ye may be able to stand against the wiles of the devil." Two other significant references to spiritual warfare are found in 2 Corinthians 10:3-6 and 6:7. In 2 Corinthians 10 the apostle made it clear that our battles were primarily spiritual battles. No doubt there are physical applications to this, but the primary manifestations of evil were in the spiritual realm. Thus, the strongholds of Satan are found in thoughts, ideas, and spiritual realities of the heart. These are defeated as every thought is brought into obedience to Christ. Paul shows that ministry against these spiritual strongholds is done with complete righteousness and integrity (2 Corinthians 6:7). The man of God does not fight with the weapons of man; rather he fights with the weapons of righteousness: prayer, obedience, and the authority of the Word of God.

B. Great Victory (vv. 4-10)

4. Pharaoh's chariots and his host hath he cast into the sea: his chosen captains also are drowned in the Red sea.

5. The depths have covered them: they sank into the bottom as a stone.

These verses return to the specific act of deliverance accomplished at the Red Sea. This is not simply a recitation of historical events. It has tremendous spiritual truth. It means that God's mighty acts are not mythological; they are real historical events in which he intervened for His people.

There are those who believe it does not matter whether God actually did these miracles or not; all that matters is that we believe them. This is a delusion of teaching. The fact that these events actually happened is crucial—the faithfulness of God to His Word is at stake. The central issue in salvation is not our faith; it is the validity of the Word of God. If God is not faithful to His Word it makes no differ-

ence what we believe. Our beliefs become nothing more than modern day versions of pagan mythology. They may sound good and be exciting ideas, but they offer no salvation from the living God and are deceptions of Satan that lead to destruction.

6. Thy right hand, O Lord, is become glorious in power: thy right hand, O Lord, hath dashed in pieces the enemy.

7. And in the greatness of thine excellency thou hast overthrown them that rose up against thee: thou sendest forth thy wrath, which consumed them as stubble.

(Exodus 15:8-10 is not included in the printed text.)

The "right hand" of God is His hand of glory, power, salvation, sustenance, might, and victory. There are at least 33 references in the Psalms to the right hand of God (for example, 16:11; 17:7; 20:6; 48:10; 80:17; see any concordance for more references). As a sign of His power, it indicated His glory. The Hebrew for "glory" is *cabod* which originally had the sense of "weight, honor, standing." Thus, the Lord's glory is His standing among us. When the glory of the Lord is upon us it impacts our standing in the world.

The "right hand" was commonly the hand of peace, honor. There are still cultures where use of the left hand is considered a personal offense. The story of Ehud, the left-handed judge (Judges 3:12-23), relates how the left hand was used to trick the Moabite king into his own death. The reference from 2 Corinthians 6:7 cited above indicates Paul was determined to be righteous in every act of life; whether he used the right or the left hand.

Verses 8-10, while not in the Printed Text, indicate the action of the sea in covering Israel's enemies. Verse 9 in particular is a powerful description of Satan's efforts to destroy, "The enemy said, I will pursue, I will overtake, I will divide the spoil; my lust shall be satisfied upon them; I will draw my sword, my hand shall destroy them." Jesus told the disciples in John 10:10, "The thief . . . [comes only] to steal, and to kill, and to destroy." It is clear Satan's efforts are to totally destroy men and women and thwart the purposes of God in human life.

The victory of this song is precisely the rejoicing that comes from those who have not been destroyed by the Evil One but who have seen the powerful right hand of God intervene for deliverance.

II. GOD'S PEOPLE REDEEMED (Exodus 15:11-17)

A. A Place for God's People (vv. 11-13, 17)

(Exodus 15:11, 12 is not included in the printed text.)

13. Thou in thy mercy hast led forth the people which thou hast redeemed: thou hast guided them in thy strength unto thy holy habitation.

17. Thou shalt bring them in, and plant them in the mountain of thine inheritance, in the place, O Lord, which thou hast made for thee to dwell in; in the Sanctuary, O Lord, which thy hands have established.

Just as verse 9 described what Satan desires to do to us; so verse 11 describes the majesty of the God of our salvation. He is "glorious in holiness, fearful in praises, doing wonders."

Not only does His victory totally defeat the enemy (v. 12), He also leads His redeemed people into His glorious future. The Hebrew for "mercy" in verse 13 is the covenant word *hesed.* It refers to God's loving kindness and steadfast love. It expresses the completeness of His love toward us and reveals His character of love. As covenant language, it expressed His commitment to this people He redeemed. He did not redeem them from Egypt because of their righteousness or numbers but because He loved them (Deuteronomy 7:6-9; this important passage is worth reading to see God's majestic love). From this we learn that God affirms His love towards us as the precondition of obedience. We are not asked to obey God on the basis of our own strength; He liberates and gives direction to our life.

Note that God guided them by His strength (v. 13). In Exodus 13:3, 14, both verses refer to the "strength" in that passage as having the sense of "firmness, strong." However, in Exodus 15:2, 13,

the Hebrew is different and the word translated "strength" has the sense of God's power, might, in action. While a sharp distinction cannot be made, it is interesting that two different words are used. The word used in Exodus 13 is used only seven times in the Old Testament; the word in Exodus 15 is used many times (including 31 in the Psalms and 6 in Isaiah).

In Exodus 15:13 the Greek translation of the Old Testament (LXX) used the same Greek word for "strength" that is used in Ephesians 6:10. In fact, three different Greek words are used in Ephesians 6:10 to indicate "power, strength, might." The King James Version offers these translations, "be strong," "in the power," "of his might." It is this last phrase, "in his might," that is paralleled in Exodus. To further illustrate God's might, I offer my own translation of Ephesians 6:10 with comments in brackets (the translation is based on the second edition, 1968, of the *Aland Greek New Testament*): "From now on, be continually strengthened [or 'empowered'; the Greek is *dunamis*] in the Lord and in the intensity [with the sense of 'strength'] of his power." Note this verse is the introduction to Paul's understanding of spiritual warfare! This warfare takes place in the context of the mighty power of God and His guiding strength. It is based on the reality that God's "holy habitation" (Exodus 15:13) is now the individual human person in whom the Holy Spirit dwells.

This leads naturally to verse 17 and its statement elaborates the "holy habitation." While the Old Testament context pointed toward the earthly Jerusalem and the Temple of Solomon, the New Testament bears witness that something "greater than the temple" is here (Matthew 12:6) and someone "greater than Solomon is here" (Matthew 12:42). It is clear this someone is Jesus Christ, as He lives personally within us (Luke 17:21).

B. Fear Among the Nations (vv. 14-16)

14. The people shall hear, and be afraid: sorrow shall take hold on the inhabitants of Palestina.

15. Then the dukes of Edom shall be amazed; the mighty men of Moab, trembling shall take hold upon them; all the inhabitants of Canaan shall melt away.

16. Fear and dread shall fall upon them; by the greatness of thine arm they shall be as still as a stone; till thy people pass over, O Lord, till the people pass over, which thou hast purchased.

It is important to keep in mind that no references to time are included in these prophecies against Israel's foes. In many instances these enemies were not defeated until the time of David and Solomon and at that they would rise again to be confronted by the prophecies of Amos, Isaiah, and Jeremiah.

The important thing to note is that the word of God's mighty deliverance would spread and cause the enemies of God's people to fear; thus giving room for God's people to inhabit the promised land.

Several other passages relate to this promise regarding the nations. The first is Exodus 23:23-33 where the Lord indicates He will slowly remove the enemies from the land. The Book of Numbers relates the return of the 12 spies sent into the land (13:25-33). Ten spies did not take seriously the word given in Exodus 15; two spies did; yet, the people failed to obey God. Numbers also records the hard-heartedness of Edom in refusing safe passage through their territory (20:14-21). Numbers records a victorious battle over the Canaanite king Arad at Hormah (21:1-3). Numbers describes other enemies who were defeated by God's might (21:21-35).

Verse 16 indicates that the nations would experience "fear and dread." The Hebrew language used several words to describe "fear" and "dread." This expression points to a paralysis of action in the face of God's arm of power. It indicates God's complete authority to subdue the nations for the sake of His covenant people.

There is a tremendous lesson for us as Christians. We know from Ephesians 6:12 that our battles today are not against "flesh and blood" but are against spiritual wickedness as manifested in our world. The message of deliverance proclaimed in Exodus 15 is that the forces of evil must be toppled in the name of Jesus. The exact timing is left as an open question; but the principles of faith and obedience are meant to be settled in the heart of every believer.

III. SONG OF VICTORY (Exodus 15:18-21)

A. Deliverance Remembered (vv. 18, 19)

18. The Lord shall reign for ever and ever.

This is an Old Testament vision of the kingdom of God. Verse 18 climaxes this song of victory by pointing to the rule of God. It affirms that the children of Israel are freed permanently from the rule of Pharaoh. It affirms that *Yahweh*, the Lord, He is their ruler.

Isaiah speaks of the messianic ruler as "a leader and commander to the people" (55:4). The idea of "leader" is that of *one who goes before*. The idea of "commander" is *one who commissions*. As the one who reigns over us, the Lord Jesus Christ accomplishes both responsibilites. He exercises His kingship in that He clears the path ahead of us. Note the hopeful sound of Psalm 23:1, 2, "The Lord is my shepherd; I shall not want. He maketh me to lie down in green pastures: he *leadeth me.*" We can follow the Lord with the inner confidence of faith and peace knowing He will never lead us anywhere that will be outside the range of His love and spiritual protection. But He also reigns over us as the One who commissions us for service. This is clearly expressed in Matthew 28:18-20, the Great Commission. When Jesus calls us to specific acts of obedience, He promises to supply the spiritual power to accomplish those tasks. It is our responsibility to obey in faith.

The reference to "for ever and ever" should not be overlooked. It is a powerful witness from God of the eternity of His kingdom. The kingdoms of this world have limited spans in serving the world; but the kingdom of our God lasts for ever.

This should be a source of hope to all believers. No nation or state is guaranteed eternal existence on this earth. Governments come and go through the course of time; yet, Christians who know their citizenship is firmly held in Christ will not be overly fearful of changes in the world, but will be free in Christ to truly minister in the world.

19. For the horse of Pharaoh went in with his chariots and with his horsemen into the sea, and the Lord brought

again the waters of the sea upon them; but the children of Israel went on dry land in the midst of the sea.

The actual hymn ended at verse 18. Verse 19 is a capsule statement repeating the main events that occurred in this mighty act of deliverance. It should be noted that the Lord brought the children of Israel across the sea with dry shoes.

B. Celebrating Our Redemption (vv. 20, 21)

20. And Miriam the prophetess, the sister of Aaron, took a timbrel in her hand; and all the women went out after her with timbrels and with dances.

Miriam was the sister of both Aaron and Moses. While not mentioned by name, it was probably Miriam who watched over the basket of the infant Moses and delivered him to his mother as a nurse (Exodus 2:4, 7, 8). Numbers records her being struck with leprosy for rebellion against Moses and her subsequent healing (chapter 12). Micah remembers her as a leader of Israel (6:4). The *Interpreter's Dictionary of the Bible* indicates that later Jewish legends "present her as the wife of Caleb, and as a prophetess who foretold the birth of Moses as a saviour." Numbers records her burial at Kadesh (20:1).

The "timbrel" was "a kind of drum, likely a hand-drum or tambourine. It was played principally by women (Exodus 15:20; Judges 11:34; 1 Samuel 18:6; Psalm 68:25) as an accompaniment to the song and dance. In its simplest form it appears to have been a hoop (sometimes with pieces of brass fixed in it to make a jingling), over which a piece of parchment was distended. It was beat with the fingers" (*The New Smith's Bible Dictionary*).

21. And Miriam answered them, Sing ye to the Lord, for he hath triumphed gloriously: the horse and his rider hath he thrown into the sea.

Along with verse 20, this verse describes a joyful scene. It is a scene of praise, thanksgiving, and worship. It is not worship out of order; rather, it is worship that knows the power of celebration and rejoicing.

One of the important aspects of corporate worship is the power that comes from large groups of the people of God gathering for worship. While small groups are valuable for individual ministry, a large celebration affirms the majesty and power of God.

REVIEW QUESTIONS

1. In what ways did the rejoicing of Israel bind itself to historical reality?

2. How do we prepare a "habitation" for God in our heart today?

3. Discuss the relationship of Exodus 15:13 with Ephesians 6:10 and the emphasis on strength.

4. What does Miriam's style of worship say about worship in your church?

GOLDEN TEXT HOMILY

"THE LORD IS MY STRENGTH AND SONG, AND HE IS BECOME MY SALVATION" (Exodus 15:2).

The whole congregation of Israel sang a song after their deliverance from Egypt. The hearts of the Israelites were filled with gratitude, and upon crossing the Red Sea they promptly engaged in praise and worship. They did not praise their leader Moses nor did they celebrate their good fortune, but each heart ascribed praise only to God and celebrated only His wonderous deliverance that He wrought for them.

First, they proclaimed the Lord as their strength and song. Their triumph was not due to their strength but to His. That called forth a song of praise. Rightly divine strength and spiritual song were joined together. The God of Israel is also our strength and our victory. Through the power of the Almighty we triumph. So the appropriate response is to rejoice in the Lord and to praise Him as Israel did.

Second, they recognized that He had become their salvation. Because He had brought them out of the land of their enemies, they could sing of salvation. They saw the salvation of the Lord at the Red Sea just as Moses assured them that they would (Exodus 14:13). Likewise the Lord has shown to us His salvation. Through Christ we have been set free from sin and death. Let us rejoice in the Lord who has become our Redeemer.

Third, they declared that they would prepare their God a habitation. A desire of their hearts was to provide Him with a dwelling place in their midst and to have fellowship with Him. God has made us, whom He has saved, His dwelling place. We have become the temple of His Spirit (1 Corinthians 6:19). It is our privilege to live in communion with our God and to enjoy His fellowship.

The congregation of Israel joined together in the praising of the living God in song, but singing praises to Him is not enough. Rejoicing in God must be followed by holy living. We must exalt Him in life as well as in song.—**French L. Arrington, Ph.D., Professor of New Testament Greek and Exegesis, Church of God School of Theology, Cleveland, Tennessee**

SENTENCE SERMONS

GOD'S REDEMPTIVE LOVE provides deliverance from the bondage of sin.

—Selected

UNDERNEATH all the arches of Bible history throughout the whole grand temple of the Scriptures, these two voices ever echo—Man is ruined! Man is redeemed!

—C. D. Foss

IT COST MORE to redeem than create us. In creation there was but "speaking a word": in redeeming us there was "shedding of the blood" of God's dear Son.

—Anonymous

EVANGELISTIC APPLICATION

GOD'S REDEMPTIVE LOVE PROVIDES DELIVERANCE FROM THE BONDAGE OF SIN.

This love is revealed in "that while we were sinners, Christ died for the ungodly" (Romans 5:5). It is also revealed in the fact that "God so loved the world that He gave His only begotten Son" (John 3:16). It is out of His deep love that His mercy is extended toward us in such a way that He not only hides our sins from His view by the blood of Jesus, He also cancels the power of those sins over our lives.

Charles Wesley's great hymn, "O For a Thousand Tongues to Sing," has these lines: "He breaks the power of canceled sin, He sets the prisoner free; His blood can make the foulest clean; His blood availed for me." The power to break the bondage of cancelled sin is part of the marvelous grace of the gospel. Even though we repent of our sins, Satan, our adversary, tries to deceive us into thinking that those sins still have a claim against us. The blood of Jesus and the witness of the Holy Spirit point to the fact that not only are sins forgiven, but their claim upon us is broken. This means the guilt and condemnation of the past can no longer enslave us. It means the new convert can truly become the new creature in Christ that he is.

ILLUMINATING THE LESSON

Jim Eby, missionary to London, England, relates that many evangelical and Pentecostal groups in European cities march in spiritual parades down the streets of the cities. While little evangelization takes place in these parades, important spiritual battles are fought in those particular cities. The marchers carry banners proclaiming the lordship of Jesus and exalting His holy name.

By doing so they take public issue with the principalities and powers (Ephesians 6) that rule those cities. This was apparently practiced by the Apostle Paul in the area of Galatia. Galatians 1 speaks of Christ being seen publicly as crucified (3:1). Some commentators believe Paul was referring to some type of parade or public exhibition proclaiming the lordship of Jesus Christ and the power of His death.

Such action is an appropriate form of spiritual warfare in our world today. Most areas of the world, especially the Western world, live under the dominate control of secularism. God is completely disregarded from our world view, and the cities of our world live as though nothing else exists except human effort and will.

It takes creative and obedient sacrifice to intercede for such a world.

DAILY BIBLE READINGS

M. Remembering Deliverance. Psalm 106: 8-12
T. Beholding God's Greatness. Isaiah 40: 9-31
W. Loosed From Infirmity. Luke 13:10-17
T. Rejoicing in Song. Ephesians 5:15-20
F. Delivered From Darkness. Colossians 1:1-14
S. Praising the Redeemer. Revelation 5: 1-13

God Provides for His People

Study Text: Exodus 15:22 through 16:21, 31-35

Supplemental References: Genesis 21:13-19; 1 Kings 17:1-9; Psalm 105: 37-45; John 4:10-15; 6:25-34

Time: Scholars differ on the time of the Exodus and related events, but the date of 1450 to 1442 B.C. is generally accepted.

Place: The Wilderness of Shur, Marah, Elim, the Wilderness of Sin.

Golden Text: "Bless the Lord, O my soul, and forget not all his benefits" (Psalm 103:2).

Central Truth: God is faithful to provide for the needs of His people.

Evangelistic Emphasis: God is able to satisfy the spiritual needs of the unsaved.

Printed Text

Exodus 15:22. So Moses brought Israel from the Red sea, and they went out into the wilderness of Shur; and they went three days in the wilderness, and found no water.

23. And when they came to Marah, they could not drink of the waters of Marah, for they were bitter: therefore the name of it was called Marah.

24. And the people murmured against Moses, saying, What shall we drink?

25. And he cried unto the Lord; and the Lord shewed him a tree, which when he had cast into the waters, the waters were made sweet: there he made for them a statute and an ordinance, and there he proved them,

16:11. And the Lord spake unto Moses, saying,

12. I have heard the murmurings of the children of Israel: speak unto them, saying, At even ye shall eat flesh, and in the morning ye shall be filled with bread; and ye shall know that I am the Lord your God.

13. And it came to pass, that at even the quails came up, and covered the camp: and in the morning the dew lay round about the host.

14. And when the dew that lay was gone up, behold, upon the face of the wilderness there lay a small round thing, as small as the hoar frost on the ground.

15. And when the children of Israel saw it, they said one to another, It is manna: for they wist not what it was. And Moses said unto them, This is the bread which the Lord hath given you to eat.

16. This is the thing which the Lord hath commanded, Gather of it every man according to his eating, an omer for every man, according to the number of your persons; take ye every man for them which are in his tents.

17. And the children of Israel did so, and gathered, some more, some less.

18. And when they did mete it with an omer, he that gathered much had nothing over, and he that gathered little had no lack; they gathered every man according to his eating.

33. And Moses said unto Aaron, Take a pot, and put an omer full of manna therein, and lay it up before the Lord, to be kept for your generations.

34. As the Lord commanded Moses, **so Aaron laid it up before the Testimony, to be kept.**

35. And the children of Israel did eat manna forty years, until they came to a land inhabited; they did eat manna, until they came unto the borders of the land of Canaan.

DICTIONARY

Wilderness of Shur—Exodus 15:22—Shur means wall and refers to a wall built by the Egyptians from the Gulf of Suez to the Mediterranean Sea for defensive purposes.

Marah (MARE-ah)—Exodus 15:23—Probably the water supply now called Ain Hawarah, close by the Wadi Amorah—a three-day journey from the Red Sea

---

LESSON OUTLINE

I. THIRST QUENCHED
   A. Human Need
   B. God's Provision
II. HUNGER SATISFIED
   A. Longing for the Past
   B. Murmuring Against God
   C. God's Answer
   D. God's Provision
   E. Lack of Faith Exposed
III. GOD'S PROVISION REMEMBERED
   A. God's Command
   B. Human Obedience

LESSON EXPOSITION

INTRODUCTION

This lesson begins the so-called "Wilderness Wanderings" of the people of Israel. It is important to remember that these people are "delivered" people. They had experienced the Passover and the mighty deliverance from death on that night of death in Egypt. They had also experienced God's delivering power in the crossing of the Red Sea and the destruction of Pharaoh's army. Thus, they came into the wilderness having personally experienced God's delivering power.

Israel's experience in the wilderness had both positive and negative dimensions. There are Old Testament passages that speak of God's constant love for Israel throughout the 40 years of wandering (Deuteronomy 32:10; Jeremiah 2:2; Hosea 2:14; 11:1; 13:4). From these passages one gets the impression that Israel was always faithful while in the wilderness.

Yet, other passages relate the negative side of Israel's wanderings (Nehemiah 9:16; Psalm 106:13-33; Ezekiel 20:10-26).

Both dimensions are accurate and indicate that Israel knew both realities: God's gracious love and her rebellious spirit in the face of His love. Thus, it should not be surprising to see many parallels between these wanderings and our life in Christ. Even though Christians have experienced deliverance from the guilt of sin, there still remains in many Christian lives a bondage to the things of the flesh and failure to walk in the Spirit.

I. THIRST QUENCHED (Exodus 15:22-25)

A. Human Need (vv. 22-24)

22. So Moses brought Israel from the Red sea, and they went out into the wilderness of Shur; and they went three days in the wilderness, and found no water.

The victorious songs of Moses and Miriam (15:1-21) were quickly forgotten in the midst of a dry land. It is likely the three-day journey had covered no more than 50 miles. It is evident that water is essential for both human and animal life. Yet, no sooner have the people been delivered by a deluge of water than they are faced with a lack of water. It is this lack that began to take charge of their thinking. They were still a people wrapped in the grave clothes of death in Egypt (compare John 11:44). They did not understand the reality of faith in God nor did they know who it was that had delivered them. They were still dominated by a "slave mind-set."

23. And when they came to Marah, they could not drink of the waters of Marah, for they were bitter: therefore the name of it was called Marah.

24. And the people murmured against Moses, saying, What shall we drink?

Verse 23 indicates the etimology of the waters of Marah. The people experienced a double attack on their faith. First, there was the lack of water. Second, water was found but was not suited for drinking.

For the first time the people "murmured" against the Lord's anointed, Moses. He was the natural target of their frustration since He had been their physical leader. It is not until later that Moses is able to see the real target of their complaint (16:8). The Hebrew for "murmuring" appears for the first time in the Bible here and is almost always used to refer to the wilderness wanderings. Brevard Childs indicates "the word denotes a grumbling and muttered complaint." But it is to be understood as more than a mere gripe. Again Childs comments it is "unbelief which has called into question God's very election of a people" (*The Book of Exodus,* Westminster Press; comment on Exodus 16:8 and further implications of the spiritual warfare behind this passage is reserved for section II of the Lesson Outline).

It is clear the people are not people of faith. They are God's people but only because of His loving grace. They are immature people and cannot fathom the things of the Spirit of God. They have minds filled with perspectives from Egypt and cannot discern the things of God. Thus, their question of verse 24 is that of the natural man, "What shall we drink?" The person who has grown in the Lord and knows His abundant grace learns that such questions are born of unbelief and are not pleasing to God. Such a person understands that God is pleased with faith (Hebrews 11:6) and that He rewards those who will trust in Him completely. For those of faith the question of doubt becomes a statement of certainty: "God will provide!"

B. God's Provision (v. 25)

25. And he cried unto the Lord; and

the Lord showed him a tree, which when he had cast into the waters, the waters were made sweet: there he made for them a statute and an ordinance, and there he proved them.

This incident is remarkably similar to 2 Kings 2:19-22. There Elisha threw salt into the spring at Jericho to heal the bitter water. In our lesson, a tree is thrown into the water that cleanses the bitterness. We can see in this the reality of the cross of Christ turning the bitterness of sin into life-transforming power through the Holy Spirit.

While not specifically part of the lesson, Exodus 15:26, 27 further indicates the miraculous power of God for His people. Verse 26 affirms that if the people would hearken to the voice of God then the diseases of Egypt would not come upon them because "I am the Lord that healeth thee." It is suggested the diseases of Egypt are related to the "slave mind-set" of Egypt. The Lord is indicating that those who will obey His Word will discover the power of His healing love in transforming the ways we think of ourselves and God's purposes among us. Verse 27 indicates that not only did God turn the Marah stream into sweetness but He also led the people to a place with 12 wells of water. Thus, did He provide abundantly for them.

From 2 Corinthians 12:9 we learn that God's grace is sufficient for every dryness of life. Even in moments of weakness (physical and spiritual) we discover His abundant strength when we come to Him in humble faith. Even though our faith may seem weak, all it takes is a little faith to begin to break through the walls of doubt with the cry, "Lord, I believe; help thou mine unbelief" (Mark 9:24).

II. HUNGER SATISFIED (Exodus 16:1-21)

A. Longing for the Past (vv. 1-3)

(Exodus 16:1-3 is not included in the printed text.)

These verses give us some idea of the time frame experienced by the Israelites. They had been out of Egypt barely 45 days. We know from Exodus 15:22 they had only been out of Egypt three days before they first murmured against God. We are not told how long they remained at Elim (15:27). They traveled some distance and were between Elim and Sinai in an area called the wilderness of Sin. It would be a mistake to read too much into the word *Sin* in this lesson. The Hebrew has nothing in common with our moral connotations of "sin, transgression." Rather, Sin is a location in the Sinai pennisula.

Verse 2 indicates the whole congregation murmured against Moses and Aaron. It seems that the spirit of murmuring did not leave with the miracle at Marah, but actually spread throughout the camp.

This spirit expressed itself in the specific longing to return to Egypt. The people looked upon their bondage as a time of satisfaction. They lacked any understanding of their mission for God. They desired only to live peaceful, satisfied lives. To them it was better to be captive in Egypt and not face the risk of faith. Although led by a man of faith, they were spiritual grasshoppers who could not see beyond their own physical needs.

B. Murmurings Against God (vv. 4-8)

(Exodus 16:4-8 is not included in the printed text.)

Moses responded with announcing God's provision. God made this provision to see if they would walk in His law (v. 4). We often think that God tests us with the dry places in life to see if we will obey. But God is also using the blessings of life to see if He can trust us with more. God desires for His people to be channels of blessings. Thus, if we prove faithful in little, He knows He can give us more. The reason many of us do not receive more from God is because we prove to be unfaithful with the blessings He gives. Jesus spoke directly to this principle when He told the disciples, "He that is faithful in that which is least is faithful also in much: and he that is unjust in the least is unjust also in much" (Luke 16:10).

Moses and Aaron told the people what God had commanded (v. 6) and made the pointed remark that the murmuring was not against man but against God (v.

8). This is similar to the Apostle Peter's rebuking words to Ananias and Sapphira (Acts 5:1-11). It should be noted that such murmuring and deception is against God.

Such murmuring indicates several things in our life. First, it indicates unbelief. It means we do not trust God to actually provide for us. Jesus' words in Matthew 6:25-34 speak directly to this unbelief. Second, such murmuring is birthed in prideful rebellion. The Israelites thought for certain they would be better off in Egypt. Wise in their own conceits, they considered their understanding to be wiser than God's promise of provision in the wilderness.

In 1 Corinthians 10:5-11 Paul identifies this murmuring spirit of the Israelites to make the point that God was not pleased with such and that those in the church are to be free of such a spirit.

C. God's Answer (vv. 9-12)

(Exodus 16:9, 10 is not included in the printed text.)

11. And the Lord spake unto Moses, saying,

12. I have heard the murmurings of the children of Israel: speak unto them, saying, At even ye shall eat flesh, and in the morning ye shall be filled with bread; and ye shall know that I am the Lord your God.

Since Moses and Aaron refused to accept the murmurings against them, they turned the people to the only One who could actually provide for their need: God. This is a marvelous principle as we minister to others. We need to learn what are those things for which we can claim an answer and those things that belong to God. Sometimes it is not as easy as it sounds. In Acts 3:1-10 Peter and John told the crippled man to "Look on us"; yet, they did this with full knowledge they had nothing to give from the perspective of natural man. But they did realize they had much to give from the perspective of the spiritual man. It was this perspective that enabled them to speak boldly for God and release, by faith, healing power.

Yet, by pointing the people in the proper direction, Moses and Aaron served them well. Verse 10 relates that the glory of the Lord appeared before the people as they came before Him. This coming before Him was done in an act of worship. Note the people were invited to come before the Lord because He had heard their complaint (v. 9).

The Lord not only heard their complaint but He provided for their need. But again, it is important to note the provision had a specific purpose: the people were to come to trust Him as their God.

D. God's Provision (vv. 13-18)

13. And it came to pass, that at even the quails came up, and covered the camp: and in the morning the dew lay round about the host.

14. And when the dew that lay was gone up, behold, upon the face of the wilderness there lay a small round thing, as small as the hoar frost on the ground.

15. And when the children of Israel saw it, they said one to another, It is manna: for they wist not what it was. And Moses said unto them, This is the bread which the Lord hath given you to eat.

In a mysterious, miraculous way, the story of the manna is simply told. Other than the description of the manna in Numbers 11:7-9, no attempt is made here to provide a natural explanation. All that mattered was that God provided a miracle in the natural order. The Book of Psalms reveals God's power over the natural order as the wind direction is changed so as to provide the quail (78:26-29). It should be noted that the dew was thought of as coming from heaven (Psalm 78:23, 24); thus, it was from heaven that the manna was provided. The word *manna* comes from the Hebrew expression, "What is it?" Moses identified it as the bread which God had for them to eat.

In John 6:25-65 Jesus used this episode of the manna to illustrate His own origin and His greater provision as the Bread of Life. The manna had a limited time for usefulness. It could not be stored (except on the Sabbath). A man could labor for hours to gather more than he needed; yet, it could not maintian its capacity to meet the need. In John 6:27 Jesus told the crowd not to labor for the food that perishes "but for the food that endures to eternal life, which the Son of Man will give you" (*New International Version*). The people desired for Jesus to perform a mighty work for them (even though He had just fed the 5000 in 6:5-14) and they appealed to the provision through Moses of the manna in the wilderness. The people misquoted Exodus 16:15 to make it appear that Moses had provided the bread. Jesus rejected their interpretation and turned the provision back to its true source: God the Father. Christ said, "Truly, truly, I say to you, it was not Moses who gave you the bread from heaven; my Father gives you the true bread from heaven. For the bread of God is that which comes down from heaven, and gives life to the world" (John 6:32, 33 paraphrased).

The crowd responded to this word with enthusiasm and expressed their desire for this bread. Yet, they expected a bread they could use to satisfy their own desires. They were looking for a miracle, not a closer relationship with the heavenly Father. In 6:35 Jesus told them, "I am the bread of life." Yet, in 6:41 the Jews began to murmur against Him because He said this. The argument expressed by Jesus in 6:41-65 centers around the meaning of Him as the Bread of Life. The Jews could not accept His relationship with the heavenly Father nor could they accept that He was the Bread.

In using John 6 in teaching this lesson, the teacher should focus upon the fact that, like Exodus 16:12, 15, the bread points to the Father. In the case of John 6, the Father has revealed Himself through His only begotten Son. The focus is thus upon fulfilling the relationship we are called to have with God and not upon a life that simply looks for miracles or divine provision. For the person who is living in relationship with God, the provision is always sufficient.

16. This is the thing which the Lord hath commanded, Gather of it every

man according to his eating, an omer for every man, according to the number of your persons; take ye every man for them which are in his tents.

17. And the children of Israel did so, and gathered, some more, some less.

Note that the people were commanded to take according to their need. God's provision was not intended to make them rich in manna. God's provision was to satisfy their need so they could continue their divine mission. If the manna could have been preserved, then the many and strong would have collected enough to initiate greed and begin selling the provision. Thus, something provided by God in grace would have been used for capitalistic profit (not that economic capitalism is wrong; rather, it becomes perverted when greed enters and that which God has graciously given is sold).

There is a word of hope regarding God's provision for a family in this lesson. We become so preoccupied with providing "a good life" that we become bogged down in the details of the actual provision. The provision itself becomes our god and we are no longer free to serve God's purposes. We often do this because we think it's the proper thing to do. While there is nothing inherently wrong with wanting life to be better for our children, it is wrong to cut short God's purposes in our life for the sake of getting more and better material possessions. For the family that seeks first the kingdom of God and His righteousness, they discover all they need is added daily so that the mission of God in their life can be fulfilled.

18. And when they did mete it with an omer, he that gathered much had nothing over, and he that gathered little had no lack; they gathered every man according to his eating.

An omer was equal to two dry quarts. The point of verse 16 is emphasized to show that God sufficiently provided. The larger family units always had enough to meet their needs and the smaller units always had enough to meet their need.

It also emphasized that the person who gathered more than he actually needed never had any left over to carry over the next day. The same applied to the one who gathered little, he never went without manna.

There is a call to discipline and simplicity in these verses. Greed and slothfulness are deadly sins because they are based on lack of trust in God. Christians who rediscover the principles of life and trust found in these verses also discover a joyful release from the competing claims of our Madison Avenue oriented world. This joyful release results in obedience. Sacrifice may be involved. But sacrifice is always involved. We can choose to sacrifice God's purposes as we seek earthly gain; or we can sacrifice this world as we seek heaven's purposes.

E. Lack of Faith Exposed (vv. 19-21)

(Exodus 16:19-21 is not included in the printed text.)

Throughout the week the children of Israel were commanded to get only enough manna for that day. To get more and then hope to have it available in the morning only left disappointment and the odor of spoiled manna. There were some who tried to hoard before God and discovered the work of worms. Those who gathered too much in the morning discovered the heat of the sun melted the manna.

God had called this people to trust completely in Him. They were accustomed to the plenty of Egypt and God's efforts to break that accommodation were hard and necessary. Jesus told us to give thanks to God for "our daily bread." This was His way of calling Christian pilgrims to the same day-to-day trust of the Lord that Israel was called to experience.

III. GOD'S PROVISION REMEMBERED (Exodus 16:31-35)

A. God's Command (vv. 31-33)

31. And the house of Israel called the name thereof Manna: and it was like coriander seed, white; and the taste of it was like wafers made with honey.

32. And Moses said, This is the thing which the Lord commandeth, Fill

an omer of it to be kept for your generations; that they may see the bread wherewith I have fed you in the wilderness, when I brought you forth from the land of Egypt.

33. And Moses said unto Aaron, Take a pot, and put an omer full of manna therein, and lay it up before the Lord, to be kept for your generations.

The description of the manna in verse 31 is similar to the description in Numbers 11:7, 8.

As we shall see from verse 34, the omer of manna collected for the Ark was for a special purpose. It was to remind the children of Israel of God's constant provision. Moses knew the time would come in Israel's national life that she would enjoy plenty (for instance, the reign of Solomon); yet, this manna was to remind her that she existed only because of God's call and provision.

Verses 32 and 33 remind us of our Lord's command at the Last Supper, "And he took bread, and gave thanks, and brake it, and gave unto them, saying, This is my body which is given for you: this do in remembrance of me" (Luke 22:19). The Lord's Supper reminds us of the body of Christ, the Bread of Life, in whom we have all life. It also reminds us that His broken body provided for our deliverance from sin and its bondage.

It is a great tragedy that in many churches the Lord's Supper is practically neglected. In a powerful essay, Swiss pastor Walter Luthi laments this neglect (and other problems) with the title "The Plight of the Lord's Supper." The late Dietrich Bonhoeffer in *Life Together* (a beautiful devotion book of Christian fellowship) wrote, "The day of the Lord's Supper is an occasion of joy for the Christian community. Reconciled in their hearts with God and the brethren, the congregation receives the gift of the body and blood of Jesus Christ, and, receiving that, it receives forgiveness, new life, and salvation. It is given new fellowship with God and men. The fellowship of the Lord's Supper is the superlative fulfillment of Christian fellowship."

In the essay mentioned above by Luthi,

he concluded with a hopeful word concerning the Lord's Table, "The meal in the pot and the oil in the jar have not run out [to use an Old Testament analogy, my note], and despite the famine in the land there goes out into this world the great call to that table which 'is prepared in the presence of all enemies' " (*Preaching, Confession, The Lord's Supper,* John Knox Press, 1960).

B. Human Obedience (vv. 34, 35)

34. As the Lord commanded Moses, so Aaron laid it up before the Testimony, to be kept.

The "Testimony" is the same as the Ark of the Covenant. It should be noticed this command was given even before the Ark was constructed. Specific instructions about the Ark are not found until Exodus 25:10-22. Also in the Ark were to be kept the tablets of the Law (not given until Exodus 20) and Aaron's budding rod (from Hebrews 9:4 we know the manna was kept in a golden urn).

Brevard Childs writes of the significance of this, "A jar of manna which is the sign of God's sustaining mercy is kept alongside the tablets of the law. Indeed, the sign of divine grace preceded the giving of the law of Sinai! . . . the point of the text focuses on the testimony that the manna and the tablets belong together before God. In New Testament terminology, the gospel and the law cannot be separated."

35. And the children of Israel did eat manna forty years, until they came to a land inhabited; they did eat manna, until they came unto the borders of the land of Canaan.

Think of it, 40 years of the same diet! The Book of Numbers relates the murmuring of the people because of the steady diet of manna (11:4-6). The Book of Joshua relates the manna ceased as the people entered the plain of Jericho and they were able to eat the produce of the land (5:12).

Note the certainty of God's provision. In spite of murmurings, rebellions, and unbelief, God was faithful to provide what was needed until they reached the Promised Land.

REVIEW QUESTIONS

1. What are ways that individuals murmur against God today?

2. What are ways that local churches murmur against God?

3. In what ways is Jesus, the Bread of Life, more sufficient than the manna in the wilderness?

4. What does the daily provision of manna teach us regarding our own lifestyles?

GOLDEN TEXT HOMILY

"BLESS THE LORD, O MY SOUL, AND FORGET NOT ALL HIS BENEFITS" (Psalm 103:2).

The Psalmist is here stirring himself up to give God thanks for the blessings of his life. It is an exercise which all of us would do well to practice. We come frequently to God with our wants and wishes. But even when He has answered our cries for help we do not always return to give Him thanks.

He then tabulates several kinds of benefits which the Lord has graciously bestowed upon him.

1. *Forgiveness of sins* (v. 3). The Hebrew word means perversity, crookedness, that which is twisted from the right. How guilty of this we all have been! But oh, the blessedness of forgiveness (Psalm 32:1, 2).

2. *Healing of disease* (v. 3). All other occurrences of the Hebrew word clearly refer to physical sickness. However the healing came to him, the psalmist attributes it to the Lord.

3. *Redemption from destruction* (v. 4). The Hebrew word rendered *destruction* may refer either to the grave or to hell. The psalmist may have either in mind—or both! And may not we? How often the Lord has delivered us from almost certain death. How wonderful to know that He will deliver us from the pains of hell!

4. *Crowned with loving kindness and tender mercies* (v. 4). The word *"loving kindness* in the King James better rendered "love and compassion" *(NIV)*. It is one of the greatest Bible words. What a beautiful crown to wear!

5. *Satisfied with good things*(v. 5). No "things" in Hebrew. "With good"—all good, especially spiritual good, God himself, the sum of all goodness.

6. *Renewal of vitality* (v. 5). This cannot be only, or even mainly, physical vitality. It is chiefly reinvigoration of mind and spirit (see 2 Corinthians 4:16).

Like the psalmist we too may pass through experiences which, as we say, "sap the life out of us," emotionally, mentally, spiritually. How good to know that there is a Source of replenishment who "fainteth not, neither is weary. . . . He giveth power to the faint; and to them that have no might he increaseth strength" (Isaiah 40:28, 29).

How can we not bless the Lord!—**Noel Brooks, D.D., Bristol, England, (Retired), Writer, *Adult Sunday School Teacher* quarterly, International Pentecostal Holiness Church, Oklahoma City, Oklahoma**

SENTENCE SERMONS

GOD IS FAITHFUL to provide for the needs of His people.
                              —Selected

TO DOUBT the providence of God is to presently wax impatient with His commandments.
                        —Edward Garrett

IN ALL THY actions think God sees thee, in all His actions labor to see Him.
                       —Francis Quarles

GOD MAKES A PROMISE
Faith believes it.
Hope anticipates it.
Patience quietly awaits it.
                    —Author Unknown

EVANGELISTIC APPLICATION

GOD IS ABLE TO SATISFY THE SPIRITUAL NEEDS OF THE UNSAVED.

There are millions of people around the world walking in their own wilderness. The people of Israel were called to walk through the wilderness. They had already been delivered from sin and the bondage of Egypt.

The tragedy for most people today is they walk through a wilderness of their own disobedience and rebellion. It is a wandering without eternal direction. It is a wilderness filled with duplicity, deceit, and the attacks of Satan upon one's eternal soul.

This wilderness is a public wilderness. Most media and most governments draw their energy from it. They see this desert-wilderness as a beautiful place; yet, the fruit it offers is filled with heartache, suffering, loss of dignity, terrible arrogance, and war. It is the world ruled by Satan.

Yet, the message of the gospel is that God seeks to deliver men and women from this terrible bondage and establish them in the might and power of His kingdom. The Apostle Paul expressed it in Colossians 1:13—"He delivered us from the domain of darkness, and transferred us to the kingdom of His beloved Son" (New American Standard). This is God's eternal provision!

ILLUMINATING THE LESSON

A marvelous truth is found in this lesson: God provided manna for 40 years. There was not a single day of drought concerning the manna. His Word is certain and can be trusted in even the most difficult circumstances.

As a pastor, I have visited with older servants of God who become prey to Satan's attacks on their salvation. Many of them never outgrew the fears of earlier days. They learned how to disguise those fears with busyness, and so forth. But in the waning years of life, with time to reflect, many of these old fears return with devastating vengeance.

Often these attacks cause tremendous pain among family and friends. They cannot understand the doubts of an aging parent who seemed to be the bulwark of the family or church.

While the particular form of ministry will vary from person to person, the same theme remains constant in this ministry: the God who provided manna every day in the wilderness is also providing the Bread of Life every day to these aging ones.

The aging ones are telling us not to forget them; not to send them off to the fringe pastures of life to die. They are crying for us to show God's providential constant love by our presence with them.

DAILY BIBLE READINGS

M. Divine Compassion. Genesis 21:13-19

T. Miraculous Provision. 1 Kings 17:1-9

W. God's Faithfulness. Psalm 105:37-45

T. Christ, the Water of Life. John 4:10-15

F. Christ, the Bread of Life. John 6:25-34

S. Christ, All-Sufficient. Philippians 4:10-20

God's People Worship

Study Text: Exodus 19:1-14; 20:18-20

Supplemental References: 1 Kings 8:1-11; Nehemiah 8:1-13; Isaiah 6:1-10; John 4:20-24; Hebrews 12:18-29

Time: Around 1450-1442 B.C.

Place: Mount Sinai and the Wilderness of Sinai

Golden Text: "God is a Spirit: and they that worship him must worship him in spirit and in truth" (John 4:24).

Central Truth: God delights in the worship of His people and manifests His glory in their midst.

Evangelistic Emphasis: People who truly worship God become effective witnesses to His redeeming love.

Printed Text

Exodus 19:3. And Moses went up unto God, and the Lord called unto him out of the mountain, saying, Thus shalt thou say to the house of Jacob, and tell the children of Israel;

4. Ye have seen what I did unto the Egyptians, and how I bare you on eagles' wings, and brought you unto myself.

5. Now therefore, if ye will obey my voice indeed, and keep my covenant, then ye shall be a peculiar treasure unto me above all people: for all the earth is mine:

6. And ye shall be unto me a kingdom of priests, and an holy nation. These are the words which thou shalt speak unto the children of Israel.

7. And Moses came and called for the elders of the people, and laid before their faces all these words which the Lord commanded him.

8. And all the people answered together, and said, All that the Lord hath spoken we will do. And Moses returned the words of the people unto the Lord.

9. And the Lord said unto Moses, Lo, I come unto thee in a thick cloud, that the people may hear when I speak with thee, and believe thee for ever. And Moses told the words of the people unto the Lord.

10. And the Lord said unto Moses, Go unto the people, and sanctify them to day and to morrow, and let them wash their clothes,

11. And be ready against the third day: for the third day the Lord will come down in the sight of all the people upon mount Sinai.

12. And thou shalt set bounds unto the people round about, saying, Take heed to yourselves, that ye go not up into the mount, or touch the border of it: whosoever toucheth the mount shall be surely put to death:

13. There shall not an hand touch it, but he shall surely be stoned, or shot through; whether it be beast or man, it

34

shall not live: when the trumpet soundeth long, they shall come up to the mount.

14. And Moses went down from the mount unto the people, and sanctified the people; and they washed their clothes.

20:18. And all the people saw the thunderings, and the lightnings, and the noise of the trumpet, and the mountain smoking: and when the people saw it, they removed, and stood afar off.

19. And they said unto Moses, Speak thou with us, and we will hear: but let not God speak with us, lest we die.

20. And Moses said unto the people, Fear not: for God is come to prove you, and that his fear may be before your faces, that ye sin not.

LESSON OUTLINE

I. CHOOSING TO OBEY
  A. Worship and Obedience
  B. Worship and God's Word
  C. Worship and Response
II. PREPARATION FOR WORSHIP
  A. Divine Revelation
  B. Divine Instructions
III. REVERENCE TOWARD GOD
  A. Worship In Awe
  B. Worship and Fear of the Lord

LESSON EXPOSITION

INTRODUCTION

Deliverance, provision, and worship are important areas in the life of the believer. The *Golden Text* is from John 4, an important place where Jesus spoke of worship. In John 4:23 we are told the Father seeks people who will worship Him in spirit and in truth. The Father seeks to be worshiped by His creatures. Worship can be defined in numerous ways; yet it seems to center around genuine submission and honor to God as He has revealed Himself and reveals how we should worship Him. The Old Testament law went to great lengths to show how God is to be worshiped and also show why He is to be worshiped.

Holy Scripture reveals God as both Creator and Redeemer. Thus, it is necessary to turn to God's revelation in the Word (Holy Scripture and Jesus Christ) in order to know we are truly worshiping the true and living God.

I. CHOOSING TO OBEY (Exodus 19:3-8)

A. Worship and Obedience (vv. 3, 4)

3. And Moses went up unto God, and the Lord called unto him out of the mountain, saying, Thus shalt thou say to the house of Jacob, and tell the children of Israel;

4. Ye have seen what I did unto the Egyptians, and how I bare you on eagles' wings, and brought you unto myself.

The context of chapters 19 and 20 is important. They surround the giving of the Law at Sinai. Chapter 19 tells of the preparation of Moses and the people and chapter 20 tells the response of the people toward God's revelation.

Worship is born from the coming together of two realities. First, the human heart longs to be in communion with its Creator. The tragedy of sin is that such loving, holy communion is lost and men have turned to their vain imaginations and substituted the one true God with idols of the human mind. Second, God desires His creatures to worship Him. To accomplish this reality, God has revealed Himself clearly through His Law and His Son, Jesus Christ. Because of sin, the revelation through the Law only brought condemnation; but because of grace, the revelation through the Son has brought eternal life and joy in the Holy Spirit.

Thus, true worship begins with obedience to God's expressed desire and way to be worshiped. Human plans, with all their pomp, do not create worship. Worship is a reality as we obey God and come into His presence through the Holy Spirit.

Note that Moses was given a specific message to tell the people. Worship presupposes communication. God has a "word" for His people in worship. His people, through words and songs, offer praise and worship to Him. He responds through His Word and the presence of His Spirit moving in the midst of the people.

The double reference in verse 3 to "house of Jacob" and "children of Israel" seems to reflect a reality that existed among the people. The "house of Jacob" refers to those Hebrews who traced their ancestral roots back to the family unit of Jacob. The "people of Israel" refers to those in Egypt, outside the family unit of Jacob's line, who fled Egyptian bondage under the banner of the Lord. Thus, worship of God is for all (to use New Testament terms, both Jew and Gentile).

Verse 4 reveals God's strength and compassion by using the metaphor "eagles' wings." It is a beautiful metaphor filled with God's desire to give the people a home. That home is to be with Him. Physically, it meant the geography called Palestine; but spiritually, it means being in His presence.

One of the wonders of worship is that it is primarily based on what God has done. One of the mistakes many moderns make is basing worship upon feelings or experience. Worship does not begin with how one feels. Worship begins with the knowledge of who God is and what He has done. The mighty, saving acts of God stand before us addressing us today with the promise of His presence.

We must be very careful that the final criteria for worship, especially in Pentecostal services, not be "feelings." Far too many people use as worship criteria whether or not they "felt" the Lord with a particular shout or song, and so forth. I am not suggesting that feelings and emotions are not important in worship; I am suggesting their importance only stands in relation to the primacy of the Word of God and His mighty acts for us.

B. Worship and God's Word (vv. 5, 6)

5. Now therefore, if ye will obey my voice indeed, and keep my covenant, then ye shall be a peculiar treasure unto me above all people: for all the earth is mine:

"Peculiar" in this verse has the sense of "God's possession." It does not mean "odd, strange" as many people have

purposedly used it. It means we belong to God personally. It also means He has a body of people worshiping in His name.

Obedience to the Word of God ("my voice") is an important component of worship. To come into His presence with words that are in conflict with our lifestyle is hypocrisy. God does not receive such worship and brings judgment upon those who do such.

It is interesting that the New Testament language for "obey" and "disobey" is formed from the word *hear*. The word *obey* is in Greek *hupakouo*. The prepositional prefix *hupo* has the meaning of "under." *Akouo* means "I hear." Thus, to obey, is to put oneself "under" the power and authority of the Word we have heard from God. In this sense obedience is both general and specific. There are commands in the Bible that are binding on all believers at all times (such as the Ten Commandments). But there are other times when God desires to speak directly to us through His Word. When we are aware we are addressed by the Word of God and place ourselves under its authority, we obey. Obedience is to do what we hear God telling us to do.

"Disobedience" is the Greek word *parakouo*. The prepositional prefix *para* means "alongside." Thus, to disobey means to either put something alongside of God's Word, or to put ourselves "beside" the Word rather than "under" the Word. The trick of the devil is to subtly get us to maintain a posture of obedience, while in our heart we are actually substituting something else for God's voice. We may deceive the church, our families, and even ourselves; but we do not deceive God. Such a life mocks God's Word.

Obeying God's voice and keeping His covenant are very similar. Both are related to blessings. Yet it seems that covenant is tied to God's promise to the patriarchs (and later to Sinai), while obeying His voice is related to specific acts of obedience.

The promise to Israel to be "a treasure above all peoples" expresses God's clear decree of election. Israel received this election because she stood in line to Abraham's believing God in Genesis chapters 12 and 15. While primarily related to the Old Covenant, this election still stands in modern history. The calling and gifts of God are irrevocable (Romans 11:29). The message of the New Covenant is that this blessing has been made available to all who come to God by faith in Christ. The church stands as the visible expression of this New Covenant community.

6. And ye shall be unto me a kingdom of priests, and an holy nation. These are the words which thou shalt speak unto the children of Israel.

This verse looks forward to Deuteronomy 7:6 which is quoted in 1 Peter 2:9. The "kingdom of priests" refers to the kingdom of God. Here we have an Old Testament prophecy that sees in the kingdom of Israel a forerunner of the kingdom of God that will not be limited by natural bloodline, but will be determined by faith in the blood of Christ. The "priests" are now every believer in Christ. Luther's dictum of "the priesthood of every believer" affirms this reality.

The "holy nation" is now all who, around the world, confess Jesus as Lord. This is limited to neither national borders nor man-made citizenship. Our citizenship is in heaven. We need to be very careful that we not equate Christianity too closely with any one political system or nation. It would be a terrible mistake for Americans to think the world can be evangelized by combining nationalism and Christianity. The "holy nation" is composed of people from all colors, nations, social levels, and educational levels, who are united together under the cross and triumph of Christ.

The meaning of this for worship is profound. It means that around the world Christians are one in Christ as they worship. He provides the unity. In the fall of 1985 I visited Ghana, West Africa with a mission team. I worshiped with Presbyterians, Methodists, and Pentecostals. Although the particular forms often differed, I was keenly aware we were worshiping the same God and Father of our Lord Jesus Christ. In the Sunday services my heart rejoiced as I knew my family in the United States was worshiping Christ even as I was worshiping Him in Ghana. I

knew our unity was in Christ and not in ourselves.

This knowledge enables us to move away from the prideful assertion that our worship style is the best. It helps steer us from the divisions that come from maintaining "you haven't worshiped unless you've done it our way." God is not bound by the form; He is present where His name is confessed in Jesus Christ, His Word is faithfully preached and heard, His table is a place of forgiveness and reconciliation, and our spirits are open to the power of His Spirit. Whether it be contemporary choruses, a printed order of worship, a hymn from Bach, or a softly delivered sermon, does not matter. What matters is our understanding of obeying His Word and submitting to His covenant as a "holy people."

C. Worship and Response (vv. 7, 8)

7. And Moses came and called for the elders of the people, and laid before their faces all these words which the Lord commanded him.

8. And all the people answered together, and said, All that the Lord hath spoken we will do. And Moses returned the words of the people unto the Lord.

The interplay between pastoral leader and congregation is clarified in these two verses. Every man of God is charged with giving the Word of God to the people of God. Most congregations can quickly ascertain whether their pastor has prepared himself mentally and spiritually for his sermon. If the man of God has consistently waited until Saturday night or Sunday morning to even begin his preparation, it will show with shallow thoughts that do not feed. When men of God are shallow with the feeding of the Word, they should not be surprised when they produce shallow disciples of Jesus.

When prayer ceases to be part of the minister's daily walk, he should not be surprised when he no longer discerns the voice of the Holy Spirit.

This is not to condemn pastors (of which I am); but it is to show that they are entrusted with the flock of God. They are held responsible for what and how they feed God's flock. It can be taken as a general rule: a local congregation will seldom go farther than its pastor in terms of faith, power, and knowledge of the Word.

Note what Moses did in verse 7. First, he came to the people. He took the initiative of going to them after being with God. He came to them *after* he had God's Word for them. His coming to them was in itself an act of obedience and humility. He did not set himself up on a pedestal and hide the Word. He loved them enough to take the Word to them. Second, he spoke to the leadership (the elders). This does not mean the whole congregation is not to be addressed! Rather, it means Moses recognized who the leadership was and the responsibility they had in sharing God's Word. Giving the Word of God is not simply the task of the "paid preacher." Deacons and elders in the churches should be some of the most active lay evangelists in the local church. Third, Moses delivered to them *all* that God had given him. Notice he did not subtract from the Word nor did he add to the Word. This means Moses was not bound by fear of what men thought. He came to please God and not strictly to please men (this should not be license for poor grammar or rudeness in the pulpit).

The response of the people in verse 8 is as important as the responsible action of Moses in verse 7. Note that "all the people answered together." That little phrase indicates (1) a unity of commitment and (2) individual responsibility for that commitment. This commitment was centered in obedience, "All that the Lord hath spoken we will do." Their commitment was to what the Lord had spoken. No congregation is called to obey that which the Lord has not given. The lessons from the Jonestown massacre in 1978 illustrates the necessity of people walking according to what the Lord has given. Any man, even when he comes in the name of the Lord, who calls us to obey something contrary to the Word of God, is a false prophet. The people also affirmed they would do "all" the Lord had spoken. There are many churches

that are willing to do *some* of what God's Word beckons. There are many who have tremendous social ministries, yet fail to evangelize the lost. There are others who go to great lengths to save lost souls, but do little for the poverty and injustice in the community. There are churches who preach solid salvation messages, yet reject the gifts of the Holy Spirit. Obedience means doing "all" that God has spoken.

Worship means that preacher and congregation obediently do what God decrees. The minister intercedes, "stands in the gap," for the congregation as he leads in worship and proclaims the Word. The congregation is called to hear God's Word as addressed personally and corporately to them. God's Word always calls for a response.

II. PREPARATION FOR WORSHIP (Exodus 19:9-14)

A. Divine Revelation (vv. 9-11)

9. And the Lord said unto Moses, Lo, I come unto thee in a thick cloud, that the people may hear when I speak with thee, and believe thee for ever. And Moses told the words of the people unto the Lord.

10. And the Lord said unto Moses, Go unto the people, and sanctify them to day and to morrow, and let them wash their clothes,

11. And be ready against the third day: for the third day the Lord will come down in the sight of all the people upon Mount Sinai.

The Bible has many references to clouds. It should be noted that in many instances the clouds are directly related to God and His various manifestations in either the Old or New Testament. Exodus, Leviticus, and Numbers all contain numerous references to clouds. From these books the clouds are the vehicles God used to hide Himself as He appeared among mortals at Mount Sinai or in the tabernacle (this is for the protection of mortals; men cannot see God and live). Here is a brief list of references: Exodus 13:21; 16:10; 19:9, 16; 24:15, 16, 18; 34:5; 40:34-38; Leviticus 16:2, 13; Numbers 9; 10 (both chapters contain numerous references to God's cloud in the tabernacle); 11:25; 12:5. Israel continued to experience this divine presence in the cloud as recorded in 1 Kings 8:10. The psalmist considered the clouds to be the chariots the Lord rode in (104:3). Isaiah pictured the Lord as riding in a swift cloud as He came to judge Egypt (19:1).

The New Testament uses the same imagery to describe God's presence among men. Luke describes the Holy Spirit as "overshadowing" Mary to bring about the miraculous conception of Jesus (1:35). This is a clear allusion to the Old Testament cloud of God's presence before the Ark of the Covenant. The gospels relate that at the Transfiguration God spoke from a cloud (Matthew 17:5). At His second coming, Jesus spoke of returning on the clouds of glory (Matthew 24:30; 26:64; Luke 21:27). In Acts 1:9 Jesus ascended back to the Father in a cloud. According to 1 Thessalonians 4:17 the dead in Christ shall rise and join those who are alive to be with Christ in the clouds. The writer of Hebrews understood we are surrounded by a great cloud of witnesses (12:1). Revelation contains several key references to clouds and they always refer to God's presence and power (1:7; 10:1; 11:12; 14:14, 15, 16).

While the presence of God is usually not visible by a literal cloud, the reference in Hebrews 12:1 to the "cloud of witnesses" points to the reality of a worshiping community that stands under the Word of God. God's presence with us in worship is related to holiness (Exodus 19:10). While holiness should not be understood as a form of self-righteousness by which we achieve merit with God, it is the basis for a holy relationship with God. The command "Be ye holy; for I am holy" (1 Peter 1:16) comes from God in order to create the spiritual/physical space for enjoying His presence. The Bible speaks of "holiness, without which no man shall see the Lord" (Hebrews 12:14). Jesus told the multitude, "Blessed are the pure in heart: for they shall see God" (Matthew 5:8). Holiness is the absence of sin and its terrible effects of

separation. Holiness is also the reality of righteousness and its joyful effects. This double side of holiness makes worship a profound liberating experience. Paul indicates "where the Spirit of the Lord is, there is liberty" (2 Corinthians 3:17). This is the glorious liberty that comes in the presence of God. It is the "Holy" Spirit in His power and righteousness that makes this possible.

The washing of clothes (v. 10) refers to the outward manifestation of God's inward work of holiness. This is also expressed in the New Testament when Paul admonished, "Put on the new self, created to be like God in true righteousness and holiness" (Ephesians 4:24). "Therefore, as God's chosen people, holy and dearly loved, clothe yourselves with compassion, kindness, humility, gentleness, and patience. Bear with each other and forgive whatever grievances you may have against one another. Forgive as the Lord forgave you. And over all these virtues put on love, which binds them all together in perfect unity" (Colossians 3:12-14, *New International Version.*)

Sadly, many people go to two extremes regarding holiness. One group thinks it is simply a matter of individual heart cleansing and what a person does in his physical life does not matter. Such an attitude breeds contempt for the inward working of the Spirit and turns the flesh loose to the dominance of fleshly passions of greed, power, and sex. The other group tries to legislate personal morality through codes that are often expressions of particular cultures and social standing. This leads to a spirit of judgment that looks only at the outward man. Both are perversions of the truth of the gospel and the power of holiness in worship.

B. Divine Instructions (vv. 12-14)

12. And thou shalt set bounds unto the people round about, saying, Take heed to yourselves, that ye go not up into the mount, or touch the border of it: whosoever toucheth the mount shall be surely put to death:

13. There shall not an hand touch it, but he shall surely be stoned, or shot

through; whether it be beast or man, it shall not live: when the trumpet soundeth long, they shall come up to the mount.

14. And Moses went down from the mount unto the people, and sanctified the people; and they washed their clothes.

Since worship is entering into the presence of the holiness of God, it is not to be entered into lightly. This does not mean that worship is not joyful and filled with excitement. It does mean that sinful lives are not to mock God by pretending worship.

Worship of the living God is not a man-made phenomenon. God has set the bounds of worship. His holiness is at stake as well as the honor of His name. This has profound implications for our attitude toward worship. To come into God's presence without spiritual preparation is to mock God. For the worship service to be planned haphazardly, on the spur of the moment without prayer and reflection, is to mock God. For the minister to lead worship without personal communion with the Holy Spirit is to mock God. Such mockery produces spiritual death in the worship service. It becomes man's efforts to appease God; that is paganism, but sadly it often happens in our services because we do not keep God's "bounds." Such spiritual death occurs in false expectations of worship. When worship is centered primarily in terms of "what God can do for *me*," we enter the realm of death. Worship focuses on God and we come to adore and magnify Him. Our receiving from Him comes in the form of blessings that originate in His gracious, loving response. Spiritual death occurs when coming to the church is simply a routine and we do not really expect to be in the presence of God. While habit is a good discipline, habit that has forgotten its purpose is boring.

III. REVERENCE TOWARD GOD (Exodus 20:18-20)

A. Worship In Awe (vv. 18, 19)

18. And all the people saw the thunderings, and the lightnings, and the noise of the trumpet, and the mountain smoking: and when the people saw it, they removed, and stood afar off.

. And they said unto Moses, Speak thou with us, and we will hear: but let not God speak with us, lest we die.

In Isaiah 6:1-9 a classic illustration of "awe" in the presence of God is found. The prophet cried, "Woe is me! For I am undone; because I am a man of unclean lips" (6:5). The encounter with "the Holy" produces a wide range of human emotions and reactions. Rudolf Otto, in his classic work *Idea of the Holy*, speaks of these emotions as "fear, terror, mystery, awe, fascination." To be in the presence of God is to literally be in "another world." William Willimon has suggested that one reason church people tend to sit near the rear pews is out of unconscious fear of being too close to the altar and the perceived presence of God near the preacher.

The Book of Hebrews gives a New Testament perspective on the experience recorded in Exodus 20:18 and the verses which follow. This perspective is one contrasting how God revealed Himself through the Law and how He has revealed Himself through His Son (12:18-21). The mount is described as one that burned with fire, blackness, darkness, and tempest (v. 18). Furthermore it was recorded "they could not endure that which was commanded." Moses experienced the scene with such awe that he said, "I exceedingly fear and quake."

While this view of worship is instructive in pointing out the seriousness of God's holiness, it also shows the limitations of the Law. The giving of the Law was God's clear statement of how His people were, and are, to live. It comes as demand, "Thou shalt not!" But since the Holy Spirit was not given in fullness, and since the Son of God had not yet paid the "once and only" price of redemption, the Law was used by sin to bring man under condemnation of death. The Law killed the spirit; it could not save. Was the Law, which came from God, then evil? No! The Law applied to human flesh and because man was disobedient the Law was abused through sinful flesh. Only the righteous flesh of the Son of God could take the full measure of the Law and become our perfection of the Law. This is why Christians are called to consider the Ten Commandments in relation to the presence of the living Christ in our heart.

The Scripture shows how this change has occurred in Christ Jesus. Christians do not worship before the mountain of fire and fear. We have come to the "city of the living God... to thousands upon thousands of angels in joyful assembly . . . to Jesus the mediator of a new covenant, and to the sprinkled blood" (Hebrews 12:22-24, *New International Version*).

B. Worship and Fear of the Lord (v. 20)

20. And Moses said unto the people, Fear not: for God is come to prove you, and that his fear may be before your faces, that ye sin not.

The "fear of the Lord" is related to obedience. This "fear" is not primarily an emotional response. Many people fear the Lord in an emotional sense and never feel they can come into His presence. They are paralyzed by this fear. Such fear is not from God. The fear of the Lord is related to obedience and respect. This fear liberates us from the fear of men. The fear of God orients the whole person toward the will of God and pleasing God. The things of the world lose their luster and dominance as the fear of the Lord enlightens our spiritual vision to the riches that are ours eternally in Christ Jesus. Sin loses its dominion in our life as the fear of the Lord sets us free from earthly passions. Obedience to the Word of God wrecks havoc on sin's claim on us. The law of God is seen through Jesus Christ and the Holy Spirit makes that Law alive through us.

REVIEW QUESTIONS

1. How does the Holy Spirit lead us in worship?

2. Using the New Testament language for "obey" and "disobey," discuss how this relates to hearing God's Word.

3. In what ways are you aware you are part of God's "holy nation"?

4. What are some responsibilities ministers and congregations have in worship?

5. How is "the fear of the Lord" liberating from "the fear of man"?

GOLDEN TEXT HOMILY

"GOD IS A SPIRIT: AND THEY THAT WORSHIP HIM MUST WORSHIP HIM IN SPIRIT AND IN TRUTH" (John 4:24).

When we speak of God as a spirit, we speak of his vital force of life necessary to mankind. God is the life breath divinely imputed unto mankind, and although He (God) cannot be looked upon, touched, or seen with the natural eye, His presence is beheld as He speaks to us through and by the Holy Spirit, and His Son Jesus Christ (John 5:19).

God is a spirit being with a personal spirit body (Daniel 7:9-14; Genesis 1:26) and can go from place to place like all other persons (Genesis 3:8).

They that worship Him through adoration and praise, must do so in and by the Holy Spirit and His Son Jesus the Christ. "The true worshippers shall worship the Father in spirit and in truth: for the Father seeketh such to worship him" (John 4:23).

When we worship God in spirit and in truth, we do so with the vital force of life through Jesus Christ our Lord. He is the way, the truth and the life, and no man can come to the Father except by Him (John 14:6).

In our spiritual worship we become a spiritual coupling of two souls, with but a single thought; two hearts that are as one with a thirsting to know that all has been forgiven and in adoration we thank and praise God for life's blessings.

The real act of worshiping a true spiritual God is as Romans 12:1 says, "I beseech you therefore, brethren, by the mercies of God, that ye present your bodies a living sacrifice, holy, acceptable unto God, which is your reasonable service." In presenting ourselves for service, we plant the word, work the field, and bring the harvest unto God;

and in offering, and praise, bear witness to the power and saving grace of His Son Jesus Christ.—**LeRoy Imperio, Th.D., (Retired), Former Pastor, Elkins, West Virginia**

SENTENCE SERMONS

GOD DELIGHTS in the worship of His people and manifests His glory in their midst.

—**Selected**

THE MAN WHO bows the lowest in the presence of God stands the straightest in the presence of sin.

—**"Speaker's Sourcebook"**

IN WORSHIP man reaches upward and finds God bending downward.

—**Rolla O. Swisher**

WORSHIP DOES NOT conclude your Christian obligation; it merely equips you to carry it out.

—**Keith Huttenlocker**

EVANGELISTIC APPLICATION

PEOPLE WHO TRULY WORSHIP GOD BECOME EFFECTIVE WITNESSES TO HIS REDEEMING LOVE.

Worship brings us into holy communion with God. We discover that He is our Creator and our Redeemer.

As our Redeemer, we discover His never ending love for us. We discover His love cannot be broken by Satan. We discover His love is related to His Word. He is faithful to His Word.

Many human vows are broken. In the United States today nearly half the marriages are shattered by broken vows and faded love. But God's love is not like that. God's love is not based on feelings; it is based on the integrity He has to His Word.

Worship also shows us that God has first loved us. Even while we were sinners we discovered His redeeming love. We discover that worship exposes the weaknesses of our life to His redeeming, healing, reconciling love. In worship we do not enter with condemnation, we enter His courts with praise and thanksgiving. We learn to bless His name because He is good.

Oral Roberts brought to national attention the message that God is good with the slogan "Something good is going to happen to you." In worship, we discover the reality of God's goodness and accept His daily provision of redeeming love.

ILLUMINATING THE LESSON

Most of us have been in a worship service that seemed to be forced, manipulative. We have felt our necks stiffen as a song leader browbeat us with another "Come on folks, let's wake up and worship the Lord!" We remember those tear-jerking altar calls that presented God as angry and deeply marred our ability to see God as good and loving.

In *Worship As Pastoral Care,* William Willimon remarks, *As C. S. Lewis said,* "The charge is 'Feed my sheep' not 'run experiments on my rats.' " When worship is reduced to a pep rally for the pastor's latest crusade or to a series of acts that contain the minister's own hidden agenda, our concern for worship is called into question.

DAILY BIBLE READINGS

M. Seeing God's Glory. 1 Kings 8:1-11

T. Responding to God's Call. Isaiah 6:1-10

W. Listening to God's Word. Nehemiah 8:1-13

T. Describing True Worship. John 4:20-24

F. Approaching God. Hebrews 12:18-24

S. Beholding His Majesty. 2 Peter 1:12-18

The Danger of Idolatry

Study Text: Exodus 32:1-35; 33:1-6

Supplemental References: Isaiah 44:9-20; Jeremiah 2:13-20; Acts 17:22-31; 1 John 5:18-21

Time: Around 1450-1441 B.C.

Place: Near the foot of Mount Sinai

Golden Text: "Consecrate yourselves to day to the Lord . . . that he may bestow upon you a blessing" (Exodus 32:29).

Central Truth: God's people must guard against evil influences that draw them away from true worship.

Evangelistic Emphasis: Sin is never excused, but God provides forgiveness and cleansing.

Printed Text

Exodus 32:1. And when the people saw that Moses delayed to come down out of the mount, the people gathered themselves together unto Aaron, and said unto him, Up, make us gods, which shall go before us; for as for this Moses, the man that brought us up out of the land of Egypt, we wot not what is become of him.

2. And Aaron said unto them, Break off the golden earrings, which are in the ears of your wives, of your sons, and of your daughters, and bring them unto me.

3. And all the people brake off the golden earrings which were in their ears, and brought them unto Aaron.

4. And he received them at their hand, and fashioned it with a graving tool, after he had made it a molten calf: and they said, These be thy gods, O Israel, which brought thee up out of the land of Egypt.

7. And the Lord said unto Moses, Go, get thee down; for thy people, which thou broughtest out of the land of Egypt, have corrupted themselves:

8. They have turned aside quickly out of the way which I commanded them: they have made them a molten calf, and have worshipped it, and have sacrificed thereunto, and said, These be thy gods, O Israel, which have brought thee up out of the land of Egypt.

9. And the Lord said unto Moses, I have seen this people, and, behold, it is a stiffnecked people:

10. Now therefore let me alone, that my wrath may wax hot against them, and that I may consume them: and I will make of thee a great nation.

30. And it came to pass on the morrow, that Moses said unto the people, Ye have sinned a great sin: and now I will go up unto the Lord; peradventure I shall make an atonement for your sin.

31. And Moses returned unto the Lord, and said, Oh, this people have

sinned a great sin, and have made them gods of gold.

32. Yet now, if thou wilt forgive their sin—; and if not, blot me, I pray thee, out of thy book which thou hast written.

33. And the Lord said unto Moses,

Whosoever hath sinned against me, him will I blot out of my book.

34. Therefore now go, lead the people unto the place of which I have spoken unto thee: behold, mine Angel shall go before thee: nevertheless in the day when I visit I will visit their sin upon them.

LESSON OUTLINE

I. WORSHIP PERVERTED
   A. False Expectations
   B. Idolatry's Folly
II. IDOLATRY CONDEMNED
   A. God's Wrath Revealed
   B. Moses' Humble Prayer
III. INTERCESSION OFFERED

LESSON EXPOSITION

INTRODUCTION

For the teacher who has access to it, Brevard Childs' commentary, *The Book of Exodus* (Westminster), provides an excellent discussion of this important chapter in Israel's history (pp. 553-381). Many of the observations in this lesson derive from insights gained from Childs.

Idolatry stands at the beginning of Israel's life under the Ten Commandments. It is significant that Moses had been on the mountain with God receiving God's definitive Law for His covenant people. As you know, that Law began with a command for complete loyalty to Yahweh and rejection of anything that would come close to idolatry. Moses was so enraged by the scene of apostasy as he descended the mountain that he broke into pieces the tablets of Law which had been given by God and actually written by God's hand (32:16, 19). Rather than understanding this as an act of Moses' rage, we should understand it as an act indicating God's covenant with His people is ended. They were violating the very first commandments that God ordained as the basis of their covenant relationship; that is, as the basis of His blessings and their obedience.

Later Jewish writers acknowledged the horror of Israel's apostasy and exclaimed, "No punishment ever comes upon Israel in which there is not a part payment for the sin of the golden calf" (quoted in Childs, who also quoted Rabbi Simeon ben Yohai who had said that Israel had been without any sickness when she stood on Mount Sinai, but these afflictions appeared after the sin of the golden calf).

This understanding of God's wrath and idolatry is expressed clearly in Romans 1:18-32. For Paul, all idolatry leads to perversion of life. All manner of disruption and distortion of human relationships is traced back to idolatry. He clearly assails the sin of homosexuality as being caused by idolatry. In our modern world, the idolatry is no longer a visible golden calf but is now the exaltation of human desire above the law of God.

Twice in the New Testament are references made to the golden calf episode of Exodus 32. The first is Acts 7:39-43. This is Stephen's sermon and he used this incident to show how Israel had always turned away from God's will. This was shown in order to validate his belief in Jesus Christ, whom the Jews had killed. The second reference is 1 Corinthians 10:7 where Paul quoted Exodus 32:4, 6. Paul used this incident to show that idolatry, immorality, and grumbling before God were all temptations that still faced the Christian but could be overcome by God's strength. "No temptation has seized you except what is common to man. And God is faithful; he will not let you be tempted beyond what you can bear. But when you are tempted, he will also provide a way out so that you can stand up under it" (10:13; *New International Version).*

I. WORSHIP PERVERTED (Exodus 32:1-6)

A. False Expectations (vv. 1-3)

1. And when the people saw that Moses delayed to come down out of

the mount, the people gathered themselves together unto Aaron, and said unto him, Up, make us gods, which shall go before us; for as for this Moses, the man that brought us up out of the land of Egypt, we wot not what is become of him.

It is instructive to read Exodus 24:12-18 regarding Moses' call to the mountain. We know that Moses and Joshua went together to the mount and Joshua remained separate from him (32:17). Aaron and Hur (both of whom had upheld Moses' arms in the defeat of the Amalekites [Exodus 17:8-13]) were left in charge of the people (why Hur is not mentioned in the account in Exodus 32 is not explained). We are told the people could see the top of the mountain as a devouring fire. For 40 days and nights Moses was on the mountain with God. The material from Exodus 25:1 through 31:18 describes the various regulations Yahweh gave Moses for the people. The account closed with the reference to the two tablets of the law written by the "finger of God," that is, the Holy Spirit.

The contrast between Moses, who had been with God, and the people and Aaron, who had not been with God, is striking. In the face of Moses' delay, the people turned from the truth of redemption into the terrible maze of idolatry. An interesting New Testament parallel is found in 2 Peter 3:3, 4, where the Apostle warns faithful Christians not to fall prey to the seductive lies of those who make jest of the delay of Christ's return. In its entirety 2 Peter 2 lambastes these seducers as immoral and compares them to "irrational animals" (see 2:12). In 3:9 Peter remarked that the delay of Christ's return is only due to the fact that God desires that all who will turn in repentance and not perish. But because His return is so certain, it is emphasized that we should be persons who live in "holiness and godliness" (see 3:11). How easy it is for us to be tempted in this modern age to turn from the truth of Christ's return toward the deceptive, easy lifestyles of our day. The turning of the children of Israel stands as a clear warning to remain faithful even when we cannot see what God's total purposes are about.

The passage in Exodus 32:1 also points to a crisis in leadership. This crisis is twofold. First, Moses is looked upon as the sole leader of Israel. The people failed to realize that their leader is Yahweh, the God who delivered from Egypt. Their eyes were fixed only on a man and when he apparently failed to return, *they returned* to the gods of Egypt. The second crisis is that of Aaron. Here was a man who had stood close to every miracle the Lord God has performed to deliver the Israelites. Here was a man who was God's mouthpiece; yet, in time of crisis he failed to stand tall for that which is right.

2. And Aaron said unto them, Break off the golden earrings, which are in the ears of your wives, of your sons, and of your daughters, and bring them unto me.

3. And all the people brake off the golden earrings which were in their ears, and brought them unto Aaron.

It is likely the golden earrings were part of the items taken from Egypt when the Israelites despoiled the Egyptians (12:35, 36). Those things which had been meant for their prosperity in the new land turned to be their downfall in the wilderness.

The people used the things of man to create worship. It should be noted that worship of the living God cannot be created. According to John 4:23 God seeks worshipers; that is, people who will worship Him in spirit and in truth. Most people have been in a service where someone, perhaps well-meaning, tried to make worship happen. It can be a coercive experience. There is no sense of freedom in the Spirit in such an atmosphere. Worship can never be forced, even in the name of Christ. Worship is birthed from hearts willing to submit to the Holy Spirit as He directs. No doubt it is important that leaders plan, pray, and truly *lead* in worship; but it is important they be submissive to the Holy Spirit and recognize the church belongs to Christ and not to them.

The title, *False Expectations,* was used to introduce this section. "Expecting" is an important part of worship. Christians should gather expecting to hear from God and expecting the Holy Spirit to be present in the services. But it is important that we not bring into the worship experience false expectations concerning God. There are many who think of God as a heavenly grandfather whose sole mission in the universe is to give us everything we want. Others come under the burden of fear as they expect God to judge them for everything they've ever done. The fact they have confessed their sins has not moved them to understand the love of God. All these false expectations make it possible for idolatry, and even forms of superstition and sorcery, to enter the worship life of an individual.

It is also important that worship be clearly directed toward God as revealed in Jesus Christ. It is not sufficient to simply worship some abstract deity known publicly as "God." There are many such "gods" who are worshiped in the world; yet, they are not real and cannot provide salvation. Christians must understand that a true knowledge of God is found in Jesus Christ. Let us not be deceived into paying lip service to a "god" who is nothing more than the ego-projection of a group or nation. We serve and worship the Lord Jesus Christ! He alone is our Savior and He alone is the true revealer of our heavenly Father.

B. Idolatry's Folly (vv. 4-6)

4. And he received them at their hand, and fashioned it with a graving tool, after he had made it a molten calf: and they said, These be thy gods, O Israel, which brought thee up out of the land of Egypt.

Idolatry is not only the worship of a false god; it is a distortion of reality. Note that the historical reality of Yahweh's deliverance from Egypt was substituted for a myth.

One of Satan's great lies is to play tricks with us regarding reality. Satan convinced Eve that reality was not found in obedience to God's Word but was found in her own questions and answers. The resulting situation was one in which humankind lost its clear standing before

God. Sin distorts the human scene. It is sin that makes the alcoholic or cocaine addict think everything is fine. The "high" of the moment blurs the terrible reality of the price that must be paid later.

This deception manifests itself in many ways. Many church-goers follow the god of materialism. The Big Lie is: God loves us when we are successful in the world. Others accept as their Big Lie: God only loves those who work hard. There are others who accept as their god: Go ahead and enjoy your life; God will not send anyone to hell.

Regardless of its manifestation, Satan is a liar and his lies distort the real truth of God and ourselves.

(Exodus 32:5, 6 is not included in the printed text.)

It was remarked above that Aaron failed in providing faithful leadership. The leadership he did provide was completely against God's will. How simple it would have been for him to have told the questioning crowd in verse 1 to "wait on the Lord." Yet, he too was filled with impatience and fear. Verse 2 revealed that he gave instructions toward the idolatry; verse 4 showed he actually made the calf with his own hand. Verse 5 showed him looking at the image and preparing to sacrifice before it. The implication of verse 5 is that Aaron was "pleased" at the god he had made. He was no different than the man in Isaiah 44:9-20 who made his god from a piece of wood. What a picture of human pride we are given! Aaron is pleased at his god! This is an ancient version of secular humanism. It is man elevating himself to the place of worship.

The conclusion of verse 5 shows Aaron seeking to justify his action by invoking the name of the Lord. It is no different from the person who uses the church as a convenient social cover for a life filled with iniquity and sin.

Verse 6 tells that the people followed Aaron. He was a leader! But tragically he was not God's leader. The people were pleased with Aaron and what he had made. In every way the biblical narrative shows the perversity of the people. Whatever gains their fancy and tickles their imagination is that thing they will do anything for. A reference is made to "peace offerings." Again, the contrast is powerful. Moses, still on the mountain with God, had in his possession God's way to a life of ordered peace with Him. The people were taking refuge in a false peace that only exercised the passions of human flesh and offered no spiritual safety.

II. IDOLATRY CONDEMNED (Exodus 32:7-14)

A. God's Wrath Revealed (vv. 7-10)

7. And the Lord said unto Moses, Go, get thee down; for thy people, which thou broughtest out of the land of Egypt, have corrupted themselves:

8. They have turned aside quickly out of the way which I commanded them: they have made them a molten calf, and have worshipped it, and have sacrificed thereunto, and said, These be thy gods, O Israel, which have brought thee up out of the land of Egypt.

9. And the Lord said unto Moses, I have seen this people, and, behold, it is a stiffnecked people:

10. Now therefore let me alone, that my wrath may wax hot against them, and that I may consume them: and I will make of thee a great nation.

God's wrath can be defined as the inevitable consequences of sin. Although the picture presented in Exodus 32 is of God personally very angry, we should not press the issue to think of God's wrath in terms of God sitting on the throne in heaven waiting for someone to sin so He can strike them with judgment. God's wrath is not primarily centered on God's response as much as it is on the fact that humanity is so blatantly sinful.

The first thing that emerges from these verses is the fact that God saw what was happening. One of Satan's lies is to make men believe that God does not see. The passage in Psalm 10:13 echoes this tendency of man, "Why does the wicked man revile God? Why does he say to himself, 'He won't call me to account'?" (NIV). In 10:4 the psalmist remarked, "In his pride the wicked does not seek him; in all his thoughts there is no room for God" (NIV). In Psalm 14:1 we are reminded, "The fool says in his heart, 'There is no God' " (NIV). In 14:2 we are told "The Lord looks down from heaven on the sons of men, to see if there are any who understand, any who seek God" (NIV). In 73:10, 11, the psalmist laments the arrogance of the wicked with: "Therefore their people turn to them [that is, they praise the wicked] and drink up waters in abundance. They say, 'How can God know? Does the Most High have knowledge?' " (NIV).

Sin causes man to distort all sense of human dignity and godly values. As the psalmist told us, not only does man think he can act without God seeing, man thinks he must act wickedly in order to be accepted among men. St. Augustine remarked, "I made myself worse than I was, that I might not be dispraised; and when in any thing I had not sinned as the abandoned ones, I would say that I had done what I had not done, that I might not seem contemptible in proportion as I was innocent" (The Confessions of St. Augustine).

But it is clear God does see the wicked intent and action of humanity. God is not blind nor has He turned His back. The first thing that emerges from Exodus 32:7-10 is that God clearly sees the evil in the world.

The second thing that emerges is God's willingness to turn humanity loose to the effects of its sin. Note throughout the verses that the people are no longer "my people" in covenant love but have become "Moses' people." In Romans 1:24, 26, 28 the expression "God gave them up" is used in relation to the wrath of God. While specifically used in reference to the Gentile world, it parallels the same reality of idolatry found among the Jews in Exodus 32. Idolatry always results in God turning people lose to experience the full effects of sin. The person who makes cocaine his god, and fails to repent from his destructive ways, is "given up" by God so the full curse of sin can run its course. This "giving up" does not mean that God's mercy cannot be found. God's desire is to save and He is near the sinner waiting to hear the heartfelt cry of confession.

It is important that the love of God be emphasized. Christian preaching/teaching for the past decades has focused on this sense of God's love. But we must never forget that God's love is costly love. It is costly love because sin is deadly expensive. "Cheap grace" (to use Bonhoeffer's phrase) fails to take sin seriously and only makes a mockery of the death of Jesus.

The third emerging fact is that the people "have corrupted themselves." They cannot blame their sin on anyone. Even Aaron, in spite of his leadership failure, is not responsible for their sin. It is the people themselves who are filled with corruption, as evidenced by their insistence upon idols.

The Hebrew for "corrupted" is *shachath.* It is used throughout the Old Testament, but here is a brief listing of some key passages and the way in which that corruption manifests itself:

1. Deuteronomy 4:16, 25—In both verses idolatry is specifically mentioned as the way in which corruption has come among the people.

2. Deuteronomy 9:12—This is the parallel account of the sin of the calf found in Exodus 32.

3. Deuteronomy 31:29—The interesting expression "through the work of your hands" is used to describe the corruption; the making of idols is clearly implied.

4. Deuteronomy 32:5—Moses contrasted the faithfulness of Yahweh with the faithfulness of Israel and her resultant corruption.

5. Ezekiel 28:17—This prophecy against the pagan city of Tyre reveals that national pride leads to corruption of wisdom.

6. Hosea 9:9—Referring to the incident of sexual abuse in Gibeah (Judges 19), Hosea compares Judah's corruption to that of sexual immorality in the forms of rape and homosexuality.

7. Malachi 2:8—This word is directed to the priests who know God's law but corrupt it in their teaching by showing partiality and failing to execute justice.

The fourth factor is God's willingness to make a new people through Moses. In no way would this violate God's promise to Abraham in Genesis 12. Moses was from the seed of Abraham and God would still prove to be faithful. It did show that God was not unilaterally bound to Israel, and whenever she proved to arrogantly assume such, God would "give her up" to the working out of her sinful corruption.

B. Moses' Humble Prayer (vv. 11-14)

(Exodus 32:11-14 is not included in the printed text.)

Moses rejected the opportunity to assert himself above the people. His act of humility stands as a powerful example of true Spirit-filled leadership. The passage in Psalm 106:23 comments on Moses, "[God] said he would destroy them [Israel] —had not Moses, his chosen one, stood in the breach before him to keep his wrath from destroying them" (*NIV*).

Moses used two primary arguments to stand in the breach with God for the people. He functioned as an intercessor (more about this in Point III of the outline) and also as one who reminded God of His character. There is precedence for this act of reminding God in Genesis 18:22-33 when Abraham argued with God over the fate of Sodom and Gomorrah.

The first argument was related to popular opinion regarding God's name in the world. The Egyptians would hear of the destruction, Moses said, and mock God's mighty power by pointing out He was capricious in His dealings with men.

The second argument centered around God's promise to Abraham, Isaac, and Jacob. Although the promise would have been maintained through Moses' line, this faithful servant called upon God to remain faithful to the entire group He had delivered from Egypt.

Verse 14 concludes this first intercession by indicating God "repented of the evil which he thought to do unto his people." Such a verse causes many Christians difficulty. While our limited perspective on God's inner nature cannot provide a complete answer, we can see that God is not a static, predetermined idea who is not responsive to humanity. Rather, we gain a picture of God who actively seeks relationship with humanity. We come to understand that He takes sin seriously and we also come to see that He is not bent toward destruction as much as He is bent toward salvation. The very tablets of law which Moses had to again receive pointed to humanity's sin and precarious standing before God. But Moses as intercessor points to the One Man Jesus Christ who stood in the gap on Calvary that the righteousness of God might be revealed in faith and power and no longer in wrath.

III. INTERCESSION OFFERED (Exodus 32:30-34)

30. And it came to pass on the morrow, that Moses said unto the people, Ye have sinned a great sin: and now I will go up unto the Lord; peradventure I shall make an atonement for your sin.

31. And Moses returned unto the Lord, and said, Oh, this people have sinned a great sin, and have made them gods of gold.

32. Yet now, if thou wilt forgive their sin—; and if not, blot me, I pray thee, out of thy book which thou hast written.

33. And the Lord said unto Moses, Whosoever hath sinned against me, him will I blot out of my book.

34. Therefore now go, lead the people unto the place of which I have spoken unto thee: behold, mine Angel shall go before thee: nevertheless in the day when I visit I will visit their sin upon them.

Moses functions as a type of Christ in the manner of his second act of intercession. Between the first and second acts stands the story of Moses' confrontation with Aaron and the judgment upon the people by the Levites. The narrative runs the emotional gamut from Aaron's remark which is ludicrously funny to the tragedy of family against family in the judgment.

Following the day of judgment Moses spoke to the people (v. 30). It is imperative to note Moses did not discount their sin. He called it "a great sin." Confession of sin still remains an important facet of redemption. Confession is not meant to embarrass people publicly; rather, its intention is for the penitent sinner to realize the seriousness of sin in his/her life. (The issue of private confession versus public confession is too broad to consider here; regardless, confession must be handled in a way that is biblical and filled with love.)

The "great sin" required atonement. Sin, whether large or small, leads to death if not covered by the blood of Christ. Moses knew that someone had to intercede for the people. He also knew that the intercessor had to be someone without sin. In this case, Moses had been with God and was not guilty of the sin the people had committed; thus, he could approach God with a pure heart and clean hands. The word "peradventure" means "perhaps." The certainty of this atonement is not evidenced. This does not mean that God cannot be trusted; rather it means that Moses was still not the perfect intercessor all humanity needed. All Moses could do was call upon the Lord with a hope and faith born of "perhaps."

That same "perhaps" regarding salvation is found in the book of Jonah. There, following Jonah's message of certain doom, the king of Nineveh called for the people to repent and said, "Who knows? God may yet relent and with compassion turn from his fierce anger so that we will not perish" (3:9, *NIV*). That proclamation of hope was based on the great "perhaps." This great "perhaps" is really another way of expressing the reality that a little faith is greater than much doubt. God can be trusted to hear the penitent cry because He desires to do good and not evil!

The word *atonement* is from the language of sacrifice. The article in Volume 1 of *The Interpreter's Dictionary of the Bible* on "Atonement" is enlightening:

"The English word 'atone' is derived from the phrase 'at one.' To be 'at one' with someone is to be in harmonious personal relationship with him. . . . In modern usage [it] has taken on the more restricted meaning of the process by which the hindrances to reconciliation are removed, rather than the end achieved by their removal. 'To atone for' a wrong is to take some action which cancels out the ill effects it has had.

"The Bible as a whole assumes the need for some 'atoning action,' if man is to be right with God. It is accepted as a fact beyond dispute that man is estranged from God, and is himself wholly to blame for this estrangement. His disobedience to the will of God—that is, his sin—has alienated him from God, and his alienation must first be remedied if right relationships are to be restored. The barrier raised by man's past sins must be removed."

The idea of "atonement" involves "covering" of sin. This "covering" is not a hiding of sin in the sense it is excused or ignored; rather, it is a covering of sin by means of a sacrificial death. This sacrificial death in the Old Testament usually involved a lamb or other pure animal. The important thing to note is that it took a life to remove the curse of death-filled separation from God caused by man's sin. Thus, in the death of Jesus we have the "once and for all" atonement (covering) made for all people and all sin.

Moses used prayer to God as his model of atonement. He offered himself to be blotted out rather than have the people blotted. He joined himself with the sinful people. This is exactly what Jesus did when He mixed with sinners and became known as a "friend of sinners." Jesus took the place of "blotting out" for us; we deserved it, He did not. Yet, out of His great love for us, He and the heavenly Father chose from eternity that Christ would pay the price of sin. Moses, in spite of his noble request, could not be used as a sacrifice for the people. The reason for his exclusion was because he was also a man of sin (in ways other than the calf). Only a perfect man could provide atonement for sinful man. This is what Jesus did!

Verse 33 spoke a principle that receives further elaboration in Ezekiel 18. That principle indicated that only those who were sinners would die; that is, the judgment upon sin is not passed down from father to son. If the father sins, then it is the father who is punished and not the son. Through verse 33 the Lord indicated to Moses He could have compassion upon those who were guiltless and would not act capriciously toward all.

Verse 34 becomes an avenue of hope and warning. The people are free to continue their journey to Canaan. They must remember that their sin has a natural course that God will allow it to run ("I will visit their sin upon them"). Thus, even though Moses had successfully brought atonement for the people, that atonement did not stop the effects of sin already set in motion.

REVIEW QUESTIONS

1. What are some of the "golden calves" that men set up today as objects of worship?

2. How would you describe the leadership shown by Aaron?

3. Why is it important that Jesus Christ be emphasized in worship?

4. What characteristics of Moses as an intercessor are important for us today?

5. Why was Moses unable to give his life for atonement?

GOLDEN TEXT HOMILY

"CONSECRATE YOURSELVES TO DAY TO THE LORD . . . THAT HE MAY BESTOW UPON YOU A BLESSING THIS DAY" (Exodus 32:29).

God hates the sin of idolatry and he always punishes it.

The thousands who waited at the foot of the mountain and became impatient because Moses did not soon come back were not ignorant of God's will in the matter of worshiping and serving only God. He had already thundered from Sinai His jealous expectations of His people. They knew they could offer sacrifice and worship only to Him.

Idolatry is a deliberate rejection of the one true God and a willful choosing of a substitute that is less than God. He will not tolerate it. On this fearful occasion, three thousand were slain by the sword because they were guilty of idolatry. This lesson lets us know that God does not treat idolatry lightly. It also teaches us that we can escape the awful punishment of those who are guilty of rejecting God and choosing a lesser god by repenting and joining those who step out on the Lord's side and consecrating ourselves to Him.

Death and judgment from a righteous God waits for idolaters; blessing is promised "this day" to those who consecrate themselves to Him.—**W. E. Johnson (Retired), Former Executive Secretary, Church of God World Missions, Cleveland, Tennessee**

SENTENCE SERMONS

GOD'S PEOPLE must guard against evil influences that draw them away from true worship
—**Selected**

IF YOU ARE swept off your feet, its time to get on your knees.—**Fred Beck**

WHEN GOD comes in the idols tumble down.
—**"Speaker's Sourcebook"**

WE EASILY FALL into idolatry, for we are inclined thereunto by nature, and coming to us by inheritance, it seems pleasant.
—**Martin Luther**

EVANGELISTIC APPLICATION

SIN IS NEVER EXCUSED, BUT GOD PROVIDES FORGIVENESS AND CLEANSING. Four important truths are found in that statement.

First, God does not deal with sin by excusing it or ignoring it. God takes sin as a matter of life and death because sin separates people from Him. He is the source of life and anything that cuts us off from Him cuts us off from eternal life.

Second, only God can provide rescue from sin. There is no salvation found outside Jesus Christ. Christ is God's complete provision. Anything, or anyone, who seeks to add to Christ's provision is frustrating the grace of God.

Third, God provides forgiveness. This forgiveness is the placing aright of our life before Him. By forgiving us He casts our sins into the sea of forgetfulness. He does not hold our sins in His memory but He treats us as new creatures in Christ Jesus.

Fourth, God provides cleansing from the effects of sin. The heart is not only forgiven but is purged of sinful desires and a life controlled by the flesh. By yielding to the Holy Spirit, God exercises lordship through Christ in our life.

ILLUMINATING THE LESSON

Many are deceived into thinking that sin does not cost. Paul called it "the wages of sin is death." The cocaine addict does not realize that, even if he breaks the habit, he has set in motion effects of sin that will alter his life. His family may be destroyed and his sources of income damaged beyond repair.

Many people turn to God thinking this will automatically keep from them the harvest they have sown in the world of sin. There are times when God mercifully limits the effects of that harvest. But it is naive to believe that the harvest will not come.

There are countless Christian leaders who fell into sin, were discovered, confessed, but whose ministries are permanently limited. This is not God's doing, this is man's doing.

An important lesson to learn is that, although God's grace is sufficient to save and forgive, grace does not mean that sin's effects will not be felt.

The encouraging word is that God will use these situations as a form of testimony to His grace. God can redeem any situation and give us the strength to walk holy in His sight.

DAILY BIBLE READINGS

M. Folly of Idolatry. Isaiah 44:9-20

T. Forsaking God. Jeremiah 2:13-20

W. Rejecting Idolatry. Daniel 3:1-18

T. Loving God. Matthew 22:34-40

F. Recognizing the True God. Acts 17: 22-31

S. Serving the True God. 1 John 5:18-21

Invitation to Serve

Study Text: Exodus 35:4 through 36:7; 40:34-38

Supplemental References: 1 Kings 12:4-16; 2 Chronicles 34:8-13; Haggai 1:3-11; Romans 12:1-3

Time: Around 1450-1441 B.C.

Place: Mount Sinai

Golden Text: "The Lord hath chosen you to stand before him, to serve him, that ye should minister unto him" (2 Chronicles 29:11)

Central Truth: God calls each of us to personal involvement in the building of His kingdom.

Evangelistic Emphasis: The invitation to salvation is God's call to service.

Printed Text

Exodus 35:4. And Moses spake unto all the congregation of the children of Israel, saying, This is the thing which the Lord commanded, saying,

5. Take ye from among you an offering unto the Lord: whosoever is of a willing heart, let him bring it, an offering of the Lord; gold, and silver, and brass,

10. And every wise hearted among you shall come, and make all that the Lord hath commanded;

21. And they came, every one whose heart stirred him up, and every one whom his spirit made willing, and they brought the Lord's offering to the work of the tabernacle of the congregation, and for all his service, and for the holy garments.

29. The children of Israel brought a willing offering unto the Lord, every man and woman, whose heart made them willing to bring for all manner of work, which the Lord had commanded to be made by the hand of Moses.

30. And Moses said unto the chil- dren of Israel, See, the Lord hath called **by name Bezaleel the son of Uri, the son of Hur, of the tribe of Judah;**

31. And he hath filled him with the spirit of God, in wisdom, in understanding, and in knowledge, and in all manner of workmanship;

32. And to devise curious works, to work in gold, and in silver, and in brass,

33. And in the cutting of stones, to set them, and in carving of wood, to make any manner of cunning work.

34. And he hath put in his heart that he may teach, both he, and Aholiab, the son of Ahisamach, of the tribe of Dan.

35. Them hath he filled with wisdom of heart, to work all manner of work, of the engraver, and of the cunning workman, and of the embroiderer, in blue, and in purple, in scarlet, and in fine linen, and of the weaver, even of them that do any work, and of those that devise cunning work.

36:1. Then wrought Bezaleel and

Aholiab, and every wise hearted man, in whom the Lord put wisdom and understanding to know how to work all manner of work for the service of the sanctuary, according to all that the Lord had commanded.

40:34. Then a cloud covered the tent of the congregation, and the glory of the Lord filled the tabernacle.

DICTIONARY

Bezalee (bee-ZAL-ee-el)—Exodus 35:30—Son of Uri (YOU-rye)—He was gifted by God to work in metals, wood and stone for the tabernacle.

Uri (YOU-rye)—Exodus 35:30—The father of Bezaleel.

Hur (her)—Exodus 35:30—Grandfather of Bezaleel of the tribe of Judah.

Aholiab (ah-HOO-li-ab)—Exodus 35:34—A man who was divinely endowed with artistic skills to construct the tabernacle.

Ahisamach (ah-HIS-ah-mack)—Exodus 35:34—A Danite, father of Aholiab.

LESSON OUTLINE

I. PERSONAL INVOLVEMENT
  A. A Worthy Cause
  B. Heartfelt Response
II. SPIRIT-ANOINTED SERVICE
  A. Filled With the Spirit
  B. Spirit-Led Instruction
III. GOD'S GLORY MANIFESTED
  A. God's Mighty Presence
  B. God's Guiding Presence

LESSON EXPOSITION

INTRODUCTION

The contrast between the lesson last week with its idolatry and judgment, and this lesson with its call to serve, is striking. It shows the marvelous grace of God. It shows God does not give up on us forever. It shows that in spite of our failures, He redeems and through the Holy Spirit enables us to work for Him. It is easy to imagine some of the same people who leaned toward the golden calf now serving the Lord with a pure heart born of true repentance.

The teacher will be wise to read Exodus 34 and also consider Exodus 35:1-3 in preparation. Exodus 34 is the renewal of the covenant of the Ten Commandments following the judgment upon the people in their sin of the golden calf. Verses 11-16 continue the strict warning against idolatry and verses 17-26 provide further insight into dimensions of Israelite law under God. Chapter 34 concludes with the manifestation of God's glory upon the face of Moses. Paul's commentary on this passage in 2 Corinthians 3 is enlightening and should be read as background.

The theme of Exodus 35 is God's "Invitation to Serve." The lesson is "work oriented" and provides insight into the dynamics of working for God in His church and among His people. That is why Exodus 35:1-3 needs to be kept in mind. Before God calls us to work, He reminds us that the Sabbath is still to be observed as a holy day. It is God's way of reminding man that even work in the Tabernacle is not man's work but God's work!

I. PERSONAL INVOLVEMENT (Exodus 35:4, 5, 10, 21, 29)

A. A Worthy Cause (vv. 4, 5, 10)

4. And Moses spake unto all the congregation of the children of Israel, saying, This is the thing which the Lord commanded, saying,

5. Take ye from among you an offering unto the Lord: whosoever is of a willing heart, let him bring it, an offering of the Lord; gold, and silver, and brass,

10. And every wise hearted among you shall come, and make all that the Lord hath commanded.

While Exodus 25:1-9 contains a similar record of the events described in our lesson, we will look exclusively at Exodus 35 for commentary.

After instructing the people concerning what constitutes a proper attitude toward work (35:1-3), Moses went on to elaborate the call of God regarding the building of the tabernacle. It is important to note this is a "command" from God. The Hebrew, tsavah, carries the sense of a "charge" given to someone. This particular form of the word was often used in matters pertaining to the Law. It can carry the sense of being "ordained" to accomplish what God has authorized. The fact that "the Lord" commanded this took it from the sphere of something Moses personally desired. He was only an instrument in what God desired. Yet, he knew this command was extremely important and had to be obeyed not only in the sense of the Law but, as the following verses showed, from a heartfelt love.

This relationship between "command" and "love" is tightly woven in the New Testament. Jesus spoke of obeying the commandment He had received from His Father, "For I did not speak of my own accord, but the Father who sent me commanded me what to say and how to say it. I know that his command leads to eternal life. So whatever I say is just what the Father has told me to say" (John 12:49, 50; New International Version). Jesus spoke to His disciples, "A new command I give you: Love one another. As I have loved you, so you must love one another" (John 13:34, NIV). "If you obey my commands, you will remain in my love, just as I have obeyed my Father's commands and remain in his love" (John 15:10, NIV); "My command is this: Love each other as I have loved you" (John 15:12, NIV); "You are my friends if you do what I command" (John 15:14, NIV). The Apostle John, in the letters written near the end of his life, "This is his command: to believe in the name of his Son, Jesus Christ, and to love one another as he commanded us" (1 John 3:23 NIV); "He has given us this command: Whoever loves God must also love his brother" (1 John 4:21, NIV); "This is how we know that we love the children of God: by loving God and carrying out his commands" (1 John 5:2, NIV); "This is love for God: to obey his commands.

And his commands are not burdensome" (1 John 5:3, NIV).

The command of the Lord was directed toward the people. They were to bring an offering to the Lord. Note in verse 5 how the offering is taken from the property of man to become God's property: "Take . . . from . . . you an offering unto the Lord . . . an offering of the Lord." That which the people brought to the Lord became His. This is the meaning of sanctification. It is that which becomes God's property; it is for His use and possession. When a person dedicates his/her talents to the Lord, those talents are no longer ours to decide how they will be used but are God's.

The command was directed to all the people; the obedience was voluntary. No one was excluded from the opportunity to give; but a precondition was established. The offering, or obedience, had to come from a willing heart. The Hebrew translated "willing" has the sense of "generous, noble, inclined." God did not coerce people to participate in the holy building. All heard the command; only those who were willing to let God control their offering were truly free to participate.

The word for "wise" in verse 10 can also mean "skilled." The focus was not meant to be exclusive but indicated a giving of talents to the Lord so that which the Lord commanded could be made. A "wise heart" is a heart that knows its gifts, affirms them, and is willing to use them. It recognizes that it belongs to God and that although there is much to do, He will provide the power to accomplish it.

B. Heartfelt Response (vv. 21, 29)

21. And they came, every one whose heart stirred him up, and every one whom his spirit made willing, and they brought the Lord's offering to the work of the tabernacle of the congregation, and for all his service, and for the holy garments.

29. The children of Israel brought a willing offering unto the Lord, every man and woman, whose heart made them willing to bring for all manner of work, which the Lord had commanded to be made by the hand of Moses.

The word *stirred* comes from a verb meaning "lift up." The heart that was stirred up was lifted up. That heart caught a vision of the future and accepted the Lord's command as an invitation. That heart was lifted because it knew that a life dedicated to God meant fulfillment and accomplishment for His glory.

The relationship between "heart" and "spirit" is interesting. "Heart" implies an emotional element; there is a joy, a leaping of the heart to be part of something important for God. "Spirit" implies a commitment of the total self. The unity is important. Action born simply from emotion wears thin in the course of work; but action birthed from a stirred heart and willing spirit has counted the cost and is prepared to see the project through. The involvement of the human spirit also indicates a "willingness" to cooperate with God. This dual usage also means that God does not manipulate people with guilt or fear. The invitation was to participate in something wonderful He has. It was an invitation that touched the heart and the spirit and brought forth a commitment to God's will.

Every person was accepted, from men to women. When it comes to working for Christ, man-made distinctions disappear and all are invited to share in the glory of God. Verse 29 remarked that the people brought "all manner of work." It was clear not everyone would be a leader and not everyone would have jobs that would be visible. But each person and his/her talents were important to the total work. Everything that was done required willing hearts and spirits for the glory of God.

II. SPIRIT-ANOINTED SERVICE (Exodus 35:30 through 36:1)

A. Filled With the Spirit (vv. 30-33)

30. And Moses said unto the children of Israel, See, the Lord hath called by name Bezaleel the son of Uri, the son of Hur, of the tribe of Judah;

31. And he hath filled him with the spirit of God, in wisdom, in understanding, and in knowledge, and in all manner of workmanship;

32. And to devise curious works, to work in gold, and in silver, and in brass,

33. And in the cutting of stones, to set them, and in carving of wood, to make any manner of cunning work.

Bezaleel, whose name means "in God's protection," was a member of the tribe of Judah. He is further described in Exodus 31:3 as a man the Lord filled "with the Spirit of God, with skill, ability and knowledge in all kinds of crafts" (*NIV*). There is no doubt Bezaleel had a special calling upon his life. Moses said that the Lord called Bezaleel by name. There is no doubt the Lord chooses certain men and women to stand forth in leadership in His kingdom. The New Testament is filled with the lives of such people who knew God had set them apart for His service.

It is important to note that Bezaleel did not set himself apart; God did that and affirmed it through the recognition of others. When a person has to fight for his claim of God's service he is walking on dangerous ground; when the people of God affirm a person as their leader it is a confirmation.

Paul twice wrote of leaders in the church who are set apart by the Holy Spirit. They were given spiritual ministry gifts for the upbuilding of the church (1 Corinthians 12:27-31; Ephesians 4:11, 12).

The manner of Bezaleel's filling with the Holy Spirit is of interest. There are four areas in which that filling manifested itself. First, he manifested wisdom. According to Deuteronomy 34:9 Joshua was a man of wisdom; Psalm 37:30 relates that the righteous speak wisdom; and Psalm 111:10 indicates "the fear of the Lord is the beginning of wisdom." In numerous instances in the Old Testament wisdom and understanding are combined: 1 Kings 4:29 (of Solomon); Daniel 1:4, 17, 20; 5:11, 14. Of special interest are the uses in Isaiah: "He will be the sure foundation for your times, a rich store of salvation and wisdom and knowledge; the fear of the Lord is the key to this treasure" (33:6, *NIV*); and especially 11:2 which prophesies the Messiah, "The Spirit of the Lord will rest upon him—the Spirit of wisdom and of understanding, the Spirit of counsel and of power, the Spirit of knowledge and of the fear of the Lord" (NIV)

Wisdom has the sense of perceiving God's purposes and plans and applying them to the future.

Second, understanding was manifested. This word has the sense of "discern, consider, perceive, give heed to, attend to." It also implied one who was able to transmit understanding; that is, a teacher. This seems to be a very practical application of what one has learned.

Third, knowledge was manifested. Knowledge deals with facts. If wisdom recognizes God's plans, and understanding saw ways to make those plans applicable, then knowledge had the necessary facts at hand to be correct in what one did.

The fourth manifestation was workmanship. This man not only knew how to think something through, he also knew how to actually do it. He could perform the task at hand.

Note that all this was from the Holy Spirit. No doubt Bezaleel had manifested these gifts for many years. He is no novice doing the Lord's work; he is a man who has prepared himself to be available for God.

The idea of "workmanship" is used in Ephesians 2:10 to describe what God has done to us in Christ Jesus: "We are his workmanship, created in Christ Jesus unto good works, which God hath before ordained that we should walk in them."

The content of Ephesians 2 shows that prior to faith in Christ, we "walked according to the course of this world, according to the prince of the power of the air, the spirit that now worketh in the children of disobedience" (v. 2). It is clear this description relates to Israel (as well as Gentiles) who followed after the course of idolatry. Paul went on to exclaim that we "were by nature the children of wrath" (v. 3).

Yet, he knew the purpose of God is to save and not to destroy. Paul understood God to be "rich in mercy" because of "His great love wherewith He loved us" (v. 4).

This love expressed in Christ is so powerful that it moves us from the sphere of making earthly tabernacles that are only a shadow of the heavenly tabernacle to the sphere of, in the spirit and through Christ, actually "sit[ting] together in heavenly places in Christ Jesus" (v. 6).

This points to a profound truth of the New Testament: we are the temple of the Holy Spirit. Twice in 1 Corinthians Paul referred to this (3:16, 17; 6:19, 20). Paul's emphasis was that individual Christians were to abstain from unholy living because the Holy Spirit dwelt within them; he also meant for the body of believers (the church) to realize that as a whole it was the temple of the Holy Spirit.

Thus, the figure of Bezaleel is a type of Christ and the Holy Spirit in that all have functions in relation to the dwelling of God. If Bezaleel was efficient in all manner of workmanship, think how much more effective Jesus is as a workman in our life! If Bezaleel had responsibility for preparing a dwelling of God made with human hands and temporal, Christ is all the more effective in preparing a dwelling of God in the human heart that will last for eternity.

The reference to "curious works" in verse 32 is better rendered "artistic designs" (NIV) and the "cunning work" of v. 33 is better rendered "artistic craftsmanship" (NIV).

B. Spirit-Led Instruction (vv. 35:34, 35; 36:1)

34. And he hath put in his heart that he may teach, both he, and Aholiab, the son of Ahisamach, of the tribe of Dan.

35. Them hath he filled with wisdom of heart, to work all manner of work, of the engraver, and of the cunning workman, and of the embroiderer, in blue, and in purple, in scarlet, and in fine linen, and of the weaver, even of them that do any work, and of those that devise cunning work.

36:1. Then wrought Bezaleel and Aholiab, and every wise hearted man, in whom the Lord put wisdom and understanding to know how to work all manner of work for the service of

the sanctuary, according to all that the Lord had commanded.

These verses form a beautiful Old Testament parallel to the New Testament's understanding of charismatic gifts. The charismatic gifts (often called spiritual gifts) are listed in Romans 12:3-8; 1 Corinthians 12:4-11, 27-30; Ephesians 4:11, 12. How these gifts operate in the church is revealed in 1 Corinthians 12 and their purpose is further revealed in Ephesians 4:12-14.

In 1 Corinthians 14:3 Paul indicates that spiritual gifts function for a threefold purpose: edification, exhortation, and comfort. Verse 12 further reveals, "forasmuch as ye are zealous of spiritual gifts, seek that ye may excel to the edifying of the church." The passage in Ephesians 4:12-14 shows that the ministry gifts (which include teaching) are used "so that the saints together make a unity in the work of service, building up the body of Christ" (v. 12 *Jerusalem Bible)*. The traditional punctuation of verse 12, found in the King James Version, does an injustice to the text. The KJV gives the impression that the manifestation of spiritual gifts are for three things: perfecting the saints, the work of ministry, and the edifying of the body of Christ. This translation implies strongly that only those who have certain spiritual gifts are to do the work of ministry. If the first comma is removed in verse 12 a much clearer understanding emerges: those who have ministry spiritual gifts (such as teaching) are to perfect the saints (the remainder of the church) so the saints can do the work of ministry!

Ephesians 4 goes on to indicate that the ultimate goal of ministry gifts is that "we all come in the unity of the faith, and of the knowledge of the Son of God, unto a perfect [mature] man, unto the measure of the stature of the fulness of Christ: That we henceforth be no more children, tossed to and fro, and carried about with every wind of doctrine, by the sleight of men, and cunning craftiness, whereby they lie in wait to deceive" (4:13, 14).

It is important that a gift of "teaching" was given Bezaleel and his coworker Aholiab. There is a common saying that "those who can, do, and those who can't, teach!" Well, the teacher finds that offensive! Note how the Word of God describes "teachers." They are people who have proven their ability to accomplish a God-given task; they are empowered by the Holy Spirit and commissioned by God to teach (disciple) others in the same fashion.

Just as these men were given special abilities in handling engraving tools, they were also to allow the Holy Spirit to use them as engravers of the human spirit and will. They were to "disciple" others for the work of building God's tabernacle! They were not to be shy in living a life that others would desire to "imitate" in the Spirit.

The fact that Bezaleel and Aholiab are named as working together is a striking picture of unity in leadership. Clearly Bezaleel is the primary leader; yet, he is not given dictatorial privilege. He is in submission to Aholiab and they must work together for the purposes of God. Every Christian leader needs to realize he/she is not the Lone Ranger for God. That is why pastors must see their elders and deacons as sources of spiritual wisdom and strength and not be in an adversary relationship. They are working together for the kingdom for the glory of Christ.

It should be noted in verse 35 that God bonded these men together "with wisdom of heart" for "all manner of work." These men had a common goal that was established by God. They accepted it as God's goal and as long as that priority was their focus they could overcome any personality differences they might have had. "Wisdom of heart" is an expression that relates to proven ability to do something. It is not an "emotional" term; it is a term of commitment to do what God has given as native or special ability. "Wisdom of heart" is humbly confident, needs no other approval than God's approval, and is focused on God's purpose.

III. GOD'S GLORY MANIFESTED (Exodus 40:34-38)

A. God's Mighty Presence (vv. 34, 35)

34. Then a cloud covered the tent of the congregation, and the glory of the Lord filled the tabernacle.

(Exodus 40:35 is not included in the printed text.)

In Exodus 36:2 through 40:33 is described the fulfillment of the command of God in 25:8, "And let them make me a sanctuary; that I may dwell among them." In response to the obedience of Moses, Bezaleel, Aholiab, and the people, God's presence moved mightily in the tabernacle. The glory of the Lord filling the tabernacle is expressed in the Old Testament in the accounts of the glory filling the Temple. Chapters 5 and 6 of 2 Chronicles relate the filling of the Solomonic Temple. "The house [of the Lord] was filled with a cloud . . . So that the priests could not stand to minister by reason [because] of the cloud: for the glory of the Lord had filled the house of God" (5:13, 14). That Solomon understood the limits of an earthly dwelling for God is evidenced by his remark in 2 Chronicles 6:18, "But will God . . . dwell [indeed] with men on the earth? behold, heaven and the heaven of heavens cannot contain thee; how much less this house which I have built!"

In his call, Isaiah had a vision of the Lord's glory in the Temple (6:1-7). Ezekiel saw the glory of the Lord depart Solomon's Temple (10:18; 11:23) but foresaw a day when the glory would return (43:4). Ezekiel's prophecy was further expanded by the post-exilic prophet Haggai who recognized that "the glory of this latter house shall be greater than of the former, saith the Lord of hosts" (2:9). This is clearly a reference to the glory that came in Jesus Christ. It is in Christ that the glory of the Lord has been most fully revealed.

The "glory of the Lord" is a powerful theme in both testaments. Old Testament theologian Gerhard von Rad observed that the root idea of "glory" is "the idea of 'weight,' of 'standing,' and of 'honour'. . . . Thus (the Lord's glory) also, that is, his power and standing, his honour, were perceptible in the world in the most varied of ways" (*Old Testament Theology,* Volume 1, pp. 239-240). Another Old Testament scholar, Walter Eichrodt, suggested that the glory of the Lord suggests that which is outwardly visible; thus, "An outward position of honour, power and success. Hence, even God's (glory) . . . includes an element of appearance, of that which catches the eye" (*Theology of the Old Testament,* Volume 2, pp. 31ff).

Eichrodt shows that the prophetic interpretation of the glory of the Lord tended toward God as ruler of the world upon a royal throne exercising power and bringing human history into conformity with His will. On the other hand, the priestly view saw God's glory in terms of the bright light and formless cloud by which He revealed His will. Both strands of thought are brought together in God's Son, Jesus Christ, as He both reveals the will of the Father and also exercises His power as the Lord Almighty!

While not part of the printed text, verse 35 shows the marked difference between the Old Covenant and the New Covenant. Under the Old, Moses was not able to enter the Tabernacle when the glory of God descended. The Book of Hebrews provides excellent commentary on this situation and the role of Moses in the house of the Lord. In Hebrews 3:5 we find that Moses was faithful in the tabernacle as a servant would be faithful. His sole purpose was "for a testimony of those things which were to be spoken after [later]." The high priest had to offer sacrifices for his own sins as well as the sins of the people (5:3; 7:27). Hebrews 9 shows that the "outer tent" (referring to the Jerusalem Temple still standing when this letter was written) is a symbol of the present age in that the things that were offered could not cleanse the conscience of the worshiper.

Jesus, as God's Son, was able to serve the purposes of redemption better than Moses could as a servant. When Jesus entered the tabernacle of God He did so sinlessly. His sacrifice was a "once for all" reality that broke down the barriers between God and humanity. His entrance into God's Holy Place has provided forgiveness of sins and purity of life for all who believe.

The beauty of what Jesus has provided is seen in the fact that the glory of God no longer separates us from God but through the blood of Christ and the Holy Spirit we can enter into the very throne room of God!

B. God's Guiding Presence (vv. 36-38)

(Exodus 40:36-38 is not included in the printed text.)

The Bible affirms we are not alone in life. God, our Creator, is also our Sustainer and Guide. Many hymns attest His guiding power. Among those hymns are "The Eternal Life" with its hope-filled message: "Lead kindly Light, amid the encircling gloom, Lead Thou me on! The night is dark, and I am far from home; Lead Thou me on! Keep Thou my feet; I do not ask to see the distant scene—one step enough for me." "The Christian Life" also speaks of the presence of God in guiding power: "Guide me, O Thou great Jehovah, Pilgrim through this barren land."

The guiding presence of God indicates several things. First, God has a goal He is leading us to. That goal is heaven. The goal is also the life of righteousness through Jesus Christ. Second, that goal is expressed in the fact that God is with us throughout life's decisions to enable us in discerning His will. That is part of the work of the Holy Spirit as the One who guides into all truth. Third, it means God will be faithful to bring us to the conclusion of that goal.

This goal is perhaps nowhere better stated than by St. Augustine, "Thou awakest us to delight in Thy praise; for Thou madest us for Thyself, and our heart is restless, until it repose in Thee."

REVIEW QUESTIONS

1. What insight does this lesson give on the use of our talents before the Lord?

2. What does this lesson teach about the use of spiritual gifts in the church?

3. Why is wisdom necessary in the use of spiritual gifts?

4. How is the glory of the Lord manifested in our life today?

GOLDEN TEXT HOMILY

"THE LORD HATH CHOSEN YOU TO STAND BEFORE HIM, TO SERVE HIM, THAT YE SHOULD MINISTER UNTO HIM" (2 Chronicles 29:11).

I do not believe there is a higher privilege than to be chosen of God. The older I become the more I am aware that God's will and way prevails in the affairs of men. How human we are when we think that the choice is exclusively ours in relation to God. Does not Scripture bear out that we have not chosen God, but God has chosen us from the foundations of the world? Space is not available for me to write about men like Abraham, Moses, and David and women like Esther and Mary who were the chosen of the Lord. For indeed all of the redeemed have been the choice of God.

To stand before Him indicates to me a place of great privilege. To stand before the King of Kings, and the Lord of Lords is the highest of all honors that could ever befall a mortal man. I sometimes shudder at how lightly we take this privilege. We are so proned to compare our standing with God to the standards of man that we cheat ourselves out of many blessings as children of the King.

The next phrase sets forth our duty, to serve Him. Being a servant of God has very little to do with actions, for anyone can act. To be a servant of God is a state of being—24 hours a day, 365 days a year we are perpetually a servant of God. My prayer is that in no way we would bring reproach on our service to God by being self-seeking or insincere in our life.

The last clause sets forth the level of service. That level of service is to minister unto Him. So many times we look upon our service to God as a duty, rather than a ministry. I sometimes frown when I think of how narrow we make the Word minister. My Bible says to do all for the glory of God. The Gospel of Matthew states, in relationship to ministering unto Christ: "As ye did it not to one of the least of these, ye did it not to me" (25:45). We always minister unto Christ by ministering unto others. To me ministry is simply seeing a need, and then filling the need for the glory of God. **—Raymond Lankford, Chaplain, A&D Unit Counselor Supervisor, Mississippi Department of Corrections, Parchman, Mississippi**

SENTENCE SERMONS

GOD CALLS EACH of us to personal involvement in the building of His Kingdom. **—Selected**

SALVATION WITHOUT SERVICE leads to stagnation.

—"Notes and Quotes"

THE FELLOW who rolls up his sleeves does not lose his shirt very often.

—Selected

SERVICE IS the outgrowth of gratitude **—"Notes and Quotes"**

EVANGELISTIC APPLICATION

THE INVITATION TO SALVATION IS GOD'S CALL TO SERVICE.

How a person responds to this invitation determines the eternal course of his life. There is no doubt God has determined that all should be saved by the death of His Son; the response to that act of His will rests with us. We make the final decision regarding our salvation by accepting or rejecting Christ.

The parable of the talents in Matthew 25:14-30 shows how important it is for the redeemed to use their talents for God. Jesus gave this parable as a warning to those who would be slack in light of the reality of His return. The parable is a demand for effective Christian service. A reading of it shows that the person who buried his talent was dominated by fear.

Salvation sets free from the power of paralyzing fear. It liberates us to the wisdom of the fear of the Lord by which

we serve Christ. The New Testament does not know of salvation without corresponding obedience to Christ. Those who accept Christ, only to continue to live under the dominion of sin, cheapen the death of Jesus. Salvation enables us to take up our cross and follow Him daily as we serve in love, righteousness, and to His glory.

ILLUMINATING THE LESSON

John Calvin wrote concerning the Lord's calling: "The Lord bids each one of us in all life's actions to look to His calling. For He knows with what great restlessness human nature flames, with what fickleness it is borne hither and thither, how its ambition longs to embrace various things at once. Therefore, lest through our stupidity and rashness everything be turned topsy-turvy, He has appointed duties for every man in His particular way of life. And that no one may thoughtlessly transgress His limits, He has named these various kinds of living 'callings.' Therefore each individual has his own kind of living assigned to him by the Lord as a sort of sentry post so that he may not heedlessly wander about throughout life."

"It is enough if we know that the Lord's calling is in everything the beginning and foundation of well-doing. . . . Your life will then be best ordered when it is directed to this goal."—*Institutes of the Christian Religion* III, 10.

DAILY BIBLE READINGS

M. Giving Which Costs. 2 Samuel 23:18-25
T. Repairing the Temple. 2 Kings 12:9-16
W. Withholding From God. Haggai 1:3-11
T. Faithful Service. Matthew 25:14-30
F. Presenting Our Bodies. Romans 12: 1-8
S. Giving Cheerfully. 2 Corinthians 9:6-15

Challenge to Believe God

Study Text: Numbers 13:1-33

Supplemental References: Psalm 11:1-7; 1 Samuel 17:31-50; 2 Chronicles 14:8-15; Hebrews 11:32-40

Time: Around 1450-1441 B.C.

Place: Wilderness of Paran and areas in the Land of Canaan

Golden Text: "Without faith it is impossible to please him: for he that cometh to God must believe that he is, and that he is a rewarder of them that diligently seek him" (Hebrews 11:6).

Central Truth: As we exercise our faith in God, He leads us in victorious living.

Evangelistic Emphasis: Through faith the repentant sinner receives salvation.

Printed Text

Numbers 13:17. And Moses sent them to spy out the land of Canaan, and said unto them, Get you up this way southward, and go up into the mountain:

18. And see the land, what it is, and the people that dwelleth therein, whether they be strong or weak, few or many;

19. And what the land is that they dwell in, whether it be good or bad; and what cities they be that they dwell in, whether in tents, or in strong holds;

20. And what the land is, whether it be fat or lean, whether there be wood therein, or not. And be ye of good courage, and bring of the fruit of the land. Now the time was the time of the firstripe grapes.

25. And they returned from searching of the land after forty days.

26. And they went and came to Moses, and to Aaron, and to all the congregation of the children of Israel, unto the wilderness of Paran, to Kadesh; and brought back word unto them, and unto all the congregation, and shewed them the fruit of the land.

27. And they told him, and said, We came unto the land whither thou sentest us, and surely it floweth with milk and honey; and this is the fruit of it.

28. Nevertheless the people be strong that dwell in the land, and the cities are walled, and very great: and moreover we saw the children of Anak there.

29. The Amalekites dwell in the land of the south: and the Hittites, and the Jebusites, and the Amorites, dwell in the mountains: and the Canaanites dwell by the sea, and by the coast of Jordan.

30. And Caleb stilled the people before Moses, and said, Let us go up at once, and possess it; for we are well able to overcome it.

31. But the men that went up with him said, We be not able to go up against the people; for they are stronger than we.

32. And they brought up an evil report of the land which they had searched unto the children of Israel, saying, The land, through which we

have gone to search it, is a land that eateth up the inhabitants thereof; and all the people that we saw in it are men of a great stature.

33. And there we saw the giants, the sons of Anak, which come of the giants: and we were in our own sight as grasshoppers, and so we were in their sight.

DICTIONARY

wilderness of Paran (PAY-ran)—Numbers 13:26—A wilderness with some uncertain identification, but generally considered to be an area in the Sinaitic Peninsula.

Kadesh (KAY-desh)—Numbers 13:26—Usually identified as Ain Qeders about 50 miles south of Beersheba.

Amalekites (ah-MAL-ek-ites)—Numbers 13;29—A nomandic, warlike people that were occupying in Canaan when Israel settled there.

Hittites (HIT-tights)—Numbers 13:29—A people who originated in Asia Minor and penetrated all parts of the ancient world.

Jebusites (JEB-u-zites)—Numbers 13:29—A mountain dwelling group who settled around Jebus, the ancient name of Jerusalem.

Amorites (AMM-oh-rights)—Numbers 13:29—A tribe of people scattered through much of Canaan. They were close kin to the Akkadians.

Canaanites (CANE-an-ites)—Numbers 13:29—One of the seven peoples to be displaced by Israel in Palestine.

LESSON OUTLINE

I. OPPORTUNITY GIVEN
   A. An Exploring Faith
   B. Wonderful Discoveries
II. FAITH OVERCOMES
   A. Human Assessments
   B. The Fear of Man
   C. The Vision of Faith
III. UNBELIEF HINDERS
   A. Loss of Faith
   B. Loss of Vision

LESSON EXPOSITION

INTRODUCTION

This powerful lesson provokes a challenge from God to each of us. We all face our decision points at Kadesh-Barnea. We all stand at the edge of great opportunity for God and must decide.

Israel's decision was to stand on the side of fear and unbelief. This lesson concludes with the sour warning of judgment for those who refuse to take advantage of the opportunities God declares in life.

I. OPPORTUNITY GIVEN (Numbers 13: 17-24)

A. An Exploring Faith (vv. 17-20)

The chapter begins with the assessment that God instructed Moses regarding this spy expedition. One leading member of each tribe was to be selected to go into the land of Canaan to search it out. The total number of men was 12 and they are named in 13:4-16.

The Jewish historian, Josephus, adds to our knowledge of this choosing and sending. His understanding of Moses' speech is: "Of the two things that God determined to bestow upon us, Liberty, and the Possession of a Happy Country, the one of them ye already are partakers of, by the gift of God, and the other you will quickly obtain; for we now have our abode near the border of the Canaanites, and nothing can hinder the acquisition of it." Moses' faith was absolutely certain in God's power to provide. He went on to say, "Not only no king nor city, but neither the whole race of mankind, if they were all gathered together could (hinder us). Let us then send spies, who may take a view of the goodness of the land, and what strength it is of; but, above all things, let us be of one mind, and let us honour God, who above all is our helper and assister."

Although not a major part of the biblical narrative, Josephus' account shows that Moses was completely in favor of God's proposal. He saw this as God's perfect will and encouraged the spies and the people to be faithful in this endeavor.

17. And Moses sent them to spy out the land of Canaan, and said unto them, Get you up this way southward, and go up into the mountain:

18. And see the land, what it is, and the people that dwelleth therein, whether they be strong or weak, few or many.

Moses instructed the twelve to go upward through the area called the *Negeb* (the Hebrew name *Negeb* means "south"). This area is south of Judah and the reference to the mountain refers to the hill country of southern Judah.

The command involved a thorough spying of the land. The land was to be analyzed in terms of geography and opportunity for harvesting and national growth. The peoples of the land were to be analyzed on the basis of their military might and the actual numbers of people.

19. And what the land is that they dwell in, whether it be good or bad; and what cities they be that they dwell in, whether in tents, or in strong holds;

20. And what the land is, whether it be fat or lean, whether there be wood therein, or not. And be ye of good courage, and bring of the fruit of the land. Now the time was the time of the firstripe grapes.

The issue of the land remained a primary concern for Moses. Note how practical is his interest: Does the land contain enough wood (forest) for cultivating trades?

He was also interested in what kinds of communal settlements the people lived in. This was necessary for making sound military decisions. If the people were tent people then they were nomadic and required great stretches of land for herding. If the land was dominated by cities then the people were more sedentary and required another type of strategy.

This is a good Old Testament illustration of counting the cost. Jesus spoke of this principle of living in Luke 14:25-33.

Two parables are used to describe the importance of understanding God's call and our commitment to the call. The first parable concerned a man who had begun a tower but failed to complete it after building the foundation. The people mocked his uncompleted effort. In terms of Christian life, it is important to realize that the end of Christian life is as important if not more so than the beginning of Christian life. There are countless people who have begun in Christ but failed to finish the course of faith. They accepted Christ only to alleviate guilt, but not to have Him exercise lordship. They are the people who want a fair share of the world and enough of Jesus to get to heaven.

The second parable related a king going to war and discovering the enemy was greater than he imagined. The wise outnumbered king finds a way to get a settled peace long before the opposing army recognizes how weak he is. Such a person is not mocked but has taken stock of reality.

Jesus introduces us to the world of *real faith* in these parables. It is the same world at work in Numbers 13. Faith is not God's invitation to an illusion; faith is not wishful thinking. Faith is rooted in God's reality expressed through His Word and command. It is not lack of faith to seriously weigh the cost of making a major move for God. That is wisdom for it commits the will and spirit together under God's promise. It becomes lack of faith when, after counting the cost, we fail to obey God's Word in spite of appearances.

God is looking for men and women who will claim hold of the future with wisdom and confidence. They are the dreamers who stake their claim in the reality of God's faithfulness. They are the people who measure success not by human standards but by divine standards. They are the people who have laid aside personal ambition for the sake of Christ.

Paul expressed this attitude in Philippians 3:7, 8: "Whatever was to my profit I now consider loss for the sake of Christ. What is more, I consider everything loss compared to the surpassing greatness of knowing Christ Jesus my Lord" (NIV).

The "land" was central in this journey of discovery. It was the land God had promised to the patriarch Abraham. It was expressed in Genesis 12:1, "Leave your country, your people and your father's household and go to the land I will show you" (NIV). Following that promise stood the theme of blessing for Abraham and the entire earth. Thus, the possession of the land was an integral part of the blessing for the world. The power of this connection of land and blessing in Israelite thought is expressed by Martin Buber: "The land is given to them (Israel) in common in order that in it and from it they may become a true national Community, a 'Holy People.' Such is the unfolding of the promise of Canaan to the Fathers, which had doubtless lived on in the Egyptians exile, even though almost forgotten. This earth, so Yahweh had promised the Fathers, He would give to their 'seed'; in order that they might become a . . . blessing power" (Moses: The Revelation and The Covenant).

Thus, to come to the land was to fulfill the ancient promise of God. To take the land was to verify that God was faithful. It put to the test the thesis: If God promises to give, He also promises the power to accomplish.

For God, the fact that Israel would be in Canaan would mean the existence of a "national Community" (to use Buber's phrase) that would be different from all the nations of the world. He, the Lord God, would be their King. Israel, living in the land God had given, would not be concerned with establishing a new land as much as being a place where God was praised for the sake of the entire world.

Verse 20 closed with Moses' words of encouragement "to be of good courage." The Interpreter's Bible suggests that "do your best" better catches the sense of the Hebrew. One thing is certain, it did take courage to go into a strange land and even return with the booty of the fruit of the land. The reference to the "firstripe grapes" indicates the season was in the month of July.

B. Wonderful Discoveries (vv. 21-24)

(Numbers 13:21-24 is not included in the printed text.)

The discoveries in the land are narrated in these verses. Coming northward through the Negeb they came to the ancient city of Hebron. This ancient city (founded about 1550 B.C.) was 19 miles south of Jerusalem and 13 miles southwest of Bethlehem. It is located in "a valley and has an unusually abundant water supply (wells and springs)" (Interpreter's Dictionary of the Bible).

There were clans of Hittites in the vicinity during the time of Abraham (2000-1800 B.C.) and the ancient site of Mamre was just north of the city (Genesis 13:18; 23:19; 35:27).

During the Israelite conquest of the land, Hebron was destroyed by Joshua. It was apparently reoccupied by clans of the Anakim and took a later action by Caleb to bring it under complete Israelite control (Joshua 14:13). It was a Levitical city and a city of refuge (Joshua 20:7; 21:10-13).

Throughout the story of David the city took on renewed prominence (2 Samuel 2:1 through 5:5; 1 Kings 2:11; 1 Chronicles 3:1-4; 29:27).

The biblical story in 13:22 indicates there were three tribes of the Anakim: Ahiman, Sheshai, and Talmai. The Interpreter's Dictionary of the Bible gives the following information of this tribe: "A tribe of pre-Israelite population in Palestine. In Hebrew tradition the Anakim are described as a tall people, whose gigantic size struck terror into the hearts of the Hebrews (Numbers 13:18; Deuteronomy 2:21; 9:2). In Numbers 13:33 they are described as descendents of the Nephilim, the offspring of the sons of God and the daughters of men (Genesis 6:4).

"The presence in Palestine about 2000 B.C. of a tribe Anak, whose princes have Semitic names, is attested by the Egyptian Execration Texts. These are pottery fragments bearing the names of the enemies of the pharaoh, who were ritually cursed with the breaking of the jar on which the curses were inscribed."

The story of their discoveries ends

with the description of the grapes the spies cut for transportation back to Kadesh. Josephus recorded concerning their findings: "They gave an account of the great quantity of the good things that land afforded, which were motives to the multitude to go to war."

The storehouse of God is filled with great and wonderful things for us in Christ. In many instances these include material blessings, but not exclusively. The primary blessings we have are spiritual and eternal in Christ. Isaiah indicates that the Lord "will be the sure foundation for your times, a rich store of salvation and wisdom and knowledge; the fear of the Lord is the key to this treasure" (*NIV*). The language in that verse points to the fact that God's storehouse is filled with all kinds of abundant treasures for our deliverance, help, and salvation. In fact, the focus is upon "salvations" in the plural. It shows God's mighty ability to deliver from any threat of sin if we will believe in Him as our stability.

II. FAITH OVERCOMES (Numbers 13: 25-30)

A. Human Assessments (vv. 25-27)

25. And they returned from searching of the land after forty days.

26. And they went and came to Moses, and to Aaron, and to all the congregation of the children of Israel, unto the wilderness of Paran, to Kadesh; and brought back word unto them, and unto all the congregation, and shewed them the fruit of the land.

27. And they told him, and said, We came unto the land whither thou sentest us, and surely it floweth with milk and honey; and this is the fruit of it.

The initial report of the twelve is couched in positive terms according to the biblical account. For the unsuspecting reader there is no hint of fear and unbelief. The land, which offered no opposition, was indeed a place of great fertility ("flowing with milk and honey"). Their 40-day journey had convinced them of its grandeur and opportunity.

Yet, there was something terribly amiss

about to interrupt the marvelous opportunity before them.

B. The Fear of Man (vv. 28, 29)

28. Nevertheless the people be strong that dwell in the land, and the cities are walled, and very great: and moreover we saw the children of Anak there.

29. The Amalekites dwell in the land of the south: and the Hittites, and the Jebusites, and the Amorites, dwell in the mountains: and the Canaanites dwell by the sea, and by the coast of Jordan.

Josephus reports, "But then they (the spies) terrified them (the people) again with the great difficulty there was in obtaining it; that the rivers were so large and deep that they could not be passed over; and that the hills were so high that they could not travel along for them; that the cities were strong with walls, and their firm fortifications round about them. They told them also, that they found at Hebron, the posterity of the giants. Accordingly these spies, who had seen the land of Canaan, when they perceived that all these difficulties were greater there than they had met with since they came out of Egypt, they were affrighted at them themselves, and endeavoured to affright the multitude also." He went on to tell how the people responded with fear and rebellion to this message. They were roused by their fear to try and kill Moses and Aaron and return back to Egyptian bondage!

There are three kinds of fear that operate in the world. The first is the "fear of the Lord" which indicates a humble attitude toward God in worship and action. It expresses adoration and obedience. From this spiritual fear comes spiritual power to walk in God's promise. The second is a natural fear that anyone should have. It expresses itself when a tire blows in a car driving 50 miles per hour. It expresses itself as a cautionary word asking for more information. Such a natural fear often operates under the direction of God. It does not paralyze human action but gives opportunity for reflection. It is often a preventative fear. The person tempted to sexual immorality in our generation might avoid the specific act because he/she is afraid of a sexually transmitted disease. Such a fear works to our benefit.

But the third fear is that which paralyzes the spirit and cast doubt upon the Word of God. It is born from Satan and has the purpose of disrupting and destroying. It is this fear which operated in the lives of 10 spies. Their natural fear of the giants was used by Satan to bring them to unbelief because the "fear of the Lord" did not control their life. They feared men more than they feared God! That is always the problem faced in unbelief. If Josephus is correct, they tried to cover their fear by inciting violence against Moses and Aaron and returning to Egypt.

There are many people who prefer to remain in the bonds of captivity rather than risk the opportunities of the future. Recently I heard a spin-off of the proverb, "Put your best foot forward." It spoke of people who "put their best foot forward but drag the other foot." They are people afraid of taking active responsibility for the future.

C. The Vision of Faith (v. 30)

30. And Caleb stilled the people before Moses, and said, Let us go up at once, and possess it; for we are well able to overcome it.

Caleb is the man who sees something and says "Why not?" He is a man of faith. His translated name is not particularly edifying: "dog of" or "slave of." Yet, it does signify a man who is bonded to his Lord. He was of the tribe of Judah and because of his faithfulness to the Lord, he was evoked as one who has "a different spirit and follows me wholeheartedly" (Numbers 14:24, NIV). Forty years later Caleb was responsible for pacifying the area of Hebron and putting an end to the feared Anakim.

He advocated immediate action. Caleb saw Canaan as ripe as the grapes insofar as conquest was concerned. He was able to see beyond the natural walls of the cities and envision the mighty presence of God. His expression, "we are well able to overcome it," does not signify pride in human terms but does indicate a confidence in the promise of God. He sensed that divine history was on his side and he was prepared to ride its wave.

There is an interesting comparison between the 12 spies and the 12 disciples of Jesus. Both groups were being introduced to a new reality. Both were given the opportunity to experience something of God never experienced before. Both were engaged in establishing a new kingdom. Both were called to possess promises from God. Both had problems with doubt; both had individuals who rose to the occasion in faith.

In James 1:2-8 we find an excellent New Testament commentary on the problem of trials and the promise of faith. The 12 spies had come across a trial. They failed to count it as joy in the Lord and receded from the opportunity. They did not accept that the testing of their faith, if they obeyed, would lead to their stable presence in the land. They feared they would be lacking in everything rather than trusting in God's promise they would "lack nothing."

In James 1:6 we are told how to ask for wisdom. The answer is to ask in faith. The wisdom of God revealed to us is our discernment of the things God is seeking to accomplish. The 10 unbelieving spies not only lacked faith; they also lacked wisdom—they could not discern God's purposes. James taught that if we ask in faith without doubting then God's purposes will be revealed to us in order that we may obey and God be glorified.

James went on to indicate that the man who lacks faith is completely out of control in life. The Greek is powerful in this passage. It shows that the double-minded person is unstable; he has no sense of control or discipline. He is the person carried by the currents of the world rather than the wind of the Spirit. It is clear from James 1:8 that the man who follows the currents of the world will not receive anything from the Lord. Such was the final result for those 10 spies, and the people of Israel, who allowed themselves to be caught in the currents of the world rather than walking in faith into the Promised Land.

III. UNBELIEF HINDERS (Numbers 13: 31-33)

A. Loss of Faith (v. 31)

31. But the men that went up with him said, We be not able to go up against the people; for they are stronger than we.

Caleb's voice was not heard in the face of fear. There comes a time when solitary voices of faith cannot carry the entire people. It becomes the responsibility of the people to bear the reproach of their continued unbelief. According to Numbers 14, Joshua continued the pleading of Caleb regarding the taking of the land. Yet, the people were stubborn and rebellious.

It should be noted that the response of the 10 spies in verse 31 indicates a setting where a debate took place. As Caleb argued, "Let's go up at once," they argued, "We are not able to go up." As Caleb argued, "We are well able to overcome it," they argued, "They are stronger than we."

The unbelief of the 10 spies is centralized in their assessment of the strength of the people. They are convinced that the Lord God is not sufficient in strength and power to give them victory. They have believed that men are stronger than God. How tragic it would have been for the gospel if Peter had felt it was more important to obey men than God (Acts 5:29). While Peter and the apostles remained faithful to the Lord in the early church, there are many in the twentieth century church who believe the ways of man are greater than the ways of God.

The New Testament teaches that "greater is he that is in you, than he that is in the world" (1 John 4:4). Paul did not underestimate the power of darkness in the world; but he did not underestimate the power of God either. In Ephesians 6:10 he instructed Christians to "grow strong in the Lord, with the strength of His power" (*Jerusalem Bible*). Paul believed that the powers of men would learn of the power of God as the church bore faithful witness to that power (Ephesians 3:10).

That God is powerful is a source of great hope to the Christian. Our hope is founded on the reality that God is almighty. Such a hope enables us to stand firm in faith regardless of the human situation. The human situation is not the final word for the Christian; God's power is that final word.

B. Loss of Vision (vv. 32, 33)

32. And they brought up an evil report of the land which they had searched unto the children of Israel, saying, The land, through which we have gone to search it, is a land that eateth up the inhabitants thereof; and all the people that we saw in it are men of great stature.

When people fail to obey God, excuses must be offered to justify the sin. Two excuses are presented in this verse. The first borders on a blatant lie. It is suggested by the spies that the land cannot support more population. The expression "eateth up the inhabitants" has the sense of a land unable to produce sufficient food for adequate living. However, their earlier report indicated just the opposite. It was indeed a land flowing with milk and honey and was everything God promised it to be.

What a terrible fix sin does to us! The very beauty of God's order is defamed because of our rebellion. We live in a world that calls the things of God "old-fashioned" and calls sin "modern." Our world takes the promised bliss of faithful marriage and offers a steady diet of television infidelity as the model of a happy life. Our world teaches that drugs and alcohol are the ways to "get all the gusto" from life and that the abstainer is some type of weakling. The world accepts that lies and deception are the real tools of business and that people who live by truth do not rise up the corporate steps.

The second lie is of the people in the land. Not only have they been described in verse 31 as too strong, they are described as simply too large. Verse 33 further clarifies this lie.

33. And there we saw the giants, the sons of Anak, which come of the giants: and we were in our own sight as grasshoppers, and so we were in their sight.

Nothing more quickly and thoroughly devastates the God-ordained human image than unbelief and the accompanying lies. To live a lie in the face of God's clear promised opportunity is to belittle oneself to the level of a grasshopper.

Their self-analysis of grasshopperitis is based on the deadly combination of fear of man and lying to God. They were men born to be great in faith but instead became insignificant wilderness rats.

It is important to notice how verse 33 presents this situation. It does not say that the giants first considered the spies to be grasshoppers; that is, insignificant. Rather, the doubt began within each of them. They first considered themselves grasshoppers and then projected that lowly image onto the giants in the land.

Self-image is extremely important. So important that the Bible does not even get past Genesis 1 before affirming that God made man in His image (vv. 26, 27). It was not God's will for these men to forget who they were. But they forgot who they were because they forgot who God was. When men forget God they also lose contact with their true humanity. The man meant for courage and obedience becomes the man struggling in fear and self-doubt. The man facing moral choices that require a noble heart becomes a man looking for the easy, quick answer.

Such loss of vision leads to a terrible form of idolatry: men of unbelief turn to other men to define their status in the world. It matters little whether it be the teenager who looks to the rock star for identity, or the successful business person who looks to the stock market for identity. Both are living in the nightmare of hell's loss of vision.

REVIEW QUESTIONS

1. Why is "counting the cost" so important in the Christian life?

2. According to Jesus, what distinguishes "faith" from "fantasy"?

3. What are three types of fear in human experience?

4. How did unbelief lead to a lying perception of the self among the spies?

GOLDEN TEXT HOMILY

"WITHOUT FAITH IT IS IMPOSSIBLE TO PLEASE HIM: FOR HE THAT COMETH TO GOD MUST BELIEVE THAT HE IS, AND THAT HE IS A REWARDER OF THEM THAT DILIGENTLY SEEK HIM" (Hebrews 11:6).

In Hebrews 11, the great chapter on faith, there are many mountain peaks of inspiration that reach high into the purified atmosphere of God's divine power. Our Golden Text is certainly one of them. This verse actually teaches us that we can bring pleasure to our heavenly Father by simply believing Him.

Verse 5 tells us of Enoch, one man who had the testimony that he pleased God. How? Enoch walked with God in faith (Genesis 5:24). It's just that simple—developing a relationship of trust and fellowship with God just as a son would have with his earthly father. This text shows us the way to do this.

First, we must believe that God really exists. There are three special ways to do this. We come to God through His Word, through worship, and through prayer.

Next, we must believe He keeps His promises; that "he is a rewarder of them that diligently seek him." Diligence in our seeking God is like Enoch walking with God continually. As Corrie ten Boon said, it is not a matter of having "great faith in God, but of having faith in a great God."

Believing God pleases Him. The passage in Hebrews 10:38 tells us that God has no pleasure in the person who shrinks back from Him in fear and unbelief. But He does have pleasure in the person who simply believes Him. In fact, He welcomes us to approach His throne with boldness, "that we may obtain mercy, and find grace to help in time of need" (Hebrews 4:16).—**F. J. May, M.Div., Associate Professor, Church of God School of Theology, Cleveland, Tennessee**

SENTENCE SERMONS

AS WE EXERCISE our faith in God, He leads us in victorious living.

—Selected

LOVE IS the crowning grace in heaven; but faith is the conquering grace on earth.

—Thomas Watson

HE WHO HAS conquered doubt and fear has conquered failure.

—James Allen

FAITH CAN PLACE a candle in the darkest night.

—Margaret E. Sangster

EVANGELISTIC APPLICATION

THROUGH FAITH THE REPENTANT SINNER RECEIVES SALVATION.

Only faith in Christ enables the sinner to see who he really is. As the Holy Spirit convicts of sin, the sinner recognizes his life is at war with God. He recognizes that there is truly a Creator and that he is not alone in this universe.

The sinner, led by the Spirit, sees Jesus as God's Son and as the Son of Man. As Son of God the sinner recognizes in Christ the power to liberate from sin; in Christ as Son of Man, the sinner sees his own sin taken on the Cross.

It is at the Cross the sinner realizes he was not destined for eternal damnation but was destined for eternal life. The longing heart realizes it is not the miserable piece of worthless soil portrayed by Satan but it is so important to its Creator God that God sent His only Son to die!

The repentant heart discovers the joy of finding its true life in Christ. It is a time of discovery; a time of humble submission to the Lord who gives true worth. It is a thankful time to be restored to glory as a person of faith.

ILLUMINATING THE LESSON

In 1858, the Reverend George Duffield wrote the hymn "Stand Up, Stand Up for Jesus" in memory of his friend Dudley Tyng. Tyng was an Episcopalian minister whose fervent preaching stirred the city of Philadelphia. On March 30 of that year Tyng preached to over 5000 men from the text "Ye that are men . . . serve the Lord" (Exodus 10:11). The message was filled with convicting power and Tyng remarked that "I must tell my Master's errand, and I would rather that this right arm were amputated at the trunk, than that I should come short of my duty to you in delivering God's message.

Barely a week later, while tending the family farm, his right arm was severely damaged in an accident. A little later it had to be amputated and, because of the shock to his body, the young minister died. On his deathbed he spoke to his godly father, "Stand up for Jesus; father, stand up for Jesus; and tell my brethren of the ministry, wherever you meet them, to stand up for Jesus!"

Duffield preached the next week from Ephesians 6:14, "Stand therefore, having your loins girt about with the truth." At the close of his sermon, he read the words of the poem he had written in memory of his friend, "Stand Up, Stand Up for Jesus."—**From *Crusader Hymns and Hymn Stories.***

DAILY BIBLE READINGS

M. Faith Answers Fear. Psalm 11:1-7

T. Faith Brings Victory. 1 Samuel 17:31-50

W. Faith Provides Confidence. 2 Chronicles 14:8-15

T. Faith Gives Boldness. Acts 4:23-31

F. Faith Inspires Endurance. Hebrews 11:32-40

S. Faith Overcomes the World. 1 John 5:1-6

Missed Opportunities

Study Text: Numbers 14:1-38

Supplemental References: Joshua 14:6-14; Psalm 95:7-11; Habakkuk 3:16-19; Hebrews 4:1-9

Time: Scholars differ on the date of the events recorded in Numbers, but a general range of dates from 1448-1441 B.C. is acceptable.

Place: Wilderness of Paran

Golden Text: "The Lord is longsuffering, and of great mercy, forgiving iniquity and transgression, and by no means clearing the guilty" (Numbers 14:18).

Central Truth: Failure to act in faith deprives the Christian of full possession of God's blessings.

Evangelistic Emphasis: Unbelief will cause a person to lose his soul.

Printed Text

Numbers 14:7. And they spake unto all the company of the children of Israel, saying, The land, which we passed through to search it, is an exceeding good land.

8. If the Lord delight in us, then he will bring us into this land, and give it us; a land which floweth with milk and honey.

9. Only rebel not ye against the Lord, neither fear ye the people of the land; for they are bread for us: their defence is departed from them, and the Lord is with us: fear them not.

10. But all the congregation bade stone them with stones. And the glory of the Lord appeared in the tabernacle of the congregation before all the children of Israel.

11. And the Lord said unto Moses, How long will this people provoke me? and how long will it be ere they believe me, for all the signs which I have shewed among them?

12. I will smite them with the pestilence, and disinherit them, and will make of thee a greater nation and mightier than they.

17. And now, I beseech thee, let the power of my Lord be great, according as thou hast spoken, saying,

18. The Lord is longsuffering, and of great mercy, forgiving iniquity and transgression, and by no means clearing the guilty, visiting the iniquity of the fathers upon the children unto the third and fourth generation.

19. Pardon, I beseech thee, the iniquity of this people according unto the greatness of thy mercy, and as thou hast forgiven this people, from Egypt even until now.

20. And the Lord said, I have pardoned according to thy word:

21. But as truly as I live, all the earth shall be filled with the glory of the Lord.

22. Because all those men which have seen my glory, and my miracles, which I did in Egypt and in the wilderness, and have tempted me now

70

these ten times, and have not hearkened to my voice;

23. Surely they shall not see the land which I sware unto their fathers, neither shall any of them that provoked me see it:

30. Doubtless ye shall not come into the land, concerning which I sware to make you dwell therein, save Caleb the son of Jephunneh, and Joshua the son of Nun.

31. But you little ones, which ye said should be a prey, them will I bring in, and they shall know the land which ye have despised.

LESSON OUTLINE

I. GOD'S PLAN REJECTED
  A. Faith in God's Promise
  B. Plea for Obedience
  C. God's Swift Judgment
II. CONSEQUENCES OF UNBELIEF
  A. Moses' Intercession
  B. God's Character Revealed
  C. God's Judgment Revealed
III. FAITH REWARDED
  A. Joy of Obedience
  B. Fruit of Obedience

LESSON EXPOSITION

INTRODUCTION

We continue the lesson of last week by looking at the missed opportunities of the children of Israel. This centers around the adoption by the people of the report of the Doubting Ten spies. The people accepted their report as a majority report when it was actually, in God's sight, a minority report. The report of Joshua and Caleb, while popularly received as a minority report, was truly the majority report of the will of God!

Much of the previous lesson examined the fears and unbelief of the Doubting Ten. A major part of this lesson will examine the basis for courage and faith. The modern Greek poet, Cavafy, wrote *Ithaka*, describing the home of Ulysses,

When you set out for Ithaka
ask that your way be long,
full of adventure, full of instruction.
The Laestrygonians and the Cyclops,
angry Poseidon-do not fear them:
such as these you will never find
as long as your thought is lofty,
as long as a rare emotion
touch your spirit and your body.
The Laestrygonians and the Cyclops,
angry Poseidon-you will not meet them

unless you carry them in your soul,
unless your soul raise them up before you.

The Laestrygonians were a savage, cannibalistic tribe defeated by Ulysses on his long journey home from the Trojan War. The Cyclops was the one-eyed monster, son of the sea-god Poseidon, who was slain by Ulysses.

Cavafy caught the spirit of faith by sensing the "rare emotion" that overcomes despair. This "rare emotion" is that "different spirit" of Caleb described in Numbers 14:24. It is the spirit of the person who carries faith in his soul. The person who carries fear and unbelief in his soul discovers that those enemies rise up to oppose the will of God.

I. GOD'S PLAN REJECTED (Numbers 14: 6-12)

Numbers 13, 14 should be read together. The poor self-image of the ten spies poured across the people as they accepted that image for themselves (13:33; 14:1). The people wept throughout the night as they lamented their plight. What wasted grief and tears poured in the wilderness that night! These were needless tears; they were shed because of unbelief. Such weeping did not lead to repentance but led to murmuring and sin. The Apostle Paul in 2 Corinthians 7:10 pointed out that "worldly grief" produces death while "godly grief" produces a repentance that leads to salvation and brings no regret."

The remorse-filled crowd wept over their lost future. Their hearts were filled with fear and doubt. The only hope they saw was to return to Egypt. Verse 4 expressed vividly their desire, "Let us make a captain, and let us return to Egypt." Their decision was not birthed in repentance but in remorse. They regretted God and His servants. Their remorse led to full-scale rebellion in God's sight. Such rebellion ignored everything of the promises of God and the actual acts of deliverance He had performed.

A. Faith in God's Promise (vv. 6-8)

(Numbers 14:6 is not included in the printed text.)

7. And they spake unto all the company of the children of Israel, saying, The land, which we passed through to search it, is an exceeding good land.

8. If the Lord delight in us, then he will bring us into this land, and give it us; a land which floweth with milk and honey.

Joshua and Caleb stood before the congregation of doubters and expressed deep repentance by tearing their clothes (v. 6). By tearing their clothes these two men expressed horror at what the ten spies had told and what the people were doing in rejecting God's will.

Joshua and Caleb rejected the lie of the ten spies that the land "eateth" the inhabitants (13:32). The Hebrew of verse 7 in describing the land as "exceeding good" is similar to God's description of His creation in Genesis 1:31, "very good." Thus, the men of faith were affirming that the goodness of the land was ultimately a reflection of the goodness of God. To challenge the land as the ten doubters did, was to challenge the goodness of God. Caleb and Joshua saw through the superficiality of the unbelief concerning the land and recognized that faith in God was the central issue.

The use of the Hebrew "delight" in verse 8 is interesting. Its further use in the Old Testament illustrates in what way God delights in us. David, in 2 Samuel 22:20, remarked that God's delight was shown in the fact that He delivered him. The passages in 1 Kings 10:9 and 2 Chronicles 9:8 both echo the praise of the Queen of Sheba who saw in Solomon's wisdom a manifestation of God's delight. The theme of deliverance expressed by David in 2 Samuel 22:20 is affirmed in Psalms 18:19 and 22:8. God's promise of restoration to defeated Judah is expressed by Isaiah 62:4. Of special note is Jeremiah 9:23, 24 where the Lord expressed that God delights in the following: (1) man understands and knows

God; (2) God practices steadfast love, justice, and righteousness. God's delight in His steadfast love is the theme of Micah 7:18.

When applied to the opportunity facing the tribes, God's delight would have been manifested in His power to give them the land, to preserve them in the land, and to reveal His steadfast love in every phase of their national and individual life. The tragedy is that these people preferred the slavery of Egypt to the delight of God's place.

But Caleb and Joshua remain for us shining models of men who trusted in God. That trust proved to be the one thing that enabled them to live to see God's promise fulfilled.

B. Plea for Obedience (v. 9)

9. Only rebel not ye against the Lord, neither fear ye the people of the land; for they are bread for us: their defence is departed from them, and the Lord is with us: fear them not.

Caleb and Joshua mustered every argument possible to sway the people to obedience. They clearly understood that the people were in rebellion. We know that those who are living in rebellion will not inherit the kingdom of God. Rebellion is man's clear decision to disregard God's will.

In our world we find pleasant expressions to cover what constitutes the reality of this rebellion. We excuse people by suggesting they are trying to "find themselves." We say that people should "make up their own minds." We indicate that it does not really matter what you do as long as it doesn't hurt anyone else and brings you pleasure. That is the philosophy of the world and it is nothing short of rebellion against God. All the excuses offered in our world will count for nothing on the day of judgment. Paul knew that God is not mocked. People who live in disregard of God's law will bring upon themselves their due penalty (Galatians 6:7; Romans 1:27).

Twice the people are admonished not to fear. The Gospels frequently tell us that Jesus commanded fear to cease (Matthew 10:26, 28, 31; Luke 5:10; 8:50; 12:7, 32). The angels also spoke God's Word in commanding fear to cease (Matthew 1:20; 28:5; Luke 1:13, 30; 2:10).

The Book of Revelation records the triumphant Christ speaking to the church concerning fear (1:17; 2:10; 14:7).

The reason the command to "fear not" was so strong for Caleb and Joshua is because they believed God's promise of victory. They spiritually discerned that the people of the land were already a defeated host. Faith enabled them to see three things: (1) their enemies are nothing more than bread to them, (2) their enemies have no defense (protection), (3) the Lord is with people of faith whom He has called. What a contrast this is between the Doubting Ten who saw themselves as grasshoppers in the land and imposed that view upon the people of the land, and Caleb and Joshua who knew they were more than overcomers in God's promise and saw the people of the land as defeated!

Each of the three insights provided by faith deserves further comment.

1. The assessment that their enemies provided bread for them illustrates the principle that the trials of life are meant to enhance our life. Paul wrote in Romans 5:3-5 that "suffering produces perseverance; perseverance, character; and character, hope. And hope does not disappoint us, because God has poured out his love into our hearts by the Holy Spirit, whom he has given us" (Romans 5:3-5; New International Version). Even the temptations that Satan brings our way are meant to be avenues of growth in that we learn to trust God who provides a way of escape that we may endure.

There are people who opt for the easy way of life. They avoid commitments and choose to live on the surface. The hurdles of life that rise before them quickly turn them away and they choose the low road of life instead of the high road of God's purposes. They avoid opportunity if it smacks of labor. They are the people who are never satisfied. They carry a spiritual and emotional hunger because the very "bread" they are to eat has been bypassed too often.

2. The two faithful spies saw the people of the land as defenseless. While the ten saw giants, the two saw giants about to fall; while the ten saw fortified cities standing firm, the two saw walls waiting

for the sounds of trumpets so they could crumble.

The Fall 1986 issue of *Leadership* has an article titled "Facing the Wreckage of Evil." In the article two pastors observed: "We don't operate *toward* victory; we operate out of victory. Christ won an absolute victory at the Cross." And "I'm impressed by Paul's attitude in Romans, his major work. Only twice does he make reference to the devil, and in both cases he is pointing to the devil's weakness. He uses the term *principalities* in Romans 8: no 'principalities . . . will be able to separate us from God's love.' And then in the sixteenth chapter: it is God's will to 'crush Satan under your feet.' "

Those quotes capture the faith expressed by Joshua and Caleb. From our New Testament perspective we know that sin has been dealt a mortal blow in the death and resurrection of Jesus Christ. Paul affirmed that Christ set aside the demands of the law of sin and death by "nailing it to the cross" and He "disarmed the powers and authorities, he made a public spectacle of them" (Colossians 2:14, 15; *NIV*). John spoke as forcefully in 1 John 5:4, 5: "For everyone born of God overcomes the world. This is the victory that has overcome the world, even our faith. Who is it that overcomes the world? Only he who believes that Jesus is the Son of God" (*NIV*).

3. "The Lord is with us" is the confessional cry of Christianity. We affirm that Jesus is truly "Emmanuel: God with us." Joshua and Caleb did not serve an abstract God who was a divine idea; they served the living God of history who controls the events of this world and beckons humanity to accept His will. That faith is our faith today as we believe that Christ is truly alive and present with us through His Word, the Holy Spirit, and the communion of saints.

C. God's Swift Judgment (vv. 10-12)

10. But all the congregation bade stone them with stones. And the glory of the Lord appeared in the tabernacle of the congregation before all the children of Israel.

11. And the Lord said unto Moses,

How long will this people provoke me? and how long will it be ere they believe me, for all the signs which I have shewed among them?

12. I will smite them with the pestilence, and disinherit them, and will make of thee a greater nation and mightier than they.

This is the second time this quarter we have seen God prepared to "give this people up" and make of Moses a new people. It is also the second time we have seen Moses intercede for the people (see Lesson 4; Exodus 32, 33). The intercession of Moses will be discussed in the next section. However, it is clear that God's wrath is a holy wrath. Verse 10 reveals that God manifested Himself in the Tabernacle. What an irony this is! The people in Exodus 35 are of a willing spirit to give for the purposes of God's dwelling. The people are given Spirit-filled and anointed leadership. They apparently obey God in every detail of the work and the presence of His glory reveals His pleasure with them. Yet, it shows that man can do all the right things on the outside but still be filled with the seeds of unbelief in his soul.

II. CONSEQUENCES OF UNBELIEF (Numbers 14:13-23)

A. Moses' Intercession (vv. 13-23)

(Numbers 14:13-16 is not included in the printed text.)

As in his previous intercession, Moses was concerned with the glory of God's name among the nations. His argument with God centered around what the nations would think of such a God who would lead people from bondage, reveal Himself to them, manifest mighty signs in their midst, lead them by the cloud of His presence, *and then* destroy them in the wilderness.

This concern for God's name is rooted in Moses' concern for the promise of God through Abraham, Isaac, and Jacob. As before, the Lord would still be faithful to that promise by making the nation great through Moses' line; yet, Moses beckoned God to remember His mighty acts of deliverance.

B. God's Character Revealed (vv. 17-19)

17. And now, I beseech thee, let the power of my Lord be great, according as thou hast spoken, saying,

18. The Lord is longsuffering, and of great mercy, forgiving iniquity and transgression, and by no means clearing the guilty, visiting the iniquity of the fathers upon the children unto the third and fourth generation.

19. Pardon, I beseech thee, the iniquity of this people according unto the greatness of thy mercy, and as thou hast forgiven this people, from Egypt even until now.

Moses turned to the heart of God to intercede for the people. He turned to God's power as the source of God's compassion. He knew that a God powerful enough to divide the Red Sea could turn aside from eternal destruction of His people.

There are two sides to God's character revealed in these verses. They are not contradictory sides; rather, they reflect the reality of God's holiness. His holiness is expressed in relation to His love and wrath. Because He is a holy and loving God, He can forgive iniquity and be of great mercy. But also, just because He is holy and loving, He cannot ignore sin and simply turn aside.

Thus, the guilty (that is, those who refuse to repent) bring upon themselves God's wrath. That wrath extends into the future. The young person who thinks he can live in the world of drugs with no effect on the future is in for a terrible shock. There are thousands of babies born as drug addicts from their mother's womb. They are innocent victims of their parents' sin that reaches into the future. There are adults who destroy their homes by infidelity or alcohol abuse and send the waves of sin's effect reaching into their children and grandchildren.

Moses began his request by calling upon the Lord to "pardon" the iniquity of the people. The Hebrew "pardon" has the sense of "pass over." It is found in several key places in the Old Testament. Among those are Exodus 34:6-9 (which parallels the language of Numbers 14 closely); Nehemiah 9:17 used it to describe God's action toward the people as they rebelled against the Lord in the wilderness; Psalm 25:11 shows the effect of this pardon upon the individual for the sake of the Lord's name. The same thought is found in Isaiah 55:7 and the passages in Jeremiah 5:1, 7; 50:20 also give important insight into the nature of God's pardon. There is a passage in 2 Kings 24:4 that shows there is a limit to God's desire to pardon. In that case the Lord vows He will not pardon the sins of the evil Judean king Manasseh.

Moses' plea did not ignore the reality of the sin of the people. He remarked in verse 19 that the people had constantly rebelled against the Lord, yet, He had faithfully forgiven and given guidance.

C. God's Judgment Revealed (vv. 20-23)

20. And the Lord said, I have pardoned according to thy word:

21. But as truly as I live, all the earth shall be filled with the glory of the Lord.

22. Because all those men which have seen my glory, and my miracles, which I did in Egypt and in the wilderness, and have tempted me now these ten times, and have not hearkened to my voice;

23. Surely they shall not see the land which I sware unto their fathers, neither shall any of them that provoked me see it.

The act of pardon from God was in relation to His initial statement to completely destroy the people and build a new people from Moses. But it should be noticed that God pardoned in response to Moses' word (v. 20).

This power of Moses' intercession points to an aspect of biblical faith seldom emphasized in evangelical circles: the power of the Christian in prayer before God. It is clearly expressed in the New Testament in Matthew 16:19 (with the power of the keys) and in John 20:22, 23 (with the power of the Holy Spirit). In both passages there is affirmed the tremendous power of the Christian to intercede in behalf of the sinner. God does listen to our prayers. Intercessory prayer is predicated on the assumption that God really does listen. If that were not the case then all prayer would be meaningless human projection upon an empty universe. But it is true: God answers prayer and we can intercede boldly for the sake of Christ and righteousness in the world.

Verses 21-23 reveal that behind God's wrath and judgment stand His glory. Israel was meant to be the people who would show God's glory on the basis of their obedience. God is so committed to the integrity of His Word and will that He even used Israel's disobedience to manifest His glory to the earth.

The beauty of that commitment is seen in the fact that God's glory was revealed in Christ Jesus. Paul's argument in Romans 9-11 shows that God's commitment will not be ultimately thwarted by the will of man. In Romans 11:28 Paul wrote that the Jews are enemies of God regarding the gospel (that is, regarding Jesus Christ); yet, God loves the Jews because of His covenant election with the patriarchs.

God was not bound to a course of redemption that depended solely on Jewish obedience. From the foundation of the world, the Son of God was prepared as the Lamb slain to come forth and use Israel's disobedience for the glory of God.

Paul was so convinced of the glory of God being revealed through Israel that he pointedly observed that if salvation came to the Gentiles through Israel's disobedience, then just imagine how much more the world will be blessed when Israel is fully included in God's kingdom (Romans 11:11, 12).

III. FAITH REWARDED (Numbers 14:24, 30, 31, 38)

A. Joy of Obedience (v. 24)

(Numbers 14:24 is not included in the printed text.)

The preceding verses concluded with the sentence of death upon all who rebelled against God in siding with the Doubting Ten. This verse shows that God does reward the obedient.

Do you remember the line from Cavafy's poem, "as long as your thought is lofty, as long as a rare emotion touch your spirit and your body"? That attitude is reflected in the biblical witness with the expression "another spirit." The *New International Version* offers the translation, "a different spirit." The spirit that Caleb had in his heart was the willingness to obey God. God spoke that Caleb had "followed me fully."

The joy that Caleb experienced was in ultimately receiving the land he had seen. According to Hebrews 12:2 Jesus "endured the cross, despising the shame," because of the joy that was set before Him.

Christian joy is not based on the instant gratification of our society. Christian joy is "eschatological" in that it looks forward to the future God has ordained. Christian joy does not rest in the stock market but abides in the promise of God. Christian joy is completely in touch with reality and understands suffering to have a greater purpose in life.

B. Fruit of Obedience (vv. 30, 31, 38)

30. Doubtless ye shall not come into the land, concerning which I sware to make you dwell therein, save Caleb the son of Jephunneh, and Joshua the son of Nun.

31. But your little ones, which ye said should be a prey, them will I bring in, and they shall know the land which ye have despised.

38. But Joshua the son of Nun, and Caleb the son of Jephunneh, which were of the men that went to search the land, lived still.

The preceding verses indicated God's specific judgment upon those who rebelled. Verses 36 and 37 show that the Doubting Ten died by a plague sent by God.

But Joshua and Caleb were promised new life in the land (v. 30).

Verse 31 reflects the view propagated by the spies that if they went into the land their children would be prey to the giants. Here God affirms that He will take care of the children and they shall indeed inherit the land of promise.

There is no doubt that obedience to God sets in motion principles that affect our life. Obedience in the family by parents will impact the lives of children. Christian parents must understand they are building a "spiritual" future for their children that is far more important than any human inheritance. When parents manifest humble, loving obedience to

the Lord, children sense it in their spirit and their hearts are turned to God.

REVIEW QUESTIONS

1. How would you describe that "rare emotion" or "different spirit" manifested by Caleb?

2. What are the ways God "delights" in us?

3. How are the problems of life confronted victoriously by people of faith?

4. How does the "wrath of God" reveal God's character?

5. How does Paul show in Romans 11 the way God turned Israel's disobedience to His advantage?

GOLDEN TEXT HOMILY

THE LORD IS LONGSUFFERING, AND OF GREAT MERCY, FORGIVING INIQUITY AND TRANSGRESSION, AND BY NO MEANS CLEARING THE GUILTY" (Numbers 14:18).

It is refreshing to read about a man who can see as clear as Moses can at this point in his life. Even in the midst of great rebellion on the part of Israel when only a few stand with him to follow God's directions, we see a man who knows what to do. He prays! Not just any prayer! This was a situation that just any prayer would not be enough.

Moses knew God and he also loved Israel. At a time when God seemed ready to let all Israel die in their rebellion and build "a nation greater and mightier than them," Moses was able to respond to God's will and pray the right prayer. He began to pray God's Word. He quoted God. He remembered what God said in Exodus 34:6, 7, "And the Lord passed before him and proclaimed, 'The Lord, the Lord God, merciful and gracious, long-suffering, and abounding in goodness and truth, keeping mercy for thousands, forgiving iniquity and transgression and sin, by no means clearing the guilty, visiting the iniquity of the fathers upon the children and the children's children to the third and the fourth generation' " (*NKJV*). God responded immediately. Then the Lord said, "I have pardoned, according to your word; but truly, as I live, all the earth shall be filled with the glory of the Lord" (Numbers 14:20, 21; *NKJV*).

The Lord God answered the prayer of Moses immediately.

There are many lessons for us from these scriptures but the one that helps the most with our walk through life in facing all the crises that come is knowing God's Word and the ability to pray the right prayer. Whenever we are able to quote God's Word as our prayer, we are praying God's will for that situation. —**Levy E. Moore, Director of Admissions, Emmanuel College, Franklin Springs, Georgia**

SENTENCE SERMONS

FAILURE TO ACT in faith deprives the Christian of full possession of God's blessings.

—**Selected**

OBEDIENCE IS the fruit of faith; patience the bloom on the fruit.

—**Christina Rossetti**

THE DOORS of opportunity are marked "push."

—**"Speaker's Sourcebook"**

OPPORTUNITY IS often lost by deliberation.

—**"Speaker's Sourcebook"**

EVANGELISTIC APPLICATION

UNBELIEF WILL CAUSE A PERSON TO LOSE HIS SOUL.

The sinner who rejects the gospel in this life is not given another opportunity after death.

There are numerous views trying to get around this unalterable fact. Some use reincarnation; others claim a just God will not allow hell to exist; others simply do not believe in life after death.

Yet the truth remains these are all deceptions of Satan. Unbelief, regardless of its rational basis, will not stand in the judgment before God.

Many have heard the gospel and have gone into eternity having missed their opportunity for eternal bliss. God in His mercy provides many opportunities for people to hear of His great love. In almost any point in the world the gospel can be heard via radio signal. Those who live in the so-called "Western world" have the advantage of television and a never-ending abundance of written communication.

Yet, in spite of that, there are thousands who fail to take seriously the gospel and will miss their opportunities for everlasting life with Christ.

ILLUMINATING THE LESSON

Most Christians know someone who simply refuses to acknowledge Christ as Savior. In a recent evangelistic outreach into local shopping centers I was amazed at the number of senior adults who did not know Christ and had no interest in the gospel.

I talked with an old farmer sitting in his truck. He knew of Jesus, having lived in the Bible belt; but, he indicated he had no desire to ask forgiveness of sins. I said, "Don't you know that if you died today you would be lost forever?" He answered yes but shrugged his shoulders.

That shrug still stands in my memory. What will God say to the shrugs of unconcern in eternity?

At a camp meeting I spoke with an older man during an altar service. He was clearly under conviction and, at eighty years old, knew his days were numbered. He also expressed knowledge of his sins but would not accept Christ as Savior. After prayer and expressing my love I walked from him fearing I would see him again in a casket—a man who missed opportunities graciously given but tragically ignored.

DAILY BIBLE READINGS

M. Accepting the Challenge. Joshua 14:6-14

T. Hearing God's Voice. Psalm 95:7-11

W. Rejoicing in God. Habakkuk 3:16-19

T. Receiving the Promise. Romans 4:13-25

F. Keeping a Responsive Heart. Hebrews 3:7-19

S. Entering Into Rest. Hebrews 4:1-9

God's Cure for Sin

Study Text: Numbers 21:1-35; John 3:14-21

Supplemental References: Deuteronomy 8:11-20; 2 Kings 18:1-4; Psalm 78:12-31; John 12:27-33; 1 Corinthians 10:1-13; Hebrews 12:1-3

Time: Around 1407 B.C.

Place: Mount Hor and surrounding wilderness

Golden Text: "As Moses lifted up the serpent in the wilderness, even so must the Son of man be lifted up: That whosoever believeth in him should not perish, but have eternal life" (John 3:14, 15).

Central Truth: Christ died on the Cross to provide deliverance from sin for all who believe.

Evangelistic Emphasis: Christ died on the Cross to provide deliverance from sin for all who believe.

Printed Text

Numbers 21:4. And they journeyed from mount Hor by the way of the Red sea, to compass the land of Edom: and the soul of the people was much discouraged because of the way.

5. And the people spake against God, and against Moses, Wherefore have ye brought us up out of Egypt to die in the wilderness? for there is no bread, neither is there any water; and our soul loatheth this light bread.

6. And the Lord sent fiery serpents among the people, and they bit the people; and much people of Israel died.

7. Therefore the people came to Moses, and said, We have sinned, for we have spoken against the Lord, and against thee; pray unto the Lord, that he take away the serpents from us. And Moses prayed for the people.

8. And the Lord said unto Moses, Make thee a fiery serpent, and set it upon a pole: and it shall come to pass, that every one that is bitten, when he looketh upon it, shall live.

9. And Moses made a serpent of brass, and put it upon a pole, and it came to pass, that if a serpent had bitten any man, when he beheld the serpent of brass, he lived.

John 3:14. And as Moses lifted up the serpent in the wilderness, even so must the Son of man be lifted up:

15. That whosoever believeth in him should not perish, but have eternal life.

16. For God so loved the world, that he gave his only begotten Son, that whosoever believeth in him should not perish, but have everlasting life.

17. For God sent not his Son into the world to condemn the world; but that the world through him might be saved.

18. He that believeth on him is not condemned: but he that believeth not is condemned already, because he hath not believed in the name of the only begotten Son of God.

19. And this is the condemnation, that light is come into the world, and men loved darkness rather than light, because their deeds were evil.

20. For every one that doeth evil hateth the light, neither cometh to the light, lest his deeds should be reproved.

21. But he that doeth truth cometh to the light, that his deeds may be made manifest, that they are wrought in God.

LESSON OUTLINE

I. SIN BRINGS DEATH
   A. Continual Complaint
   B. Serpents of Death
II. REMEDY PROVIDED
III. LOOKING TO CHRIST
   A. Type of Christ
   B. God's Love Revealed
   C. God's Light Revealed

LESSON EXPOSITION

INTRODUCTION

While the primary focus of our lesson is upon Numbers 21, the previous chapter records several key events that help us understand the natural state of the people in their complaint.

First, we learn that both Miriam and Aaron are dead. Numbers 20 begins with her death and ends with his death. These were national losses and resulted in mourning as well as a question of leadership.

Second, we learn that Moses, in the face of the people's complaint concerning water, produced water from the rock. Unfortunately, he disobeyed God's specific command and struck the rock twice. In God's sight this was an unholy act born out of Moses' frustration and not his confidence in God.

Third, we learn that Israel faced a political conflict with Edom that could not be resolved to mutual satisfaction. Israel was forced to back down in the face of the Edomite threat.

Thus, coming into Numbers 21 we have a people filled with disappointment, loss of national leaders, and loss of national esteem. It's no wonder their frustration was taken out on the Canaanites in Numbers 21:1-3.

I. SIN BRINGS DEATH (Numbers 21:4-7)

A. Continual Complaint (vv. 4, 5)

4. And they journeyed from mount Hor by the way of the Red sea, to compass the land of Edom: and the soul of the people was much discouraged because of the way.

5. And the people spake against God, and against Moses, Wherefore have ye brought us up out of Egypt to die in the wilderness? for there is no bread, neither is there any water; and our soul loatheth this light bread.

Because of Edom's refusal to allow Israel to march along the King's Highway (which led up the eastern side of the Dead Sea to the Jordan River) the people, after defeating the Canaanites and rescuing the captives (21:1-3), turned back towards the Red Sea. It is the northeastern branch of the sea the Israelites crossed in the Exodus.

In the introductory remarks it was seen that the people had experienced a series of discouraging events. The account in Numbers 21:4 further reveals the extent of their discouragement. The collective "soul" of the people was burdened by defeat and failure.

Many people experience setbacks in life. There are many cliches like "when the going gets tough, the tough get going" and the like. Yet, in most instances in life a pep-rally atmosphere does little good. There are genuinely discouraging moments that stifle creativity and suffocate life from the future. These encounters are often so serious they lead to depression.

Such discouragement must be taken seriously. When people do not feel they are taken seriously in the struggles of life, they lose the ability to receive and express care. One of the seven deadly sins is "sloth." But the Greek for "sloth" is *acedia* and really has the sense of "not caring."

The children of Israel expressed to

God and Moses their feeling that no one cared. All people need a sense of accomplishment. The tragedy in the wilderness wanderings is that the people failed to operate under principles of accomplishment that God had given. They were living under a terrible judgment because of unbelief. There is no doubt God still cared; but the effects of their sin could not be removed except by death.

Sin seeks to wreck havoc in our life. Often this is done by willful acts of disobedience by which we inherit the whirlwind. There are countless marriages and families destroyed by infidelity and various kinds of abuse in which the survivors live in discouragement and failure. Such persons may have received divine forgiveness, but the effects of sin still haunt their lives.

For others sin lurks as a vague feeling of guilt. Recently an elderly woman wept in my office of the guilt she felt. She was so discouraged because life had not turned out the way she thought it would. She loved Christ and knew all her sins were covered by His precious blood; yet, there remained a nagging guilt manifested in feeling worthless to her family, her church, even the Lord.

This is why there is a need for a "double cure," to use Charles Wesley's words, for sin. Not only do we need forgiveness for specific acts; but we also need deliverance from Satan's fiery darts of fear, discouragement, and pain.

B. Serpents of Death (vv. 6, 7)

6. And the Lord sent fiery serpents among the people, and they bit the people; and much people of Israel died.

7. Therefore the people came to Moses, and said, We have sinned, for we have spoken against the Lord, and against thee; pray unto the Lord, that he take away the serpents from us. And Moses prayed for the people.

It is common for humanity to turn to God in times of crisis. The children of Israel quickly realized the dimensions of their complaint against God. Complaining resulted in physical death among the Israelites; among believers today complaining results in spiritual death. A complaining person can bring a cloud of doom over any gathering. That person is so filled with self-doubt and hurts he is unable to see the possibilities offered in Christ. Complaining is a symptom of eyes taken off Christ. The complainer initiates all his thoughts from within himself. Complainers are not filled with the Spirit; rather, they are filled with mistrust and feelings of inadequacy.

It is important to learn the difference between complaining and genuine criticism. A genuine criticism will not center around a person(s) but rather around an idea. A genuine criticism will also offer an alternative idea. Complainers will often carry personal grudges behind their specific complaint.

The use of the serpents in this lesson is interesting. The Old Testament uses three main words to describe serpents of which only two concern us in this lesson. The first is *nachash* which is used in Genesis 3 to describe the evil tempter of Eve. That is the same word used in Numbers 21:6, 7, 9 (our lesson). It is interesting that another word, *seraph* is used in Numbers 21:8, to describe the fiery serpent made by Moses and placed upon the pole. There does seem to be a certain relationship between seraph and the seraphim (which is the plural) who surround the throne of God in worship (Isaiah 6:2).

The predominate use of serpent in the Bible points to Satan. The passage in Revelation 12:9 refers to "that old serpent, called the Devil" (also used in 20:2).

The Apostle Paul used this lesson from Israel's history to describe the power of temptation. In 1 Corinthians 10:9 he remarked, "We should not test the Lord, as some of them did, and were killed by snakes" (New International Version), and then further observed, "These things happened to them as examples and were written down as warnings for us" (v. 11, NIV). The warning is specifically addressed to those who might think they can stand before God on past achievements or human merit. Such persons are prey to the stinging effects of temptation.

We must remember, Satan knows our weaknesses better than we ourselves. We are not tempted at places where we are strong spiritually; rather, in his vile ways he tempts us at the places of moral and spiritual weakness. We are called to be "on guard" regarding the efforts of Satan to destroy our lives. Paul encouraged the Corinthian Christians with the assurance that they would not face any temptations from Satan that were not common to all humanity. This meant there was not a special kind of temptation for those in Christ in which Satan was more powerful. Rather, the fact that God is faithful serves as the necessary knowledge to realistic faith that enables us to overcome the temptations of Satan.

The closing part of verse 7 tells that Moses "prayed for the people." This is a beautiful picture of intercession. We know from Hebrews 2:18 that Christ makes intercession for us in the midst of our temptations. Another passage that shows the power of Christ as a prayer warrior for us in the face of temptation is in Luke 22:31, 32. The setting is the Last Supper and the disciples are engaged in an argument over who will be the greatest. Apparently Simon Peter was a center of this discussion as Jesus turned to him and said, "Simon, Simon, Satan has asked to sift you as wheat" (v. 31, *NIV*). It should be noted that first, Satan had to ask permission to attack one of Christ's children. This is significant for us in that it shows that an attack from Satan upon us is not outside the sphere of God's control. God allows it for one of two purposes: (1) To break down a place of rebellion and unbelief in our life; or (2) To reveal His glory for the purposes of redemption that extends beyond us. The second thing to be noted is that the "you" of verse 31 is plural, indicating Jesus was speaking about all the disciples being sifted.

But the key phrase is in verse 32, "But I have prayed for you [singular], Simon, that your faith may not fail" (*NIV*). What a marvelous thing to know that Jesus is praying for our faith. No one could have a greater intercessor than Jesus himself. He not only knows about every sin, temptation, and weakness, He has also experienced all the fury of those enemies and rose triumphant!

II. REMEDY PROVIDED (Numbers 21:8, 9)

8. **And the Lord said unto Moses, Make thee a fiery serpent, and set it upon a pole: and it shall come to pass, that every one that is bitten, when he looketh upon it, shall live.**

9. **And Moses made a serpent of brass, and put it upon a pole, and it came to pass, that if a serpent had bitten any man, when he beheld the serpent of brass, he lived.**

One of the liberating themes of the gospel is that God does not leave us without hope of deliverance. In this generation of "cheap grace" it is important we emphasize that God meets us in our condition of sin and accepts us there so that He may move us into the life of obedience. There are many who think confession and forgiveness means that "Christ accepts me just as I am" and this is all that is needed. But this is not the case. For us to think of God as accepting us in our sin so we may continue in that sin is to make a mockery of the grace of God. We are accepted in Christ so we can come under the rulership of the Holy Spirit.

Thus, the fiery serpent was set up so that any man could find deliverance and be led to full life. All that was required was that a man "look." This act of looking indicated faith. It meant that the bitten person believed his only hope was in God's promised way of healing (in biblical thought healing and salvation are closely related). As is vividly expressed in verse 8, to look is to live. It is faith that appropriated the life-giving power of Christ into our life. Note that this act of looking-faith required an act of obedience on the part of the bitten person. Thus, James's admonition that "faith without works is dead" is not violated here. The bitten person actually turned to look at bronze serpent and thus "actualized" his faith.

From 2 Kings 18:4 we discover that the bronze serpent was given a special place in Israel's worship life. It was preserved throughout the remainder of the wilderness wandering and the crossing into the Promised Land. It was secured during the conquest under Joshua and the instability of the judges. It made its way into Israel's monarchial history through Saul, David, Solomon, and was a special shrine during the time of Hezekiah. The passage in 2 Kings 18:4 tells that Hezekiah "broke into pieces the bronze snake Moses had made, for up to that time the Israelites had been burning incense to it" (*NIV*).

It is very easy for a symbol to take the

place of faith. God never intended for the bronze serpent to be worshiped; it was simply a point of visible contact for faith. As happens so often, what was meant as an avenue of contact becomes a sacred spot. This is not only true of Catholicism but is true of Evangelicals. We do this whenever we bind ourselves to certain places or songs or phrases that worked once. We insist they continue to be used and in our insistence close the doors of real faith. We offer the incense of tradition rather than walk in relationship with the Lord of Glory.

III. LOOKING TO CHRIST (John 3:14-21)

A. A Type of Christ (vv. 14, 15)

14. And as Moses lifted up the serpent in the wilderness, even so must the Son of man be lifted up:

15. That whosoever believeth in him should not perish, but have eternal life.

Alfred Edersheim writes that "a rite which has a present spiritual meaning is a symbol; and if, besides, it also points to a future reality, conveying at the same time, by anticipation, the blessing that is yet to appear, it is a type" (*The Temple,* Eerdmans Publishing Company, p. 106). Our Lord himself used the bronze serpent as a type of Himself.

The context of John 3 is the longing question of Nicodemus concerning his relationship with God. Nicodemus was a Pharisee who was sympathetic to the ministry of Jesus. The gospel record presents his relationship with Christ as genuine. Jesus led him into a broader understanding of the meaning of the New Birth. This was new to Nicodemus and until the Holy Spirit enlightened his vision he would not be able to fully comprehend.

In response to what Jesus said concerning being born again, Nicodemus asked, "How can these things be?" (v. 9). It is in response to the question of "how" that Jesus speaks in verses 10-15. Jesus answered the query by talking about revelation. In verse 12 He spoke of how difficult it is for natural man (even a religious man) to understand the things of heaven. Jesus went on to observe that only He, the Son of Man, had descended from heaven so that He could again ascend into heaven.

This rising to heaven is not only a reference to Christ's ascension, but is primarily a reference to His being raised up on the Cross of Calvary.

Thus, verse 14 shows that Christ will take the place of the serpent. The serpent could only heal from the physical wounds of the people; Christ is able to heal and save the entire person. In referring to the serpent raised by Moses, Christ was showing that in Himself, someone greater than Moses was present. Moses could not raise himself for the healing of the people; it took a substitute. But Christ became the substitute for all humanity as He bore the curse of sin.

In his commentary on John, Rudolf Schnackenburg observes that this typology from Numbers 21 shows three things in relation to John 3:14. First, it shows the exaltation of Jesus. This exaltation is not confined to His ascension but is rather a powerful interpretation of His death. What was meant as the most humiliating of deaths has become glory and exaltation because God has revealed the majesty and power of His salvation through the Cross. Second, the saving power of the Cross extends across time, peoples, cultures, and generations. The bronze serpent, although worshiped by the Jews, could not continue to provide healing. The cross of Christ continues to provide complete salvation for all who will believe. Third, the Cross upon which the Son of Man was lifted was in the perfect plan of the heavenly Father. From the foundation of the world the Son of God had been prepared as the Lamb slain. God was not caught by surprise at Adam's fall. God was prepared because He knew the power of His love. God knew that love was always called upon to be sacrificial. Thus, His only Son was prepared regardless of what man would do.

The reality of this exaltation is further illustrated in John 12:28-32. There Jesus asked the Father to glorify His holy name. The answer in verse 28 is that the Father has glorified His name once and will do it again (this glorification took place at the death of Jesus). In verse 31 Jesus revealed that this glorification would be the way that judgment would come upon the world and the ruler of this world (Satan) would be cast out. The passage then finds comparison with 3:14 by the words of Jesus in verse 32, "And I, if I be lifted up from the earth, will draw all men unto me."

The fact that Christ was lifted up as God's sacrifice for sin makes possible the reality of atonement. That is the focus of verse 15. Anyone who will have faith in Christ and receive the benefits of His death will escape eternal damnation and obtain eternal life.

B. God's Love Revealed (vv. 16-18)

16. For God so loved the world, that he gave his only begotten Son, that whosoever believeth in him should not perish, but have everlasting life.

17. For God sent not his Son into the world to condemn the world; but that the world through him might be saved.

18. He that believeth on him is not condemned: but he that believeth not is condemned already, because he hath not believed in the name of the only begotten Son of God.

John 3:16 can be quoted by most people who have any connection with Christianity. It is a powerful expression of the love of God and His commitment to seek and save the lost.

The world is the cosmos. It points to God's desire to bring deliverance to humanity and our earth. The Apostle Paul understood that creation itself was longing for the revealing of the sons of God (Romans 8:19-22). The death of Jesus thus not only addresses the individual human soul but also extends to the full redemption of this earth.

The expression of God's love is seen in the fact that "He gave." This divine "giving" was in the person of Jesus. Every person can bear witness that the greatest gifts at Christmas are not material gifts but the actual presence of family and friends. Thus, God manifested His great love though the person of Jesus Christ. What a mighty confession this is: God is a Giver! The love of the heavenly Father flows freely through Christ toward His creation. Note that both verses 15 and 16 conclude with the same promise of eternal life. Those who believe in Christ are blessed with the gift of eternal life.

Verse 17 shows God's intention toward humanity. That intention is that we not live under condemnation. The New Testament teaches that we are under condemnation because of sin. The Greek used for "condemn" in John 3:17, 18, 19 all have the basic meaning of "sentence of death, punishment." It is Satan who brings condemnation and accusation against the people of God. God does bring judgment upon us; but as a father disciplines his children (Hebrews 12:3-11). This "divine discipline" or "divine judgment" is meant to lead us to repentance for the fruit of righteousness to be produced in us. But Satan brings condemnation in order to destroy the spirit; his words attack and discourage; his words crush our will to stand firm as men and women of faith. Christ disciplines our life so as to produce more life; Satan condemns so as to produce death.

Paul, in Romans 8:1-4, illustrated the practical applications of this to the Christian life. In that marvelous passage, he showed (from Romans 7) that although sin is at work in our mortal body, taking advantage of the law and the flesh, that our mind and heart are committed to serve God. He did not mean that we are thereby free to sin freely! No! His emphasis in Romans 6 showed that in Christ we were no longer under the "dominion" of sin but rather under the "dominion" of Christ. Because of this change of "dominion" (or "ruling force") over our life, we were to take the act of obedience from the heart (will) and no longer "yield to sin" but now "yield to God."

But, even though we yielded to Christ, we still are aware of sin's effort to destroy the work of God. We still face temptations; we still are oppressed by the Evil One. Paul wrote these words of victory and encouragement in Romans 8:1 that in Christ Jesus "there is therefore now no condemnation" or "sentence of death." This freedom from condemnation is possible because Jesus himself has done in human flesh (His own) what the tablets of law could not do. Christ, on the Cross, condemned sin. This is a powerful picture: Christ does not condemn *me;* He condemns *sin!*

Thus verse 17 points to our glorious liberty in Christ. If the Son did not come to condemn, then there is only one other thing He could possibly do: *come to save!*

Verse 18 shows how this freedom from sin's condemnation is possible only through faith in Jesus as the Son of God. It is not sufficient to believe that Jesus was a good man. When we confess Him as our Savior we must also understand we are accepting His divinity as the Son of God. This settles the quest for God. The person who truly believes that Jesus is the Son of God, that He is the Word of God incarnate, has ceased his quest to find God in human philosophy. That person has come to the restful place of faith in Jesus. Such a person is truly freed from the paralyzing, condemning work of Satan.

C. God's Light Revealed (vv. 19-21)

19. And this is the condemnation, that light is come into the world, and men loved darkness rather than light, because their deeds were evil.

20. For every one that doeth evil hateth the light, neither cometh to the light, lest his deeds should be reproved.

21. But he that doeth truth cometh to the light, that his deeds may be made manifest, that they are wrought in God.

The words of Jesus in this address to Nicodemus end with verse 21. They further clarify what is the origin of this condemnation and how it actually manifests itself in the world.

The origin, in verse 19, is in man's unbelief. While it is important we recognize the work of Satan, we must never forget that each person is responsible before God for accepting or rejecting Jesus, the Light. Our disobedience, while occasioned by Satan, is still *our* disobedience. God did not make us as robots to either love Him or follow Satan. We follow sin because we refuse to believe in Christ and because we love the darkness. We allow ourselves to accept the deception that fulfillment of this human life in the world is the only real way to happiness.

But the person who moves into the Light moves into the sphere of truth. Jesus made it clear that "the truth will set you free." But this truth is the truth about Himself. It is not scientific or philosophical truth. Only the truth of Christ liberates us from the darkness of our deeds and enables the deeds of righteousness to become manifest.

REVIEW QUESTIONS

1. How can a Christian distinguish between God's discipline in his life and an attack of condemnation by Satan?

2. How did the bronze serpent become a source of idolatry for Israel? Do such things still happen today?

3. How does faith in Christ break the power of sin?

4. How does Christ compare to Moses as an intercessor?

GOLDEN TEXT HOMILY

"AS MOSES LIFTED UP THE SERPENT IN THE WILDERNESS, EVEN SO MUST THE SON OF MAN BE LIFTED UP: THAT WHOSOEVER BELIEVETH IN HIM SHOULD NOT PERISH, BUT HAVE ETERNAL LIFE" (John 3:14, 15).

In these two verses the Lord Jesus calls the attention of Nicodemus to the incident of Moses lifting up the serpent in the wilderness. Many people were dying because of disobedience. They had asked God to take away the serpents, but He did not choose to do so—instead He gave to them a remedy that involved the exercise of their faith.

A close look at the Scripture indicates that the event recorded in Numbers is clearly a type of the lifting up of the Son of Man. We note in both cases that death is the punishment for sin: the first as the result of the Israelites' disobedience and the second as the result of the sin of mankind. Again, we note that it is God himself who, in His sovereign grace, provides a remedy in both instances.

The lifting up of the Son of Man is presented as a "must" (compare Mark 8:31; Luke 24:7). However, it is not just a remedy, it is the only way for man to meet the demands of God's holiness, righteousness, and love. The remedy in both cases consisted of a public display. Though Jesus was lifted up in the sight of all, He does not save all. It is only those who with a believing heart are able to avail themselves of salvation. In order for the Israelites to receive deliverance they had to do two things: they first had to become aware of their need; then they had to be attentive to what God said. We, too, must follow the same steps.—**Luther E. Painter, D. Min., Assistant Professor of Religion, Lee College, Cleveland, Tennessee**

SENTENCE SERMONS

CHRIST DIED on the Cross to provide deliverance from sin for all who believe.
—Selected

HE THAT HATH slight thoughts of sin never had great thoughts of God.
—"Speaker's Sourcebook"

IN DARKNESS there is no choice. It is light that enables us to see the difference between things; and it is Christ that gives us light.
—Mrs. C. T. Whitnell

ALL THE WORLD'S joy comes from the grave of our risen Lord.
—J. R. Miller

EVANGELISTIC APPLICATION

CHRIST DIED ON THE CROSS TO PROVIDE DELIVERANCE FROM SIN FOR ALL WHO BELIEVE.

That deliverance is meant to be a total deliverance from sin's ruling power. Romans 6 provides tremendous insight in helping the Christian overcome sin's claim.

Sin seeks to make its claim upon us by making us believe a lie. That lie is: Satan still has authority over our life and we are still under his dominion. It is imperative we realize that in Christ Jesus we have "died" to sin and it no longer has a place of authority over us. The only authority Satan has is that which we give him.

But the Christian is called to flee from Satan and come under the lordship of Jesus Christ. His authority sets free and by His Word breaks the walls of sin's slave camps.

The world is longing for men and women to truly live as sons of God. It is longing to see us walk triumphant over sin. This walk is not one of arrogance or show-off power; rather it is a walk of humble love. Such a humble love is strong. It is able to be the "servant of all" for the sake of God's delivering message.

ILLUMINATING THE LESSON

Recently a young Christian told me of how he had to "break up" with his girlfriend. She did not want to leave her ways of drinking, immorality, and other sins. As he sat across the table, his eyes filled with tears, he remarked, "I see what she can be in the Lord. I love her. But I told her I could not live with that kind of life."

I remarked that was a good description of God's love for us. He loves us; but He can't live with our sin.

Sinners are led to believe that since God hates their sin, He hates them. They accuse God of not being a God of love because of the consequences of their actions. But the truth is that God does deeply love; so much that He gave His own Son. But because His love is so holy and pure, He cannot "live with" our rebellion.

What a marvelous change occurs when we recognize that to live with God is far more fulfilling and has eternal rewards than to live against Him.

DAILY BIBLE READINGS

M. Warning Against Disobedience. Psalm 78:12-31

T. Evil Practices Abandoned. 2 Kings 18:1-7

W. Salvation Offered. Mark 16:14-18

T. Dangers of Murmuring. 1 Corinthians 10:1-13

F. Jesus the Son of Man. John 12:27-36

S. The Exalted Christ. Hebrews 12:1-3

God Provides Leaders

Study Text: Numbers 27:12-23

Supplemental References: Deuteronomy 34:1-12; Joshua 1:1-9; Isaiah 45:1-6; Mark 3:12-19; Acts 1:15-26; 9:1-9

Time: Probably early in 1406 B.C.

Place: The Plains of Moab, east of the Jordan River.

Golden Text: "Feed the flock of God which is among you, taking the oversight thereof, not by constraint, but willingly" (1 Peter 5:2).

Central Truth: God calls and commissions individuals to lead His people.

Evangelistic Emphasis: As leaders faithfully serve the Lord, they will be used to lead the lost to Christ.

Printed Text

Numbers 27:12. And the Lord said unto Moses, Get thee up into this mount Abarim, and see the land which I have given unto the children of Israel.

13. And when thou hast seen it, thou also shalt be gathered unto thy people, as Aaron thy brother was gathered.

14. For ye rebelled against my commandment in the desert of Zin, in the strife of the congregation, to sanctify me at the water before their eyes: that is the water of Meribah in Kadesh in the wilderness of Zin.

15. And Moses spake unto the Lord, saying,

16. Let the Lord, the God of the spirits of all flesh, set a man over the congregation,

17. Which may go out before them, and which may go in before them, and which may lead them out, and which may bring them in; that the congregation of the Lord be not as sheep which have no shepherd.

18. And the Lord said unto Moses, Take thee Joshua the son of Nun, a man in whom is the spirit, and lay thine hand upon him;

19. And set him before Eleazar the priest, and before all the congregation; and give him a charge in their sight.

20. And thou shalt put some of thine honour upon him, that all the congregation of the children of Israel may be obedient.

21. And he shall stand before Eleazar the priest, who shall ask counsel for him after the judgment of Urim before the Lord: at his word shall they go out, and at his word they shall come in, both he, and all the children of Israel with him, even all the congregation.

22. And Moses did as the Lord commanded him: and he took Joshua, and set him before Eleazar the priest, and before all the congregation:

23. And he laid his hands upon him, and gave him a charge, as the Lord commanded by the hand of Moses.

DICTIONARY

Abarim (AHB-ah-rim)—Numbers 27:12—The name of the mountain range northwest of Moab.

Zin—Numbers 27:14—A wilderness near the border of Canaan.

Meribah (MAIR-ah-bah) in Kadesh (KAY-desh)—Numbers 27:14—A place near and to the northwest of Sinai.

Eleazor (eh-lih-AY-zer)—Numbers 27:19—The third son of Aaron. After the death of the two older brothers, he became chief priest.

Urim (YOU-rim)—Numbers 27:21—Perhaps stones in the breastplace of the high priest. One theory is that they served as a symbol of the high priest's authority to seek counsel of Jehovah.

LESSON OUTLINE

I. VISION OF THE FUTURE
   A. Divine Opportunity
   B. Limits of Earthly Life

II. GOD'S LEADER REVEALED
   A. Leadership Qualifications
   B. A Man of the Spirit

III. GOD'S LEADER ORDAINED
   A. Spiritual Leadership
   B. Authority to Lead

LESSON EXPOSITION

INTRODUCTION

There are two lessons in Spring Quarter 1987 that will be of value in this lesson. The first illustrates the qualities of Moses as a leader. It is titled "A Great Leader" and begins on page 333 of the *Evangelical Commentary*. The second lesson concerns the death of Moses from the account in Deuteronomy 31 and 34. It is titled "Moses' Last Days" and begins on page 340. Your lesson this week will be enriched by referring back to the Spring Quarter as you study.

Leadership is a quality we look for in people throughout life. Perhaps the most basic definition of a leader is someone who is able to influence people to accomplish certain tasks. Most people have some degrees of leadership. Some are able to mobilize a Sunday school class; others can work with larger groups in the church; still others have pastoral leadership gifts that inspire people to follow the Lord and build a significant church for His kingdom.

Jesus indicated that spiritual leadership is modeled after a servant. Spiritual leadership does not seek power nor position. It flows in the righteous power of the Holy Spirit and recognizes that Jesus is the true Authority in His position as King of Kings and Lord of Lords.

As the topic suggests, God knows best the leader we need. That leader for all of us is Christ. Yet, throughout His church there are other leadership positions that must be filled by capable men and women. It is the responsibility of each believer to hear God's call to leadership and obey; it is also each Christian's responsibility to recognize the leaders God sends and submit in responsible obedience to their leadership.

I. VISION OF THE FUTURE (Numbers 27:12-14)

A. Divine Opportunity (v. 12)

12. And the Lord said unto Moses, Get thee up into this mount Abarim, and see the land which I have given unto the children of Israel.

It should be noted that Numbers 27 records a striking example of female leadership as the daughters of Zelophehad, with humility, wisdom, and courage, addressed an injustice. The law allowed for property to be transferred from the father to his sons; in the case where there were no sons, no provision was made for surviving daughters. These women boldly argued they should receive their father's inheritance. Moses sought the counsel of the Lord and in this instance a biblical stance for treating women as people was established. In the ancient world most women had few, if any, rights and were often treated as property. This decision to regard the daughters as women of legal status places the living God on the side of liberation and affirmation of womanhood. The Bible is not a sexist document; when believers use the Bible to put down others, then God's Word is misappropriated. God's Word speaks for justice and human dignity under the banner of God's love and truth.

The mountains of Abarim—of which Mount Nebo, upon which Moses actually died, is in the northeast section—are located on the northeastern side of the Dead Sea just east of the plains of Moab. Mount Nebo is about 12 miles east of the Jordan River, 20 miles east of Jericho, 30 miles east of Jerusalem, and 70 miles east of the Mediterranean Sea. From his vantage point on Mount Nebo, Moses was able to see the entire length and breadth of the land the people of Israel would soon inherit. The passage in Deuteronomy 34:1-3 reveals that Moses went "to the top of Pisgah" to view the land. Pisgah probably refers to a viewing area on Mount Nebo that gave an unobstructed view across the entire Jordan Valley. Mount Nebo is 2,740 feet above the Mediterranean Sea and 4,030 feet above the Dead Sea.

While the next verses will tell why Moses was not able to enter the land, it is important to note that God did not deny Moses an opportunity to envision the future. This in itself is a marvelous blessing. Moses was late in years, being 120 years old when he died. His days were numbered and his time of leadership was coming to an end. The particular leadership style the people had in the wilderness was not sufficient for the new opportunities of conquest and settling the land. God, in His marvelous wisdom, matches leadership styles with the situations His people are facing and will face. That is why change is necessary and often good. A change made in God's will provides a leader with a new vision and special gifts to see the vision through.

We are told in Proverbs 29:18, "Where there is no vision, the people perish." The New English Bible reads, "Where there is no one in authority, the people break loose," while the New Internationals Version offers, "Where there is no revelation, the people cast off restraint." It is clear that a vision is necessary for the people of God. It is also clear, as deduced by the NEB translation, that the vision must be established in the truthfulness of God in order for a claim or authority to exist. Moses was able to act with vision, authority, and trust in God for the sake of the people.

One illustration of his leadership suffices to show this. It is related in Exodus 32 (Lesson 4 of this quarter) how the children of Israel fell into idolatry while Moses was absent on the mountain receiving the Ten Commandments. Even though they murmured while he was present, Moses' leadership functioned as a restraining reality while he was present. But note how quickly the people "broke loose" and "perished" when they lost the source of their vision.

What Moses saw of the land was concretely related to the promise of God. Note that the land is not called anything but "the land which I [the Lord] have given." It is important to remember that "the earth is the Lord's, and the fulness thereof" (Psalm 24:1). The notion of private property that is so important in American society is not as important in biblical thought. In fact, our notions of private property often stand in contrast to the biblical affirmation quoted above. The land is God's land. It is the Lord's to give to whom He pleases. It is our land only in that we are given stewardship responsibilities over it. The land still belongs to the Lord.

The New Testament parallel to "the land" is found in the spiritual blessings of Christ. The man and woman of faith can recognize these blessings and have a vision for God's fullness in their life. These "blessings" are God's to give. They become "our" blessings insofar as we use them for the betterment of those around us and the glory of God.

B. Limits of Earthly Life (vv. 13, 14)

13. And when thou hast seen it,

thou also shalt be gathered unto thy people, as Aaron thy brother was gathered.

14. For ye rebelled against my commandment in the desert of Zin, in the strife of the congregation, to sanctify me at the water before their eyes: that is the water of Meribah in Kadesh in the wilderness of Zin.

The passage in Deuteronomy 32:48-52 has a parallel account to our record in Numbers 27. The basic aspects of both passages are identical in that Aaron is mentioned and the sin at the water of Meribah is mentioned.

It is interesting that death is described as being "gathered unto thy people." Although the covenant people traced their lineage to Abraham, it was Moses who established them as a people for God's purpose. Through Moses the liberation from Egypt had happened; through Moses the eternal law was revealed that bound the people together under one code; through Moses provision was made as they journeyed; through Moses the people had a leader with vision and compassion. Thus, at the end of his life, death is not a separation from God's eternal purposes through Israel but death becomes a uniting with God's people. We must remember that the understanding of life after death, which we possess since the resurrection of Jesus, was not truly revealed in Moses' time. Thus, to be gathered to "thy people" was a statement of eternal life.

There are three places where the death of Aaron is recorded in more detail. Two passages are brief announcements: Numbers 33:38, 39, which also tells he was 123 years old when he died (thus, we are able to reckon he was three years older than his younger brother Moses who died at 120 years, assuming they died in the same year); and Deuteronomy 10:6 where it is recorded he died at Moserah and his son Eleazar ministered in his stead.

The major passage of his death is Numbers 20:22-29. The same expression "gathered unto his people" is used to describe Aaron's death (v. 24). As will be discussed in more detail in a follow-

ing paragraph, neither Aaron nor Moses was able to enter the land because of the incident at the waters of Meribah. Aaron died on the summit of Mount Hor. On the mount, Moses undertook the transfer of the priestly role from Aaron to Eleazar. They then left the mountain and Aaron died before the Lord. Thus, Moses knew the general circumstances he would face on Mount Nebo when he was "gathered unto his people."

Verse 14 records the reason why Moses died. He rebelled against the Lord in the incident at the waters of Meribah. There are two accounts of water coming from a rock during the wilderness experience of Israel. The first is recorded in Exodus 17:1-7 where Moses was commanded by the Lord to actually strike the rock at Rephidim. He obeyed the Lord completely and water came forth. There is no hint that Moses disobeyed the Lord in this incident. In fact, Aaron is not even mentioned! Although the same name is used, *Meribah* in Hebrew means "contention" or "rebellion." Thus, it could have been used at any number of sites and times to describe the attitude of the children of Israel toward God. Therefore, we are compelled to consider these two incidents as separate events and not a double narrative of the same event (as is sometimes the case in the Bible).

Moses was not allowed to see the Promised Land because he "rebelled" against the Lord's commandment. The Hebrew for *rebel* has the sense of "provoke, make bitter." Thus, we are given some insight into the spiritual nature of Moses' rebellion. The rebellion was precisely against the commandment of the Lord. The account in Numbers 20:2-13, which describes this rebellion, reveals that the Lord specifically told Moses to "speak" to the rock. He was instructed to take the rod and hold it in his hand as a sign of divine authority; but he was expressly forbidden to "strike" the rock as in the earlier incident recorded in Exodus 17. It was this express command from the Lord that he violated. It is of value for the teacher to read the Numbers 20 passage closely in relation to what constituted the sin of Moses. Lesson 13 of Spring Quarter, 1987, contains a section of the Lesson Outline that describes this anger of Moses.

It is important to note that Moses' rebellion constituted unbelief before the Lord. By failing to completely trust the Lord even with a rebellious people, Moses violated the holiness of God. This is a powerful statement to spiritual leaders. In Numbers 20:10 we discover two things that manifested this unbelief. First, Moses (and Aaron) spoke harshly to the people calling them "you rebels" (NEB). This name-calling indicated Moses had forgotten they were God's people, God's flock, and not his own. We have a picture of a man who has allowed his own ego needs to be so closely tied with the people that he is unable to clearly relate to them in God's will. Second, Moses turned the focus of the miracle from God to himself and Aaron, "Must we get water out of this rock for you?" (NEB). While God honored the request, it was because of the holiness of His name and not because of Moses' obedience.

Spiritual purity and humility are essential qualities in any leader in the church. It is imperative we remember that we are called to lead God's flock. The pastor or church-school teacher who continually berates his people is ministering death and condemnation. He is lording his spiritual power over them and manipulating out of his own frustrations. Only when we accept that it is God's flock we are serving are we free to minister life, even when we must speak with judgment and authority.

II. GOD'S LEADER REVEALED (Numbers 27:15-18)

A. Leadership Qualifications (vv. 15-17)

15. And Moses spake unto the Lord, saying,

16. Let the Lord, the God of the spirits of all flesh, set a man over the congregation,

17. Which may go out before them, and which may go in before them, and which may lead them out, and which may bring them in; that the congregation of the Lord be not as sheep which have no shepherd.

We are given tremendous insight into Moses' spiritual maturity in these verses. How many of us, after struggling for years and then discovering we will not inherit what we worked so hard for, would remain faithful to God as Moses? Would we not rather argue and complain and assert that God is unfair? Would we not protest our innocence? Would we not weep our confession and assume that God owes it to us since we confessed? But what a different man is Moses!

He immediately accepted the Lord's will. He knew his future rested in God's perfect provision. Although sin, however unintentional, had marred his understanding of the future, God's provision for the future was marvelous.

There is a profound humility and meekness in his remarks in verse 16. "Now the man Moses was very meek, above all the men which were upon the face of the earth" (Numbers 12:3). His assertion in verse 16 is that Yahweh, the Lord God, is Lord of all humanity. It is God who has breathed life into all flesh. He asserts that God is Lord over Israel and also over the entire world. All flesh is created by God and thus the Creator can assert His lordship upon us.

Moses, who easily could have blamed the people for causing him to rebel at Meribah, asked the Lord to give the people a leader. Moses remained consistent as an intercessor for the people (see Lesson 4 of this quarter).

These qualities of leadership are evidenced throughout the Bible. The men whom God has used most effectively have been men (and women) of humility, obedience, and intercession. Such leaders are caring leaders because they take God's Word, God's call, and people seriously. Leaders who are manipulative use people only for their own gain. Pastor Jack Hayford of the Church on the Way in Van Nuys, California, wrote that the Lord convicted him of a tendency he had to use people. Like many pastors, Hayford would see a new couple come into the church. They were talented and could make a wonderful contribution to the church. He remarked that he would find himself asking the Lord to help those people become part of his church because "I can use folks like that." The Lord revealed how that attitude was not birthed in genuine care for those people but rather birthed in manipulation.

In 1 Peter 5 we have an interesting inner relationship revealed concerning leadership and caring. The first six verses of that chapter speak of godly leadership among God's people. The emphasis of feeding "the flock of God" is developed in verses 2-4. Verses 5 and 6 are addressed to younger leadership that is being developed in the church. These verses call for the younger leadership to "submit . . . unto the elder." Such submission takes place in an atmosphere of humility. The passage closes in verse 7 with, "Casting all your care upon him; for he careth for you." While that verse provides comfort to many, the context points to its primary interpretation as being toward those in leadership. That God *cares* means He takes us seriously. He takes sin seriously; He takes redemption seriously; He takes the fulfilling of His will seriously.

Thus, leaders are people who care (take others seriously). Qualifications that add to this are found in 1 Timothy 3:1-13 and Titus 1:5-9. While these specific passages refer to specific leadership positions in the church, the principles of leadership are implicit for all.

Moses was concerned that the people would be left without a shepherd. Jesus was moved with compassion (another way of caring) when He saw the multitudes because they were "as sheep having no shepherd" (Matthew 9:36). In the famous words of our Lord, "The harvest truly is plenteous, but the labourers are few; Pray ye therefore the Lord of the harvest, that he will send forth labourers into his harvest" (Matthew 9:37, 38), stand in relationship to the multitude of people around the world who are God's sheep but without the leadership of a shepherd. As this passage reveals so clearly, the Lord is still looking for laborers who will lead the lost sheep into the fold of eternal life!

B. A Man of the Spirit (v. 18)

18. And the Lord said unto Moses,

Take thee Joshua the son of Nun, a man in whom is the spirit, and lay thine hand upon him.

Joshua is a wonderful illustration of what it is to be a man of the Spirit. It should be noted that he was already recognized by God as a man of the Spirit before Moses laid his hand upon him. The laying on of hands is important in the reception and affirming of the Holy Spirit. In Acts 8:14-17 we read that the apostles had spiritual power to enable the Samaritans to receive the Holy Spirit as they laid their hands upon them. We should not think there was any power in their hands (see the false understanding of this by Simon Magus in 8:18-25); rather, their hands became a point of contact with faith by which the Samaritans believed God and thus received the Spirit.

Paul in 2 Timothy 1:6 encouraged Timothy to keep alive the gift of the Spirit he had received through the laying on of hands. In this sense we should think of apostolic commissioning to a work God has ordained. This laying on of hands implied authority and affirmation.

In the case of Joshua we have a man who is already filled with the Spirit. The laying on of hands became the recognizable transferring of authority from Moses to Joshua. By this was the community of Israel able to see that Joshua was to be their leader. Further description of this laying on of hands occurs in Point III of the Lesson Outline.

As a man of the Spirit, we find in Joshua a man who has a vision for the things of God. He was a man willing to obey that vision. The clearest expression of his vision and obedience is found in the positive report he brought back from the Promised Land. But his obedience to God is also found in Exodus 17:8-16 when he led an Israelite army against the Amalekites and soundly defeated them. The theme of that battle became "The Lord is my banner" and that clearly reflects the work of God's Spirit in Joshua's life.

III. GOD'S LEADER ORDAINED (Numbers 27:19-23)

A. Spiritual Leadership (vv. 19, 21)

(Verse 20 will be considered in the next section of this passage.)

19. And set him before Eleazar the priest, and before all the congregation; and give him a charge in their sight. 21. And he shall stand before Eleazar the priest, who shall ask counsel for him after the judgment of Urim before the Lord: at his word shall they go out, and at his word they shall come in, both he, and all the children of Israel with him, even all the congregation.

Eleazar, whose name means "God has helped," was the third son of Aaron (Exodus 6:23). The land of Ephraim memorialized him at his death by his burial there. His son was Phinehas who lived at Gibeah (Joshua 24:33). Eleazar and Joshua divided the Promised Land among the tribes (Numbers 32:28, 29; 34:17). It was through his line that Zadok and Ezra traced their lineage to Aaron (1 Chronicles 6:3-15; Ezra 7:1-5).

It is important to note that Moses fully obeyed God in this matter. It was critical that Moses bring Joshua before Eleazar to be anointed. Eleazar functioned as the priest of God. The various functions of prophet, priest, and king, found divided in the Old Testament, are unified in Jesus Christ. Thus, while Joshua had to go before Eleazar and Moses, we only go before Jesus Christ for all the blessings of the heavenly Father to be lavished upon us.

It was Eleazar's responsibility to give Joshua a "charge" before all the people. This charge Joshua took was made before the people so that they would see and thus accept the new leadership. It affirmed that Joshua was God's chosen instrument for leadership.

The charge given Joshua has the sense of God's order that was laid upon him. It is God's burden to be a leader. The Hebrew word used here has the sense of "command, order, install, appoint."

But Joshua was not left alone before the Lord in his position of leadership. He was united with Eleazar who would function to assist in gaining God's decisions in matters. Reference is made in verse 21 to the Urim. Usually the Urim is men-tioned in connection with the Thummim. With these two words we enter into a very simple way of revealing the will of God. Eichrodt writes this was "the one technical means of inquiring the will of God" (*Theology of the Old Testament*, Vol. 1, pp. 113, 114). These two items were kept on the breastplate of the high priest. The two words *Urim* and *Thummim* are usually understood as meaning "light" and "truth." Thus, the will of God is understood to be a "light" or "revealing" of God's purposes for us as well as corresponding to that which is true. Thus, the will of God always corresponds to truth as revealed by God.

It is uncertain exactly how these holy items actually worked. They were either stones or pieces of wood that were cast by lot. Eichrodt suggests, on the basis of 1 Samuel 14:41-52, that "a little stick jumped out when the container of the lots was shaken." On the basis of which stick came forth it was determined whether God had said yes or no to the query regarding His will.

Whatever the case (and the teacher should not try to make too much out of the Urim and Thummim; there is simply not enough historical data available to clearly understand how they operated), it is clear that the knowledge of God's will is essential for effective Christian living. Books too numerous to name have been published to try and establish how we can truly know His will. Even experienced Christians still struggle in prayer over the will of God. Even Jesus labored over God's will in the Garden of Gethsemane.

Today, the primary sources for God's will in our life are the Bible, the inner testimony of the Holy Spirit, and the confirmation of others regarding God's call upon us. How these three are worked out is still a matter that each person must decide. We do know it is God's will for all who will repent to be saved; thus, evangelism is always the will of God. We also know it is God's will we live holy lives; thus, righteousness is never a point of debate. We know we can have the mind of Christ; this comes through know-ing His words in the Gospels and allow-ing the Holy Spirit to minister them to us.

We do know it is His will that we obey once we have ascertained the specific call in our life.

B. Authority to Lead (vv. 20, 22, 23)

20. And thou shalt put some of thine honour upon him, that all the congregation of the children of Israel may be obedient.

22. And Moses did as the Lord commanded him: and he took Joshua, and set him before Eleazar the priest, and before all the congregation:

23. And he laid his hands upon him, and gave him a charge, as the Lord commanded by the hand of Moses.

Most of the details of these verses are discussed in the above section. Note that Moses was instructed to "put some of thine honour upon" Joshua. This indicated that in public Moses was to begin sharing the leadership. It meant that Moses was called to relate to Joshua in a different way. It was Moses' place to begin to decrease so that Joshua could increase.

In this fashion Moses and Joshua stand as types of the relationship between John the Baptist and Jesus. John the Baptist stands on the side of the law, just as Moses did as the great lawgiver. Joshua, whose name means "the Lord saves," is the one who leads God's people into the Promised Land. Jesus, whose name in Hebrew was "Joshua," is the One who leads all humanity into God's eternal heaven of glory and righteousness.

REVIEW QUESTIONS

1. What is your definition of *biblical leadership?*

2. In what way did Moses' striking the rock at Meribah constitute rebellion?

3. How did Moses show humility even after God's judgment for striking the rock?

4. What characteristics did Joshua have that made him fit for leadership?

5. How can leaders today discern the will of God?

GOLDEN TEXT HOMILY

"FEED THE FLOCK OF GOD WHICH IS AMONG YOU, TAKING THE OVER-SIGHT THEREOF, NOT BY CONSTRAINT, BUT WILLINGLY" (1 Peter 5:2).

I believe the most significant word in this verse is "willingly." The scripture bears out the fact that our attitude toward Christian service plays an important role in our relationship with Jesus Christ. Service and giving is an attitude that is common among Christian people. Moreover, these virtues are not solely relegated to pastors and church leaders. The Bible clearly addresses all of us when it states, "It is more blessed to give than to receive" (Acts 20:35).

Giving and service breathes the very air of our spiritual kingdom. It puts into language the very spirit of Jesus Christ. He points out to us that those who are only interested in receiving are living on a lower plane of human accomplishment.

When we accept Jesus Christ as our Savior we take on a Christian character and personality that is uncommon to the world. Our life should exemplify compassion and service. We should think of others, care for others, and strive to proclaim the message of Christ to the world. Such an attitude is a Christian virtue that comes from the heart of God.

Again Jesus is our example, as He lived to enlighten, to bestow, and to redeem. It was very little that He received. He simply gave everything to mankind.

Such an attitude is contrary to a worldly mentality. Obsession with personal gain will only lead to selfishness and the manipulation of others. But to be serving and concerned about others opens the door to everything that is noble and pure. To receive is to be superficial and momentarily happy, whereas a giving person is inwardly happy and blessed.

It can be said that the person who is always concerned with receiving will be a debtor to many people; but the one who gives will owe nothing to any man.
—Jerry Puckett, Plant Superintendent, Church of God Publishing House, Cleveland, Tennessee

SENTENCE SERMONS

GOD CALLS and commissions individuals to lead His people.
—Selected

TACT IN LEADERSHIP is the ability to give a person a shot in the arm without letting him feel the needle.
—**"Notes and Quotes"**

A TASK WITHOUT vision is drudgery. A vision without a task is a dream. A task with a vision is victory.
—**"Notes and Quotes"**

A LEADER IS an ordinary person with extraordinary determination.
—**"Southwestern Advocate"**

EVANGELISTIC APPLICATION

AS LEADERS FAITHFULLY SERVE THE LORD, THEY WILL BE USED TO LEAD THE LOST TO CHRIST.

This evangelistic mission is critical for every Christian leader. Many leaders have administrative and speaking abilities. Often these are spiritual gifts of the Holy Spirit. Yet, we must never forget that personal evangelism is part of every Christian's responsibility.

It is also important for leaders to be faithful to the Lord. This faithfulness manifests itself in many areas: reading of the Word; continual study of the Word; faithfulness in worship; and lives that are morally pure.

Leaders are "in front" of people. They are "in front" in terms of actually going ahead with thoughts and plans. But they are also "in front" in terms of being visible. People are watching Christian leaders to see if their walk is up to par with their talk! Leaders do not have private lives. Our lives are meant to be examples to the flock of God. As examples, we inspire God's people and motivate them to greater service.

Thus, leaders are in need of a growing spiritual life and humility before the Lord.

ILLUMINATING THE LESSON

Leaders are people who influence us. One of my special memories as a boy in Sunday school is of Mr. Rose.

Mr. Rose was a grandfather figure to his class of ten-year-olds. As an adult I do not remember any of the Sunday school lessons he taught, although I am sure they were all done quite well. What I do remember is that Mr. Rose loved us boys. He always greeted us personally and we each knew he cared.

He would take the time to have us over to his house for fellowship. He knew how to plan activities that would appeal to ten-year-olds.

Mr. Rose was a Sunday school teacher. Sometimes he helped lead the singing at church and sang in church groups. But, for us ten-year-old boys, he was *our* teacher. He led us to the love of Christ and commitment to His church. As a leader, he was faithful to the church and thus influenced us to be faithful also.

What kind of leader are you as a Sunday school teacher? Whether you teach ten-year-olds, or whatever, do your students really know you care?

DAILY BIBLE READINGS

M. Leadership Changes. Deuteronomy 34:1-12

T. An Obedient Leader. Judges 7:15-22

W. Spiritual Ministry. 2 Kings 2:9-22

T. Chosen Disciples. Mark 3:13-19

F. Selected to Serve. Acts 1:15-26

S. Commissioned by Christ. Acts 9:1-9

A Place of Refuge

Study Text: Numbers 35:9-34

Supplemental References: Deuteronomy 19:1-13; Joshua 20:2-6; 1 John 3:11-18

Time: Probably early in 1406 B.C.

Place: Probably in the Arabah (Plain) east of the Jordan River

Golden Text: "God is our refuge and strength, a very present help in trouble" (Psalm 46:1).

Central Truth: Christ provides a place of refuge for all who seek deliverance from the curse of sin.

Evangelistic Emphasis: The unsaved will find mercy and salvation through faith and repentance.

Printed Text

Numbers 35:14. Ye shall give three cities on this side Jordan, and three cities shall ye give in the land of Canaan, which shall be cities of refuge.

15. These six cities shall be a refuge, both for the children of Israel, and for the stranger, and for the sojourner among them: that every one that killeth any person unawares may flee thither.

16. And if he smite him with an instrument of iron, so that he die, he is a murderer: the murderer shall surely be put to death.

17. And if he smite him with throwing a stone, wherewith he may die, and he die, he is a murderer: the murderer shall surely be put to death.

18. Or if he smite him with an hand weapon of wood, wherewith he may die, and he die, he is a murderer: the murderer shall surely be put to death.

19. The revenger of blood himself shall slay the murderer: when he meeteth him, he shall slay him.

20. But if he thrust him of hatred, or hurl at him by laying of wait, that he die;

21. Or in enmity smite him with his hand, that he die: he that smote him shall surely be put to death; for he is a murderer: the revenger of blood shall slay the murderer, when he meeteth him.

22. But if he thrust him suddenly without enmity, or have cast upon him any thing without laying of wait,

23. Or with any stone, wherewith a man may die, seeing him not, and cast it upon him, that he die, and was not his enemy, neither sought his harm:

24. Then the congregation shall judge between the slayer and the revenger of blood according to these judgments:

25. And the congregation shall deliver the slayer out of the hand of the revenger of blood, and the congregation shall restore him to the city of his refuge, whither he was fled: and he shall abide in it unto the death of the high priest, which was anointed with the holy oil.

26. But if the slayer shall at any time come without the border of the city of his refuge, whither he was fled;

27. And the revenger of blood find him without the borders of the city of his refuge, and the revenger of blood kill the slayer; he shall not be guilty of blood:

28. Because he should have remained in the city of his refuge until the death of the high priest: but after the death of the high priest the slayer shall return into the land of his possession.

LESSON OUTLINE

I. REFUGE PROVIDED
A. Safeguards of Justice
B. Cities of Life

II. JUSTICE EXACTED
A. The Death Penalty
B. The Avenger of Blood

III. SAFETY ASSURED
A. Accidental Homicide
B. Hope for the Future

LESSON EXPOSITION

INTRODUCTION

The Bible is deeply interested in the matter of justice. The laws given to ancient Israel show a dual concern that justice and mercy walk side by side. The blood avenger is not given complete liberty to exact justice; neither is the murderer given a host of technical ways of avoiding his crime.

The notion of sanctuary is very ancient. Many ancients, including the Phoenicians, Syrians, Greeks, and Romans, provided sacred shrines that were understood to provide absolute protection regardless of the crime. In these places of refuge all were "beyond the reach of revenge and justice alike" (*Interpreter's Dictionary of the Bible*, Vol. 1). But such absolute provisions could not serve the entire community well. The biblical concern to combine justice and mercy flows from the fact that the acts that violate human rights and integrity are moral violations; thus, violations are against God himself.

In teaching this lesson it will be of value to read the United States Constitution and accompanying Bill of Rights. Sections that refer specifically to individual rights in regards to justice are as follows: Article I, Section 9; Article III; Amendment III; Amendment IV; Amendment V; Amendment VI; Amendment VIII; Amendment XIV, Section I. While this lesson should not become a discussion

of criminal and civil law in America, some of the references in the Constitution may serve to illustrate how one modern society deals with matters of justice.

I. REFUGE PROVIDED (Numbers 35:9-15)

A. Safeguards of Justice (vv. 9-13)

(Numbers 35:9-13 is not included in the printed text.)

The first eight verses of this chapter provide the background for understanding the significance of the six cities of refuge. From these verses we learn the cities were part of 48 cities assigned to the Levites. The Levites were given cities in the tribal districts of all Israel. While the entire land was considered "God's possession," these 48 cities were in a particular way the territory of God. The Levites ministered to the Lord God and were not allotted one particular tribal district. They were in a unique way God's possession and, by being distributed among the tribes, manifested His priestly presence among all Israel.

Of particular note is the reference in verse 8 that the number of Levitical cities in each tribe was based on the population of that tribe. Thus, the larger tribes provided more cities than the smaller tribes. The principles of land reform and justice were clearly entrenched in Israelite life. The land was and is God's land. While private property was not discarded, there was a much more liberating view of the nature of property possession. A man's land was his by inheritance and this inheritance was not to be violated over the course of generations. Yet, this principle was co-established with the fact that certain portions of the producing land were meant for the poor.

Other references to the Levitical cities are found in Exodus 21:13 where Moses was instructed that a place of refuge would be created to protect the accidental homicide perpetrator. The passage in

Deuteronomy 19:1-13 provides a parallel account to our Numbers 35 passage. However, the Deuteronomy account adds the information that the three cities in Canaan would be placed in equal thirds of the country and that roads would be clearly established so the manslayer could flee quickly to the city of refuge. An added note in Deuteronomy 19:8, 9 shows that three more cities were to be added within Israel as her borders were enlarged by the Lord. This is a marvelous description of divine grace expanding to meet every need of sinful man! The third reference is the entire chapter of Joshua 20. There the six cities are actually named (see section B below).

In these opening verses of the study text the general principles of justice regarding homicide are laid down. It is made clear from the beginning that the slayer who accidentally kills another is provided refuge. Apparently this implied that if the "revenger" (see section II, B for more information on this particular role of the go'el) met the person before he was safe in the city of refuge, then the slayer could be avenged. How this actually worked itself out in day-to-day Israelite life is difficult to ascertain; yet, it seems likely that forces of restraint were at work so as to allow the accused to flee to the city of refuge. This was probably imposed by the entire community so as to avoid the blood of the innocent from being spilled in the rage of revenge.

The accused found refuge in the city until a time could be established for a true judicial hearing (the meaning of the phrase "until he stand before the congregation in judgment," (v. 12).

With this in mind, it becomes even more noteworthy that the cities of refuge were Levitical cities. As Keil and Delitzsch remarked, "Levitical or priests' towns were selected for all six, not only because it was to the priests and Levites that they would first of all look for an administration of justice, but also on the ground that these cities were the property of Jehovah . . . where the manslayer, when once received, was placed under the protection of divine grace. . . ."

B. Cities of Life (vv. 14, 15)

14. Ye shall give three cities on this side Jordan, and three cities shall ye give in the land of Canaan, which shall be cities of refuge.

15. These six cities shall be a refuge, both for the children of Israel, and for the stranger, and for the sojourner among them: that every one that killeth any person unawares may flee thither.

From Joshua 20:7-9 we learn the names of these cities. Note that verse 14 speaks of the cities "on this side." It must be remembered that Numbers is describing the children of Israel before they cross the Jordan into the land of Canaan. Thus, the narrative reflects a pre-Jordan crossing perspective.

The cities on the east side of Jordan ("this side") were Bezer, Ramoth-gilead, and Golan. Bezer was probably located to the east of Mount Pisgah in the tribe of Reuben. It was located about 20 miles east of the Jordan River. The second city, to the north but still on the east bank of the Jordan, was Ramoth-gilead. This city was about 25 miles east of the Jordan River and located in the northern part of the tribe of Gad. It was the city midway between the north and south of Israelite territory running parallel to the Jordan River. The third city was Golan in the northern tribe of Manasseh. Manasseh was the only tribe that was found on both sides of the Jordan River. It was about 20 miles east of the Sea of Galilee and in the area known today as the Golan Heights.

The cities on the west side of the Jordan (Canaan) are found in Joshua 20:7. Kedesh, in the northern tribe of Naphtali, was in the region known as Galilee and about 15 miles north of the Sea of Galilee. The middle city on the western side was Shechem. It was in the northern part of the tribe of Ephraim, about 15 miles west of the Jordan River. The southernmost city was Hebron in the tribe of Judah, about 20 miles west of the Dead Sea.

A look at a good map of Canaan during the time of the conquest will reveal how these cities covered the entire country.

Again, it should be mentioned that Deuteronomy 19:8, 9 shows that even more cities were to be added as the nation grew and expanded her boundaries. Thus, God's intention was for justice and peace among His people. No one was excluded by territory from having a place of refuge!

Verse 15 shows that the cities of refuge were for three groups of people. The first were the "children of Israel." The second were the so-called "strangers." They are very similar to the "sojourners" who are mentioned third. The stranger probably refers to someone who is visiting within the borders of Israel. Regardless, the stranger is afforded the same protective rights as the Israelite citizen. The sojourner encompasses a large group of people of non-Israelite background who are part of the inhabitants of the land. The Hebrew *ger* has parallel meanings in Aramaic which give the meaning "proselyte." It basically refers to a person who is a newcomer with no inherited rights. Some of these groups included the mixed multitude that followed the Israelites out of Egypt (Exodus 12:38); Canaanites who remained in the land; prisoners of war; and a variety of other people who would have reason to dwell in the land. The *New Smith's Bible Dictionary* records that "the Hebrews were commanded by law to show respect and provide protection (to the sojourner) because they themselves were once sojourners on foreign soil (Genesis 15:13; Exodus 20:10; 22:21; 23:9)."

II. JUSTICE EXACTED (Numbers 35:16-21)

A. The Death Penalty (vv. 16-18)

16. And if he smite him with an instrument of iron, so that he die, he is a murderer: the murderer shall surely be put to death.

17. And if he smite him with throwing a stone, wherewith he may die, and he die, he is a murderer: the murderer shall surely be put to death.

18. Or if he smite him with an hand weapon of wood, wherewith he may die, and he die, he is a murderer: the murderer shall surely be put to death.

Three different kinds of weapons are named as possible weapons of violent death. Verse 16 implies strongly that a weapon of iron is likely to kill someone quickly. Note that verse 16 does not contain the additional clause found in verses 17 and 18: "and he die." This additional clause indicates that it is likely someone may be struck by a thrown stone or a piece of wood in the hand and not die immediately. A person may be wounded severely and only die later as a result of the blow. Regardless, the principle is established that the perpetrator is held responsible for taking the life of the victim whether the victim dies quickly or slowly.

Throughout this passage the word used for "kill" and "murderer" is *ratsach*, the same Hebrew word used in the commandment, "Thou shalt not kill" (Exodus 20:13; the Sixth Commandment). From the various words used in the Old Testament, it seems Israel knew of at least four different perspectives of homicide:

1. Premeditated murder. In this case the killer lay in wait or carried enmity in his heart toward a person. A murderous weapon was used. Keil and Delitzsch indicate that such enmity would be strong feelings of hatred that were older than three days. They offered a paraphrase, ". . . hating him from yesterday and the day before yesterday." It is this form of murder that is the concern of this part of the lesson.

2. Accidental homicide. This is unintentional and the six cities of refuge were for persons who had accidentally killed someone.

3. The goring ox of Exodus 21:28-32. An important principle is established in these verses regarding responsibility for one's possessions. In the biblical story, if the ox was known to be violent then the owner was personally responsible. The implications of this reach far beyond the individual in our modern world. Can we suggest that morally the tobacco industry is guilty of murder by knowingly producing a product that has been shown to kill? Can we suggest that chemical companies are guilty of murder for know-

ingly polluting our atmosphere and water? Can we suggest that governments and private industry are guilty of murder for knowingly failing to be careful with nuclear power plants?

Obviously, this could become a very delicate issue. Yet, it is important to note the moral responsibility that transcends personal ownership.

4. Justifiable homicide. It seems that Israel allowed as justifiable the taking of a life if one's house was broken into at night. This provision also included slayings that occurred in the course of battle.

While some taking of life is justifiable, it is important to note that it still constitutes a violating of what God originally intended. Murder is prohibited because man has been made in the image of God. To slay a man is to cast murderous intentions upon God. John Calvin wrote that we "violate the image of God" when a murder occurs. This means the neighbor is sacred, holy.

The New Testament pushes us to understand murder as a spiritual act. Obviously a murder takes an individual human life; but it is predicated upon a death of the spirit. Jesus taught that anger and degrading one's fellows with destructive language was in danger of the same judgment that came upon murderers (Matthew 5:21, 22). He also referred to Satan as "a murderer from the beginning" (John 8:44) and connected the spirit of murder to the spirit of lying. In 1 John 3:15 we find additional commentary on the spiritual nature of murder: "Whosoever hateth his brother is a murderer: and ye know that no murderer hath eternal life abiding in him." Verses 16 and 17 show the practical applications of this principle in the need to be responsible for the legitimate welfare of others.

Finally, Psalm 42:10, 11 give special insight into the terrible reality of a murderous spirit. The psalmist is lamenting the fact that accusers are against him. He is oppressed by an enemy (v. 9). His enemies are striking against him with hard words of rejection and jeer (note the jeering is theological in v. 10; also note how this is a prophecy of the scene at the cross of Christ). In verse 11 the

psalmist asks of himself, "Why art thou cast down, O my soul?" The stinging effect of murderous words is to break the human spirit. The old childhood saying, "Sticks and stones can break my bones but words can never hurt me" is simply not true. Jesus taught that words are extremely powerful. There are murderous words that break the spirit and cast it down in order to crush and wound.

There is much debate over capital punishment. It is clear both testaments allow it as an acceptable form of punishment. The Old Testament is very clear. The New Testament can only be inferred. Yet, it is clear from Romans 13:1-7 that Paul recognized the power of the state to take life as a legitimate power. This is not to say there may not be compelling theological and moral objections raised to the continued use of capital punishment. It is important to remember that these words from Israel's ancient codes cannot simply be carried into our society without serious theological interpretation. These codes were specifically for a covenant community who accepted Yahweh as their Lord. Such is not the case for our society. But the principles are important and it is especially noteworthy that the church take seriously the New Testament's expanding teaching on what constitutes ultimate murder!

B. The Avenger of Blood (vv. 19-21)

19. The revenger of blood himself shall slay the murderer: when he meeteth him, he shall slay him.

20. But if he thrust him of hatred, or hurl at him by laying of wait, that he die;

21. Or in enmity smite him with his hand, that he die: he that smote him shall surely be put to death; for he is a murderer: the revenger of blood shall slay the murderer, when he meeteth him.

The King James Version of verses 20 and 21 does not read clearly. The use of "but" in verse 20 may lead one to think that verses 20 and 21 refer to "the revenger of blood." That is not the meaning of the text. Verses 20 and 21 refer to the murderer and emphasize again how he has murdered someone with premeditated thought. The reading of the *New International Version* is clearer: "The avenger of blood shall put the murderer to death; when he meets him, he shall put him to death. If anyone with malice aforethought shoves another or throws something at him intentionally so that he dies or if in hostility he hits him with his fist so that he dies, that person shall be put to death; he is a murderer. The avenger of blood shall put the murderer to death when he meets him" (vv. 19-21).

It is significant to note that the repetition of premeditated murder is found in this passage as a powerful reminder that accidental homicide must await due process of the law.

The avenger of blood is called in Hebrew, the *go'el*. This same word is used to describe Boaz in the transaction by which he secured Ruth as his wife. In that passage the *go'el* is the kinsman-redeemer (Ruth 4). Keil and Delitzsch write, "Redeemer is that particular relative whose special duty it was to restore the violated family integrity, who had to redeem not only landed property that had been alienated from the family, or a member of the family that had fallen into slavery, but also the blood that had been taken away from the family by murder."

In the New Testament, Jesus is our kinsman-redeemer. He is the One who has paid the price for our salvation. He is the One who allowed Himself to be slain as the Lamb of God so that the power of Satan could be broken. He is the One who will slay Satan by the power of His Word.

It should be noted that the avenger of blood is given license to get vengeance wherever he meets the murderer. Although it was important that the murder be premeditated, it is easy to see how passions could inflict injustice if the killing was accidental but the avenger failed to consider that as a reality.

Just as the New Testament made a powerful shift in the issue of murder, so it also shows a powerful shift in the issue of vengeance. The notion of the blood avenger is replaced by forgiveness. The

Apostle Paul wrote to the Roman Christians, "Do not repay anyone evil for evil. Be careful to do what is right in the eyes of everybody. If it is possible, as far as it depends on you, live at peace with everyone. Do not take revenge, my friends, but leave room for God's wrath, for it is written: 'It is mine to avenge; I will repay,' says the Lord. On the contrary: 'If your enemy is hungry, feed him; if he is thirsty, give him something to drink. In doing this, you will heap burning coals on his head.' Do not be overcome by evil, but overcome evil with good" (Romans 12:17-21; *NIV*).

Paul quoted from Deuteronomy 32:35, thus recognizing an element of Old Testament truth that was dormant until the time of the Spirit. It is very important that Christians remember Paul's words are how we live today, not the words of Numbers 35:19-21. Our task is not to find someone and "put him in his place," thus verbally slaying him. We may feel we have a right, yea, even an obligation. But that is not our calling. We are people led by the Spirit of Christ and controlled by love. Vengeance belongs only to God. It is impossible for us to know the hidden things of the heart. What we see and hear is only the surface; God knows the intentions of the heart. We are called to be reconcilers in this world. We are ambassadors of the gospels of peace and reconciliation (see 2 Corinthians 5:20). Thus, the words of forgiveness take priority over our feelings of vengeance. We obey not because we feel like it, but because God's Word is true and commands it. Such obedience will make possible the marvelous flow of redemptive power in our life.

III. SAFETY ASSURED (Numbers 35:22-28)

A. Accidental Homicide (vv. 22-24)

22. But if he thrust him suddenly without enmity, or have cast upon him any thing without laying of wait,

23. Or with any stone, wherewith a man may die, seeing him not, and cast it upon him, that he die, and was not his enemy, neither sought his harm:

24. Then the congregation shall judge

between the slayer and the revenger of blood according to these judgments.

Earlier remarks have been made concerning accidental homicide. These verses show that blood vengeance was not left to the passions of the avenger of blood. As is obvious, there are many unfortunate ways that someone may be accidentally killed. Each year many are killed in hunting accidents. Yet, there is no intent to murder and the law is cognizant of that absence of malice. The personal suffering of realizing we have been party to the death of another is sufficient enough punishment for anyone.

The law provided several safeguards besides the cities of refuge. First, note that only a designated member of the deceased family could function as the avenger of blood. This is not legalized vigilante justice. It is carefully controlled so as to preserve rights of the accused and yet offer justice to the offended family. Second, the reality of intent must be proved in order for the avenger of blood to have community sanction to avenge.

Verse 24 is given more detail in verse 25. Yet, it is clear that the community remains a part of the process. This is not a license for individual revenge. The vengeance is either sanctioned or restrained by the judges of the community. The language of the "congregation" is a reference to elders in each community that would function to determine if a slaying were either accidental or premeditated.

B. Hope for the Future (vv. 25-28).

25. And the congregation shall deliver the slayer out of the hand of the revenger of blood, and the congregation shall restore him to the city of his refuge, whither he was fled: and he shall abide in it unto the death of the high priest, which was anointed with the holy oil.

26. But if the slayer shall at any time come without the border of the city of his refuge, whither he was fled;

27. And the revenger of blood find him without the borders of the city of his refuge, and the revenger of blood

kill the slayer; he shall not be guilty of blood:

28. Because he should have remained in the city of his refuge until the death of the high priest: but after the death of the high priest the slayer shall return into the land of his possession.

From these verses we gain a perspective of how this form of justice actually functioned. If a slaying occurred, the slayer fled to the city of refuge in order to avert immediate retribution. At the city of refuge he had to plead his case of accidental manslaughter before the city would actually become sanctuary. Once the elders of the city (Levites) accepted his claim, he was granted limited protection until a full hearing could be made back in the community where the killing took place.

We are told in Numbers 35:30, 31 that it took more than one witness to the intentionality of the crime before the avenger of blood was released to exact vengeance. These witnesses were called together and if it was proved the killing was premeditated, then no ransom was available and the killer would die.

However, if the charge was not proved and the killing was seen to be accidental, it was the responsibility of the community to provide protection for the slayer back to the city of refuge. Once in the city of refuge, he was safe from the vengeance of the blood avenger.

The passage in Numbers 35:1-8 shows that the legal property for these cities included the actual city within the walls as well as the surrounding fields for a distance of 1,000 cubits (approximately 1,500 feet or 500 yards, the length of five football fields).

If the slayer ventured out of this protective zone before the death of the high priest, he was no longer under the legal protection and, if found by the avenger of blood, could be killed with immunity. This sounds harsh in our day. Yet, it recognized that even accidental killings leave wounds in the community. It provided a way for time to work healing among all the parties. It separated the slayer from the offended family so that continual contact would not open the door to more slayings of revenge. It was important that the slayer, under the protection of the refuge cities, realize this and maintain his security until the allotted time.

The slayer's property was not confiscated, neither was he under forced separation from his family. His family could move to the city of refuge and upon his release he was restored to his legal property.

The form of release for the slayer is the death of the high priest. This would be the high priest who was ruling at the time of the actual killing. On the Day of Atonement the high priest entered the Holy of Holies for the only time that year. While not actually sacrificing himself, he did carry the sins of the entire nation, including himself, into the altar to be atoned. Thus, at his death, the high priest functioned in an atoning way to set free all who were living in the cities of refuge for protection. Keil and Delitzsch wrote concerning the anointing oil: "The anointing with the holy oil was a symbol of the communication of the Holy Ghost, by which the high priest was empowered to act as mediator and representative of the nation before God, so that he alone could carry out the yearly and general expiation for the whole nation, on the great Day of Atonement. But as his life and work acquired a representative signification through this anointing with the Holy Ghost, his death might also be regarded as a death for the sins of the people, by virtue of the Holy Ghost imparted to him, through which the unintentional manslayer received the benefits of the propitiation for his sins before God, so that he could return cleansed to his native town, without further exposure to the vengeance of the avenger of blood."

The Book of Hebrews makes plain that Jesus, as our high priest, has entered the Holy of Holies "once and for all" through His atoning death. The vengeance that is rightfully ours because of our violations of the law of God are now removed through His shed blood! We are indeed people who have passed from death to life and have found "a city . . . whose builder and maker is God"

(Hebrews 11:10). Our city of refuge is found in Jesus Christ. As the great High Priest, He has died "once for all" and because of His one death on Calvary we are truly free people. We are not destined for wrath in Christ Jesus but are destined for glory through Him.

REVIEW QUESTIONS

1. Why were the six cities of refuge "Levitical" cities?

2. Why were the cities located throughout the land inhabited by Israel?

3. In what other ways did the *go'el* function besides avenger of blood? Name an Old Testament example.

4. What constitutes murder that is punishable by death in the Old Testament?

5. What is the significance of the death of the high priest for the person residing in the cities of refuge?

GOLDEN TEXT HOMILY

"GOD IS OUR REFUGE AND STRENGTH, A VERY PRESENT HELP IN TROUBLE" (Psalm 46:1).

Refuge means: (1) protection or shelter as from danger or hardship; (2) place providing protection or shelter; haven or sanctuary; (3) anything to which one may turn for help, relief or escape.

God instructed the leaders of Israel to provide six cities of refuge for those who would need a place to escape to for involuntary murder of someone. The establishing of the cities of refuge were an act of God's mercy to those who had committed the sin of involuntary murder.

The next of kin's duty to the one who was murdered was to spill the blood of the murderer. But God had these cities of refuge so the ones who committed this sin would have a place of refuge. God has always provided covering for man's sins. In the Garden of Eden, God killed animals to make clothing for Adam and Eve's sin because they were naked. "For all have sinned, and come short of the glory of God" (Romans 3:23).

Man has no escape from the penalty of his sins in himself. We all fall short in our own refuge for our sin. God's plan of redemption is the only refuge for the sinner and the saint to keep the judgment of God from being poured out on mankind because of their sins. "For the wages of sin is death; but the gift of God is eternal life through Jesus Christ our Lord" (Romans 6:23). This gift of God is our refuge now and forever.—**Charles G. Wiley, Evangelist, Weatherford, Texas**

SENTENCE SERMONS

CHRIST PROVIDES a place of refuge for all who seek deliverance from the curse of sin.

—Selected

GOD'S WRATH comes by measure; His mercy without measure.

—"Notes and Quotes"

WHEN THE PSALMIST wrote "Hope thou in God," he gave the world the only ground for hope that exists.

—Leslie D. Weatherhead

THE DYING JESUS is the evidence of God's anger toward sin; but the living Christ is the proof of God's love and forgiveness.

—Lorenz Eifert

EVANGELISTIC APPLICATION

THE UNSAVED WILL FIND MERCY AND SALVATION THROUGH FAITH AND REPENTANCE.

This comes only through faith and repentance in Jesus Christ. He is the Son of God who has revealed the purposes of eternal redemption. He is the only begotten of the Father.

The tragedy is that many turn to other gods and systems of thought for their salvation. Those who seek refuge in anything or anyone else do not escape the wrath of God.

Paul, in Romans 1, pointed out that the wrath of God is revealed because humanity has turned from Him as the true source of life and refuge. Man is an idolater in sin. Man turns to himself in order to establish faith; he turns to himself in order to establish lasting laws.

Yet, these all fail and the human heart is left destitute and longing for a Savior.

The reality of the gospel is that the Savior has appeared. The Book of Hebrews tells us that Christ first appeared to deal with sin. By dealing with sin Christ has become our refuge. This refuge is certain, for nothing can penetrate the protecting blood of Jesus. This refuge is certain, for His blood protects us from Satan's accusations. Those who turn in faith and repentance to Christ move from the realm of the unsaved to the glorious liberty of the saved!

ILLUMINATING THE LESSON

Martin Luther, in his *Table Talk*, remarked of Jesus, " 'There is but one God,' says St. Paul, 'and one mediator between God and man: namely, the man Jesus Christ, who gave Himself a ransom for all.' Therefore let no man think to draw near unto God or obtain grace of Him, without this mediator, high priest, and advocate.

"It follows that we cannot through our good works, honesty of life, virtues, deserts, sanctity, or through the works of the law, appease God's wrath, or obtain forgiveness of sins; and that all deserts of saints are quite rejected and condemned, so that through them no human creature can be justified before God. Moreover, we see how fierce God's anger is against sins, seeing that by none other sacrifice or offering could they be appeased and stilled, but by the precious blood of the Son of God."

DAILY BIBLE READINGS

M. Refuge Provided. Genesis 6:12-18

T. A Place of Safety. Deuteronomy 19:1-13

W. Justice Assured. Joshua 20:2-6

T. Need for Reconciliation. Matthew 5:21-26

F. Discipline in the Church. Matthew 18:15-17

S. The Power of Love. 1 John 3:11-18

The Almighty God

Study Text: Deuteronomy 4:31-40; 7:6-11

Supplemental References: Genesis 15:1-6, 17-21; Psalms 8:1-9; 9:7-12; Luke 11:5-13; 1 Peter 2:6-10; 1 John 4:7-21

Time: Probably early in 1406 B.C.

Place: Probably in the Arabah (Plain) east of the Jordan River

Golden Text: "Know therefore this day, and consider it in thine heart, that the Lord he is God in heaven above, and upon the earth beneath: there is none else" (Deuteronomy 4:39).

Central Truth: God's power to accomplish His will is a source of comfort and hope for all believers.

Evangelistic Emphasis: God is able to save all who come to Him through faith in Christ.

Printed Text

Deuteronomy 4:32. For ask now of the days that are past, which were before thee, since the day that God created man upon the earth, and ask from the one side of heaven unto the other, whether there hath been any such thing as this great thing is, or hath been heard like it?

33. Did ever people hear the voice of God speaking out of the midst of the fire, as thou hast heard, and live?

34. Or hath God assayed to go and take him a nation from the midst of another nation, by temptations, by signs, and by wonders, and by war, and by a mighty hand, and by a stretched out arm, and by great terrors, according to all that the Lord your God did for you in Egypt before your eyes?

35. Unto thee it was shewed, that thou mightest know that the Lord he is God; there is none else beside him.

36. Out of heaven he made thee to hear his voice, that he might instruct thee: and upon earth he shewed thee his great fire; and thou heardest his words out of the midst of the fire.

37. And because he loved thy fathers, therefore he chose their seed after them, and brought thee out in his sight with his mighty power out of Egypt.

7:6. For thou art an holy people unto the Lord thy God: the Lord thy God hath chosen thee to be a special people unto himself, above all people that are upon the face of the earth.

7. The Lord did not set his love upon you, nor choose you, because ye were more in number than any people; for ye were the fewest of all people:

8. But because the Lord loved you, and because he would keep the oath which he had sworn unto your fathers, hath the Lord brought you out with a mighty hand, and redeemed you out of the house of bondmen, from the hand of Pharaoh king of Egypt.

9. Know therefore that the Lord thy God, he is God, the faithful God, which keepeth covenant and mercy with them that loved him and keep his commandments to a thousand generations;

10. And repayeth them that hate him to their face, to destroy them: he will not be slack to him that hateth him, he will repay him to his face.

11. Thou shalt therefore keep the commandments, and the statutes, and the judgments, which I command thee this day, to do them.

LESSON OUTLINE

I. GOD'S FAITHFULNESS
  A. Mercy Creates Newness
  B. God's Unique Provision
II. GOD'S PROMISE OF BLESSING
  A. God's Mighty Power
  B. Benefits of Trusting God
III. GOD'S COVENANT OF LOVE
  A. God's Chosen People
  B. God's Great Love
  C. Loving Obedience

LESSON EXPOSITION

INTRODUCTION

One of the most powerful books in the Bible, Deuteronomy, stands at the threshold of God's people entering the Land of Promise. Numbers closed with the people at the end of the wilderness wandering preparing to enter the land. The Book of Joshua picks up the action of the crossing the Jordan and the military conquest. It is Deuteronomy that serves as an important interlude as Moses teaches the children of Israel a series of "last things" before he dies and before they enter the land. It stands as a powerful concise statement of Israel's history and God's unique purposes in her life. It is so revealing of God that it is quoted 83 times in the New Testament, making it one of the top books quoted in the New Testament (only the Gospel of John, Colossians, 1 Thessalonians, 2 Timothy, and 1, 2 Peter fail to quote from Deuteronomy; see the opening article in *The Interpreter's Bible* for more information).

This recitation of God's law is composed of three major speeches by Moses. The first speech is found in 1:6 through 4:40 (thus the closing part of this first speech is found in our lesson). The second speech (or sermon) is found in 5:1 through 28:68. The third sermon is found

in 29:1 through 30:20. At the beginning and end of the book stand an introduction and appropriate conclusion. The third part of our lesson outline is from the second major sermon of Moses.

It is likely that Deuteronomy was lost as a historical document after Israel's entrance into the land. In 2 Kings 22 and 23 we learn of Josiah's reform of religious life in 621 B.C. It is likely that the book of the Law found in the Temple was Deuteronomy. On the basis of this discovery and the reading and hearing of its marvelous message, a great revival swept the nation.

What a wonderful example this is for revival! As God's people rediscover the Word of God and apply it to their lives it results in spiritual renewal and genuine revival.

I. GOD'S FAITHFULNESS (Deuteronomy 4:31-35)

A. Mercy Creates Newness (vv. 31, 32)

(Deuteronomy 4:31 is not included in the printed text.)

As noted in the introduction, these verses constitute the climax of Moses' first speech. At the end of Deuteronomy 3 we find Moses reciting the events by which he was disallowed entry into the land. We discover there that he did beseech the Lord to allow him to enter (vv. 23-25) but the Lord did not relent of His decision regarding Moses.

Because of this incident, Moses was profoundly aware of the significance of total obedience to God's Word. His remarks in 4:1-39 emphasize the terrible folly of idolatry. The polemic against idolatry includes warnings against cult prostitution (4:3, 4); warnings against making images of people or animals (4:16-18); a clear warning against worship of the stars, sun, and moon—astrology (4:19).

In 4:26 he calls for "heaven and earth to witness against" Israel if she turned to graven images rather than worshiping the holy God. This compares with covenant curses that were pronounced upon those who broke the covenant in ancient treaties made between a king and a vassal. In this case the king was none other than the King of the Universe, the Lord God. The entire world was called to bear witness against Israel if she disobeyed His Word. Thus, even from the framework of the witnesses, Israel had a worldwide ministry of blessing if she would only obey the Lord.

The context leading to verse 31 is that after rebellion and punishment by the Lord, Israel, although few in number and scattered, will "seek the Lord thy God" and "shalt find him, if thou seek him with all thy heart and with all thy soul" (4:29). In the times of tribulation and terrible suffering Israel will return to the voice of the Lord and obey. The reason she will obey is given in verse 31:

31. For the Lord thy God is a merciful God;) he will not forsake thee, neither destroy thee, nor forget the covenant of thy fathers which he sware unto them.

With the language of "covenant," we enter the world of the sovereign will of God being worked out in the midst of sin, rebellion, and unbelief. Yet, we also discover God's power to take a few who are faithful and use them as the source of His glorious might. We discover that a covenant means God is committed to creating, maintaining, and saving His people. The reason this is so is found in verse 32:

32. For ask now of the days that are past, which were before thee, since the day that God created man upon the earth, and ask from the one side of heaven unto the other, whether there hath been any such thing as this great thing is, or hath been heard like it?

God's covenant with the fathers (Abraham, Issaac, and Jacob) is the new, marvelous thing by which God has chosen to manifest His glory. In making the covenant with Abraham (see Genesis 15:1-16; 17:1-14) God committed Himself to the future of the seed of Abraham. The Jews were birthed in a miracle of new life in the womb of Sarah. They were from Abraham's seed and thus were heirs of the promises of God's Word. This miracle event, based on the fact that Abraham believed God, became the foundation of the integrity of God's Word. Israel knew she could trust God to be faithful. The tragedy is that she failed to trust Him to be faithful to her with blessings and forced Him, by her rebellion, to be faithful to her through His judgment. Yet, even in His judgment, His covenant word to Abraham was constant.

The New Testament picks up this reality and shows that in Jesus Christ we have Israel truly obedient before the Lord. Thus, the promises to the patriarchs are found in Christ and we are heirs of mercy and grace if we believe even as Abraham believed. The theology of the Apostle Paul is crystal clear on the point that the covenant with Moses is not a covenant by which the blessings of God come to the entire world. The covenant with Abraham is the covenant by which God's mercy is manifest in Christ. Thus, the early church learned quickly that faith in Christ was the key to receiving God's blessings of eternal life and life in the Spirit.

Yet, Paul also understands that "the gifts and calling of God are without repentance," or, as the *New International Version* reads, "God's gifts and his call are irrevocable" (Romans 11:29). This shows that God still has a purpose for Israel, for the Jew, that has yet to be fulfilled. Yet, even this will be fulfilled in Christ as the Jews recognize Him as their Messiah and Savior.

Verse 32 points to the profound newness of this relationship between Israel and her God. The invitation is to look all through heaven and try and find another example. There is no other example! Even Adam and Eve in the Garden of Eden are not heirs of such a unique relationship as God has decreed He will have with Israel.

In 2 Corinthians 5:17-21 Paul described the reality of this newness that we have in Christ. Please try to follow the logical connection of biblical theology at this point: God's unique love for Israel through His covenant with Abraham is now available to all who will believe. This newness is expressed by Paul, "If anyone is in Christ, he is a new creation; the old has gone, the new has come!" (v. 17, *NIV*). When the Christian takes delight in being a "new creation" in Christ it is important to remember we are heirs of the blessings and promises of God. We as Christians now have the responsibility of blessing the world by faith and obedience. Only at the end will the world be overwhelmingly blessed as the Jews return back to their historic mission and accept Christ.

Paul's vision of this blessing is further expressed in Romans 11:15-36. In speaking of the Jews he wrote, "If their rejection is the reconciliation of the world [that is, if by rejecting Christ and offering Him on the Cross, the Jews helped to make possible His atoning, reconciling death], what will their acceptance be but life from the dead? [that is, if their rejection brought reconciliation, just imagine what their acceptance of Christ will bring!]" (v. 15, *NIV*).

The reason it is important for Christians to understand this is far more than just intellectual curiosity. It means that Christians and Jews are brothers in Christ. The Christian already shares in the brotherly fellowship with Christ; the Jew does not yet share in that brotherly fellowship but will. It means that since we are brothers in Christ, as Christians we have a tremendous responsibility to the Jew to respect, protect, and love him, even when he rejects Christ. Anti-Semitism of any kind is to be rejected by Christians as completely contrary to the will of God. Anti-Semitism is ultimately ungodly and anti-Christ because it places us against our brothers in Christ.

B. God's Unique Provision (vv. 33-35)

33. Did ever people hear the voice of God speaking out of the midst of the fire, as thou hast heard, and live?

34. Or hath God assayed to go and take him a nation from the midst of another nation, by temptations, by signs, and by wonders, and by war, and by a mighty hand, and by a stretched out arm, and by great terrors, according to all that the Lord your God did for you in Egypt before your eyes?

35. Unto thee it was shewed, that thou mightest know that the Lord he is God; there is none else beside him.

A series of questions serve to show the special work that God did for Israel. The "ever" of verse 33 is better rendered "did any." The voice of God heard from the midst of the fire refers to God's presence on Mount Sinai. In Exodus 19:16 we read of thunder and lightning on the mountain. The mountain was wrapped in smoke because the Lord descended in the form of fire according to Exodus 19:18. In the Psalm 68:8 account we learn that the mountain quaked at the presence of God. We also understand that God was present through fire on the mountain in Deuteronomy 5:4, 5. An interesting New Testament remembrance of this is found in Hebrews 12:18-24 where the revelation of God on Sinai is contrasted with His revelation in Jesus Christ. This incident concludes in Deuteronomy 4:33 concludes by drawing attention to the fact that such a revelation by God generally meant death. Yet, for Israel, they had lived. One cannot help but wonder if Moses is making reference to other revelations of God in which nations were destroyed as God appeared, such as the fire storm that fell on Sodom and Gomorrah (Genesis 19).

While verse 33 focused on the revelation at Sinai as a unique revelation, verse 34 focuses on the deliverance from Egypt as a unique manifestation of His presence. The "assayed" is old English which means "attempted." It was unheard of that any god would deliver a weak people from oppression, especially from a power as great as Egypt. Even more astounding was the manner in which the deliverance was wrought: by signs, wonders, temptations, and so on. The "temptations" must be understood as being trials that proved the character of Pharaoh. Note that Moses, in both instances of events so crucial in Israel's life, is calling the people to remember something that is part of their immediate experience, "before your eyes."

The purpose of these revelations is revealed in verse 35: that Israel might truly know that Yahweh (the Lord) is God; "there is none else beside him." Moses was rightfully concerned that idolatry would be Israel's downfall. He knew the severe temptations to trust in gods of the visible realm rather than trust in the God of the Spirit. The recitation of these marvelous acts of God's revelation were to remind Israel of the special love God had for her.

This central belief in the absolute supremacy of God runs throughout the Bible. The holy preaching of the prophets is predicated upon its reality. The passages in Isaiah 43:10-13; 44:9-20; 45:5, 6, 9-12 all speak forcefully to this point.

II. GOD'S PROMISE OF BLESSING (Deuteronomy 4:36-40)

A. God's Mighty Power (vv. 36-38)

(Deuteronomy 4:38 is not included in the printed text.)

36. Out of heaven he made thee to hear his voice, that he might instruct thee: and upon earth he shewed thee his great fire; and thou heardest his words out of the midst of the fire.

37. And because he loved thy fathers, therefore he chose their seed after them, and brought thee out in his sight with his mighty power out of Egypt.

It is by His great power that the Lord delivered Israel from the hands of the Egyptians and while verse 37 confirms the Lord's love for Israel's fathers (the patriarchs). As was seen earlier, this love was a covenant love based on God's faithful word. Verse 38 is a promise, based on that same covenant love, that Israel, though weak when compared to the nations around her, will be victorious in the land because the Lord will drive the enemies away.

B. Benefits of Trusting God (vv. 39, 40)

(Deuteronomy 4:39, 40 are not included in the printed text).

Israel is commanded to "know" what the Lord has said. This "knowing" is not primarily intellectual; it is a knowing that results in action. It is a knowing that

leads to obedience. It is a knowing that accepts the challenge of the future and God's provision of strength and wisdom.

This knowledge is primarily a spiritual knowledge. It is based upon the fact, birthed in revelation and reared in faith, that God is Lord over all creation and there are no other gods.

This spiritual knowledge understands that God as Creator and God as Redeemer are life-changing ideas. It understands that since the Lord God is the Lord of all, what He says must be true and will be accomplished. This spiritual knowledge breaks the strongholds of doubt and fear. This spiritual knowledge feeds on God's Word and the marvelous manifestations of His love. This spiritual knowledge informs me that demonic power is broken in God through Christ and that the very gates of hell cannot withstand the truth of the living God.

III. GOD'S COVENANT OF LOVE (Deuteronomy 7:6-11)

As mentioned in the introduction, this part of the lesson is found in the second major speech (or sermon) by Moses. The theme of warning against idolatry becomes more specific in Deuteronomy 7:1-5. Various groups that the Israelites will encounter in the land are named: Hittites, Girgashites, Amorites, Canaanites, Perizzites, Hivites, and Jebusites. Moses told Israel that these seven nations were greater than them (7:1); yet, they would be delivered to the Israelites by the divine intervention of God.

The command is that these groups are to be totally destroyed. The Hebrew word to describe this "holy war" has the sense of "devoting" them to the Lord. It means they were to be destroyed as an act of sanctification to purify the land for the things of God. This is holy war born from obedience and not birthed in hatred. It is easy to see how this can be distorted (as in the case of some versions of Islamic fundamentalism). The spiritual principle remains true today: we are to utterly destroy those things in our life that keep us from obeying the Lord in faith.

The reason they were to be removed was so they would not be present for intermarriage and thus pollute the integrity of the faith. Intermarriage meant that foreign gods would be introduced into the households of Israel. Verse 5 gives specific instructions on how these foreign gods were to be dealt with.

A. God's Chosen People (v. 6)

6. For thou art an holy people unto the Lord thy God: the Lord thy God hath chosen thee to be a special people unto himself, above all people that are upon the face of the earth.

This verse describes a profound responsibility as well as a marvelous opportunity. Several things should be noted:

1. Israel is holy unto the Lord. After all the murmurings and times of disobedience, this people is still holy to God. This kind of holiness is not based on personal obedience or morality; it is based on the fact that God has separated Israel unto Himself for a particular purpose in human history. Thus, Israel's holiness was always dependent upon God's holiness. She was not holy because of anything she did or was; rather, she was holy because of who He was and His commitment to her.

2. Second, Israel is a "holy people." It is important that not only were the Levites holy, but all in Israel were holy to the Lord. The idea that God wants only a few people to be holy in the church is totally false. God calls for all to be holy, even as He is holy. Holiness is not an option in Christian living; it is the essence of Christian living.

3. God chose Israel. This is divine election. We should distance ourselves from double predestination that says God has chosen some for heaven and some for hell. This is not taught in the Word of God. People go to hell because of their disobedience to the Word of truth. People go to heaven because they accept God's loving and merciful provision of eternal life in Christ Jesus.

However, let us not fail to underscore the reality of God's election of us in Christ. In Christ, God has chosen all for eternal life. The invitation to respond to this election is given to "whosoever will." It is man who chooses to reject God's grace. God has chosen eternal life for all

who will believe. To enter into questions like "Since God knows all things, then He must know who will accept and who will not" is to utterly miss the point of divine election and to beg the question that cannot be answered.

Election means that God has chosen to make the impossible possible. The impossible is man's efforts to save himself. God, in Christ, has made the only provision for man's lost condition.

4. This election is an election to be a "special people." The term "special people" reminds us of 1 Peter 2:9, "But ye are a chosen generation, a royal priesthood, an holy nation, a peculiar people." While 1 Peter likely reflects Isaiah 43:21, the term "special" or "peculiar" has caused many people serious misunderstandings. *The Interpreter's Bible* on 1 Peter shows that the English word for "peculiar" comes from a Latin word referring to a slave held as private property. Thus, a better way to translate both 1 Peter 2:9 and Deuteronomy 7:6 is by an expression such as "a people for God's own possession." Thus, Israel was set free from the bondage of Egypt's terrible slavery so she could become God's "slave" for righteousness in the world.

B. God's Great Love (vv. 7, 8)

7. The Lord did not set his love upon you, nor choose you, because ye were more in number than any people; for ye were the fewest of all people:

8. But because the Lord loved you, and because he would keep the oath which he had sworn unto your fathers, hath the Lord brought you out with a mighty hand, and redeemed you out of the house of bondmen, from the hand of Pharaoh king of Egypt.

God's ways in the world are not man's ways. It is the way of man to look to power and might as the ultimate authorities. God's way is to confound the wise and use the foolish and weak things of the world to manifest His glory (1 Corinthians 1:18-31). Paul had to learn this lesson personally. In 2 Corinthians 12:1-10 he wrote of his discovery that "when I am weak, then I am strong" (v. 10, *NIV*) and that Jesus had told him, "My grace is sufficient for you, for my power is made perfect in weakness" (v. 9, *NIV*).

The reason God chose Israel and loved her greatly is because of His word made to Abraham. Again, we return to the reality of covenant as the basis for this liberating relationship between God and His people. God will keep His word! It is because of this covenant love that God delivered Israel from the hands of the Egyptians.

It is important to note that God's love is always expressed in actions that affect people. The deliverance from Egypt and destruction of Pharaoh's army was a clear manifestation of the action of His love. That is exactly the meaning of John 3:16, "For God so loved the world, that he gave his only begotten Son." Note that *love* means "God gave!" The incarnation of Jesus, as the Word made flesh, expresses itself in the reality of His divine love on the Cross. It is the Cross that reveals the depths of the love of God. No form of sin, no human suffering, is greater than the suffering of Jesus on the Cross.

C. Loving Obedience (vv. 9-11)

9. Know therefore that the Lord thy God, he is God, the faithful God, which keepeth covenant and mercy with them that love him and keep his commandments to a thousand generations;

10. And repayeth them that hate him to their face, to destroy them: he will not be slack to him that hateth him, he will repay him to his face.

11. Thou shalt therefore keep the commandments, and the statutes, and the judgments, which I command thee this day, to do them.

In verse 9 the word "mercy" is the Hebrew *hesed*. It is a very important biblical word that is sometimes translated as "steadfast love" or "lovingkindness." It comes from the language of *covenant* and refers to "the obligations involved in a covenant relationship" (*The Interpreter's Bible*). Gerhard von Rad in *Old Testament Theology* comments that *hesed* "designates an attitude required by fellowship and includes a

disposition and an attitude of solidarity." It is also interesting that von Rad discusses *hesed* under the heading of righteousness as seen in His fidelity (faithfulness) to His covenant word. God's inner disposition toward humankind through the covenant is expressed by *hesed*. Thus, God is not grudgingly remaining faithful for the sake of a legal principle; rather, His heart is filled with love and He longs to share the blessings of that love with humanity.

But the sharing of this great love takes place within the context of the covenant. Israel had a role to obey the covenant stipulations so that God's holiness would not be defamed and thus life could flow freely. Since God kept the promise of His word, and did so with the lovingkindness expressed in *hesed*, then Israel should obey His word and do so with pure hearts of love and reverence.

REVIEW QUESTIONS

1. Why did Moses speak so forcefully concerning the threat of idolatry in Canaan?

2. How are the promises to Abraham fulfilled in Christ Jesus?

3. Are all Christians called to live holy lives?

4. In what way can we understand election for us in Jesus Christ?

GOLDEN TEXT HOMILY

"KNOW THEREFORE THIS DAY, AND CONSIDER IT IN THINE HEART, THAT THE LORD HE IS GOD IN HEAVEN ABOVE, AND UPON THE EARTH BENEATH: THERE IS NONE ELSE" (Deuteronomy 4:39).

This intriguing text is drawn from a powerful exhortation to obedience delivered to the children of Israel by Moses. As the days of his leadership drew ever nearer to the end, he carefully documented reasons why Israel should honor and obey God. From their own historical perspective, he reminded them over and over again of God's intervention in their national affairs. Nothing else could account for the fact that a young upstart nation had appeared on the horizon of history and supplanted established nations and kingdoms, driving them before their onslaught as the last lingering leaves of fall before the blustery winds of winter. The omnipotent God had been behind the scene orchestrating every development for this fledgling nation.

Moses did not appeal to the proof of history alone, however. He challenged them to consider in their heart the strength of his claim. The Lord of heaven and earth alone controlled the destinies of men and nations. The still, small voice of the heart bore witness to the supremacy of the Almighty God. He was attempting to draw out from them a national confession of this powerful revelation so that Israel could proclaim to the world of its day the existence of this one all-knowing, all-powerful Supreme Being.

How well Moses knew the fickle nature of this gainsaying people! How often had the people of God attempted to reduce the Almighty to just another god among many gods? As they stood on the threshold of the Promised Land, their venerable leader reminded them of God's miraculous delivery from Egypt's oppressive bondage.

May Moses' warning resound to our generation. We too have been called from the bondage of sin and promised our own Canaanland. We must not allow the gods of this present age to dull our spiritual perception of God. He is still the God of heaven and earth. There is no other God. The universe declares it; history supports it; and we must believe it!—**Jimmy D. Wood, Associate Pastor, Church of God, Martinsville, Virginia**

SENTENCE SERMONS

GOD'S POWER TO ACCOMPLISH His will is a source of comfort and hope for all believers.
Selected

NOTHING IS SO HIGH and above all danger that is not below and in the power of God.
"Encyclopedia of Religious Quotations"

GOD IS big enough to be everywhere but small enough to be anywhere.
"Notes and Quotes"

GOD HEARS no sweeter music than the cracked chimes of the courageous human spirit ringing in imperfect acknowledgment of His perfect love.
Joshua Loth Liebman

EVANGELISTIC APPLICATION

GOD IS ABLE TO SAVE ALL WHO COME TO HIM THROUGH FAITH IN CHRIST.

This is the marvelous good news of the gospel! "God is able" means that nothing is impossible with Him. All who are burdened under the weight of sin are invited to the God who is able! All who carry the terrors of uncontrollable passions are invited to the presence of the God who is able. The message rings true: He is able to deliver thee!

Not only is God able to save; He is also willing to save. God desires that all come to Him and receive His bountiful gift of life in Christ Jesus. From eternity it was the will of the heavenly Father that the eternal Son be prepared to suffer and die for our sin. God did not will sin in the Garden of Eden. That came through man's disobedience. God willed fellowship and communion with His creatures. He is so committed to that will that Christ has come to die so the power of sin can be broken over all who believe. But God is not content to simply leave it for those who will believe. The time is coming when Christ will appear the second time to establish God's perfect will on this earth.

The tragedy will rest upon all who refuse to accept the gift of God and condemn themselves to an eternal separation from God's love.

ILLUMINATING THE LESSON

"Come, Thou Almighty King" is a hymn familiar to many. Although a beautiful melody that sounds a rich, triumphant note, knowledge of its background is scarce. It is first found in an English hymnal of 1757 with a hymn by Charles Wesley. If Wesley wrote it, that claim has never been substantiated.

When we consider the message of this hymn, perhaps it is good that no one person can claim fame to it. The four verses magnify the glory and power of the Holy Trinity. It almost demands that human attention be slighted so that only praise to God remains.

The first verse is a tribute to God, the Father. He is called the "Almighty King" and "Ancient of Days." His victorious might is remembered and His kingship is affirmed.

The second verse praises Jesus Christ. He is called the "Incarnate word." His power is manifested through His "mighty sword." In relationship to Christ, three things emerge: (1) the effects of prayer; (2) the success of Christ's word; (3) the power of holiness resting upon us.

The third verse praises the Holy Spirit as the "Holy Comforter." Through His presence the almighty power of God is manifested in exercising "rule in every heart." The verse closes with Him being called "Spirit of power."

The final stanza affirms the unity of this one God, "To Thee, great One in Three." The "sovereign majesty" of God is revealed for us to praise and glorify for all eternity.

Yes, this is indeed a powerful prayer of the believing church, "Come, Thou Almighty King"!

DAILY BIBLE READINGS:

M. God's Power to Bless. Genesis 12:1-3

T. God's Power in Creation. Psalm 8:1-9

W. God's Power in Righteousness. Psalm 9:7-12

T. God's Power to Deliver. Luke 1:46-55

F. God's Power for Believers. Ephesians 1:15-23

S. God's Power for Love. 1 John 4:7-21

Possessing God's Promises

Study Text: Deuteronomy 11:1-32

Supplemental References: Deuteronomy 30:11-20; 1 Samuel 17:41-49; 2 Kings 4:1-7; Romans 6:12-19; 2 Corinthians 6:3-10

Time: Probably early in 1406 B.C.

Place: Probably in the Plain of Moab, east of the Jordan River.

Golden Text: "Therefore shall ye keep all the commandments which I command you this day, that ye may be strong, and go in and possess the land" (Deuteronomy 11:8).

Central Truth: Obedience to the will of God makes us heirs of His eternal promises.

Evangelistic Emphasis: Eternal life is found in the promises of God manifested in Christ.

Printed Text

Deuteronomy 11:13. And it shall come to pass, if ye shall hearken diligently unto my commandments which I command you this day, to love the Lord your God, and to serve him with all your heart and with all your soul,

14. That I will give you the rain of your land in his due season, the first rain and the latter rain, that thou mayest gather in thy corn, and thy wine, and thine oil.

15. And I will send grass in thy fields for thy cattle, that thou mayest eat and be full.

16. Take heed to yourselves, that your heart be not deceived, and ye turn aside, and serve other gods, and worship them;

17. And then the Lord's wrath be kindled against you, and he shut up the heaven, that there be no rain, and that the land yield not her fruit; and lest ye perish quickly from off the good land which the Lord giveth you.

22. For if ye shall diligently keep all these commandments which I command you, to do them, to love the Lord your God, to walk in all his ways, and to cleave unto him;

23. Then will the Lord drive out all these nations from before you, and ye shall possess greater nations and mightier than yourselves.

24. Every place whereon the soles of your feet shall tread shall be your's: from the wilderness and Lebanon, from the river, the river Euphrates, even unto the uttermost sea shall your coast be.

25. There shall no man be able to stand before you: for the Lord your God shall lay the fear of you and the dread of you upon all the land that ye shall tread upon, as he hath said unto you.

26. Behold, I set before you this day a blessing and a curse;

27. A blessing, if ye obey the com-

mandments of the Lord your God, which I command you this day:
28. And a curse, if ye will not obey the commandments of the Lord your God, but turn aside out of the way which I command you this day, to go after other gods, which ye have not known.

DICTIONARY

wilderness of Lebanon (LEB-uh-nun)—Deuteronomy 11:24—Lebanon's mountain range extended for 100 miles along the Syrian Coast. The wilderness possibly refers to the forest area.

river Euphrates (You-FRAY-teez)—Deuteronomy 11:24—The longest and most important river of Western Asia. It was the boundary between Assyria and the Hittite country after Solomon's time.

LESSON OUTLINE

I. THE REWARDS OF OBEDIENCE
  A. Strong in the Lord
  B. Joy of the Lord
  C. Bountiful Provision
  D. Divine Warning

II. THE VICTORY OF OBEDIENCE
  A. God's Powerful Word
  B. God's Promised Victory

III. THE BLESSINGS OF OBEDIENCE
  A. Human Choices
  B. Mandatory Decisions

LESSON EXPOSITION

INTRODUCTION

The introductory remarks concerning Deuteronomy made in lesson 11 should be read again in preparation for this lesson.

The lesson this week shows the relationship between obedience and possessing God's promises. It shows that God demands obedience if we are to share in the manifold blessings He has provided by His grace. This obedience is not something we bargain over; rather, it is born out of humble gratitude for what God has done to deliver us from sin.

Many people turn from obedience because they do not desire to be compelled to serve God. They fail to understand that obedience is birthed in love. We read in 1 John 4:19 that we love God "because he first loved us." The manifestation of our love is found in obedience.

I. THE REWARDS OF OBEDIENCE (Deuteronomy 11:8-17)
A. Strong in the Lord (vv. 8, 9)
(Deuteronomy 11:8, 9 is not included in the printed text.)

Deuteronomy 11 brings together two events in Israel's history to contrast the rewards of God's mercy and the tragedy of disobedience. As we have noted in earlier lessons, the deliverance from Egypt stands as the clear example of God's saving mercy (vv. 2-5). Note the reading of the King James Version in your Bible. In these verses the emphasis falls upon what God (He) did. In verses 2-4 the third person singular (he, his) is used eight times to emphasize what God has done.

On the other hand, verses 6 and 7 show what happened to Dathan and Abiram when they disobeyed the Lord. Their rebellion and deaths are recorded in Numbers 16. The revolt is the same as Korah's revolt in which God's divine authority in Moses was challenged. It was a terrible scene of judgment as entire families were destroyed by the wrath of God. The enormity of their sin consisted in the arrogance in offering themselves as leaders without divine authority and anointing.

It is with these critical events in mind that verses 8 and 9 call the people to a life of obedience. Obedience has its rewards. These rewards are enumerated in verses 8 and 9.

The first reward is found in the promise "that ye may be strong." Biblical Hebrew has nearly a dozen different words that speak of "strong, strength."

The word used here is *chazaq* which has the sense of "grow firm." There is a sense of gaining strength in this verb. It is used of royal power (2 Samuel 3:1; 2 Chronicles 26:15; Daniel 11:5); of the power of a king's word to prevail over the word of another (2 Samuel 24:4); of growth in courage and confidence (Deuteronomy 31:6, 7, 23); of the growth in strength necessary to make repairs (Nehemiah 3:19); of the power of someone to take hold of something in order to master or complete it (Nehemiah 5:16). It is also used to describe the power of the hand of the Lord (Deuteronomy 6:21; 7:8; 9:26).

It should be noted that not all uses of this word are positive. It is also used to describe that the heart of Pharaoh was hardened, rigid, opposed to God's will (Exodus 7:13, 22; 8:15).

From this contrast it appears that obedience to the Lord is a key factor in keeping the heart on the right track. There is a sense in which people can grow strong in their desire to control other people and circumstances of life. Such control is usually not in harmony with the work of the Holy Spirit. The "strength" required of the Lord is a growing strength. It is the strength that provides spiritual victory in times of battle. An excellent New Testament illustration is found in Ephesians 6:10. The context of the passage is Paul's description of the Christian and his spiritual warfare against the "wiles of the devil" (v. 11). My own translation of Ephesians 6:10 offers a dynamic look at the use of "growing in strength": "From now on, be continually strengthened in the Lord and in the intensity of His might." The Greek for "intensity" has the sense of the strength by which a person "does" something." The Greek for "might" is the strength that a person has inherently; it is the strength that He actually *is*.

When we bring this passage to bear on the strength mentioned in Deuteronomy 11:8, we see that the word of the Lord provides the strength by which we can possess the blessings of God. But we must note that this strength for the Christian is not the "strength" of human power,

human personality, human effort. This strength is the power of the Holy Spirit who births in us the strength of humility, forgiveness, reconciliation, mercy, and love. It is the strength witnessed by the fruit of the Spirit (Galatians 5:22, 23).

Verse 9 also shows that obedience to the Lord brings long-term blessings. The Bible speaks of a principle which is applicable to all life: "Whatsoever a man soweth, that shall he also reap" (Galatians 6:7). If a person sows disobedience and rebellion, he reaps that throughout his entire life. If a person sows obedience, then the blessings of God are reaped over the course of life. This principle is established in Galatians 6:7 because "God is not mocked." God has ordained that people who go by His name live a certain way—the way of faith and obedience. The person who disregards the ways of God makes mockery of His Word of life and places himself in the sphere of judgment and discipline from the Lord.

Many people think that because there are no immediate negative results of sin they are "free" from the consequences of their actions. That is far from the case. Because sin is primarily a spiritual matter, it extends into the spiritual future. Thus, we may reap the consequences of our actions through our children or other circumstances. This is not because God is capricious and is out there causing us problems! It is because we have sinned and that sin has a spiritual life of its own that penetrates into the future. If not manifested in this life, it will be clearly manifested in hell's eternity.

The only hope we have from this clinging power of sin is repentance, and where necessary and possible, restitution. While there may be consequences of our sinful actions that still seek to work themselves out in our redeemed lives; as forgiven people in Christ, we can be assured God's purposes will be accomplished through our lives and His name glorified regardless of the sins of the past.

Just as God will not be mocked by our rebellion; God will also not allow Satan to rob Him of His due glory as we repent and submit to His Word.

B. Joy of the Lord (vv. 10-12)

(Deuteronomy 11:10-12 is not included in the printed text.)

Obedience brings us into a richness of life that is incomparable to anything we have ever experienced. We know from Exodus 14:10-12 that the Israelites immediately began to clamor for the comfort of Egypt.

This memory of Egypt continued to be part of their life in the wilderness (16: 2, 3; 32:1-6). The heart not circumcised (sanctified), even though forgiven of sin, still considers the world of sin to have its attraction. This memory of the world's "better life" must be removed so the whole self can be given to God's glory. This memory is not removed by any magic or irrational action; rather, the world is revealed in its sinfulness and the self recognizes the truth of God's Word. This happens at the cross of Jesus where both sin and grace are most clearly revealed. At the cross of Christ, God's glory is revealed and we discover in the depths of our heart that we truly belong to Him. Sanctification reveals the glory of eternity (Romans 6:22) and thus our hearts are turned from dependence upon this world to genuine dependence and trust in God.

Verse 10 reveals that the supposed glory of Egypt is an illusion. It was a place where constant irrigation was absolutely essential. Even today, Egypt is only fertile along the Nile River Valley (a very small strip of land surrounded by desert). Note that the sowed seed had to be watered by foot. We are not exactly sure what this referred to in the ancient world. However, it clearly shows that water was not easily available and required more than the usual effort. The verse concludes by observing that after all that effort the result was little more than a garden of herbs. The smallness of Egypt's crop is commented upon to remind Israel that the world truly has "little" to offer in the light of God's abundant provision.

The comparison is vividly made in verses 11 and 12. The reference of "hills and valleys" indicates diversity of land. Such diversity is able to sustain large groups of people as well as provide for diversity of life skills. Finally, verse 12 reveals that this land is the land God cares for. His eyes are always upon it. The beauty of God's provision is thus seen in the fact that God considers it "the apple of His eye."

C. Bountiful Provision (vv. 13-15)

13. And it shall come to pass, if ye shall hearken diligently unto my commandments which I command you this day, to love the Lord your God, and to serve him with all your heart and with all your soul,

14. That I will give you the rain of your land in his due season, the first rain and the latter rain, that thou mayest gather in thy corn, and thy wine, and thine oil.

15. And I will send grass in thy fields for thy cattle, that thou mayest eat and be full.

The list of blessings continues in these verses with references to the early and latter rain. This came to be representative of the outpouring of the Holy Spirit. There are nine clear references in the Old Testament to the first or early rain, and the latter rain. There is one New Testament reference. The early, or autumn, rain came from mid-October to mid-December. Following the dry period of the summer, it was the rain that softened the ground for plowing and planting of the fields. While it usually rained through most of the winter, the latter rains came from late February to early April that brought the grain to full growth. This full growth manifested itself in the barley harvest of April and May and the wheat harvest of May and June.

Among Pentecostals, the early rain is seen to represent the time of the ministry of Christ and the outpouring of the Holy Spirit on the Day of Pentecost. It was the work of the Spirit that prepared the harvest for planting and reaping that would follow. The latter rain is understood today to refer to the current outpouring of the Holy Spirit (a reality that has existed since the first of this century) and the anticipated return of the Lord. This outpouring of the Holy Spirit is God's work of preparing the harvest for His glorious return.

The Old Testament passages mentioned above and some comments about them are listed below:

1. Leviticus 26:4—The "rains in their season" (*New American Standard Bible*) clearly refer to the early and latter rains. The context deals with obedience (much like Deuteronomy 11) and the increase of the harvest.

2. Job 29:23—In summing up his life, Job remembered that once men listened to him like thirsty men waiting for water. His words were words of wisdom like the spring rain (latter rain) that brought the harvest.

3. Proverbs 16:15—The favor that comes from the king of righteousness is like the blessing that comes from the spring rain (latter rain).

4. Jeremiah 3:3—The latter rain (spring) has been withheld from Judah because of her idolatry.

5. Jeremiah 5:24—A clear reference is made to both rains. Yet, there is no respect of the God who gives these rains; the people live in open rebellion against Him.

6. Hosea 6:3—Those who repent can turn to the Lord and expect His grace-filled blessings to come to them as the latter rain.

7. Joel 2:23—The atmosphere is one of gladness and joy as the early rains have come as a sign of God's love and the latter rain will arrive as promised.

8. Zechariah 10:1—God calls for His people to ask for the latter rain (spring) rather than trust in the deceivers of their generation. The call is for God's people to call for the Holy Spirit to be poured out upon them; the Spirit of truth and righteousness.

9. Deuteronomy 11:14—This verse in our lesson is the promise of great blessings as a result of the first and latter rains.

The passage from the New Testament is James 5:7. In this context the return of the Lord is specifically related to the latter rain. His return is certain; as certain as the latter rain in Palestine.

It is important that we recognize the relationship between the Holy Spirit and

God's blessings to us. The Holy Spirit, the third person of the blessed Trinity, is alive in the world today. He is present to reveal the glory of Christ and to fill our life with the presence of Christ. He does the work of revealing Christ's words to us. He is the divine Teacher who leads us into all truth. He applies the blood of Jesus to our heart in sanctifying power. He manifests Himself to His church in tongues, miracles, revelations, and prophecies. He upbuilds and empowers the church for service to Christ. He convicts the world of sin.

All these things are elements of God's blessings to us as we live obediently in the world. While there may be some correlation between material blessings and the work of the Holy Spirit, we must not make that correlation too strong. The blessing of the Holy Spirit is for greater power to serve Christ.

D. Divine Warning (vv. 16, 17)

16. Take heed to yourselves, that your heart be not deceived, and ye turn aside, and serve other gods, and worship them;

17. And then the Lord's wrath be kindled against you, and he shut up the heaven, that there be no rain, and that the land yield not her fruit; and lest ye perish quickly from off the good land which the Lord giveth you.

In the previous section it was noted in the two passages from Jeremiah (3:3; 5:24) that judgment was manifested in withholding the rains. That judgment, while foretold in Deuteronomy, was remembered during the early days of Solomon's reign. During his prayer at the dedication of the newly-built Temple (recorded in both 1 Kings 8:35 and 2 Chronicles 6:26) the word of the Lord spoke through him making it plain that sin on the part of Israel/Judah would cause the early and latter rains to cease.

It should be noted from Jeremiah 3:3 and 5:24 that the specific sin that most concerned the Lord was that of idolatry. Verse 16 makes plain that the serving of other gods brings God's judgment upon His people.

In verse 17 the wrath of God is manifested in the natural world. This is consistent with Paul's interpretation of the wrath of God in Romans 1. There the apostle makes plain the fact that sin bears its fruit in destruction of humankind. It was noted that sexual immorality (especially that of homosexuality) brings its error to fruition in the lives of those who live such immoral lives.

II. THE VICTORY OF OBEDIENCE (Deuteronomy 11:18-25)

A. God's Powerful Word (vv. 18-21)

(Deuteronomy 11:18-21 is not included in the printed text.)

God's final word to Israel was not that of wrath, but the reward and hope found in obedience. These verses reveal that man has a part to play in warding off the wrath of God. Man's part is to "lay up" God's Word in his heart. The Hebrew word translated "lay up" has the meaning of "put, place, set." There is a sense in which the Word of God is "set, established" in the heart. This is not some form of Bible idolatry; rather, it is an awareness that the living God of creation has spoken His definitive word of life in Christ Jesus and the revelation of Him is found in the Bible. The *heart* in biblical thought is the place of willful decision making. It is that place where the self is confronted with the choice of life or death.

By binding the Word of God to the hands and eyes, God's Word is made central to life. All life is meant to focus upon the Word. This is not a naive focus that discounts human achievement in science, the arts, and technology; rather, it is a placing of God's Word as the ultimate priority by which all other words are measured for their eternal value.

This Word is so important that it is commanded to be passed down from one generation to the next. The most unfaithful act any Christian parent can commit is to fail to pass down the Word of God to their children. To fail to pass along the Word as God's living Word in our life is to leave our children defenseless in a world where Satan seeks to devour and destroy. It would be just as foolish to give a teenager license with the family car on interstate highways without first teaching them how to drive and control a speeding vehicle. No parent in his/her right mind would allow such a thing. Yet, numerous Christian parents spend more time watching evening television than making time for the Word of God to be heard, memorized, and understood in the lives of their children. It is little wonder many children born and reared in the church depart from it when they become adults; they have seen the superficiality of our adult lives and how carelessly we have handled the Word of God.

B. God's Promised Victory (vv. 22-25)

22. For if ye shall diligently keep all these commandments which I command you, to do them, to love the Lord your God, to walk in all his ways, and to cleave unto him;

23. Then will the Lord drive out all these nations from before you, and ye shall possess greater nations and mightier than yourselves.

24. Every place whereon the soles of your feet shall tread shall be your's: from the wilderness and Lebanon, from the river, the river Euphrates, even unto the uttermost sea shall your coast be.

25. There shall no man be able to stand before you: for the Lord your God shall lay the fear of you and the dread of you upon all the land that ye shall tread upon, as he hath said unto you.

The keeping of the Lord's commandments (v. 22) is composed of four distinct things. It should be noted that to *keep* these commandments means we are to "observe" them, to "take heed." So that no one will misunderstand the nature of "observing," these four elements are specified to show the intimacy this "keeping" will bring between the Lord and His obedient children.

The first is to "do" the commandments. This refers to specific acts of obedience. It means that God's law is not a law for "someone else." It means that the attitude "do what I say, not what I do" is not applicable to the child of God. God's law is very specific; we are called to specifically obey.

The second thing is to "love the Lord." This love bespeaks a relationship of trust. It shows that *doing* is not the sum of total obedience. There are many who *perfectly* obey; yet, their love relationship with Christ is nonexistent. They obey the law but only to show their own rightness; genuine compassion and love for others is missing. They know how to *do*; but they know little of mercy.

The third aspect is to "walk in all his ways." If *doing* connotes specific obedience, then *walking* denotes an attitude of obedience that is reflected in the totality of life. The New Testament has much to say about "walking" with the Lord: Romans 6:4; 8:4; 2 Corinthians 5:7; Galatians 5:16; Ephesians 4:1; 5:2; Colossians 1:10; 2:6; 4:5. The person who "walks" with another has made a fundamental decision regarding an attitude of cooperation and friendship. There are many Christians who obey the Lord and love Him; yet, they need an attitude adjustment in order to daily be obedient in joy and thanksgiving.

The final aspect is to "cleave" unto the Lord. Its usage in the Old Testament gives us insight into the nature of the relationship this has to keeping His commandments. It is first used in Genesis 2:24 to describe the marriage relationship between man and woman. It is important to note that to "cleave" to one's wife is to eliminate all other women from exercising power and compelling influence in a man's life. In the Genesis passage the burden of "cleaving" falls upon the man. It is his responsibility to make certain no other woman, including his earthly mother, interferes with the divinely ordained plan.

"Clave" is used in Genesis 34:3 to describe the strong love Shechem felt for Jacob's daughter, Dinah. While the significance of that story in Genesis 34 lies elsewhere, it cannot be overlooked that the passion necessary for married love does exist in the story.

These two passages give us a perspective on cleaving to the Lord that is filled with passion and obedience. How many of us have been "turned off" by those Christians who have a blasé relationship with Christ? There is no enthusiasm as they speak of the Lord, if they speak of Him at all. Their participation in worship is bland. They hover near the rear of the congregation in order to avoid the intensity of the front. When the Spirit of God is moving and many have uplifted hands in praise, they have their arms folded and are watching the praises as spectators. When challenged, they argue, "This is my way of worshiping!"

In Deuteronomy 11:22 we find a call for Christians who are filled with excitement for God. It calls for Christians who have a holy passion for His name and glory. It calls for a passion for responsible living, for excellence among the things of the church, and for a passion that loves the lost and bears love as Paul described it in 1 Corinthians 13.

Such a life of keeping God's commandments results in God's divine activity. Verses 23-25 show the extent of His victory in our behalf. Each verse contains elements of that victory that can be easily applied to our Christian lives today.

Verse 23 shows that even when we are confronted with circumstances of the enemy that are bigger than us, our God is able to overcome and provide the victory.

Verse 24 shows that God seeks to expand our horizons in faith and responsible action. It shows His victory will be accomplished as we trust and obey.

Verse 25 shows that we will not be dominated by fear but that the demons themselves will recognize the power of God in our life and they will tremble (see James 2:19).

III. THE BLESSINGS OF OBEDIENCE
    (Deuteronomy 11:26-32)

A. Human Choices (vv. 26-28)

26. Behold, I set before you this day a blessing and a curse;

27. A blessing, if ye obey the commandments of the Lord your God, which I command you this day:

28. And a curse, if ye will not obey the commandments of the Lord your

God, but turn aside out of the way which I command you this day, to go after other gods, which ye have not known.

God gives us a choice: a life filled with blessings or a life filled with curses. There is no middle ground. The person who thinks he is postponing a decision is only choosing the life of curses.

It is sometimes difficult for us to accept the notion of blessings and curses as real. We should not enter the world of superstition and rub some kind of spiritual "rabbit's foot." That is not at all what is being discussed in God's Word.

The issue of blessings and curses centers around God's clear revelation and clear choice to us whether we will obey. There is no supernatural mystery out there that must be gained by a seer. There is nothing hidden; God has made clear His will in these matters. Thus, the realm of magic does not exist in our relationship with God.

The curse is real because sin is real. The curse is activated by our disobedience. God desires that His people live under the joy of blessings; it is rebellious sin that causes His people to live under the realm of curses. The blessings and curses are further clarified in Deuteronomy 28-30. The blessings of obedience are spelled out in 28:1-14; the curses of disobedience are detailed in 28:15-68 and 29:16-28. While the curses are greater in number, they are not the final word. We find in Deuteronomy 30:1-10 the blessings of repentance and obedience, and in vv. 15-20 the reminder that man has a choice from God.

Verse 28 of chapter 11 makes clear that the blessings and curses are related concretely to the issue of idolatry. It would be a terrible distortion of the biblical witness for us to think that any particular act of disobedience unleashes a hidden, yet waiting, torrent of demonic curses upon our life. That is not the case at all and the lesson should not be taught so as to leave the class with that impression.

What is clear is the reality of the threat of idolatry. Idolatry is simply allowing someone, or something, to take the place of the living God revealed in Israel's history and in Jesus Christ. It is not sufficient for someone to say "I believe in God." Their "god" may be an idea, a philosophy, even themselves. The God of life is clearly revealed in Jesus Christ.

But such a belief in the God of life, revealed in Jesus Christ, brings one to the point of keeping His commandments (see comments on verse 22). Thus, affirming the reality of God is not merely an intellectual exercise; it is a placing of ultimate trust in His goodness and love so that our lives are shaped in obedience to His will for our purpose in life.

B. Mandatory Decisions (vv. 29-32)

(Deuteronomy 11:29-32 is not included in the printed text.)

It has previously been noted the covenant nature of the Book of Deuteronomy. Biblical covenants reflect patterns of ancient suzerainty treaties where an agreement is made between a major power and a lesser power. It is clear the agreement has mutual benefits; but it is also clear the major power receives the greater blessing!

There are usually six parts to these ancient treaties. These parts have parallels in the covenants found in the Old Testament. These parts are (1) preamble; (2) historical prologue; (3) stipulations; (4) provisions for storing the treaty and public readings; (5) a list of divine witnesses to the treaty; and (6) blessings and curses (from Delbert Hillers, *Covenant: The History of a Biblical Idea*).

In this last part of Deuteronomy 11, we have reference to the storing of the covenant and public readings as well as the list of blessings and curses. The blessings were to be placed on Mount Gerizim which stood to the south and faced north. The curses were placed on Mount Ebal which was north of Gerizim. These two mountains were in the center of the country and became places whereby the entire land was called to submit to the lordship of the God of Israel.

Toward the close of the conquest, in Joshua 24, stands an account of Israel and the peoples of the land coming together at Shechem, which was strategically located between the two mountains mentioned above. Here a covenant-making ceremony was performed by which the people affirmed their allegiance to the God of Israel. Joshua gave the people a choice; but he clearly affirmed that he and his house would serve the Lord (24:15).

REVIEW QUESTIONS

1. What does it mean to be "strong" in the Lord?

2. What are signs today that we are experiencing the "latter rain"?

3. How are we to "keep" the commandments of the Lord?

4. How does idolatry break the bond of blessing which the Lord has for us?

GOLDEN TEXT HOMILY

"THEREFORE SHALL YE KEEP ALL THE COMMANDMENTS WHICH I COMMAND YOU THIS DAY, THAT YE MAY BE STRONG, AND GO IN AND POSSESS THE LAND" (Deuteronomy 11:8).

Divorced from its context, Deuteronomy 11:8 would impose a legal demand cold as ice and hard as steel—a covenant without heart with a promise unfulfilled. But, contrary to modern misconceptions, the Old Testament Jehovah does not thunder without love to a loveless people.

God's demand in Deuteronomy 11:8 parallels Jesus' imperative in John 14:15 ("if ye love me, keep my commandments") when read in light of Deuteronomy 6:4, 5, a passage which mandates loving God with the entire being and keeping His commandments ever on the heart.

Chapters 6 to 11 of Deuteronomy place these twin imperatives *love* and *obey* in the context of Israel's recent history. Under God's loving oversight, His people had relentlessly disobeyed; *their* love, never His, had proved defective. They had also suffered divine judgment. God's covenant, nevertheless, still operated: He loved them (7:13); He remained faithful (7:9, 10). They had experienced the stern side of divine love—divine justice.

In the three discourses composing Deuteronomy, Moses, in God's stead,

called Israel to renewal of covenant. The terms were clear-cut: love, obey, and prosper in a covenant community under the direction and protection of a loving God; or rebel, disobey, and feel His just wrath, a negative provision of that same covenant.

Today we still express our love for God within a covenant relationship which presupposes voluntary obedience to moral and spiritual principles. Out of God's will, we reap an unhappy harvest—unfulfilled lives, spiritual stagnation, and, potentially, judgment. In loving obedience to God we experience fellowship and fulfillment—in time and eternity.—**Sabord Woods, Ph.D., Professor of English, Lee College, Cleveland, Tennessee**

SENTENCE SERMONS

OBEDIENCE TO THE WILL of God makes us heirs of His eternal promises.
—Selected

IT IS A GREAT DEAL easier to do that which God gives us to do, no matter how hard it is, than to face the responsibility of not doing it.
—J. R. Miller

OBEDIENCE IS NOT idle holiness.
—"Notes and Quotes"

IT IS VAIN THOUGHT to flee from the work that God appoints us, for the sake of finding a greater blessing, instead of seeking it where alone it is to be found—in loving obedience.
George Eliott

EVANGELISTIC APPLICATION

ETERNAL LIFE IS FOUND IN THE PROMISES OF GOD MANIFESTED IN CHRIST.

The reality of eternal life is expressed in Ephesians 1 in terms of the "blessings" we have received in Christ.

The word "blessed" is used three times in Ephesians 1:3 to describe the manifold richness of His glory. Paul understood that God was so rich in love that He should first be blessed. This blessing is a form of praise from us because of His great love. This praise-blessing we offer God is because of what God has done: He has brought us into marvelous fellowship with Himself in Christ Jesus. Thus, we are blessed to be in Christ. Finally, because we are in Christ, we are heirs of the spiritual blessings that exist in God's heaven. We are heirs of life, joy, peace, love, and so forth.

These blessings provide the basis for sharing the good news of Christ. We bless and praise God by sharing these blessings with others. We bless others by telling them of the goodness of God and His love for them.

Blessings are not meant to be counted and hoarded; blessings are meant to be shared. By sharing God's blessing of eternal life, we participate in the glory of God and His praise.

ILLUMINATING THE LESSON

C. S. Lewis, in his little book describing a journey from hell to heaven on a bus (*The Great Divorce*), relates an episode where the issue of choice is evidenced:

"Ye cannot fully understand the relations of choice and time till you are beyond both. . . . What concerns you is the nature of the choice itself: and that ye can watch them making.

" 'Well, Sir,' I said, 'that also needs explaining. What do they choose, these souls who go back? And how *can* they choose it?'

" 'Milton was right,' said my teacher. 'The choice of every lost soul can be expressed in the words *Better to reign in hell than serve in heaven.* There is always something they insist on keeping, even at the price of misery. There is always something they prefer to joy—that is, to reality. Ye see it easily enough in a spoiled child that would sooner miss its play and its supper than say it was sorry and be friends. Ye call it the sulks. But in adult life it has a hundred fine names— Achilles' wrath and Coriolanus' grandeur, Revenge and Injured Merit and Self-Respect and Tragic Greatness and Proper Pride.' "

DAILY BIBLE READINGS

M. The Word Is Near. Deuteronomy 30: 11-14

T. To Obey Is Life. Deuteronomy 30:15-20

W. Obedience Rewarded. 2 Kings 4:1-7

T. Call to Obedience. Isaiah 1:18-20

F. Results of Obedience. Romans 6:12-19

S. Precious Promises. 2 Peter 1:1-4

God's Faithful Guidance

Study Text: Psalm 78:1-72

Supplemental References: Exodus 12:21-27; 1 Samuel 16:6-13; 1 Kings 11:6-8; Matthew 13:34, 35; Hebrews 11:8-16

Time: Although they existed earlier, the Psalms in their present form were compiled in the third century B.C.

Place: Uncertain

Golden Text: "Thou art my rock and my fortress; therefore for thy name's sake lead me, and guide me" (Psalm 31:3).

Central Truth: As we obey God, He will lead us in the paths of righteousness.

Evangelistic Emphasis: Believers are called to bear witness to the power of God that saves from sin.

Printed Text

Psalm 78:5. For he established a testimony in Jacob, and appointed a law in Israel, which he commanded our fathers, that they should make them known to their children:

6. That the generation to come might know them, even the children which should be born; who should arise and declare them to their children:

7. That they might set their hope in God, and not forget the works of God, but keep his commandments.

56. Yet they tempted and provoked the most high God, and kept not his testimonies:

57. But turned back, and dealt unfaithfully like their fathers: they were turned aside like a deceitful bow.

58. For they provoked him to anger with their high places, and moved him to jealousy with their graven images.

59. When God heard this, he was wroth, and greatly abhorred Israel:

60. So that he forsook the tabernacle of Shiloh, the tent which he placed among men.

68. But chose the tribe of Judah, the mount Zion which he loved.

69. And he built his sanctuary like high palaces, like the earth which he hath established for ever.

70. He chose David also his servant, and took him from the sheepfolds:

71. From following the ewes great with young he brought him to feed Jacob his people, and Israel his inheritance.

72. So he fed them according to the integrity of his heart; and guided them by the skilfulness of his hands.

DICTIONARY

Shiloh (SHY-low)—Psalm 78:60—A city in the tribe of Ephraim about 12 miles NE of Bethel. A place of great importance because the Ark was there for a period of time. When David made Jerusalem the capital of Israel, the ark was removed from Shiloh, and the importance of the area dwendled.

Judah (JOO-duh)—Psalm 78:68—The name of the Hebrew tribe that descended from Judah, fourth son of Jacob.

Zion (ZY-uhn)—Psalm 78:68—The meaning of the word Zion is uncertain, but probably refers to one of the hills on which Jerusalem stood.

LESSON OUTLINE

I. KNOWING GOD'S WAYS
   A. Hope for the Future
   B. Sins of the Past

II. TRAGEDY OF REBELLION
   A. Sin Manifest
   B. Judgment Revealed
   C. Judgment Ends

III. GOD GUIDES HIS PEOPLE
   A. God's Preserving Power
   B. The Good Shepherd

LESSON EXPOSITION

INTRODUCTION

The Psalms comprise some of the most inspiring devotional literature in the world. Dietrich Bonhoeffer, in *Life Together*, remarks that "the Psalter is the prayer book of Jesus Christ in the truest sense of the word. He prayed the Psalter and now it has become His prayer for all time. Jesus Christ prays through the Psalter to His congregation. The Psalter is the vicarious prayer of Christ for His church."

Bonhoeffer went on to write, "The Psalter is the great school of prayer." He saw that we learned several things concerning prayer from this marvelous collection of prayers, laments, and praises from God's people. First, we learn that true prayer consists of praying according to the Word of God. "Christian prayer takes its stand on the solid ground of the revealed Word and has nothing to do with vague, self-seeking vagaries." Second, "we learn from the prayer of the Psalms what we should pray." Third, it is through the Psalms we learn that fellowship with the people of God is the basic of our unity in prayer. Thus, while we may pray individually, we are aware of our fellowship with the larger body of faith.

The 150 psalms are divided into five sections (or books). The first is 1-41;

second, 42-72; third, 73-89; fourth, 90-106; and fifth, 107-150. As is clear, Psalm 78, which is the focus of our lesson, is found in the third book. It is in this third book that most of the psalms ascribed to Asaph are found (an exception is Psalm 50). Asaph is mentioned in 1 Chronicles 6:39 and 15:17. These two passages name the temple musicians who served in the tabernacle until the building of the Temple under Solomon. They were given their assignments by David after he returned the ark of the Lord (2 Samuel 6). We learn that Asaph was the son of Bereckiah and that Asaph served at the right hand of Heman the musician (1 Chronicles 15:17, 19). Asaph was naturally a member of the tribe of Levi. The account of David's moving the ark to Jerusalem (1 Chronicles 15; 2 Samuel 6) tells that the Levites were given special jobs in this exercise as "singers to sing joyful songs, accompanied by musical instruments: lyres, harps and cymbals" (1 Chronicles 15:16, *NIV*). From 1 Chronicles 15:19 we learn that Asaph was one of the three men chosen to sound the bronze cymbals. His father, Bereckiah, was a doorkeeper for the ark (v. 23), and in 16:4, 5 we learn that once the ark was presented in Jerusalem, Asaph was one of the men named to minister before the ark of the Lord, "to make petition, to give thanks, and to praise the Lord" (v. 4, *NIV*). Asaph was appointed the "chief" or head of this special group of ministers and he was also given the honor of playing the cymbals before the ark on a regular basis. The remainder of 1 Chronicles 16 relates a psalm of thanks to the Lord that David gave Asaph (vv. 7-36).

Psalm 78 is relatively lengthy. Because of this, our lesson only concentrates on a portion of the first section and the final sections. The psalm can be divided into seven sections: (1) vv. 1-8 which calls the people to listen to the Lord; (2) vv. 9-20 which remembers the disobedience of Israel; (3) vv. 21-31 which is a specific memory of the manna and quail in the wilderness; (4) vv. 32-39 describes Israel's continued sin before the Lord; (5) vv. 40-55 reflects upon the Exodus experience; (6) vv. 56-66 is Israel in Canaan; (7) vv. 67-72 is assurance of God's continued guidance. (These divisions and headings are taken from *The Interpreter's Bible*).

The psalm is called a *maschil* or *maskil*. This title is used in 12 other psalms besides Psalm 78. This technical term may mean "to have understanding" or signifies accompaniment by some special music or used at a particular festival (*Interpreter's Dictionary of the Bible*).

I. KNOWING GOD'S WAYS (Psalm 78:5-8)

A. Hope for the Future (vv. 5-7)

5. For he established a testimony in Jacob, and appointed a law in Israel, which he commanded our fathers, that they should make them known to their children:

6. That the generation to come might know them, even the children which should be born; who should arise and declare them to their children:

7. That they might set their hope in God, and not forget the works of God, but keep his commandments.

As noted earlier, this first part of Psalm 78 is a summons to Israel to hear of the Lord's commandments. At the close of Matthew 13 (which contains a series of parables by Jesus), Psalm 78:2 is loosely quoted by Matthew to show how Christ fulfilled this prophecy of opening His "mouth in parables" (13:35).

The pattern is established early (Psalm 28:4) regarding the importance of passing on to our children the "praises of the Lord, and his strength, and his wonderful works that he hath done."

It is in this light that the "testimony" and "law" are to be made known to each generation. *Testimony* comes from the Hebrew that means "witness." It is used 32 times in the Psalms (also in 78:56 of our lesson). It seems to refer to the "testimony of the Ten Words on the

tables as a solemn divine charge" (Brown, Driver, and Briggs, *Hebrew-English Lexicon of the Old Testament*). It should be noted this testimony has been "established." This means it has been "raised up" as a witness rises to speak. The Hebrew word is used only here in the Psalms and, from its usage throughout the Old Testament, refers to the establishing of a covenant. It is used in the Noah story (Genesis 6-9) four times to show how God has established a covenant that affirms He will not destroy humanity again by water. This covenant form is directed to all humanity. The second major use in Genesis is three uses in chapter 17 in the covenant-making ceremony with Abraham. This covenant affirms the new people of God created through the faith of Abraham.

Even as the testimony was established, so also the law was appointed. The law is the *torah*. Interestingly, torah comes from a verbal root meaning "throw, shoot." The meaning shifts toward "point unto" or "point out." Thus, we move to the idea of "direct, teach, instruct." As a noun, *torah* means "direction, instruction, law." From the previously cited Brown, Driver, and Briggs (BDB), we discover that it could be used to describe the teaching that parents give their children; instructions from the priest in relation to sacred things; instruction concerning the messianic age; special laws of Israel (such as Sabbath, and so forth); the laws of the "covenant" (in which case it parallels "testimony"); and customs and manners. This law has been "appointed" by God, and has the sense of "set, ordained." It is used only here in the Psalms. Its other usages imply a more specific form of "setting." Thus, while God's testimony is established as a general revelation of His covenant love (as manifested in the Ten Commandments), His law is a more precise application of His covenant love and is thus "appointed" throughout various areas of life.

The reason for this intense desire for the children of Israel to be reared in the knowledge of God is set forth in verse 7. The revelation of God's law and testimony creates the basis of hope in God.

Hope, in the biblical sense, is not wishful thinking. It is not "pie-in-the-sky" preaching. It is not positive thinking or confession. Hope, while not seeing the results, is confident in who God is! Thus, hope does not express itself on the basis of God's revelation through His testimony and law. Those who set their hope in God do so with the confidence that He is faithful to His Word. Thus, the very person of God becomes the basis for hope.

Hope that is founded upon God, and is thus able to hope in God, will not forget His works. The Hebrew word for "works" is not used extensively in the Bible. These "works" refer to the specific acts of God, His practices, His actual doings. These "works" are thus not some general recognition of God's works in the universe (for instance, as expressed in Psalm 8:3); rather, these are the works of God that a person recognizes as God's practices in his own life. It is the knowledge that events and circumstances in our life are ordered by God. Thus, hope and His works stand together in forming an obedient life as we keep His Word.

B. Sins of the Past (v. 8)

(Psalm 78:8 is not included in the printed text.)

The contrast between parents, children, and forefathers is marked. Remember that verses 5-7 described the significance of God's testimonies and law in establishing hope and obedience for the future.

The former generation is described as being "stubborn and rebellious." Their heart was not right and their spirit was not faithful to God. The fact that the heart was not "aright" refers to the fact that the heart was not directed toward doing right. It indicates that the intention of the heart was toward violation of God's law. Thus, this is not a lament of people who meant to do good but failed; this lament speaks of people whose very intention was to violate God's law.

The analysis of the Hebrew writers concerning generations is of interest. They often speak of the past or present generation as rebellious. One seldom reads of concern over the future generation; espe-

cially the young. This is just the opposite of what is often heard today. It is the older generations that make accusation against the younger. The biblical sense of reversing this order shows that the younger generation is only inheriting what it has been given by either example or mind-set. This may be important in helping us understand how to minister to the future. Perhaps such ministry to the young generations can occur only as we of the older generation publicly repent of our stubborn and rebellious hearts. I have often thought that the key to genuine "youth revival" is a genuine "adult revival."

II. TRAGEDY OF REBELLION (Psalm 78: 56-66)

A. Sin Manifest (vv. 56-58)

56. Yet they tempted and provoked the most high God, and kept not his testimonies:

57. But turned back, and dealt unfaithfully like their fathers: they were turned aside like a deceitful bow.

58. For they provoked him to anger with their high places, and moved him to jealousy with their graven images.

Even as verses 5-8 provided contrast between the older generation and the younger generation, the sins of rebellion and stubbornness of the older were cataloged in verses 9-55. That catalog continued into this part of our lesson. The "they" of these verses is the older generations who had the special calling and blessing of God, yet failed to be obedient.

The ways they "tempted" the Lord are described in Exodus 17:2, 7; Numbers 14:22; Deuteronomy 6:16; and four other key places in the Psalms. These Psalms passages are revealing:

1. 78:18—the correlation of asking for meat in the wilderness with lust;

2. 78:41—another reference to the wilderness temptations by which they limited God's power in their behalf;

3. 95:8, 9—the context is the wilderness temptation where the people "hardened" their hearts even though they saw the works of God;

4. 106:14, 15—the context is the wil-

derness and the lust of the flesh in the wilderness. This lust manifested itself in their failure to receive God's counsel and the leanness they received in their souls.

In (Psalm 78:56) the idea of *provoke* has the sense of "bitterness." In verse 58 *provoked* carries the sense of "anger, wrath, jealousy." The context of the verses gives light to how these two words operate. Note first that verse 56 indicates that bitterness is related to failing to keep God's testimonies. In this sense we suffer the bitterness of sin and brokenness as we reject the covenant stipulations and promises of God. The *provoking* of verse 58 is related to God's jealousy at the people's idolatry. This is a clear violation of the first and second commandments.

The "deceitful bow" of verse 57 refers to a twisted bow an archer would use. The archer was not able to shoot an arrow straight because the bow was twisted. The *Anchor Bible* reads, "they recoiled like a treacherous bow." By turning from God they became of little good for His redemptive purposes. While the message they had about God was good (like an arrow), the method of delivering that message (the bow) was twisted and filled with lies.

The "high places" refer to pagan shrines kept by the Israelites. These high places were already in place when they arrived in the land. They were instructed to destroy them and remove all traces of idolatry. But, they failed to be obedient. They allowed these high places to remain and ultimately began to worship them. In many instances, they tried to make them appear right by seeking to transform them through combining the worship of the living God with the rites of the pagan gods. Needless to say, this syncretism did not please God and His wrath was brought upon them.

B. Judgment Revealed (vv. 59-64)

(Psalm 78:61-64 is not included in the printed text.)

59. When God heard this, he was wroth, and greatly abhorred Israel:

60. So that he forsook the tabernacle of Shiloh, the tent which he placed among men.

The idea of "wroth" is part of the wrath of God. The same Hebrew expression is used in Psalms 78:21, 62; 89:38. It suggests that sickening turning away; an inability to look any longer at someone or something. It is amplified with the use of "abhor." Several Hebrew words are translated by our English "abhor." Some of those words suggest "cast away, loathe" (Leviticus 26:11, 15, 30, 43, 44); "nauseate" (Job 33:20); "wearied with" (Isaiah 7:16). The word used in our passage has the sense of "despise, reject" and is also found in Job 42:6; Psalms 36:4; 89:38.

The reference to Shiloh is important. This ancient site was about 25 miles north of Jerusalem. It was an early center of the true worship and the ark resided there. A reference to its destruction is found in Jeremiah 7:14 and 26:6. *Smith's Bible Dictionary* relates that archaeological evidence points to a destruction of Shiloh about 1050 B.C. It was probably destroyed during a Philistine uprising during the time of Eli (1 Samuel 4:1-22) in which the corrupt sons of Eli were killed and the ark was taken by the Philistines (1 Samuel 5). The ark was later recovered (1 Samuel 6) and remained for 20 years at Kirjath-jearim under the care of Eleazar (1 Samuel 7:1, 2). Apparently the destruction of Shiloh was so complete that the prophet Samuel centered his ministry in Ramah (1 Samuel 7:17)

The use of Shiloh in Psalm 78 stands as clear warning that God will remove His presence if His people persist in rebellion. The New Testament speaks of this same warning in Hebrews 10:26-31 and warns not to quench the Spirit. While God's mercy abounds to those repentant, His mercy is limited by our rebellion and rejection of His love.

C. Judgment Ends (vv. 65, 66)

(Psalm 78:65, 66 in not included in the printed text.)

All of Israel's history is the story of God's love, Israel's rebellion, God's judgment, and God's provision for the future. This part of the lesson concludes with the assurance that His wrath will end for His people and restoration will occur. This restoration is possible because

God's people repent of their sins and humble themselves in His presence. While in sin and while suffering His judgment we often feel that He is asleep and distant. Yet, the time comes when we are aware of His great love and provision for life.

III. GOD GUIDES HIS PEOPLE (Psalm 78:67-72)

A. God's Preserving Power (vv. 67-69; verse 67 is not in the Printed Text).

68. But chose the tribe of Judah, the mount Zion which he loved.

69. And he built his sanctuary like high palaces, like the earth which he hath established for ever.

The previous verses in Psalm 78 show that God rejected Shiloh because of Israel's disobedience (v. 60) and He rejected Joseph and Ephraim (v. 67). These verses seem to reflect the attitude of Judeans against the Northern Tribes who left during the reign of Jeroboam (1 Kings 12ff).

Verse 68 shows that God had a special purpose for Judah and Zion. It was through Judah that the Messiah, Jesus Christ, was born. This fulfilled the Messianic prophecies and maintained God's freedom of election. Zion was especially loved because of its role in the worship of the Most High. It was David who made Zion into the royal city for the Lord to dwell in.

B. The Good Shepherd (vv. 70-72)

70. He chose David also his servant, and took him from the sheepfolds:

71. From following the ewes great with young he brought him to feed Jacob his people, and Israel his inheritance.

72. So he fed them according to the integrity of his heart; and guided them by the skilfulness of his hands.

Earlier in the lesson it was noted that Asaph was appointed by David to his position in ministering to the ark of the Lord. This portion of the psalm seems to reflect Asaph's love for God's anointed, David. One can almost feel the personal love and respect manifested in these words.

David is the servant of the Lord (v. 70). This assessment came from a priest of the Lord. There is no human jealousy here! There is an inspired recognition of God's hand in the life of this shepherd boy from Bethlehem.

Verse 71 establishes a principle of faithfulness in little which leads to opportunity for faithfulness in much. David is seen taking care of ewe lambs. The image is that of a sensitive and caring provider. Further, the image conveys one who can protect the defenseless lamb and her unborn. The unborn lamb represents the future. David is the man given a vision for all his people and a vision for the future. While an effective shepherd, his vision, love, and abilities were not restricted by himself or others. Rather, he accepted the call of God, in spite of serious opposition from his brothers and King Saul, and obeyed God.

This picture of David, as vivid as it is, dims in comparison to our Good Shepherd, Jesus Christ. David's work was limited by time; the work of Jesus was eternal. David had blemishes of sin upon his record; Jesus was sinless in heart and deed. David was not able to build the Temple for God; Jesus lives in the heart of all who believe. David died and remains buried; Jesus died but rose from the grave with an indestructible life.

REVIEW QUESTIONS

1. From references in the Old Testament and Psalm 78, what do you think of the relationship between Asaph and David?

2. What is the true ground of hope for the people of God?

3. In what ways do we tempt God today?

GOLDEN TEXT HOMILY

"THOU ART MY ROCK AND MY FORTRESS; THEREFORE FOR THY NAME'S SAKE LEAD ME, AND GUIDE ME" (Psalm 31:3).

This precious psalmist has known so much adversity in his lifetime. In times of distress, whether it be from his own failings or the enemy, he cried to his heavenly Father for help.

There is the possibility that God had not answered his prayers for guidance and care as soon as he felt He should. We all find ourselves in these same circumstances at times. We fear God is not listening. Yet, by Scripture, we know He knows even our thoughts.

Whoever the enemy may be at this time, David again pleads for protection and guidance. Numerous are the times he has found the rocks to be a fortress. So, in his petition, he asks God to be a shelter. Could it be that he has run so long that it seems there is no other rock in which to hide? He realizes only God can be to him his protection and guide now.

David implores God for direction lest he miss the way. He is not just concerned for himself personally. His God has been ridiculed by his enemies. He wishes God to lead and guide him because God's name is at stake in it all.

David gives personal testimony to his relationship to God as He is *my* rock and guide. This is of primary importance. Later in this psalm we learn he gets an answer to his petition. And so will we if He is *our* rock and guide.

It is in times of struggle that God's wise counsel is needed even more so than His strong arm.—**Fred H. Whisman, Cost Analyst, Church of God Publishing House, Cleveland, Tennessee**

SENTENCE SERMONS

AS WE OBEY GOD, He will lead us in the paths of righteousness.

—**Selected**

IF YOU WOULD HAVE God's guidance, you must listen as well as talk to the Guide.

—**"Speaker's Sourcebook"**

WHEN GOD SHUTS and bolts the door, don't try to get in through the window.

—**"Speaker's Sourcebook"**

GOD NEVER ALTERS the robe of righteousness to fit man, but the man to fit the robe.

—**"Speaker's Sourcebook"**

EVANGELISTIC APPLICATION

BELIEVERS ARE CALLED TO BEAR WITNESS TO THE POWER OF GOD THAT SAVES FROM SIN.

Part of that power is revealed in His prevenient grace. That is grace at work in our life while we are sinners. It is the work of God to lead us to the point of salvation and confession of Christ.

We must always remember that we cannot save ourselves. We cannot decide by our own will to "be saved." We are saved as the Holy Spirit touches our heart with the truth of Christ.

That is why it is so important that the sinner not reject the wooing of the Holy Spirit. Many sit under anointed gospel preaching and say to themselves, "I'll wait until a later time, then I'll get saved." What a tragedy. We can only be saved as the Holy Spirit can birth saving faith.

In this quarter we have studied various ways that God leads His people. As Christians awaiting the return of the Lord, we must resolve to be led by God into effective evangelism. More than ever must we speak to the unsaved concerning His marvelous grace and eternal life.

ILLUMINATING THE LESSON

William Williams (1717-1791) was instrumental in some of the great revivals the Lord sent to Wales. This great layman-preacher traveled throughout the countryside during 40 years of ministry. His travels logged over 100,000 miles as he preached and sang of the goodness of God.

The Welsh were known for their singing of God's love. Often music was more influential than preaching in bringing the lost to Christ. Of the eight hundred hymns that Williams wrote, the one most remembered is *Guide Me, O Thou Great Jehovah*. The words of this great hymn and its ringing melody are fitting conclusion to this quarter of study. The words beckon us to remember that the same Lord who guided Israel is also guiding us through Christ!

Guide me, O Thou great Jehovah,
Pilgrim through this barren land;

I am weak, but Thou art mighty;
Hold me with Thy powerful hand;
Bread of heaven, Bread of heaven,
Feed me till I want no more.
Open now the crystal fountain,
Whence the healing stream doth flow;
Let the fire and cloudy pillar
Lead me all my journey through;
Strong Deliverer, strong Deliverer,
Be Thou still my strength and shield.
When I tread the verge of Jordan,
Bid my anxious fears subside;
Death of death, and hell's destruction,
Land me safe on Canaan's side;

Songs of praises, songs of praises,
I will ever give to Thee.

(From *Crusader Hymns and Hymn Stories* by the Billy Graham Team)

DAILY BIBLE READINGS

M. Godly Instruction. Exodus 12:21-27

T. Anointed for Service. 1 Kings 16:6-13

W. The Power of God. Psalm 44:1-8

T. Led by God. Isaiah 43:1-7

F. Led by the Spirit. Acts 13:1-4

S. A Better Country. Hebrews 11:8-16

INTRODUCTION
TO WINTER
QUARTER

The month of December begins the winter quarter and marks a departure from Old Testament studies that have occupied us for the last three months.

The lessons for the winter quarter (December, January, February) which are presented under the theme "The Teachings of Christ" are drawn from Matthew and Mark. The two Gospel writers, although unique in their own way of giving the accounts of Christ's teachings, present a well-rounded, Spirit-inspired narrative of the messages of the Master.

The study of Christ's teachings is the most soul-searching and faith-building study anyone can undertake. To the Christian it is more than just a study, it is an inexhaustible fountain of refreshment, and a coffer of immeasurable treasures. To the unregenerate person, the teachings of Christ can be a new vista of hope to set him free from sin and bondage.

The eternal Christ pitched His tent of flesh among men. He was God as though He were not man. Yet He became man that He might both identify Himself with man and fully reveal the Father to men by the things He taught and the life that He lived.

These lessons are certain to challenge the student to greater love and understanding of the Word. They will also inspire greater devotion to the One who gave His life for the human family.

PALESTINE IN THE
TIME OF CHRIST

THE GREAT SEA
(Mediterranean)

SYRIA

ARABS

Sidon

Damascus

Tyre

Dan

(Philip)

GAULANITIS

BASHAN

PHOENICIA

Ptolemais

(Herod
Antipas)

Capernaum

Sea of
Galilee

Cana

Gergesa (?)

GALILEE

Nazareth

Yarmuk River

Caesarea

Dothan

Bethabara?

Beth-shan

DECAPOLIS

Samaria

Shechem

Jabbok River

SAMARIA

Jordan River

(Archelaus)

(Pilate)

PEREA

Joppa

Jericho

Jerusalem

Bethany beyond Jordan?

Bethlehem

Azotus

(Herod
Antipas)

Ascalon

Machaerus

JUDEA

Salt
Sea

Gaza

Hebron

WILDERNESS
OF JUDEA

Arnon River

Beersheba

ARABIA

Christ's Mission Announced

Study Text: Mark 1:1-39
Supplemental References: Isaiah 9:6, 7; 53:1-12; Matthew 8:14-17; Luke 4:31-41
Time: Early in A.D. 28
Place: In Galilee by the Sea of Galilee and in Capernaum
Golden Text: "Come ye after me, and I will make you to become fishers of men" (Mark 1:17).
Central Truth: Jesus Christ came to preach the good news of the Kingdom.
Evangelistic Emphasis: Through Christ, the church must minister to the total needs of people.

Printed Text

Mark 1:14. Now after that John was put in prison, Jesus came into Galilee, preaching the gospel of the kingdom of God,

15. And saying, The time is fulfilled, and the kingdom of God is at hand: repent ye, and believe the gospel.

21. And they went into Capernaum; and straightway on the sabbath day he entered into the synagogue, and taught.

22. And they were astonished at his doctrine: for he taught them as one that had authority, and not as the scribes.

23. And there was in their synagogue a man with an unclean spirit; and he cried out,

24. Saying, Let us alone; what have we to do with thee, thou Jesus of Nazareth? art thou come to destroy us? I know thee who thou art, the Holy One of God.

25. And Jesus rebuked him, saying, Hold thy peace, and come out of him.

26. And when the unclean spirit had torn him, and cried with a loud voice, he came out of him.

27. And they were all amazed, insomuch that they questioned among themselves, saying, What thing is this? what new doctrine is this? for with authority commandeth he even the unclean spirits, and they do obey him.

28. And immediately his fame spread abroad throughout all the region round about Galilee.

29. And forthwith, when they were come out of the synagogue, they entered into the house of Simon and Andrew, with James and John.

30. But Simon's wife's mother lay sick of a fever, and anon they tell him of her.

31. And he came and took her by the hand, and lifted her up; and immediately the fever left her, and she ministered unto them.

35. And in the morning, rising up a great while before day, he went out, and departed into a solitary place, and there prayed.

36. And Simon and they that were with him followed after him.

37. And when they had found him, they said unto him, All men seek for thee.

38. And he said unto them, Let us go into the next towns, that I may preach there also: for therefore came I forth.

39. And he preached in their synagogues throughout all Galilee, and cast out devils.

DICTIONARY

Galilee (GAL-uh-lee)—Mark 1:14—The northern most part of Palestine in Roman times.

Capernaum (Ka-PER-na-um)—Mark 1:21—A town on the northwestern shore of Lake Galilee.

synagogue (SIN-ah-gog)—Mark 1:21—Taken from the Greek word meaning "a gathering" or "congregation." It probably had its rise during the exile when there was no Temple at Jerusalem, and became a social, religious, and educational gathering of the Jews for instruction and religious service. They perhaps met originally in the open air, then in houses, and later in buildings constructed for that purpose. The synagogue at Capernaum has been rebuilt on the old foundation from ancient ruins.

LESSON OUTLINE

I. CHRIST'S AUTHORITY
   A. The Gospel of God
   B. The Kingdom of God
   C. The House of God
   D. The Authority of God
II. CHRIST'S POWER
   A. The Unclean Spirit
   B. The Holy One of God
   C. The Amazed Congregation
   D. The Vanishing Fever
   E. The Seeking Crowd
III. CHRIST'S MISSION
   A. The Praying Savior
   B. The Search Party
   C. The Larger Mission

LESSON EXPOSITION

INTRODUCTION

Historians say that Mark was Peter's interpreter, and that his gospel is based on the preaching material of Peter. Certainly there are, in Mark's Gospel, vivid details which read very much as if they were the memories of someone who was there. Also, his style reminds us of what we know of Peter. It is sometimes said that a story marches; but Mark's story gallops—event following event with breathless rapidity.

Mark begins his Gospel abruptly by announcing the good news found in Je-sus Christ, who is the Son of God. Then, with no account of the Virgin Birth, no genealogy, and no history of the childhood years of Jesus, Mark gives a brief synopsis of the ministry of John the Baptist. This is followed by an account of the baptism of Jesus in the Jordan by John, the heavens opening, the Spirit like a dove descending upon Christ, and the voice of the Father saying, "Thou art my beloved Son, in whom I am well pleased" (1:11). Mark, then, covers the wilderness experience and temptation in two verses.

Throughout his Gospel, Mark employs this rapid fire approach to reporting events in the life of Jesus. And yet, more than any of the other Gospel writers, he established the pattern of the life of Jesus. He presented that drama in four acts. Act One involved the preparation of Je-sus including His baptism, His temptations, and His call of the disciples. Act Two covered the long conflict recorded in the first 13 chapters. Act Three presented the bitter tragedy of the passion and the Cross. And Act Four portrayed the triumph of the Resurrection.

Mark presents the true human personality of Jesus in all its originality and power. His aim was to give a picture of Jesus as He was. He offers an incomparable touch of reality.

I. CHRIST'S AUTHORITY (Mark 1:14, 15, 21, 22)

A. The Gospel of God (v. 14)

14. Now after that John was put in prison, Jesus came into Galilee, preaching the gospel of the kingdom of God.

Several events transpired before Jesus began His first tour of Galilee. After His temptation in the wilderness, Jesus went to Jerusalem to celebrate the Passover. While He was there He cleansed the Temple, driving out the money changers (see John 2:13-22). He also carried on a conversation with Nicodemus by night (see John 3:1-21). Then, Jesus returned to Galilee. On the way, He stopped in Samaria to talk with a woman at a well (see John 4:1-42). In Galilee, He healed a nobleman's son (see John 4:46-54). He also preached in His hometown synagogue in Nazareth where the people tried to kill him (see Luke 4:16-31).

Jesus preached some in the Lower Jordan area (see John 3:22-24). Two circumstances caused Him to leave that region: the growing hostility of the Pharisees (see John 4:1-3) and Herod's imprisonment of John the Baptist (see Mark 1:14). On another level, it seems that God's purpose was being fulfilled in John's arrest and that the time for Jesus' ministry in Galilee had now come.

Against a background of hope that Jesus would establish an earthly kingdom and free the people from Roman domination, He proclaimed His purpose was to establish a spiritual kingdom. His followers never fully understood this during His earthly ministry. His message was the good news of the kingdom of God. By the kingdom of God, He meant that kingdom over which Jesus rules. It is not confined to heaven, nor limited to a certain time or place. In fact, after encouraging His followers to seek the kingdom first, Jesus said, "Fear not, little flock; for it is your Father's good pleasure to give you the kingdom" (Luke 12:32). In this kingdom, Jesus is Lord; Jesus reigns supreme; Jesus is sovereign.

B. The Kingdom of God (v. 15)

15. And saying, The time is fulfilled, and the kingdom of God is at hand; repent ye, and believe the gospel.

After quoting the prophecy of Isaiah in the synagogue in Nazareth, Jesus declared, "This day is this scripture fulfilled in your ears" (Luke 4:21). By this statement He meant that the season had come, that the door was open, that the threshold to a great future had been reached, and that the concluding drama could now start. The purposes of God for the Old Testament era had been fulfilled and a new day was dawning.

The Jews were familiar with the term "kingdom of God." They expected the establishing of a messianic kingdom. So when Jesus spoke of the kingdom being near, they were acquainted with the term. The word *kingdom* carries the thought of kingship, kingly rule, reign, or sovereignty. The expression *kingdom of God* denotes the sovereign lordship of God over His people or over the world which He has made (*A Theological Word Book of the Bible*). Jesus spoke of the kingdom as near until the blood of the Cross was shed, and the Spirit had come.

Jesus called men to repentance. To repent involves both a turning from sin and a turning to God. The parable of the prodigal son is an outstanding illustration of this (see Luke 15:11-32). Isaiah expressed it this way: "Let the wicked forsake his way, and the unrighteous man his thoughts: and let him return unto the Lord" (55:7).

The Lord also called upon men to believe the gospel. The call is to believe that Jesus is the Messiah, the Son of God. There is no other means by which one can enter into the kingdom of God. Peter said, "There is none other name under heaven given among men, whereby we must be saved" (Acts 4:12).

C. The House of God (v. 21)

21. And they went into Capernaum; and straightway on the sabbath day he entered into the synagogue, and taught.

After His rejection at Nazareth, Jesus moved to Capernaum. Capernaum was about 20 to 25 miles from Nazareth and was located on the northwest shores of the Sea of Galilee. It was a thriving area where international trade routes crossed. A Roman centurion and a Roman garrison were stationed there. This would underscore the importance of the area. Also, Matthew (or Levi) was the customs official in Capernaum. Today, the entire town is in ruins, even as Jesus foretold that it would be (see Matthew 11:23, 24).

Jesus probably lived in Peter's home in Capernaum. In the fifth century, a church was built on the site where it is believed Peter's house stood. Its ruins can still be seen there today.

On His very first Sabbath day in Capernaum, Jesus went to the synagogue. In the second century, a beautiful synagogue was built only a few feet from Peter's house. The ruins of this synagogue still remain there. It is believed to have been built on the ruins of the synagogue where Jesus worshiped. The synagogue was, of course, a Jewish place of assembly and worship. It was a lifelong custom of Jesus to be present each Sabbath day in the synagogue.

Mark says that Jesus not only attended the synagogue on the Sabbath, but He taught the lesson. Of Jesus' teaching, Craig Skinner wrote: "He spoke with a divine dynamic that had such force that the crowds often burst into excited comment. . . . The force of this impact came . . . from the manner of His revelation of truth. His command came most from the use of apt illustration, in the truly prophetic manner, in distinction from the command of the current religious teachers, who depended on arguments based on the legal minutiae of Scripture."

D. The Authority of God (v. 22)

22. And they were astonished at his doctrine: for he taught them as one that had authority, and not as the scribes.

The listeners contrasted the manner of presentation which Jesus used with the approach the scribes made and they were amazed. The message of the scribes centered around additions that had been made to the commandments. They left

their hearers with a feeling of guilt. Also, they never spoke their own convictions. Instead, they quoted various scribes on the subject.

What gives authority to teaching and preaching?

In contrast to this, Jesus made no reference to any authority other than Himself. A familiar expression of His was: "You have heard that it was said . . . But I say unto you." The people were not accustomed to that kind of authoritative teaching. They were astonished. It blew them out of their reserve. They dropped their cautious religious reservations and got excited.

"His words were so insightful," wrote Ray C. Stedman, "so true to the experience and inner convictions of the men and women there that they nodded their heads, 'Of course!' and knew what He said was true. . . . His words had that ring of truth, acknowledged by all who heard Him speak. It was self-authenticating truth, corresponding to an inner conviction in each person who heard Him, so that they knew that He knew the secrets of life. . . . This is important, because it means that we ought to measure every teaching by what Jesus has said about the subject. . . . We need the insights of this amazing Man, as we study our lives, and human lives in general."

II. CHRIST'S POWER (Mark 1:23-34)

A. The Unclean Spirit (v. 23)

23. And there was in their synagogue a man with an unclean spirit; and he cried out.

Demons, as well as men, took note of the message and mission of Jesus. As soon as He had finished speaking, a man possessed by an unclean spirit, provoked by what He had heard, responded with a strong outburst. The man was so totally dominated by demonic power that his personality was lost to that of the evil spirit.

"In the New Testament," Norval Geldenhuys wrote, "demon possession means that a person is dominated by the spirit of a demon and tormented by him. . . . That the unclean spirits were personal beings is evident from what is related about their leaving a possessed person, talking or crying out, possessing knowledge concerning Jesus, as well as other supernatural knowledge—showing fear, and the like. . . . Those possessed are depicted throughout as unfortunate sufferers who, by no fault of their own, are dominated by evil spirits and who, when the spirits are cast out by Jesus, accept their deliverance with joy and gratitude (see Mark 5:18-20; Luke 8:2)."

There are 23 references to unclean spirits in the New Testament. Demons often caused blindness (see Matthew 12:22), muteness (see Matthew 9:32, 33), defects and deformities (see Luke 13:11-13), and suicidal tendencies (see Mark 9:22).

Mention of demon possession is limited to two passages in the Old Testament (see 1 Samuel 16:14; 1 Kings 22:22). Also, only two references appear in the New Testament outside the Gospels (see Acts 16:16; 19:13). But demon possession is a phenomenon that appeared on an amazing scale while Jesus was on the earth. There is a reason for this.

"The Son of God came out of the invisible, eternal, divine world for the purpose of destroying the works of the devil (see 1 John 3:8)," Geldenhuys wrote. "This was fully realized by the members of the kingdom of the evil one (see Mark 1:24; Luke 4:34). Accordingly it goes without saying that the power of darkness would attempt everything to conquer Christ or at any rate to hamper Him as much as possible. . . . Demon possession was one of the means used by the kingdom of darkness in this struggle. . . . The rage of Satan and his satellites was clearly reflected in this. In order to be truly the Redeemer, Jesus had . . . to prove that He had indeed overcome the power of the evil one."

B. The Holy One of God (vv. 24-26)

24. Saying, Let us alone; what have we to do with thee, thou Jesus of Nazareth? art thou come to destroy us? I know thee who thou art, the Holy One of God.

25. And Jesus rebuked him, saying, Hold thy peace, and come out of him.

26. And when the unclean spirit had torn him, and cried with a loud voice, he came out of him.

The demon spoke through the man and said, "What do we have to do with You, Jesus of Nazareth?" By this, he meant that they had nothing in common. There was a total incompatibility between them. They had entirely opposite interests.

Then, the demon posed another question, "Have You come to destroy us?" Their business was to destroy their hapless victims and they dreaded the day when Jesus would turn the tables on them and bring them to ruin. They perceived that their power was permitted and temporary, and that Jesus had come to destroy their works. His presence was a threat to all demonic forces.

Then, the demon identified Jesus, "I know who You are—the Holy One of God!" Drawing an expression from Psalm 16:10, a messianic psalm, the demon realized that he had an explanation for Jesus' authority. He acknowledged Christ's true character and identity as the One empowered by the Holy Spirit. How strange that the demon knew that He was God's Son, but the religious leaders of the day could not recognize that!

Jesus sharply rebuked the demon and ordered him to be silent and to come out of the man. Submitting to Jesus' authority, the evil spirit threw the man into convulsions, gave a deafening shriek, and left him. This action represented a last fling, an attempt to show what he would have done had he been permitted. However, he found himself impotent before the restraint of the Lord, so he could not hurt the man.

C. The Amazed Congregation (vv. 27, 28)

27. And they were all amazed, insomuch that they questioned among themselves, saying, What thing is this?

what new doctrine is this? for with authority commandeth he even the unclean spirits, and they do obey him.

28. And immediately his fame spread abroad throughout all the region round about Galilee.

The people—already astonished at the teaching of Jesus— were amazed by the expulsion of a demon with only a word of command. When this demon was confronted by Jesus, he was forced to leave the person he was inhabiting. The demon was reluctant to go, but he had to leave. He was overwhelmed by a superior power. (Through all the centuries since, the only name demons have ever feared is the name of Jesus. It is Jesus who sets men free and delivers the oppressed, *Stedman.*) The people had not seen or heard anything like this before. They realized that the miracle was wrought to illustrate the teaching and display the character and glory of the Teacher.

Within a few hours, the word of what had happened in the synagogue spread throughout the whole region of Galilee. By evening, the people were bringing the sick and the demon possessed into the city to be healed by Jesus.

The people began to speculate, "What does all this mean?" "What sort of new teaching is this?" "He even tells unclean spirits what to do and they do what He says." Is it any wonder that His reputation spread like wildfire?

The kingdom of darkness breeds horrible things and fosters impure powers. These things, however, shrivel up and die when they are exposed to the light of God's glory. When the light of the Pure One, Jesus Christ, touches them, they must draw back and disappear. How awesome is His power!

D. The Vanishing Fever (vv. 29-31)

29. And forthwith, when they were come out of the synagogue, they entered into the house of Simon and Andrew, with James and John.

30. But Simon's wife's mother lay sick of a fever, and anon they tell him of her.

31. And he came and took her by the hand, and lifted her up; and im- mediately the fever left her, and she ministered unto them.

Why are not more miracles of healing effected today?

After a synagogue service where everybody went home talking about the miraculous deliverance of a demon-possessed man, Jesus walked down the street to Peter's house. The house was situated near the synagogue in one of the better sections of town, indicating that Peter was at least moderately prosperous. Jesus was accompanied to the house by Peter, James, John, and Andrew.

When they arrived at the house, they found Peter's mother-in-law sick and in the bed. She was running a high fever. Remembering what had happened in the synagogue service, they immediately told Jesus about her condition. Jesus walked into the room where she was, stood over her, and rebuked the fever. Then He took her by the hand and lifted her up, and the fever left her.

Peter, James, and John were eyewitnesses to this supernatural cure. They were selected from among the rest of the disciples to be a threefold cord of testimony to certain events in the life of Jesus. (In this case, Andrew was also present.)

The healing of Peter's mother-in-law was perfect, immediate, and complete. As evidence of this, she began to prepare a meal for them. Her service to them was also an expression of gratitude to the lovely Lord for His healing touch.

E. The Seeking Crowd (vv. 32-34)

(Mark 1:32-34 is not included in the printed text.)

To bring the sick to Jesus for a cure on the Sabbath day would have been regarded as unlawful. But as soon as the Sabbath was over—it ended at sundown— they began to bring their sick and demon possessed to Him. A clear distinction is made between physical illness and demon possession. This distinction is maintained in Mark 6:13, "And they cast out many devils, and anointed with oil many that were sick, and healed them."

A large crowd gathered at Peter's door including the infirm, those who had brought them, and those who came to see what was going to happen. It seemed to those in the house that everybody in town was there.

These sick ones were afflicted with various types of disease. This did not matter to the compassionate Christ. He healed many of them. The word translated *many* carries the meaning, "all who were brought." The same word is used with reference to the number for whom Christ died: "For even the Son of man came not to be ministered unto, but to minister, and to give his life a ransom for *many*" (Mark 10:45).

Jesus also drove out *many* demons. He did so with a word of command (see Matthew 8:16). He forbade them to speak thereby silencing their cries of recognition. They were utterly powerless to do anything before Him.

III. CHRIST'S MISSION (Mark 1:35-39)

A. The Praying Savior (v. 35)

35. And in the morning, rising up a great while before day, he went out, and departed into a solitary place, and there prayed.

Can you imagine how physically exhausted Jesus must have been after this Sabbath day Mark has described? He preached the sermon in the synagogue and delivered the demon-possessed man; He healed Peter's mother-in-law; and He healed and delivered the sick and demon possessed that were brought to Him in the evening. Yet, Mark says that Jesus got up very early the next morning, while it was still dark and went out to an uninhabited place, where he spent time praying.

Mark gives three such accounts of Jesus in prayer. Each time He is alone and under the cover of darkness. The occasions are found near the beginning of his book (1:35), near the middle (6:46), and near the end (14:32-42).

Why did Jesus seek the face of His Father in this manner? It seems to have been in anticipation of the work that lay before Him. These were times when He poured out His soul to the One who had sent Him. What an experience it would have been to have been within hearing distance of Him on these solemn occasions.

Also, Jesus is teaching us the source of His authority through these prayer times. He did not act on His own authority; He received His authority from the Father (see John 5:19; 14:10). Jesus' power came from Him who dwelt in Him.

B. The Search Party (vv. 36, 37)

36. And Simon and they that were with him followed after him.

37. And when they had found him, they said unto him, All men seek for thee.

The popularity which Jesus gained in the synagogue service and which resulted in virtually the whole community coming to Peter's house in the evening, continued the next morning. When Peter awoke, he found that Jesus was gone and that the multitudes were back expecting to find the Lord there. They expected the miraculous manifestations of the day before to continue on this day.

Peter and his companions formed a search party to track Jesus down. Andrew, James, and John were probably included in this group. When they found Jesus, they told Him that everyone was looking for Him. The implication was that He was missing a great opportunity in Capernaum. This was no time for Him to be away. He should capitalize on His opportunities. A chance like this doesn't come every day.

Jesus' perspective was quite different from that of Peter and the townspeople. He understood the importance of being alone with God in order to be effective with men. He understood the principle of praying in secret and seeing the Father honor Him openly.

Some of the most important time a pastor spends is when no one but God sees him. It may appear that he should be out doing other things, but those other things will be done better after he has spent time alone with God.

C. The Larger Mission (vv. 38, 39)

38. And he said unto them, Let us go into the next towns, that I may preach there also: for therefore came I forth.

39. And he preached in their synagogues throughout all Galilee, and cast out devils.

Jesus did not respond as Peter and his companions had expected Him to. Although all of Capernaum was clamoring for more, Jesus said that He must go into the nearby towns and preach the gospel there. The easy course would have been to go back to Capernaum and bask in the sunshine of this newfound popularity. But His sense of mission would not allow Him to turn away from the purpose for which He had come.

The mission of the church is more than a *local mission.* It is that, first and foremost. But it is also a *universal mission.* The church must reach out to other towns and to other communities. It must ultimately reach around the world. Jesus' instructions are to preach the gospel to every creature, disciple every nation, and teach the ways of Christ to every believer (see Mark 16:15; Matthew 28:19, 20).

True to His calling, Jesus journeyed to other towns and preached the gospel to them. He also cast out demons. The mighty works He did served to heighten His fame. But He never performed these miracles to impress His audience. They served to confirm and authenticate His message. And this was His message: "The time is fulfilled, and the kingdom of God is at hand: repent ye, and believe the gospel" (Mark 1:15)

REVIEW QUESTIONS

1. What was there about Jesus' teaching, as compared to other teachers, that astonished those who heard Him?

2. What did the man with the unclean spirit say about Jesus?

3. What did Jesus demand of the unclean spirit?

4. How did the people who saw the miracle of the demon exorcism react?

5. How did Peter's mother-in-law show her gratitude for the healing she received?

GOLDEN TEXT HOMILY

"COME YE AFTER ME, AND I WILL MAKE YOU TO BECOME FISHERS OF MEN" (Mark 1:17).

The call from Jesus to you and me is to come. To come requires no special ability, only a willingness and the putting forth an effort to move toward Him. Then, following in His steps (after me) and not after the flesh (self) He takes charge and He makes us. The Creator who made us now, through a move to Him, makes us anew. The Potter molds those of us who are but clay yielded to Him into what He wants us to be (Jeremiah 18:6). He did not make us to be a vessel beautiful to behold, but one to be useful to Himself, sanctified and meet for the Master's use (2 Timothy 2:21).

Our business is to fish for souls and to win them to Christ. All men have sinned and have "come short of the glory of God" (Romans 3:23). They are lost in the sea of life. Like the disciples on one occasion, fishermen sometimes fish all night and catch nothing, but we must launch out into the deep, follow Jesus' instructions, and keep fishing until we catch (Luke 5:4-6). There are often dangers and disappointments but the fisherman continues to fish. He has left the world behind. He continues in the work of His Lord. He knows that his labor is not in vain (1 Corinthians 15:58) and the angels will rejoice with him in his catch (Luke 15:7).—**Terry A. Beaver, Pastor, West City, Illinois**

SENTENCE SERMONS

FAITH IS the pencil of the soul that pictures heavenly things.
—T. Burbridge

MIRACLES MAY be denied, but healings are not . . . Christ produces a sound faith, and faith has a theraputic value.
—John H. Gerstner

THE HEAD OF MEDICAL services in a great university hospital once said, "One should send for his minister as he sends for his doctor when he becomes ill." That is to say, God helps the sick in two ways, through the science of medicine and surgery and through the experience of faith and prayer.

—**Norman Vincent Peale**

EVANGELISTIC APPLICATION

THROUGH CHRIST, THE CHURCH MUST MINISTER TO THE TOTAL NEEDS OF PEOPLE.

In the second chapter of Colossians, Paul condemned the false philosophies of his day calling them empty and deceitful. In order for men to find fulfillment they must turn to Christ, he contended. Of Christ, Paul wrote: "For in him dwelleth all the fulness of the Godhead bodily (2:9).

One philosopher, Jean Paul Sartre wrote: "Life is an empty bubble on the sea of nothingness." With him, Solomon agreed: "I have seen all the works that are done under the sun; and, behold, all is vanity and vexation of spirit" (Ecclesiastes 1:14).

These attitudes represent life without Christ. What a different perspective Christ brings. Paul wrote: "Ye are complete in him" (2:10). All the treasures of wisdom and knowledge are hidden in Christ (see 2:3). He is the Head over all rule and authority. The fullness of life which we experience comes from His fullness. The touch of the divine nature which we enjoy comes through Him (see 2 Peter 1:4). The marvelous grace which we have received has come from His hand (John 1: 16). Does it not follow then that through Him the church may minister to the total needs of men?

DAILY BIBLE READINGS

M. A Confirmed Ministry. Matthew 3:13-17

T. A Criticized Ministry. Matthew 9:1-8

W. A Rejected Ministry. Matthew 13:53-58

T. A Powerful Ministry. Mark 2:1-12

F. A Compassionate Ministry. Mark 6: 30-44

S. A Self-Giving Ministry. Mark 8:31-37

Principles of the Kingdom

Study Text: Matthew 5:1-16
Supplemental References: Psalm 24:3-6; Luke 6:20-26; Romans 12:1-3, 9-21
Time: Early in A.D. 28
Place: On a hill or mountain near Capernaum in Galilee
Golden Text: "Blessed are they which do hunger and thirst after righteousness: for they shall be filled" (Matthew 5:6).
Central Truth: God's blessings rest on those who understand and apply Kingdom principles to daily living.
Evangelistic Emphasis: Christians living by principles of the kingdom of God are lights in the world.

Printed Text

Matthew 5:1. And seeing the multitudes, he went up into a mountain: and when he was set, his disciples came unto him:

2. And he opened his mouth, and taught them, saying,

3. Blessed are the poor in spirit: for their's is the kingdom of heaven.

4. Blessed are they that mourn: for they shall be comforted.

5. Blessed are the meek: for they shall inherit the earth.

6. Blessed are they which do hunger and thirst after righteousness: for they shall be filled.

7. Blessed are the merciful: for they shall obtain mercy.

8. Blessed are the pure in heart: for they shall see God.

9. Blessed are the peacemakers: for they shall be called the children of God.

10. Blessed are they which are persecuted for righteousness' sake: for their's is the kingdom of heaven.

11. Blessed are ye, when men shall revile you, and persecute you, and shall say all manner of evil against you falsely, for my sake.

12. Rejoice, and be exceeding glad: for great is your reward in heaven: for so persecuted they the prophets which were before you.

13. Ye are the salt of the earth: but if the salt have lost his savour, wherewith shall it be salted? it is thenceforth good for nothing, but to be cast out, and to be trodden under foot of men.

14. Ye are the light of the world. A city that is set on an hill cannot be hid.

15. Neither do men light a candle, and put it under a bushel, but on a candlestick; and it giveth light unto all that are in the house.

16. Let your light so shine before men, that they may see your good works, and glorify your Father which is in heaven.

LESSON OUTLINE

I. THE PRINCIPLES DESCRIBED
   A. The Occasion
   B. The Principles Explained
     1. Character
      a. Poor in Spirit
      b. Those Who Mourn
      c. The Gentle
      d. Searchers for Righteousness
      e. The Merciful
      f. The Pure in Heart
      g. The Peacemakers
     2. Persecution
II. THE PRINCIPLES APPLIED
   A. The Salt of the Earth
   B. The Light of the World
   C. The Life That Glorifies

LESSON EXPOSITION

INTRODUCTION

A division of opinion exists as to the exact location where the Sermon on the Mount was delivered. Some identify the Horns of Hattin, a short distance south of the Sea of Galilee as the place. Others say a hilly region not far from Capernaum, toward the west, a place that is now called the Mount of Beatitudes, is the spot. However, we cannot be certain about the exact location.

What is the purpose of the Sermon on the Mount? It was not an effort to present the way of salvation. It was rather a message to those who are members of the family of God. In *The Bible Knowledge Commentary,* Louis A. Barbieri, Jr., succinctly writes: "The sermon showed how a person who is in right relationship with God should conduct his life."

The standard of righteousness set forth in Jesus' sermon applies to believers today. Only those who are a part of the kingdom of God are capable of walking in obedience to these precepts. The benefits of this manifesto are reserved for them. To build one's life on these principles is to live life on the highest possible plane. It is to taste heaven while still on earth.

I. THE PRINCIPLES DESCRIBED (Matthew 5:1-12)

A. The Occasion (vv. 1, 2)

1. And seeing the multitudes, he went up into a mountain: and when he was set, his disciples came unto him:

2. And he opened his mouth, and taught them, saying.

The more Jesus preached and performed miracles the larger the crowds became that gathered to hear Him. On this occasion, He went up on a mountain to teach His followers the principles of the kingdom of God. What followed is a masterpiece of ethics and righteous living unequaled by any other person.

In *A Few Buttons Missing,* J. T. Fisher, an outstanding American psychiatrist wrote: "If you were to take the sum total of all authoritative articles ever written by the most qualified of psychologists and psychiatrists on the subject of mental hygiene, if you were to combine them and refine them and leave out the excess verbiage, if you were to take the whole of the meat and none of the parsley, and if you were to have these unadulterated bits of pure scientific knowledge concisely expressed by the most capable of living poets, you would have an awkward and an incomplete summary of the Sermon on the Mount. And it would suffer immeasurably through comparison. For nearly two thousand years the Christian world has been holding in its hands the complete answer to its restless and fruitless yearning. Here rests the blueprint for successful human life, with optimum mental health and contentment."

B. The Principles Explained (vv. 3-12)

1. Character

a. Poor in Spirit (v. 3)

3. Blessed are the poor in spirit: for their's is the kingdom of heaven.

The Beatitudes have a twofold significance. They describe the inner condition of a believer and they promise him blessings in the future. Their standards are unattainable by personal effort, but may be attained by the work of the Holy Spirit within.

Each beatitude begins with the word *blessed. The New International Dictionary* of New Testament Theology, Volume One defines blessed as "free from daily cares and worries . . . describes the condition of the gods and those who share their happy existence." It involves more than just being happy; it includes being in harmony with God and the security and blessedness that spring from that relationship.

This first Beatitude speaks of the "poor in spirit." Who are they? William Barclay says they are those who have fully realized their own inadequacy, their own worthlessness, and their own destitution, and who have put their whole trust in God. They have discovered that the way to power is through the realization of helplessness. The way to independence is through dependence.

The "poor in spirit" are assured a place in the kingdom of heaven, a society in which God's will is as perfectly done on earth as it is in heaven.

b. Those Who Mourn (v. 4)

4. Blessed are they that mourn: for they shall be comforted.

When a man realizes his poverty of spirit, his unworthiness before God, it leads him to mourn over his sin. The impact of the realization of his own sin and his helplessness to do anything about it is devastating. In his sense of helplessness, a man turns to God. As Neville Talbot wrote: "When you come to the bottom, you find God."

The road to God is marked by a broken heart. The psalmist declared: "For I will declare mine iniquity; I will be sorry for my sin" (38:18). The Apostle Paul wrote: "For godly sorrow worketh repentance to salvation" (2 Corinthians 7:10). The first step, then, toward the Christian life is utter dissatisfaction with life apart from Christ. That dissatisfaction leads to a brokenness that produces repentance and ultimately results in salvation.

Those who are truly sorry for their sins shall be comforted, Jesus said. The word that is translated comforted is related to the word that Jesus used when He promised the coming of the Holy Spirit (see John 14:16-18). The Holy Spirit

as an ally, a helper, a counselor will bring comfort to those who mourn.

c. The Gentle (v. 5)

5. Blessed are the meek: for they shall inherit the earth.

The meek person is truly humble and gentle. He has a proper perspective of himself and his position. He is an imitator of Jesus Christ who said, "I am meek and lowly in heart" (Matthew 11:29). He shows kindness to all men because he remembers that he too was one time alienated from God (see Titus 3:1-7). The meek person no longer takes matters into his own hands. Mistreatment and suffering do not call up revenge. Rather, he commits himself to Him who deals righteously (see 1 Peter 2:19-22). Pride, wrath, and revenge have no place in his life. He is submitted to God's guidance and accepts whatever God sends to him.

Who are the really "meek?" In what sense do they and will they inherit the earth?

To the meek a promise is given: they shall inherit the earth. Many years before the time of Christ, the psalmist had made that same promise (see 37:11). He listed several other promises in combination with this one: the meek will dwell in the land; they will be fed; they will have the desires of their heart; they will see evildoers cut off; and they will enjoy abundance of peace (see Psalm 37:1-11). In their Commentary on the Whole Bible, Jamieson, Fausset, and Brown wrote: "Thus are the meek the only rightful occupants of a foot of ground or a crust of bread here, and heirs of all coming things."

d. Searchers for Righteousness (v. 6)

6. Blessed are they which do hunger and thirst after righteousness: for they shall be filled.

What the heart hungers for tells you much about the person. If the desire is only for possessions and material things, the person is out of step with the kingdom of God. If the desire is for righteousness and spiritual things, the person is moving in the right direction.

When this inner longing for righteousness is satisfied, it is reflected in outward character and conduct. It also responds to the need for righteousness is the lives of others. Martin Luther expressed the thought well: "The command to you is not to crawl into a corner or into the desert, but to run out, if that is where you have been, and to offer your hands and your feet and your whole body, and to wager everything you have and can do." What is needed, he adds, is "a hunger and thirst for righteousness that can never be curbed or stopped or sated, one that looks for nothing and cares for nothing except the accomplishment and maintenance of the right, despising everything that hinders this end."

God honors those who have a healthy, hearty spiritual appetite. Ultimately their hunger and thirst will be fully satisfied in that land where we "shall hunger no more, neither thirst any more; . . . For the Lamb . . . shall feed them, and shall lead them unto living fountains of waters" (Revelation 7:16, 17).

e. The Merciful (v. 7)

7. Blessed are the merciful: for they shall obtain mercy.

The first three Beatitudes deal with man's spiritual awareness in approaching God. The fourth Beatitude speaks of the promise of God's provision. The last three Beatitudes address the character of the believer. Each of these characteristics is an essential, divine quality.

Those who have obtained God's righteousness are to show mercy. It is to God that mercy belongs (see Isaiah 16:5) and He is rich in mercy (Ephesians 2:4). To be merciful, therefore, is to "bear toward others that outgoing love which reflects and reproduces the outgoing love of God." It "is to have the same attitude to men as God has, to think of men as God thinks of them, to feel for men as God feels for them, to act toward men as God acts toward them" (Barclay).

Those to whom mercy has been shown are themselves to show mercy. When this quality characterizes one's life it is much easier to be tolerant toward others, to freely forgive others, and to lend a helping hand wherever there is a need. These Christlike traits are the product of an attitude of mercy.

f. The Pure in Heart (v. 8)

8. Blessed are the pure in heart: for they shall see God.

Those to whom Jesus was speaking were more familiar with ceremonial purification than they were with purity of heart. This purity of heart is obtained only through the blood of Christ. The writer of Hebrews declares: "How much more shall the blood of Christ, who through the eternal Spirit offered himself without spot to God, purge your conscience from dead works to serve the living God?" (9:14).

Something that is pure has nothing mixed with it; it is untainted in any way. A heart that is pure is a heart whose thoughts, motives, desires, and attitudes are completely genuine and absolutely unmixed with anything that would defile in any way.

Even the psalmist understood the pure in heart will see God. He wrote: "As for me, I will behold thy face in righteousness: I shall be satisfied, when I awake, with thy likeness" (17:15). Certainly, the vision of the future in the Book of Revelation foretells a time when the Lord's "servants shall serve him: and they shall see his face; and his name shall be in their foreheads" (22:3, 4). John says that believers will see Jesus as He is and be like Him (see 1 John 3:2).

g. The Peacemakers (v. 9)

9. Blessed are the peacemakers: for they shall be called the children of God.

The word peace occurs 88 times in the New Testament. It appears in every book except First John. Most of the Epistles begin or end with a prayer for peace for their readers. Jesus' departing words to His disciples were, "Peace I leave with you, my peace I give unto you" (John 14:27).

Discuss the role of "peacemakers." How can they best function in today's world?

The promise is to the peacemaker. "Peacemaker" is not a negative term. It is not speaking of someone who evades trouble and allows a matter to drift until the situation becomes harder to solve. A peacemaker takes positive action to bring about the highest good for another. He is willing to face difficulty, unpleasantness, and unpopularity in order to produce peace. A peacemaker works for right relations between persons.

The peacemakers shall be called the children of God. Literally, they are called *sons of God*. This expression carries with it a certain virtue or quality. For example, Barnabas was called the "son of consolation." This meant that he was a consoling and a comforting man. To say that a man is a son of God is to say that he is a godlike man doing a godlike work, which, in this instance, is making peace.

2. Persecution (vv. 10-12)

10. Blessed are they which are persecuted for righteousness' sake: for their's is the kingdom of heaven.

11. Blessed are ye, when men shall revile you, and persecute you, and shall say all manner of evil against you falsely, for my sake.

12. Rejoice, and be exceeding glad: for great is your reward in heaven: for so persecuted they the prophets which were before you.

Jesus never tried to conceal the difficulties and problems His followers would face. Thus, He tells them that they will be reviled, persecuted, and have all manner of evil said against them falsely because they are following Him. The world hated Him and it will feel no different toward them (see Matthew 10:16-22)

One of the chief reasons that believers in the early church faced persecution was the spread of emperor worship. The time came when all men under the pro-

vince of Rome were expected to declare: "Caesar is Lord." No Christian could ever do that. To him Jesus Christ and He alone was Lord. Rome felt threatened by this refusal to bow to its demands and severely persecuted the believers.

There is a positive side to persecution. To persecute a person is to show that he and his claims are taken seriously. Persecution offers an opportunity to demonstrate loyalty. To endure persecution is to walk with the saints, the prophets, and the martyrs. To suffer for Christ means that we will also reign with Him (see 2 Timothy 2:12). For this reason, we can rejoice in persecution.

II. THE PRINCIPLES APPLIED (Matthew 5:13-16)

A. The Salt of the Earth (v. 13)

13. Ye are the salt of the earth: but if the salt have lost his savour, wherewith shall it be salted? it is thenceforth good for nothing, but to be cast out, and to be trodden under foot of men.

When Jesus said that believers are the salt of the earth, He meant that we are to influence our world in a positive way. The various uses of salt illustrate how we are to be effective. For instance, salt preserves. This quality was of special importance in Jesus' day. The tropical climate, without cooling systems, made salt essential to keep things from spoiling. In a world that is bad and getting worse, there is a need for believers to allow God to work through them in a preserving way. This calls for Christians to be Christians at work, in politics, at home, and everywhere else. This work of preservation is desperately needed.

Then, salt provides flavor. Others need to see the life of God in us. They need to perceive us as a people who possess within us the Spirit of the living God. Also, salt makes one thirsty. Do we make anyone thirsty for Jesus Christ? Do we give such evidence of peace and joy that others say, "That's what I want to be like."

The down side of this verse is that if the salt has lost its strength, it is worthless. Have we been guilty of losing our spiritual strength?

B. The Light of the World (v. 14, 15)

14. Ye are the light of the world. A city that is set on an hill cannot be hid.

15. Neither do men light a candle, and put it under a bushel, but on a candlestick; and it giveth light unto all that are in the house.

A man on a business trip was complimented by a client on his spectacular advancement in his company. He simply replied radiantly, "I am very thankful for the gifts I have received." "What do you mean? You did it by hard work!" the client insisted. "Yes, that's true," he replied, "but the strength, wisdom, and love were gifts with which to work hard." Later the client pressed him further to know the source of the remarkable joy and confidence the man had. Quietly, simply, but powerfully, he told him what had happened to him after he had let Christ control his life (*A Life Full of Surprises,* Lloyd John Ogilvie).

Are we living such a radiant life that it causes others to ask, "Why are you the way you are?" Is the manifestation of God at work in the painful, practical, personal areas of life so obvious that all can see? Are we living and letting the light of our life shine? Are we living in such a way that others are pressing us for the key to our life? If not, are we really alive?

C. The Life That Glorifies (v. 16)

16. Let your light so shine before men, that they may see your good works, and glorify your Father which is in heaven.

The believer is to be like the beacon in a lighthouse that points the ships toward the harbor. He is to be a beacon who points the way to God. He does not point to himself; he points beyond himself to God.

How does the Christian point men to God? This happens in the things he does and by the beauty of his living.

He is to "adorn the doctrine of God our Savior in all things" (Titus 2:10). He "adorns the doctrine" by the purity and consistency of his living. Nothing attracts men to Christ like the virtues of Christ seen in the believer.

Bishop Westcott wrote: "We lose the light if we do not follow Christ, and move as He moves . . . But the Light, which lightens because it lives . . . burns on with changeless splendour. And this only is required of us if we would know its quickening, cheering, warming energies, that we should follow it." Let us walk in the light that we may bring glory to our heavenly Father.

REVIEW QUESTIONS

1. What was the occasion for Jesus' discourse on principles of Christian living?

2. What is the meaning of the introductory word "blessed" used with each beatitude?

3. What does it mean to hunger and thirst after righteousness?

4. Why are the persecuted considered blessed?

5. What spiritual truths are set forth in the metaphors of salt and light?

GOLDEN TEXT HOMILY

"BLESSED ARE THEY WHICH DO HUNGER AND THIRST AFTER RIGHTEOUSNESS: FOR THEY SHALL BE FILLED" (Matthew 5:6).

These words undoubtedly had a much greater impact upon those who heard them directly from Jesus upon the mount than they do to most of us today. We who live in modern society rarely, if ever, know what it means to be really hungry or really thirsty. However, this was a common experience to many who lived in ancient Israel. Wages were low and laborers often lived near the edge of starvation. In a dry country without modern plumbing, water was not always readily available and thirst was a frequent experience.

Jesus pronounced a blessing upon those whose desire for righteousness could be compared to hunger and thirst. These are very basic drives. When one is truly hungry or thirsty other needs and desires lose their importance until the hunger is satiated or the thirst quenched. Our desire for righteousness should have precedence over all other desires.

The meaning of this beatitude is that we should aspire to total righteousness not merely some righteousness.

It is not the realization of righteousness that is to be blessed but the strong desire for it. However, if one desires to do right and please God, as a hungry man desires food and a thirsty man craves water, he or she will come close to achieving that goal. Such a person will be blessed; because the knowledge that you have done your best to do what is right contains its own satisfaction. —**Richard Y. Bershon, Chief, Chaplain Service, V. A. Medical Center, Tomah, Wisconsin.**

SENTENCE SERMONS

THE PRINCIPLES of the Bible are the groundwork of human freedom.
                              —**Horace Greely**

THE GREATER THING in this world is not so much where we stand, as in what direction we are going.
                    —**Oliver Wendell Holmes**

GOD IS PREPARING His heroes; and when the opportunity comes, He can fit them into their place in a moment, and the world will wonder where they came from.
                              —**H. B. Simpson**

PRINCIPLES OF LIFE are like tuning forks; sound them often to bring your life up to a standard pitch.
                              —**S. D. Gordon**

EVANGELISTIC APPLICATION

CHRISTIANS LIVING BY PRINCIPLES OF THE KINGDOM OF GOD ARE LIGHTS IN THE WORLD.

A man with a conviction must do one of two things; as Robert E. Speer used to put it: "Change it or spread it. If it is not true, he must give it up. If it is true, he must give it away. He must propagate it if it is true, or repudiate it if it is false."

We find ourselves facing this challenge with our knowledge of Christ. If what we know of Him is true, and it is, then we must spread it. We must find a way to give it away. And the best way to communicate this truth is by living according to the principles of the kingdom of God.

No matter who you are, if you are a follower of Christ, you can reflect His light to the world. Paul wrote: "But God hath chosen the foolish things of the world to confound the wise; and God hath chosen the weak things of the world to confound the things which are mighty; And base things of the world, and things which are despised, hath God chosen, yea, and things which are not, to bring to nought things that are: That no flesh should glory in his presence" (1 Corinthians 1:27-29).

ILLUMINATING THE LESSON

In Melville's classic story, *Moby Dick*, Captain Ahab hates the great whale, Moby Dick, who has crippled him. He's obsessed with killing the whale no matter what. Every waking hour, Ahab is consumed with tracking him down.

As the plot unfolds, it becomes obvious that Ahab, not Moby Dick, is the real victim. Ahab is the one who is imprisoned, hunted, and driven by hatred. In the end, he kills everything around him—the whale, the crew, and himself.

How different things would have been for Ahab had he discovered the beauty of mercy. Hating someone is hard work. Being merciful allows one to grow and be creative. If you give mercy, you receive mercy. If you give no mercy, you receive no mercy.

DAILY BIBLE READINGS

M. Need Acknowledged. Mark 9:17-24
T. Sorrow Expressed. Romans 9:1-5
W. Meekness Rewarded. Psalm 37:3-11
T. Righteousness Sought. Proverbs 11 1-6, 18, 19
F. Mercy Shown. Romans 12:1-8
S. Persecution Endured. Luke 6:22, 23

December 20, 1987

The Birth of Christ

(Christmas Lesson)

Study Text: Matthew 1:1-25

Supplemental References: Isaiah 7:10-14; 11:1-9; Luke 2:1-20

Time: 5 B.C.

Place: Nazareth

Golden Text: "Behold, a virgin shall be with child, and shall bring forth a son, and they shall call his name Emmanuel" (Matthew 1:23).

Central Truth: Jesus Christ is the divinely conceived, virgin born, Son of God.

Evangelistic Emphasis: Jesus came to be the Savior of the world.

Printed Text

Matthew 1:1. The book of the generation of Jesus Christ, the son of David, the son of Abraham.

16. And Jacob begat Joseph the husband of Mary, of whom was born Jesus, who is called Christ.

17. So all the generations from Abraham to David are fourteen generations; and from David until the carrying away into Babylon are fourteen generations; and from the carrying away into Babylon unto Christ are fourteen generations.

18. Now the birth of Jesus Christ was on this wise: When as his mother Mary was espoused to Joseph, before they came together, she was found with child of the Holy Ghost.

19. Then Joseph her husband, being a just man, and not willing to make her a publick example, was minded to put her away privily.

20. But while he thought on these things, behold, the angel of the Lord appeared unto him in a dream, saying, Joseph, thou son of David, fear not to take unto thee Mary thy wife: for that which is conceived in her is of the Holy Ghost.

21. And she shall bring forth a son, and thou shalt call his name JESUS: for he shall save his people from their sins.

22. Now all this was done, that it might be fulfilled which was spoken of the Lord by the prophet, saying,

23. Behold, a virgin shall be with child, and shall bring forth a son, and they shall call his name Emmanuel, which being interpreted is, God with us.

24. Then Joseph being raised from sleep did as the angel of the Lord had bidden him, and took unto him his wife:

25. And knew her not till she had brought forth her firstborn son: and he called his name JESUS.

149

LESSON OUTLINE

I. JESUS' ANCESTRY
  A. From Abraham to David
  B. From David to the Deportation
  C. From the Deportation to Jesus
II. DIVINE ASSURANCE
  A. His Mother
  B. His Legal Father
  C. His Name
  D. His Divinity
III. JOSEPH'S RESPONSE
  A. Joseph's Obedience
  B. The Child's Birth

LESSON EXPOSITION

INTRODUCTION

It is not easy to understand how the Almighty God could become a Babe in Bethlehem. And yet Jesus was the Son of God before He ever became Jesus of Nazareth. Jesus is the only person who lived before His birth and decided for Himself to come into the world. He existed from all eternity.

Jesus was born of a virgin. Both Matthew and Luke attest this fact. There was nothing ordinary about His birth. He was conceived of the Holy Spirit and born of the Virgin Mary. Thus this Man, Jesus, was also the Son of God.

The Savior lived in submission to the Father's will. He declared that He could do nothing apart from the Father. Never is His submission more clearly revealed than in Gethsemane. He was even willing to be shut away from the presence of His Father in order to atone for man's sin. He yielded Himself so totally to the Father's mission for Him that He became obedient even to death.

The glory which Christ had with the Father before the world began was not manifest in His earthly walk. Only on the Mount of Transfiguration was His glory revealed and that for a few moments (Matthew 17:1-9). This true glory of the Son of God of which Peter, James, and John were given a glimpse, believers will observe throughout eternity.

Jesus came into the world that He might show us the love of God and that we might put our trust in Him that we might be redeemed.

I. JESUS' ANCESTRY (Matthew 1:1-17)

A. From Abraham to David (vv. 1-6)

1. The book of the generations of Jesus Christ, the son of David, the son of Abraham.

(Matthew 1:2-6 is not included in the printed text.)

Matthew wrote with the Jews in mind. He was aware of their expectation that the Messiah would be born of a certain family. Therefore, he began his book with a genealogy. He shows that Jesus was a descendant of Abraham, who was the head of the covenant nation, and to whom the promise had been given that in his seed all the nations of the earth should be blessed (Genesis 22:18). Jesus also descended from David, the founder of the royal line. The Jews looked for the Ruler of Israel to be among David's descendants (see 2 Samuel 7:13-16).

Matthew refers to the Lord as Jesus Christ. The name *Jesus* means "the Lord is salvation." The name *Christ* means "anointed One."

Another genealogy appears in Luke 3:23-38. Evidently, it is that of Mary. What Matthew gives us is a genealogy that is traced through Joseph, Jesus' legal (though not natural) father. It established His claim and right to the throne of David.

The term *begat* is used to identify the natural descent of the son from his father. However, in the case of Jesus the terminology changes. Matthew simply says, "Joseph the husband of Mary, of whom was born Jesus, who is called Christ" (v. 16).

Besides Mary, four other women are mentioned in the genealogy in Matthew 1:2-16; they are Tamar, Rahab, Ruth, and Bathsheba. All but one of these were noted for the sinful stain upon her life, and two of them were Gentiles. Perhaps the inclusion of them in this list pictures the redemptive work of the Savior, and His offer of mercy to Gentiles as well as to Jews.

Why was the recording of Christ's genealogy so necessary for the Scripture writers?

B. From David to the Deportation (vv. 6-11)

(Matthew 1:6-11 is not included in the printed text.)

Between Joram and Ozias (literally Uzziah), three names are omitted: Ahaziah, Joash, and Amaziah (see 1 Chronicles 3:11, 12). The reason for their omission probably rests in the fact that they descended from Jezebel. Their connection with the house of Ahab would have been justification enough in the mind of any Jew for removing their names from the list.

Another interesting character listed here is Jechonias (literally Jeconiah). Of him Jeremiah wrote: "As I live, saith the Lord, though Coniah . . . were the signet upon my right hand, yet would I pluck thee thence. . . . Is this man Coniah a despised broken idol? is he a vessel wherein is no pleasure? wherefore are they cast out, he and his seed, and are cast into a land which they know not? . . . Thus saith the Lord, Write ye this man childless, a man that shall not prosper in his days: for no man of his seed shall prosper, sitting upon the throne of David, and ruling any more in Judah" (Jeremiah 22:24, 28, 30). This curse pronounced upon Jeconiah declared that none of his descendants would prosper sitting on the throne of David. This meant that if Jesus had been a physical descendant of Joseph, He would not have been successful on the throne of David. But since He came through Mary's lineage, He was not affected by this curse.

Matthew does not refer to the deportation of the Jews as their "captivity." That word carried with it bitter recollections, so Matthew studiously avoided its use.

C. From the Deportation to Jesus (vv. 12-17)

(Matthew 1:12-15 is not included in the printed text.)

16. And Jacob begat Joseph the husband of Mary, of whom was born Jesus, who is called Christ.

17. So all the generations from Abraham to David are fourteen generations; and from David until the carrying away into Babylon are fourteen generations; and from the carrying away into Babylon unto Christ are fourteen generations.

This list concludes with a reference to the birth of Jesus. The *New American Standard Bible* renders the announcement this way: "Joseph the husband of Mary, *by whom* was born Jesus, who is called Christ" (v. 16). The expression "by whom" is "feminine singular, indicating clearly that Jesus was born of Mary only and not of Mary and Joseph. It is one of the strongest evidences for Jesus' virgin birth (*The Ryrie Study Bible*).

In various verses, the Bible makes it clear that Jesus was born of Mary; He was not the son of Joseph; He had no earthly father. Joseph was the husband of Mary, but not the father of Jesus; He was born of *her*. The first mention of His birth points at once to other than a human origin. He who is the Son of Abraham is also the Son of God (*The Pulpit Commentary*).

In compiling this genealogy, the names were arranged that there should be the same number in each of the three divisions. This made the list easier to remember. If the reader expected all the persons listed to be perfect, he will be disappointed. Some of them were people of the highest caliber: Abraham, Isaac, Jacob, David, Asa, Jehoshaphat, Hezekiah, Josiah, Zerubbabel. Others of them were less reputable: Rehoboam, Abijah, Uzziah, Ahaz, Manasseh, Amon, Jeconiah.

Unmistakably, the messiahship of the Master is set forth in this genealogy. He is the son of Abraham, the Son of David and therefore entitled to the throne.

II. DIVINE ASSURANCE (Matthew 1:18-23)

A. His Mother (v. 18)

18. Now the birth of Jesus Christ was on this wise: When as his mother Mary was espoused to Joseph, before

they came together, she was found with child of the Holy Ghost.

Matthew now explains the circumstances surrounding the birth of Jesus. His "explanation can best be understood in the light of Hebrew marriage customs. Marriages were arranged for individuals by parents, and contracts were negotiated. After this was accomplished, the individuals were considered married and were called husband and wife. They did not, however, begin to live together. Instead, the woman continued to live with her parents and the man with his for one year. The waiting period was to demonstrate the faithfulness of the pledge of purity given concerning the bride. If she was found to be with child in this period, she obviously was not pure, but had been involved in an unfaithful sexual relationship. Therefore the marriage could be annulled. If, however, the one-year waiting period demonstrated the purity of the bride, the husband would then go to the house of the bride's parents and in a grand processional march lead his bride back to his home. There they would begin to live together as husband and wife and consummate their marriage physically. Matthew's story should be read with this background in mind" (*The Bible Knowledge Commentary*).

During this one-year waiting period, Mary was found to be with child. Paradoxically, Matthew explains that Mary is still a virgin and has been faithful to her vows. The child to be born of her was conceived of the Holy Spirit.

B. His Legal Father (vv. 19, 20)

19. Then Joseph her husband, being a just man, and not willing to make her a publick example, was minded to put her away privily.

20. But while he thought on these things, behold, the angel of the Lord appeared unto him in a dream, saying, Joseph, thou son of David, fear not to take unto thee Mary thy wife: for that which is conceived in her is of the Holy Ghost.

Very little is known about Joseph the husband of Mary. He was a descendant of David and he acted as a father to-

ward Jesus. Most biblical scholars believe that he died young and was not alive during the ministry of Jesus.

Matthew describes Joseph as a righteous man. He endeavored to live by the divine precepts set forth in the Law. He wanted to do what was right in all things. Now he faced a dilemma. Mary told him that she was pregnant. If he reported her condition to the judges at the city gate, it would result in a public scandal. It could even mean that Mary could be stoned to death (Deuteronomy 22:23, 24). Joseph was unwilling to expose her to such public shame. He decided to adopt the most private form of legal divorce. This involved handing the letter to her privately in the presence of only two witnesses, to whom he need not convey his reasons. He intended to preserve his personal and family purity, and at the same time not be insensitive to the one whom he loved.

While Joseph pondered on the best course of action for himself, an angel of the Lord appeared to him in a dream. Thus, there entered into his reasoning an element he did not expect. As He so often does, the Lord sent His messenger just when Joseph needed to hear from him. The angel confirmed the divine nature of Mary's conception. He urged Joseph not to be afraid to take Mary as his wife because the expected child within her was conceived by the Holy Spirit.

C. His Name (v. 21)

21. And she shall bring forth a son, and thou shalt call his name JESUS: for he shall save his people from their sins.

The angel gave Joseph the gender of the child which Mary would bring forth. The child would be a son and this would be one way of testing the accuracy of the angel's statement.

As the legal father, Joseph is charged with naming the child. The name which he must give the child is Jesus. The Hebrew form of the name means "Jehovah the Savior." It expresses Jesus' whole saving office and work. It is, to the awakened and anxious sinner, the sweetest and most fragrant of all names.

The angel added that it is He who shall save His people from their sins. The empathic nature of the expression conveys the thought that "He, and no other, is the expected Savior." Later, the Apostle Peter confirmed this truth: "Neither is there salvation in any other: for there is none other name under heaven given among men whereby we must be saved" (Acts 4:12).

The angel said that Jesus would come to save *His people:* the lost sheep of the house of Israel. Later, the Apostle Paul confirmed that the message was given to the Jews first: "For I am not ashamed of the gospel of Christ: for it is the power of God unto salvation to every one that believeth; to the Jew first, and also to the Greek" (Romans 1:16). While the hope of redemption began with the Jew, it reaches to all mankind. Jesus has redeemed men to God by His blood "out of every kindred, and tongue, and people, and nation" (Revelation 5:9).

Jesus came to save His people *from their sins.* Deliverance from their sin leads to a restoration to their rightful position. His redeeming work is comprehensive, resulting in full salvation from sin. He washes "us from our sins in his own blood" (Revelation 1:5).

D. His Divinity (vv. 22, 23)

22. Now all this was done, that it might be fulfilled which was spoken of the Lord by the prophet, saying,

23. Behold, a virgin shall be with child, and shall bring forth a son, and they shall call his name Emmanuel, which being interpreted is, God with us.

Although Matthew expresses these two verses in his own words, some biblical scholars believe they are part of the angel's message to Joseph. As such, they would offer him more assurance and encouragement.

Do you think Isaiah fully grasped the significance of the message he gave concerning Jesus? Support your answer.

That a Savior is to be born; that He is to be born of a virgin; and that He is conceived of the Holy Spirit: all these things were foretold by the Hebrew prophets. While the prophecy was spoken by men, it came from the Lord. The prophets were merely instruments in His hand.

The Old Testament passage to which these verses allude is Isaiah 7:14, "Therefore, the Lord himself shall give you a sign; Behold, a virgin shall conceive, and bear a son, and shall call his name Immanuel."

The nature and character of Jesus will be such that men will call Him *Immanuel,* meaning God is with us. This is the same thought which John had in mind when he wrote: "In the beginning was the Word, and the Word was with God, and the Word was God. . . . And the Word was made flesh, and dwelt among us, (and we beheld his glory, the glory as of the only begotten of the Father,) full of grace and truth" (John 1:1, 14).

In Luke 7, we are given the account of Jesus raising the son of the widow of Nain from death to life. Those who were present praised and glorified God for what was done. Of Jesus, they observed that God had come to help His people (see Luke 7:11-17).

III. JOSEPH'S RESPONSE (Matthew 1:24, 25)

A. Joseph's Obedience (v. 24)

24. Then Joseph being raised from sleep did as the angel of the Lord had bidden him, and took unto him his wife.

This dream in which an angel visited him meant much to Joseph. His fears and anxiety about the true state of affairs with Mary were allayed. With this clear view of what had happened, his course of action was easier to determine. He no longer had to decide between his personal integrity and his love for Mary.

This angelic visit, in a dream to Joseph, was equally important to Mary. Now, the one she cared most about had no reason to be suspicious that she had been unfaithful. Though she had bestowed upon her the highest honor ever brought to any woman, other people were not aware of these circumstances. But now Joseph is. And what peace of mind this must have meant for Mary.

Upon awaking from his sleep, Joseph did as the angel of the Lord directed him. The thought is that immediately upon arising, he obeyed. Thinking of what was best for Mary, he violated all custom by taking Mary into his home without waiting for the one-year period of betrothal to pass.

Joseph is a shining example of the obedience every believer should display. When a man is sure that he has heard God's Word, there should be no further argument. His ears should be closed to any reasoning that would dispute the message of God. No wonder the Scriptures say that "to obey is better than sacrifice." Service to God is rendered gladly when one acts in obedience to His voice.

B. The Child's Birth (v. 25)

25. And knew her not till she had brought forth her firstborn son: and he called his name Jesus.

Although Joseph took Mary to his home, they continued their obedient self-restraint. There was no sexual relationship between them until after the birth of Jesus.

That a son was born to Mary fulfilled the angel's promise. The reference to her "firstborn son" does not necessarily address the question as to whether there were other children born to her. J. B. Lightfoot wrote: "The law, in speaking of the firstborn, regarded not whether any were born *after* or no, but only that none were born before."

In obedience to the command given him by the Lord through the angel, and as a sign of his faith in Him and His work, Joseph named the child Jesus.

Charles Hodge wrote: "There is more power to sanctify, elevate, strengthen, and cheer in the word *Jesus* than in all the utterances of man since the world began." Believers have discovered this grand truth. The secret of our joy rests in the knowledge that Jesus is with us. He is a present, not an absent, Jesus. He is the Son of God, the King of Kings, the Lord of lords, and our daily companion. If Christ is with us, what temptation or difficulty cannot be conquered? What victory cannot be won through Him?

REVIEW QUESTIONS

1. What kind of a man does verse 19 describe Joseph as being?

2. How was Joseph convinced that Mary's pregnancy was in order?

3. What name did Isaiah say Jesus would carry?

4. What does the name "Emmanuel" mean?

5. What did Joseph do after awakening from his sleep?

GOLDEN TEXT HOMILY

"BEHOLD, A VIRGIN SHALL BE WITH CHILD, AND SHALL BRING FORTH A SON, AND THEY SHALL CALL HIS NAME EMMANUEL" (Matthew 1:23).

Halley's Bible Handbook states that Matthew is said to be the "most widely read book in all the world." Thus, the fact of the Virgin Birth of Jesus becomes knowledgeable to all the world. From the miraculous union of the divine and human natures, Jesus, the Son of God, was born (Matthew 1:20; Luke 1:34, 35) Mary is the only virgin that ever became or ever shall become, a mother in this fashion. The Jews, and even some (so-called) Christians, try desperately to refute this miracle birth; but the Scriptures leave no room for doubt in the Christian believer as to the authenticity of the Virgin Birth of Jesus—Emmanuel (Isaiah 7:14; Matthew 1:23; Luke 1:27 34, 35).

Emmanuel—"God with us," God with us then, God with us now! In the Old Testament ages God manifested Himself as Jehovah; in the Gospels God manifested Himself—"God with us"—in the Person of Jesus Christ the Son; and after the Ascension, He manifests Himself in the indwelling, empowering Holy Spirit (John 14:16-18; 1 John 4:4).

God is *with* us, and *in* us, through the miracle of faith; God with us:

- saving from sin
- comforting us
- defending us
- enlightening us
- protecting us from Satan's darts
- guiding us
- keeping us from yielding to Satan's temptations and sinning
- sanctifying us
- infilling us with the Holy Spirit

- healing us
- empowering us for service for God and mankind

Jesus was born of God's nature and human nature; He is very God and perfect man. Because of His humanity He relates with humankind. He experienced all the temptations that we do. He felt pain, loneliness, hunger, thirst, weariness; He was poor; He shed tears (Hebrews 4:15).

We live in a sinful, sick, strife-ridden, suffering, cruel, revengeful world. So did Jesus! He understands our every need. He is all-knowing, ever-present, all-powerful to meet our every need.

Emmanuel—"God with us" and in us, and we with Him now and eternally! —**Karl W. Bunkley, (Retired), Former General Sunday School President, International Pentecostal Holiness Church, Oklahoma City, Oklahoma**

SENTENCE SERMONS

THE MESSAGE of Christmas is that the visible material world is bound to the invisible spiritual world.

—**Anonymous**

EVERY LITTLE CHILD in all the world has been a little safer since the coming of the Child of Bethlehem.

—**Selected**

THE SON OF GOD became a man to enable men to become the sons of God.

—**C. S. Lewis**

SELFISHNESS MAKES Christmas a burden: love makes it a delight.

—**"The Encyclopedia of Religious Quotations"**

EVANGELISTIC APPLICATION

JESUS CAME TO BE THE SAVIOR OF THE WORLD.

When his bed caught fire, Edward Sweeny, of New York City, awakened, ran to the door, opened it, went through it, and slammed it behind him only to discover that he was in a clothes closet and could not get out. Meanwhile other tenants smelled smoke and sounded the alarm. The firemen extinguished the blaze and released Mr. Sweeny from from the closet when they heard him pounding on the door.

How like human beings! Caught in the sleep of death, they race to any door and rush through only to be trapped in their false hope. Is it any wonder that the Lord cries through the prophet, "Turn you to the strong hold, ye prisoners of hope" (Zechariah 9:12)? Christ is the stronghold and the only door. Any man who attempts to find safety by any other door will find himself trapped forever (*Let Me Illustrate,* Donald Grey Barnhouse).

Jesus said: "I am the door: by me if any man enter in, he shall be saved" (John 10:9).

ILLUMINATING THE LESSON

Until the track gauge was standardized in 1881, Illinois Central Railroad trains running between Cairo and New Orleans had to be jacked up and their wheels exchanged because of a difference in width of the northbound and southbound tracks.

But it was not as difficult to jack up these trains, exchange the wheels, and put a train from a broad gauge road onto a narrow gauge, as it is now to get people to leave the broad road and travel on the narrow road about which Jesus so wisely spoke.

He said, "Enter ye in at the strait gate: for wide is the gate, and broad is the way, that leadeth to destruction, and many there be which go in thereat: Because strait is the gate, and narrow is the way, which leadeth unto life, and few there be that find it" (Matthew 7:13, 14). (From *Sourcebook of 500 Illustrations,* Robert G. Lee.)

Through faith in the lovely name of Jesus, men can find the right road and travel securely therein. There is hope in Him.

DAILY BIBLE READINGS

M. Foretold by Prophets. Isaiah 7:10-14
T. Sent by God. Galatians 4:1-6
W. Born of a Virgin. Luke 1:26-31
T. Sought by Shepherds. Luke 2:8-18
F. Worshiped by Kings. Matthew 2:1-11
S. Protected by Angels. Matthew 2:13-20

The Way of Righteousness

Study Text: Matthew 5:17-48

Supplemental References: Exodus 20:1-17; Psalm 106:1-3; Romans 14:17-19

Time: Probably summer A.D. 28

Place: On a high hill or mountain near Capernaum in Galilee

Golden Text: "Love your enemies, bless them that curse you, do good to them that hate you, and pray for them which despitefully use you, and persecute you" (Matthew 5:44).

Central Truth: A right attitude evidenced by right action is the biblical pattern of true righteousness.

Evangelistic Emphasis: Those made righteous through Christ will escape the coming judgment.

Printed Text

Matthew 5:17. Think not that I am come to destroy the law, or the prophets: I am not come to destroy, but to fulfil.

18. For verily I say unto you, Till heaven and earth pass, one jot or one tittle shall in no wise pass from the law, till all be fulfilled.

19. Whosoever therefore shall break one of these least commandments, and shall teach men so, he shall be called the least in the kingdom of heaven: but whosoever shall do and teach them, the same shall be called great in the kingdom of heaven.

20. For I say unto you, That except your righteousness shall exceed the righteousness of the scribes and Pharisees, ye shall in no case enter into the kingdom of heaven.

21. Ye have heard that it was said by them of old time, Thou shalt not kill; and whosoever shall kill shall be in danger of the judgment:

22. But I say unto you, That whosoever is angry with his brother without a cause shall be in danger of the judgment: and whosoever shall say to his brother, Raca, shall be in danger of the council: but whosoever shall say Thou fool, shall be in danger of hell fire.

23. Therefore if thou bring thy gift to the altar, and there rememberest that thy brother hath ought against thee;

24. Leave there thy gift before the altar, and go thy way; first be reconciled to thy brother, and then come and offer thy gift.

43. Ye have heard that it hath been said, Thou shalt love thy neighbour, and hate thine enemy.

44. But I say unto you, Love your enemies, bless them that curse you, do good to them that hate you, and pray for them which despitefully use you, and persecute you;

45. That ye may be the children of your Father which is in heaven: for he maketh his sun to rise on the evil and on the good, and sendeth rain on the just and on the unjust.

46. For if ye love them which love you, what reward have ye? do not even the publicans the same?

47. And if ye salute your brethren only, what do ye more than others? do not even the publicans so?

48. Be ye therefore perfect, even as your Father which is in heaven is perfect.

DICTIONARY

scribes—Matthew 5:20—Professional writers who, in Israel, became the official interpreters and teachers of the law of Moses and who served as judges in the administration of that law.

Pharisees (FAIR-ah-sees)—Matthew 5:20—A religious party, or school of the Jews, in the time of Christ, so called from an Aramic form of the Hebrew word meaning "separated." Their theology was conservative, holding to the supernatural, the law of Moses, and the tradition of the elders.

Raca (RAY-kah)—Matthew 5:22—A term of contempt, but its exact meaning is uncertain. Some suggest it means "vain" or "worthless."

LESSON OUTLINE

I. FULFILLING GOD'S LAW
  A. Abolish or Fulfill
  B. Surpass or Perish
II. TEACHING TRUE RIGHTEOUSNESS
  A. Peaceableness
    1. Murder
    2. Reconciliation
  B. Purity
    1. Adultery
    2. Preservation
  C. Harmony
  D. Honesty
  E. Kindness
    1. Nonresistance
    2. Compliance
  F. Love
    1. Sons
    2. Perfect

LESSON EXPOSITION

INTRODUCTION

In the previous passage we studied, the Lord set forth the ideal character of His followers (see Matthew 5:3-10). He also spoke to them of letting that character shine out into the world to the glory of God the Father (see Matthew 5:11-16). Now, He addresses the great theme of His sermon: the righteousness which His followers must possess and display in the Kingdom for the saving of the world.

What Jesus calls upon His disciples to do is in absolute harmony with the Old Testament Scriptures. He was not presenting a rival system to the law of Moses and the teachings of the Prophets, but a true fulfillment of them. On the other hand, Jesus' message was in glaring disharmony with the righteousness advocated by the scribes and Pharisees. He contradicted the traditions of the Pharisees completely in principle and in detail. While He did this, He did not intend to abolish or even modify the Old Testament teachings, but rather to fulfill them in reality and in truth.

I. FULFILLING GOD'S LAW (Matthew 5:17-20)

A. Abolish or Fulfill (vv. 17-19)

17. Think not that I am come to destroy the law, or the prophets: I am not come to destroy, but to fulfil.

18. For verily I say unto you, Till heaven and earth pass, one jot or one tittle shall in no wise pass from the law, till all be fulfilled.

19. Whosoever therefore shall break one of these least commandments, and shall teach men so, he shall be called the least in the kingdom of heaven: but whosoever shall do and teach them, the same shall be called great in the kingdom of heaven.

Since Jesus opposed the traditions of

the Pharisees, there was the danger that His disciples might conclude that He intended to abolish the Old Testament. He wanted them to understand that His mission was not to destroy but to fulfill. The Law and the Prophets refer to the entire Old Testament, and Jesus is come to fulfill them completely. When His Word is done, the whole Old Testament will be fulfilled.

Jesus' fulfillment would extend to the smallest Hebrew letter, the "jot," and even to the smallest stroke of a Hebrew letter, the "tittle." In English "a jot would correspond to the dot above the letter 'i' (and look like an apostrophe), and a tittle would be seen in the difference between a 'P' and an 'R'. The small angled line that completes the 'R' is like a tittle. These things are important because letters make up words and even a slight change in a letter might change the meaning of a word" (*The Bible Knowledge Commentary*).

Further, Jesus taught that anyone who made the Old Testament teaching invalid by a vicious system of misinterpretation, and taught others to do the same would be relegated to a degrading position in the kingdom of heaven. On the other hand, those who exalt the authority and honor of God's law, shall be esteemed great in the kingdom of heaven.

B. Surpass or Perish (v. 20)

20. For I say unto you, That except your righteousness shall exceed the righteousness of the scribes and Pharisees, ye shall in no case enter into the kingdom of heaven.

The scribes were the most learned men of Israel and the Pharisees the most zealous. Some of them were extremely earnest and equally conscientious. The most familiar examples are Gamaliel and Saul of Tarsus. And yet, something was lacking in their relationship to God and His kingdom.

What did Jesus mean when He said that the righteousness of His disciples was to surpass that of the scribes and Pharisees? Did He mean that the disciples were to observe the ceremonies and rituals of the Law more earnestly

than they? Were they merely to work harder at keeping the Law?

The commitment of the scribes and Pharisees was to the observance of external rules without an accompanying change of heart. Entrance into the kingdom of heaven, however, is not dependent merely on observing external rules, but rather on finding true inner righteousness through faith in God's Word (see Romans 3:21, 22). This is what Jesus was telling Nicodemus, "Except a man be born of water and of the Spirit, he cannot enter into the kingdom of God" (John 3:5). Our righteousness, then, must be inward, vital, and spiritual to surpass that of the scribes and Pharisees.

II. TEACHING TRUE RIGHTEOUSNESS (Matthew 5:21-48)

A. Peaceableness (vv. 21-26)

1. Murder (vv. 21, 22)

21. Ye have heard that it was said by them of old time, Thou shalt not kill; and whosoever shall kill shall be in danger of the judgment:

22. But I say unto you, That whosoever is angry with his brother without a cause shall be in danger of the judgment: and whosoever shall say to his brother, Raca, shall be in danger of the council: but whosoever shall say, Thou fool, shall be in danger of hell fire.

Six times Jesus said, "Ye have heard that it was said . . . But I say unto you" (5:21, 22; 27, 28; 31, 32; 33, 34; 38, 39; 43, 44). In each instance, what Jesus says is vastly different from what the scribes and Pharisees taught. He shows what Moses really meant in contrast to the way his words had been interpreted.

In this passage Jesus dealt with the sixth commandment. He sought to show that this is more than a civil law for a civil court to administer. It has rather to do with the heart.

While the Pharisees viewed murder as taking someone's life, Jesus taught that the internal attitude behind the act was involved as well. Anger and its most common manifestation of calling ugly names is also sin. John wrote: "Whosoever hateth his brother is a murderer: and ye know that no murderer hath eternal life abiding in him" (1 John 3:15).

Beginning with anger and calling another by derogatory names and continuing on to murder, each is sin and gives evidence of a sinful heart. Jesus said the destiny of all such sinners is hell. Sin is a violation against God and will be judged in His court, not in some civil court. Who but God could sentence anyone to the fire of hell? No civil court could do that!

2. Reconciliation (vv. 23-26)

23. Therefore if thou bring thy gift to the altar, and there rememberest that thy brother hath ought against thee;

24. Leave there thy gift before the altar, and go thy way; first be reconciled to thy brother, and then come and offer thy gift.

(Matthew 5:25, 26 is not included in the printed text.)

Now Jesus illustrates the proper conduct of a believer toward others where reconciliation is needed whether the believer is the innocent party or the offending party. The setting for the account is a public worship service after the Old Testament order. The believer brings his offering to the altar and as he prepares to worship God he remembers that his brother has something against him. It may be something he did or did not do, something he said or did not say. He knows in his heart that he has done his brother wrong, whether or not his brother holds it against him, and he must make it right.

Do you think there is a tendency in churches today for people to avoid reconciliation even when that action would solve problems? Explain.

When he goes to his brother, confesses his sin, and asks his brother's pardon, he has done what he can do. If his brother accepts, then full reconciliation is achieved. If the brother refuses to forgive, the believer has done what he could. He may then return to the altar

with a clear conscience and proceed with his offering.

If a dispute is headed for the courts for resolution, every effort should be made to find a means of reconciliation outside of court. This calls for confession on the part of the one who has done wrong and forgiveness on the part of the wronged.

B. Purity (vv. 27-30)

1. Adultery (vv. 27, 28)

(Matthew 5:27, 28 is not included in the printed text.)

The treatment given to the sixth commandment Jesus now gives to the seventh. The Pharisees interpreted this commandment only in terms of the outward act. Jesus said that adultery begins in the heart and is followed by the act. "The man who casts lustful looks," Lenski wrote, "is an adulterer to begin with. The sin is already 'in his heart' and only comes out in his lustful look. If the heart were pure, without adultery, no lustful look would be possible. . . . The man's very heart and nature must be so changed by divine grace that lustful looks will become impossible for him."

What is said of a man in this passage may also be said of a woman. And what applies to a married man also applies to an unmarried man.

James affirmed that sin begins in the heart: "Let no man say when he is tempted, I am tempted of God: for God cannot be tempted with evil, neither tempteth he any man: But every man is tempted, when he is drawn away of his own lust, and enticed. Then when lust hath conceived, it bringeth forth sin: and sin, when it is finished, bringeth forth death" (James 1:13-15).

2. Preservation (vv. 29, 30)

(Matthew 5:29, 30 is not included in the printed text.)

Jesus underscores the fact that the lust problem is a heart problem. He addresses the idea that the problem is in the eye or the hand or the foot (see Matthew 18:8, 9). If that is where the problem is, He declares, then get rid of that part of the body. If some part of the body is so diseased with sin as to sink one into hell, then pluck it out or have it amputated. That is a small price to pay to save you from hell.

But where does the amputation end? If the right eye looks lustfully and is plucked out, what about the left eye? Is it not capable of sin as well? Is this not also true of the left hand and the left foot? If sin is in the members of the body will not the whole body be mutilated eventually?

Is not Jesus seeking to teach that the seat of lust and sin is in the heart? His call is for a pure heart which keeps even the eyes pure. Such a pure heart is the result of regenerating and sanctifying grace alone. When a new heart is created in us, it will take care of any eye problem or hand problem or any other problem.

C. Harmony (vv. 31, 32)

(Matthew 5:31, 32 is not included in the printed text.)

Jesus addressed the matter of divorce against the background of two schools of thought. The school of Rabbi Shammai allowed divorce only for a major offense; the laxer school of Hillel, whom the Jewish practice followed, made divorce permissible for anything which displeased the husband. Both schools appealed to the words of Moses in Deuteronomy 24:1-4.

The Jews failed to realize that Moses did not command divorce, but only sought to regulate an existing practice. He was not even professing to state the grounds of divorce, but accepting it as an existing fact.

But Jesus is not here addressing the words of Moses in Deuteronomy 24 so much as He is concerned with Moses' words in Exodus 20:14 as quoted in verse 27. Jesus gave the divine norm for marriage in Matthew 19:6, "What therefore God hath joined together, let not man put asunder." This divine union which is to be severed by God alone is severed by man when the seventh commandment is violated.

D. Honesty (vv. 33-37)

(Matthew 5:33-37 is not included in the printed text.)

In these verses, Jesus speaks to a

misapplication of the third commandment. Leaving the heart out of the fulfillment of this commandment, the Jews referred to this law to justify the use of all sorts of oaths. They argued about the degree of binding force the different forms of oaths had, and concluded that those which did not directly name God had no binding force. They argued that oaths made by heaven, or by the earth, or by Jerusalem, or by one's own head were not binding since God himself was not included. Jesus reminded them that the heavens are God's throne, the earth His footstool, Jerusalem His city, and the color of the hair on their head was determined by Him.

Having shown the futility of their argument, Jesus then called upon them to let their life be sufficient to back up their words. If their heart was true to God, every statement they make should be made as though they were in the very presence of God. If their heart was thus pledged to truth, their lips will reflect that. Their yes will always mean yes, and their no will always mean no.

E. Kindness (vv. 38-42)

1. Nonresistance (vv. 38, 39)

(Matthew 5:38, 39 is not included in the printed text.)

The Pharisees looked at one side of Moses' teaching of the law of retaliation, but failed to see the other side. They remembered that he said, "Burning for burning, wound for wound, stripe for stripe. . . . Breach for breach. . . . hand for hand, foot for foot (Exodus 21:25; Leviticus 24:20; Deuteronomy 19:21). They somehow forgot that Moses also said: "Thou shalt not avenge, nor bear any grudge against the children of thy people, but thou shalt love thy neighbour as thyself" (Leviticus 19:18).

What can the church do to promote acts of kindness, love, and harmony?

The law of retaliation was designed to protect the innocent and to make sure that retaliation did not occur beyond the offense. The Pharisees, however, interpreted it to mean that in his dealings with others every man should retaliate in kind and should insist on his full rights. In contrast to this, Jesus said that the believer "need not necessarily claim his rights. Instead he might go 'the extra mile' to maintain peace. When wronged by being struck on a *cheek,* or sued for his *tunic* (undergarment: a *cloak* was the outer garment), or forced to travel with *someone a mile,* he would not strike back, demand repayment, or refuse to comply. Instead of retaliating he would do the opposite, and would also commit his case to the Lord who will one day set all things in order" (see Romans 12:19-21 *[The Bible Knowledge Commentary]).*

2. Compliance (vv. 40-42)

(Matthew 5:40-42 is not included in the printed text.)

Let me illustrate the beauty of the Christ-like life which foregoes the right of retaliation. The black evangelist Tom Skinner was converted to Christ while he was leader of the largest, toughest, teenage gang in New York City, the Harlem Lords. His conversion was so real that he left the gang the next day, turning from a life of fighting and violence to preach the gospel.

Several weeks after his conversion he was playing a football game in which, as his assignment on one play, he blocked the defensive end while his own halfback scored a touchdown. As he headed back to the huddle, the boy whom he had blocked jumped in front of him in a rage and slammed him in the stomach. As he bent over from the blow he was hacked across the back. When Skinner fell the boy kicked him, shouting, "You dirty black nigger! I'll teach you a thing or two."

Skinner said that under normal circumstances the old Tom Skinner would have jumped up from the ground and pulverized the white boy! But, instead, he got up from the ground and found himself looking the boy in the face and saying, "You know, because of Jesus Christ, I love you anyway." Later the defensive end came to Skinner and said, "Tom, you've done more to knock prejudice out of me by telling me that you loved me than you would have if you'd socked my

jaw in" (Adapted from *The Sermon on the Mount,* by James Montgomery Boice).

F. Love (vv. 43-48)

1. Sons (vv. 43-45)

43. Ye have heard that it hath been said, Thou shalt love thy neighbour, and hate thine enemy.

44. But I say unto you, Love your enemies, bless them that curse you, do good to them that hate you, and pray for them which despitefully use you, and persecute you;

45. That ye may be the children of your Father which is in heaven: for he maketh his sun to rise on the evil and on the good, and sendeth rain on the just and on the unjust.

The Pharisees took the teaching of Leviticus 19:18—"Thou shalt love thy neighbour as thyself"—and added the thought that you shall hate your enemies. They ignored the portion of the verse that admonished not to avenge or hold a grudge. They interpreted their neighbor to be their fellow Israelites. All others were regarded as their enemies and were subject to their hatred.

Now Jesus tells them that this is a flagrant perversion of what Moses meant. His message is that we are to love our enemies. In spite of their wickedness and hatefulness, they are to be loved. Even if they are actively persecuting us, we are to love them. Jesus is our best example. Even on Calvary, He prayed for His executioners. Likewise, we should pray that the grace of God will reach our enemies, convict them of their sins, and bring them to repentance and pardon.

We should not forget that God causes His sun to rise on all men, and He sends rain to produce their crops: the evil and the good; the righteous and the unrighteous. Since His love reaches out to all men, so should we love all men. In doing so, we are demonstrating that we are sons of God.

2. Perfect (vv. 46-48)

46. For if ye love them which love you, what reward have ye? do not even the publicans the same?

47. And if ye salute your brethren

only, what do ye more than others? do not even the publicans so?

48. Be ye therefore perfect, even as your Father which is in heaven is perfect.

The superior principle embedded in Christianity is not evidenced in loving those who love you. Even the worst of men will do that. To bring this truth home forcefully to the Pharisees, Jesus told them that even the tax collectors and pagans would do that. Can you imagine what a blow to the ego of the Pharisees this must have been?

In contrast to the murder, lust, hate, deception, and retaliation condemned by our Lord, believers are to be like their Father. We are to make God our model and follow Him in spirit and in truth. We are to be completely devoted to the will of God as revealed in His Word. As we put our trust in Him, He reproduces His righteousness in us. His greatest saints are found among the common believers who respond to His grace and strive to live by His standards.

REVIEW QUESTIONS

1. How, according to verse 17, is Christ's coming and mission related to the Law and prophets?

2. What does Christ say, in verse 18, about the inspiration and authority of the Holy Scriptures?

3. What kind of righteousness does Christ demand of Kingdom subjects?

4. How, in verses 21 and 22, does Jesus emphasize the sacredness of human life and personality?

5. What is a Christian's responsibility with regard to an offended brother?

GOLDEN TEXT HOMILY

"LOVE YOUR ENEMIES, BLESS THEM THAT CURSE YOU, DO GOOD TO THEM THAT HATE YOU, AND PRAY FOR THEM WHICH DESPITEFULLY USE YOU, AND PERSECUTE YOU" (Matthew 5:44).

As a chaplain, I deal, on a daily basis, with drug addicts, robbers, pimps, and murderers—those scarred by life, those whose language is profane, and those filled with hate. Ninety percent are non-Christians. If and when they get out of prison our churches tend to exclude them.

Effective rehabilitation must come from the Christian community; however, we tend to reject those whose skin is a different color, those whose upbringing is different, those who have been in prison or live in the streets. But the Bible says for us to love our enemies, bless those that curse us. If the church is to win those that have despitefully used us, we must reevaluate our priorities.

Do we make a non-Christian feel comfortable and welcome at church? Will this person, be he an ex-offender or a man off the street, see love from the body, or will he see only the preacher and a few other professionals?

Since God is love, He sent His Son to earth to fill our heart with love for others. If we have His love there is no room for hatred. Where there is love, kindness, honesty, harmony, purity, and peace, there is no room for hatred and racism. The lost enter the churches—yes they have robbed, murdered, raped, cursed us, hated us, done all matter of evil against us; but the Bible says *love them anyway*.

Jesus launched the Christian movement with 12 people who were to love one another, demonstrating that we should love all men. As Christ's disciples, we must open our heart so that His love can reach those that are our enemies, bless those that curse us; do good to them that despitefully use us.—**James L. Durel, Senior Chaplain, Cook County Department of Corrections, Chicago, Illinois**

SENTENCE SERMONS

A RIGHT ATTITUDE evidenced by right action is the biblical pattern of true righteousness.

—Selected

NO ONE CAN live wrong and pray right. And no one who prays right can live wrong.

—David C. Hall

LET US LIVE as people who are prepared to die, and die as people who are prepared to live.

—James S. Stewart

WHAT MEN NEED today in this time of trouble is not a way out so much as a way of high and manly living within.
—**Wilmont Lewis**

EVANGELISTIC APPLICATION

THOSE MADE RIGHTEOUS THROUGH CHRIST WILL ESCAPE THE COMING JUDGMENT.

The Pearl Harbor Report demonstrated that not only were an admiral and a general unprepared, the authorities were unprepared and the whole nation was in a lethargy of self-satisfaction. In spite of all the evidence that an attack would come, people were amazed when it did. Thus is the approaching judgment of God going to come upon the world; the Bible informs us that judgment is coming. Men are warned to flee from the wrath of God. They are warned that sudden destruction will come upon them, that it will come suddenly as a stroke of lightening from the east and the west and as unexpectedly as a thief in the night. In spite of all these warnings the world sinks in its lethargy of self-satisfaction. It will be awakened by a blow far more rude than Pearl Harbor, for just as the gifts and calling of God are without repentance, so are His judgments.

There is only one escape from the judgment to come: Jesus Christ. Our sins were judged in Him on Calvary. He alone is our hope.—**Adapted from Let Me Illustrate, by Donald Grey Barnhouse.**

ILLUMINATING THE LESSON

Carl Bates, respected pastor and seminary professor, once wrote about an experience of Michelangelo as related by a tour guide. The great artist was explaining his current work to a visitor. He pointed out how he had retouched one part, softened certain features, given more expression to a muscle, and more energy to a limb. The visitor commented that those things seemed to be mere trifles. The master replied that trifles made perfection, and perfection was no trifle.

Striving for Godlikeness brings tension into Christians' lives, but it is a tension that is needful and productive. Perhaps, as Michelangelo indicated, growing into what God wants us to be does not come by large leaps but by careful attention to the seemingly trivial activities and responsibilities of life (Ernest D. Standerfer).
—**From Illustrating the Gospel of Matthew, by James E. Hightower, Jr.**

DAILY BIBLE READINGS

M. Live Peaceably. Genesis 13:5-18

T. Be Pure. Psalm 24:1-5

W. Encourage Harmony. 1 Corinthians 1: 10-17

T. Practice Honesty. Isaiah 33:15, 16

F. Show Kindness. Colossians 3:12-15

S. Manifest Love. Romans 12:9-13

Establishing Proper Motives

Study Text: Matthew 6:1-18

Supplemental References: Psalm 139:1-24; Matthew 23:23-33; Luke 20:45-47

Time: Early in A.D. 28

Place: On a high hill or a mountain near Capernaum in Galilee

Golden Text: "Take heed that ye do not your alms before men, to be seen of them" (Matthew 6:1).

Central Truth: Giving, praying, and fasting must be done with proper motives in order to please God.

Evangelistic Emphasis: The Lord saves those who come in sincerity and with faith in Christ's redemptive work.

Printed Text

Matthew 6:1. Take heed that ye do not your alms before men, to be seen of them: otherwise ye have no reward of your Father which is in heaven.

2. Therefore when thou doest thine alms, do not sound a trumpet before thee, as the hypocrites do in the synagogues and in the streets, that they may have glory of men. Verily I say unto you, They have their reward.

3. But when thou doest alms, let not thy left hand know what thy right hand doeth:

4. That thine alms may be in secret: and thy Father which seeth in secret himself shall reward thee openly.

5. And when thou prayest, thou shalt not be as the hypocrites are: for they love to pray standing in the synagogues and in the corners of the streets, that they may be seen of men. Verily I say unto you, They have their reward.

6. But thou, when thou prayest, enter into thy closet, and when thou hast shut thy door, pray to thy Father which is in secret; and thy Father which seeth in secret shall reward thee openly.

7. But when ye pray, use not vain repetitions, as the heathen do: for they think that they shall be heard for their much speaking.

8. Be not ye therefore like unto them: for your Father knoweth what things ye have need of, before ye ask him.

9. After this manner therefore pray ye: Our Father which art in heaven, Hallowed be thy name.

10. Thy kingdom come. Thy will be done in earth, as it is in heaven.

11. Give us this day our daily bread.

12. And forgive us our debts, as we forgive our debtors.

13. And lead us not into temptation but deliver us from evil: For thine is the kingdom, and the power, and the glory, for ever. Amen.

14. For if ye forgive men their trespasses, your heavenly Father will also forgive you:

15. But if ye forgive not men their trespasses, neither will your Father forgive your trespasses.

16. Moreover when ye fast, be not as the hypocrites, of a sad countenance

for they disfigure their faces, that they may appear unto men to fast. Verily I say unto you, They have their reward.

17. But thou, when thou fastest, anoint thine head, and wash thy face;

18. That thou appear not unto men to fast, but unto thy Father which is in secret: and thy Father which seeth in secret, shall reward thee openly.

LESSON OUTLINE

I. MOTIVES FOR HELPING OTHERS
   A. Practicing Righteousness
   B. Giving Alms
   C. Acting Secretly

II. MOTIVES FOR PRAYER
   A. Proper Prayer
   B. The Lord's Prayer
      1. His Name
      2. His Will
      3. His Provision
      4. His Grace
      5. His Protection
   C. Divine Forgiveness

III. MOTIVES FOR SELF-DISCIPLINE
   A. Fasting Ostentatiously
   B. Fasting Privately

LESSON EXPOSITION

INTRODUCTION

In the previous chapter, Jesus dealt with the Law and the false teachings which the Pharisees had added to it. In this chapter, He deals with a holier-than-thou attitude toward certain religious practices. Three perfectly legitimate practices—almsgiving, prayer, and fasting— were reduced to hypocritical exercises by many. Although they were encouraged by Old Testament example (see Deuteronomy 26:12-15), there were no guidelines about their practice in ordinary and daily life. Since these were matters of custom and tradition, the Law did not directly address them. The scribes and Pharisees, therefore, added instructions which sometimes resulted in acting out of the wrong motives. Jesus seeks in this passage to correct any wrong views they had been taught, and to bring them to a relationship with God which is rich and rewarding. Although they had been missing the mark because they were improperly motivated, they could enter into a new and meaningful relationship through giving, praying, and fasting.

I. MOTIVES FOR HELPING OTHERS
   (Matthew 6:1-4)

A. Practicing Righteousness (v. 1)

1. Take heed that ye do not your alms before men, to be seen of them: otherwise ye have no reward of your Father which is in heaven.

Jesus admonished His followers that their righteousness should surpass that of the scribes and Pharisees (see Matthew 5:20). He also charged them to aim at perfection and to avoid mere pretense. In these verses, He shows them how both these goals can be achieved.

The righteousness Jesus speaks of is not the imputed righteousness which we have from Him, but the acts of righteousness which we may do. They must be acts which spring from a regenerated heart and which are done unto God and not as a display before men.

This does not mean that our works are not to be seen of men. Jesus said that we should let our light shine before men (see Matthew 5:16). But these works are to be seen in such a way as to glorify our Father who is in heaven. If we do our works in front of men for the purpose of having them gaze upon them that we may have glory of them, we are acting out of the wrong motivation. Even great and wonderful deeds done to impress men will not be rewarded in God's sight. The choice the believer faces is to do his deeds to gain the empty praise of men, or to do them in a fashion that will bring the blessing and praise of the heavenly Father.

B. Giving Alms (v. 2)

2. Therefore when thou doest thine alms, do not sound a trumpet before thee, as the hypocrites do in the synagogues and in the streets, that they

may have glory of men. Verily I say unto you, They have their reward.

The word *therefore* refers to the principle Jesus set forth in the previous verse. The specific act which must be governed by this principle is almsgiving or acts of charity. The disciples of Jesus were not to follow the example of the Pharisees. The Pharisees were known for blazoning or advertising their deeds before men. They chose the public places—the synagogues and the streets—to show off their deeds of charity. Much of what they did was good and needed to be done, but they did it for the wrong reasons.

Jesus called them hypocrites. Hypocrisy is "the assumption of a part which masks (men's) genuine feelings, and makes them appear otherwise than they are." It is to "willfully and continuously attempt to produce a false impression." It is the opposite of the attitude one should have in relation to a truth-loving God.

Those who do their deeds to gain the applause of men may receive that applause—but that is all they will ever get. If any man having this attitude thinks that he will receive glory from God, he is only fooling himself. His final end will be the same as those to whom Jesus said, "ye did it not to me" (Matthew 25:45).

C. Acting Secretly (vv. 3, 4)

3. But when thou doest alms, let not thy left hand know what thy right hand doeth:

4. That thine alms may be in secret: and thy Father which seeth in secret himself shall reward thee openly.

The hands are usually so close together that, if they could see, each would be fully aware of what the other is doing, Lenski wrote. He added that when one hand does what even the other fails to see, that is doing a thing "in secret" indeed. When Jesus said that in giving one should not so much as let his left hand know what his right hand is doing, He meant that it should be so secret that the giver readily forgets what he gave. In contrast to making a public display of his giving, the giver does not even dwell upon it in his own thought, lest it should

lead to spiritual pride. In doing this, he shows that his giving is before God and not before men.

The current "you-owe-me" attitude has no place in Christian charity. If we help others with the idea that they are then under obligation to return the favor, we have missed the point Jesus is making. Our acts of charity must be with no strings attached.

Those who seek the applause of men may gain that reward immediately. Those who do their good works for God alone so that they may please Him may receive their reward now or it may come when they pass before the judgment seat of Christ. But God will render unto them their due and He will do it openly for all to see.

II. MOTIVES FOR PRAYER (Matthew 6:5-15)

A. Proper Prayer (vv. 5-8)

5. And when thou prayest, thou shalt not be as the hypocrites are: for they love to pray standing in the synagogues and in the corners of the streets, that they may be seen of men. Verily I say unto you, They have their reward.

6. But thou, when thou prayest, enter into thy closet, and when thou hast shut thy door, pray to thy Father which is in secret; and thy Father which seeth in secret shall reward thee openly.

7. But when ye pray, use not vain repetitions, as the heathen do: for they think that they shall be heard for their much speaking.

8. Be not ye therefore like unto them: for your Father knoweth what things ye have need of, before ye ask him.

Jesus warned His disciples to avoid the practice of the hypocrites in prayer. The hypocrites loved to pray while standing in public places. Their prayers were offered for the ears of men, not the ears of God. They hoped to impress men with their devotion and righteousness. That men were impressed constituted their reward.

On the other hand, believers are encouraged to go into a room by themselves and fasten the door and pray to their Father privately. Thus is the worshiper alone with His God. Such private communion will aid the believer in his participation in public prayer. Also, the Father will hear and answer openly his prayer offered in secret.

If God knows our needs in advance, why do we need to spend time and effort in reminding Him of our needs?

Jesus also cautioned against repeating empty phrases or the same words over and over again. Some think that long prayers spoken with an unctuous tone indicate true spirituality. Jesus denied that. He said that God knows our needs even before we ask. It is not necessary to inform Him of every detail. He is omniscient. Yet He does encourage us to pray to Him, to draw near Him and to stay near to Him, indeed to talk and walk with Him.

B. The Lord's Prayer (vv. 9-13)

1. His Name (v. 9)

9. After this manner therefore pray ye: Our Father which art in heaven, Hallowed be thy name.

Having mentioned some approaches that should not be used in prayer, Jesus offered positive guidance in prayer. The model prayer He gave is perfect in every respect; not a word of it is superfluous. It has no equal.

Jesus opened the prayer by referring to God as "Our Father." In thinking of Him as Father, we picture His nearness and we remember His holy, loving intimacy. What warmth and serenity the thought of the Father brings. How encouraged we feel to open our heart and mind to Him and to share with Him our deepest feelings. Then, we are minded that the Father is in heaven. Thus do we think of His majesty and glory, and approach Him with an awesome reverence.

The name of God is that description of Him which embraces all He really is. It is God himself revealed to us. To hallow, or honor, or revere His name is to set it apart from everything that is common and profane. It means to esteem, prize, and adore as divine and infinitely blessed. How meaningful prayer must be when it is entered upon in such a spirit of worship and reverence.

2. His Will (v. 10)

10. Thy kingdom come. Thy will be done in earth, as it is in heaven.

The kingdom of God is described by Jamieson, Fausset, and Brown as that moral and spiritual kingdom which the God of grace is setting up in this fallen world. Its subjects consist of as many as have been brought into subjection to His gracious scepter. His Son Jesus is the glorious Head of the Kingdom. There is a sense in which the Kingdom has existed in inward reality ever since men have walked with God and waited for His salvation. There is another sense in which the Kingdom is still to come. As long as there is one subject of the Kingdom to be brought in, we should pray, "Thy Kingdom come." This petition longs for the establishment of "the everlasting kingdom of our Lord and Saviour Jesus Christ" (2 Peter 1:11).

This prayer expresses the desire that God's will be done on earth, as it is done in heaven. His will is done fully and willingly in heaven. No opposition such as the devil, the world, and the flesh interfere there. And in this prayer, believers put their own will into complete harmony with their Father's will. Thus may we come to follow Him cheerfully, constantly, and completely. Jesus left us the ultimate example of submission to God's will in the Garden of Gethsemane.

3. His Provision (v. 11)

11. Give us this day our daily bread.

The Lord's Prayer includes a petition for the daily necessities of life. It encourages us to bring our basic needs to Him. Nothing that concerns the believer is too insignificant for the Father's attention. He cares!

The request is for daily bread, that is, bread sufficient for today. Although God often and generally gives us far more than enough for the day, our prayer is for our daily needs. Every believer may echo the desire of the wise man who said: "Two things I ask of you, O Lord; do not refuse me before I die: Keep falsehood and lies far from me; give me neither poverty nor riches, but give me only my daily bread" (Proverbs 30:8, *New International Version*).

Since our real security rests in the Father alone, this is a prayer which may be repeated on a daily basis. In seeking provision day by day, we are displaying a spirit of childlike dependence upon the Lord. And it is a dependence that is never disappointed. David testified to this truth: "I have been young, and now am old; yet have I not seen the righteous forsaken, nor his seed begging bread" (Psalm 37:25). Many other believers could affirm David's conclusion.

4. His Grace (v. 12)

12. And forgive us our debts, as we forgive our debtors.

Not only does this prayer include a petition for physical needs, it also makes requests for spiritual needs. God's mercy and forgiveness are indeed an area which should be a part of our prayer life. Spiritual matters should have a high priority in our terms of communion with the Lord.

The only way we can have our debts, or sins, dismissed is by the grace of God. Our debts to God are so great that we can never hope to pay them. Our only hope is that God through Christ will freely remit them. Through Christ we can be assured that "as far as the east is from the west, so far hath he removed our transgressions from us" (Psalm 103:12). How richly have we been forgiven!

This prayer implies that the believer has already forgiven those who have sinned against him. When we consider the nature of what we are asking for, our heart must be rid of any resentment toward others. Their debts to us are as nothing compared with what we owe God. Therefore, our forgiveness of them is so complete that we no longer consider them as debtors. What beautiful evidence of the work of God's grace in our heart and of our having become His children.

5. His Protection (v. 13)

13. And lead us not into temptation, but deliver us from evil: For thine is

the kingdom, and the power, and the glory, for ever. Amen.

This prayer also has an eye to the future. The writers of Scripture agree that we will face trials and temptations in this life. Paul wrote: "There hath no temptation taken you but such as is common to man: but God is faithful, who will not suffer you to be tempted above that ye are able; but will with the temptation also make a way to escape, that ye may be able to bear it" (1 Corinthians 10:13). James admonished: "My brethren, count it all joy when ye fall into divers temptations; Knowing this, that the trying of your faith worketh patience. But let patience have her perfect work, that ye may be perfect and entire, wanting nothing" (1:2-4). Peter added: "Beloved, think it not strange concerning the fiery trial which is to try you, as though some strange thing happened unto you: But rejoice, inasmuch as ye are partakers of Christ's sufferings; that, when his glory shall be revealed, ye may be glad also with exceeding joy" (1 Peter 4:12, 13).

In view of the obstacles we will face in life, this prayer includes a request for divine protection and for rescue from the Evil One.

C. Divine Forgiveness (vv. 14, 15)

14. For if ye forgive men their trespasses, your heavenly Father will also forgive you:

15. But if ye forgive not men their trespasses, neither will your Father forgive your trespasses.

Jesus teaches that we are to be forgiving toward those who have offended us. But He is not teaching that our forgiveness of others is the basis of God's forgiveness of us. The opposite is true. A Christian forgives because he has been forgiven. Paul wrote: "And be ye kind one to another, tenderhearted, forgiving one another, even as God for Christ's sake hath forgiven you" (Ephesians 4:32).

At the same time, "no one can reasonably imagine himself to be the object of divine forgiveness who is deliberately and habitually unforgiving towards his fellowmen . . . God sees His own image reflected in His forgiving children; but to ask God for what we ourselves refuse to men, is to insult Him" (*Jamieson, Fausset, Brown*).

The importance of forgiving is underscored by these words from John Owens: "Our forgiving of others will not procure forgiveness for ourselves; but our not forgiving others proves that we ourselves are not forgiven."

III. MOTIVES FOR SELF-DISCIPLINE (Matthew 6:16-18)

A. Fasting Ostentatiously (v. 16)

16. Moreover when ye fast, be not, as the hypocrites, of a sad countenance: for they disfigure their faces, that they may appear unto men to fast. Verily I say unto you, They have their reward.

Fasting, which usually means total abstinence from food, frequently accompanied the practice of prayer in Bible times. It was practiced in times of mourning, as a sign of repentance, and as a kind of reinforcement for urgent supplication. At certain times, prophets called an entire nation to a solemn fast (see Joel 2:12, 15). Devout Pharisees fasted twice a week (see Luke 18:12). The disciples of John the Baptist engaged in fasting (see Mark 2:18). Inasmuch as Jesus gave His followers instructions about fasting, we may conclude that He assumed that they would fast, just as He assumed that they would pray.

Jesus did not condemn the practice of fasting any more than He condemned the practice of praying. He only condemned the hypocrisy connected with it. The fasting He addressed was to be of a private and voluntary nature and was to be regulated by each individual. But the Pharisees practiced private fasting as a means to secure the reputation of great holiness among the people. It was not the deed, but reputation for the deed which they sought. To make sure people were aware they were fasting, they disfigured their faces with ashes and maintained a gloomy countenance. This recognition by men was all the reward they would ever get.

B. Fasting Privately (vv. 17, 18)

17. But thou, when thou fastest, anoint thine head, and wash they face;

18. That thou appear not unto men to fast, but unto thy Father which is in secret: and thy Father, which seeth in secret, shall reward thee openly.

In contrast to the open display of the hypocrites in fasting, Jesus instructs His followers to give no external sign of fasting. They were to dress and appear as usual, thereby attracting no notice to themselves. Christ's teaching that they were to anoint their head indicates that instead of appearing sad, they were to maintain a countenance of special joy and gladness.

Discuss the importance of fasting. Is there enough emphasis on the practice of fasting? Discuss.

In all three examples of the self-righteous acts of the Pharisees—almsgiving (vv. 1-4), praying (vv. 5-15), and fasting (vv. 16-18)—Jesus spoke of hypocrites (vv. 2, 5, 16), public ostentation (vv. 1, 2, 5, 16), receiving their reward in full when their actions are done before men (vv. 2, 5, 16), acting in secret (vv. 4, 6, 18), and being rewarded by the Father, who sees or knows, when one's actions are done secretly (vv. 4, 6, 8, 18). By the use of repetition, Jesus drives home to His hearers the valuable lessons contained in this passage. We will do well to heed what He said.

REVIEW QUESTIONS

1. What is the principle concerning "piety" laid down by Christ in this lesson?

2. How did the hypocrites do alms, and with what intent?

3. With what motive should the true believer do alms?

4. In what way, according to the example Jesus used, should a Christian pray?

5. What motives should we have when we fast and pray?

GOLDEN TEXT HOMILY

"TAKE HEED THAT YE DO NOT YOUR ALMS BEFORE MEN, TO BE SEEN OF THEM" (Matthew 6:1).

Some years ago my brother Bill and I spent the day together in Tampa, Florida. Except for some telephone work and some incidentals we both did the same things all day. Our motives, however, were different. His desire was to impress me as to how well he could get along without embracing the Christian faith. My desire was to impress him as to the imperative of being born again.

Two opposite motives are seen in this text. One is self-seeking for personal gratification. He was doing right for wrong reasons. The other was self-giving for the glory of God. He was doing right for right reasons.

In the case of the one who desired to be seen of men, it seems evident that there was an inner void which he hoped would find fulfillment in the applause of men.

Of this our Lord said, "Take heed." Please notice four reasons why one should take heed:

1. Popular applause may becloud one's judgment and cause him to make unwise decisions.

2. The applause is temporary.

3. Applause is often treacherous. The same crowd that applauded Christ on His triumphal entry into Jerusalem, just a few days later, cried out, "Crucify him! Crucify him!"

4. The applause of men is the only reward such a one will get. How sad!

Now consider the one who does right for right reasons. It is evident that such a person is inwardly fortified with the basics of faith which recognizes our purpose for being: We are created for the glory and pleasure of God (Isaiah 43:7; Revelation 4:11).

With this knowledge and faith one's primary motive is to first please God and second his motive is to encourage others to join in glorifying God.

A warm glow of joy comes to a child when he or she is approved by the parents for good attitudes and conduct. The Father affirmed His pleasure in His Son when at Jesus' baptism He spoke from heaven, "This is my beloved Son, in whom I am well pleased" (Matthew 3:17).

One minister paraphrased these words in a very earthly manner, "This is My boy and I am proud of Him."

Such approbation is in itself copious reward but Jesus said, "Thy Father which seeth in secret himself shall reward thee openly" (v. 4). Both here and in eternity we will be involved in unwrapping a lot of surprise reward packages which will be expressions of our Father's pleasure in us. "Godliness is profitable unto all things, having promise of the life that now is, and of that which is to come" (1 Timothy 4:8).

There is a big payoff for doing right for right reasons.—**David Lemons, D.D., Faculty Member, Church of God School of Theology, Cleveland, Tennessee**

SENTENCE SERMONS

THOUGH THEY MAY NOT be visible to the eye, motives are the best measure of character.

—Selected

THE MORALITY of an action depends upon the motive from which we act.

—J. Johnson

THE MOTIVE OF love makes service out of what would otherwise be selfishness.

—Selected

IT IS STRANGE that in our praying we seldom ask for a change of character, but always a change in circumstances.

—"Bits and Pieces"

EVANGELISTIC APPLICATION

THE LORD SAVES THOSE WHO COME IN SINCERITY AND WITH FAITH IN CHRIST'S REDEMPTIVE WORK.

Myron Augsburger was asked one day if he had seen a painting which depicted the broad and narrow way which Jesus portrayed in Matthew 7:13, 14. When he said yes, he was asked to describe it. He recounted a painting with the broad road leading downhill filled with people on it. The narrow road was over at the edge of the picture winding up a mountain to the golden city in the distance.

"But that is wrong," his friend interrupted.

"The narrow road is right in the middle of the broad road—just heading the other way." Dr Augsburger had to agree. With their back toward God, many travel the broad road away from God. Those seeking to follow God find that the narrow road often runs head-on into the stream of humanity going the wrong way! To walk in the way of Jesus is demanding, but Christians take that path unashamedly because they know it is the way which leads to life in all its fullness (William P. Tuck).—**From *Illustrating the Gospel of Matthew* by James E. Hightower, Jr.**

ILLUMINATING THE LESSON

The word *hypocrite* is a difficult word for translators of the Bible to describe. But nearly all use the idea of deceit.

The Indians of Latin America refer to hypocrites as persons with "two faces," "two hearts," "two heads," and "two sides." A man with "a straight mouth and a crooked heart" characterizes the hypocritical person to the Thai people. In Madagascar, a hypocrite is a person who "spreads out a clean raffia mat." The mat is how the negligent housekeeper hides a dirty floor.

Duplicity is an obvious ingredient in hypocrisy. Abraham Lincoln told of a man who murdered both his parents and then, when sentence was about to be pronounced, begged for mercy on the grounds that he was a helpless orphan! (Robert D. Dale).

"A hypocrite," says Oren Arnold, "is a man who writes a book praising atheism, then prays that it will sell" (Jack Gulledge).—**From *Illustrating the Gospel of Matthew* by James E. Hightower, Jr.**

DAILY BIBLE READINGS

M. Blind Hypocrisy. Isaiah 29:9-16
T. Foolish Counsel. Job 2:7-10
W. Deceptive Friendship. Psalm 55:12-18
T. Repentant Prayer. Luke 18:9-14
F. Acceptable Worship. Genesis 4:1-7
S. Self-Giving Love. Philippians 2:5-8

Freedom From Worry

Study Text: Matthew 6:19-34

Supplemental References: Psalm 104:14-24; Matthew 11:28-30; Luke 12:22-34; 2 Corinthians 9:8-10; 1 Timothy 6:17-19

Time: Early in A.D. 28

Place: On a high hill or mountain near Capernaum in Galilee.

Golden Text: "Behold the fowls of the air: for they sow not, neither do they reap, nor gather into barns; yet your heavenly Father feedeth them" (Matthew 6:26).

Central Truth: By trusting in God and doing His will we find freedom from the oppression of worry.

Evangelistic Emphasis: Christ calls all people to come to Him for spiritual rest.

Printed Text

Matthew 6:19. Lay not up for yourselves treasures upon earth, where moth and rust doth corrupt, and where thieves break through and steal:

20. But lay up for yourselves treasures in heaven, where neither moth nor rust doth corrupt, and where thieves do not break through nor steal:

21. For where your treasure is, there will your heart be also.

22. The light of the body is the eye: if therefore thine eye be single, thy whole body shall be full of light.

23. But if thine eye be evil, thy whole body shall be full of darkness. If therefore the light that is in thee be darkness, how great is that darkness!

24. No man can serve two masters: for either he will hate the one and love the other; or else he will hold to the one, and despise the other. Ye cannot serve God and mammon.

25. Therefore I say unto you, Take no thought for your life, what ye shall eat, or what ye shall drink; nor yet for your body, what ye shall put on. Is not the life more than meat, and the body than raiment?

26. Behold the fowls of the air: for they sow not, neither do they reap, nor gather into barns; yet your heavenly Father feedeth them. Are ye not much better than they?

27. Which of you by taking thought can add one cubit unto his stature?

28. And why take ye thought for raiment? Consider the lilies of the field, how they grow; they toil not, neither do they spin:

29. And yet I say unto you, That even Solomon in all his glory was not arrayed like one of these.

30. Wherefore, if God so clothe the grass of the field, which to day is, and to morrow is cast into the oven, shall he not much more clothe you, O ye of little faith?

31. Therefore take no thought, saying, What shall we eat? or, What shall we drink? or, Wherewithal shall we be clothed?

32. (For after all these things do the Gentiles seek:) for your heavenly Father

knoweth that ye have need of all these things.

33. But seek ye first the kingdom of God, and his righteousness; and all these things shall be added unto you.

34. Take therefore no thought for the morrow: for the morrow shall take thought for the things of itself. Sufficient unto the day is the evil thereof.

LESSON OUTLINE

I. SET RIGHT PRIORITIES
   A. Treasures in Heaven
   B. Full of Light
   C. Two Masters
II. TRUST GOD'S CARE
   A. Anxious for Nothing
   B. Solomon in His Glory
   C. Men of Little Faith
III. SEEK GOD'S KINGDOM
   A. Things Gentiles Seek
   B. The Kingdom of God
   C. Anxious for Tomorrow

LESSON EXPOSITION

INTRODUCTION

In the preceding passage, almsgiving, prayer, and fasting are presented as righteous acts which should be done in a righteous manner. In the portion of Scripture we study today, Jesus continues to emphasize the importance of righteousness in the conduct of our life. For example, He addresses the matter of our attitude toward wealth. He teaches that God should have first place in this area of our life too, and that we should be concerned with acquiring true wealth rather than those things that will perish.

Hypocrisy is a form of deception. To this point, Jesus has spoken of deceiving others. Now He turns His attention to self-deception. We deceive ourselves, He says, when we seek perishable items, instead of the imperishable. We deceive ourselves when we think that life consists only of what we eat, what we drink, and what we wear. We deceive ourselves when we concern ourselves with those things which people outside of Christ seek, and neglect the things of the Lord.

The cure for the problem of deception is to keep our eyes upon God. He takes care of the birds of the air and the lilies of the field. He knows what we need before we ask Him. He asks only

that we seek His Kingdom and His righteousness, and He will add the other things that we need. The Lord holds the future in His hands. We can trust Him for tomorrow. He would have us live one day at a time. Each day will have problems of its own. But the Lord is mightier than any difficulty we will face. Trusting Him, He will bring us through.

I. SET RIGHT PRIORITIES (Matthew 6:19-24)

A. Treasures in Heaven (vv. 19-21)

19. Lay not up for yourselves treasures upon earth, where moth and rust doth corrupt, and where thieves break through and steal:

20. But lay up for yourselves treasures in heaven, where neither moth nor rust doth corrupt, and where thieves do not break through nor steal:

21. For where your treasure is, there will your heart be also.

Earthly treasures are subject to destructive forces. In the Middle East, treasures often took the form of costly dresses and other fine garments. These items were liable to be consumed or at least damaged by the clothes moth. Other treasures might rust away. The thought here is of any power that eats, corrodes, or wastes. Then, treasures could be lost by thieves digging through the houses made of mud or sunburned bricks and carrying the goods off. James comments on this subject in his book (5:1-6).

Treasures which are laid up in heaven are unassailable and imperishable. What are these treasures? Luke quotes Jesus as saying: "Sell that ye have, and give alms; provide yourselves bags which wax not old, a treasure in the heavens that faileth not, where no thief approacheth, neither moth corrupteth" (Luke 12:33). Paul commented: "Set your affection on things above, not on things on the earth" (Colossians 3:2). The treasures we lay up in heaven are not fine garments or abundant food or earthly valuables, but deeds we do for others and for the Lord.

Discuss the matter of "financial security." Are Christians wrong to plan for their future? Explain.

"What really makes a treasure valuable," Lenski wrote, "is the affection of the heart. He whose treasures are on the earth has his heart anchored to the earth; he whose treasures are in heaven has his heart anchored there. The earth and all its treasures must pass away; what, then, about the heart that loses all its treasures? Heaven alone abides forever; the heart whose treasures are there will never lose them." Where is your treasure—on earth or in heaven?

B. Full of Light (vv. 22, 23)

22. The light of the body is the eye: if therefore thine eye be single, thy whole body shall be full of light.

23. But if thine eye be evil, thy whole body shall be full of darkness. If therefore the light that is in thee be darkness, how great is that darkness!

The eye is the one member of the body which acts as a lamp by which a man sees. Our perspective, then, depends on the spiritual quality of the eye. If the eye gazes constantly upon the things of the world, the soul will tend to respond to those things. If, on the other hand, the eye is fixed upon heavenly things, the soul will move toward those things. Therefore, Jesus urged His disciples to find the proper object and with singleness of purpose, to pursue that objective. Solomon said: "Let thine eyes look right on, and let thine eyelids look straight before thee. Ponder the path of thy feet, and let all thy ways be established. Turn not to the right hand nor to the left: remove thy foot from evil" (Proverbs 4:25-27). When the eye is sound and the object is clear, the path is easy to follow. Likewise, when one resolves to serve and please God in everything, his whole character and conduct will give evidence of it. The Lord is looking for that kind of simple and persistent purpose.

On the other hand, if the eye is bad, that is, wicked and godless, the entire body will be full of darkness. When that is the case, the individual puts everything ahead of God and His kingdom. In such darkness, the soul perceives nothing as it is but is deceived into thinking that earthly treasures are more important than heavenly treasures.

A man's inward purpose, his scope, his aim in life, determines his character. If that light within him has become darkness, distorting his perspective, what kind of direction will his life take? What kind of character will he develop? How terrible is the nature and effects of that darkness? The total absence of light leaves room only for sin and evil—nothing positive, only negative.

C. Two Masters (v. 24)

24. No man can serve two masters: for either he will hate the one, and love the other; or else he will hold to the one, and despise the other. Ye cannot serve God and mammon.

It is in the nature of slavery that a slave's person and his work belong wholly to his master. It is in the nature of man that no man is his own master; "it is ingraved in our very nature that our heart, will, and work be governed by another. The only question is who this other shall be" (Lenski). The choice of this verse is God or money.

"What you own, owns you" is a slogan used by a large insurance company in its advertising compaign. The sad thing about the slogan is that it is true for many, if not most, Americans. The people that once had a goal of "a chicken in every pot" seem now to want a steak on every grill, a car for every member of the family, a home and a cottage on the lake, and on and on. Any honest observer would be hard put to deny that ours is among the most materialistic cultures the world has ever known. Many appear to have more faith in their business, their trade union, their stocks and bonds, their property, or even the "American way" than they do in Christ. Even the poor are not free of this malady of materialism; for those who have it want to keep it, and those who don't, want to get it.

We could learn a great deal from the colonial Quaker Christian, John Woolman. Woolman was a successful merchant, but he operated his business each year only long enough to accumulate enough money to care for his family's needs for the year. The rest of the time he gave to the service of the Lord, traveling about the young nation at his own expense to share the good news (Raymond H. Bailey) —*Illustrating the Gospel of Matthew* by James E. Hightower, Jr.

II. TRUST GOD'S CARE (Matthew 6:25-30)

A. Anxious for Nothing (vv. 25, 26)

25. Therefore I say unto you, Take no thought for your life, what ye shall eat, or what ye shall drink; nor yet for your body, what ye shall put on. Is not the life more than meat, and the body than raiment?

26. Behold the fowls of the air: for they sow not, neither do they reap, nor gather into barns; yet your heavenly Father feedeth them. Are ye not much better than they?

If a person sets his mind upon spiritual things and becomes occupied with them, how will he care for the ordinary needs in life, such as food, clothing, and shelter? It seems that Jesus' disciples were worrying about these things. The concern about drink alludes to the hot climate of Palestine and to the lack of water in that region. Food and drink represent daily needs. Clothes last longer and are mentioned last. Will He who gave us our life and the body fail to give us the little food we need and the few garments we require? Where is our faith?

The word *thought* has a different meaning today than it had in 1611 when the King James Version of the Bible was translated. When Jesus said to take no thought about these things, He meant not to be anxiously concerned about them. He did not mean that we were to give no forethought or consideration to temporal things. What we are to avoid is anxiety and doubtful misgivings. Paul summed it up beautifully, "Be anxious for nothing, but in everything by prayer and supplication with thanksgiving let your requests be made known to God" (Philippians 4:6, *New American Standard Bible*).

Discuss the matter of anxiety and worry. Why do we get anxious and worry? What is the cure for this practice?

Jesus called attention to the birds of the air. He pointed out that they do not sow, reap, or gather food into barns, yet God takes care of them. We, He said, are worth much more than they. As men and as His children, we are much more valuable in God's eyes. Will He not, therefore, take care of us, if we trust in Him?

B. Solomon in His Glory (vv. 27-29)

27. Which of you by taking thought can add one cubit unto his stature?

28. And why take ye thought for raiment? Consider the lilies of the field, how they grow; they toil not, neither do they spin:

29. And yet I say unto you, That even Solomon in all his glory was not arrayed like one of these.

Most translators see verse 27 as referring to one's life span rather than to one's height. That interpretation is consistent with the context. The prolonging of life by the supply of its necessities of food and clothing is the subject being discussed. Unless one is a midget, the thought of adding a foot and a half to one's height is not very appealing. But adding days to one's life is. However, Jesus cautions, all the worry in the world cannot add so much as a step to the length of your life's journey. Worry does not lengthen life, it usually shortens life.

Having used the birds of the air to illustrate God's provision of food, Jesus turns again to nature, using the lilies of the field to show how God provides clothing. He said that it is needless and useless to worry about what we will wear for the best we can make or purchase cannot compare to a single lily. Of the lily someone has written that it is "the most gorgeously painted, the most conspicuous in spring, and the most universally spread of all the floral treasures of the Holy Land." So, Jesus said, there is something to be learned from the lily. It grows wild, without human care, without labor of any kind and without spinning a thread. Yet they come to wear garments so exquisite that they exceed all that Solomon at the height of his royal glory ever wore. Dressed in a regal robe, Solomon did not compare in splendor with the lily of the field.

C. Men of Little Faith (v. 30)

30. Wherefore, if God so clothe the grass of the field, which to day is, and to morrow is cast into the oven, shall he not much more clothe you, O ye of little faith?

Jesus calls the attention of His disciples back to God. God is responsible for the origin, development, and results in clothing the lilies of the field. Yet, gorgeous as is the array of the flowers that deck the fields, they are only there for a short time. Then, they are cut and wither and are used for fuel. With their own hands, men cast them into the oven. If God so beautifully dresses the grass which is green today but dry tomorrow, how much more likely is He to clothe His followers. They are of much greater worth to Him. His disciples should trust in His faithfulness. The writer of Hebrews admonished: Let your conversation be without covetousness; and be content with such things as ye have: for he hath said, I will never leave thee, nor forsake thee" (Hebrews 13:5).

On four different occasions in Matthew's Gospel, Jesus referred to His disciples as men of little faith. The first reference was the occasion of the text we are studying. The second time was when He and His disciples were caught in a great temptest on the Sea of Galilee (8:26). Next, He used this term when Peter attempted to walk on the water and failed (14:31). Then, He used this expression when His disciples did not understand His warning to beware of the leaven of the Pharisees (16:8). In each instance, their lack of faith came under the pressure of earthly trials. It was His way of gently chiding them to shake off the spirit of unbelief and put their trust in Him.

III. SEEK GOD'S KINGDOM (Matthew 6:31-34)

A. Things Gentiles Seek (vv. 31, 32)

31. Therefore take no thought, saying, What shall we eat? or, What shall we drink? or, Wherewithal shall we be clothed?

32. (For after all these things do the Gentiles seek:) for your heavenly Father knoweth that ye have need of all these things.

In verse 25, Jesus called upon His disciples to stop worrying. In this verse, He urges them not to worry at all. No matter what need may arise including the three things He mentioned—food, drink, and raiment—nothing is ever to trouble our heart.

Worry is *irreverent,* wrote Myron S. Augsburger, for it fails to recognize the God who gave us life and is sustaining it. Worry is *irrelevant;* it does not change things, nor does it help us in coping with problems. And worry is *irresponsible;* it burns up energy without using it to apply constructive action to the problem.

To worry about these things, and a thousand others, is to do as the Gentiles do. They are unacquainted with proper dependence on divine Providence, and so their chief anxiety centers around life-sustaining objects. Believers, on the other hand, have a knowledge of the heavenly Father and know that He will provide for their needs. Therefore, they have no cause to be anxious.

With an authority only He could claim, Jesus said: "No man knoweth the Son, but the Father: neither knoweth any man the Father, save the Son, and he to whomsoever the Son will reveal him" (Matthew 11:27). Now, to His disciples, Jesus says, "Let Me tell you something about the Father whom I know so well. He knows very well that you have need of all these things. What a word of encouragement!

B. The Kingdom of God (v. 33)

33. But seek ye first the kingdom of

God, and his righteousness; and all these things shall be added unto you.

While the Gentiles are seeking things that pertain to this life, believers are to be seeking the kingdom of God. This quest for the Kingdom, described earlier as hunger and thirst, is the mark of all true disciples. It consists of a longing to enter ever more fully into union with God. It recognizes God's royal rule which is a rule of grace leading to a rule of glory. This seeking acknowledges Him "who is the blessed and only Potentate, the King of kings, and Lord of lords; Who only hath immortality, dwelling in the light which no man can approach unto; whom no man hath seen, nor can see: to whom be honour and power everlasting. Amen" (1 Timothy 6:15, 16).

Believers are also to seek to be righteous and to obtain the favor of the Father. They are to bring themselves, by His grace, to personal conformity to God's standard of righteousness. Righteousness is the character trait of all those who are spiritually recovered from sin and are subjects of the King.

To seek first God's kingdom and His righteousness does not mean that believers are to seek nothing more. They do seek other things from the Father, but they seek in the right way, by humble and submissive prayer, without worry, and without a false estimate of these things. God has control over all things, and He can give us everything we need. He will give us that which He deems best for us.

C. Anxious for Tomorrow (v. 34)

34. Take therefore no thought for the morrow: for the morrow shall take thought for the things of itself. Sufficient unto the day is the evil thereof.

This verse calls for a life of daily faith, a life committed to God, and a life in which there is no room for anxiety. It offers the same advice Paul gave in Philippians 4:6, when he said in effect, "Don't worry about anything, but pray about everything." This is the thought Peter had in mind when he wrote: "Casting all your care upon him; for he careth for you" (1 Peter 5:7).

Jesus also warns against borrowing trouble from the future. Every day brings its own cares, and to anticipate is only to double them. It is not even certain that you will live to see another day. If you do, that day will bring its own troubles and needs. God will be the same Father then as He is today, and He will make then, as He does now, the proper supply of your needs.

Each day will have cares and anxieties of its own, but it will also bring the proper provisions for those cares. Though you have needs, yet God will provide for them as they occur. Do not, therefore, increase the cares of this day by borrowing trouble from the future. Do your duty faithfully now, and depend on the mercy of God and His divine help for the troubles which are yet to come. As you care each day for the things God has trusted to you, your heavenly Father cares for your daily needs. God is faithful and will not fail to meet your needs.

REVIEW QUESTIONS

1. What attitude should one have toward earthly treasures?

2. Discuss the matter of divided loyalties, as indicated by verse 24. How do we cope with the problem?

3. What does Christ say about anxiety and our future?

4. Can you give examples of persons who seriously applied the principles of verse 33 to their lives?

5. Review practical values this lesson has provided for you.

GOLDEN TEXT HOMILY

"BEHOLD THE FOWLS OF THE AIR: FOR THEY SOW NOT, NEITHER DO THEY REAP, NOR GATHER INTO BARNS; YET YOUR HEAVENLY FATHER FEEDETH THEM. ARE YE NOT MUCH BETTER THAN THEY?" (Matthew 6:26).

In Matthew 6:19-34, we read a very familiar passage of Scripture, but one that is very hard for modern man to accept and follow. The verse being considered in Matthew 6:26 is plainly linked with the preceding verses and a continued warning against the lure of self-service. The words of Jesus came as a warning to those involved in the business of serving self, "Be on guard, that your hearts may not be weighted down with dissipation and drunkenness and the worries of life, and that day come on you suddenly like a trap" (Luke 21:34, New American Standard Bible).

Verse 26 calls our attention to "the fowls of the air and reminds us "they sow not, neither do they reap, nor gather into barns; yet your heavenly Father feedeth them." Jesus asks us the question, "Are you not worth much more than they?" (NASB). Verse 31 tells us, "Do not be anxious then, saying, 'What shall we eat?' or 'What shall we drink' or 'With what shall we clothe ourselves?' " (NASB). In 1 Peter 5:7, the apostle is telling us to cast all our cares (or anxieties) upon Him (Jesus) for He cares for us.

The reasons against "being anxious" are not enumerated, but they are given, and are not hard to find. First, man's plans must always err, for man does not own or rule the earth. Second, it is a fair assumption that God, having given the great gift of life, will not fail to provide its temporal needs. If God cares so much for the birds and even the grass, we can be assured He cares much more for us.

Third, in all the preceding scriptures there is ample evidence of God's providential care: the birds are fed, the flowers are clothed, and even the grass is sustained. These "creatures" all fulfill their nature, and God provides for them. If man fulfills his nature (not idleness, but trustful and faithful work) God will not fail him, for He has promised never to leave us or forsake us.

Fourth, a person whose central focus is on the material things of this world has a pagan (or sinner's) attitude. (Read Matthew 6:31, 32.) God already knows what we have need of, and He tells us in Matthew 6:33, to seek first the kingdom of God and His righteousness, and all these things will be added unto us.

"Be anxious for nothing, but in everything by prayer and supplication with thanksgiving let your requests be made known to God" (Philippians 4:6, NASB).

"Casting all your care [or anxieties] upon him; for he careth for you" (1 Peter 5:7).—**Ronald M. Padgett, Chaplain, Director of Chaplaincy Services, Mississippi Department of Corrections, Parchman, Mississippi**

SENTENCE SERMONS

BY TRUSTING IN GOD and doing His will, we find freedom from the oppression of worry.

—Selected

WORRY IS a thin stream of fear trickling through the mind. If encouraged it cuts a channel into which all other thoughts are drained.

—A. S. Roche

BLESSED IS the person who is too busy to worry in the daytime, and too sleepy to worry at night.

—Leo Aikman

WORRY DOESN'T EMPTY tomorrow of its sorrow, it empties today of its strength.

—Corrie Ten Boom

EVANGELISTIC APPLICATION

CHRIST CALLS ALL PEOPLE TO COME TO HIM FOR SPIRITUAL REST.

A man bought a picture and asked Whistler to assist him in hanging it in the right place. When Whistler walked into the room, the man held up the picture in one place and then in another. Finally, Whistler said, "You are going about this all the wrong. What you need to do is to move all the furniture out, hang the picture where you want it, and then arrange all the furniture in relationship to the picture."

We often treat God as a nice addition to the furniture of our life. What we really need to do is to remove all the furniture, put God in the central place, and then arrange all the furniture of our life in relationship to Him.

God demands the place of priority in our life. This was what Jesus meant when He said, "But seek first His kingdom and His righteousness; and all these things shall be added to you" (Matthew 6:33, *New American Standard Bible*). —**Brian L. Harbour, from** *Illustrating the Gospel of Matthew* **by James E. Hightower, Jr.**

ILLUMINATING THE LESSON

Our concern for our physical well-being may link humanity to monkeys more strongly than any theory of evolution. A story out of World War II tells about how natives trapped monkeys on their island. The natives took earthen jars with long narrow necks and secured them to the trees that were the habitat of the monkeys. They partially filled these jars with grain. At night the monkeys came down from the trees and reached into the jars to get the grain; but when they tried to take their hands out of the jars,

they found it impossible because they had fists full of grain. All the monkeys needed to do was to turn loose of the grain; but by refusing to do so, they lost their freedom. The passage in Matthew 6:31 helps us keep material possessions in the proper perspective (Bill Bruster) .—*Illustrating the Gospel of Matthew,* **by James E. Hightower, Jr.**

DAILY BIBLE READINGS

M. Needs Supplied. 1 Kings 17:1-7

T. Miraculous Provision. 1 Kings 17:8-16

W. Sharing Good News. 2 Kings 7:1-9, 16

T. God's Providence. Psalm 104:14-24

F. God Will Supply. 2 Corinthians 9:8-10

S. Sufficient Through Christ. Philippians 4:10-20

Choosing the Right Way

Study Text: Matthew 7:13-29

Supplemental References: Deuteronomy 30:15-19; Luke 6:43-49; 13:24-30; Romans 8:6

Time: Early in A.D. 28

Place: On a high hill or mountain near Capernaum in Galilee

Golden Text: "Not every one that saith unto me, Lord, Lord, shall enter into the kingdom of heaven; but he that doeth the will of my Father which is in heaven" (Matthew 7:21).

Central Truth: Following Christ requires true commitment.

Evangelistic Emphasis: Jesus Christ is the only way to eternal life.

Printed Text

Matthew 7:13. Enter ye in at the strait gate: for wide is the gate, and broad is the way, that leadeth to destruction, and many there be which go in thereat:

14. Because strait is the gate, and narrow is the way, which leadeth unto life, and few there be that find it.

15. Beware of false prophets, which come to you in sheep's clothing, but inwardly they are ravening wolves.

16. Ye shall know them by their fruits. Do men gather grapes of thorns, or figs of thistles?

17. Even so every good tree bringeth forth good fruit; but a corrupt tree bringeth forth evil fruit.

18. A good tree cannot bring forth evil fruit, neither can a corrupt tree bring forth good fruit.

19. Every tree that bringeth not forth good fruit is hewn down, and cast into the fire.

20. Wherefore by their fruits ye shall know them.

21. Not every one that saith unto me, Lord, Lord, shall enter into the kingdom of heaven; but he that doeth the will of my Father which is in heaven.

22. Many will say to me in that day, Lord, Lord, have we not prophesied in thy name? and in thy name have cast out devils? and in thy name done many wonderful works?

23. And then will I profess unto them, I never knew you: depart from me, ye that work iniquity.

24. Therefore whosoever heareth these sayings of mine, and doeth them, I will liken him unto a wise man, which built his house upon a rock:

25. And the rain descended, and the floods came, and the winds blew, and beat upon that house; and it fell not: for it was founded upon a rock.

26. And every one that heareth these sayings of mine, and doeth them not, shall be likened unto a foolish man, which built his house upon the sand:

27. And the rain descended, and the floods came, and the winds blew, and beat upon that house; and it fell: and great was the fall of it.

28. And it came to pass, when Jesus had ended these sayings, the people were astonished at his doctrine:

29. For he taught them as one having authority, and not as the scribes.

LESSON OUTLINE

I. CHOOSE THE WAY OF LIFE
  A. The Broad Way
  B. The Narrow Way
II. BEWARE OF DECEIVERS
  A. False Prophets
  B. Good Fruit
  C. The Will of God
  D. The Lawless
III. OBEY CHRIST'S WORD
  A. The Wise Man
  B. The Foolish Man
  C. The Teaching of Jesus

LESSON EXPOSITION

INTRODUCTION

In this section of the Sermon on the Mount, Jesus employed a teaching method that was common in Judaism and Greco-Roman philosophy. It is the "two ways method. Thus, He speaks of the two ways (vv. 13, 14), two trees (vv. 15-20), two professions (vv. 21-23), and two builders (vv. 24-29).

In the previous verses, Jesus dealt with two negatives that show who we are. We will not judge (vv. 1-5), and we will not give what is holy to dogs (v. 6). He also dealt with two positives. We will ask with trust (vv. 7-11), and we will do unto others (v. 12). In the remainder of the chapter, He presents a positive plus a negative. We will enter the narrow gate and will keep away from the broad gate, and so forth.

To follow the principles set forth by Jesus may involve a separation from the majority of men (vv. 13, 14). Many men will claim to know and reveal the Lord's mind, but their true nature will be made known by their actions (vv. 15-20). Those who practice lawlessness have neither present nor future union with Christ (vv. 21-23). Those who build on a weak and wrong foundation are solemnly warned of the inevitable consequences (vv. 24-27).

At every turn in this passage, the reader is faced with a decision. Will he follow the path of ease and self-indulgence which will end in ruin? Or will he take the way that leads to eternal safety no matter what the cost? Each person must

decide for himself. Therefore, each individual bears personal responsibility for the course and consequence of his own life.

I. CHOOSE THE WAY OF LIFE (Matthew 7:13, 14)

A. The Broad Way (v. 13)

13. Enter ye in at the strait gate: for wide is the gate, and broad is the way, that leadeth to destruction, and many there be which go in thereat.

Every man faces two portals in life. One is wide; the other is narrow. He must decide which doorway he will enter. No one remains outside. All enter one or the other portal. The passageways correspond to the portals. The wide gate opens to a broad way; the narrow gate opens to a narrow way. The wide gate may be entered with any baggage we care to carry. Sins, self-righteousness, false notions, vices, and follies: All will pass through this portal easily. But this entrance leads to utter, final ruination.

One reason some people have difficulty deciding which portal to enter is the negative influence of false teachers. Each such teacher has his own formula for what is best for men. They were heard in Jesus' day from the housetops and in the streets. They are heard today through newspapers, magazines, radio, and television. Their message is always the same, "We have discovered the truth. Walk this way." Their teaching often appears at first sight to bear resemblance to the truth. Therefore, they leave many people confused. There is a great need to share the simple gospel message that points to life everlasting.

The Bible makes a clear distinction of destiny between those who enter the narrow gate and those who enter the broad gate. Those destinies are graphically described in Jeremiah 21:8, "And unto this people thou shalt say, Thus saith the Lord; Behold, I set before you the way of life, and the way of death" (see also 1 Corinthians 1:18).

B. The Narrow Way (v. 14)

14. Because strait is the gate, and narrow is the way, which leadeth unto life, and few there be that find it.

In his *Institutes,* published in 1561, John Calvin has a picture of two portals. One is narrow and has a thornbush in the entrance and a crown over the top. The other one is broad with a flower in the entrance and flames flaring over the top.

Entrance through the narrow gate leads to life. This gate must be approached with contrition and faith. This passageway is bounded on either side by the principles of Christianity. The life this entrance offers begins in regeneration, and culminates in a blessed and eternal existence in heaven.

The narrow gate is not as obvious to the view of man as is the wide gate. A person does not just drift into it, he has to find it. And what an astonishing discovery it is when suddenly it appears before one. We do not find it by our own searching; we are brought to it by the marvelous grace of our God. His great grace draws us by its attracting power. Jesus declared: "No man can come to me, except the Father which hath sent me draw him: and I will raise him up at the last day" (John 6:44).

Jesus said that only a few find the narrow gate, the majority enters the wide gate. This is another case where the majority is wrong. The majority has been wrong many times in history. They were wrong in the days of Columbus. The majority believed the earth was flat; Columbus believed it was round. They were wrong in the days of Robert Fulton. The majority called his steamboat "Fulton's Folly." And they are wrong in their attitude toward Jesus Christ. The majority is not on the narrow road.

II. BEWARE OF DECEIVERS (Matthew 7:15-23)

A. False Prophets (vv. 15-17)

15. Beware of false prophets, which come to you in sheep's clothing, but inwardly they are ravening wolves.

16. Ye shall know them by their fruits. Do men gather grapes of thorns, or figs of thistles?

17. Even so every good tree bringeth forth good fruit; but a corrupt tree bringeth forth evil fruit.

In the Old Testament, the people of God were constantly subjected to the pernicious influence of false prophets. Moses warned the people that if any prophet arose who sought to draw them away from God, they were not to heed his message. Further, they were to put him to death (see Deuteronomy 13:1-5). God gave Ezekiel a vision of the abominations that the house of Israel committed at the hand of false prophets. In the house of God, he saw every form of creeping thing, and abominable beasts, and all the idols of the house of Israel, portrayed upon the wall. In response, God said that He would deal with them in fury. He would not spare them nor pity them. Even though they cried to Him, He would not hear them (see Ezekiel 18:1-18).

How can the church help guard against false teachers and prophets?

False prophets continued to pester God's people in New Testament days. Paul described them in this way: "For such are false prophets, deceitful workers, transforming themselves into the apostles of Christ" (2 Corinthians 11:13). Peter warned: "But there were false prophets also among the people, even as there shall be false teachers among you, who privily shall bring in damnable heresies, even denying the Lord that bought them and bring upon themselves swift destruction. And many shall follow their pernicious ways. . . . And through covetousness shall they with feigned words make merchandise of you" (2 Peter 2:1-3). Jesus also warned of the presence of false prophets in the last days (see Matthew 24:24).

B. Good Fruit (vv. 18-20)

18. A good tree cannot bring forth evil fruit, neither can a corrupt tree bring forth good fruit.

19. Every tree that bringeth not forth good fruit is hewn down, and cast into the fire.

20. Wherefore by their fruits ye shall know them.

False prophets are always deceitful Verse 15 says that they come to you in sheep's clothing, but inwardly they are ravenous wolves. They make it their business to come to you, but they are never sent by God. In reality, they are fierce wolves, but they pretend to be gentle, harmless sheep. They are as the wolf who snatches the sheep, and separates him from the flock (see John 10:12). They are as savage as the wolves who come in and spare not the flock (see Acts 20:29). They are as destructive as men who with smooth and flattering speech deceive the hearts of the unsuspecting (see Romans 16:18). They are as harmful as those who deceive with empty words (see Ephesians 5:6) and persuasive arguments (see Colossians 2:4).

Jesus said that we are to recognize a false prophet by his fruits. The fruits of the prophets have reference to his teaching. You cannot always tell by his works (see Matthew 24:24). But his teaching can be measured by the Word of God. John said that if a man does not abide in the teaching of Christ, he is not of God. The believer, therefore, is not to receive him into his house, or to greet him (see 2 John 9-11). Every prophet, true or false, appeals to the Word. The worst heresy claims the Word as its source. Therefore, the prophet is judged as to his teaching by the Word to which he himself is constrained to appeal. If his teaching is true, you will find grapes and figs, true spiritual food; if not, you will find briars and thistles, man's wisdom.

C. The Will of God (v. 21)

21. Not every one that saith unto me, Lord, Lord, shall enter into the kingdom of heaven; but he that doeth the will of my Father which is in heaven.

Not everyone who addresses Jesus as Lord will enter the kingdom of heaven. Some will because they have experienced the relationship to Jesus that this title expresses. In fact, Jesus expects His disciples to address Him in this fashion. When He washed their feet, He said: "Ye call me Master and Lord: and ye say well; for so I am" (John 13:13). The duplication of the title, "Lord, Lord, denotes zeal and is for the purpose of urgency in prayer and in worship. The

objection which Jesus registers is toward those who, using this title, claim a connection with Him which does not exist except in their imagination. Since there is no real relationship to Christ, there can be no entrance into the kingdom of heaven.

On the other hand, Jesus said that those who obey the heavenly Father, thus doing His will, will enter the kingdom of heaven. Doing the will of God shows that the relationship with Jesus is real. Doing the will of God begins with repentance and faith, and leads to works that please the Lord. Jesus Christ is the source of this new life (see John 6:39, 40). Those who have walked and worked to glorify Him benefit from His gracious, saving will (see John 6:29).

In this verse, Jesus referred to God as "My Father." Thus, for the first time, He used the pronoun that identified Him as the Son of the Father. What authority this claim gives to everything He has said or He will say!

D. The Lawless (vv. 22, 23)

22. Many will say to me in that day, Lord, Lord, have we not prophesied in thy name? and in thy name have cast out devils? and in thy name done many wonderful works?

23. And then will I profess unto them, I never knew you: depart from me, ye that work iniquity.

Jesus gives further proof that a false prophet is to be judged by his words rather than by his works. A day of judgment is coming when all pretenders and false prophets will be tried. In that day, many will parade their works before the Lord as evidence that they belong to Him. Their approach to Him will be in that zealous double designation, "Lord, Lord." As they made His name prominent to give credibility to their earthly activities, then they will use His name to gain His favor.

These pretenders will mention that they prophesied in His name. Again, they clothed their pretense in the name and revelation of God. They proclaimed their false doctrines to be true and appealed to the Word for support. In so doing, they deceived many people. Also, they will say that they cast out demons and performed many miracles in Christ's name. In Matthew 24:24, these miracles are described as being so astonishing they would deceive, if it were possible, the very elect. This is further proof that the apparent miracle is not the criterion of a true prophet, but the Word is.

These false prophets will stand before Jesus, the Son of God, as their Judge in the last day. They have abused His name and His Word, now they must answer to Him. He will tell them that though they used His name, He never acknowledged them at any time. He orders them out of His sight and labels them practitioners of lawlessness.

III. OBEY CHRIST'S WORDS (Matthew 7:24-29)

A. The Wise Man (vv. 24, 25)

24. Therefore whosoever heareth these sayings of mine, and doeth them, I will liken him unto a wise man, which built his house upon a rock:

25. And the rain descended, and the floods came, and the winds blew, and beat upon that house; and it fell not: for it was founded upon a rock.

Jesus concluded the Sermon on the Mount with a powerful illustration which called for a personal application of the truths He taught. They must not only hear what He says, but act upon His words. This same response is required toward all of God's Word. James wrote: "But be ye doers of the word, and not hearers only, deceiving your own selves. For if any be a hearer of the word, and not a doer, he is like unto a man beholding his natural face in a glass: For he beholdeth himself, and goeth his way, and straightway forgetteth what manner of man he was. But whoso looketh into the perfect law of liberty, and continueth therein, he being not a forgetful hearer, but a doer of the work, this man shall be blessed in his deed" (1:22-25).

The man who builds his life on the Word is likened to the man who builds his house on a rock. In either case, one has a solid foundation. Paul had the wise man in mind when he wrote: "For other foundation can no man lay than that is laid, which is Jesus Christ" (1 Corinthians 3:11). When one has built properly on the right foundation, the house or the life will withstand the severest tests. Let the rains fall in torrents, let the floods rise, let the winds lash and beat upon the house; it will stand. Likewise, when a man has grounded and founded his life on the words of Jesus, he will overcome life's obstacles.

B. The Foolish Man (vv. 26, 27)

26. And every one that heareth these sayings of mine, and doeth them not, shall be likened unto a foolish man, which built his house upon the sand:

27. And the rain descended, and the floods came, and the winds blew, and beat upon that house; and it fell: and great was the fall of it.

There is only one difference in the two men described in this parable. One acted upon the word of Jesus, and one did not. Both heard the Word. Also, in the parable, both built a house. And there is no indication that one house was less elaborate than the other. It is only that one built upon the rock, and the other built upon the sand.

What are some of the "sands" that undisciplined lives are built on in the modern era?

The sand may be described as all teaching and doctrines that are not "these words of mine." As the songwriter expressed it: "All other ground is sinking sand." The irony is that the folly of building upon the sand may not be immediately apparent. As long as the sun is shining and the winds are calm, no danger appears. On the contrary, everything may be rosy and blissful. But when the tempest stirs, the house will not stand and great will be its fall. It will come down with a crash of utter wreck and ruin. It will even be swept away by the swirling flood waters.

The same thing is true in life. A life built on false teachings may not feel their damaging effects immediately. As long as things are going well, it may appear that one is on solid ground. But all of that changes when tests and trials and temptations assail one. Then the false foundation will crumble. A person needs to ask about the teachings upon which he has based his life, "Will they sustain me in the most difficult moments of life?"

C. The Teaching of Jesus (vv. 28, 29)

28. And it came to pass, when Jesus had ended these sayings, the people were astonished at his doctrine:

29. For he taught them as one having authority, and not as the scribes.

Can you picture the scene at the conclusion of Jesus' sermon? Throughout the message, every eye and every ear have been fixed on Him in undivided attention. They did not want to miss a single word. Perhaps now a hush fell over the audience. Maybe they expected something more from Him. When they realized that this mighty warning was His last word in this message, an amazement swept over the multitude. They were dumbfounded at what they had heard.

Jesus' hearers were not accustomed to hearing anyone speak so clearly, and with such authority. He spoke as One who was filled with authoritative power. His deity revealed itself in all that He said. The scribes had to rely on tradition for authority; Christ's authority was His own.

Every preacher and teacher should study the messages of Jesus as models of effective communication. He spoke with accuracy, clarity, and practicality. His messages were not only interesting; they were captivating. He was easily understood. There was none of the mumbo-jumbo gobbledygook that came from other pulpits or lecterns. Some of the descendants of those who left the truth cloudy and fuzzy and indefinite are still around. We need to hear again the clear message of the Master delivered as the authoritative, infallible Word of God.

REVIEW QUESTIONS

1. What Christian principle is emphasized in this lesson?

2. What constitutes the "broad way" mentioned in verse 13?

3. What conditions are necessary for entrance to the "narrow way?"

4. List some of the major ways people are deceived today?

5. What illustration did Jesus use in the conclusion of the Sermon on the Mount to emphasize the personal application of principles He shared?

GOLDEN TEXT HOMILY

"NOT EVERY ONE THAT SAITH UNTO ME, LORD, LORD, SHALL ENTER INTO THE KINGDOM OF HEAVEN; BUT HE THAT DOETH THE WILL OF MY FATHER WHICH IS IN HEAVEN" (Matthew 7:21).

Being a follower of Christ is more than just professing obedience to Him. It requires action: *doing* the will of God.

A personal relationship with Christ is the beginning of all good work.

Individuals may deceive other people with their profession of obedience. However, no one fools Christ. Under His eyes all disguises must drop off, and persons will be known for what they really are.

Everything we do short of doing the will of God is merely saying, "Lord, Lord!"

All of us have known persons who are glib speakers, even to the extent of moving congregations with their oratory. Yet, they did not do the will of God.

Today some people are deceived into saying of a man, "He must be a good man; see how successful he is." We must remember, however, that success may be won on purely human principles and may have nothing *divine* about it. The real test is, "Is the individual doing the will and work of God?"

In the days this scripture was written, the term "miracle worker" was often used. Today the reference is "successful men in religious work." Then, it seemed to be a great thing to have the gift of prophecy and the power of working miracles, but we must always bear in mind that these gifts will not *save* the soul.

There is a need of something deeper: the hidden life of holiness which the

Father only sees; the submission of the human will in love and faith to the holy will of God.

Putting the sayings of Christ into action is the *only* way to build a Christlike life.

We must learn to do our Father's will here on earth so that one day we may enter into that blessed place where everyone does His will, *lovingly* and *perfectly.*

The final goal of all sincere Christians is to enter into the kingdom of heaven. God is the King of heaven, and only those who do His will can enter therein.

What a disaster it will be for persons who *think* they can gain entrance into heaven by some other means.—**O. W. Polen, D.D., Editor in Chief, Church of God Publishing House, Cleveland, Tennessee**

SENTENCE SERMONS

FOLLOWING CHRIST requires true commitment.

—Selected

IT IS NO FAULT of Christianity if a hypocrite falls into sin.

—Jerome

THE CHRISTIAN is a person who makes it easy for others to believe in God.

—Robert M. McCheyne

A FEW CHRISTIANS want the spiritual maturity that comes through testings; the rest want to take life easy.

—Henry Jacobsen

EVANGELISTIC APPLICATION

JESUS CHRIST IS THE ONLY WAY TO ETERNAL LIFE.

The federal government erected a new multimillion dollar courthouse in Philadelphia. The building was almost completed when inspectors noticed cracks in the brick facing the inner walls. Tests determined the building was beginning to tilt on its foundation. The cause was a decision to shorten the foundation pillars.

An extra ten million dollars was spent repairing the damage and providing adequate support for the building.

The foundation is crucial in construction and in life. The wise build "upon a rock," which will provide stability in the storm. The wise person will build on the sayings of Jesus and be obedient to His Word (Bill D. Whittaker)—*Illustrating the Gospel of Matthew* by James E. Hightower, Jr.

Peter declared: "Neither is there salvation in any other: for there is none other name under heaven given among men, whereby we must be saved" (Acts 4:12).

ILLUMINATING THE LESSON

"Button, button, who's got the button?" may be more than child's play. A woman bought a coat in a shop in Brooklyn for ninety dollars and soon lost a button from it. The shop did not have an extra button, so the woman wrote to the factory. The factory recognized the button as one that matched from a stolen coat. The woman led detectives to the shop, and the owner was jailed as a fence for receiving stolen goods from shoplifters. From button to coat, from theft to thief—the chain led to judgment.

With man it takes detective work, but to God all things are naked and open. All missing buttons will be located in that day—every wrong will be brought home to the doer unless he has let the Savior settle out of court for him.—*Let Me Illustrate,* by Donald Grey Barnhouse.

DAILY BIBLE READINGS

M. Blessing or Cursing? Deuteronomy 30:15-19

T. Death or Life? Romans 8:6-14

W. Choose the Lord. Joshua 24:14-18

T. Righteous Leadership. 2 Kings 18:1-7

F. The Right Way to Live. 1 Peter 2:11-16

S. Follow the Right Way. Proverbs 2:10-22

Called to Discipleship

Study Text: Matthew 10:5-42
Supplemental References: Daniel 6:4-10; Mark 13:9-13; Luke 12:2-12; 14:25-33; 21:12-18; Acts 4:13-20
Time: Probably summer A.D. 28
Place: Uncertain. Jesus had just finished visiting a number of towns in Galilee
Golden Text: "He that findeth his life shall lose it: and he that loseth his life for my sake shall find it" (Matthew 10:39).
Central Truth: The believer is called to a life of total commitment to Jesus Christ.
Evangelistic Emphasis: Sinners are called to be saved and to live as Christ's disciples.

Printed Text

Matthew 10:24. The disciple is not above his master, nor the servant above his lord.

25. It is enough for the disciple that he be as his master, and the servant as his lord. If they have called the master of the house Beelzebub, how much more shall they call them of his household?

26. Fear them not therefore: for there is nothing covered, that shall not be revealed; and hid, that shall not be known.

27. What I tell you in darkness, that speak ye in light: and what ye hear in the ear, that preach ye upon the housetops.

28. And fear not them which kill the body, but are not able to kill the soul: but rather fear him which is able to destroy both soul and body in hell.

29. Are not two sparrows sold for a farthing? and one of them shall not fall on the ground without your Father.

30. But the very hairs of your head are all numbered.

31. Fear ye not therefore, ye are of more value than many sparrows.

32. Whosoever therefore shall confess me before men, him will I confess also before my Father which is in heaven.

33. But whosoever shall deny me before men, him will I also deny before my Father which is in heaven.

34. Think not that I am come to send peace on earth: I came not to send peace, but a sword.

35. For I am come to set a man at variance against his father, and the daughter against her mother, and the daughter in law against her mother in law.

36. And a man's foes shall be they of his own household.

37. He that loveth father or mother more than me is not worthy of me: and he that loveth son or daughter more than me is not worthy of me.

38. And he that taketh not his cross, and followeth after me, is not worthy of me.

39. He that findeth his life shall lose it: and he that loseth his life for my sake shall find it.

LESSON OUTLINE

I. MISGUIDED FEAR
  A. What to Expect
  B. Whom to Fear
II. CONFESS CHRIST BEFORE MEN
  A. Mutual Loyalty
  B. Divine Mission
  C. Worthiness Determined
III. DISCIPLESHIP REWARDED

LESSON EXPOSITION

INTRODUCTION

In our lesson today, we move from the series of studies of the Sermon on the Mount to the more practical application of principles to the Christian life. William Barclay gives a good summation of the contents of the Gospel According to Matthew "In the story of the Baptism Matthew shows us Jesus accepting His task. In the story of the Temptation Matthew shows us Jesus deciding on the method which He will use to embark upon His task. In the Sermon on the Mount we listen to Jesus' words of wisdom. In Matthew 8 we look on Jesus' deeds of power. In Matthew 9 we see the growing opposition gathering itself against Jesus. And now we see Jesus choosing His men" (*The Gospel of Matthew,* by William Barclay, Vol. 1).

As a leader about to embark upon a great undertaking, it was natural for Jesus to choose His staff. On them a great deal of the present effect and the future success of His work would depend.

Two things stand out about the helpers Jesus chose: (1) They were ordinary persons; and (2) They were a most extraordinary mixture. Yet these men, simple men with no unusual background, men from many different spheres of belief, were the very foundation stones by which the church was built. It is on the confession, dedication, and service of common men and women that the church, to this day, is moved forward for the glory of God.

After the twelve disciples were commissioned (vv. 5-15), Jesus talked with the disciples about the coming persecution of both Himself and His followers. True discipleship is faced with the reality of persecution but ultimate rewards also.

I. MISGUIDED FEAR (Matthew 10:24-31)

A. What to Expect (vv. 24, 25)

24. The disciple is not above his master, nor the servant above his lord.

25. It is enough for the disciple that he be as his master, and the servant as his lord. If they have called the master of the house Beelzebub, how much more shall they call them of his household?

Beginning with verse 16 of Matthew 10, there is recorded the message Jesus spoke to the disciples with the intention of putting them in the right frame of mind for their task. They are warned of the persecutions awaiting them and are reminded that they answer ultimately to God and not to man.

The nature of the disciple (learner)-master (teacher) relationship dispells any idea that the disciple is superior to the master. In fact the disciple-master relationship was a sort of apprenticeship that aimed to help prepare the disciple to take on the characteristics of the master. So it was inevitable that they, having fulfilled that objective, could expect reaction from the world much like that directed to the master. The disciples could never hope to be equal with Jesus, but they could emulate His qualities and be willing to suffer with Him.

Among the abuse directed to Jesus by the Jewish people was the assigning of His miracle deeds to Satan. They called Jesus Beelzebub whom they designated as the "prince of demons." They were saying in effect that satanic power was behind Jesus' supernatural deeds. Jesus here assured the disciples that similar accusations would be directed to them.

B. Whom to Fear (vv. 26-31)

26. Fear them not therefore: for there is nothing covered, that shall not be revealed; and hid, that shall not be known.

27. What I tell you in darkness, that speak ye in light: and what ye hear

in the ear, that preach ye upon the housetops.

The Lord assured the disciples that any fears they had of their persecutors should be overshadowed by their knowledge that in due time the full truth about all matters would be disclosed. For instance, the just character of Jesus and the divine power behind His miraculous works would come to light. It might take a long time but "truth will triumph."

When James the Sixth threatened to hang or exile Andrew Melville, Melville's answer was: "You cannot hang or exile the truth." When the Christian is involved in suffering and sacrifice and even martyrdom for his faith, he must remember that the day will come when truth will triumph and things will be seen as they really are.

In verse 27 Jesus told the disciples that the information He shared with them, in the darkness, or in whispered tones, was not merely for their edification, but was God's saving grace to be shared with all mankind. Jesus would have all disciples share the truth with fallen humanity.

What is the greatest fear present-day Christians have about sharing the gospel? What can be done to help with the problem?

---

28. And fear not them which kill the body, but are not able to kill the soul: but rather fear him which is able to destroy both soul and body in hell.

29. Are not two sparrows sold for a farthing? and one of them shall not fall on the ground without your Father.

30. But the very hairs of your head are all numbered.

31. Fear ye not therefore, ye are of more value than many sparrows.

There are persons without proper eternal values who might be fearful before magistrates, but Jesus' disciples need not tremble before those whose power is merely over the physical properties of mankind. Jesus' disciples knew who was the final power and what He would

do to persons who defy His Word and ignore His will. The disciples were admonished to fear Him whose power was not limited to the present life and who could indeed "destroy both soul and body in hell."

The disciples were instructed to be encouraged by the assurance that this heavenly Father would care for them. He knew of the fall of the sparrow and took note of the smallest portions of the body—the hairs of the head—of His children.

If God notes the fall of the sparrow, certainly He will be constantly attentive to the needs of the human family. Man is central to God's purpose on earth, and He will not ignore a single legitimate concern.

II. CONFESS CHRIST BEFORE MEN (Matthew 10:32-38)

A. Mutual Loyalty (vv. 32, 33)

32. Whosoever therefore shall confess me before men, him will I confess also before my Father which is in heaven.

33. But whosoever shall deny me before men, him will I also deny before my Father which is in heaven.

In these verses is laid down the double loyalty of the Christian life. If a Christian is loyal to Jesus Christ in this life, Christ will be loyal to that person in the life to come.

The church of today is built on the unbreakable loyalty of those who held fast to their faith regardless of circumstances. Indeed, it is a plain fact of history that if there had not been men and women in the early church who in the face of death and agony, refused to deny their Master, there would be no Christian church today.

There is something fascinating about those saints of the early church and the catacombs. It has intrigued our writers and showed up in QUO VADIS (WHO GOES THERE?) years ago and in similar books today. We cannot forget this fellowship of simple believers who loved Jesus Christ more than their life, who were in the world but not of it, whose blood was the seed of the church. It was said of them long ago: "They live, each in his native land but as though they were not really at home here. They share in all duties like citizens and suffer all hardships like strangers. Every foreign land is for them a father land and every father land a foreign land. They dwell on earth but are citizens of heaven. They obey the laws that men make, but their lives are better than the laws. They love all men but are persecuted by all men" (*A History of the Christian Church,* Qualben).

These soldiers of God's underground were on fire with a passion which swords could not kill nor water drown nor fire destroy. Their blood was spilled so freely in the arena that a traveler has asked, "Do you want a relic? Take a handful of sand from the Coliseum. It is all martyrs."

Our fathers, chained in prisons dark,
Were still in heart and conscience free;
How sweet would be their children's fate,
If they, like them, could die for Thee!

Is there a de-emphasis on confessing Christ today? Explain.

B. Divine Mission (vv. 34-36)

34. Think not that I am come to send peace on earth: I came not to send peace, but a sword.

35. For I am come to set a man at variance against his father, and the daughter against her mother, and the daughter in law against her mother in law.

36. And a man's foes shall be they of his own household.

That Jesus had come on a divine mission there can be no doubt. His purpose in redeeming men from the forces of evil would cause a clash with the demonic forces of the world. Likewise, His disciples would encounter the possessive ungodly forces coming against them as they attempted to set at liberty those bound by Satan.

In stating that He had "not come to send peace, but a sword," it appears at first glance that His words are a contradiction to Isaiah 9:6 "Prince of Peace," Luke 2:14 "on earth peace . . . toward men," and John 14:27 "Peace I leave with you." Luke's version gives us the meaning of the word *sword.* "Suppose ye that I am come to give peace on earth? I tell you, Nay; but rather division" (Luke 12:51).

It is true Christ came to bring peace—peace between the believer and God, and peace among men. Yet the inevitable result of Christ's coming is conflict (sword)—between Christ and the Antichrist; between light and darkness, between Christ's children and those who give their allegiance to the devil.

The spirit of Christ can have no union with the spirit of the world. Even a father, while unconverted, will oppose a godly child, wife, or daughter-in-law. A mother and daughter might be out of harmony because one is aligned with Christ, and the other with the forces of evil. The same is true of a daughter-in-law/mother-in-law relationship, as well as any combination of relationships in a household.

C. Worthiness Determined (vv. 37, 38)

37. He that loveth father or mother more than me is not worthy of me: and he that loveth son or daughter more than me is not worthy of me.

38. And he that taketh not his cross, and followeth after me, is not worthy of me.

The divine mission of Christ made necessary a total commitment of His disciples. The disciples were to choose between love of Christ and love of the family. Although children should love their father and mother, they are not to love them more than they love Jesus. Parents should love their children, they should not love them more than they love Christ, or they are not worthy of Christ.

The first mention of the cross in Matthew's Gospel appears in verse 38. The cross was an instrument of death and here symbolizes the necessity of total commitment—even unto death—on the part of Jesus' disciples.

Perhaps we have become so accustomed to the expression—"taking up one's cross"—in the sense of being prepared for trials in general for Christ's sake, that we are apt to lose sight of its primary and proper sense as used here—a preparedness to go forth even to crucifixion as when our Lord had to bear His own cross to Calvary.

Is there reason to believe that "cross bearing" to us in our day has a different connotation than it did for Christ's disciples? Explain.

III. DISCIPLESHIP REWARDED (Matthew 10:39-42)

39. He that findeth his life shall lose it: and he that loseth his life for my sake shall find it.

(Matthew 10:40-42 is not included in the printed text.)

Jesus reminded the disciples that the person who found his life would lose it; and the man who lost his life would find it. As paradoxical as that turn of events seems, again and again it has been proven in the most literal way. John the Baptist, Martin Luther, and John Bunyan could have denied their convictions, but in so doing the real life (eternal life) would have been lost.

There is no place for a life of ease and safety in the Christian life. Those who seek first ease, comfort, security and fulfillment of personal ambition may well get all these things—but will not be a happy person; for they were sent into this world to serve God and fellow human beings. An individual can hoard life, if he desires, but that way he will lose all that makes life valuable to others and worth living for himself. The way to serve others, the way to fulfill God's purpose for us, the way to true happiness is to spend life selflessly, for only thus will we find life both here and hereafter.

40. He that receiveth you receiveth me, and he that receiveth me receiveth him that sent me.

41. He that receiveth a prophet in the name of a prophet shall receive a prophet's reward; and he that receiveth a righteous man in the name of a righteous man shall receive a righteous man's reward.

When Jesus spoke the words of verses 40-42, He was using a way of speaking that the Jews regularly used. The Jews felt that to receive a person's envoy or messenger was the same as to receive the person himself. To pay respect to an ambassador was the same as to pay respect to the king who sent him. This was particularly true in regard to wise men and to those who taught God's truth. The rabbis said: "He who shows hospitality to the wise is as if he brought the first-fruits of his produce unto God." If a man is a true man of God, to receive him is to receive the God who sent him.

William Barclay suggests that this passage sets out the four links in the chain of salvation: "(1) There is God out of whose love the whole process of salvation began. (2) There is Jesus who brought that message to men. (3) There is the human messenger, the prophet who speaks, the good man who is an example, the disciple who learns, who in turn all pass on to others the good news which they themselves have received. (4) There is the believer who welcomes God's men and God's message and who thus finds life to his soul (*The Gospel of Matthew,* Vol. 1).

42. And whosoever shall give to drink unto one of these little ones a cup of cold water only in the name of a disciple, verily I say unto you, he shall in no wise lose his reward.

The "little ones" are Christ's disciples, setting forth on their mission of Kingdom service. Christ foresaw the hardships of the disciples, as He foresees the hardships of His servants in our day. They are like lambs in the midst of wolves.

Christ also foresaw that some would minister to the needs of these "little ones"—at the risk of unpopularity and perhaps bitter loss. The hospitality to the servants of the Lord is not mere charity for it is motivated by the fact that these are messengers of Christ. The word "cool" is in contrast to the heat of the sunstruck land. A cup of cold water meant more than a trip to an underground cistern, even when that meant no small journey, for cistern water was not very cold and was generally not the best for drinking. The cup of cold water more often meant a trip to the well, with the expenditure of energy. It was done in honor of the one who came in the name of Christ.

It seems certain that Christ had heaven in mind as the reward for hospitality. The reward is that God will quench the soul's thirst in the donor, even as the donor has been willing to risk to minister to the lowly messenger of Christ.

REVIEW QUESTIONS

1. What emphasis is given in this lesson about the disciple/master and the servant/lord relationships?

2. What admonition did Christ give about fear?

3. What promise is given to those who are willing to confess Christ before men?

4. What is meant by the term "sword," used in verse 34?

5. Discuss the need for hospitality to the "little ones" (servants of God).

GOLDEN TEXT HOMILY

"HE THAT FINDETH HIS LIFE SHALL LOSE IT: AND HE THAT LOSETH HIS LIFE FOR MY SAKE SHALL FIND IT" (Matthew 10:39).

Nowhere else in Scripture is the honesty of Christ more exemplified than in this passage. It is the intention of Jesus to attract people to the kingdom of heaven, but never with false impressions. The way to the kingdom is by way of the cross, and the cross is by no means identified with easy achievement or access. Listen to the words of Christ in Matthew 10:38, "And he that taketh not his cross and followeth after me, is not worthy of me." Again in Matthew 16:24, "If any man will come after me, let him deny himself, and take up his cross, and follow me." Christ is explicit in stating the hardships for all who accept His invitation to follow Him.

Jesus suggests the possibility of warfare, and may include conflict in the home with the family being divided. The Jews believed at "the day of the Lord," the day when God would directly involve Himself in the world events, would be a time of family divisions. The rabbis state it, and Christ later confirmed it. "For I am come to set a man at variance against his father, . . . and the daughter in law against her mother in law. And a man's foes shall be they of his own household" (Matthew 10:35, 36).

There is always the possibility that one may eventually have to choose between his dearest earthly asset and Jesus Christ. People in every generation since Christ came have been confronted with this dilemma. John Bunyan was forced to make a choice of either remaining with his wife and children, including a blind child, or going to prison for preaching without license. He went to prison.

There are divided houses today, brought about because some members have chosen to follow Christ and others refuse to follow Him. Jesus even inferred that a person's life might be in jeopardy by following Him. Again the Golden Text: "He who finds his life will lose it, and he who loses his life for My sake, will find it" (New King James Version). The life one loses may be only the old life of sin, and the life he finds is the life of joy in Christ, but it might mean losing physical life while finding new life. However severe the hardships, whatever price to pay, living in Christ is worth what one may have to pay.—**Wayne S. Proctor, Pastor, Lexington, Kentucky**

SENTENCE SERMONS

THE BELIEVER is called to a life of total commitment to Jesus Christ.

—Selected

GOD IS MORE INTERESTED in making us what He wants us to be than giving us what we ought to have.

—Walter L. Wilson

ONLY A BURDENED heart can lead to fruitful service.

—**Alan Redpath**

WHAT WE CAN DO for Christ is the test of service. What we can suffer for Him is the test of love.

—**"Speaker's Sourcebook"**

EVANGELISTIC APPLICATION

SINNERS ARE CALLED TO BE SAVED AND TO LIVE AS CHRIST'S DISCIPLES.

A Christian blind woman became concerned regarding a blind friend who had never heard the gospel. She took a journey of two days over high mountains to bring her the good news of salvation. The friend was saved, and in answer to prayer her blind eyes were opened. Within an hour after her healing the whole city knew that she could see. All day she received visitors, to whom she testified about Christ. Later she learned to read, and the Lord has greatly used her in the women's evangelistic band. As a result of her work, there is now a self-supporting church of a hundred members. Other remarkable healings are on record, enough to assure to any reasonable person the certainty of miracles.

—**"Sunday School Times"**

ILLUMINATING THE LESSON

When Paganini died, he left his marvelous violin to his native city of Genoa with the instructions that it never be played upon. In time it became a worm-eaten and a worthless relic. As long as wood is used and cared for, it wears little. But when it is discarded, it begins to decay.

We must be active in the service of Christ or face spiritual decay.

The Duke of Wellington asked a British officer who was standing in a slack manner, "Why do you stand in such an unbecoming attitude?" "I'm off duty, sir," the officer replied. But the duke answered, "A British officer is never off duty; so resume your military standing."

Nor is a Christian ever off duty.

An Arab faithfully fed a beggar at his gate. One day when he needed to have an urgent errand run he asked the beggar to do it. He replied, "I ask alms; I do not run errands."

DAILY BIBLE READINGS

M. Courageous Faith in God. Daniel 3:8-18

T. Bold Witness to Christ. Acts 4:13-20

W. Unashamed for Christ. 1 Peter 4:12-19

T. Steadfast in Christ. Acts 21:8-14

F. Fearless Devotion to God. Daniel 6:4-10

S. Live the Faith. 2 Timothy 4:1-8

God's Kingdom in the World

Study Text: Matthew 13:1-43

Supplemental References: Daniel 2:36-44; Matthew 13:44-52; Mark 4:1-34; Luke 13:18-21; Romans 14:17

Time: Probably, A.D. 28

Place: A ship just off shore in the Sea of Galilee. Also, on shore in the Galilee area.

Golden Text: "He that received seed into the good ground is he that heareth the word, and understandeth it; which also beareth fruit, and bringeth forth, some an hundredfold, some sixty, some thirty" (Matthew 13:23).

Central Truth: Wherever the gospel is received and obeyed, the kingdom of Christ is established.

Evangelistic Emphasis: Christ calls men to forsake the kingdom of Satan and become citizens of His everlasting kingdom.

Printed Text

Matthew 13:18. Hear ye therefore the parable of the sower.

19. When any one heareth the word of the kingdom, and understandeth it not, then cometh the wicked one, and catcheth away that which was sown in his heart. This is he which received seed by the way side.

20. But he that received the seed into stony places, the same is he that heareth the word, and anon with joy receiveth it;

21. Yet hath he not root in himself, but dureth for a while: for when tribulation or persecution ariseth because of the word, by and by he is offended.

22. He also that received seed among the thorns is he that heareth the word; and the care of this world, and the deceitfulness of riches, choke the word, and he becometh unfruitful.

23. But he that received seed into the good ground is he that heareth the word, and understandeth it; which also beareth fruit, and bringeth forth, some an hundredfold, some sixty, some thirty.

24. Another parable put he forth unto them, saying, The kingdom of heaven is likened unto a man which sowed good seed in his field:

25. But while men slept, his enemy came and sowed tares among the wheat, and went his way.

26. But when the blade was sprung up, and brought forth fruit, then appeared the tares also.

27. So the servants of the householder came and said unto him, Sir, didst not thou sow good seed in thy field? from whence then hath it tares?

28. He said unto them, An enemy hath done this. The servants said unto him, Wilt thou then that we go and gather them up?

29. But he said, Nay; lest while ye gather up the tares, ye root up also the wheat with them.

30. Let both grow together until the harvest: and in the time of harvest I will say to the reapers, Gather ye together first the tares, and bind them in bundles to burn them: but gather the wheat into my barn.

LESSON OUTLINE

I. PROCLAIMING THE WORD
  A. The Wayside Hearer
  B. The Stony Hearer
  C. The Thorny Hearer
  D. The Good Hearer

II. RECOGNIZING THE ENEMY
  A. The Kingdom of Heaven
  B. An Evil Deed
  C. A Wise Decision

III. REAPING THE HARVEST
  A. The Parable Explained
  B. The Parable Applied

LESSON EXPOSITION

INTRODUCTION

Chapter 13 of Matthew shows an important pattern in the gospel, since it reflects a definite turning point in the ministry of Jesus.

At the beginning of His ministry He taught in the synagogues, but now we find Him teaching on the seashore. It is not that the door of the synagogue was completely shut to them, but it was closing. In the open countryside and seashores He chose to use unique methods in teaching.

Even before the use of parables, Jesus used a way of teaching which had the germ of the parable in it. The simile of the salt and light (5:13-16), the picture of the birds and lilies (6:26-30), and the story of the wise and foolish builder (7:24-27) are embryo parables, but in this chapter we find Jesus' way of using parables fully developed.

The thirteenth chapter contains seven parables of the Kingdom. Each parable portrays an aspect of the Kingdom and each begins with the formula: "The Kingdom of Heaven is like."

Our lesson today focuses on only two parables—the parable of the sower and the parable of the tares. In each case, the disciples persisted in having an explanation of the parables.

The parables of Jesus speak to us today. They challenge us to soul searching and watchfulness as we claim our place in the Kingdom of God.

I. PROCLAIMING THE WORD (Matthew 13:18-23)

18. Hear ye therefore the parable of the sower.

The parable of the sower is really a parable about four kinds of soil or four kinds of listeners. Indeed, the emphasis in the parable is upon the hearer and his responsibility of hearing and nurturing the Word of God.

A. The Wayside Hearer (v. 19)

19. When any one heareth the word of the kingdom, and understandeth it not, then cometh the wicked one, and catcheth away that which was sown in his heart. This is he which received seed by the way side.

The wayside hearer is characterized by lack of desire for spiritual perception. Such persons never allow the Word to penetrate beyond the intellect. It never penetrates to the heart and soul where action bubbles forth. Duty is recognized in word, but is not felt.

The religious life of the wayside hearers is couched in a framework of social acceptability. They feel nothing in their religion beyond a safeguard for common decency and political advantage.

The seed (Word) is subject to failure in such hearts. The failure can happen because of being trodden down or crushed out by passing feet or the wheels of traffic or pleasure. F. W. Robertson speaks of the wayside hearer in relationship to a single sermon. "Scarcely has its [the sermon's] last tone vibrated on the ear, when a fresh impression is given by the music which dismisses the congregation. That is succeeded by another impression, as your friend puts his arm in yours and talks of some other matter, irrelevant, obliterating any slight seriousness which the sermon produced. Another, and another, and another—and the Word is *trodden down.* Observe, there is nothing wrong in these impressions. The farmer's cart which crushes the grain by the wayside is rolling by on rightful business, and the stage and the pedestrian are in their place; simply the seed is not. It is not the wrongness of the impressions which treads religion down, but only this, that outside religion yields in turn to other outside impressions which are stronger" (Sermons Preached at Brighton).

Jesus also said of the wayside hearer "fowls came and devoured them up" (v. 4). The picture suggests that the winged thoughts come when we pray, or read, or listen in our inattentive wayside hours, and before we can be upon our guard, the very trace of holy purposes disappears.

Discuss the difficulties which surround the efforts to pray around the altar. Are you ever bombarded by thoughts not related to that prayer?

B. The Stony Hearer (vv. 20, 21)

20. But he that received the seed into stony places, the same is he that heareth the word, and anon with joy receiveth it;

21. Yet hath he not root in himself, but dureth for a while: for when tribulation or persecution ariseth because of the word, by and by he is offended.

The stony ground meant those places in the field where there were large ledges of rock embedded in the ground and covered with a thin layer of soil. Such soil is shallow and unable to retain moisture for normal growth of the seed.

This illustrates clearly the shallow experience of many who are quick to accept the Word. Such persons are easily swayed by emotional appeals. They are caught up in the excitement of the occasion, but they have no deep down roots in the Word of God. Therefore, tribulations or persecutions strike them and they are offended and give up. Not having the inner strength of the Holy Spirit to draw upon, they die never bearing fruit.

C. The Thorny Hearer (v. 22)

22. He also that received seed among the thorns is he that heareth the word; and the care of this world, and the deceitfulness of riches, choke the word, and he becometh unfruitful.

It appears that there is nothing basi-

cally wrong with the soil in this case. It is good and the seed sinks deeply into it. But there was also the seed of thorns that had been left in the gound. Consequently, as the good grain began to grow, so did the thorns which stole the nourishment and grew above the grain, taking away the needed light and heat.

The hearer that Jesus is thinking about here is not a superficial or thoughtless person, but one that exhibits character, purpose, and depth of thought. The Word stays in the heart of such a hearer and perhaps he makes a contribution to the Kingdom.

But the care of the world and the deceitfulness of riches choke the Word in such soil. Perhaps the thorns choke out the nourishment of God's Word by not allowing time for study, prayer, and the times of public worship. Eventually he lives only for himself and forces God's will out of his life, His spiritual life is choked and he becomes unfruitful.

D. The Good Hearer (v. 23)

23. But he that received seed into the good ground is he that heareth the word, and understandeth it; which also beareth fruit, and bringeth forth, some an hundredfold, some sixty, some thirty.

The rich soil of this type hearer knows no inner defilement or outward restrictions. When the seed is planted in such soil it does not have to struggle with thorny roots, rocky surface, shallow or hardened surface. Rather the seeds bring forth fruit "some an hundredfold, some sixty, some thirty."

What can be done to help the soil become fruitful?

II. RECOGNIZING THE ENEMY (Matthew 13:24-30)

A. The Kingdom of Heaven (v. 24)

24. Another parable put he forth unto them, saying, The kingdom of heaven is likened unto a man which sowed good seed in his field.

Again Jesus is making use of a parable to teach about the "kingdom of heaven." Just as a harvest comes with sowing seed, plowing ground, and a growing season, so does the kingdom of God. The gospel must be planted in the hearts of men; they must respond with acceptance and love. This begins life and starts the growth process toward the mature stages.

The man mentioned as the sower had planted good seed in his field. All he had to do then was to wait for the grain to grow and ripen for the harvest. When the harvest is ready, he would send his reapers to gather the grain.

B. An Evil Deed (vv. 25-26)

25. But while men slept, his enemy came and sowed tares among the wheat, and went his way.

26. But when the blade was sprung up, and brought forth fruit, then appeared the tares also.

The parable vividly illustrates both how an enemy can frustrate the natural harvest of grain and the development of the kingdom of heaven.

In verse 25 the enemy's strategy of operation is unfolded. He does his work while men sleep. Also, the enemy takes advantage of the labors of others. The hard labor of preparing the ground had already been done. All the enemy had to do was scatter the bad seed.

But the enemy's strategy also includes deception. This is evidenced by the use of "tares." The word *tares* is a translation of a Greek word meaning "darnel," a poisonous plant or spurious wheat.

The pictures in this parable would be clear and familiar to Palestinian farmers. Tares were one of the curses against which they had to labor.

In their early states the tares so closely resembled the wheat that it was impossible to distinguish the one from the other. When both had ripened, it was easy to distinguish them; but by that time the roots were so intertwined that the tares could not be removed without uprooting the wheat.

C. A Wise Decision (vv. 27-30)

27. So the servants of the house-holder came and said unto him, Sir, didst not thou sow good seed in thy field? from whence then hath it tares?

28. He said unto them, An enemy hath done this. The servants said unto him, Wilt thou then that we go and gather them up?

29. But he said, Nay; lest while ye gather up the tares, ye root up also the wheat with them.

30. Let both grow together until the harvest: and in the time of harvest I will say to the reapers, Gather ye together first the tares, and bind them in bundles to burn them: but gather the wheat into my barn.

From the characteristics of the tares, it is apparent that the growing was well under way when the servants detected an unusual amount of tares growing in the wheat. When the tares were noticed, the servants questioned the householder about the possible contamination of the seed that had been sown. The householder explained that he had sown only good seed and that an enemy had sown the bad seed.

Who do you think is charged with the responsibility of recognizing the works of the enemy? Does the enemy work in churches?

The servants appear to have been ready to go gather the tares but were cautioned by the householder to let them grow together till harvest. A. M. Hunter suggests the point as this: "The parable sounds like Jesus' reply to a critic— probably a Pharisee (the very name means 'separatist')—who had objected: "If the kingdom of God is really here, why has there not been a separating of sinners from saints in Israel?" (*Interpreting the Parables*).

At the harvest the tares would be gathered, bound in bundles and burned. The wheat would be gathered and stored in the barn. What makes for a good harvest is not the absence of tares, but the presence of rich, golden grain.

III. REAPING THE HARVEST (Matthew 13:36-43)

A. The Parable Explained (vv. 36-39)

(Matthew 13:36-39 is not included in the printed text.)

After some intervening parables and the dismissing of the multitudes, Jesus entered into a home—probably Peter's in Capernaum—perhaps for some rest and privacy. There the disciples requested an explanation of the parable of the tares. Again Jesus gave an allegorical interpretation as in the case of the parable of the sower.

1. The Sower

Jesus identified the sower of the good seed. The sower is Jesus himself, here called the "Son of man." Several things about the Kingdom are revealed with this statement. Christ is the householder—the owner of the field. He was responsible for beginning the Kingdom by sowing the good seed, for preparing the soil into which the good seed would fall and grow.

This parable reveals the method of how the kingdom of God grows. It does not come by military conquest, political revolution, or social change. It was begun and continues to grow because the truth of God is sown in the world. The truth of God's Word, when sown, produces more good seed which in turn is planted and produces more good seed. The more the seed is sown, the more the Kingdom grows.

2. The Field

Jesus followed His explanation of the sower with an identification of the field as the world. Here on earth is the field where the sowing and reaping takes place, where the contest is waged between the forces of evil and Jehovah, and where the enemy, bent on his vicious efforts to frustrate the redemptive plan, sows evil seed in the field.

3. The Good Seed

Jesus explained that the good seed are the children of the Kingdom. They are the redeemed who have responded in faith and obedience to the Word of God by the power of the Holy Spirit.

The children of the Kingdom follow Christ and are identified with Him. They live and grow in the same field as the wicked, but they are different and distinct from the tares. They are a part of the golden harvest of good seed, and each mature stalk has the potential of yielding abundantly.

As one grain of wheat has the power to make a stalk on which will grow many grains, so the Christian has the power and potential to produce a life which will multiply many times into other Christians for the great harvest.

How important is it for church leaders to encourage sound biblical evangelism programs?

---

4. The Tares

Jesus identified the tares as the children of the wicked one. They are the people whose fruit is produced from the seeds sown by the enemy. The children of the wicked one have refused to respond to the gospel of Christ but are rather influenced by Satan.

The tares live, grow, and produce their own kind of fruit— fruit which is worthless and poisonous. Their active cooperation with the forces of evil explains why the kingdom of Satan expands. The most serious tragedy about the tares is the fact that such lives are a complete waste in this world and they are doomed to final destruction.

5. The Enemy

Jesus makes it clear that the enemy is the devil. This evil one attempts to frustrate God's plan and is active in deceiving the human family. He uses every possible means not only to open new roads of attack on the children of the Kingdom, but also to assure the keeping of those who have sided with the forces of evil.

Jesus identified Satan as the enemy that sowed the tares— which frustrate the full harvest. As people respond to the evils of Satan, they become hardened to the mercy of God and spread their evil seed to aid in building the kingdom of evil.

6. The Harvest

Jesus explained that the harvest is "the end of the world." The word *world* used here is better translated "age." Consequently, He was speaking of the harvest at the end of the age. At that point there will be a final separation of the evil from the righteous. The tares will be separated from the wheat at harvest-time.

B. The Parable Applied(vv. 40-43)

(Matthew 13:40-43 is not included in the printed text.)

Jesus indicated that the harvest would take place at the end of the age, and the angels of God would be sent forth as reapers to gather the tares. Those tares are identified in verse 41 as "all things that offend, and them which do iniquity."

Those who have helped to further the growth of the kingdom of the devil and joined in the rebellion against the laws of God will be gathered, bound, and cast into "a furnace of fire: there shall be wailing and gnashing of teeth" (v. 42). Such is the description Jesus gives of the destiny of the wicked one.

In contrast to the end of the evil persons is the reward of the righteous. "Then shall the righteous shine forth as the sun in the kingdom of their Father" (v. 43). Human minds cannot conceive the happiness and eternal peace that awaits those who have cast their lot with the kingdom of God, but Jesus assures us such splendor awaits the righteous.

REVIEW QUESTIONS

1. What is your definition of the term "parable"?

2. Why did Jesus initiate the parable approach to His teaching?

3. What is the central idea expressed in the parable of the sower?

4. What is the central idea expressed in the parable of the tares?

5. Summarize the practical applications you have gained from this lesson.

GOLDEN TEXT HOMILY

"HE THAT RECEIVED SEED INTO THE GOOD GROUND IS HE THAT HEARETH THE WORD, AND UNDERSTANDETH IT; WHICH ALSO BEARETH FRUIT, AND BRINGETH FORTH, SOME AN HUNDREDFOLD, SOME SIXTY, SOME THIRTY" (Matthew 13:23).

Farmers invest heavily and work hard all year to be able to produce a crop and experience the rewards of reaping a harvest. Most farmers understand that there are three basic essentials to be able to harvest a crop: (1) prepared soil; (2) good seed; and (3) sufficient water. Jesus understood these principles very well and related them to the spiritual harvest.

The person who hears and understands the Word of God is like good soil that has been properly prepared and fertilized. Sometimes we plant seed in unprepared lines that will not produce the proper harvest. Other times we fail to sow the seed because we do not recognize the opportunity that is there.

In the pioneer days, my grandfather homesteaded in Saskatchewan, Canada. He and the other homesteaders had broken the virgin prairie soil in preparation to seed flax. It was very dry and most of the homesteaders questioned the wisdom of planting seed in dry soil where it would not germinate. The seed was costly and there was no money to buy more. Perhaps it would be better to wait until after it rained to sow the seed. Grandfather, who was not an experienced farmer, asked a neighbor who had more experience if it was advisable to sow or not. His neighbor told him that it was impossible to reap a harvest if you do not sow the seed. That made sense to Grandfather and he proceeded to plant the seed. Later on, the rains came, his crop grew, and he reaped a good harvest. Those who waited until after the rain to sow did not reap a crop as it was too late in the season and their crops froze before they were ripe. Grandfather prepared the soil, planted the seed, and reaped a harvest!

The exciting fact that Jesus was communicating is that if the seed, which is the Word of God, is sown in prepared lives there will be a harvest! Seed that produces 30 or 60 times is a good crop but that which produces a hundred times is a bumper crop that farmers only dream about. Jesus promised that kind of harvest for us if we will sow the Word in prepared lives. He that goeth forth and weepeth, bearing precious seed, shall doubtless come again with rejoicing, bringing his sheaves with him" (Psalm 126:6). Remember that it is God who gives the increase.—**Philip Siggelkow, Pastor, Surrey, Canada**

SENTENCE SERMONS

WHEREVER THE GOSPEL is received and obeyed, the kingdom of Christ is established.

—**Selected**

THE KINGDOM OF GOD does not exist because of your effort or mine. It exists because God reigns. Our part is to enter this Kingdom and bring our life under His sovereign will.

—**T. Z. Koo**

WHEREVER GOD RULES over the human heart as King, there is the kingdom of God established.

—**Paul W. Harrison**

SIN WILL KEEP you from the Word of God, but the Word of God will keep you from sin.

—**Dwight L. Moody**

EVANGELISTIC APPLICATION

CHRIST CALLS MEN TO FORSAKE THE KINGDOM OF SATAN AND BECOME CITIZENS OF HIS EVERLASTING KINGDOM.

It is a fact that God is always interested in our welfare and well-being. He never makes any requirement, allows any burden, or permits any sorrow that is not for our own best interest. On the other hand, the devil is bent on our destruction. Every act he motivates, every sin he encourages, and every circumstance he causes is totally and invariably to destroy our influence, to ruin our bodies, and eventually to destroy our souls.

From the time of his expulsion from heaven to the present time, the devil has spent every moment of his day to "get even" with God; and, since mankind is the crowning achievement of God's creation, Satan knows that every man he can turn from God pains the heart of the Creator. If we please God, we are the most benefited; if we please the devil, we are our own worst enemy.

ILLUMINATING THE LESSON

An irreligious farmer in one of our western states, who gloried in his irreligion, wrote a letter to a local newspaper, saying: "Sir, I have been trying an experiment with a field of mine. I plowed it on Sunday. I planted it on Sunday. I cultivated it on Sunday. I reaped it on Sunday. I hauled it into my barn on Sunday. And now, Mr. Editor, what is the result? I have more bushels to the acre in that field than any of my neighbors have had this October." He expected some applause from the editor, who did not, perhaps, himself profess to be a specially religious man. But underneath the letter the editor published a line or two of comment as follows: "God does not always settle His accounts in October." —**The Expositor**

DAILY BIBLE READINGS

M. The Everlasting Kingdom. Daniel 2:36-44

T. Christ's Kingdom. Isaiah 9:6, 7

W. The True King. John 18:33-37

T. The Kingdom Within. Luke 17:20, 21

F. Unshakable Kingdom. Hebrews 12:18-29

S. The Kingdom to Come. Revelation 11:15-19

Jesus, the Son of God

Study Text: Matthew 16:13-27
Supplemental References: Psalm 2:1-12; Isaiah 11:1-5; Matthew 18:18-20; John 1:11-14; 20:24-31
Time: Perhaps in autumn, A.D. 29
Place: Caesarea Philippi in northern Palestine
Golden Text: "Simon Peter answered and said, Thou art the Christ, the Son of the living God" (Matthew 16:16).
Central Truth: God reveals Himself to men through Jesus Christ.
Evangelistic Emphasis: Salvation comes through repentance and faith in Christ as Lord.

Printed Text

Matthew 16:13. When Jesus came into the coasts of Caesarea Philippi, he asked his disciples, saying, Whom do men say that I the Son of man am?

14. And they said, Some say that thou art John the Baptist: some, Elias; and others, Jeremias, or one of the prophets.

15. He saith unto them, But whom say ye that I am?

16. And Simon Peter answered and said, Thou art the Christ, the Son of the living God.

17. And Jesus answered and said unto him, Blessed art thou, Simon Barjona: for flesh and blood hath not revealed it unto thee, but my Father which is in heaven.

18. And I say also unto thee, That thou art Peter, and upon this rock I will build my church; and the gates of hell shall not prevail against it.

19. And I will give unto thee the keys of the kingdom of heaven: and whatsoever thou shalt bind on earth shall be bound in heaven: and whatsoever thou shalt loose on earth shall be loosed in heaven.

20. Then charged he his disciples that they should tell no man that he was Jesus the Christ.

21. From that time forth began Jesus to shew unto his disciples, how that he must go unto Jerusalem, and suffer many things of the elders and chief priests and scribes, and be killed, and be raised again the third day.

22. Then Peter took him, and began to rebuke him, saying, Be it far from thee, Lord: this shall not be unto thee.

23. But he turned, and said unto Peter, Get thee behind me, Satan: thou art an offence unto me: for thou savourest not the things that be of God, but those that be of men.

24. Then said Jesus unto his disciples, If any man will come after me, let him deny himself, and take up his cross, and follow me.

25. For whosoever will save his life shall lose it: and whosoever will lose his life for my sake shall find it.

26. For what is a man profited, if he shall gain the whole world, and lose his own soul? or what shall a man give in exchange for his soul?

27. For the Son of man shall come in the glory of his Father with his angels; and then he shall reward every man according to his works.

DICTIONARY

Caesarea Philippi (sez-ah-REE-ah PHIL-ah-pie)—Matthew 16:13—A city in northern Palestine was rebuilt by Herod-Philip, who called it by his own name to distinguish it from Caesarea Stratonis, the seat of the Roman government on the Mediterranean coast. The Greek name for Caesarea Philippi was Paneas, which survives in the present name of Baniyas. It was the most northerly point reached by our Lord.

Elias (ee-LYE-us)—Matthew 16:14—The Old English translation of the Greek form of the word **Elijah**

Jeremias (jer-eh-MY-us)—Mat-thew 16:14—The Old English translation of the Greek form of the word **Jeremiah**

Bar-jona (bar-JON-ah)—Matthew 16: 17—That is, son of Jonah—**bar** is Aramaic for "son." The Hebrew word **Jonah** means "dove."

LESSON OUTLINE

I. DIVINE REVELATION
   A. Important Question
   B. Christ, the Son of God
   C. The Church
II. HUMAN MISUNDERSTANDING
   A. Suffering Foretold
   B. Heartfelt Protest
   C. Divine Rebuke
III. CHALLENGED TO FOLLOW
   A. A Cross to Bear
   B. A Life to Give
   C. A Reward to Gain

LESSON EXPOSITION

INTRODUCTION

In several previous lessons we observed the reactions of various people to the ministry of Jesus. On the one hand, we have seen an increasing number of common people rising to different levels of faith and understanding as they accepted and believed in Christ. These heard the Lord gladly and rejoiced in His blessings.

On the other hand, we have seen the religious leaders—the scribes, the Pharisees and the Sadducees—reacting to the person and ministry of Jesus with growing hostility and rejection. Merrill Tenney in his book, *John, the Gospel of Belief,* describes this development in the

following terms. First, there seemed to be a period of "consideration," when the religious leaders were taking a rather casual look at Christ. Next, there was a period of "controversy," when they were constantly testing Jesus with questions concerning points of the Law. We have discussed some of those controversies and listed many others. Then, there was a period of genuine "conflict," where they tried to find reasons to put Christ to death. Finally, came the "crisis" of Calvary and the "consummation."

This outline by Tenney clearly presents the developing hostilities of the religious leaders to the ministry of Christ. Our lesson today comes at a very important turning point in that outline. "Controversy" is changing to open, bitter "conflict." Most New Testament scholars agree that the confession at Caesarea Philippi marked a decisive turning point in the ministry of Jesus. As we study this lesson, we will try to understand why this is true.

Also, in this lesson we will see that a divine revelation from God is necessary for us to understand who Jesus Christ really is. Once we have this enlightenment, we are to grow in our relationship with Christ until we can accept the responsibilities He places upon His church. Through consecration and commitment we are to follow Him, doing His will, until He comes to reward us.

I. DIVINE REVELATION (Matthew 16:13-20)

The time had come when Jesus needed to determine the depth of understanding in His disciples and in people in general. This was not necessary for His own benefit, but for the sake of the disciples. It is clear that at this point, the disciples were filled with misunderstandings about the true nature and purpose of the mission of Jesus. Therefore, the Lord began a new stage in their training by asking them the most important question in the world.

A. Important Question (vv. 13-15)

13. When Jesus came into the coasts of Caesarea Philippi, he asked his disciples, saying, Whom do men say that I the Son of man am?

14. And they said, Some say that thou art John the Baptist: some, Elias; and others, Jeremias, or one of the prophets.

15. He saith unto them, But whom say ye that I am?

Among all the people who had seen and heard Jesus, there had developed many different opinions about Him. Evidently, Jesus was the topic of conversation everywhere—among young and old, rich and poor, among the religious and the nonreligious. Consequently, there was much speculation as to His identity and His ministry. The time had come when Jesus must make certain that His disciples understood His true identity and mission. Thus, in the region of Caesarea Philippi He began to question His disciples.

First, He asked, "Whom do men say that I the Son of man am?" Their answers revealed the many different opinions concerning Christ. Everyone seemed to think that He was a great prophet. Some said that He was Elijah; others thought Him to be Jeremiah. A few, like Herod, thought that He was John the Baptist, risen from the dead. Evidently, the general public, at this point, saw Jesus in a prophetic role only, and not as the Messiah.

Turning from the opinions of others,

Jesus next pinpointed His question to the disciples: "But whom say ye that I am?" Here was the most important question the disciples would ever face. They had been with Jesus for a long time—hearing His teachings, seeing His miraculous works, hearing some of His claims. The testing time had come to determine their understanding, their faith, and their commitment.

Is the purpose and mission of Jesus still a problem in the world? Among Christians?

B. Christ, the Son of God (vv. 16, 17)

16. And Simon Peter answered and said, Thou art the Christ, the Son of the living God.

17. And Jesus answered and said unto him, Blessed art thou, Simon Bar-jona: for flesh and blood hath not revealed it unto thee, but my Father which is in heaven.

In answer to the question of Jesus, Peter answered, "Thou art the Christ, the Son of the living God." This confession of Peter was very important because it affirmed two great truths. First, Peter referred to Jesus as the "Christ." Being a Hebrew, this meant that Peter recognized Jesus as the Messiah, the Anointed of God, the One who would fulfill all the promises of the Hebrew prophets. Throughout the Old Testament the inspired writers had pointed toward the age when the Messiah would come, emerging from the lineage of David, and establish a kingdom on the earth. He would overthrow the enemies of the Jews and exalt the people of God to a place of glory and power. This is what Peter saw in Jesus when he said, "Thou art the Christ."

Second, Peter's confession reveals that he saw in Jesus more than the Hebrew Messiah or Davidic King; he saw Him also as "the Son of the living God." This meant that Peter saw Jesus as more than a Jew, or as a member of the human race; but he recognized Him as having come from God on high.

In response to this confession of Peter, Jesus spoke with blessing and authority. He said, "Blessed art thou, Simon Barjona." This beatitude pronounced upon Peter meant that Christ recognized what had happened to the Apostle. He had received a revelation concerning the identity of the Lord. Jesus knew whose son Peter was, and He was saying that this revelation did not come from any natural source; in other words, it was not from his own "flesh and blood" father. Instead, Jesus explained that Peter's understanding came as divine enlightenment from the heavenly Father.

What does it mean in terms of conviction and consecration to confess Jesus as Christ, the Son of God?

C. The Church (vv. 18-20)

18. And I say also unto thee, That thou art Peter, and upon this rock I will build my church; and the gates of hell shall not prevail against it.

19. And I will give unto thee the keys of the kingdom of heaven: and whatsoever thou shalt bind on earth shall be bound in heaven: and whatsoever thou shalt loose on earth shall be loosed in heaven.

20. Then charged he his disciples that they should tell no man that he was Jesus the Christ.

Here is one of the most controversial passages in the entire Bible among the many branches of Christianity. The point in question has to do with Peter's relationship to the church and what Jesus meant when He said, "Upon this rock I will build my church." Several observations should be made.

First of all we need to keep in mind that Jesus gave to Simon the name of *Peter,* which is the Greek word for "rock." It corresponds to the Aramaic word *Cephas,* used by Jesus in John 1:42, where He said, "Thou art Simon the son of Jona: thou shalt be called Cephas, which is by interpretation, A stone" (or *Petros*). We may assume that Jesus gave Simon this nickname as a symbol of what

Simon was to become. It is quite evident that Peter was not a rocklike individual at that time.

Thus Jesus said, "Thou art Peter [*Petros*], and upon this rock [*Petra*] I will build my church." The use of the two forms of the word is significant. The first form *Petros* is masculine and therefore proper when applied to a man. The second form *Petra* is feminine and is proper when applied to a great rock as a whole and not just a fragment or stone.

All scholars do not agree on the meaning of "this rock." Some say that it means Peter himself; others say the faith of Peter; still others say the confession of Peter; and many others say "this rock" refers to Christ himself. Although Peter and all the apostles are referred to as being a part of the foundation of the church, it is clear that Jesus Christ is "the chief corner stone" (Ephesians 2:20). This leads to the conclusion that the rock on which the church is built can be none other than Christ our Lord. Frank Stagg in the Broadman Bible Commentary expresses this idea clearly: "There could be a church without Peter, none without Christ. Peter is neither the head nor foundation of the church. Jesus founded it; it stands or falls with Him; and He is yet its living Lord and head."

How can we answer the Roman Catholic Church for the preeminence of Peter in light of verse 19?

This brings us to the Lord's great declaration of authority and power: "I will build my church; and the gates of hell shall not prevail against it."

With this statement Christ introduced a new term, "church" (*ecclesia*), into His teaching. The disciples had been looking for an earthly kingdom with Christ as king. They were told that Christ was the founder and the foundation of the church that He would build. *Ecclesia* means "the called-out assembly" or people of God. It can refer to the church in a universal sense or as a local assembly. Therefore, Jesus was preparing His disciples to understand the nature and mission of the church, not for a literal, earthly, political kingdom.

Jesus also declared that the "gates of hell" (Hades) would not overcome or prevail against the church. This Greek word *Hades* like the Old Testament Hebrew word *sheol* means "the realm of the dead." It does not mean the same as *Gehenna,* "the place of torment." Jesus was saying that the powers of death could not overthrow or stop the advance of the church. In a few moments Jesus would announce His own sufferings and death. Some of His followers would soon give their lives for the gospel. Despite this, Jesus was saying that His church would survive and fulfill its mission in the world.

Following that declaration of great power and purpose, Jesus laid upon Peter and all the apostles a very solemn responsibility (compare Matthew 18:18); they were to use "the keys of the kingdom of heaven." This expression symbolizes the spiritual authority placed upon the apostles in matters of church teachings and discipline. Men who had been with Jesus and who would be empowered by the Holy Spirit would be able to determine God's will in matters of ethical conduct and religious practice. It would be their responsibility as leaders in the church to interpret the Scriptures, and to pass on to other Christians what was "binding" in the sight of God. *Binding* and *loosing,* as used by Jesus, were terms used by the rabbis when setting forth practices which could be permitted or forbidden. Therefore, the Lord was beginning to prepare His apostles to be leaders of authority in the church. Their responsibility would be to answer to God for the souls placed under their care.

As Jesus ended this solemn charge to His disciples, He went a step further in His explanation. From then on, He would work with them somewhat in secret, preparing them for His death and eventual departure from the earth. They were not to publicize the fact that Jesus was the Messiah. If they openly proclaimed Him Messiah, political consequences could develop which would cut short the Master's work with them.

II. HUMAN MISUNDERSTANDING (Matthew 16:21-23)

As alluded to earlier in the lesson, Jesus had reached a turning point in His approach to teaching and preparing the disciples for the final dastardly deeds of the religious leaders. His death was approaching and the need to spend more time in preparing the disciples to carry on the ministry was essential. In particular, He wanted them to fully understand His purpose and mission as well as the kind of Messiah He was to be.

A. Suffering Foretold (v. 21)

21. From that time forth began Jesus to shew unto his disciples, how that he must go unto Jerusalem, and suffer many things of the elders and chief priests and scribes, and be killed, and be raised again the third day.

One great task had been accomplished; the disciples had been brought to the full realization of the divine person of Jesus as Peter voiced this conviction for the twelve in his confession (v. 16). It remained yet for Jesus to explain to His disciples His destiny. He indicated He would go to Jerusalem as the great religious leader but He would be rejected by the religious leaders of the Jews and suffer many things at their hands. He would enter Jerusalem as a king; yet, He would be mocked and scoffed and treated as a political revolutionist. He would enter Jerusalem having given life to others, only to yield to death Himself. Following the words, "I am the way, the truth, and the life," He would be dead in 24 hours.

Immediately following the confession of Peter—this great revelation of God that Jesus was the Christ, the Son of the living God—Jesus had to explain that He was to take upon Himself the form of a servant, humble Himself, and become obedient unto death, even the death of the Cross. Suffering and death would not be all; He would "be raised again the third day."

B. Heartfelt Protest (v. 22)

22. Then Peter took him, and began to rebuke him, saying, Be it far from thee, Lord: this shall not be unto thee.

Although Peter had so clearly and boldly confessed Christ and had been commended for the expression, he now exposed his lack of understanding about Christ's saving mission.

With the light of divine revelation enlightening his mind— visions of the glory of the kingdom of God with Jesus as the Messiah—it was extremely difficult for the Apostle Peter to comprehend and accept the words he heard Jesus say. Christ was to be Lord and King soon. The Romans would be driven out and the kingdom of Israel reestablished. The disciples were to ascend in power with Christ and share in His glorious reign. These must have been the kind of thoughts burning in the mind of Simon Peter. The ideas of shame, reproach, weakness, suffering, and death, he just could not accept.

Therefore, he began to rebuke Christ: "Lord: this shall not be unto thee." Peter thought surely there was a way to have power without being weak; a way to reign without being humble; a way to glory without sufferings; a way to have wonderful life without death. The idea of a suffering Messiah was too much for him.

C. Divine Rebuke (v. 23)

23. But he turned, and said unto Peter, Get thee behind me, Satan: thou art an offence unto me: for thou savourest not the things that be of God, but those that be of men.

The response of Christ to Peter was prompt and stern. According to Christ's reproof, Peter the apostle had taken the place of the tempter, Satan the adversary of God and His Son. Of course, it is not certain that Jesus meant Peter was actually being used as Satan's instrument. The word *Satan* means "adversary," one opposed to what is being said or done. Jesus may have used the term in its general sense, meaning that Peter was now opposing God's design in redemption and thus contradicting Jesus' announcement of its accomplishment.

It is, however, not impossible that Peter may have been used by Satan at the moment. In any case, Peter became a

temporary stumbling block to Christ in His moving toward His redeeming death and triumphant resurrection. Peter had fallen a long way— he who had been the recipient of a divine revelation concerning Christ had now fallen to the level of mere human reasoning. For his mind now was not on the things of God, but on the things of men.

Some of the most formidable instruments of temptation are well-meaning friends who care more for our comfort than for our character and spiritual progress.

In what way may a Christian friend become a hindrance to God's plan for our Christian life and service?

III. CHALLENGED TO FOLLOW (Matthew 16:24-27)

Christ realized that the disciples did not fully understand His meaning when He rebuked Peter. Consequently, He explained further that there was a price to pay to share in the glory of God. He indicated by His own submissiveness that suffering for God is not to be ruled out, and He outlined important steps in the life of consecration.

A. A Cross to Bear (v. 24)

24. Then said Jesus unto his disciples, If any man will come after me, let him deny himself, and take up his cross, and follow me.

Jesus made it clear that consecration begins with self-denial. Christians must realize that this means saying *no* to our own selfish will and *yes* to the will of God. Strangely enough, it is at the point where the will of God cuts across our own will that our cross is formed. In plain, simple language, Jesus presented the conditions by which we may follow after Him. We must deny ourselves and take up our own cross. He knew that it would be impossible for Him to give guidance to any disciple who would refuse to obey Him. There must be obedience and commitment to the will of God.

Discuss the matter of crossbearing. What does it mean to you as a Christian?

B. A Life to Give (vv. 25, 26)

25. For whosoever will save his life shall lose it: and whosoever will lose his life for my sake shall find it.

26. For what is a man profited, if he shall gain the whole world, and lose his own soul? or what shall a man give in exchange for his soul?

Verse 25 presents a mysterious paradox which sets forth the terms of true consecration. It is a mind-set the world cannot understand.

In order for a person to truly find his life, he must be willing to lose it in the will of God. That is, the very things we value the most—peace of mind, fulfillment in our vocation, a sense of achievement in our work, the richness of our family and human relationships—are found when our will is surrendered to God's will. To hold on selfishly to our own desires, refusing to allow God to bring out the best in us will only lead to the loss of all those things we value and cherish most. This is God's way of helping us find ourselves.

The parable of the prodigal son is a very good illustration of this principle. All the things he really wanted when he left home—friends, love, joy, happiness, good clothes, family, and satisfying employment—he found only when he returned to his father's house. He left saying, "Give me"; he returned saying, "Make me." He found his life.

Verse 26 explains the apparent paradox concerning loss and gain in the previous verse. It requires an understanding of spiritual values. The whole world, with all its wealth and power, can never compensate for the eternal loss of one's soul. Nothing in this world—not man himself—can pay the ransom for a man's soul.

C. A Reward to Gain (v. 27)

27. For the Son of man shall come in the glory of his Father with his angels; and then he shall reward every man according to his works.

Consecration and devotion to the Lord include as their incentive the hope of reward for service rendered. This will be realized at the second coming of Christ. In verse 28, which is beyond the basic text of this lesson, Christ reassures His disciples of His coming to inaugurate His kingdom, and that some of them would live to see a foregleam of that glorious kingdom in the Transfiguration, and then Christ's resurrection, and the Pentecostal affusion.

REVIEW QUESTIONS

1. What answer did the disciples give Jesus in response to His question: "Whom do men say that I the Son of man am?"

2. What great confession did Peter make concerning the identity of Jesus?

3. What did Jesus mean by the expression "Thou art Peter, and upon this rock I will build my church"?

4. What authority did Christ indicate He would give to Peter concerning the kingdom of heaven?

5. What request concerning His identity did Jesus make of the disciples in verse 20?

GOLDEN TEXT HOMILY

"SIMON PETER ANSWERED AND SAID, THOU ART THE CHRIST, THE SON OF THE LIVING GOD" (Matthew 16:16).

Man can receive no greater revelation than the fact that Jesus Christ is our salvation. This comes to us when we acknowledge the invitation of the Spirit to receive Jesus as our Savior. Jesus said to Peter, "Flesh and blood hath not revealed it unto thee, but my Father which is in heaven" (Matthew 16:17). Paul also stated in 1 Corinthians chapter 2 that God reveals the mysteries of promise by His Spirit. We must determine that Jesus is Christ, our Messiah, Savior, and eternal Lord. This is accomplished only by our submission to the lordship of Christ and a willing heart to do the will of Christ in our lives. The real beauty of Peter's testimony is the positive declaration of knowledge, "Thou art the Christ, the Son of the living God."

The question now comes to us, "Whom do you say Christ is?" When we have fully settled in our minds and hearts that He is Christ, Christian living in word and deed will be a natural response. The question of eternal life will be settled and our temptations from the enemy will be easily overcome. Trials and temptations become difficult when we question who Jesus is. Even though Peter was a disciple and had occasion to know Jesus, it was the Father who revealed the truth to him. By reading God's Word, praying, and worshiping regularly in God's house, you will receive the great revelation that Jesus is the Savior, the Son of the living God.—**Marion H. Starr, Pastor, Portland Oregon**

SENTENCE SERMONS

GOD REVEALS HIMSELF to men through Jesus Christ.

—Selected

ANYTHING THAT one imagines of God apart from Christ is only useless thinking and vain idolatry.

—Martin Luther

CHRIST IS NOT valued at all—unless He is valued above all.

—Augustine

NO QUESTION is ever settled until it is settled right.

—Ella Wheeler Wilcox

CHRIST DIED for us. Now He, and we, live for others.

—Malcolm Cronk

EVANGELISTIC APPLICATION

SALVATION COMES THROUGH REPENTANCE AND FAITH IN CHRIST AS LORD.

Dr. Donald Grey Barnhouse says that many years ago he rode the streetcar home from one of the suburbs of Los Angeles late at night. There were only half a dozen passengers in the car—all men—when a young man got on the car at an intermediate stop. The new passenger paid his fare, lifted his hands and

cried out, "I'm engaged to be married. My girl just said, 'Yes.' " Everyone laughed; there was joshing and wisecracks. Love from his heart had found a response and he could not keep still about it.

Is it possible for an interchange of love between the Lord God and His creature without a great desire to acknowledge it? Is it possible to realize that Christ is the Son of God without sharing that glorious truth with others? The most beautiful discovery that the soul can make is that Jesus lives and not only that He lives but also that He lives within. What peace and joy that knowledge brings to the heart! Have you experienced that happiness? Have you accepted and confessed Christ as the Son of God?

—Selected

ILLUMINATING THE LESSON

Victorinus, a great man at Rome, who had many rich heathen friends and relatives, was converted to the Christian religion. He visited a friend of his and told him secretly that he, too, was a Christian. "I will not believe thee to be a Christian," said the other, "until I see thee openly profess it in the church."

"What," said Victorinus, "do the church walls make a Christian?" But directly the answer came to his own heart. "Whosoever shall be ashamed of Me and My words, of him also shall the Son of Man be ashamed when He cometh in the glory of His Father with the holy angels."
—Augustine's "Confessions."

DAILY BIBLE READINGS

M. God's Anointed Son. Psalm 2:1-12
T. Accepting His Authority. Isaiah 1:1-5
W. Understanding His Mission. John 1: 11-14
T. Trusting His Knowledge. Colossians 2:1-3
F. Recognizing His Power. Matthew 28: 16-20
S. Confessing His Deity. John 20:24-31

Jesus Is Coming

Study Text: Matthew 24:1-51
Supplemental References: Matthew 25:31-34; 1 Thessalonians 4:13-18; 5:1-11; 2 Peter 3:10-15
Time: April A.D. 30
Place: The Mount of Olives, the great hill immediately east of Jerusalem.
Golden Text: "Watch therefore: for ye know not what hour your Lord doth come" (Matthew 24:42).
Central Truth: All should take heed to Christ's warning and prepare for His soon return.
Evangelistic Emphasis: All should take heed to Christ's warning and prepare for His soon return.

Printed Text

Matthew 24:35. Heaven and earth shall pass away, but my words shall not pass away.

36. But of that day and hour knoweth no man, no, not the angels of heaven, but my Father only.

37. But as the days of Noe were, so shall also the coming of the Son of man be.

38. For as in the days that were before the flood they were eating and drinking, marrying and giving in marriage, until the day that Noe entered into the ark,

39. And knew not until the flood came, and took them all away; so shall also the coming of the Son of man be.

40. Then shall two be in the field; the one shall be taken, and the other left.

41. Two women shall be grinding at the mill; the one shall be taken, and the other left.

42. Watch therefore: for ye know not what hour your Lord doth come.

43. But know this, that if the goodman of the house had known in what watch the thief would come, he would have watched, and would not have suffered his house to be broken up.

44. Therefore be ye also ready: for in such an hour as ye think not the Son of man cometh.

45. Who then is a faithful and wise servant, whom his lord hath made ruler over his household, to give them meat in due season?

46. Blessed is that servant, whom his lord when he cometh shall find so doing.

47. Verily I say unto you, That he shall make him ruler over all his goods.

48. But and if that evil servant shall say in his heart, My lord delayeth his coming;

49. And shall begin to smite his fellowservants, and to eat and drink with the drunken;

50. The lord of that servant shall come in a day when he looketh not for him, and in an hour that he is not aware of,

51. And shall cut him asunder, and appoint him his portion with the hypocrites: there shall be weeping and gnashing of teeth.

LESSON OUTLINE

I. TIME OF HIS COMING
  A. The Discernment of Signs
  B. The Fulfillment of Christ's Words
  C. The Unknown Future
II. NATURE OF HIS COMING
  A. The Example of Noah's Day
  B. The Example of Separation
III. BE READY FOR HIS COMING
  A. The Exhortation to Watchfulness
  B. The Reward of Faithful Stewardship
  C. The Judgment of Forfeited Stewardship

LESSON EXPOSITION

INTRODUCTION

The prophetic discourse of today's study was uttered in response to the disciples' threefold question (Matthew 24:3). Their question was evidently prompted by Christ's prediction concerning the Temple and His second coming (23:37-24:2). In His discourse, Christ first describes the course of events during the time of His absence (vv. 4-14); second, the destruction of Jerusalem (Luke 21:20-24); third, the Great Tribulation (Matthew 15-28); and fourth, His coming in glory (vv. 29-31).

It is to be expected that the doctrine of the Second Coming should affect the lives of those who believe in the Lord Jesus. A doctrine of this nature may quite easily become a ridiculous thing and lead to ridiculous practices, if it is not properly safeguarded by authoritative instructions. The applications which Christ makes are designed to prevent such dangers. Therefore, Christ takes up such matters as the believer's patience, stewardship, and expectancy. He also warns against the excessiveness of some practices which may arise.

I. TIME OF HIS COMING (Matthew 24:32-36)

A. The Discernment of Signs (vv. 32, 33)

(Matthew 24:32, 33 is not included in the printed text.)

Our Lord, the master Teacher, uses here a picture common to the experience of His hearers to illustrate the truth He desires to communicate to them. The fig tree's indication of approaching spring was considered highly dependable and is used here as a symbol of all the signs by which the progression of time toward the return of Christ may be judged. Consequently, this parable should be interpreted in relation to all the prophecies that Christ had just given.

By the use of this figure in relation to approaching spring and its application to His own second coming, Christ is teaching an important lesson. The message which He gives to believers here is that they should be as alert to spiritual signs as the natural man is to the signs of spring. By such attentiveness to signs of Christ's return the believer remains ever vigilant. It is clear that this is Christ's intention by His warning, "Know that it is near, even at the doors" (v. 33). The sense of immediacy is conveyed and is essential to every generation of Christians.

Do you feel there is a de-emphasis on the coming of Christ in modern times? Discuss the need for an emphasis on the doctrine.

B. The Fulfillment of Christ's Words (vv. 34, 35)

34. Verily I say unto you, This generation shall not pass, till all these things be fulfilled.

35. Heaven and earth shall pass away, but my words shall not pass away.

Verse 34 is variously understood by Bible scholars. The difficulty hinges on the interpretation of the word *generation*. Some understand this to mean "race, nation, kind, family, breed"; hence they interpret this to mean the Jewish race. Others believe the word refers to the people to whom Jesus was speaking. Still others see it to mean the generation that will be living at the end of the age when Christ will return.

Christ's statement that the generation in which He lived would not pass away till all these things were fulfilled needs some interpretation if we are to understand it.

If He referred to a generation in the usual sense, then His prediction here is applicable primarily to the destruction of Jerusalem. If the term is used in the sense of an age, then it is applicable directly to the signs of the times since Christ's First Advent and until His Second Advent. Probably the correct interpretation is to apply this scripture first to the destruction of Jerusalem. The generation to which Christ spoke did see this event occur. In the broader sense, however, the destruction of Jerusalem was a prophetical type of the events leading up to the Second Advent of Christ. By interpreting this development as a type and prophecy, the lesson is applicable to the second coming of Christ.

Of special assurance and security in these statements of Christ is the authority of the divine Word. Christ is by this statement claiming to speak the divine Word because He contrasts His Word with all things temporal. When He says that heaven and earth will pass away, He refers to the temporal, physical universe. He is not referring to heaven as the dwelling place of God, because this concept of heaven does not pass away. The physical universe is by nature decaying, changing and is doomed for destruction. The Word of God issues from an eternal God and is not at all subject to time and its changes. It is by its nature permanent. Christ, by making this claim of His Word, claims to speak the Word of God.

C. The Unknown Future (v. 36)

36. But of that day and hour knoweth no man, no, not the angels of heaven, but my Father only.

By directly pointing to "that day and hour" Christ shows that He makes specific reference to the time of His return. The statement is emphatic and it indicates that this area of knowledge is reserved from the reasoning and speculation of the creature. All creatures are excluded, specifically angels and men. This exclusion shows the futility of speculation and it also indicates that speculation in this area is spiritually offensive.

It should be pointed out that even broad speculation (such as attempts to speculate concerning the century in which Christ will return) is contrary to this instruction. According to Mark 13:32 knowledge is reserved even from the authority of the Son Himself. The intention is not to make Christ less than God, but to show that Christ as the messenger of God does not hold the authority of this decree. This decree is appropriate only to the work of the Father.

It is clear that the attempt to set dates is damaging to the spirituality of the church. It is a presumptuous thing for men to pry into knowledge that is specifically reserved to God. Speculations lead to vanity and away from the centrality of Christ. If this knowledge were available, it would have a damaging effect; for whenever men attempt to make speculations, they do damage to the vigilance of the church.

II. NATURE OF HIS COMING (Matthew 24:37-41)

A. The Example of Noah's Day (vv. 37-39)

37. But as the days of Noe were, so shall also the coming of the Son of man be.

38. For as in the days that were before the flood they were eating and drinking, marrying and giving in marriage, until the day that Noe entered into the ark,

39. And knew not until the flood came, and took them all away; so shall also the coming of the Son of man be.

This passage of Scripture shows that the period preceding the Flood was a period of self-centeredness, and self-indulgence for mankind. The activities that are listed here are not in themselves illegitimate activities. However, a study of the Genesis account of the days preceding the Flood indicates that it was a time of excess to the point of licentiousness, and a time of drunkenness. This was the time in which mankind was completely preoccupied with his own affairs. It was also a time in which individuals were completely preoccupied with their own satisfactions and self-indulgences.

Because of man's preoccupation with himself and with the pursuit of pleasure, he was taken by surprise in the Flood. Noah had been a faithful minister of God and had preached the warnings of divine wrath. The people had not heard because of their self-centeredness. They had no idea of the nature of the judgment that was to come or of its imminence.

Discuss some of the parallels between Noah's day and the days preceding the coming of Christ.

It is not so much the conduct of the people that the Lord has in mind in Matthew 24:39 but rather the suddenness of His return. "For yourselves know perfectly that the day of the Lord so cometh as a thief in the night. For when they shall say, Peace and safety; then sudden destruction cometh upon them, as travail upon a woman with child; and they shall not escape" (1 Thessalonians 5:2, 3).

B. The Example of Separation (vv. 40, 41)

40. Then shall two be in the field; the one shall be taken, and the other left.

41. Two women shall be grinding at the mill; the one shall be taken, and the other left.

The first aspect of Christ's return is the Rapture of the church. The word *Rapture* does not occur in the Scriptures; however, the truth expressed by this word is clearly a doctrine of the Bible. The word *Rapture* comes from a Latin word meaning, "to seize, to snatch," and it refers to removal from one place to another by forcible means. According to 1 Thessalonians 4:16, 17, those that shall be taken shall be "caught up together

with them [the resurrected dead in Christ] in the clouds, to meet the Lord in the air. "And so shall they "ever be with the Lord."

As the Lord first delivered Noah before He sent the flood; so likewise He shall catch up into the heavens those that "love" and wait for His "appearing" (2 Timothy 4:8).

This act of God—the taking away of the one group, while leaving behind another—expresses approval upon the one and disapproval and judgment upon the other. The separation of these people from one another is to be expected as characteristic of the coming of Christ. This is one of the identifying points of His return.

It is clear from this passage of Scripture that this separation will be sudden ("in the twinkling of an eye," 1 Corinthians 15:52), unexpected, and physical. It is expected in the sense that neither the believer nor the unbeliever could predict the time of its occurrence. The physical character of the bodily resurrection from the fact that Christ describes here is a physical situation in which one of a pair is suddenly snatched away.

III. BE READY FOR HIS COMING (Matthew 24:42-44)

A. The Exhortation to Watchfulness (vv. 42-51)

42. Watch therefore: for ye know not what hour your Lord doth come.

43. But know this, that if the goodman of the house had known in what watch the thief would come, he would have watched, and would not have suffered his house to be broken up.

44. Therefore be ye also ready: for in such an hour as ye think not the Son of man cometh.

The exhortation to watch is a strong one. It means to be alert and to watch with meticulous care. This watchfulness requires attention to details.

The warning "for ye know not what hour your Lord doth come" carries the meaning "in what sort of an hour." The watchman cannot afford to make a judgment concerning the "likely hours" or "unlikely hours" of danger. He must assume that every hour is an hour of danger. The attempt to make this decision by human ingenuity in relation to the coming of Christ is to apply human wisdom to a divinely determined decree.

What, in your opinion, does it mean to "watch" for the return of Christ?

Christ illustrated the futility of man's attempt to discern the times of watchfulness by the parable of the goodman of the house. The steward of this house was responsible that it and its treasures be kept safely. Continual watching was the only approach to safety because the thief would attempt to figure out the times of vulnerability.

B. The Reward of Faithful Stewardship (vv. 45-47)

45. Who then is a faithful and wise servant, whom his lord hath made ruler over his household, to give them meat in due season?

46. Blessed is that servant, whom his lord when he cometh shall find so doing.

47. Verily I say unto you, That he shall make him ruler over all his goods.

The steward in this illustration is responsible to run the household and to see that all its responsibilities are met. Both the owner and all the dependents of the household are dependent upon the steward and upon the rendering of his services. This position is one of great trust and it demands faithfulness—faithfulness in the absence of the owner. This, the very time of the steward's greatest temptation, is no time for him to be slack. The demand of faithfulness increases with the extension of the owner's absence. In this manner Christ is illustrating to the believers the pattern of responsibility and of temptation which they will face in His physical absence.

The servant who is faithful under these trying circumstances is blessed because of his faithfulness. He has the happiness of the approval of his master and the consequent reward. The reward takes the form of increasing the trust given to

this servant because of his faithfulness to the trust. The final result is an appointment over all the master's property.

The main application of this parable is the spiritual principle of faithfulness in adversity and in spite of the extended absence of our Lord.

C. The Judgment of Forfeited Stewardship (vv. 48-51)

48. But and if that evil servant shall say in his heart, My lord delayeth his coming;

49. And shall begin to smite his fellowservants, and to eat and drink with the drunken;

50. The lord of that servant shall come in a day when he looketh not for him, and in an hour that he is not aware of,

51. And shall cut him asunder, and appoint him his portion with the hypocrites: there shall be weeping and gnashing of teeth.

In referring to the evil servant, Christ uses most emphatic words in order to show the heinousness of presumptuousness in stewardship. The decision of the evil servant that the lord of the house delayed his coming, assumed that he was away at a great distance. He further assumed that the distance was too great to bring about any immediate accounting of his stewardship. This assumption also ignored the master's promise to return.

Having made this presumptuous decision, the evil servant began to use the estate in a way contrary to the wishes of the owner. He began a program of abuse of his fellow servants and of squandering the wealth of the household. Thus the servant revealed his wasteful and sadistic character. It is clear that he thought he could correct his error at a time of his own choosing. However, he was caught at a time that he could not.

The judgment of this servant is described in harsh tones. The expression "cut him sunder" means literally to cut him in two. However, the language here doubtlessly intends to convey the severity probably of a fierce lashing and then a rejecting of this servant from the household. Christ further describes this judgment in language which conveys the sense of eternal damnation. The reason for this language is the parallel between the judgment of the parable and the judgment of God upon the wicked.

The hope of the return of Christ is an exercise in faith and in holiness. It is an experience in faith because the believer is asked to keep on believing in this promise of our Lord Jesus in spite of the course of the world. The course of the world takes the fact that the return has not yet taken place, as proof that the promise is of no value; it is a mistaken hope of zealous but mistaken men. These scoffers reason saying, "Where is the promise of his coming? for since the fathers fell asleep, all things continue as they were from the beginning of the creation" (2 Peter 3:4).

It is the privilege and obligation of faith to resist this reasoning and to proclaim fearlessly that Christ will come.

REVIEW QUESTIONS

1. What is the application of the parable of the fig tree?

2. How does the Lord illustrate the uncertainty of the precise time of His second coming?

3. What will be the conditions on earth at the Lord's return?

4. What is the lesson of the unexpected coming of the thief?

5. What two contrasting attitudes and actions are presented in the parable of the servant?

GOLDEN TEXT HOMILY

"WATCH THEREFORE: FOR YE KNOW NOT WHAT HOUR YOUR LORD DOTH COME" (Matthew 24:42).

God is not playing a "cat and mouse" game with His followers. The exact day and hour for the return of Jesus depends upon a number of variables. Of course God knows, for He knows everything including the outcome of the variables. The mystery of the time of His coming is reduced in proportion to the spiritual sensitivity of the individual believer. His return will be a greater surprise to some than it will be to others. If this were not the case then the admonition to "watch" would be mockery. Exactly what does Jesus mean when He tells us to watch? Of course it means to stay awake, but it means much more than that.

To *watch* means to expand one's range of vision. We may watch to the extent of the reach of the arm or we may broaden the range as much as several miles. In the sense of watching for His coming, the implication is the observation of a broad spectrum of data. What do we see in the world of economics, science, education, politics, and morals? As we observe the church, do we see signs pointing to His coming? It is so easy for "church people" to have tunnel vision. We see signs in our small frame of reference. This is good, but it is not enough. Watching as Jesus instructs us means "total alert."

To *watch* also means the sharpening of our perceptive skills. It is one thing to see a body of data and yet another to organize it into meaningful information. Being able to see the long hand of the clock on 12 and the small hand on 3 does not mean we know what time it is. It is possible to be always learning, but never getting any smarter. Perception enables us to make sense out of what we see.

Watching requires keen discrimination. There are so many things that resemble other things. Deception is a danger Jesus warned us about over and over again. A watchman on the wall (Nehemiah 7:3) must have the ability to distinguish between a friend or a foe. Unless he can do this, he is a liability and not an asset. The inability to tell the difference between the true or the false Christ can be spiritually fatal. Jesus said that His sheep know His voice and a stranger they would not follow. Our safety and security depend upon our ability to discriminate.
—R. B. Thomas, D.Min., Pastor, Bloomington, Minnesota

SENTENCE SERMONS

HE WHO receives scars for Christ here will wear stars with Christ there.
—Anonymous

GOD IS not looking for ornamental but fruit-bearing Christians.

—Harold W. Erickson

CHRISTIANITY IS either relevant all the time or useless anytime. It is not just a phase of life; it is life itself.

—Richard C. Halverson

I SINCERELY BELIEVE, and if I can study the Scriptures aright and read current events, that we are living in the latter days. I believe that the coming of the Lord draweth nigh.

—Billy Graham

EVANGELISTIC APPLICATION

ALL SHOULD TAKE HEED TO CHRIST'S WARNING AND PREPARE FOR HIS SOON RETURN.

We know that Christ is coming! We know that His coming is near! We do not know the exact hour, day, or week, or even the exact year; but we do know the era of time. The similarity of our present world to that of "the days of Noe" is very apparent as we "behold the fig tree."

Our soon-coming King tells us in this scripture—which is supported by many other scriptures—that we should learn from the experience of the householder. Not knowing the exact time of night that the thief was coming, the householder was unprepared. Shall we learn from this? We cannot afford to guess that Christ will not come today, for it is in "such an hour" that He will come. Here we have the important guiding principle for those who await His return: constant readiness.

From this guiding principle of constant readiness for Christ's return, we are urged to win the lost and to nurture and retain the converted, so that together we may meet the Lord in the air. Am I asleep to His coming? Are you?

—R. Terrell McBrayer

ILLUMINATING THE LESSON

If He should come today
And find my hands so full
Of future plans, however fair,
In which my Saviour has no share,
    What would He say?

If He should come today
And find my love so cold;
My faith so very weak and dim
I had not even looked for Him,
    What would He say?

If He should come today
And find that I had not told
One soul about my heavenly Friend
Whose blessings all my way attend,
    What would He say?

If He should come today,
Would I be glad, quite glad?
Remembering that He died for all
And none through me had heard His call
    What would He say?

—Selected

DAILY BIBLE READINGS

M. Saved Through Christ. John 12:44-50

T. Living Righteously. 2 Peter 3:10-15

W. Waiting for Christ's Coming. 1 Thessalonians 4:13-18

T. Watching for Christ's Coming. 1 Thessalonians 5:1-11

F. Glorified in Christ. 2 Thessalonians 1:6-12

S. Inheriting the Kingdom. Matthew 25:31-34

The Stewardship of Life

Study Text: Matthew 25:1-46

Supplemental References: Proverbs 16:1-9; Luke 19:12-27; Romans 14:7-13; 1 Timothy 6:20, 21

Time: Probably April, A.D. 30

Place: The Mount of Olives, just east of the city of Jerusalem

Golden Text: "Well done, good and faithful servant; thou hast been faithful over a few things, I will make thee ruler over many things" (Matthew 25:23)

Central Truth: God holds us accountable for all He gives us.

Evangelistic Emphasis: Eternal life is promised to all who accept Christ, but eternal judgment awaits those who reject Him.

Printed Text

Matthew 25:14. For the kingdom of heaven is as a man travelling into a far country, who called his own servants, and delivered unto them his goods.

19. After a long time the lord of those servants cometh, and reckoneth with them.

20. And so he that had received five talents came and brought other five talents, saying, Lord, thou deliveredst unto me five talents: behold, I have gained beside them five talents more.

21. His lord said unto him, Well done, thou good and faithful servant: thou hast been faithful over a few things, I will make thee ruler over many things: enter thou into the joy of thy lord.

22. He also that had received two talents came and said, Lord, thou deliveredst unto me two talents: behold, I have gained two other talents beside them.

23. His lord said unto him, Well done, good and faithful servant; thou hast been faithful over a few things, I will make thee ruler over many things: enter thou into the joy of thy lord.

24. Then he which had received the one talent came and said, Lord, I knew thee that thou art an hard man, reaping where thou hast not sown, and gathering where thou hast not strawed:

25. And I was afraid, and went and hid thy talent in the earth: lo, there thou hast that is thine.

26. His lord answered and said unto him, Thou wicked and slothful servant, thou knewest that I reap where I sowed not, and gather where I have not strawed:

27. Thou oughtest therefore to have put my money to the exchangers, and then at my coming I should have received mine own with usury.

28. Take therefore the talent from him, and give it unto him which hath ten talents.

29. For unto every one that hath shall be given, and he shall have abundance: but from him that hath not shall be taken away even that which he hath.

30. And cast ye the unprofitable servant into outer darkness: there shall be weeping and gnashing of teeth.

34. Then shall the King say unto them on his right hand, Come, ye blessed of my Father, inherit the kingdom prepared for you from the foundation of the world.

LESSON OUTLINE

I. PERSONAL ACCOUNTABILITY
 A. The Distribution of the Talents
 B. The Response of the Servants
 C. The Day of Reckoning

II. FAITHFULNESS COMMENDED
 A. The Reward of the Man of Five Talents
 B. The Reward of the Man of Two Talents

III. SLOTHFULNESS CONDEMNED
 A. The Complaints and Default of the Man of One Talent
 B. The Will of the Master
 C. The Judgment of the Man of One Talent

IV. INHERITING THE KINGDOM
 A. The Throne of Judgment
 B. The Separation Between the Righteous and the Wicked
 C. The Reward and Commendation of the Righteous

LESSON EXPOSITION

INTRODUCTION

In last week's lesson we were instructed in the necessity of an inner readiness of character in order to be ready for the return of our Lord. Today's lesson has to do more with the activity of the believer while he waits the return of the Lord. External works are in view in this lesson, while inner spiritual condition was the main subject of the last one. It will be seen that these are both closely related; works to be acceptable must be joined with sincere motives and a true Christian character.

The parable of the talents implies that there is actual diligence in the work and the service of the Lord. The key point is that every individual, regardless of his talent (Matthew 25:21), is held accountable or responsible for the use of that talent. The action of the workmen (managers, administrators) will be evaluated, and those who are faithful will receive a reward, whereas those who are faithless will receive judgment. Throughout this parable, the principle of the sovereignty of the master over all his goods is central.

I. PERSONAL ACCOUNTABILITY (Matthew 25:14-19)

A. The Distribution of the Talents (vv. 14, 15)

14. For the kingdom of heaven is as a man traveling into a far country, who called his own servants, and delivered unto them his goods.

15. And unto one he gave five talents, to another two, and to another one; to every man according to his several ability; and straightway took his journey.

The Lord Jesus, about to leave the earth and return to His Father in heaven, represents Himself as a man traveling into a far country. However, before leaving he called his servants (bond servants) to him and made them stewards of his kingdom. His delivering unto them his goods represents our Lord giving gifts unto His servants. The abilities are given as a sacred trust. This distribution of gifts (ministries or abilities) is divided or given "to every man severally as he [the Holy Spirit] will" (1 Corinthians 12: 11). (See also Ephesians 4:7-16.)

The servants in this parable were men of the household whom the master had come to know and trust. Doubtlessly their previous performances had been the basic of the master's evaluation of them. He trusted them to the extent of dividing among them his entire material wealth in that country. This act completely entrusted his fortunes and personal welfare to these stewards.

The word *talent* originally meant "a weight of silver or gold"; but because of our Lord's use of the word in the parable, it has come to mean "one's gifts, abilities, and endowments." The Lord never gave the apostles any money; however, we hear Peter after Pentecost saying to the lame man at the entrance to the Temple, "Silver and gold have I none; but such as I have give I thee: In the name of Jesus Christ of Nazareth rise up and walk" (Acts 3:6). Peter was exercising the gift of healing.

Does the Lord assign the work of His kingdom to a select few, or is there a job to be performed by all of His children?

God does not assign responsibilities to all men alike, but in the manner and to the extent that each man is able to bear them according to his own ability. His knowledge of people governs the assignments. The infinite variety in men's dispositions, intellects, wills, opportunities, positions, and so on, are all taken into account, and these modify and condition their responsibilities. "For unto whomsoever much is given, of him shall be much required" (Luke 12:48).

B. The Response of the Servants (vv. 16-18)

16. Then he that had received the five talents went and traded with the same, and made them other five talents.

17. And likewise he that had received two, he also gained other two.

18. But he that had received one went and digged in the earth, and hid his lord's money.

The two servants who were faithful, who invested their master's money profitably, responded immediately to their responsibility. This response reveals an eagerness to please the master, even though they knew he would be away for a long time. The laggard could well have said there is plenty of time left for the investment of this money. This responsiveness also reveals the sense of stewardship that required him to use this money in terms of the trust in which it had been given him.

The eagerness with which the first two servants responded was matched by the ability of each. They were able to gain

five talents and two talents respectively. This fact shows that the man of two talents revealed the same zeal and proportional ability with proportional results as that of the five-talent man.

The response of the man with one talent is the opposite of all that is said about the other two. He made no attempt to increase his stewardship; instead, he buried the money. He insured the safety of the one talent but destroyed the possibility of increase. This was a violation of his master's wishes for his servant and for his money. It was a forfeiture of the servant's own initiative and ultimately of his opportunity.

C. The Day of Reckoning (v. 19)

19. After a long time the lord of those servants cometh, and reckoneth with them.

As the lord of the servants in this parable came to call their stewardship into account, so shall the Lord Jesus come again and call His stewards into account. The "long time" is suggestive of the many centuries which have already elapsed since our Lord's ascension into glory.

How much longer before our Lord returns is known only to the Father. We do know He promised: "Behold, I come quickly; and my reward is with me, give to every man according as his work shall be" (Revelation 22:12). "Wherefore we labour, that, whether present or absent, we may be accepted of him. For we must all appear before the judgment seat of Christ; that every one may receive the things done in his body, according to that he hath done, whether it be good or bad" (2 Corinthians 5:9, 10).

II. FAITHFULNESS COMMENDED (Matthew 25:20-23)

A. The Reward of the Man of Five Talents (vv. 20, 21)

20. And so he that had received five talents came and brought other five talents, saying, Lord, thou deliveredst unto me five talents: behold, I have gained beside them five talents more.

21. His lord said unto him, Well

done, thou good and faithful servant: thou hast been faithful over a few things, I will make thee ruler over many things: enter thou into the joy of thy lord.

The day of reckoning alluded to in verse 19 implies the possibility of either reward or punishment, depending upon one's faithfulness. The man who had received five talents came boldly to his lord. His confidence and pleasure at meeting the lord was due to his faithfulness in service. To those who have been diligent in their service and perfect in their love, the coming of the Master is the great day for which they yearn.

While his lord tarried, this man did not allow himself to become careless and negligent; but rather, by "redeeming the time" he enjoyed a 100 percent increase.

The commendation by the master is a form of reward: "Well done, thou good and faithful servant." This is an emphatic and emotional utterance of approval. The reward continues in the fact that he is promised rulership over many things. In relation to the master's wealth in all of his kingdom, this was but a small thing; but he is now promised great rulership. This reward also involves a larger stewardship.

The chief reward appears in the statement, "Enter thou into the joy of thy lord." This is the fellowship of joy with the master and it implies spiritual blessedness in terms of the application of the parable. This statement also indicates that the master is placing the servant in the position of rulership in company with him.

To what extent and in what way may faithfulness in the Lord's work be rewarded in the present life?

B. The Reward of the Man of Two Talents (vv. 22, 23)

22. He also that had received two talents came and said, Lord, thou deliveredst unto me two talents: behold, I have gained two other talents beside them.

23. His lord said unto him, Well done, good and faithful servant; thou hast been faithful over a few things, I will make thee ruler over many things: enter thou into the joy of thy lord.

The pattern of this servant's approach to the master is virtually identical with the pattern noted above. There is the same evident eagerness to be judged and the same eagerness for an opportunity to present his stewardship to the master.

It is important to note that the master's response to this servant is identical with his response to the man who had received five talents. The reward is identical in proportion. In the basic and most important aspects of the reward, he receives the same assurances and invitations that the man of five talents had received.

There is a hero frontiersman of early America who illustrates the principle of the employment of one's abilities. His name is John Chapman, commonly referred to as Johnnie Appleseed. He was not a man of such ability that he could take his place in political circles with his contemporaries, such as George Washington and Benjamin Franklin. However, because he dedicated himself to one task, his name has lived alongside of theirs. The one talent for which he lives in history is his talent as an orchardist and spiritual leader. There are orchard monuments of his work still growing to this day.

III. SLOTHFULNESS CONDEMNED (Matthew 25:24-30)

A. The Complaints and Default of the Man of One Talent (vv. 24, 25)

24. Then he which had received the one talent came and said, Lord, I knew thee that thou art an hard man, reaping where thou hast not sown, and gathering where thou hast not strawed:

25. And I was afraid, and went and hid thy talent in the earth: lo, there thou hast that is thine.

When the one-talent servant came before the lord, the first thing he did was to try to justify his conduct. He blames his failure on what he supposes to be the character of his master.

The sincerity of this man is immediately open to question. The first basis of questioning his sincerity is the fact that this master did not seem to be the type of person described here. We judge this from his dealings with the other servants. The second basis of questioning this servant's sincerity is that he was seeking an excuse for his own failure. These accusations brought by one who was not already under condemnation for failure would carry greater weight.

How does a person either consciously or unconsciously avoid blaming another individual for his own shortcomings?

The accusations are quite severe. This servant accused his master of being a hard man: self-seeking, and accepting nothing but the most severe demands of his servants. He accused the master of being unethical in that he reaped where he had not sown. The implication is that the master by shrewd overbearing and questionable business practices had taken the crops of other less wealthy men. The servant also accused the master of oppressiveness of his servants in gathering where he had not planted. The accusation here is that he had not given a fair share of the fruit of labor to those who did the labor. He claimed the labor of other men for himself.

The self-conviction of this man appears in his statement, "I was afraid." This is also a basic point of his failure. He had feared to take the risk of investment. This fear does not excuse him because it was not properly founded, and he still knew what the will of his master was. The master had not dictated that he be oppressive and unethical, but that he should use the money for investment.

B. The Will of the Master (vv. 26, 27)

26. His lord answered and said unto him, Thou wicked and slothful servant, thou knewest that I reap where I sowed not, and gather where I have not strawed:

27. Thou oughtest therefore to have put my money to the exchangers, and then at my coming I should have received mine own with usury.

The rebuke of the master is the exact opposite of his manner in the commendation of the other servants. In describing this servant he assesses his character and his faithfulness. As the servant had accused the master of being evil, the master now assesses the servant as being both evil and slothful.

The servant had convicted himself by acknowledging that he knew what the master desired in the use of this talent. The master relates this fact to the servant. Verse 26 probably should be translated as a question rather than as a statement. The master is not admitting that the accusations are true. Instead he is showing how the servant had convicted himself in that he had shown that he understood the master to want one thing and he had done the exact opposite.

As we have noted, the desire for increase on the part of the master did not dictate unethical practices. This desire only dictated faithfulness in stewardship.

C. The Judgment of the Man of One Talent (vv. 28-30)

28. Take therefore the talent from him, and give it unto him which hath ten talents.

29. For unto every one that hath shall be given, and he shall have abundance: but from him that hath not shall be taken away even that which he hath.

30. And cast ye the unprofitable servant into outer darkness: there shall be weeping and gnashing of teeth.

The first aspect of judgment of this servant was the fact that the one talent, previously committed to him, was taken away. This talent was given to the man who had used faithfully the five talents. The proverbial statement (v. 29) is a principle universally employed and recognized. Those who show themselves most trustworthy in the heaviest responsibilities are the ones who are further rewarded and burdened with extra duty. This statement is the master's answer to any who might object to this redistribution.

The second and most severe part of the judgment of the slothful servant is that he was cut off from the household and cast out of the kingdom. Verse 30 mixes the parable itself with the application. The application is to be understood in relation to divine and eternal judgment; therefore, the language of the parable here is "there shall be weeping and gnashing of teeth." The exposure of the servant is analogous to the position of those who are eternally damned.

This one-talent man was condemned, not for the great crimes, but for omitting to do what he knew was required of him. "Therefore to him that knoweth to do good, and doeth it not, to him it is sin" (James 4:17).

He not only lost his reward, but from verse 30 it is clear that he lost his soul in hell as well. Our Lord frequently described hell as a place of "outer darkness" where "there shall be weeping and gnashing of teeth."

IV. INHERITING THE KINGDOM (Matthew 25:31-36)

A. The Throne of Judgment (v. 31)

(Matthew 25:31 is not included in the printed text.)

The coming of Christ and the subsequent judgment are taken as facts already established. These are the presuppositions that lie behind Christ's statement, "when the Son of man shall come."

A part of this glory of the Son of Man which is described in this passage is that He is accompanied by His angels. They are a part of His kingdom and they are subject to His sovereignty. When the Son of Man appears in such glory, He will sit upon the throne of His inheritance from the Father. It is a throne appropriate to His nature, majesty, and eternal and universal dominion. By its employment it is also the throne of judgment.

B. The Separation Between the Righteous and the Wicked (vv. 32, 33)

(Matthew 25:32, 33 is not included in the printed text)

The term translated in verse 32 as

"nations" is a term comprehensive of all peoples. It especially points out the gathering of the Gentiles. This should not imply however that the judgment of God relates only to the Gentile nations. The emphasis here is that though the Gentiles are not commonly associated with the covenant, they are, nevertheless, the subjects of the Kingdom. The King's sovereignty is universal whether the nations acknowledge Him or not. The will of the nations is not considered in determining whether they shall come before the judgment. They will be gathered by the authority of the King (Matthew 13:47-50).

It is by the King's decree that the people of the nations will be separated. By this statement we know that the judgment which is executed from the throne is an act of the sovereignty of the Son of Man and a display of His kingship. The act of separation is an act of judgment in itself. It is according to the pattern and the clear-cut distinctives of a shepherd who is able to go through his flock and cut the goats off from among the sheep. The people of Christ's audience knew what it was to drive the goats away at night when the sheep were taken into the fold.

The Lord uses the sheep as a type of the innocent, the obedient, and the good; while He uses the goats to represent the unruly, the proud, and the evil. In the Greek the diminutive is used for goats and should read "little goats." This is used to express their worthlessness. In the symbolism the sheep are placed in a position of favor; namely, the right hand of the King. The goats are placed in the position of disfavor: namely, the left hand of the King.

C. The Reward and Commendation of the Righteous (vv. 34-36)

(Matthew 25:35, 36 is not included in the printed text.)

34. Then shall the King say unto them on his right hand, Come, ye blessed of my Father, inherit the kingdom prepared for you from the foundation of the world.

In verse 34 the term "King" is introduced. It is clear from this statement that the King is identical with the Son of Man. It is also clear that it is the King who serves in the position of judgment.

Having established two basic facts—that Christ will sit upon the throne as judge, and that He shall separate the righteous from the unrighteous as illustrated by the shepherd dividing his sheep from the goats—Christ now moves to establish the basis for both the reward and the punishment.

His attention immediately is turned to those who are on His right hand and hold a position of honor, respect, and acceptance. To those individuals, the King says: "Come, ye blessed of my Father, inherit the kingdom prepared for you from the foundation of the world." There are three aspects or significant points about this verse. First, He addresses Himself to those who are blessed of His heavenly Father. This is the highest honor which could be placed upon any Christian. It means that not only the believer's relationship but also his actions and theology have been in conformity with that which the Father has projected for his life. Second, Christ invites them to inherit the Kingdom which has been prepared for them. At this point, we can see the consummation of being adopted as sons of God and made joint-heirs with Jesus Christ.

Those on the right hand then fall heir to the Kingdom which has been prepared for the righteous to inherit. This means that heaven is theirs, that all of its privileges, opportunities, and enjoyments now belong to them. They have not only been grafted into the family of God but they also now take their rightful place as the inheritors of the kingdom of God. Third, the Kingdom was prepared from the foundation of the world for the righteous, for those who are judged righteous in the eyes or evaluation of God.

The commendation of the righteous was based on the fact that they had ministered to Christ when He was in need. Christ commends these deeds as having been done to Him personally. The nature of these deeds is important inasmuch as they represent human suffering

with which Christ identifies Himself and to which Christ's love must address itself. These needs cannot be met by materialistic giving alone. They must be met by self-giving. Only in this manner can love exist and act.

It is a serious weakness to see someone in any condition of need and to turn away from him. Our obligation extends as far as our ability to help; for "whoso hath this world's good, and seeth his brother have need, and shutteth up his bowels of compassion from him, how dwelleth the love of God in him? My little children, let us not love in word, neither in tongue; but in deed and in truth" (1 John 3:17, 18).

REVIEW QUESTIONS

1. How does the parable of the talents differ from the parable of the pounds in Luke 19:11-27?

2. How did the five-talent and two-talent servants utilize their talents?

3. What excuse did the one-talent servant give for his handling of the talent?

4. What reward is given to the people represented by the sheep in verse 34?

5. What practical lessons did you gain from the study today?

GOLDEN TEXT HOMILY

"WELL DONE, GOOD AND FAITHFUL SERVANT; THOU HAST BEEN FAITHFUL OVER A FEW THINGS, I WILL MAKE THEE RULER OVER MANY THINGS" (Matthew 25:23).

In our land of democracy and personal freedom, it is difficult to comprehend the true context of the word "servant" used here in this passage. Most often a servant was not a paid worker such as one may hire to care for their home or children in today's world, but a slave, a bond servant. In relationship to a servant, the master exercised full authority, absolute judgment regarding life or death.

Jesus is here giving examples of how different types of servants invest themselves in their work for their master's benefit. He is speaking a parable, an illustration regarding the kingdom of God.

The slothful servant is condemned for his fearfulness (vv. 25, 26) and considered to be unfaithful to his master. But the servant who takes what has been placed into his care and gains even more is to be considered worthy in his master's eyes. "Well done, because you have not only benefited yourself by making good use of your time and talent, but you have also added to my kingdom." The master is pleased with the faithful servant and rewards his efforts, his willingness to serve.

Jesus is speaking of the judgment of God. There is no benefit for God if a Christian is ruled by fear and hides himself. God is seeking people who will invest themselves in the building of the Kingdom, people who consider themselves as slaves of righteousness, people who will risk living out their Christian experience in the face of a hostile world which offers little reward.

The Christian does not have an option whether to serve God or not! This may sound harsh, but look at the price paid at Calvary to set us free—free from sin, free from fear, free from death. We cannot hold back; we must invest ourselves in telling someone about the Good News of Jesus Christ. The desire of every Christian believer's heart should be to hear these words, "Well done, good and faithful servant." Our Master is alive from the grave and coming soon to give His reward to every one of His faithful servants!—**Eugene Wigelsworth, Coordinator of Student Services, Church of God School of Theology, Cleveland, Tennessee**

SENTENCE SERMONS

GOD HOLDS US accountable for all He gives us.

—**Selected**

JESUS WILL NEVER say "well done" to anyone unless his work had been well done.

—**G. Campbell Morgan**

MAKE THE BEST use of today; you will find yourself prepared for tomorrow.

—**Selected**

THE DEEDS WE do, the words we say,
Into still air they seem to fleet,
We count them ever past;
But they shall last—
In the dread Judgment they
And we shall meet.

—**John Keble**

EVANGELISTIC APPLICATION

ETERNAL LIFE IS PROMISED TO ALL WHO ACCEPT CHRIST, BUT ETERNAL JUDGMENT AWAITS THOSE WHO REJECT HIM.

I have a rendezvous with Christ,
And that time not far away,
When all I am and do and say
Shall counted be, and weighed by Him.
I have a rendezvous with Christ
Ere days are run and eyes grow dim.
It seemed 'twere better far
To follow the career I'd chose
Than to become a mighty power.
Turn my course at His high will,
And all for self my own days fill:
But I have a rendezvous with Christ!
All other aims in that must pale,
For fatal is it if I fail.
And I to my pledged word am true,
I shall not fail that rendezvous!

—**Betty Thornton,
in "Sunday School Times"**

DAILY BIBLE READINGS

M. Stewards of Earth's Resources. Genesis 1:26-31

T. Choosing Priorities. Proverbs 16:1-9

W. Warning Against Slothfulness. Proverbs 24:30-34

T. Living in God's Will. Colossians 1:9-13

F. Giving Account to God. Romans 14:7-13

S. Receiving God's Blessing. Psalm 1:1-3

The Great Commission

Study Text: Matthew 28:16-20; Mark 16:14-20

Supplemental References: Jonah 3:1-10; John 3:11-18; Acts 1:1-8; Romans 15: 20-32

Time: Spring A.D. 30

Place: In the mountain region of Galilee, or the near vicinity of Jerusalem, Mount of Olives

Golden Text: "Ye shall be witnesses unto me both in Jerusalem, and in all Judea, and in Samaria, and unto the uttermost part of the earth" (Acts 1:8).

Central Truth: God has a purpose for every member of His church on earth.

Evangelistic Emphasis: Those who accept the gospel shall be saved.

Printed Text

Mark 16:14. Afterward he appeared unto the eleven as they sat at meat, and upbraided them with their unbelief and hardness of heart, because they believed not them which had seen him after he was risen.

15. And he said unto them, Go ye into all the world, and preach the gospel to every creature.

16. He that believeth and is baptized shall be saved; but he that believeth not shall be damned.

17. And these signs shall follow them that believe; In my name shall they cast out devils; they shall speak with new tongues;

18. They shall take up serpents; and if they drink any deadly thing, it shall not hurt them; they shall lay hands on the sick, and they shall recover.

19. So then after the Lord had spoken unto them, he was received up into heaven, and sat on the right hand of God.

20. And they went forth, and preached every where, the Lord working with them, and confirming the word with signs following. Amen.

Matthew 28:16. Then the eleven disciples went away into Galilee, into a mountain where Jesus had appointed them.

17. And when they saw him, they worshipped him: but some doubted.

18. And Jesus came and spake unto them, saying, All power is given unto me in heaven and in earth.

19. Go ye therefore, and teach all nations, baptizing them in the name of the Father, and of the Son, and of the Holy Ghost:

20. Teaching them to observe all things whatsoever I have commanded you: and, lo, I am with you alway, even unto the end of the world. Amen.

LESSON OUTLINE

I. THE CHURCH'S TASK

A. Appearance and Rebuke of Unbelief

B. The Commission Given

C. Ascension and the Disciples' On-
   going Mission
II. THE LORD'S POWER
   A. Jesus and the Disciples Meet on
      the Mountain
   B. Christ's Claim of Authority
III. THE LORD'S PRESENCE
   A. The Great Commission
   B. The Great Promise

LESSON EXPOSITION

INTRODUCTION

Under the theme "Teachings of Christ,"
our studies this quarter have given us
wide exposure to principles for personal
spiritual growth as well as to admonitions that speak to us about our relationship and service to others. It is a fitting
conclusion to the series of lessons,
therefore, that the final words of our Lord
would speak to us about our responsibility as members of His body—the church.

In the company of His disciples, Jesus
made a number of post resurrection
appearances. But no appearance had
greater impact on those He had trained
to carry on the work than the final moments
of the Master's earthly life when the
Great Commission was given.

Our lesson today focuses on the task
of the church to extend its arms of
service into the harvest field through the
power of the Holy Spirit and with the
assurance of Chirst's continued presence.
It was a mandate the early church gladly
accepted. It can be given no less priority
in our day.

I. THE CHURCH'S TASK (Mark 16:14-20)

The main duty of the church is to win
the lost whether they are far or near and
whether they have heard or have not
heard the gospel. The good news must
be proclaimed throughout the world. This
is, or at least should be, the primary
concern of the church.

The heart of the New Testament message is evangelism and missions; the
prime interest of our Lord is the same.
He tells Zacchaeus, "For the Son of man
is come to seek and to save that which
was lost" (Luke 19:10). He says to those
around Him, "I am come that they might

have life, and that they might have it
more abundantly" (John 10:10). The Great
Commission is rooted and grounded in
our Lord's desire that fallen man be
reconciled to God, for the marching command to the church is found in this great
statement of Jesus just prior to His ascension (Mark 16:15-20; Matthew 28:19, 20).

What can the church do to more effectively reach sinners?

The passage of Scripture from Mark
16 has been the subject of controversy
through the centuries since verses 9-20
were not found in some of the ancient
manuscripts. Also, some critics suggest
that the passage does not follow well
with the flow from verse 8. Regardless of
the objections to the passage, it has
been accepted into the canon and the
verses are consistent with the rest of the
Scripture. (For those interested in examining further the "longer ending of Mark," a
scholarly work is presented in *The Bible
Knowledge Commentary*, edited by John
F. Walvoord and Roy B. Zuck.)

A. Appearance and Rebuke of Unbelief
   (v. 14)

**14. Afterward he appeared unto the
eleven as they sat at meat, and
upbraided them with their unbelief and
hardness of heart, because they believed
not them which had seen him after he
was risen.**

Earlier in this chapter, Mark records
the appearance of the angelic being to
the women who had gone to the burial
tomb of Jesus. They were told that Christ
had arisen and were invited to view the
place where He had been laid. The
messenger also told the women that Christ
had gone into Galilee and there they
would see Him. In verses 12 and 13 the
account is given of Christ's appearance
to two of the disciples as they walked
and went into the country.

The news of Christ's resurrection was
told by the two men and the response
was one of unbelief. Whether the disciples were a part of the "residue" referred
to in verse 13 is not clear. What is clear

is the fact that Christ appeared to the eleven disciples "as they sat at meat" and He "upbraided them with their unbelief and hardness of heart, because they believed not them which had seen him after he was risen" (v. 14).

The Greek word used here for the rebuke is *oneidisen* and is a strong term not used by Jesus elsewhere. Perhaps the rebuke was strong since the matter of believing eyewitness reports of the Resurrection was essential in the spread of the gospel—a factor which is still essential in sharing the gospel. By hearing about Jesus' resurrection before seeing Him, they learned what it was like to believe the testimony of eyewitnesses. This acceptance of the Resurrection story on the basis of an eyewitness report was exactly what they would depend on as they preached in their coming missionary outreach.

B. The Commission Given (vv. 15-18)

15. And he said unto them, Go ye into all the world, and preach the gospel to every creature.

16. He that believeth and is baptized shall be saved; but he that believeth not shall be damned.

17. And these signs shall follow them that believe; In my name shall they cast out devils; they shall speak with new tongues;

18. They shall take up serpents; and if they drink any deadly thing, it shall not hurt them; they shall lay hands on the sick, and they shall recover.

In these verses, which correspond to Matthew 28:16-20, we have the great missionary Magna Charta. It speaks of the universality of grace. No human being is shut out from the gospel by Jesus. And absolutely all are to hear the gospel with the one divine purpose that they are to believe.

It is important to note that the phrase "to every creature" is best translated "to the whole creation," and in that connotation cannot mean only the generation of persons then living. Rather the expression reaches to the end of time. If it is asked how the apostles could share the gospel that far, the answer is that they

did it through the New Testament and through the voice of every person who preaches and teaches the message of the New Testament.

The Commission is immediately sealed by a promise "He that believeth and is baptized shall be saved" (v. 16). The connection is evident because believing is the one purpose of preaching. Faith and baptism are combined here because both are essential parts of the conversion experince. The moment a person believes, he will want and will have baptism. By believing, the person clings to the gospel and part of the gospel is baptism.

Jesus also adds the opposite of believing since many who hear the gospel do not respond as believers. "He that believeth not shall be damned." This involves the fact that the person hears the gospel preached, for only then can he answer it with unbelief. R. C. H. Lenski writes: "Nothing is said about those who never hear the gospel and thus never get to believe or not believe; the Scriptures leave their fate in God's hands, and it is in vain for us to speculate. Only the general statement is given, hence nothing is said of a believer who afterwards falls into unbelief or of a disbeliever who finally comes to faith. But both cases are clear as to their fate." (*The Interpretation of St. Mark's Gospel*)

In verse 17 miraculous signs are promised to the disciples as they carry the message into the harvest. Jesus calls these miracles "signs" and uses a term for them which is far higher than "wonders" or "power works," for a sign points beyond itself to something that is far greater. Signs were, therefore, credentials for the apostles and their gospel message. They were seals that authenticated the message and gave evidence that the risen living Lord was present with them in their Kingdom work.

The sign of speaking in tongues was evidence of the coming and present reality of the Holy Spirit in their midst. Casting out of demons had already been part of the experience of the disciples (Mark 6:13).

To "take up serpents" was not characteristic of the early Christians so far as Bible scholars can determine. The passage in Acts 28:2-6 records the event of Paul having been bitten by a viper and when Paul had no ill effects from the bite, the people of Malta regarded it as a sign of divinity.

The drinking of deadly poisons with no ill effects is not mentioned in the New Testament. But some early church fathers mention an account of Justus Barsabbas drinking poison with no harm to himself. New Testament writers such as James anticipated miracle healings (James 5:14, 15). Also, there are numerous accounts of the disciples being involved with a healing ministry (Mark 6:13; Luke 10:17-19, and others).

The Commission given to the disciples and hence to the church is crystal clear about Kingdom service: (1) The church has a preaching task. That means it is the duty of every Christian to share the gospel story. (2) The church has a healing task. A great deal of emphasis is given to healing of bodies and minds. Jesus wished to bring health to the body, mind, and soul. The soul healing has been documented as being the root source of total body healing. (3) The church has a source of power. Perhaps we are not to think of deliberately picking up snakes or drinking deadly poison, but at the back of this picturesque language is the conviction that the Christian is filled with a power to cope with life that others do not possess. And (4) The church is never left to do its work alone. Always Christ works with it in the power of the Holy Spirit.

Discuss the role of the church in ministry of healing. Is physical healing the only factor in the Commission?

C. Ascension and the Disciples' Ongoing Mission (vv. 19, 20)

19. So then after the Lord had spoken unto them, he was received up into heaven, and sat on the right hand of God.

20. And they went forth, and preached every where, the Lord working with them, and confirming the word with signs following. Amen.

Mark indicates the time of the Ascension in general terms while Luke reports the time of the Ascension as being 40 days after the Resurrection (Acts 1:3). Luke, also, identifies the place as Olivet or the Mount of Olives near Jerusalem (Luke 24:50).

The passive makes God the Agent in the act, "He was received up into heaven." The bodily form of Jesus rose visibly toward heaven until it was hidden in a cloud. For the last time the disciples had seen Jesus in bodily form as they gazed into the heavens.

In Mark's words there is the evidence of Christ's exaltation, "and sat on the right hand of God." To speak of God's right hand is an anthropomorphic usage of body components, but it is evidence of the omnipotent majesty and authority of the risen Lord.

Mark says the disciples "went forth," presumably from Jerusalem, and preached everywhere. The promise of the Lord's presence was evidenced by signs that accompanied their ministry.

The Lord of the church is still in the church and is still the Lord of power. The limits placed on the Great Commission are always on the human side, but never on the side of the Lord of glory.

II. THE LORD'S POWER (Matthew 28:16-18)

A. Jesus and the Disciples Meet on the Mountain (vv. 16, 17)

16. Then the eleven disciples went away into Galilee, into a mountain where Jesus had appointed them.

17. And when they saw him, they worshipped him: but some doubted.

Matthew alone places Jesus' first appearance to the eleven in Galilee, but Mark 14:28 and 16:7 may imply the same. Although the details are impossible to correlate, the reality of the appearance to His followers is solidly supported in all of the Gospels and in the writings of Paul. The mountain is not identified nor is the exact time mentioned here.

When the Eleven saw Jesus they responded in two different ways: some worshiped and some doubted. It is possible that a dual response was the action of some of the disciples. Luke reports that the apostles discredited the report of the women looking upon it as "idle tales" (24:11). He also reported that when Jesus appeared among the Eleven there were questions in their hearts and that they still disbelieved for joy (24:38, 41).

"While the doubts of the disciples cannot be justified, they can be understood in light of the trauma they had gone through. Perhaps honest doubt is resident in most of us" (George A. Buttrick).

"Some measure of doubt is almost inevitable. We all sin, and sin clouds our faith. Meanwhile our minds are dim at best, and the ways of God are a great depth of mystery. Perhaps the conviction that Jesus lived beyond death came slowly to some of His followers. Perhaps some saw, but counted the news too good to be true. Perhaps others saw, and denied that they had seen Jesus. Our life of fitful faith and doubt is here seen in two words—*worshiped* and *doubted.*

"Doubt is perhaps not the opposite of faith, but only faith's misgiving. We could hardly doubt what does not exist: if we doubt God, we have perhaps therefore already glimpsed Him. We need not fear doubt unless it comes from sin: there is faith in honest doubt. 'Who never doubted never half believed. Where doubt there truth is—'tis her shadow.' " (*The Interpreter's Bible*, Vol. 7).

How should we handle doubt? Is a willingness to recognize doubt part of the solution?

B. Christ's Claim of Authority (v. 18)

18. And Jesus came and spake unto them, saying, All power is given unto me in heaven and in earth.

The Gospel of Matthew ends with a claim (v. 18), a commission (v. 19), and a promise (v. 20). The last two will be considered under point III of the lesson outline.

Although the disciples had recognized the power and authority of Christ during His ministry with them, it was important to Christ and the disciples that a post-resurrection claim should preceed the Great Commission. This claim left no doubt as to Christ's supreme right to appoint to service those He had chosen. The claim also meant a right to require obedience because of love poured out even to death. It meant a right to govern and head the church for which He came.

What does Christian service mean in relationship to Christ's authority in the church?

III. THE LORD'S PRESENCE (Matthew 28:19, 20)

A. The Great Commission (vv. 19, 20a).

19. Go ye therefore, and teach all nations, baptizing them in the name of the Father, and of the Son, and of the Holy Ghost:

20a. Teaching them to observe all things whatsoever I have commanded you.

The Great Commission serves as a summary and fitting conclusion to the Gospel according to Matthew. In the book he introduced Jesus as the Son of David, Son of Abraham, and the Christ Child in a Jewish genealogy. In the Great Commission He is presented as the One with all authority and with credentials as sovereign over the nations. The covenants with Abraham and David, with the promise of a universal and everlasting Kingdom in a sovereignty of righteousness, are now fulfilled in Christ.

The responsibility was to be universal—"teach all nations." The disciples were admonished to "make disciples." Accordingly, the idea is presented that as they go they were to bring all nations under His discipline. Perhaps this is a reference to a broader ministry, since Jesus had almost restricted His personal ministry to "the lost sheep of the house of Israel" (15:24).

Jesus admonished the disciples to teach others the things He had taught them

The believer is not at liberty to make up his own message. Rather he is to speak the message of Christ. The Apostle Paul said that even if an angel came and taught a message other than that centered in Christ, he was not to be given an audience.

The message of Christ is the answer to the deep needs of humanity. If that message is shared through a loving, caring church, the mission of Jesus will have accomplished its purpose.

B. The Great Promise (v. 20b)

20b. And, lo, I am with you alway, even unto the end of the world. Amen.

Christ's last words on earth, as far as we know, were the words of His promise to be with them as they go. They were assured that commission would not be carried out without His help and presence even to the "end of the age."

The reality of Christ's presence is a source of strength today. For our tasks become heavy and directions fuzzy without the sustaining power and guidance of the Holy Spirit. Although the Great Commission places a heavy responsibility on the church, it can joyfully work with the assurance of Christ's continued presence.

REVIEW QUESTIONS

1. What is the setting of the lesson?

2. What admonition did Jesus give the disciples just before He ascended into heaven?

3. What signs were to follow the preaching ministry of the disciples?

4. What action, according to Mark 16:20, did the disciples take following the ascension of Christ?

5. How does the Great Commission speak to you?

GOLDEN TEXT HOMILY

"YE SHALL BE WITNESSES UNTO ME BOTH IN JERUSALEM, AND IN ALL JUDEA, AND IN SAMARIA, AND UNTO THE UTTERMOST PART OF THE EARTH" (Acts 1:8).

Jesus cared so much for His followers that He would not leave them until He had equipped them with the full message of the gospel. In the wake of His ascension, He first corrects His disciples about their concern whether the kingdom would be immediately restored to Israel. In His last words on earth, He tells them to have nothing to do with the times or seasons, of dates or predictions, but their care is to be His witness.

What then were they to do? Instead of foreasting the future or seeking political power, Jesus offers them the assurance of heavenly power. They are to await the power from on high which will fill their service and their preaching with the power of God. Jesus tells them again of their dependency upon the Holy Spirit.

It is this promise that our Lord extends to each of us, His disciples. We will never be alone, without comfort or without hope. Although Jesus was bodily received up into a higher life, a life not made with human hands or limits of materialism, He did not go away! Jesus is even with us now as the Holy Spirit takes what belongs to Him and testifies of His presence. It is the Holy Spirit who fills the life of the believer and gives power to be His witness.

Several New Testament principles are revealed in this scene of Christ and His disciples: (a) witnessing is a universal obligation—Jesus has gathered the whole earth into His declaration of purpose; (b) witnessing is centered in the fact and meaning of the earthly ministry of Christ—His will be done on earth as it is in heaven; (c) witnessing depends upon the saving grace of what Christ has done in the life of the believer—the child of God has only to tell the truth of what God has done; (d) and finally, as Christian witnesses we are to be faithful regardless of the circumstances that confront us.

It is necessary for the Christian church to realize that Christ has commissioned His followers to be witnesses; this is their purpose, their mission. Effective witnessing will always find power in being dependent upon and being led by the Spirit of God.

How effective is your witness? Do you

see yourself dependent upon the Holy Spirit? Let Him give you daily guidance. Wait each day until you know the power from on high has refreshed your soul for this day's task of being a witness for Christ's sake.—**Florie Brown Wigelsworth, M.Div., Cleveland, Tennessee**

SENTENCE SERMONS

GOD HAS A PURPOSE for every member of His church on earth.

—Selected

THE GLORY of the local church is that it is not local.

—"This Day"

THE CHURCH IS not a dormitory, it is a workshop.

—"Speaker's Sourcebook"

THE CHURCH EXISTS for the double purpose of gathering in and sending out.

—"The Encyclopedia of Religious Quotations"

EVANGELISTIC APPLICATION

THOSE WHO ACCEPT THE GOSPEL SHALL BE SAVED.

Somebody thought this out. A mechanic can take five dollars worth of material and make it worth fifty dollars. That's skill. The government can stamp a piece of paper, and it becomes a hundred-dollar bill. That's money. An artist may take a cheap canvas and paint a picture worth one thousand dollars. That's art. A poet may take a piece of paper and write a poem worth two thousand dollars. That's genius. A rich man may sign his name to a check and make it worth a million dollars. That's capital. God can take a sinful life, transform it, and make it an asset to humanity. That's salvation!

—Selected

A phrenologist examined a man's head in the presence of a crowd and declared him to be a rough, unreliable fellow. The crowd laughed, for they knew him to be a kind man. But the man said, "That description fits me exactly before I was saved."

—"Notes and Quotes"

ILLUMINATING THE LESSON

One day the telephone rang in the clergyman's office of the Washington church which President Franklin Roosevelt attended. An eager voice inquired, "Do you expect the President to be in church Sunday?"

"That," answered the clergyman, "I cannot promise. But we expect God to be there and we fancy that should be incentive enough for a reasonably large attendance."

—"Together"

Jesus said, "And I, if I be lifted up from the earth, will draw all men unto me" (John 12:32).

If you take a common magnet, place it under a piece of white paper, and sprinkle iron filings on the paper, they will fall into a discernible pattern. Without the magnet, the filings become a shapeless mass.

It is the power of Christ that gives the church its basic organizational structure. It exists only by virtue of His magnetic power. He is the head. We are the body.

—Elmer Chase

DAILY BIBLE READINGS

M. Willing to Obey. 1 Samuel 3:1-10

T. A Pattern for Ministry. Luke 10:1-12

W. Diligent in Service. Romans 15:20-32

T. Faithful to God's Call. 1 Timothy 4:1-8

F. Proclaiming Christ's Mission. John 3:11-18

S. Salvation for All. Acts 13:46-49

INTRODUCTION TO SPRING QUARTER

The month of March begins the spring quarter of studies and marks a departure from the lessons on the "Teachings of Christ" that have occupied our thoughts for the last three months. On April 3, however, we will return to the Gospel According to Mark for the Easter lesson.

The lessons for the spring quarter (March, April, May) are presented under the theme "The Pauline Epistles," and are drawn from four of the writings of Paul—Ephesians, Philippians, Colossians, and 1 Thessalonians. Other Pauline writings are considered under several headings during the seven-year cycle.

With the exception of 1 Thessalonians, the Epistles we study this quarter are referred to as Prison Epistles. Only one Epistle—Philemon—is missing from the four Prison Epistles. In these letters Paul writes for the first time as a prisoner. He calls himself "the prisoner of Jesus Christ" (Ephesians 3:1).

The Pauline Epistles which we study this quarter are marked by their special emphasis on the person of Christ, and are aptly characterized as Christological. Two of the books—Ephesians and Colossians—are referred to as twin Epistles. Ephesians highlights the church as the body of Christ while Colossians emphasizes Christ as the Head of the church.

Philippians is the most personal of all the Pauline Epistles not written to individuals. Two topics predominate in the text of the Philippians. One is the "gospel" with its two aspects: Christ died for men, and men can possess His righteousness before God. The second topic which Paul stressed is joy.

May the Christ of Calvary, who is the essential theme of these lessons, become increasingly real and near to you as the studies unfold.

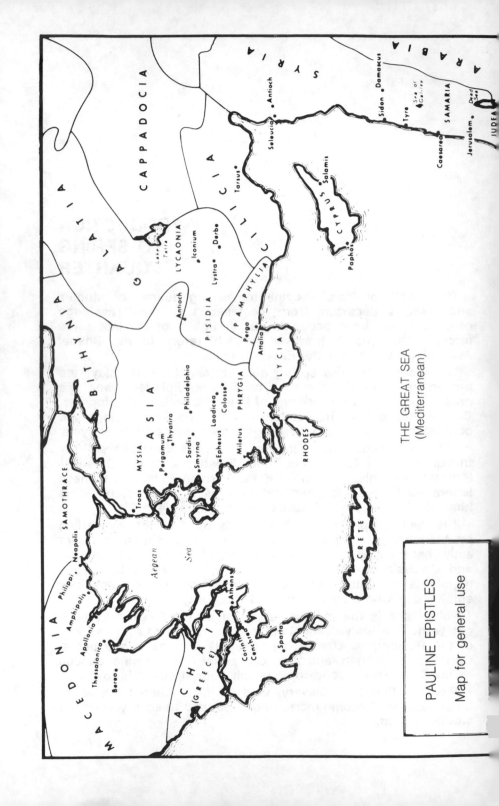

THE GREAT SEA
(Mediterranean)

PAULINE EPISTLES
Map for general use

Chosen in Christ

Study Text: Ephesians 1:1-23
Supplemental References: Genesis 12:1-3; Deuteronomy 7:6-8; 2 Samuel 7:8-16; Isaiah 53:1-11; John 15:16; Galatians 4:4-7
Time: Probably in A.D. 61
Place: Written from a Roman prison
Golden Text: "Blessed be the God and Father of our Lord Jesus Christ, who hath blessed us with all spiritual blessings in heavenly places in Christ (Ephesians 1:3).
Central Truth: Through faith in Jesus Christ, a person enters into a new life of fellowship with God.
Evangelistic Emphasis: God's plan of redemption provides forgiveness of sins through the blood of Christ.

Printed Text

Ephesians 1:3. Blessed be the God and Father of our Lord Jesus Christ, who hath blessed us with all spiritual blessings in heavenly places in Christ:

4. According as he hath chosen us in him before the foundation of the world, that we should be holy and without blame before him in love:

5. Having predestinated us unto the adoption of children by Jesus Christ to himself, according to the good pleasure of his will,

6. To the praise of the glory of his grace, wherein he hath made us accepted in the beloved.

7. In whom we have redemption through his blood, the forgiveness of sins, according to the riches of his grace;

8. Wherein he hath abounded toward us in all wisdom and prudence;

9. Having made known unto us the mystery of his will, according to his good pleasure which he hath purposed in himself:

11. In whom also we have obtained an inheritance, being predestinated according to the purpose of him who worketh all things after the counsel of his own will:

12. That we should be to the praise of his glory, who first trusted in Christ.

13. In whom ye also trusted, after that ye heard the word of truth, the gospel of your salvation: in whom also after that ye believed, ye were sealed with that holy Spirit of promise,

14. Which is the earnest of our inheritance until the redemption of the purchased possession, unto the praise of his glory.

15. Wherefore I also, after I heard of your faith in the Lord Jesus, and love unto all the saints,

16. Cease not to give thanks for you, making mention of you in my prayers;

17. That the God of our Lord Jesus Christ, the Father of glory, may give unto you the spirit of wisdom and revelation in the knowledge of him:

18. The eyes of your understanding being enlightened; that ye may know

233

what is the hope of his calling, and what the riches of the glory of his inheritance in the saints,

19. And what is the exceeding great- **ness of his power to us-ward who believe, according to the working of his mighty power.**

LESSON OUTLINE

I. BLESSINGS IN CHRIST
  A. Worship of the Father
  B. Description of Christ's Part
II. INHERITANCE IN CHRIST
  A. Description of the Inheritance
  B. Purpose of the Christian's Inheritance
  C. Description of the Holy Spirit's Work in the Believer
III. SPIRITUAL UNDERSTANDING
  A. Conditions Leading to Paul's Prayer
  B. Paul's Thanksgiving and Prayer

LESSON EXPOSITION

INTRODUCTION

The lessons in this quarter focus upon the writings of the Apostle Paul. Paul was one of the most profound individuals presented in the New Testament. He played a pivotal role in early Christianity. The Bible documents his Christian character and ministry. He was a true Christian and a major apostle. His writings articulated many of the doctrines of the Christian faith. This quarter of lesson material provides the opportunity to look at the apostle and many of his writings which have decisively contributed to Christianity.

The passages in this quarter will come from Ephesians, Philippians, Colossians, and 1 Thessalonians. With the exception of the latter, these Epistles were written while Paul was imprisoned in Rome. Paul was under house arrest in Rome awaiting the outcome of his appeal to Caesar. His imprisonment probably covered the years from A.D. 59 to 61. Colossians and Ephesians, along with Philemon, were probably delivered by Tychicus to their various destinations (Ephesians 6:21-22 and Colossians 4:7). Philippians was delivered by Epaphroditus (Philippians 2:25-30).

This first lesson is from the Book of Ephesians. Paul had been to Ephesus on his second missionary journey. He spent three years there as part of his third missionary journey. Timothy ministered there after Paul left. Ephesus was a major metropolitan area with a population of approximately 500-750 thousand people.

There does not appear to be any major crisis or theological struggle occurring at Ephesus at the occasion of Paul's writing to the Ephesians. Rather, the Epistle seems to be a description of the life of faith as Paul had experienced it. He expresses his hope that the Ephesians would experience this life of faith. In fact, the Scripture text of this lesson includes a prayer on the part of Paul for the faith of the Ephesians. Paul prefaces his prayer with words of praise to the Father and Christ. Also, he includes a description of the work of the Spirit in the life of the believer.

I. BLESSINGS IN CHRIST (Ephesians 1:3-10)

A. Worship of the Father (vv. 3-6)

3. Blessed be the God and Father of our Lord Jesus Christ, who hath blessed us with all spiritual blessings in heavenly places in Christ.

In verses 3-6 Paul offers an utterance of praise unto God, the Father, who has made provision for the believer through Jesus Christ. The first part of verse 3 expresses a blessing to the Father. Paul uses a familiar word and expression when he uses the word "blessed." It was not a commonplace expression. On the contrary, it was an utterance recognizing God as the source of all blessings. Paul knew that what he received had come from God. He was saying, "Blessed be the giver of all blessings" (*Linguistic Key to the Greek New Testament* by Rienecker and Rogers, pp. 450, 521).

The rest of verse 3 down through verse 6 is a description of God's blessing upon the believer, primarily through

Jesus Christ. The initial statement of the blessing upon the believer is in the latter portion of verse 3. God's blessing upon the believer has been by means of "all spiritual blessings" coming from within the heavenly realm. "Heavenly" emphasizes that the blessings are not based upon this world. They come from a sphere that is beyond this corrupt world. The term "all" assures the believer that God does not keep any good thing from those that love Him.

4. According as he hath chosen us in him before the foundation of the world, that we should be holy and without blame before him in love.

The first part of verse 4 extends the idea of blessing from verse 3 and indicates the reason God's blessing is evident in the life of the believer. God has "chosen" anyone who will believe in Christ. This is the first indication of God's blessing upon the believer presented by Paul. *Chosen,* according to the Greek text, indicates a definite time in which God spoke for, or selected the believer. It also indicates that God chose the believer as opposed to those who do not believe. Finally, the word indicates that God chose the believer for Himself, to be in vital fellowship with Him.

"Before the foundation of the world" indicates the time at which God chose anyone who would trust in Christ for their salvation. The phrase refers to time before natural and earthly time. The decision came from God alone. It was not dependent upon this world. It was a decision made in eternity.

"In him" is an extremely important phrase. It distinguishes the nature of God's choosing. "Him" refers to Christ who was mentioned just previously in the latter part of verse 3. The phrase indicates that the choosing is not exclusive. It does not select particular persons to be saved. Rather, the choosing is done "in Christ." The decision is made in and by the criterion of Christ himself. The choice is of whomsoever will believe in Christ and live in Him.

The latter part of verse 4 indicates the purpose of God for choosing the believer

in Christ. The purpose is that the believer "should be holy and without blame before him in love." "Holy" indicates separation and is highlighted in the phrase, "without blame." The phrase meant that which is unblemished and was used in reference to sacrificial animals in the Old Testament. The call to vital relationship with God is stressed in the phrase, "before him in love." "Before" emphasizes being continually within the presence of God. The believer's life is to be completely involved in a loving relationship with God.

5. Having predestinated us unto the adoption of children by Jesus Christ to himself, according to the good pleasure of his will,

6. To the praise of the glory of his grace, wherein he hath made us accepted in the beloved.

Verses 5 and 6 indicate the condition of the believer as a result of being chosen in God. "Adoption" is the result of God's choosing. "Predestinated" reaffirms God's act of choosing. "Predestinated" came from a Greek word which was used for someone marking out a boundary in preparation for something. In this verse the word refers to God's prior planning and arrangements for the adoption of the believer.

"Adoption" is a very important concept for the Christian. The Greek word used here for *adoption* literally meant to "place someone as a son." It carried a very important legal concept in the Roman world. Adoption was a "legal action by which a person takes into his family a child not his own, with the purpose of treating him as and giving him all the privileges of an own son" (*Studies in the Vocabulary of the Greek New Testament* by Wuest, p. 78). God gives the regenerated sinner who believes in Christ as Savior the eternal privileges and responsibilities of His kingdom. Though not born into the family of God, the believer is fully "adopted."

The latter portion of verse 5 gives the extent of the adoption. The adoption extends as far as the "good pleasure of his [God's] will." Rather than being guaranteed by an earthly legal process, the adoption is secured by the "good pleasure of his will." The adoption is the result of a loving God. The terms of the adoption are as strong as that love.

Verse 6 conveys the purpose of the believer's adoption. That purpose is "the praise of the glory of his grace." God's adoption of the believer is directed toward this end. The manifestation and glory of God's marvelous grace is displayed by the act of adoption into the family of God. The believer's adoption in Christ is an event which demonstrates the abundant love of God.

Paul adds that adoption makes the believer "accepted in the beloved." *Accepted* came from a Greek term which meant to "bestow grace upon someone with an act of grace." Rather than a judgmental kind of acceptance, the term emphasizes an act of unmerited favor.

"In the beloved" indicates the person in which the bestowing of grace takes place. The "beloved" refers to Christ. This act of grace is possible within the scope of Christ's work. In the act of adoption into the family of God, the believer is given grace.

B. Description of Christ's Part in Our Redemption (vv. 7-10)

7. In whom we have redemption through his blood, the forgiveness of sins, according to the riches of his grace.

Paul expands his reference to the work of Christ. In verse 7 he states the work of Christ twice and gives the means and extent of Christ's work. Paul first describes Christ's work as "redemption." Paul states that in Christ the believer possesses "redemption." The particular Greek word used here for *redemption* meant "to set someone free or ransom someone, usually for a certain ransom price." The phrase "forgiveness of sins" indicates the thing from which the believer is redeemed. The believer is redeemed from the bondage of sin.

"Through his blood" indicates the means and purchase price which made redemption possible. This refers to Christ's sacrificial death in behalf of sinners.

"The forgiveness of sins" is a specific restatement of Christ's work. It compliments the earlier use of "redemption" by demonstrating the particular bondage a person is redeemed from, the bondage of sin. "Forgiveness" referred to an action dismissing someone from bondage and prison. It meant not only freedom from captivity, but also the cancellation of obligations attached to the imprisonment. Freedom from guilt as well as from bonds occurs.

"According to the riches of His grace" indicates the extent of Christ's redemption and forgiveness of sins. Rather than exhibiting a portion of God's grace, Christ's redemptive work displays the fullness of the riches of God's grace. "Riches" emphasizes the fullness of God's provision. God's goodness in Christ is a full measure of His good pleasure and grace unto mankind.

8. Wherein he hath abounded toward us in all wisdom and prudence;

9. Having made known unto us the mystery of his will, according to his good pleasure which he hath purposed in himself.

(Ephesians 1:10 is not included in the printed text.)

Verses 8-10 convey the benefits the believer acquires in redemption. These benefits are generally stated in verse 8. These benefits extend from the "riches of his grace" mentioned in the latter part of verse 7. These benefits have "abounded" toward the believer. "Abounded" emphasizes that the quantity of God's action toward the believer is above and beyond minimal amounts. God's action in Christ is not only sufficient for redemption, it far exceeds what was required for forgiveness of sins.

The phrase "in all wisdom and prudence" indicates that divine intelligence and understanding brings about the redemption of lost humanity. "All" is an important word. It indicates the wisdom and prudence exercised were not minimal or natural. God encompasses wisdom and prudence in His divine intelligence. Rather than being illogical or unreasonable, redemption was the most reasonable and prudent event in history. It displayed "all" wisdom and prudence. It resulted from the work of the Creator of intelligence and understanding Himself.

The revelation of the mystery of God's will is a primary benefit made possible by the redemption of Christ. This is the topic of verse 9. It presents another aspect of God's benefits to the redeemed, the other aspect being the abounding nature of His grace.

The phrase "having made known" indicates that the mystery has definitely been revealed. It is no longer hidden. The mystery of God's will has already been revealed in Christ.

"Mystery" came from a Greek word which referred to something that was unknown. It only became known to those who had been given rights and privileges to know the mystery. The content of the mystery is completely hidden except to those with the special, confidential rights to the information. The access to the content of the mystery was something granted. It was acquired only by the privilege of revelation. The mystery of God's will in Christ was completely unaccessable to mankind. The knowledge of the mystery came to humanity only through the revelation of God.

The revelation of the mystery of God's will was an act of love by God. *Will* in this verse comes from a Greek word, *thelema,* which emphasizes a "determination stemming from the emotions." If it had been a will based purely on reason, a different Greek term, *boule,* would have been used. The revelation of God's will was a privileged insight into the depths of God's loving desire for mankind. The last phrase of verse 9, "according to his good pleasure which he hath purposed in himself," is a further indication of the depth of this heartfelt love and desire.

Verse 10 indicates the purpose of Christ's work in redemption. It refers to the gathering of all things in Christ. The verse emphasizes the scope of Christ's work of redemption. Christ's redemption encompasses all things in heaven and earth.

What does Paul have in mind when he says, "Blessed be God"? What is involved in God's choosing the believer? How important was the act of adoption in the Roman world? What is the means of Christ's redemption of lost humanity? To what extent did God forgive sins in the sacrifice of Christ?

II. INHERITANCE IN CHRIST (Ephesians 1:11-14)

A. Description of the Inheritance (v. 11)

11. In whom also we have obtained an inheritance, being predestinated according to the purpose of him who worketh all things after the counsel of his own will.

The phrase "obtained an inheritance" came from a single Greek word which highlighted the special provisions appointed to the believer by Christ. The term refers to a definite action which has already taken place. The believer's inheritance has already been secured by Christ. The Greek word for this phrase was used in Greek culture for the casting of lots in order to appoint certain things to individuals. In similar fashion, Christ's work of redemption has appointed and destined the believer to obtain the things of the will of God.

"Predestinated" is the same word used earlier in verse 5. The term here stresses God's prior determination of the believer's life. The criterion of this determination is the "purpose" of God. The boundaries God has predetermined for the Christian are not arbitrary. They are according to His purposes. The standard is God himself.

Paul explains the manner in which God arranges that purpose. God "worketh" all things, including the believer's life, according to the "counsel of his own will." "Worketh" emphasizes the effective work of God. Every determination God makes for the life of the believer is beneficial for the believer and not wasteful or harmful. "Counsel" emphasizes careful deliberation by God. God's purposes and plans for the believer are not careless and haphazard. They are reasonably and deliberately made.

"Of His own will" indicates the source from which all of the deliberation and planning of God is derived God's will. "Will" is the same word used in verse 9. It indicates the heartfelt love of God. God's purposes for the believer stem from deep within the loving desire and will of God.

B. Purpose of the Christian's Inheritance (v. 12)

12. That we should be to the praise of his glory, who first trusted in Christ.

The ultimate purpose of God's work of redemption in the life of the believer, and all of the circumstances which accompany that redemption are for bringing praise to the glory of God. This was the purpose God had in mind when He brought about His glorious plan of redemption. This purpose is not the result of man's efforts. It is a principle of the redemption itself. The inevitable conclusion of redemption is that God be glorified. God is glorified in His redemption of lost humanity.

C. Description of the Holy Spirit's Work in the Believer (vv. 13, 14)

13. In whom ye also trusted, after that ye heard the word of truth, the gospel of your salvation: in whom also after that ye believed, ye were sealed with that holy Spirit of promise,

14. Which is the earnest of our inheritance until the redemption of the purchased possession, unto the praise of his glory.

The first half of verse 13 is a description of the believer's trust in Christ. Paul ended verse 12 with the theme of trust. He continues it in verse 13. Paul recognizes the trust of the Ephesian believers in the simple statement, "In whom ye also trusted." He next indicates the timing of that trust. It came after they heard "the word of truth, the gospel of your salvation."

The act of initial believing, according to Paul, involved the actions of hearing and trusting. *Hearing* is the reception of the gospel and *trusting* is the required response to the gospel. The "word of truth" is the essential message to all persons. The gospel is God's truth available equally to all persons. The gospel is applied to each trusting individual and becomes their salvation. Personal application of the gospel is the emphasis of the phrase, "the gospel of *your* salvation."

The latter portion of verses 13 and 14 describes the work of the Holy Spirit in the believer. Having described the believer's reception of salvation, Paul now focuses upon the Spirit's role in redemption. The Spirit's work is to "seal" the believer. "Seal" referred to the ancient practice of sealing and securing a document. The "seal" guaranteed ownership claims and the authenticity of the contents. The Holy Spirit acts as the guarantor of the presence and ownership of God in the redeemed. The Holy Spirit also guarantees the authenticity of salvation for the believer.

The Holy Spirit also serves as the "earnest" of the inheritance of the believer. *Earnest* came from a Greek word indicating the "down payment, pledge, or deposit" which served as a guarantee that the full amount would be paid. This concept complements the guaranteeing concept in "sealing." Both highlight the title given to the Holy Spirit as the "holy Spirit of promise." The primary function of the Holy Spirit described here is to assure the believer of the reality of the salvation they have received upon trusting in Christ.

How does Paul describe the predestination of God as it relates to the inheritance of the believer in redemption? What is the purpose of the Christian's inheritance? What actions are involved in initial believing? What is the role of the Holy Spirit in redemption as described in this passage by Paul?

III. SPIRITUAL UNDERSTANDING (Ephesians 1:15-23)

A. Conditions Leading to Paul's Prayer (v. 15)

15. Wherefore I also, after I heard of your faith in the Lord Jesus, and love unto all the saints.

The remainder of this passage, verses

15-23, concerns a prayer by Paul for the Ephesian Christians. Paul offers this prayer from a positive perspective. He had heard of their faith and love. Based upon this, he offers the following prayer. His prayer is in response to their Christian maturity.

B. Paul's Thanksgiving and Prayer (vv. 16-23)

16. Cease not to give thanks for you, making mention of you in my prayers.

Verse 16 is a statement of the fact that Paul had been praying for the Ephesian believers. His prayers have been unceasing. The Ephesians had been a constant source of thankfulness for Paul. They had also been part of Paul's continual petition before God. They had evoked both gratitude and intercession. The content of his thanksgiving and petitions is in verses 17-23.

17. That the God of our Lord Jesus Christ, the Father of glory, may give unto you the spirit of wisdom and revelation in the knowledge of him:

18. The eyes of your understanding being enlightened; that ye may know what is the hope of his calling, and what the riches of the glory of his inheritance in the saints,

19. And what is the exceeding greatness of his power to usward who believe, according to the working of his mighty power.

(Ephesians 1:20-23 is not included in the printed text.)

Paul prays that the Ephesian believers would receive insight into four primary areas—the knowledge of Christ (v. 17), the hope of Christ's calling (v. 18), the "riches of the glory of His inheritance" (v. 18), and God's power (vv. 19-22).

Paul's request for the believers to receive insight into the knowledge of Christ is found in verse 17. Paul desires that God would give them the "spirit of wisdom and revelation in the knowledge of him [Christ]." "What Paul is praying for is that God might so work in the lives of the Ephesian saints that they will have the spiritual wisdom and a revelation from Him that is the result of the Holy Spirit energizing their human spirit" (*Ephesians*

and Colossians in the Greek New Testament by Wuest, p. 52).

Paul's request for the believers to receive insight into the hope of Christ's calling is in the first part of verse 18. This petition refers back to the concepts of inheritance and the role of the Holy Spirit in guaranteeing the inheritance of the believer. Paul's prayer is that the reality of the hope of redemption in Christ would continue to be made known unto them.

Paul's request that they have insight into the "riches of the glory of his inheritance" is in the latter portion of verse 18. It stresses the depth of their inheritance in salvation. This refers back to Paul's earlier discussion of the "riches" of God's grace (v. 7), the abounding of the work of God (v. 8), the gathering of "all things" in accomplishing His will (v. 10). The inheritance of God is not measured by the riches of God. Paul prayed that the Ephesian believers would have insight into the depth of those riches.

Paul's request that they have insight into God's power is found in verses 19-22. Paul describes this power as having "exceeding greatness," measured by the standard of God's own "mighty power." "Exceeding greatness" emphasizes the superiority of the power which Paul desired for the Ephesians. This power is determined, supplied, and controlled by God himself. It is a power established by Christ. It is a power which serves the purposes of Christ. It is a power which encompasses all things and puts them under the command and authority of Christ.

Paul ends the prayer by referring to the vital relationship between Christ and the church (vv. 22, 23). The church is an extension of Christ in the world. Paul's emphasis in verse 23 is the manner in which the church is to be the fullness of Christ. The church is, by its very nature, the body of Christ in the world.

In chapter 1 Paul has given a description of the work of redemption wrought in Christ. Paul declared that the source of the work is God. The standard by which the effects of the work are measured is God. The guarantee of the reality of the work is God. Paul's faith that the work of redemption be fully applied to the believer rests in God. Redemption is rooted in the grace and love of God. It was carried out in the work of Christ. It is applied to an individual's life as he trusts in God for his salvation.

REVIEW QUESTIONS

1. What is the occasion that prompted Paul's prayer for the Ephesian believers?

2. How often did Paul give thanks and make petitions in behalf of them?

3. What were the four main points of Paul's prayer?

4. In what ways does the prayer refer to Paul's previous descriptions of the work of redemption?

5. What is the redemption of God rooted in?

6. How is redemption applied to an individual's life?

GOLDEN TEXT HOMILY

"BLESSED BE THE GOD AND FATHER OF OUR LORD JESUS CHRIST, WHO HATH BLESSED US WITH ALL SPIRITUAL BLESSINGS IN HEAVENLY PLACES IN CHRIST" (Ephesians 1:3).

There are certain words in the Authorized King James Version that are no longer in current use. One such word is "blessed." Very seldom do you hear anyone called "blessed" nowadays. A pity, too, for there is a wealth of meaning in this word that the substitute "happy" by modern translators cannot convey.

The word *blessed* as used in the New Testament has several meanings. The ancient Greeks ascribed the quality of blessedness to deity, which means "to bless," "to praise," or "to speak well of." It is in this sense that Paul speaks of God in our golden text and ascribes to Him the highest possible honor. As we recognize the greatness and faithfulness of God in our lives, we too join the chorus of praise in declaring that "The Lord is a great God, and a great King above all gods" (Psalm 95:3).

Paul also announces that God has blessed us in the heavenly realms with every spiritual blessing in Christ. All that we long for or hope for is found in personal relationship with Jesus Christ, and because that relationship is so intimate and real, we have in Jesus himself the abundant life for which we yearn and which God has ever yearned to give straying mankind.

What a wonderful truth that we are "blessed . . . with all spiritual blessings in heavenly places." We are told that "our citizenship is in heaven" (Philippians 3: 20, *New International Version*), where our High Priest is ever "blessing" us. Our "treasures" are there (Matthew 6: 20, 21). Our hopes (Colossians 1:5; Titus 2:13), our aims and affections (Colossians 3:1, 2) are also there. Our inheritance (1 Peter 1:4) is there. Spiritual blessings in heavenly places! We are truly blessed. Blessed by God!—**J. Ralph Brewer, Pastor, Cramerton, North Carolina**

SENTENCE SERMONS

THROUGH FAITH in Jesus Christ, a person enters into a new life of fellowship with God.

—Selected

YOU CANNOT be a son of God over there, unless you are a son of God down here.

—"Notes and Quotes"

IF WE ARE GOING to a prepared place, we must make necessary preparations for it.

—William Ellis

THE LORD JESUS CHRIST loves to reveal Himself to those who dare to take the bleak side of the hill with Him.

—"This Day"

EVANGELISTIC APPLICATION

GOD'S PLAN OF REDEMPTION PROVIDES FORGIVENESS OF SINS THROUGH THE BLOOD OF CHRIST.

God's plan of redemption provides for an abundant supply of blessings, but primary among these blessings is the forgiveness of sins. Sin holds an individual in bondage. The darkness of sin imprisons a person in fear, depression, frustration, guilt, and shame. The redemption which God offers to those who repent of their sins and accept Christ as Savior releases a person from bonds and fetters of sin.

God's forgiveness is not only a release from bondage but a freedom from guilt. The sins which caused the person to be in bondage are forgiven. An individual, once forgiven, is released from the requirements and punishments required of their sins. They are free from guilt as well as bondage.

This marvelous forgiveness of God is made possible by the blood of Christ. The shedding of blood in His sacrifice was necessary according to God to satisfy His judgment and justice. Christ was the only person worthy and pure enough to be offered as a blood sacrifice in behalf of the sins of mankind. Christ offered Himself willingly that those who would trust in Him as Savior would be saved.

God's almighty plan of redemption has already accomplished the salvation of those who would accept Christ as Savior. All that remains is the application of that work to individual lives. A person can receive forgiveness of sins through the blood of Christ if he will repent of his sins and accept Christ as his Lord and Savior.

ILLUMINATING THE LESSON

Eilert Rogerned, a taxi driver of Oslo, Norway, on four occasions took a seventy-year-old woman to her desired destination. On the fifth time he was asked to take her to a mountain resort, she gave him what amounted to a $4,000.00 tip, because he was "extremely helpful, polite, and cheerful." She gave him legal documents making him the owner of an acre of ground and a cottage at the resort. He checked with authorities and found the papers to be legal.

God offers you a great gift. It's yours for the claiming. Check on it in God's Word.

A Christian lady on her deathbed was visited by a brother who lived a great distance away. He told her that he probably would never see her again in the land of the living as he prepared to return home. She answered, "Brother, I trust we shall meet in the land of the living; we are now in the land of the dying."

DAILY BIBLE READINGS

M. A Blessing Promised. Genesis 12:1-3

T. Faith Rewarded. Genesis 15:1-6

W. Christ Our Sin-Bearer. Isaiah 53:1-11

T. Salvation Provided. John 3:16-18

F. God Is for Us. Romans 8:31-39

S. Christ's Love for Us. Revelation 1:1-6

God's Mercy in Christ

Study Text: Ephesians 2:1-22

Supplemental References: Exodus 20:1-6; Leviticus 16:2-19; Psalm 86:1-7; Romans 10:6-13; Titus 2:11-14

Time: Probably in A.D. 61

Place: Written from a Roman prison

Golden Text: "By grace are ye saved through faith; and that not of yourselves: it is the gift of God" (Ephesians 2:8).

Central Truth: God's mercy toward us is expressed by Christ's death on the cross.

Evangelistic Emphasis: God's message to sinners is reconciliation through faith in Jesus Christ.

Printed Text

Ephesians 2:4. But God, who is rich in mercy, for his great love wherewith he loved us,

5. Even when we were dead in sins, hath quickened us together with Christ, (by grace ye are saved;)

6. And hath raised us up together, and made us sit together in heavenly places in Christ Jesus:

7. That in the ages to come he might shew the exceeding riches of his grace in his kindness toward us through Christ Jesus.

8. For by grace are ye saved through faith; and that not of yourselves: it is the gift of God:

9. Not of works, lest any man should boast.

10. For we are his workmanship, created in Christ Jesus unto good works, which God hath before ordained that we should walk in them.

13. But now in Christ Jesus ye who sometimes were far off are made nigh by the blood of Christ.

14. For he is our peace, who hath made both one, and hath broken down the middle wall of partition between us;

15. Having abolished in his flesh the enmity, even the law of commandments contained in ordinances; for to make in himself of twain one new man, so making peace;

16. And that he might reconcile both unto God in one body by the cross, having slain the enmity thereby:

17. And came and preached peace to you which were afar off, and to them that were nigh.

18. For through him we both have access by one Spirit unto the Father.

19. Now therefore ye are no more strangers and foreigners, but fellow-citizens with the saints, and of the household of God;

20. And are built upon the foundation of the apostles and prophets, Jesus Christ himself being the chief corner stone;

21. In whom all the building fitly framed together groweth unto an holy temple in the Lord:

22. In whom ye also are builded together for an habitation of God through the Spirit.

LESSON OUTLINE

I. CHRIST OUR SAVIOR
   A. Description of the Believer's Former Condition
   B. Contrasting Action of God Toward the Sinner
   C. Summary of the Actions of God Toward the Believer
II. CHRIST OUR PEACE
   A. Description of the Gentiles
   B. The Work of Christ's Blood
   C. Christ's Work of Peace
III. CHRIST OUR FOUNDATION
   A. Access to the Father
   B. Description of Gentiles as Part of the Household of God
   C. Christ Our Foundation

LESSON EXPOSITION

INTRODUCTION

In the first three chapters of Ephesians, Paul presents some important doctrinal teachings. They represent principles about the nature of God the Father, the Son, and the Holy Spirit. These principles instruct the believer about God's plan of salvation. They give insight into God's intention for the believer's present life on earth.

Chapter 1 of Ephesians emphasizes God's work of redemption. Chapter 2 stresses the manner in which God's mercy has transformed the believer, especially the Gentile. Chapter 3 focuses upon the revelation of the mystery of God hid in Christ Jesus. The underlying theme of all three chapters is the work of God in the life of the believer.

Chapter 2 emphasizes God's mercy as revealed in Christ. Christ's work as Savior makes peace possible for the believer and lays the foundation for the household of God. Believers are part of that household and the Holy Spirit inhabits it.

I. CHRIST OUR SAVIOR (Ephesians 2:1-10)

A. Description of the Believer's Former Condition (vv. 1-3)

(Ephesians 2:1-3 is not included in the printed text.)

In verses 1-3 Paul describes the believer as someone previously "dead in tres-

passes and sins." Further, the believer before conversion is led by the "course of this world" and is an offspring of sinfulness. This brief description is a good reminder to the reader of the reality and depth of their corruption before they accepted Christ as Savior. Paul moves from this section to a description of God's action toward lost humanity.

B. Contrasting Action of God Toward the Sinner (vv. 4-7)

4. But God, who is rich in mercy, for his great love wherewith he loved us,

5. Even when we were dead in sins, hath quickened us together with Christ, (by grace ye are saved;)

6. And hath raised us up together, and made us sit together in heavenly places in Christ Jesus.

Paul begins verse 4 by noting that God's action is in contrast to the sinful condition of man. The believer was previously dead in sin, "but God" brought him to newness of life. Verses 4-7 explain the nature of God's response to the sinfulness of man.

Paul describes God as One who is "rich in mercy." Mercy "indicates the emotion aroused by someone in need and the attempt to relieve the person and remove his trouble" (*Linguistic Key to the Greek New Testament* by Rienecker and Rogers, p. 525). The Greek text emphasizes the richness of God's mercy. Rather than being hesitant to redeem lost sinners, God is abundant and rich in His merciful desire to save the lost.

God's love makes His redemption of the lost possible. It was "for His great love" that God extended His redemption. His love was the means and instrument which made redemption possible. The Greek text emphasizes the greatness of God's love. As with the richness of His mercy, the greatness of His love responds to the sinfulness of mankind.

The phrase "wherewith He loved us" indicates that God's love has been applied to mankind. It is not just a theoretical love. It is not just a feeling that has not been turned into action. God's love is a love that has already been extended to the lost. It is a love that was given even in the midst of the sinner's lost and spiritually dead condition.

Paul describes three aspects of God's action in redemption. The first is that God "hath quickened us together with Christ." This action brings the sinner, who is dead, into life. It is an action emphasizing close fellowship with the life of Christ. The existence of the life of the Christian is vitally associated and dependent upon Christ.

There is a paranthetical statement emphasizing the dependent nature of the believer's new life. The transformation from spiritual death to newness of life is not the result of anything the sinner is or does. It is "by grace." The theme of grace is expanded later in verse 8. "Saved" in the Greek text here refers to a salvation experience which was previously received and has a continuing reality. God's grace completed the work of salvation for the believer and continues to apply its power in that life.

The second aspect of God's action in redemption is that He "hath raised us up together" in Christ. This aspect of redemption emphasizes the effects of salvation beyond this earthly life. God's work toward the believer goes beyond newness of life on earth. God provides for the eternal life of those who trust Him. This eternal life is vitally dependent upon and in fellowship with Christ. Hence, the believer is raised "together" with Christ.

The third and final aspect of God's action in redemption mentioned in verse 6 is that He has "made us sit together in heavenly places in Christ Jesus." The emphasis of this action is upon the authority and position of the believer apart from the trivialities and evils of this world. The believer is in a position in Christ which is not governed by the spirit of this world. He is governed by things "in heavenly places in Christ Jesus." God's provision of redemption includes a new order of life that is controlled by Christ.

7. That in the ages to come he might shew the exceeding riches of his grace in his kindness toward us through Christ Jesus.

Having given a description of various aspects of God's action in redemption, Paul gives the reason and purpose for those actions. "That" at the beginning of verse 7 is a word indicating that what follows is the reason for what was just discussed. God's purpose in His redemptive activity is to "shew the exceeding riches of his grace in his kindness toward us through Christ Jesus."

The phrase "ages to come" indicates the time in which God will display His riches. God intends His redemptive activity to be an eternal witness to the measureless riches of His grace. Salvation is not just something for a few individuals in a particular age of time. Persons who accept salvation enter into an eternal plan which gives unending witness of God's grace.

"Shew" in this context means to "demonstrate, display, or show." "Exceeding" comes from a Greek term *huperbalonta* which literally means "to throw beyond." It describes something that surpasses ordinary standards. The term here refers to the outstanding superiority and excellence of God's grace. Paul climaxes his discussion of grace in verse 8.

The demonstration of God's grace is found in His action of "kindness toward us through Jesus Christ." "Kindness" comes from a Greek term *chrestotes* which refers to "effective kindness." This kindness is used to benefit another person, not just a nice emotion within someone. God's "kindness" is effective because of Christ Jesus. God is rich in grace. This is demonstrated in His kindness toward sinful man through Christ.

C. Summary of the Actions of God Toward the Believer (vv. 8-10)

8. For by grace are ye saved through faith; and that not of yourselves: it is the gift of God:

9. Not of works, lest any man should boast.

The theme of grace which Paul began focusing on in verse 5 is climaxed in verses 8 and 9. "Grace" comes from the Greek word *charis*. The term was used in classical secular Greek to refer to things which delight and create beauty for others. These were "gracious" things or persons who were beautiful enough to elicit a positive response from others. The word was used to refer to the graciousness of an individual or ruler which caused them to be gracious to others. However, the emphasis was often upon being gracious in a pleasing circumstance to a favorable person.

Charis, as used by Paul and others in the New Testament, radically departed from much of the classical secular usage of the word "grace." The New Testament writers attributed "grace" to God as an act and attribute that spontaneously responded to those who were unfavorable, even unjust. The grace of God is an act that is not motivated by the external beauty of the one receiving grace. God's grace comes from the loving character of God and extends to the most undeserving individuals.

The grace of God makes salvation possible. The repenting sinner is saved "by grace." "Faith" is the channel through which salvation is administered. The repenting sinner is saved "through faith." Human dependency for salvation is secondary. Salvation is not of man. It is a "gift" coming from God and God alone.

The meaning of salvation as a "gift" from God is amplified in the latter portion of verse 9. As a gift, salvation is freely given. It is not earned by "works." Because salvation is not earned, no one can "boast" of the salvation they have received. Not even the act of faith by an individual creates salvation. Redemption's source is completely an act of God's grace. Faith is the channel which applies God's grace. Nothing is done in salvation that would allow man to boast and rob God of the praise and glory due Him (see v. 7).

10. For we are his workmanship, created in Christ Jesus unto good works, which God hath before ordained that we should walk in them.

Verse 9 ends with the impossibility of man's work being the basis of salvation. Verse 10, in contrast, emphasizes the work of God done in salvation. Rather than the creator of salvation, the believer becomes the "workmanship" of redemption. "Workmanship" refers to the action of God that has been done in the repentant sinner in salvation. The means by which salvation is accomplished is Christ Jesus. The purpose for God's workmanship in the believer is "good works." "Good works" emphasizes those things which are eternally good in the plan of God. They are not good because of the action of man. They are good because they result from God's salvation. The Christian is not void of works. The Christian's good works are not for salvation (v. 9), but the Christian's good works are the result of salvation.

God has already established the "good works" which are the result of salvation. God has also "ordained" that the Christian should "walk in them." Good works are not originated in man. They ultimately originate in the grace of God. God's plan is that the Christian live and walk in the works of God.

How did Paul describe the former condition of the believer before salvation? What was God's response to the sinner while he was still dead in trespasses and sin? In what ways does Paul describe God's action toward sinners? How did the New Testament writers radically change the secular usage of the word "grace" when they applied it to God's salvation?

II. CHRIST OUR PEACE (Ephesians 2:11-17)

A. Description of the Gentiles (vv. 11, 12)   (Ephesians 2:11, 12 is not included in the printed text.)

In verse 11 Paul reminds the Ephesian believers that they were once outside of God's provision through the Jewish nation. In verse 12 Paul explains that this meant they were "without Christ," "aliens from the commonwealth of Israel," did not have the "covenant of promise," they had "no hope," and they were "without God in the world." Paul is emphasizing how far removed they were as Gentiles from God's salvation.

B. The Work of Christ's Blood (v. 13)

13. But now in Christ Jesus ye who sometimes were far off are made nigh by the blood of Christ.

In contrast to the great distance separating the Gentiles and God's salvation through the nation of Israel is the total provision of Christ. Salvation is "now" made available to the Gentiles through Christ. Specifically, the means by which this salvation became possible is the "blood of Christ." The sacrifice of the Messiah on the Cross was the fulfillment of the requirements of the provisions described in verse 12. The terms of the commonwealth, the covenant, and the hope—all established by God—required a blood sacrifice for the sins of mankind. Christ became that sacrifice. As a result, salvation became available to Gentiles as well as Jews. Paul explains that availability given to Gentiles in verses 14-17.

C. Christ's Work of Peace (vv. 14-17)

14. For he is our peace, who hath made both one, and hath broken down the middle wall of partition between us;

15a. Having abolished in his flesh the enmity, even the law of commandments contained in ordinances.

In verses 14-17 Paul explains the reason why Christ's work accomplished salvation for all persons. Specifically, he explains the manner in which Christ's work brought salvation to the Gentiles as well as the Jews. Verse 14 through the first portion of verse 15 emphasizes the work of Christ itself. The latter portion of verse 15 and verse 16 emphasize the purpose for Christ's work as it relates to Gentiles and Jews.

In the beginning of verse 14 Paul introduces the theme of "peace." This is the central accomplishment of the work of Christ regarding the Jews and Gentiles. "Peace" emphasizes the opposite of conflict. Reconciliation and genuine relationships are stressed. Christ not only makes this possible but is Himself peace. The peace of Christ is the result of who Christ is first of all. From the character of peace within Christ came His work accomplishing peace for the lost.

Christ's work made Jews and Gentiles "one." This work "broke" the separation between them. "Broken" comes from the Greek word *lusas* meaning "to destroy." The thing destroyed was the "middle wall of partition." The word order of the Greek text places "enmity" as a further description of the nature of the dividing wall between Jews and Gentiles.

"Enmity" comes from a Greek term *ekthron* meaning "hostility." The division between Jews and Gentiles before the sacrifice of Christ was hostility. By nature, the two were hostile and opposed to one another. The Jewish law commanded separation from Gentiles. The Gentile way of life cared nothing for Jewish law. They were opposed to one another.

Christ's own "flesh" was the means of "abolishing" the enmity maintained by the "law of commandments contained in ordinances." "Abolished" comes from the Greek term *katargesas* which meant to "render a work inoperative and ineffective." It did not mean to annihilate. Christ's work so dominated the effect of the Jewish law that it rendered the commandments no longer effective in God's plan of salvation. The work of God's salvation was fulfilled through Christ, not the law.

15b. For to make in himself of twain one new man, so making peace;

16. And that he might reconcile both unto God in one body by the cross, having slain the enmity thereby:

17. And came and preached peace to you which were afar off, and to them that were nigh.

In the latter portion of verse 15 and in verse 16 Paul presents the purpose of Christ's work as it relates to Jews and Gentiles. Christ's purpose was to bring the two peoples into "one new man." "Make" is actually "create." "New" is not something redone but something totally new. Therefore, this "new man" is different from the Jew and from the Gentile. This person is of a new order of existence, created by Christ himself. This new reality is one of peace. It is one in which persons are not at enmity, hostile to one another. The "new man," the Christian, is the product of reconciliation.

Verse 16 explains that this reconciliation is not just between the Jew and the Gentile. More importantly, it is a reconciliation established between them and God. The enmity between God and man has been *slain*. Slain means "to put to death." Hostility is killed and reconciliation is created at the Cross between God and man. Just as Jew and Gentile were opposed to one another, the sinful nature of man is opposed to God. That enmity between God and man is put to death in Christ's work at the cross.

Verse 17 refers to the central role peace played in the preaching of Jesus. Christ is the One who came and preached peace. Christ not only established the reality of reconciliation between God and man, He proclaimed it. This emphasizes the necessity of proclamation. Reconciliation must be carried one step further in the act of preaching. Christ himself felt the need to proclaim peace, both to the Gentile and the Jew.

In what ways does Paul describe the Gentiles in comparison to those of the nation of Israel? What made salvation available to the Gentiles? What was "broken" by Christ? What was "abolished" or rendered ineffective? What does Paul mean by "new man" in verse 15? What did Christ do besides establishing reconciliation?

III. CHRIST OUR FOUNDATION (Ephesians 2:18-22)

A. Access to the Father (v. 18)

18. For through him we both have access by one Spirit unto the Father.

In verse 18 Paul further explains the result of Christ's work of reconciliation. Christ provides "access . . . unto the Father." "Access" comes from the Greek word *prosagogen* which in ancient times referred to a "landing stage" area (*The Vocabulary of the Greek New Testament* by Moulton and Milligan, p. 545). It was

a receiving area. The word came to refer to the privilege, especially in divine and royal courts, of being received by a supreme authority. The word in this verse refers to "that friendly relation with God whereby we are acceptable to him and have assurance that he is favorably disposed towards us" (*Greek-English Lexicon of the New Testament* by Grimm and Thayer, p. 544).

B. Description of Gentiles as Part of the Household of God (vv. 19, 20a)

19. Now therefore ye are no more strangers and foreigners, but fellowcitizens with the saints, and of the household of God;

20a. And are built upon the foundation of the apostles and prophets.

Paul gives two illustrations of the reconciled position of the Gentile believer to God. The first is that of *citizens*. The second is that of a *household* or *family*. The idea of citizenship is enlarged and enriched with the deeper idea of family.

Before conversion, the believer was a "stranger" and "foreigner" with no access (see v. 18) to the Father. "Strangers" comes from the Greek word *xenoi* referring to someone who was not a natural citizen. "Foreigner" comes from the Greek word *paroikoi* meaning someone who resided in a country but did not have the rights of citizenship. These terms give a rather complete description of someone who had none of the rights or privileges of citizenship in a country.

In contrast, the believer is now a "fellowcitizen with the saints." "Fellowcitizens" emphasizes that the redeemed has the same origin and privileges of citizenship as the "saints." "Saints" is a descriptive term of those who have been set apart from sin unto God. The Christian has a holy citizenship giving him full authority and privilege in the kingdom of God.

To deepen the relationship of the believer with God, Paul adds that the Christian is of the "household of God." "Household" comes from a term *oikeioi* which can also be translated here as "members of the family." The term does not refer to servants, but actual family members in the household.

Paul develops the illustration of household by referring to the apostles and prophets as the *foundation* of the household. Apostles highlight the patriarchs of the early church. Prophets emphasize the role of the prophets of the Old Testament.

C. Christ Our Foundation (vv. 20b-22)

20b. Jesus Christ himself being the chief corner stone;

21. In whom all the building fitly framed together groweth unto an holy temple in the Lord:

22. In whom ye also are builded together for an habitation of God through the Spirit.

Paul climaxes this chapter on the redemption of God by giving a final description of the vital role of Christ. Paul's description centers around the concept of the "chief corner stone" of a building. The chief cornerstone is the most important stone in the masonry of a building. The stone must be carefully and permanently laid. It is usually laid by the best mason available. The rest of the stones in a building are measured and set straight by the measurement and straightness of the chief cornerstone. If that stone is not plumb and precise, the building will be crooked and insecure. The accuracy and strength of an entire masonry project depends upon the position and durability of the chief cornerstone. The chief cornerstone determines the development of the rest of the stonework.

With this background, Paul says that it is in Christ, or according to Christ, as the chief cornerstone, that the rest of the building is "fitly framed together." The household of God is built around Christ as the chief cornerstone. The result is that the household becomes a "holy temple in the Lord." The temple was the place where God was worshiped and praised. Similarly, the household of believers becomes a place of worship and praise unto God.

The temple was also the place where God was to have maintained His habitation on earth. With Christ as the chief

cornerstone, the household of God becomes the habitation of God as well. "Through the Spirit" is a brief reference to the role of the Spirit. God inhabits the household of believers through the Spirit. His habitation is a spiritual habitation.

With this climactic reference to God inhabiting the believer, Paul has come from the other end of the spectrum that he used at the beginning of the chapter. The chapter began with references to the former life of the believer when he was dead in trespasses and sin. In contrast, Paul presents the present condition of the believer in which the Spirit of God dwells within the Christian. In between, Paul has explained how God has made this possible through Christ. It is an act solely of God's grace received through the channel of faith.

REVIEW QUESTIONS

1. How did Paul describe the former condition of the believer before salvation?

2. In what ways does Paul describe the Gentiles in comparison to those of the nation of Israel?

3. What is meant by Paul's reference to the Christian's "access" to the Father?

4. What is the importance of a "chief cornerstone" in the masonry of a building?

5. What is the contrast between the way Paul began chapter 2 and ended it?

GOLDEN TEXT HOMILY

"BY GRACE ARE YE SAVED THROUGH FAITH; AND THAT NOT OF YOURSELVES: IT IS THE GIFT OF GOD" (Ephesians 2:8).

While serving as a missionary in Japan, I was often faced with the difficult task of trying to explain the grace of God to young people steeped in the teachings of Buddhism. On one occasion a university student witnessed my reaction to an accident involving a car load of students. A large dump truck hit my car while on a steep mountain road and it speeded away leaving us dangling over a thousand foot drop off.

I was so filled with praises to God because no one was injured that I never thought to be angry over the actions of the truck driver or the damage done to the car.

Following this episode the university student continued to come to the Bible class but watched me very closely. About six weeks later he came to me in tears of frustration because he had been practicing extreme control of his emotions since the episode of my accident. He had admired what he thought was disciplined self control in my life. At the accident, he reasoned, he would have been so angry over the truck driver and the damaged car that he would have exploded with rage. When he witnessed my reaction of praise and worship he thought that I, too, was boiling inside but was able to control those feelings. Using me as a model he had miserably tried to achieve this type of self control through his own efforts. Of course he failed.

Now in frustration he said, "Teach me how you do this," I could only turn with him to Paul's writings and tell him that becoming a new creature with the life and emotions of Christ flowing throughout was not achieved by man's effort but by God's grace. While love is an attribute of God that love becomes mercy and grace when it is related to sinners. God gives freely to us what we can never earn or deserve and this is possible by the death of His Son, Jesus, at Calvary.

By grace are ye saved through faith . . . Frank Gabelein in his commentary on Ephesians stated, "Faith, however, is not a quality, a virtue or a faculty. It is simply a trustful response that is itself evoked by the Holy Spirit." Therefore, it is all a gift of God and man is left with nothing wherein he can boast.—**Edward E. Call, Head Librarian, West Coast Christian College, Fresno, California**

SENTENCE SERMONS

GOD'S MERCY toward us is expressed by Christ's death on the cross.
—**Selected**

JESUS LIVED that He might die and died that we might live.
—**"Speaker's Sourcebook"**

CHRIST'S LIMITLESS RESOURCES meet endless needs.
—**"Speaker's Sourcebook"**

GOD'S WRATH comes by measure; His mercy without measure.
—**Selected**

EVANGELISTIC APPLICATION

GOD'S MESSAGE TO SINNERS IS RECONCILIATION THROUGH FAITH IN JESUS CHRIST.

God is aware of sinners and has a message He wishes to communicate to them. God knows every sin that is committed. He knows the origin and nature of sins committed by man. He has full knowledge of the circumstances and feelings behind every sin committed. God knows the wickedness and evil in the sinner's heart. Yet, God has a message of love and redemption He desires to proclaim to sinners.

The life of sin represents a hostile departure from the natural desires of God. The sinner does not fellowship with God. In fact, the life of the sinner is principally set in confrontation against God.

Despite the separation between God and the sinner, God has made reconciliation possible through faith in Jesus Christ. God's love does not respond to the confrontation of the sinner with alienation and bitterness. God's love gives reconciliation and peace. God earnestly desires fellowship and communion with the sinner.

This fellowship and communion with God is received through faith. It is already available, but it can only be received through faith in Jesus Christ as Lord and Savior. If the sinner is repentant before God and trusts Christ for his salvation, God will reconcile the sinner unto Himself. The sinner will be transformed from a stranger to a family member in the household of God.

DAILY BIBLE READINGS

M. God's Blessings. Genesis 1:26-31

T. God's Instructions. Genesis 2:8, 9, 15-17

W. God's Promise. Genesis 9:8-17

T. God and Man Reconciled. 2 Corinthians 5:17-21

F. Abiding in God's Love. Jude 20-25

S. Promise to the Overcomer. Revelation 21:1-7

God's Eternal Purpose

Study Text: Ephesians 3:1-21
Supplemental References: Isaiah 11:1-16; 12:1-6; 45:22; Daniel 2:28-45; Habakkuk 2:1-4; Matthew 4:12-17; Acts 13:44-49; Revelation 5:9-13
Time: Probably in A.D. 61
Place: Written from a Roman prison
Golden Text: "Unto him be glory in the church by Christ Jesus throughout all ages, world without end" (Ephesians 3:21).
Central Truth: Through God's redemptive plan, all believers become one in Christ.
Evangelistic Emphasis: God desires that all be saved and share in His glory.

Printed Text

Ephesians 3:1. For this cause I Paul, the prisoner of Jesus Christ for you Gentiles,

2. If ye have heard of the dispensation of the grace of God which is given me to you-ward:

3. How that by revelation he made known unto me the mystery; (as I wrote afore in few words,

6. That the Gentiles should be fellowheirs, and of the same body, and partakers of his promise in Christ by the gospel:

7. Whereof I was made a minister, according to the gift of the grace of God given unto me by the effectual working of his power.

8. Unto me, who am less than the least of all saints, is this grace given, that I should preach among the Gentiles the unsearchable riches of Christ;

9. And to make all men see what is the fellowship of the mystery, which from the beginning of the world hath been hid in God, who created all things by Jesus Christ:

10. To the intent that now unto the principalities and powers in heavenly places might be known by the church the manifold wisdom of God,

11. According to the eternal purpose which he purposed in Christ Jesus our Lord:

12. In whom we have boldness and access with confidence by the faith of him.

13. Wherefore I desire that ye faint not at my tribulations for you, which is your glory.

14. For this cause I bow my knees unto the Father of our Lord Jesus Christ,

15. Of whom the whole family in heaven and earth is named,

16. That he would grant you, according to the riches of his glory, to be strengthened with might by his Spirit in the inner man;

17. That Christ may dwell in your hearts by faith; that ye, being rooted and grounded in love,

18. May be able to comprehend with all saints what is the breadth, and length, and depth, and height;

19. And to know the love of Christ, which passeth knowledge, that ye might be filled with all the fulness of God.

20. Now unto him that is able to do

exceeding abundantly above all that
we ask or think, according to the power
that worketh in us,

21. Unto him be glory in the church by
Christ Jesus throughout all ages, world
without end. Amen.

LESSON OUTLINE

I. GOD'S PURPOSE IN CHRIST
 A. Stewardship of the "Mystery" and Purpose of God in Christ
 B. Revelation of the "Mystery" of God in Christ
II. PROCLAIMING THE GOSPEL
 A. Origin of Paul's Ministry
 B. Description of Ministry
 C. Purpose of the Ministry
III. EXPERIENCING GOD'S FULLNESS
 A. Introduction of Paul's Prayer
 B. Prayer to Experience the Fullness of God
 C. Summary Desire for God's Power to Work in the Believer

LESSON EXPOSITION

INTRODUCTION

In this powerful chapter Paul summarizes his doctrinal exposition of the gospel of Christ. The last three chapters of Ephesians will deal with practical concerns. The first three chapters deal with foundational truths which provide the basis for the Christian life. Paul summarizes the first three chapters dealing with principles which enable a Christian to live pleasing before God.

Paul proclaims, in chapter three, that God's power gives the Christian the ability to live acceptably to God. Paul begins the chapter by stressing the purposes and power in Christ which were hidden to mankind prior to the coming of Christ. Paul then explains the glorious revelation and subsequent proclamation of God's power and purpose revealed in Christ. Paul concludes by praying that the fullness of the revelation and power of God in Christ would be applied in their life.

The climactic emphasis of Paul's message in this chapter is that the power of God would work in the believer. Paul expresses this in verse 20. The description of the revelation and power of God in Christ is important. However, the fact that God's power exists does not enable the believer to walk pleasing before God. God's power must be appropriated within the believer. This appropriation is necessary for persons to be able to live the Christian life. It comes through faith in Christ.

I. GOD'S PURPOSE IN CHRIST (Ephesians 3:1-6)

A. Stewardship of the "Mystery" and Purpose of God in Christ (vv. 1-4)

1. For this cause I Paul, the prisoner of Jesus Christ for you Gentiles.

Paul continues his emphasis in the second half of chapter 2 which has been upon the message of God's ministry to the Gentiles. "For this cause" refers to the message about the Gentiles developed in 2:11-22. Paul describes himself as a "prisoner of Jesus Christ" for the Gentiles. Paul is referring to his present imprisonment in Rome. His ministry of God's truth for the Gentiles led to his imprisonment. Paul will refer to his imprisonment again in 3:13.

2. If ye have heard of the dispensation of the grace of God which is given me to you-ward:

3. How that by revelation he made known unto me the mystery; (as I wrote afore in few words.

(Ephesians 3:4 is not included in the printed text.)

In verses 2-4 Paul describes the stewardship of the "mystery" of God that was given to him. The word *if* at the beginning of verse 2 indicates assurance. The word might be translated "surely." Paul is not instructing them about new information. He is only affirming their knowledge.

Paul assures them of the "dispensation" that had been given to him. *Dispensation* comes from a Greek word *oikonomion* which literally means "stewardship of a house." The emphasis of the word is upon stewardship and administration of something. God had given Paul the administration of God's grace to the Gentiles.

"Dispensation" does not mean "origin." God's grace did not originate with Paul. The origin of God's grace was discussed by Paul in chapter 2. Paul is merely the channel of the administration of God's grace to the Gentiles.

The particular way that God had given the administration of His grace to Paul is explained beginning in verse 3. God began Paul's ministry of the administration of God's grace by "revelation." Neither the grace of God nor the ministry of that grace came to Paul by common knowledge. It was divinely revealed to Paul. It was made known only by the provision of God. Without God's revelation Paul would not have known God's grace nor the capacity to minister that grace.

The thing revealed to Paul was "the mystery." This was not some magical or mystical formula. The content of the mystery will be discussed by Paul in verse 6. Paul used the word *mystery* because it meant something that was completely hidden from human perception or comprehension without the revelation of God. It was sealed knowledge that could only be acquired through God.

In the latter part of verse 3 and in verse 4 Paul refers to a previous correspondence he had sent to the Ephesians. The correspondence has been lost to us in contemporary time. However, Paul indicates that the letter did cover his knowledge of the "mystery of Christ" (v. 4).

B. Revelation and Statement of the "Mystery" of God in Christ (v. 5, 6)

(Ephesians 3:5 is not included in the printed text.)

6. That the Gentiles should be fellowheirs, and of the same body, and partakers of his promise in Christ by the gospel.

In verse 5 Paul indicates from whom the mystery was hidden and to whom the mystery had been revealed. The mystery had been hidden from "the sons of men." In contrast, "now" the mystery has been revealed by God—not only to Paul, but also to the prophets and other apostles.

The instrument by which the mystery has been revealed is the Person of the Holy Spirit.

In verse 6, Paul states the "mystery" he has referred to since verse 3. The Gentiles are the subject of the mystery. These were the various nations which stood outside the nation of Israel. The mystery is that, even though the Gentiles were outside of the nation of Israel (compare 2:12, 19), they were now to receive the same blessings and salvation available to the Israelites in Christ.

Paul describes the blessings Gentiles now had in common with Israel in a threefold manner. First, the Gentiles were fellowheirs. *Fellowheirs* comes from a Greek word which literally means "to have the same allotment." The word emphasized the apportionment and assignment of blessings. Gentiles, in Christ, received the same allotment of blessings.

The second blessing was to have *the same body*. This phrase emphasized the intimate relationship they had in Christ as members of the same body of God's new creation in the Messiah. They were vitally joined to the body of Christ, God's people, the church.

The third blessing was to be partakers of his promise. *Partakers* comes from a Greek word *summetocha* which means to have the "same possessions." The word was used in ancient literature to describe "joint-possessors" of a house (*Linguistic Key to the Greek New Testament* by Rienecker and Key, P. 528). This word emphasizes use and possession. Gentiles have full authority in Christ to possess and live in God's salvation.

All of these blessings take place "in Christ." The Gentile who is "in Christ" receives the same allotment, body, and promise given to the nation of Israel. The blessings are given "by the gospel." The proclamation of salvation in Christ is the vital means by which the blessings are appropriated to the Gentiles. Paul continues in verse 7 to explain the nature of God's call to him as it relates to the proclamation of the gospel.

Why was Paul a prisoner in bonds? What does the word *dispensation* mean in verse 2? How was the *mystery* made known to Paul? What was the *mystery* revealed to Paul, other apostles, and the prophets? What blessings did Gentiles receive? What does each part of those blessings emphasize?

II. PROCLAIMING THE GOSPEL (Ephesians 3:7-13)

A. Origin of Paul's Ministry (v. 7)

7. Whereof I was made a minister, according to the gift of the grace of God given unto me by the effectual working of his power.

"Whereof" indicates the content of the mystery of God discussed in verse 6. Paul says that he was made a "minister" of the mystery. *Minister* comes from a Greek word *diakonos,* with a special use in the New Testament. The word is usually translated "servant." In the New Testament, the term "is always one who serves on Christ's behalf and continues Christ's service for the outer and inner man" (*Dictionary of New Testament Theology,* vol. 3, p. 548). Paul was called to minister in light of God's work bringing Jews and Gentiles into a new being in Christ.

The criterion by which Paul received this special call was the "gift of the grace of God" which had been given to him. The means by which his ministry came was the "effectual working of his [God's] power." God's power dominated and controlled Paul's ministry. It was "effectual" power. *Effectual* comes from a Greek concept meaning to be "energized" and was used only of power greater than human power. The power which energized Paul's ministry was divine in origin. In fact, Paul recognizes the power as being God's power.

B. Description of Ministry (8, 9)

8. Unto me, who am less than the least of all saints, is this grace given, that I should preach among the Gentiles the unsearchable riches of Christ;

9. And to make all men see what is the fellowship of the mystery, which from the beginning of the world hath been hid in God, who created all things by Jesus Christ.

Paul describes his ministry in these verses by noting how unworthy he was to receive this ministry. *Grace* refers to the "gift of the grace of God" mentioned in verse 7. Paul highlights the fact that his ministry is the result of the grace of God and not by his own means.

Paul stresses his unworthiness by creating an unusual expression. The words "less than the least" in Greek is probably an expression created by Paul. "Least" already refers to the smallest possible variable. He is the least of all saints. Paul further describes himself as being "less than the least of all saints." This is not to minimize his ministry or God's grace. However, it underscores his unworthiness as a recipient of the ministry by God's grace.

The ministry Paul had been given was directly to the Gentiles. Paul played a pivotal role in God's plan of salvation for the Gentiles. The message and ministry God had given Paul was not of salvation alone. God had commissioned Paul to proclaim the "unsearchable riches of Christ" to the Gentiles. Paul's message was that salvation was for the Gentiles as well as for the Israelites.

"Make all men see" comes from a single Greek word *photisai* which means "to illuminate or enlighten." Paul's ministry was to illuminate the mystery revealed by God that Gentiles and Jews were partakers of the same salvation in Christ. "Fellowship" comes from a Greek term *koinonia* which actually means "stewardship." In this verse it refers to the way God administers His salvation to both Gentiles and Jews.

Proclamation is an important part of God's commission to Paul. God gave a specific revelation of the mystery that Gentiles may receive salvation. Following that, God gave him the gift of grace in a ministry. That ministry was to proclaim the revelation of the mystery he had received. Knowledge of the revealed mystery was not in itself Paul's ministry. His ministry was to proclaim the good news of salvation to the Gentiles.

C. Purpose of the Ministry (vv. 10-13)

10. To the intent that now unto the principalities and powers in the heavenly places might be known by the church the manifold wisdom of God.

In verse 7, Paul states the intent or purpose for which God had granted the ministry Paul received to the Gentiles. "Now" indicates when the purpose was to be accomplished. It stresses the present accomplishment of the purpose. The central purpose is that knowledge of a certain thing might be made known. Paul eventually indicates that the thing to be made known is the "manifold wisdom of God." The receivers of the knowledge are "principalities and powers in heavenly places." God's desire in the proclamation of the gospel to the Gentiles is that even the most supreme rulers and authorities, in places that are spiritual and beyond this world, would know of His wisdom.

A translation of this verse following the word order of the Greek text would be, "In order that it might be made known now to the rulers and to the authorities in the heavenlies through the church the manifold wisdom of God."

The word order and changing "by the church" to the more proper "through the church" is important. They highlight the role of the church in the gospel to the Gentiles. The church is the means by which God's wisdom is made known. Paul's personal ministry is important. However, the purpose of his ministry was to help fulfill the larger purpose of the church becoming the means through which God's wisdom is made known.

The thing that is made known is the "manifold wisdom of God." "Manifold" comes from the Greek word *polupoikilos*, meaning "many sided or many colored." The word emphasizes the spectacular display coming from God's wisdom. His wisdom holds eternal beauty and power. It is on display through the church as part of God's message of salvation to the Gentiles.

11. According to the eternal purpose which he purposed in Christ Jesus our Lord:

12. In whom we have boldness and access with confidence by the faith of him.

The revealing of God's manifold wisdom through the church is controlled by the greater and "eternal purpose" of God in Christ. The first word in the King James Version translated "purpose" comes from a Greek term *prothesin* which means "design." Christ is the pattern of God's work to the Gentiles. The second word translated "purposed" comes from a Greek word *epoiesen*, different from the earlier "purpose," and can be translated "made" or "accomplished" (*New International Version*). Christ is not only the content of the message of salvation, He also controls the communication of the gospel.

Christ is the One in whom the believer has "boldness" and "access." "Boldness" refers to the right and ability to speak freely without being inhibited or hindered. "Access" refers to the privilege of coming before someone, usually of high rank. This boldness and access are acquired in the midst of great "confidence." The emphasis of the term "confidence" is upon what occurs within an individual. It refers to confidence as it infills someone. These are the attributes Christ gives to the person who has faith in Him.

In verse 12 Paul stresses the application of the blessings of God. Christ not only makes the proclamation of the message of salvation possible, He empowers the believer. The message of salvation is about the Savior who empowers whosoever has faith in Him.

13. Wherefore I desire that ye faint not at my tribulations for you, which is your glory.

Paul extends the theme of Christ's power for the believer by making a personal request in verse 13. He wants the Ephesian believers to "faint not" because of his imprisonment in their behalf. Paul states in verse 1 that he is in prison because of his ministry to the Gentiles. He spends the majority of the chapter discussing that ministry. It is a ministry from Christ which bears the news of Christ's power for the believer. Paul hopes this power, as part of the message of salvation, will give them the ability to be strong in the midst of his weakness.

The message of salvation to the Gentile is not the only privilege of salvation. It is a message of the ability that God gives to stand in full authority and privilege in His kingdom. It is a message communicating the strength available for the Gentile believer, even in the midst of extreme hardship such as Paul experienced in prison.

What did Paul mean by the "effectual working" of God's power in verse 7? In what ways did Paul describe his ministry? What does the phrase, "fellowship of the mystery," in verse 9 mean? What was the purpose of the ministry of Paul concerning the gospel to the Gentiles? What role does the church play in making known the wisdom of God?

III. EXPERIENCING GOD'S FULLNESS (Ephesians 3:14-21)

A. Introduction of Paul's Prayer (vv. 14, 15)

14. For this cause I bow my knees unto the Father of our Lord Jesus Christ,

15. Of whom the whole family in heaven and earth is named.

In verses 16-19 Paul prays for the Ephesian believers. In the prayer he summarizes what he has said concerning God's purpose of bringing salvation to the Gentiles as well as to the Jews. Before he offers the content of the prayer, he gives an introduction glorifying God.

The introduction offers Paul's humble approach before Christ. Paul "bows his knees" in humility as he petitions the Father. Further, Paul recognizes the supremacy of God the Father. Verse 15 is in reference to the Father. "Family" is from the Greek word *patria* for "father" and can also be translated "fatherhood." It speaks of family relationships, with stress upon the authority and leadership of the father. Paul recognizes the suprem-

acy of God by praising His Fatherhood in all the heaven and earth.

B. Prayer to Experience the Fullness of God (vv. 16-19)

16. That he would grant you, according to the riches of his glory, to be strengthened with might by his Spirit in the inner man;

17a. That Christ may dwell in your hearts by faith.

Based upon the Greek text of verses 16-19, there are three primary requests in Paul's prayer. The first is that God would "grant" (v. 16) certain things to the believers. The second is that the saints would be "able to comprehend" (v. 18) certain things. The final primary request is that the believers would "be filled with all the fulness of God" (v. 19).

The requests have criteria, conditions, and purposes mentioned by Paul. All of the requests concern the appropriation of the principles of the gospel which Paul discussed earlier in the chapter. Paul wants the gospel to be appropriated to their life. The first request focuses upon *God's action.* The second request focuses upon the *action of the believer.* The final request focuses upon *God's action and power within the believer.*

The full account of the first request, that God would "grant" them certain things, is in verses 16 and 17a. The emphasis of this request is that God would be gracious enough to "grant" His blessings upon them. Paul knew the importance of receiving from God rather than from the corrupt supplies of the world.

The controlling factor of God's giving would be "the riches of glory." The importance of the phrase is not "riches" but *his.* It was important, again, that God be the One giving the riches and blessings.

There are two purposes mentioned for God giving the riches of His glory to the believer. The first is strength for the inner man. "Strengthened" comes from a Greek word *krataiothenai,* meaning "to fortify or brace." The emphasis of the concept is upon stability. The second purpose is that Christ would dwell in their hearts. The benevolent giving of God to the believer results in stability and the presence of Christ in the Christian life.

17b. That ye, being rooted and grounded in love,

18. May be able to comprehend with all saints what is the breadth, and length, and depth, and height;

19a. And to know the love of Christ, which passeth knowledge.

Verses 17b-19a present the second request of Paul along with its purposes and one condition. The request is that the believer may be able to *comprehend* certain things. Before the request, one condition which accompanies "comprehension" is stated. The accompanying condition is *love*. Love is the abiding condition in which the believer should be rooted and grounded as he "comprehends" the things of God.

"Comprehend" comes from a Greek word *katalabesthai,* meaning "strength and ability to complete or perfect." The emphasis of the word was upon completion and sufficiency. The emphasis was to not only receive from God, but the ability to completely grasp the fullness of what the Christian has received.

The believer needs grace from God to be able to comprehend the full measure of what God has given. This measure includes the "breadth, and length, and depth, and height" of God's blessings. If the Christian only receives from God, but never comprehends the value and glory of what he has received, God will not be known as He should by that Christian. Further, the Christian will not "know the love of Christ."

Knowledge of the love of Christ is an essential purpose in comprehending what God has given to the Christian. However, though the Christian seeks to be able to comprehend what he has received from God, it is still not entirely knowable. As with the love of God that results, it is that which passes knowledge. It is a love and comprehension beyond mere knowledge and it reaches into the soul and spirit of man.

19b. That ye might be filled with all the fulness of God.

The third and final request is the shortest of the three. It is that the believer be "filled with all the fullness of God." This request combines the two and climaxes their intent. The believer needs to receive all that God gives: "the fulness of God." This is an extension of the first request. The believer also needs to comprehend the things of God to the point of being "filled." This is another extension of the first request. Paul has been presenting the gospel plan by which persons may be saved. The believer is given salvation and can be filled with all that God has to offer as well.

C. Summary Desire for God's Power to Work in the Believer (vv. 20, 21)

20. Now unto him that is able to do exceeding abundantly above all that we ask or think, according to the power that worketh in us,

21. Unto him be glory in the church by Christ Jesus throughout all ages, world without end. Amen.

Paul ends this prayer (verses 16-21), as well as the first three chapters of Ephesians which have been emphasizing doctrine, by proclaiming two themes. The first theme is a glorious praise of the sufficiency of Christ. Christ's ability is abundant and far greater than the measure of human thinking. Christ, the all-sufficient Savior, is due eternal praise.

The second theme is shorter, but is an important climax to the message of the gospel. It says that the power of God "worketh *in* us." The gospel is the message of God's sufficiency, but not that alone. It is the message of the appropriation of God's power working *in* the Christian. The power of the gospel is that God has chosen, by His grace, to work His power *in* those who will trust Christ as Lord and Savior.

REVIEW QUESTIONS

1. What was the "mystery" that Paul mentioned?

2. How did Paul describe his ministry?

3. What three requests did Paul make for the believers when he prayed?

4. How are the requests related and climaxed?

5. What is the important message about God's power in verse 20?

GOLDEN TEXT HOMILY

"UNTO HIM BE GLORY IN THE CHURCH BY CHRIST JESUS THROUGH-OUT ALL AGES, WORLD WITHOUT END" (Ephesians 3:21).

In studying the doxologies of the New Testament, it seems that they usually followed a passage of Scripture in which the writer has either proclaimed some aspect of the greatness of God's person, or some aspect of the greatness of God's work among men (Romans 11:32-36; Jude 24, 25; Revelation 5:11-14). Our golden text follows the writer's statement (in verse 20) concerning God's power and ability to do things, even beyond man's comprehension. Therefore, because of the greatness of God's power which is involved in the redemption of man, God is to receive glory in the church.

Just how God receives "glory in the church" we're not told in this verse, except it is "by Christ Jesus." It would seem that glory is to be given by the church to God, because of what was accomplished for it through the Cross work of Jesus Christ. When one realizes that because of Christ's death, resurrection, and ascension a sinner can come to God, an heir of God, and joint-heir with Christ, a well of praise and glory should spring out of the heart to God.

Not only is God to receive glory from the church during this present age, but throughout all ages, world without end. Little is said in Scripture concerning the activities of the church during the ages to come. Yet two times in this Epistle, God seems to allow us a fleeting glimpse of some things that will exist for the church throughout eternity. First, "in ages to come" God will show "the exceeding riches of his grace in his kindness toward us through Christ Jesus" (Ephesians 2:7). And second, the church will give glory to Him "by Christ Jesus throughout all ages, world without end. Amen" (3:21).—**Kenneth K. Foreman, D.Min., Executive Director of Messenger Publishing House, Joplin, Missouri**

SENTENCE SERMONS

THROUGH GOD'S redemptive plan, all believers become one in Christ.
—**Selected**

CHRIST SENDS none away empty but those who are full of themselves.
—**"Speaker's Sourcebook"**

THE HEAD that once was crowned with thorns, is crowned with glory now.
—**Thomas Kelley**

ALL THAT IS necessary to salvation is contained in two virtues: faith in Christ and obedience to the laws of God.
—**Thomas Hobbes**

EVANGELISTIC APPLICATION

GOD DESIRES THAT ALL BE SAVED AND SHARE IN HIS GLORY.

God demonstrated through Jesus Christ that salvation is available to everyone. Before Christ, salvation was through God's chosen people, the Israelites. Christ made it possible for both Gentiles and Israelites to receive salvation. God did not desire that only a few elite persons of special national origin or ability be saved. The only criterion is Jesus Christ. Salvation through Christ is available to anyone who will repent and serve Him as Lord.

God's salvation not only offers redemption from sin, it gives believers the privilege of receiving power and ability that comes from God. God will not keep any good thing from those who love and serve Him. According to His goodness and mercy He freely gives what is best for man. His power is sufficient to effectively live as God intends for us to live. God desires to give this ability and power to whosoever will trust Him.

A sinner may receive salvation and participate in the glory of God by repenting of his sins and believing by Christ as Lord and Savior. God desires to give His fullness to those who fully believe in Christ.

DAILY BIBLE READINGS

M. God's Word Is Sure. Joshua 23:8-14

T. Wise Counsel. 1 Chronicles 28:1-13

W. God's Greatness. 1 Chronicles 29:10-17

T. Spiritual Truth Revealed. Matthew 13:16-23

F. Hearing God's Voice. John 10:27-29

S. True Freedom. Romans 8:1-4

Spiritual Maturity

Study Text: Ephesians 4:1-32

Supplemental References: Psalm 68:17-20; Ezekiel 36:25-27; Malachi 2:4-7; Luke 2:49-52; 2 Peter 1:5-11

Time: Probably in A.D. 61

Place: Written from a Roman prison

Golden Text: "Grow in grace, and in the knowledge of our Lord and Saviour Jesus Christ" (2 Peter 3:18).

Central Truth: The ultimate goal of spiritual maturity is Christlikeness.

Evangelistic Emphasis: Spiritual maturity equips a person for ministry to both the saved and lost.

Printed Text

Ephesians 4:1. I therefore, the prisoner of the Lord, beseech you that ye walk worthy of the vocation wherewith ye are called,

2. With all lowliness and meekness, with longsuffering, forbearing one another in love;

3. Endeavouring to keep the unity of the Spirit in the bond of peace.

4. There is one body, and one Spirit, even as ye are called in one hope of your calling;

5. One Lord, one faith, one baptism,

6. One God and Father of all, who is above all, and through all, and in you all.

11. And he gave some, apostles; and some, prophets; and some, evangelists; and some, pastors and teachers;

12. For the perfecting of the saints, for the work of the ministry, for the edifying of the body of Christ:

13. Till we all come in the unity of the faith, and of the knowledge of the Son of God, unto a perfect man, unto the measure of the stature of the fulness of Christ:

23. And be renewed in the spirit of your mind;

25. Wherefore putting away lying, speak every man truth with his neighbour: for we are members one of another.

26. Be ye angry, and sin not: let not the sun go down upon your wrath:

27. Neither give place to the devil.

28. Let him that stole steal no more: but rather let him labour, working with his hands the thing which is good, that he may have to give to him that needeth.

29. Let no corrupt communication proceed out of your mouth, but that which is good to the use of edifying, that it may minister grace unto the hearers.

30. And grieve not the holy Spirit of God, whereby ye are sealed unto the day of redemption.

31. Let all bitterness, and wrath, and anger, and clamour, and evil speaking be put away from you, with all malice:

32. And be ye kind one to another tenderhearted, forgiving one another even as God for Christ's sake hath forgiven you.

LESSON OUTLINE

I. CALL TO UNITY
   A. Call to Walk Worthy
   B. Characteristics of the Walk
   C. Statement of the Unity of God
II. SPIRITUAL GROWTH
   A. Recognition of the Grace God has Given
   B. Grace Enabled by Christ's Victory
   C. Listing of Gifts Given to the Church
   D. Purpose of Gifts
III. NEW ATTITUDES
   A. Contrasting Walks Between the Old and New Life
   B. Description of the Old Life
   C. Description of the New Life
IV. GODLY BEHAVIOR
   A. General Call to Truthfulness With One's Neighbor
   B. Specific Commands to Fulfill the Call to Truthfulness
   C. Call to Grieve Not the Spirit
   D. Summary Call to Relate With Others in a Godly Manner

LESSON EXPOSITION

INTRODUCTION

In the first three chapters of Ephesians, Paul has been giving a doctrinal treatment of the position of the believer. He has described the life of the believer in Christ by primarily using theological terms. Here in chapter 4, Paul moves from the theological and doctrinal to the practical. He begins to speak specifically about how life in Christ is actually lived. This is the emphasis of the last three chapters of Ephesians.

At this transitional point in the book, Paul speaks of the lifestyle of the Christian. He conveys the importance of personal change in the believer. He also emphasizes the change in one's relationship with God. And, he stresses the new way the believer relates to those around him.

Paul translates his doctrine into actual practice. He does this elsewhere in his writings. Ephesians is no exception. Paul's message is decisively community oriented. Life in Christ for Paul is by no means merely a private affair. Paul emphasizes Christian community in discussing the practical side of the Christian's faith.

I. CALL TO UNITY (Ephesians 4:1-6)

A. Call to Walk Worthy (v. 1)

1. I therefore, the prisoner of the Lord, beseech you that ye walk worthy of the vocation wherewith ye are called.

In this opening verse to the section about practical matters, Paul begins with a warm exhortation. "Beseech" comes from a Greek word which means to "call someone alongside." Paul calls the readers to his side to offer them this exhortation.

The center of his exhortation is that they "walk worthy." "Walk" indicates their manner and conduct of life. It emphasizes the practical side of life. "Worthy" is from the Greek word *axios.* The word deals with weights and balances. To be worthy meant to be weighed or balanced in relationship to some measurement. In this verse, that measurement was the "vocation" by which they had been called.

Vocation referred to their "calling." The origin of that calling is God. The Christian has been divinely called by God. The Christian, according to Paul, is to conduct himself in a manner which "weighs" or "balances" in accordance with that calling. The nature of this divine call has been the topic of Paul's discussion in chapters 1-3. The implications of this call for the life and "walk" of the Christian is the topic of Paul's discussion in chapters 4-6.

B. Characteristics of the Walk (vv. 2, 3)

2. With all lowliness and meekness, with longsuffering, forbearing one another in love;

3. Endeavoring to keep the unity of the Spirit in the bond of peace.

In the first part of verse 2 Paul indicates the kind of walk they were to live. This description of the kind of walk is threefold. First, it was to be with "all lowliness." The word for "lowliness" in Greek means "humility in heart or understanding." The item referred to the subjecting of "oneself to others and to be more concerned about their welfare than one's own" (Walter Grundmann, *Theological Dictionary of the New Testament,* VIII, pp. 21-2).

The second description of the kind of walk they were to follow was "meekness." "Meekness" comes from a Greek word which essentially means "mild." In this context it meant "the humble and gentle attitude which expresses itself in a patient submissiveness to offense, free from malice and desire for revenge" (*Linguistic Key to the Greek New Testament,* p. 530).

The final description of the kind of walk they were to follow was "longsuffering." This word in Greek was constructed from two Greek words which mean "long, length" and "rush, rage." It referred to a person's long endurance in the face of raging opposition and anger from other persons.

After this threefold description, Paul gives a twofold description of the circumstances which should accompany this kind of walk. These are "forbearing" and "endeavoring to keep the unity." "Forbearing" refers to the ability to continue relationships with others despite hindrances to do so, God calls the Christian to a persistent love which "forbears" with others in order to maintain unity.

"Endeavoring" emphasized eagerness and diligence of effort. This stressed the intensity with which the believer was to strive for unity of the Spirit. The sphere in which this was to be accomplished was peace. Unity was a goal to be accomplished vigorously yet peacefully.

C. Statement of the Unity of God (vv. 4-6)

4. There is one body, and one Spirit, even as ye are called in one hope of your calling;

5. One Lord, one faith, one baptism,

6. One God and Father of all, who is above all, and through all, and in you all.

The description of the kind of walk and manner of life the Christian should have is climaxed in verse 3 with the theme of unity. This theme is extended by Paul in a discussion of the unity of God. God's

unity permeates the call and life of the Christian. It is a motivation for Christians to be unified.

Paul gives seven aspects of God and the godly life in these verses. They are the unity of body, Spirit, hope, Lord, faith, baptism, and God (intending God the Father). The trinity is indicated here by Paul's reference to the Spirit, the Lord (Christ), and God (the Father). Critical aspects of the Christian life are listed: the body, meaning the body of believers; hope, emphasizing the calling of God unto salvation; faith, the means of salvation; and baptism, implying the symbolic initiation of the Christian into new life in Christ.

What is Paul's exhortation unto the believers? What characteristics describe the kind of walk the Christian is to have? What are the circumstances which should accompany the walk of the Christian? How important is unity and especially the unity of God to the walk of the Christian?

II. SPIRITUAL GROWTH (Ephesians 4: 7, 11-16)

A. Recognition of the Grace God Has Given (v. 7)

(Ephesians 4:7 is not included in the printed text.)

In verse 7 Paul stresses God as the source of the ability to function in unity. Paul does not overemphasize the unity of the body to the exclusion of the contribution each individual makes. To each believer God gives "grace." This grace is the unmerited favor of God which enables the believer to perform the will of God. The emphasis of this verse is upon the source of the grace. The grace comes from God according to the standard or "measure" of Christ. The "measure" of Christ is unto all who believe without human partiality or favoritism. The Christian is empowered by the grace of Christ.

B. Grace Enabled by Christ's Victory (vv. 8-10)

(Ephesians 4:8-10 is not included in the printed text.)

Verses 8-10 continue the emphasis of

verse 7 upon the source of God's enabling grace. Verses 8-10 recount the scene of Christ's actual victory in which he redeemed all who would believe on Him. The phrase "gave gifts unto men" in verse 8 indicates the vital connection between grace and gifts. The enabling power of grace is to be utilized by believers in the gifts God has given through Christ.

C. Listing of Gifts Given to the Church (v. 11)

11. And he gave some, apostles; and some, prophets; and some, evangelists; and some, pastors and teachers.

The theme of gifts to men is continued in verse 11. Here Paul lists specific gifts given to individuals in the body of Christ. These have been considered offices and positions in the church. Yet, they are described here as gifts. This emphasizes the source of these offices. Their source is God. He is the Giver of the gift and office. That God is the source of these gifts has been the emphasis of Paul since verse 7, and he continues to stress this in verse 11.

Paul says that God "gave" some the gift of apostle. "Apostle" meant "a delegate, messenger, one sent forth with orders." The word was originally formed from two Greek words *apo* and *stello*. *Stello* means to "set in order or place." *Apo* intensified the sense of mission and being sent from one to some designated place, person, or group. The emphasis of the word here by Paul is that those given the gift of apostleship are those sent from God to set things in order. Historically, these were the first things of the church. These were the original apostles of the church.

The second gift given is that of "prophet." "Prophet" comes from the combination of two Greek words *pro* and *phami*. *Pro* meant "before" and *phami* meant "to say." Together they meant to speak before. This gift can refer to foretelling of the future. However, *pro* when used in combination with other words also meant "to set before others." Therefore, the prophet would be the one who proclaims things before, in front of,

others. This appears to be the emphasis of the word here. The prophet, as indicated by Paul here, is the one who proclaims or preaches before others.

The third gift given is that of "evangelist." Two evangelists are named in the New Testament: Philip (Acts 21:8) and Timothy (2 Timothy 4:5). There were certainly others in the early church besides these. They were the proclaimers of the good news of the gospel. They continued the work of the apostles in the church but especially beyond the church in missionary, evangelistic preaching.

The final gift is that of "pastor and teacher." The grammar of the Greek text indicates that these two areas are listed as one item. They are a single gift with two aspects. The first aspect is that of "pastor." The Greek word here is the same word used for shepherd. The image of a shepherd leading a flock is intended. A pastor was to function as a shepherd. This was marked by care for the spiritual welfare of the flock and seeking those lost from the flock.

Besides the function of shepherding, this final gift carried the aspect of "teaching." The emphasis of the Greek word, *didasko*, used here for "teacher," stresses the imparting of knowledge and skills. It does not exclude the imparting of character and virtue, but the stress is on communication of essential information. That information was the content of the gospel.

Another Greek word for teacher, *paidagogos*, stressed the discipline of the teacher and the relationship between the teacher and the learner. This word is used elsewhere in the New Testament and is pictured as a vital aspect of ministry. However, the stress in this verse is upon the gospel content which is taught.

C. Purpose of the Gifts (vv. 12-16)

12. For the perfecting of the saints, for the work of the ministry, for the edifying of the body of Christ:

13. Till we all come in the unity of the faith, and of the knowledge of the Son of God, unto a perfect man, unto

the measure of the stature of the fulness of Christ.

(Ephesians 4:14-16 is not included in the printed text.)

The word "for" in verse 12 indicates that what follows is the purpose for what preceded in verse 11. That is, the gifts listed in verse 11 are for the reasons cited in verses 12 and 13. Paul presents the perfecting of the saints as the general purpose of the gifts. Following this he gives a fivefold description of this perfecting work.

These gifts given by God are to the saints. "Perfecting" comes from the Greek word *katartismos*. It is a different word from the one used later in verse 13. The word in verse 12 means "to have something or someone prepared and ready at the suitable time." The word was used for the outfitting of buildings, furniture, or persons. It was even used as a medical term in reference to properly preparing or setting a broken bone. The gifts were to be used for preparing and furnishing the saints.

This "perfecting" was to extend into five different areas. The first area was the "work of ministry." This is the Christian service given by believers. The second area was the "edifying of the body of Christ." "Edifying" is literally "housebuilding." It emphasized building up others. The third area was the "unity of the faith and the knowledge of the Son of God." The emphasis here is not just upon unanimity itself, but unanimity which is characterized by faith and the knowledge of Christ. The fourth area was the goal of a "perfect man." "Perfect" here refers to "maturity, completeness, or being full grown." The reference here is to spiritual growth and ultimate maturity.

The final area the gifts were to be used for was furnishing the believer unto "the measure of the stature of the fullness of Christ." This is the climactic goal of the gifts, the believer being fashioned in the image of Christ. Paul is careful to describe the degree to which the believer is to strive. This "measure" is the "stature" or "full age" of the "fullness of Christ." The standard of maturity for the Christian

is Christ. Further, the standard is the full measure of all that Christ calls us to be as Christians.

Verses 15 and 16 continue the topics of maturity and growth. Verse 15 refers to the immaturity which results from following men rather than Christ. Verse 16 calls the Christian in love to focus upon Christ as the goal of full spiritual maturity.

What is the purpose of the grace God has given to the believer? What is the source of this grace? What measure should the gifts given to the church strive for? What substitute goals do believers sometimes have in place of spiritual maturity in Christ?

III. NEW ATTITUDES (Ephesians 4:17-24)

A. Contrasting Walks Between the Old and New Life (v. 17)

(Ephesians 4:17 is not included in the printed text.)

Verses 1-16 focus upon unity and spiritual growth. Verses 17-24 continue the theme of the Christian's "walk" highlighted in verse 1. However, Paul begins to contrast between the believer's walk and the way of the unbeliever. Paul says, in verse 17, that the Gentile, the unbeliever, walks in the "vanity" of his mind. Rather than being based in Christ, the unbeliever is self-centered.

B. Description of the Old Life (vv. 18, 19)

(Ephesians 4:18, 19 is not included in the printed text.)

These two verses give a rather thorough description of the person who does not walk after Christ. The major theme is in verse 18. It is the phrase "having their understanding darkened." The phrase indicates the development of a darkened condition and the symptoms which follow.

The symptoms of a darkened understanding are described in verses 18 and 19. "Understanding" comes from a Greek word which emphasizes their ability to "think through" something. Verses 18 and 19 indicate that the result of not being able to "think through" properly is moral corruption. These verses indicate that mental judgment affects morality. Paul was stressing the importance of developing the mind around godly things.

C. Description of the New Life (vv. 20-24)

(Ephesians 4:20-22, 24 is not included in the printed text.)

23. And be renewed in the spirit of your mind.

Paul contrasts the mentality of the old, sinful man with that of the new man in Christ. In verses 20 and 21 he stresses the things that were "learned" (v. 20) and "taught" (v. 21) by Christ. Just as verses 18 and 19 connected the mind with morality, verses 20 and 22 do the same. Teaching and learning the things of Christ are for the purpose of putting off the corruption of the old man (v. 22).

Verse 23 states the positive result of learning the ways of Christ. This benefit is *renewal*. The word in Greek means "to be made new again." This is something done in the Christian by Christ. It is not done by the Christian's own power or ability. The concept involves renewal of the person and his ability.

The area of the Christian that is renewed is the "spirit of the mind." The emphasis in this phrase is "spirit." It refers to the human spirit, the spiritual part of man. The renewal of the Christian is spiritual. Nevertheless, the phrase "of the mind" indicates that it does involve the ability of persons to judge and make determinations of the mind. As the "spirit of the mind" functions in the Christian, it is renewed by Christ. It is given renewed ability and godly content.

Verse 23 is a command to the believer. The Christian is to allow renewal to go on within them by the power of Christ. The word "renewal" as it occurs here in Greek indicates a continuing action. Submission to the renewing power of Christ should be a continuing part of the Christian walk.

Verse 24 stresses God as the originator of the new man in Christ. Like verse 23, it is a command to the Christian.

How strong should the contrast be between the old man and the new man in Christ? How is this contrast described by Paul? Where in man does Christ do the work of renewal? Does this renewal of the spirit of the mind affect man's morality?

IV. GODLY BEHAVIOR (Ephesians 4:25-32)

A. General Call to Truthfulness With One's Neighbor (v. 25)

25. Wherefore putting away lying, speak every man truth with his neighbour: for we are members one of another.

The word "wherefore" is from a Greek word which indicates strong results. Paul is strongly emphasizing the implications of the renewed walk and the believer being in Christ.

Paul speaks of this lifestyle by first emphasizing the Christian's relationship with his neighbor. "Neighbor" is from the Greek word *plasion*. The central idea of the word is simply "one who is near." The word does not refer to persons the Christian may choose to relate with. It refers to any person found near to the Christian. In other words, a "neighbor" is simply someone we come in contact with.

The issue between the Christian and anyone near him is "truth." The Christian is commanded to stop "lying" and begin to "speak truth." This is the first result of the Christ-centered walk. The Christian's relationships with other persons are to be characterized by truthfulness. Paul was not necessarily speaking of the gospel when he referred to the "truth." If he intended this he would probably have said *"the* truth." The absence of "the" means that Paul is probably emphasizing truthfulness as a quality and way of living.

The reason the Christian needs to be truthful is unity. Paul had earlier discussed the unity of believers in verses 3-6. He says the Christian is to put away lying and speak truthfully because "we are members one of another."

"Members," as used in this verse,

comes from a Greek word primarily referring to parts of the human body. The image created here is of various parts joined together to form one body. Each part is distinctive, but each is part of the same body. Paul exhorts the believer to be truthful with his neighbor in Christ because they are joined together in the same way that parts of a body are joined together.

B. Specific Commands to Fulfill the Call to Truthfulness (vv. 26-29)

26. Be ye angry and sin not: let not the sun go down upon your wrath:

27. Neither give place to the devil.

28. Let him that stole steal no more: but rather let him labour, working with his hands the thing which is good, that he may have to give to him that needeth.

29. Let no corrupt communication proceed out of your mouth, but that which is good to the use of edifying, that it may minister grace unto the hearers.

In this section there are three primary areas Paul addresses. They are anger (vv. 26, 27), stealing (v. 28), and corrupt communication (v. 29). There are specific commands within each of these general headings.

The first general area is anger. The first phrase of verse 26, "Be ye angry," has created controversy among interpreters. The question is whether this is a direct command to be angry or a concession admitting that people do get angry.

The form of the word "anger," as it appears in the Greek text of this verse, could be either a command or a concession. In the majority of the occurrences of this word, it would be translated a command. However, there is room for a concession. There are several grammatical arguments involved and many authorities treat this phrase as a concession. In fact, the *New International Version* translates this phrase as, "In your anger."

Anger may be considered as a positive virtue here by Paul. In this sense, it would be similar to righteous zeal a person might have for a just cause. In

this case, "Be ye angry" might be considered a worthy command. However, anger may also be considered a bad virtue, with detrimental effects. In this case, "Be ye angry" may be considered a concession in which Paul was recognizing the fact that anger does occur.

In either case, positive or negative, command or concession, Paul identifies three perils that are possible when a person is angry. The first peril is sin. The threat of evil is present in anger. Therefore, Paul says, "sin not." The second peril is allowing anger to be prolonged. Permitting anger to persist and grow is addressed when Paul says, "let not the sun go down upon your wrath."

The third peril in anger is the intervention of Satan. It is the most lethal of the three. Paul commands the believer to avoid the peril of "giving place to the devil." The emphasis in this command is upon a place being provided or developed in which Satan may be allowed to work. This is the ultimate peril of anger. If anger is allowed to persist, Satan is able to do more of his work.

Given the stress Paul has been making upon unity and the community of believers, anger is especially lethal to the fellowship of believers. It is, in fact, a "place" through which the devil can intrude into Christian fellowship.

The second general area Paul discusses in verses 26-29 is stealing. Paul refers to a habit some in the Ephesian Church had retained from their sinful past. It may sound odd to us today that some in the early church may have been given to this practice. However, in the pagan culture of that day, stealing was frequent, even allowable in some pagan areas. The Ephesian Christians were obviously having difficulty adjusting to their new walk in Christ.

The call away from stealing was a call unto honest labor. The purpose of their labor was to do that which was good and give to others who were in need. The second purpose is part of the overall emphasis of Paul in this section, unity.

The third general area Paul addresses in verses 26-29 is "corrupt communication."

He commands them to stop their corrupt communication. The first part of verse 29 in the Greek text can be translated, "Each corrupted, worthless word out of your mouth, let it not come out." "Corrupt" means to be "no longer fit for use, worthless." The emphasis in this verse is upon the fact that not a single, worthless word is to come out of the Christian's mouth. Rather, Paul calls the believer to words which edify others.

This call to edification matches the theme of unity Paul has been building upon throughout this chapter. Paul adds the dimension of "grace" at the end of this verse. Words can become the actual channels through which God's grace can be ministered.

C. Call to Grieve Not the Spirit (v. 30)

30. And grieve not the Holy Spirit of God, whereby ye are sealed unto the day of redemption.

Extending the idea of the ministry of grace from verse 29, Paul adds the idea of the work of the Holy Spirit in verse 30. It is a familiar verse. The concepts of "grieving" and "sealing" are often highlighted. While they are critical to interpreting this verse, the context of the chapter and verses just preceding verse 30 are important. The context is Christian unity. Paul has been giving commands about things which either cause or hinder the unity of believers.

Paul gave three general commands in verses 26-29. He gives another command in verse 30. All of these commands deal with the preservation of unity in the Christian's walk and the life of the church.

The work of the Holy Spirit in this verse is "sealing" the believer unto the day of redemption. "Seal" comes from a Greek term which refers to guaranteeing something. It was a stamp or imprint used to close a document. It authenticated ownership and the correctness of the contents. Any claims made in the document were guaranteed by the institution or person represented on the seal. The believer's redemption is sealed by the Spirit. This means the Holy Spirit guarantees and authenticates that salvation.

D. Summary Call to Relate with Others in a Godly Manner (vv. 31, 32)

31. Let all bitterness, and wrath, and anger, and clamour, and evil speaking be put away from you, with all malice:

32. And be ye kind one to another, tenderhearted, forgiving one another, even as God for Christ's sake hath forgiven you.

In verse 31 Paul summarizes the commands he has been giving since verse 26. He lists five things to be "put away." The first is "bitterness." This refers to a "fretted and irritable state of mind that keeps a man in perpetual animosity that inclines him to harsh and uncharitable opinions of men and things" (*Linguistic Key to the Greek New Testament* by Rienecker, p. 534).

The second area is "wrath." This refers to heated anger. The third area is "anger" which emphasizes deep rooted emotions. The fourth area is "clamour" which refers to loud outcries. The fifth and final area is "evil speaking." The emphasis here is upon speech which is injurious to others.

Paul commands the believer to "put away" these five things. The command refers to a removal and cleaning of oneself from these five things. "With all malice" is an accompanying phrase which summarizes the five areas previously mentioned in verse 31. "Malice" referred to the evil resulting in the five areas. Each of the five areas was marked by bad intentions and evil results.

Verse 32 is a summary admonition to do those things which support the unity of the believers. Paul lists three things which enhance unity: kindness, tenderheartedness, and forgiveness. "Kindness" refers to actions beyond cordial gestures. This word in Greek refers to actions which are useful and beneficial for others. "Tenderhearted" refers to heartfelt compassion. "Forgiveness" is from a Greek word which actually means "to be obliging in relationship with others." It emphasizes having a favorable disposition toward other persons.

Paul's theme throughout the chapter is unity among believers in their Christian walk. In emphasizing this Paul applies the work of Christ to the development of godly character. The work of Christ must be applied to daily living. The critical area where this application must take place is the unity of the believers among themselves. As Christ said in John 13:35, "By this shall all men know that ye are my disciples, if ye have love one to another."

REVIEW QUESTIONS

1. What characteristics describe the kind of walk the Christian is to have?

2. What is the purpose of the grace God has given to the believer?

3. How strong should the contrast be between the old man and the new man in Christ?

4. What is Paul's summary call to the believer in verses 31 and 32?

5. What five things did Paul command the believer to put away?

GOLDEN TEXT HOMILY

"GROW IN GRACE, AND IN THE KNOWLEDGE OF OUR LORD AND SAVIOUR JESUS CHRIST" (2 Peter 3:18).

There are people who base their whole Christian philosophy and life on the observance of the Ten Commandments. That is all well and good provided that they don't come to a full stop there. There are many commandments in the New Testament that carry the same authority and demands as do those of the Old Testament.

Let us read 2 Peter 3:10-14, 17, 18: "But the day of the Lord will come as a thief in the night; in which the heavens shall pass away with a great noise, and the elements shall melt with fervent heat, the earth also and the works that are therein shall be burned up. Seeing then that all these things shall be dissolved, what manner of persons ought ye to be in all holy conversation and godliness. Looking for and hasting unto the coming of the day of God, wherein the heavens being on fire shall be dissolved, and the elements shall melt with fervent heat? Nevertheless we, according to his promise,

look for new heavens and a new earth, wherein dwelleth righteousness. Wherefore, beloved, seeing that ye look for such things, be diligent that ye may be found of him in peace, without spot, and blameless. Ye therefore, beloved, seeing ye know these things before, beware lest ye also, being led away with the error of the wicked, fall from your own steadfastness. *But grow in grace, and in the knowledge of our Lord and Saviour Jesus Christ. To Him be glory both now and forever. Amen."*

There is a one word commandment in the eighteenth verse of the reading above: Grow! Grow in grace, and the knowledge . . . of our Saviour Jesus Christ! This verse mentions two Christian aspects, grace and knowledge, and then demands that we grow in them.

One simple definition for the word grow is to increase. Humans and plants grow by a process of ingesting materials and assimilating them. To grow is simply to mature from a child to adulthood. Men grow beards. Women grow roses. Growth is a gradual process. Our friendships grow stronger and more precious when we are truly Christian. God's love grows in Christian friendship. Christian graces and holiness are apparent in growing Christians.

No child (babe) of God can afford to ignore this imperative, powerful, and unchanging demand of the Lord. Those who do grow in grace have the prospect of becoming fully matured and maximum Christians, but those who do not will find themselves stunted and on the diminutive side of the dividing line. No one dishonors God more than dwarfed Christians, (Hebrews 10:38). Nobody can blame the midget for his stature, but it is shameful when babes in Christ never grow out of their "babes in Christ" state.

Christ said, "My words are spirit and they are life" (John 6:63). Christ and New Testament writers repeatedly call His words milk, bread, meat, wine, water, and honey. The words of Christ are our all sufficiency and they will grow stalwart, healthy children of God when they pursue this strict diet. We start on milk, grow to like bread (Bread of Life) and eventually grow stronger on meat (1 Peter 2:2).

Maybe the analogy of humans and plants over simplifies this great spiritual lesson, but Christ made continual use of the same. He mentioned the corn of wheat that dies before it grows. Some seeds produce more than others—some a hundredfold, some sixtyfold, and some thirtyfold (Matthew 13:8). Christ used himself and us to illustrate the thriving vineyard and the vinedresser. In John 15:1-5 Jesus said, .".without me you cannot grow." Trees by the riverside are continually nourished. These grow naturally, we grow in the grace and knowledge of God by the Holy Spirit. Paul thought as a child and spoke as a child until he increased to manhood and he put away childish things.

If you have any ambition, or if you have aspirations to imitate Christ in your life, there is strong implication that to do so, you will have to start early in the Christian life to do as He did.

"And the child grew, and waxed strong in spirit, filled with wisdom: and the grace of God was upon Him," (Luke 2:40).

If we are blameless and beautiful now, because of grace, we shall be faultless presently when we finally all speak the Truth in love, and *Grow Up* in him in all things in Christ (Ephesians 4:7).—**C. E. French, Associate Pastor, North Cleveland Church of God, Cleveland, Tennessee**

SENTENCE SERMONS

THE ULTIMATE GOAL of spiritual maturity is Christ likeness.

—**Selected**

GROWTH IN CHRIST is shown by one's desire for unity and self-giving service to the body of Christ.

—**Selected**

LIFE IS LIKE a game of tennis; the player who serves well seldom loses.

—**Anonymous**

CHRISTIANS MAY NOT see eye to eye, but they can walk arm in arm.

—**Selected**

EVANGELISTIC APPLICATION

SPIRITUAL MATURITY EQUIPS A PERSON FOR MINISTRY TO BOTH THE SAVED AND THE LOST.

Spiritual maturity is required in order to grow into the likeness of Christ. If this were not so, Paul would not have had to admonish the Christians at Ephesus away from negative and evil works. He would not have had to encourage them to do works which reflect Christ within them. The Ephesian believers needed to constantly mature in Christ. The same is true of believers today.

Maturing in the Christian walk and becoming like Christ is important because the heart of effective witnessing involves the sinner being able to see Christ within the Christian. If the image of Christ within the believer is weak or distorted, the testimony will be ineffective. Also, without a clear and mature image of Christ in the Christian's life, witnessing only reflects the person witnessing and not Christ.

Lack of maturity in the believer results in an ineffective ministry to other Christians. Christians must edify one another. Spiritual maturity allows the believer to become a channel through which the ministry of Christ can flow from one Christian to another. Bitterness, strife, anger, and other immature characteristics stop this flow. Christian maturity is essential for ministry in the body of Christ.

DAILY BIBLE READINGS

M. Blessings Bestowed. Psalm 68:17-20

T. Light for the Journey. Psalm 119:97-105

W. Deliverance Promised. Isaiah 61:1-3

T. Exhortation to Holiness. 2 Corinthians 6:14-18; 7:1

F. Right Motives. 1 Thessalonians 2:3-12

S. A Right Choice. Hebrews 11:24-26

Christ Is Risen

(Easter)

Study Text: Mark 16:1-20; Revelation 1:17, 18

Supplemental References: Psalm 16:7-11; Acts 2:22-36; 1 Corinthians 15:1-8, 12-25; Revelation 1:17-20

Time: A.D. 30

Place: A garden near Calvary, possibly in the city of Jerusalem.

Golden Text: "Now is Christ risen from the dead, and become the firstfruits of them that slept" (1 Corinthians 15:20).

Central Truth: Christ's resurrection provides a sure basis for the salvation of man and his resurrection.

Evangelistic Emphasis: The power of the risen Christ brings life to those dead in sin.

Printed Text

Mark 16:1. And when the sabbath was past, Mary Magdalene, and Mary the mother of James, and Salome, had bought sweet spices, that they might come and anoint him.

2. And very early in the morning the first day of the week, they came unto the sepulchre at the rising of the sun.

3. And they said among themselves, Who shall roll us away the stone from the door of the sepulchre?

4. And when they looked, they saw that the stone was rolled away: for it was very great.

5. And entering into the sepulchre, they saw a young man sitting on the right side, clothed in a long white garment; and they were affrighted.

6. And he saith unto them, Be not affrighted: Ye seek Jesus of Nazareth, which was crucified: he is risen; he is not here: behold the place where they laid him.

7. But go your way, tell his disciples and Peter that he goeth before you into Galilee: there shall ye see him, as he said unto you.

8. And they went out quickly, and fled from the sepulchre; for they trembled and were amazed: neither said they any thing to any man; for they were afraid.

9. Now when Jesus was risen early the first day of the week, he appeared first to Mary Magdalene, out of whom he had cast seven devils.

10. And she went and told them that had been with him, as they mourned and wept.

11. And they, when they had heard that he was alive, and had been seen of her, believed not.

12. After that he appeared in another form unto two of them, as they walked, and went into the country.

13. And they went and told it unto the residue: neither believed they them.

14. Afterward he appeared unto the

eleven as they sat at meat, and upbraided them with their unbelief and hardness of heart, because they believed not them which had seen him after he was risen. **Revelation 1:17.** And when I saw him,

I fell at his feet as dead. And he laid his right hand upon me, saying unto me, Fear not; I am the first and the last: **18. I am he that liveth, and was dead; and, behold, I am alive for evermore, Amen; and have the keys of hell and of death.**

LESSON OUTLINE

I. A GREAT ANNOUNCEMENT
   A. Approaching the Tomb
   B. The Great Announcement
II. GREAT AMAZEMENT
   A. Great Amazement
   B. Appearance to Mary Magdalene
   C. Appearance to Two Walking in the Country
   D. Appearance to the Disciples
III. THE VICTORIOUS CHRIST

LESSON EXPOSITION

INTRODUCTION

The resurrection of Christ is a cornerstone of Christian faith. It provides a source of hope and strength for the believer. Through the resurrection Christ demonstrated his superiority over sin and death. Christ made the resurrection and new life of the Christian a reality when He arose. Christ's resurrection makes possible the eventual resurrection of the believer.

Mark had a very devout view of Christ as the "Son of God." He presents this strong view of Christ beginning with the first verse of Mark 1 where he identifies Jesus Christ as "the Son of God." Mark continues this emphasis throughout his Gospel. It continues to the description of the resurrection. Here Christ conquers death, affirming His deity.

Mark realistically deals with the death of Christ. Forty percent of his Gospel is devoted to Jesus' journey to Jerusalem and the events connected with His death and resurrection" (*An Introduction to the New Testament, Volume One, The Gospel and Acts* by D. Edmond Hiebert, p. 100).

Mark also presents the reality of the resurrection, including the amazement of

those who first discovered the absence of Christ's body from the tomb, the glorious announcement concerning His resurrection, and the affirmation of Christ's post-resurrection appearances.

I. A GREAT ANNOUNCEMENT (Mark 16: 1-7)

A. Approaching the Tomb (16:1-4)

1. And when the sabbath was past, Mary Magdalene, and Mary the mother of James, and Salome, had bought sweet spices, that they might come and anoint him.

2. And very early in the morning the first day of the week, they came unto the sepulchre at the rising of the sun.

The day of the week on which the Resurrection took place has raised questions among scholars. The most generally accepted view places the resurrection of Christ on Sunday. Some scholars place the Resurrection on Saturday. This alternate view results from the opinion that Christ was crucified on Wednesday or Thursday. However, most scholars feel Christ was crucified on Friday and arose on Sunday.

The most generally accepted sequence of events begins with Christ being crucified on Friday and buried on the same day. This was the day before the Jewish Sabbath, Saturday (Matthew 27:62; 28:1; Mark 15:42; Luke 23:54, 56; John 19:31, 42). Following this the women returned home and rested on the Jewish Sabbath (Luke 23:56).

Friday, the day of the crucifixion, was the "first day." The Jewish Sabbath, Saturday, was the "second day." Early on the third day, the day following the Jewish Sabbath, the women went to the tomb (Matthew 28:1). This would have been Sunday. It is described in Mark 16:2 as the "first day of the week," meaning the first day after the Jewish Sabbath. (For more on the sequence of the Crucifixion and Resurrection see *Chronological Aspects of the Life of Christ* by Harold W. Hoehner.)

"And when the Sabbath was past" does not necessarily refer to the morning. The Sabbath days in the Jewish calender were marked from sunset to sunset (Leviticus 23:32). Therefore, the Sabbath ended at the sunset. After the Jewish Sabbath day, possibly after sunset, the women bought spices to further prepare Jesus' body.

According to Mark 16:1, the three women were "Mary Magdalene, and Mary the mother of James, and Salome." Mary Magdalene was given the name *Magdalene* because she was from Magdala, a small fishing village on the shores of Galilee. Mark will later note in verse 9 that Jesus had cast seven devils out of her. This is mentioned also by Luke (8:2). Some scholars feel "Magdalene" refers to the Hebrew word, *Magdala,* which referred to one who plaits hair.

Mary Magdalene is an important figure in the death, burial, and empty tomb of Christ. She is the primary witness of all three events. All four Gospel writers mention her as being present at each of these events. No other person is referred to as frequently (and directly by name) as she is concerning these events.

She is first mentioned in John 19:25 as being present at the foot of the cross. She is mentioned in Mark 15:40 and Matthew 27:56 as viewing the cross from afar. She is named in Mark 15:47 and Matthew 27:61 as being present at the tomb when Christ was buried. In Matthew 28:1 and John 20:1 she is named as being present when the empty tomb was discovered. And finally, Christ appears to her first after His resurrection according to John 20:14 and Mark 16:9.

The other two women mentioned in Mark 16:1 are "Mary the mother of James, and Salome." The exact identity of these two women is debated. A trio of women is identified and named in several descriptions of the events surrounding Christ's death, burial, and resurrection. The events

at which the trio is identified are at the foot of the Cross (John 19:25), viewing the Cross from afar (Mark 15:40; Matthew 27:56; Luke 23:49), purchasing the spices for Jesus' body after the Sabbath (Mark 16:1), and the report of the empty tomb (Luke 24:9, 10).

Mary Magdalene is clearly identified in each of these events. A second woman mentioned seems to have been consistently the mother of Jesus or a woman identified as "Mary the mother of James the less and of Joses" (Mark 15:40). She was also present at the tomb with Mary Magdalene when they buried Jesus (Mark 15:47; Matthew 27:61).

A third woman mentioned in Mark 16:1 and in the events mentioned earlier was a different woman each time or the same woman being referred to in different ways. At the Cross she is called Jesus' "mother's sister, Mary the wife of Cleophas" (John 19:25). While viewing the Cross from afar she is called "Salome" in Mark 15:40 and the "mother of Zebedee's children" in Matthew 27:56. While purchasing the spices in Mark 16:1 she is called "Salome." While reporting the empty tomb to the disciples in Luke 24:9, 10 she is called "Joanna."

Despite the debate as to the identity of the other two women throughout the above events, it is significant that the initial witnesses of the events surrounding the death, burial, empty tomb, and post-resurrection appearance of Christ were women. The gospel is certainly not biased toward male dominance. The fact that these important witnesses are women demonstrates the truth of the gospel is without bias as to male or female.

3. And they said among themselves, Who shall roll us away the stone from the door of the sepulchre?

4. And when they looked, they saw that the stone was rolled away: for it was very great.

After the three women purchased the spices to anoint Jesus' body, they approached the tomb. Only Matthew mentions Mary Magdalene and "the other Mary" at this point (28:1). It is reasonable to assume from the context of Mark

16:1 that all three women approached the tomb initially that morning.

Mary Magdalene and Mary, the mother of Joses, had witnessed the burial of Jesus earlier. Therefore, they were aware of the giant stone that had been placed in front of the tomb. However, they were not aware that the tomb had been officially sealed and a guard posted (Matthew 27:62-66). They were simply concerned about the physical difficulty of removing the stone.

Mark does not explain how the stone had been rolled away. Matthew gives an account of the rolling away of the stone (28:2-4). Mark emphasizes the moment when the women discovered the tomb was empty. Upon approaching the opened tomb, Mark does not indicate any surprise by the women. They simply proceed into the tomb.

Guards are mentioned in Matthew 28:4 as becoming as "dead men" at the rolling away of the stone. Whether they are still present is not mentioned by Mark or the other Gospel writers.

B. The Great Announcement (16:5-7)

5. And entering into the sepulchre, they saw a young man sitting on the right side, clothed in a long white garment; and they were affrighted.

According to Mark's description, the sepulchre was large enough to walk into. As the women walked in they were neither afraid nor surprised by any of the circumstances, according to Mark's description. The Greek text indicates they were in the sepulchre chamber when they saw the young man sitting.

Mark stresses what the women saw after they entered the tomb. Matthew identifies the man sitting as the angel who rolled away the stone (28:2, 5). Mark is careful to note several facts about the angel. He appears as a "young man." He is "sitting on the right side." And, he is "clothed in a long white garment." This description serves to document and enrich the event for the reader.

"Young man" was not an unusual form or appearance for an angel. "Garment" comes from a Greek word which is especially used to refer to long, flowing robes.

"White" was a typical color associated with angelic beings and events in which the salvation of the Lord during the end times was stressed.

Mark has been dramatically describing the movements of the women and what they saw. Luke includes the fact that the women bowed down their faces to the earth (24:5). Mark's description climaxes with the last word of verse 5 describing the reaction of the women to the man they saw.

Mark says they were "affrighted." The word comes from a Greek word which means to be "startled, amazed, or terrified." The latter definition is probably the most descriptive of what the women felt at the sight of the young man in the tomb, sitting no doubt where Christ should have been lying.

6. And he saith unto them, Be not affrighted: Ye seek Jesus of Nazareth, which was crucified: he is risen; he is not here: behold the place where they laid him.

7. But go your way, tell his disciples and Peter that he goeth before you into Galilee: there shall ye see him, as he said unto you.

The mere appearance of the angelic being was not enough to let the women know what had happened that glorious morning. This highlights the importance of the Word of God and proclamation which declares His miraculous activity upon earth. Without the declaration of the angel, the women would not have known that Christ had risen. The declaration and explanation of God's Word is necessary for people to know what has occurred when God moves within a life.

The angel's initial concern was for the terrified condition of the women. He comforts them by exhorting them to "be not affrighted." Matthew also records this declaration to fear not (28:5). The resurrection event is not intended to frighten the believer. It is an occasion for joy and rejoicing.

The angel's reference to Christ, "Jesus of Nazareth, which was crucified," highlights the earthly existence of Christ and the treatment He received from men.

These two themes were echoed several times by the early Church in its preaching. Peter used this description of Christ in his sermon at the Day of Pentecost (Acts 2:22, 23).

In contrast to the earthly existence of Christ and especially the treatment He received at the Crucifixion stands the Resurrection. The angel declares that Christ is risen. This was the message of the early church, as indicated in Peter's message in Acts 2. Christ is risen from this earth in contrast to the attempt of men to destroy Him in the Crucifixion.

The angel presents the evidence of Christ's resurrection and then commands the women to declare the news that Christ will be seen again. The evidence is the empty place where Christ had once lain. The fact of the empty tomb is confirmed by all four Gospels and was never disputed by Jews who later questioned the Resurrection itself (*The Gospel According to Mark* by William L. Lane, P. 588). The angel's command to tell the disciples not only concerned the Resurrection, but specifically that the disciples would see Jesus shortly. They were to not simply say, "He is risen," but further that, "You will see Him again."

The fact of the Resurrection is fulfilled and even more glorious when the message of the appearance of Jesus is declared. This was the message of the angels when Christ ascended into heaven in Acts 1. Christ did not just ascend into the clouds, but the angels declared that Christ would appear again "in like manner as ye have seen him go into heaven" (Acts 1:11). The women ran to the disciples primarily for the purpose of declaring Christ's appearance. The church today should also declare the reappearance of Christ as well as the fact of His resurrection.

What are some of the chronological aspects surrounding the death, burial, and resurrection of Christ? What are some of the significant points regarding the women present that day at the tomb? What were some of the emotions felt by the women as they encountered the angel in the tomb? What did the angel instruct the women to do? Describe the reaction of the women as they fled from the tomb.

II. GREAT AMAZEMENT (Mark 16:8-14)

A. Great Amazement (v. 8)

8. And they went out quickly, and fled from the sepulchre; for they trembled and were amazed: neither said they any thing to any man; for they were afraid.

Throughout this portion of Scripture Mark has communicated the drama of the event. He has captured the alarm and surprise of the women at their encounter of the opened tomb and the meeting with the angel. In verse 8 Mark strongly communicates the emotions the women were feeling as they raced to tell the disciples.

In verse 8 there are no less than eight references which communicate the drama of the event. The first reference is in the word *quickly*. It meant to do something "speedily and without delay." The second reference is the word *fled*. Some ancient references poetically used this word to refer to a "flight" away from something (*The Vocabulary of the Greek New Testament* by Moulton and Milligan, p. 666). The women were fleeing with as much speed as they could muster feeling a variety of emotions. Mark describes these emotions in the next references.

The next reference to this emotional scene is the word *trembled*. This was the reason why they were moving so quickly. *Trembled* comes from a Greek word which means "to shake with fear." This fear resulted from a sense of being overwhelmed by an encounter with God.

The next reference also describes emotion, "amazed." This word in Greek emphasizes the importance of an event. They were awe stricken but it was because of the amazing event that had taken place. They were feeling the wonder produced by the event.

The next reference indicates the duration of their shaking and amazement. They did not speak to any of the other travelers on the road that day during the entire time they traveled. They were so taken by the event and the command of the angel that they went directly to the disciples and spoke to them only.

The final reference to what was occurring to the women is a summary of what they were feeling. "For" indicates the reason for what they were feeling and doing is given. They were "afraid." The Greek word for "afraid," as it is used in this verse, indicates "reverential awe." They were neither doubting nor apathetic, but they were consumed by the importance and reverence of what had taken place.

Others on the road did not feel what they felt. But, the women had an encounter with a divine messenger and had come in contact with the reality of the Resurrection. They were anticipating the reappearance of Christ. No doubt Mark wanted to capture the excitement and reverence of the moment because this response is similar to what Christian's should feel today. The impact of the Resurrection message and the anticipation of Christ's reappearance should compel Christians to be committed to carrying out the commands of Christ.

B. Appearance to Mary Magdalene (vv. 9-11)

9. Now when Jesus was risen early the first day of the week, he appeared first to Mary Magdalene, out of whom he had cast seven devils.

10. And she went and told them that had been with him, as they mourned and wept.

11. And they, when they had heard that he was alive, and had been seen of her, believed not.

The Gospel of Mark turns its attention to the appearance of Christ to Mary Magdalene at the tomb. The other Gospels give details of the various events which were taking place during this time: Luke includes the report of the empty tomb by the women (24:9-11); Matthew records an appearance by Jesus to the women as they went to the disciples (28:8-10); Luke records the visit of Peter to the empty tomb (24:12); and John gives a detailed description of Christ's appearance to Mary Magdalene (20:11-18).

Mark does not give a description of the encounter between Jesus and Mary Magdalene, but he does add a significant point regarding Mary Magdalene. She

had seven demons cast out of her by Jesus. Mark is the only Gospel writer to note this about Mary Magdalene's past in the sequence of descriptions concerning the death, burial, and resurrection of Jesus.

Mary Magdalene is the only primary witness mentioned in all the Gospels as being present at the death, burial, and empty tomb of Christ. Further, she was the first person to whom the risen Christ appeared. The glory of her witness and the depth from which Christ had saved her is a profound image of the power of Christ. Christ can redeem the vilest sinner and reveal Himself in His glory to that same person. This is what Mark is noting when he reminds the reader of Mary Magdalene's past (v. 9).

Mary Magdalene gives her report to those who had been with Christ. Mark records that the disciples were in unbelief. The verse emphasizes their condition of unbelief and that they did not believe Christ was alive and had been seen by Mary Magdalene. The verse does not indicate whether they questioned Mary herself or the message. It was perhaps the latter.

C. Appearance to Two Walking in the Country (vv. 12, 13)

12. After that he appeared in another form unto two of them, as they walked, and went into the country.

13. And they went and told it unto the residue: neither believed they them.

Mark describes Jesus' appearance to two travelers going to the village of Emmaus. Luke describes this encounter in detail (24:13-35). The account of Mark is much more brief. Mark simply notes that after the reports of the women, Jesus appeared to the two travelers in the country.

Mark emphasizes the fact that the disciples did not believe this report. This is, no doubt, an extension of the theme of unbelief mentioned in verse 11. Mark may have been adding credibility to the report of Mary Magdalene, reinforcing the idea that they did not believe her report, rather than her personally.

D. Appearance to the Disciples (v. 14)

14. Afterward he appeared unto the eleven as they sat at meat, and upbraided them with their unbelief and hardness of heart, because they believed not them which had seen him after he was risen.

Verse 14 describes Jesus' first appearance to the disciples after His resurrection. This incident is recorded also in Luke 24:36-49 and John 20:19-25. In this appearance Thomas was absent. Later, Christ would appear to the disciples with Thomas present (John 20:26-29). Christ would also appear after that to His disciples by the shore of the Sea of Tiberias (John 21:1-23). Jesus would make another appearance in Galilee recorded in Matthew 28:16-20. The ascension is mentioned in Mark 16:19, 20 and Luke 24:50-53.

The emphasis of Mark's description of Christ's first appearance to His disciples involves their skepticism of previous reports that He was alive and had appeared to others. Christ "upbraided" them. "Upbraided" was a strong word referring to the shame involved in their unbelief. "With" indicates that their unbelief was the thing Jesus used to upbraid or shame them. Mark adds that they were also hardened in their heart. This indicates the severity of their unbelief.

Mark's description highlights the need to believe the events of the Resurrection and the testimony of those to whom Christ had appeared. Mark's Gospel emphasizes repentance and belief. His description of the post-resurrection appearances of Christ fits those themes. Those who had encountered the risen Christ were fearful and reverent. Those who did not believe the reality of the risen Christ are strongly rebuked by Christ.

The risen Christ and the anticipation of His reappearance are not to be taken lightly, much less not believed. Mark persuasively presents the Resurrection story with a strong case for a reverent and believing heart. The risen Christ challenges a unbelieving world to believe that He is alive.

How does Mark describe the reaction of the women in verse 8 as they raced to convey the news of the reappearance of Christ? What was significant about Jesus appearing first to Mary Magdalene? What does Mark mention about her past? What does Mark highlight about the disciples in this passage? What does Christ do when He appears to the disciples? What themes are evident in Mark's account of the post-resurrection appearances of Christ?

III. THE VICTORIOUS CHRIST (Revelation 1:17-18)

17. And when I saw him, I fell at his feet as dead. And he laid his right hand upon me, saying unto me, Fear not; I am the first and the last:

18. I am he that liveth, and was dead; and, behold, I am alive for evermore, Amen; and have the keys of hell and of death.

These verses complement Mark's description of the post-resurrection appearances of Christ. Mark highlighted the fearful, reverent responses of the women to the reality of the risen Christ. John does the same in these two verses when he describes his reaction to the risen Christ. Mark presented the declaration of the risen Christ calling for belief in Christ. John presents the declaration of the risen Christ as given by Christ himself and an amplification of what belief in the risen, victorious Christ actually means.

These two verses are in two sections. The first section is in verse 17 and is John's reaction to the sight of the risen Christ. John says that he "fell at his feet as dead" when he saw Christ. This is similar to the response by the women when they saw the angel in the tomb (Mark 16:5 and Luke 24:5). John was not merely acting out of ritual or homage. He was truly captured by the event. He was in the glorious presence of the risen Christ and he suddenly gained perspective of how minute he was in comparison.

The second section of these two verses is the larger of the two sections. It is Christ's reaction and declaration to John.

This section is in the remainder of verse 17 and in verse 18.

Christ responds to John by first laying His right hand upon him. "The laying on of the right hand communicated power and blessing. It is a commissioning hand which restores John's confidence and prepares him to hear the words of consolation and command" (*The Book of Revelation* by R. H. Mounce, p. 80). These words of command and consolation are to follow in the remainder of verses 17 and 18. The Greek text indicates that Christ's hand remained upon John while Christ spoke to him.

Christ first exhorted John to "fear not." The Greek text indicates that John was currently in fear and Christ was admonishing him to stop his fear. "Fear" comes from a Greek word which means in this context "to be afraid or frightened." John no doubt had a sense of reverence and awe. However, Jesus perceived an inordinate sense of terror being felt by John. This required Christ's calm assurance to not fear. The Christian should reverence the risen Christ, but should not feel terror or personal apprehension.

The rest of Christ's address to Paul is a declaration of His position and power as the risen Christ. This declaration may be analyzed in three parts. In the latter portion of verse 17, it is a declaration of His position in the universe. In the first part of verse 18 it is a declaration of His position in relationship to the earth and earthly existence. The final part is in the latter portion of verse 18 and is a declaration of the power of Jesus' ministry regarding man.

The declaration regarding the universe is that Christ is sovereign. He is the "first and the last." This was a citation from Isaiah 44:6 where God declares that, "I am the first, and I am the last; beside me there is no God." Christ is the sovereign God who stands before all things in power and in dominion, and stands beyond even the end of all things as Lord.

The declaration regarding His position in relationship to the earth and His earthly existence is that He was once dead but is now alive. Christ told John, "I am he

that liveth, and was dead; and, behold, I am alive for evermore, Amen." Christ was recounting the story of His life, death, and Resurrection. He was comparing the treatment He had been given by men and the power He displayed by rising in the glory of His resurrection.

The declaration of the power of Jesus' ministry regarding man is in the phrase, "And have the keys of hell and of death." "And" indicates that Christ's possession of the keys is an extension of His resurrection reality. The "keys of hell and death" indicate that Christ has ultimate authority to determine the ultimate destiny of persons beyond death. Christ's ministry and sovereignty is not in this life only. He is Lord of the eternal destiny of each individual. He demonstrates this to John by claiming possession of the "keys of death and hell."

The fact and appearance of the risen Christ should evoke reverential fear and fervent belief on the part of all Christians. This response is described by Mark concerning the women who encountered the reality of the risen Christ. It is described by John concerning his own reaction to the risen Lord. Christ himself, as the risen Savior, declares that He is the almighty One who conquered the powers of death and is ready to minister eternal life to all who would serve Him.

REVIEW QUESTIONS

1. What were some of the emotions felt by the women as they encountered the angel in the tomb?

2. How does Mark describe the reaction of the women in verse 8 as they raced to convey the news of the reappearance of Christ?

3. How does John complement Mark's description of the post-resurrection appearance of Christ?

4. What are the three parts of Jesus' declaration to John?

5. What response should the Christian have to the risen Lord?

GOLDEN TEXT HOMILY

"NOW IS CHRIST RISEN FROM THE

DEAD, AND BECOME THE FIRSTFRUITS OF THEM THAT SLEPT" (1 Corinthians 15:20).

Having concluded his masterful argument, Paul makes a powerful statement of fact. "Now is Christ risen from the dead, and become the firstfruits of them that slept." He is referring to Leviticus 23:10, 11, "Ye shall bring a sheaf of the firstfruits of your harvest unto the priest: And he shall wave the sheaf before the Lord, to be accepted for you: on the morrow after the sabbath the priest shall wave it." A clear explanation of this passage is offered by William Barclay in his *Letters to the Corinthians*:

"The law laid it down that some sheaves of barley must be reaped from a common field. They must not be taken from a garden or an orchard or from specially prepared soil. They must come from a typical field. When the barley was cut, it was brought to the temple. There it was threshed with soft canes so as not to bruise it. It was then parched over the fire in a perforated pan so that every grain was touched by the fires. It was then exposed to the wind so that the chaff was blown away. It was then ground in a barley mill, and the flour of it was offered to God. That was the firstfruits. And it is very significant to note that not until after that was done could the new barley be bought and sold in the shops and bread be made from the new flour. The firstfruits were a sign of the harvest to come; and the resurrection of Jesus was a sign of the resurrection of all believers which was to come."

So even as the new barley could not be used until the firstfruits had been offered, so our resurrection could not occur until Jesus was first raised from the dead and offered as the firstfruits.
—Thomas Griffith, Jr., D.Min., Pastor, Salinas, California

SENTENCE SERMONS

CHRIST'S RESURRECTION provides a sure basis for the salvation of man and his resurrection.

—Selected

FAITH CANNOT LONG keep death in view. Resurrection is that which fills the vision of faith and in the power thereof, it can rise from the dead.
—Charles Mackintosh

THE RESURRECTION IS a true sunrising, the inbursting of a cloudless sky on all the righteous dead.
—Horace Bushnell

YOU CAN'T WRECK the Resurrection by open attack, deliberate denial, or intentional ignorance.
—"Notes and Quotes"

EVANGELISTIC APPLICATION

THE POWER OF THE RISEN CHRIST BRINGS LIFE TO THOSE DEAD IN SIN.

The resurrection of Christ means life for the sinner. The sinner dwells in darkness and has no hope outside of Christ to find eternal life and blessings. The way of the sinner is destined for nothing except eternal destruction and torment. However, the resurrection of Christ brings life to those in sin.

The risen Christ conquered death so that the sinner may have life. Christ was crucified by man. Man tried to put the life of Christ to an end by subjecting Jesus to the violent death of the cross. However, by contrast, God raised Christ from the dead. The risen Christ holds the keys to death and hell. He has eternal power and sovereignty to give new life to those in sin.

Eternal life is available by faith in Christ. If the sinner is repentant and humble before the risen Christ, eternal life can be his by the power of the risen Christ. The power is available through Christ. The option is either eternal life in Christ or eternal punishment for those who choose to remain in their sins.

DAILY BIBLE READINGS

M. Fullness of Joy. Psalm 16:8-11
T. Wisdom's Blessings. Proverbs 3:13-18
W. The Scriptures Interpreted. Luke 24:25-32
T. The Exalted Christ. Acts 2:29-36
F. Motivated to Steadfastness. 1 Corinthians 15:51-58
S. All Things New. Revelation 21:1-5

Followers of God

Study Text: Ephesians 5:1-33

Supplemental References: Leviticus 18:1-5; Deuteronomy 14:1, 2; Romans 1:18-32; 1 Corinthians 6:9-11; 1 Peter 2:1-12; 3:1-7

Time: Probably in A.D. 61

Place: Written from a Roman prison

Golden Text: "Be ye therefore followers of God, as dear children" (Ephesians 5:1).

Central Truth: The reality of one's faith in God is reflected in a changed life.

Evangelistic Emphasis: Christ's death makes it possible for anyone to walk in fellowship with God.

Printed Text

Ephesians 5:1. Be ye therefore followers of God, as dear children;

2. And walk in love, as Christ also hath loved us, and hath given himself for us an offering and a sacrifice to God for a sweetsmelling savour.

8. For ye were sometimes darkness, but now are ye light in the Lord: walk as children of light:

9. (For the fruit of the Spirit is in all goodness and righteousness and truth;)

10. Proving what is acceptable unto the Lord.

11. And have no fellowship with the unfruitful works of darkness, but rather reprove them.

12. For it is a shame even to speak of those things which are done of them in secret.

13. But all things that are reproved are made manifest by the light: for whatsoever doth make manifest is light.

14. Wherefore he saith, Awake thou that sleepest, and arise from the dead, and Christ shall give thee light.

15. See then that ye walk circumspectly, not as fools, but as wise,

16. Redeeming the time, because the days are evil.

17. Wherefore be ye not unwise, but understanding what the will of the Lord is.

18. And be not drunk with wine, wherein is excess; but be filled with the Spirit;

19. Speaking to yourselves in psalms and hymns and spiritual songs, singing and making melody in your heart to the Lord;

20. Giving thanks always for all things unto God and the Father in the name of our Lord Jesus Christ;

21. Submitting yourselves one to another in the fear of God.

22. Wives, submit yourselves unto your own husbands, as unto the Lord.

23. For the husband is the head of the wife, even as Christ is the head of the church: and he is the saviour of the body.

24. Therefore as the church is subject unto Christ, so let the wives be to their own husbands in every thing.

25. Husbands, love your wives, even as Christ also loved the church, and gave himself for it;

33. Nevertheless let every one of you in particular so love his wife even as himself; and the wife see that she reverence her husband.

LESSON OUTLINE

I. WALK IN LIGHT
  A. Command to Walk in Love
  B. Command to Walk in the Light of the Lord
II. LIVE IN THE SPIRIT
  A. Call to Wisdom
  B. Summary Call and Description of Life in the Spirit
III. SUBMIT TO ONE ANOTHER
  A. Theme of Submission/Part of Life in the Spirit
  B. Command for Wives to Submit
  C. Command for Husbands to Love
  D. Summary Command to Husbands and Wives

LESSON EXPOSITION

INTRODUCTION

This lesson emphasizes Paul's concern for converting the doctrinal side of Christianity into practical living. Paul began the Book of Ephesians by giving doctrinal foundations in the first three chapters. Paul turned in chapter 4 to a concern for applying those doctrinal principles into actual practice. In chapter 5 Paul continues to apply doctrine to practice.

Chapters 4 and 5 discuss the Christian's walk. Both are concerned with relationships between Christians. Chapter 4 highlights the theme of unity. Chapter five continues this theme and expands into several areas: love, reproving unclean actions, the light of the Lord, reproving darkness, life in the Spirit, wisdom, Christian community, and submission.

Chapter 5 is very specific, especially in three areas. The first is wine drunkenness. The second surrounds various practices of worship in the church. The last area focuses specifically on relationships between husbands and wives.

Paul will continue in chapter 6 to enumerate specific ways the Christian needs to apply doctrine to living. This application process throughout Ephesians is typical of Paul. In his writings he rejects a

Christianity which only "talks" and never puts that talk into action. According to Paul, a fundamental characteristic of Christianity is putting belief into action.

I. WALK IN LIGHT (Ephesians 5:1-14)

A. Command to Walk in Love (vv. 1-7)
  1. Call to Follow God as Children (v. 1)
  1. Be ye therefore followers of God, as dear children.

Paul begins chapter 5 by appealing to the readers to be "followers" of God. "Followers" is from the Greek word, *mimatas*. The English word *mimic* is derived from this word. The word means to "imitate." Every occurence of the word in the New Testament is in the context of moral living (*The Vocabulary of the Greek New Testament* by Moulton and Milligan). Therefore, the emphasis in verse 1 is upon morality. Christians are to follow God, especially in morality.

"As" indicates that what is to follow is the "characteristic quality" (*A Greek English Lexicon of the New Testament* by Bauer) of what it means to be a "follower of God." The primary trait of a follower of God is that he follows as a "dear child" would lovingly follow and obey his parents.

  2. Call to Walk in Love (v. 2)
  2. And walk in love, as Christ also hath loved us, and hath given himself for us an offering and a sacrifice to God for a sweetsmelling savour.

In verse 2, Paul extends his command to be followers of God with a command to "walk in love." The expanded translation of the opening phrase would be "walk/conduct your lives in the sphere/realm of love." The Christian's life is to be lived within the boundaries of love.

The Christian's walk is to be conducted in comparison to the way in which Christ conducted Himself in the sphere of love. The action of Christ Paul specifies is the giving of Himself "for us an offering and a sacrifice to God for a sweetsmelling savour." Christ's action was giving of self in behalf of others as an act of worship before God. Christ's action of love involved others and God. This is the manner in which Christians should walk in love.

"Offering" and "sacrifice" were words typically used in reference to plant and animal sacrifices in worship offerings in Israel. The acceptance of the offering was marked by the fragrance of the burning of the sacrifice. Unacceptable offerings had an abominable odor (Isaiah 1:13). In Ephesians 5:2, giving of oneself in behalf of another person, as demonstrated by Christ, is an acceptable, sweet-smelling savor in the judgment of God.

3. Call Against Unclean Actions (vv. 3, 4)

(Ephesians 5:3, 4 is not included in the printed text.)

Verses 3 and 4 give the contrast and opposite of walking in love and giving of oneself in behalf of another. These actions are fornication, all uncleanness, covetousness, filthiness, foolish talking, and jesting which is not convenient. Paul admonishes that these should not even be named among Christians. Rather, Paul exhorts the Christian to be giving thanks among themselves.

4. Call to Not Partake With Sinners (vv. 5-7)

(Ephesians 5:5-7 is not included in the printed text.)

Whereas in verses 3 and 4 Paul spoke of actions, he now discusses types of people in verses 5-7. The types of persons he cites are whoremongers, unclean persons, covetous persons, idolators. These, Paul warns, have no inheritance in the kingdom of God.

The word *and* in the latter part of verse 5 is intended to connect Christ and God. They are one and the same. The word *and* neither divides them into two separate beings nor makes Christ less than God. Christ is God. This phrase indicates Paul's trinitarian theology and belief that Christ is divine.

B. Command to Walk as Light in the Lord (vv. 8-14)

1. Command to Walk as Light (vv. 8-10)

8. For ye were sometimes darkness, but now are ye light in the Lord: walk as children of light.

The command to walk in the light is given in this verse. The reason for the command will be given in verse 9. The circumstance which accompanies the following of the command is given in verse 10. In verses 11-13 Paul gives the same pattern of command, reason for the command, and circumstance following obedience to the command. In those verses the theme is the complement of the theme of light. The theme is repelling the darkness.

The believer is to personify light and darkness. The believer is "light" rather than "in the light" or "of the light." The believer was "darkness" and not "in darkness" or "out of darkness" before accepting the Lord as Savior.

Paul's references to being "light" or being "darkness" refer to the condition in which the believer once lived and should now live. "Darkness" refers to an immoral and obscure existence. More will be said about it in verses 11-13. "Light" was a term used by Paul and other religions of his day such as the gnostic cults. It referred to a lifestyle that receives the perception needed to master living. Existence in this sphere of living is marked by special insight into answers for the mysteries which often make life unbearable.

The phrase *in the Lord* in verse 8 is decisive to properly understanding what Paul means by "light." Unlike pagan sects which based their "light" upon a variety of sources, Paul bases the "light" of the Christian "in the Lord." The Christian's "light" is within the power, authority, and origin of Christ. The Christian's light in life is rooted "in the Lord."

The light to which Paul refers is demonstrated in living—the walk of the Christian. The realization of being light is revealed in the conduct of the Christian. Being light is not a matter of theory but practice in living. This is why Paul exhorts at the end of verse 8, "walk [live, conduct yourselves] as children of light."

9. (For the fruit of the Spirit is in all goodness and righteousness and truth.)

The vast majority of ancient manuscripts of the New Testament translate the first part of this verse, "fruit of the light." This is the translation in some modern versions. These versions include the *New International Version* and the *New American Standard Version.* "Light" fits the immediate context of verses 8-14.

The word *for* indicates that what follows is the reason why the believer should "walk as children of light" (v. 8). They should do so because *the* Light, the Lord, exists in the midst of all goodness, righteousness, and truth. There is no action in the midst of *the* Light which is not of these three characteristics. Therefore, Paul admonishes the believer to walk in a manner befitting the Lord, *the* Light.

10. Proving what is acceptable unto the Lord.

The circumstance accompanying obedience is given in this verse. Walking as children of light "proves" what is "acceptable" unto the Lord. "Proving" means to receive something and then by using it find it to be of good quality. "Acceptable" indicates things which are of good pleasure to the Lord. These are things that are of personal interest and of advantage to the Lord. When the Christian is obedient, he experiences ("proves") those things which are already of good pleasure to the Lord.

2. Command to Reprove the Darkness (vv. 11-13)

11. And have no fellowship with the unfruitful works of darkness, but rather reprove them.

Verse 11 gives the command to reprove darkness. Verse 12 will give the reason for the command. Verse 13 will give the circumstance which accompanies obedience to the command. This pattern of command, reason, and resulting circumstance was followed earlier in verses 8-10.

"And" at the beginning of verse 11 indicates that in addition to walking in the light (vv. 8-10), the believer is to reprove the darkness (vv. 11-13). These are coordinating activities which complement each other. Walking in light indicates that the Christian must also reprove darkness and reproving darkness must be accompanied by walking in the light.

"Fellowship" means, in this verse, to be in common together with someone. In contrast to common association and bond with darkness, the believer is to "reprove" darkness. "Reprove" is from a Greek word which meant to "bring to light, to expose, to reveal hidden things, to convict or convince, to reprove, to correct, to punish, to discipline" (*Linguistic Key to the Greek New Testament,* p. 536). The emphasis in this verse is upon convicting and exposing the nature of darkness. At the same time the Christian is walking in the light, that light exposes and passes judgment upon the works and character of darkness.

12. For it is a shame even to speak of those things which are done of them in secret.

The reason for reproving darkness is in the depth of the shame within the darkness. "Shame" comes from a Greek word which means "base, dishonorable, immodest." Derivatives of the word in ancient literature referred to someone who was foulmouthed. Early church writings used derivatives of the word to refer to evil, obscene, or abusive speech. In Colossians 3:8 a derivative of the word is used to mean "filthy communication."

Paul indicates here that even speaking of the evil, dark deeds done in a hidden way is an abuse and shame. The believer should reprove darkness because of the depths of shamefulness these deeds represent.

13. But all things that are reproved are made manifest by the light: for whatsoever doth make manifest is light.

In this verse Paul indicates what occurs as a result of the believer reproving darkness. Light fulfills it's true nature when it reproves darkness. Evil is brought under conviction through the process of reproving. God's justice and goodness is carried out. The means of this reproving is light. When a Christian walks in the light, he or she becomes an instrument of God's justice and goodness.

3. Command to Awake (v. 14)

14. Wherefore he saith, Awake thou that sleepest, and arise from the dead, and Christ shall give thee light.

Paul gives a summary command in this verse. In this command he indicates the conditions necessary to walk in the light and reprove darkness. He also indicates the conditions which keep Christians from walking in the light and reproving darkness. The conditions which make these actions possible are awaking from sleep, arising from death, and the giving of light by Christ. The conditions which keep the Christian from walking in light and reproving darkness are sleep and death.

"Sleep" refers to "spiritual laziness and indifference" (*A Greek English Lexicon,* by Bauer, p. 389). "Death" refers to their lifeless spiritual condition. The Christian is to awake and arise from this condition. However, the source of the light in which the Christian walks is not of themselves. Their source is Christ. The last part of verse 14 indicates that Christ will shine on the believer and give him light. In verse 14 Paul has utilized Isaiah 26:19 and 61:1.

What are the commands to the Christian in verses 1-14? Can the Christian only be concerned with the things of "love" and "light," or must he also be concerned about unclean actions and darkness? What is the Christian response to unclean actions and darkness?

II. LIVE IN THE SPIRIT (Ephesians 5:15-20)

A. Call to Wisdom (vv. 15-17)

1. Call to Wisdom (v. 15)

15. See then that ye walk circumspectly, not as fools, but as wise.

In light of the call to walk in the love and light of Christ (vv. 1-14), Paul calls the believer to walk "circumspectly." "Circumspectly" comes from a Greek word which means "exactly, accurately, or carefully." The steps of the Christian are to be chosen carefully with the goal of precision in mind. The Christian must not walk carelessly or foolishly. Wisdom

must be applied in the walk of the Christian. The word *wisdom* as it occurs here emphasizes the careful application of principles for living.

2. Accompanying Circumstance (v. 16)

16. Redeeming the time, because the days are evil.

In this verse Paul says the quality or nature of the Christian's wisdom should be displayed by effective use of one's time. "Redeeming" comes from a Greek word which means to "buy from or take an opportunity to buy." The emphasis of the word was especially in "buying back." A full definition of the word in this verse would be "buying back [at the expense of personal watchfulness and self-denial] the present time, which is now being used for evil and godless purposes" (*The Vocabulary of the Greek New Testament* by Moulton and Milligan, p. 220).

3. Call to Understand the Lord's Will (v. 17)

17. Wherefore be ye not unwise, but understanding what the will of the Lord is.

Since the "days are evil" and the time must be redeemed back, Paul further exhorts the believer to not be unwise but understand the will of the Lord. "Unwise" comes from a Greek word which indicates failure to use proper judgment and reason. The word indicates a foolish and haphazard lifestyle. "Unwise" stands in contrast to "circumspectly" in verse 15. The contrast is between a careless life and one which is careful and wise.

"Understanding" was a command using a special concept in Greek. The particular word for "understanding" used here emphasizes "putting things together" in one's mind. The word indicates that the "will of the Lord" is to be the focus of putting things together in one's mind. These understandings result from the thought processes concerning the will of the Lord.

B. Summary Call and Description of Life in the Spirit (vv. 18-20)

1. Call to Be Filled with the Spirit (v. 18)

18. And be not drunk with wine,

wherein is excess; but be filled with the Spirit.

In verses 1-17 Paul has been exhorting the believer to walk in love, light, and wisdom. He summarizes this section by calling the believer to be filled with the Spirit. This summary is in conjunction with the earlier exhortations of verses 1-17. A life filled with the Spirit is by nature the climactic reflection of walking in love, light, and wisdom.

The reference to drunkenness with wine was used by Paul to epitomize a life which was out of control. Drunkenness depicts someone who has allowed folly and senselessness to control his life. Paul is commanding those becoming drunk to stop and those who might acquire the habit to stop.

The construction of the verse in Greek indicates that within wine itself is "excess." "Excess" comes from a Greek word which is used to describe persons who are abusive, violent, dishonest, and riotous. They are without any preservation or safety from danger and destruction. On the contrary, they produce danger and destruction for others. These attributes are latent within wine.

In contrast to the above, Paul admonishes the believer to be "filled with the Spirit." The emphasis of the word "filled" in the Greek text is "control." Rather than reckless and careless, the believer is to be controlled and guided by the Spirit. The factor controlling the life of the believer should be the Spirit of God.

2. Attending Circumstances of the Spirit-Filled Life (vv. 19, 20)

19. Speaking to yourselves in psalms and hymns and spiritual songs, singing and making melody in your heart to the Lord;

20. Giving thanks always for all things unto God and the Father in the name of our Lord Jesus Christ.

In the remaining verses of the chapter Paul presents actions which come as a result of being filled with the Spirit (v. 18). There are four main areas of action presented by Paul. The first is "speaking" to one another in public worship. The second is "singing" within oneself in private worship. The third is giving thanks to God. The fourth is submitting to one another. Paul greatly expands and emphasizes the last area as it applies to husbands and wives.

In verse 19, "speaking" refers to an act of declaration to one another in public worship. Worship is something done to honor God. Paul further indicates here that it is beneficial for members of the body of Christ as well. "Psalms" refers to songs which had musical accompaniment. "Hymns" comes from a Greek word highlighting the sacred beauty and praise a song offered to God. "Songs" comes from a Greek word referring to songs known for lyric and poetic beauty. Paul adds that the last category, "songs," should be "spiritual" in nature.

The second action which results from being filled with the spirit is private worship. Paul refers to the impact of singing within an individual's "heart." "Singing" refers to the singing of a song and "making melody" refers to instrumental accompaniment. These were symbolic references of what is to occur within the individual believer. Paul encourages the believer that in addition to public worship, worship should be a deeply personal experience as well.

The third act resulting from being filled with the Spirit is giving thanks to God. The grammer of the Greek text indicates that giving of thanks is to be a continual part of the believer's life. The final action, submitting to one another, is discussed in the rest of the chapter.

What does it mean to walk "circumspectly"? How is this contrasted with foolishness? What climaxes Paul's description of the walk of love, light, and wisdom? What actions result from being filled with the Spirit?

III. SUBMIT TO ONE ANOTHER (Ephesians 5:21-32)

A. Theme of Submission (v. 21)

21. Submitting yourselves one to another in the fear of the Lord.

The final action resulting from being filled with the Spirit is "submitting" oneself to another person. "Submitting" comes from a Greek word which means to "place under authority." The use of the word by Paul in this verse means to "place *oneself* under the authority of another." This is an action initiated and enacted within an individual. It is not an action resulting from force or coercion. The emphasis of the word is upon giving up one's own position and rights in order to favor and edify another person.

The authority referred to comes from God. Christians are to submit "one to another." Paul does not mention human authority by itself. Standing behind human authority is the authority of God. He indicates the authority of the Lord with the phrase, "In the fear of the Lord." Their submission to human authority is to be done because the Christian is within the sphere of God's authority.

B. Command For Wives to Submit (vv. 22-24)

22. Wives, submit yourselves unto your own husbands, as unto the Lord.

23. For the husband is the head of the wife, even as Christ is the head of the church: and he is the saviour of the body.

24. Therefore as the church is subject unto Christ, so let the wives to be to their own husbands in every thing.

Paul expands the command to be submissive to one another by referring to wives subjecting themselves to their husbands. "Submit" in verse 22 is from the same Greek word which was used in verse 21. The reason for submitting one to another is the same for wives in verse 22 as it was for Christians in general in verse 21. That reason is the Lord.

"Submit" in verses 21 and 22 refers to putting oneself under the authority of another. "Submit" does not simply refer to a general attitude of servitude. In both verses, by virtue of the particular Greek word Paul uses, he has in mind the concept of authority. Paul describes the specific form of authority he has in mind. This authority is the husband's in relationship to the wife. The word "head" is

another concept which refers to authority.

The spiritual relationship of Christ and the believer is the motivation and reason why wives should be submissive to their husbands. This is not only true for the general idea of "submission," it is also true for the specific idea of authority.

The phrase "and he is the saviour of the body" indicates the function of Christ as the authority ("head") over the church. Christ is the savior of the church and this is a motivation for the church to submit itself under Him. Likewise, Paul presents wives in a similar role under their husbands. While husbands do not "save" their wives as Christ "saves" the church, a husband is a means for the improvement of his wife's spiritual life as she submits herself under his authority.

C. Command for Husbands to Love (vv. 25-32)

25. Husbands, love your wives, even as Christ also loved the church, and gave himself for it.

(Ephesians 5:26-32 is not included in the printed text.)

Paul departs from direct reference to the theme of "submission." In verses 25-32 he speaks directly about a husband's love for his wife. However, the themes of submission and love are related and interdependent. Paul discusses love in particular from this point to the end of the chapter. He moves back to more references about submission in chapter 6. In 6:1-9 he discusses children and servants being obedient, a theme directly related to submission. The overall theme of 5:21-6:9 must be viewed as "submission." Therefore, when Paul speaks of love in 5:25-32, it is within the goal of "submitting yourselves one to another in the fear of God" (5:21).

The motivation and reason for a husband's love for his wife is the work of Christ in behalf of the church. This work is described as love and giving of Himself. Christ's giving of Himself in behalf of the church represents the nature of His love for the church. The emphasis of His giving and consequently His love was the sacrifice of Himself. Paul amplifies sacrifice of oneself as it applies to husbands in verses 28-32.

Before focusing upon self-sacrifice, Paul highlights the results of Christ's love and self-sacrifice. This description of Christ's work parallels an earlier reference to Christ being the "saviour of the body" in verse 23. Christ's authority over the church helps make the salvation of the church possible. In a similar way, Christ's sacrifice of self results in the sanctification and cleansing of the church (v. 26) and the glorious and holy presentation of the church before the Father (v. 27).

Self-sacrifice is emphasized in verse 28-32. This is the central feature of the love a husband should have for his wife. Self-sacrifice is commanded in verse 28. Three reasons for self-sacrifice follow. These are nourishment (v. 29), the unity of the church in Christ (v. 30), and the unity within marriage (v. 31). Paul completes the section on self-sacrifice and unity in verses 28-32 by referring to the mystery of those principles. Their accomplishment and reality is hidden as a mystery except as they have been revealed by the example of Christ and the church. Christ displayed the ultimate answer to the mystery of self-sacrifice and unity by loving the church and giving Himself for it.

D. Summary Command to Husbands and Wives (v. 33)

33. Nevertheless let every one of you in particular so love his wife even as himself; and the wife see that she reverence her husband.

Paul repeats his earlier references regarding husbands and wives. The theme of love as displayed in self-sacrifice is repeated in the phrase "love his wife even as himself." The theme of submission of oneself under the authority of another is repeated in the phrase "that she reverence her husband."

REVIEW QUESTIONS

1. How important is submission to a life filled with the Spirit? Are the two related?

2. How important is submission in describing Christ's relationship with the church?

3. In what ways are a husband and wife to demonstrate submission and love for one another?

4. In what ways did Christ provide the reason and motivation for love and submission between husbands and wives?

GOLDEN TEXT HOMILY

"BE YE THEREFORE FOLLOWERS OF GOD, AS DEAR CHILDREN" (Ephesians 5:1).

Why should we be imitators (followers) of God. First, it is our natural duty. Nothing short of this will satisfy the claims of right. It is not enough that we follow the best men and conform with the utmost propriety to the pious fashions of the times, nor even that we obey our own consciences. We have to make our conduct agree with God's conscience. Duty is infinite—a ceaseless climbing to higher and yet higher regions of holiness. We cannot reach the pinnacle of perfection at once, and we are not guilty for not doing what lies beyond our present powers. But we are blameworthy if we aim at less than perfection and if we ever rest contented with any lower state of progress. "Ye therefore shall be perfect, even as your Father which is in heaven perfect" (Matthew 5:48).

Second, we are under obligations of gratitude to become imitators of God. The word "therefore" calls our attention to these obligations. It points back to the previous words, wherein we are exhorted to forgive one another, even as God also in Christ forgave us.

Third, our highest blessedness will be found in our resemblance to God. He is ever blessed. Everything ungodlike must be ultimately a source of pain and death. Though the imitation of God begins in toil and sacrifice, it grows into the deepest peace and the richest gladness. —**Excerpts from** The Pulpit Commentary, **Vol. 20**

SENTENCE SERMONS

THE REALITY of one's faith in God is reflected in a changed life.
—**Selected**

THE LOVE that unifies Christians is stronger than the differences that divide them.
—**Selected**

THE FELLOW who is pulling the oars usually hasn't time to rock the boat.
—**"Speaker's Sourcebook"**

LOVE MAKES all hard hearts gentle.
—George Herbert

EVANGELISTIC APPLICATION

CHRIST'S DEATH MAKES IT POSSI-
BLE FOR ANYONE TO WALK IN FEL-
LOWSHIP WITH GOD.

The walk of the Christian is a high
calling. It challenges the Christian to put
his relationship with Jesus Christ into
action. Paul makes it abundantly clear in
Ephesians 5 that the high calling of the
Christian walk is made possible only by
the death and work of Christ.

God calls all people to the Christian
walk. Whether or not a person should
become a Christian and walk in fellowship with God is not optional. God desires
and calls all people to be in fellowship
with Him.

God does not call a special select
group to a lifestyle to be lived only by a
few. Anyone may have fellowship with
Him, and the godly life is required of all.
The death of Christ guarantees the availability and possibility of this fellowship
with God.

Christ's sacrificial death is the pass-
port to life in God. Fellowship with God
is not made possible by anything else.
This fellowship is not earned by heroic or
superlative works. This fellowship is not
merited by virtue of a person's position
in society. This fellowship is not deserved
by the high standard of living someone
may maintain. Fellowship with God is
available to anyone by only one specific
means, Christ's sacrificial death. This death
and resulting fellowship is appropriated
by faith in Christ.

ILLUMINATING THE LESSON

The true Christian is the true citizen,
lofty of purpose, resolute in endeavor,
ready for a hero's deeds, but never
looking down on his task because it is
cast in the day of small things; scornful
of baseness, awake to his own duties as
well as to his rights, following the higher
law with reverence, and in this world
doing all that in his power lies, so that
when death comes he may feel that
mankind is in some degree better because
he lived.**—Theodore Roosevelt**

In an engine room it is impossible to
look into the boiler to see how much
water is there. So on the outside of the
boiler there is a tube of glass which
serves as a gauge. As the water stands
in the gauge, so it stands in the boiler. A
tube half full means the boiler is half full.

This is true of our love for God. To half
love our neighbor is to half love God; to
neglect our neighbor is to neglect God.
—Rolla O. Swisher

DAILY BIBLE READINGS

M. Walking With God. Genesis 5:21-24
T. Obeying God. Genesis 12:1-5
W. Hearing God's Voice. 1 Samuel 3:1-10
T. Following the Lord. Matthew 4:18-22
F. Cost of Discipleship. Luke 9:23-26
S. Rewards for Following Christ. Luke
18:28-30

Christ, the Believer's Example

Study Text: Philippians 2:1-30
Supplemental References: Psalm 2:1-12; Isaiah 42:1-4; Matthew 20:20-28; 1 Peter 2:19-25
Time: Probably near the end of Paul's first Roman imprisonment, in early A.D. 63
Place: Roman prison
Golden Text: "Christ also suffered for us, leaving us an example, that ye should follow his steps" (1 Peter 2:21).
Central Truth: A life patterned after Christ's example brings glory to God.
Evangelistic Emphasis: The measure of God's desire for sinners to be saved is the gift of His Son on the cross.

Printed Text

Philippians 2:1. If there be therefore any consolation in Christ, if any comfort of love, if any fellowship of the Spirit, if any bowels and mercies,

2. Fulfil ye my joy, that ye be likeminded, having the same love, being of one accord, of one mind.

3. Let nothing be done through strife or vainglory; but in lowliness of mind let each esteem other better than themselves.

4. Look not every man on his own things, but every man also on the things of others.

5. Let this mind be in you, which was also in Christ Jesus:

6. Who, being in the form of God, thought it not robbery to be equal with God:

7. But made himself of no reputation, and took upon him the form of a servant, and was made in the likeness of men:

8. And being found in fashion as a man, he humbled himself, and became obedient unto death, even the death of the cross.

9. Wherefore God also hath highly exalted him, and given him a name which is above every name:

10. That at the name of Jesus every knee should bow, of things in heaven, and things in earth, and things under the earth;

11. And that every tongue should confess that Jesus Christ is Lord, to the glory of God the Father.

12. Wherefore, my beloved, as ye have always obeyed, not as in my presence only, but now much more in my absence, work out your own salvation with fear and trembling.

13. For it is God which worketh in you both to will and to do of his good pleasure.

14. Do all things without murmurings and disputings:

15. That ye may be blameless and harmless, the sons of God, without rebuke, in the midst of a crooked and perverse nation, among whom ye shine as lights in the world;

16. Holding forth the word of life; that I may rejoice in the day of Christ that I have not run in vain, neither laboured in vain.

LESSON OUTLINE

I. ATTITUDES TOWARD OTHERS
  A. Foundation of Christian Attitudes
  B. Attitude of Unity
II. THE MIND OF CHRIST
  A. Example of Christ
  B. Humility of Christ
  C. Exaltation of Christ
III. GOD'S WORK IN US
  A. God's Work in the Believer
  B. Shining in the World
  C. Labour That Is Not in Vain

LESSON EXPOSITION

INTRODUCTION

In Philippians 2 Paul makes a strong challenge to the believers in Philippi. Paul knew the importance of a life that is pleasing to God. With such a great responsibility, the task of living for God could seem impossible. However, God calls the believer to a life that is pleasing before Him knowing that it is possible.

The center of Paul's appeal is the example set by Christ. The life that is pleasing to God is a life that is patterned after the example Christ set. Again, this is a strong challenge. However, it is possible. The example of Christ is not an ideal that was given without the expectation that it be followed. On the contrary, Christ left an example with the expectation that it be followed.

The description Paul gives in this passage of Christ's example is one of the loftiest images of Christ in all of the New Testament. The passage describes the sacrifice made by Christ in the Incarnation. Christ is presented as One who was obedient even unto the death of the Cross. He becomes a servant and eventually sacrifices Himself for lost sinners.

The two dominant themes in the sections directly addressing the believer are unity and God working within the believer. Following the example of sacrifice and servitude, portrayed by Christ, makes the work of God possible in the believer. God not only makes the challenge to live an acceptable life for Him, He provides the example and means to do so.

I. ATTITUDES TOWARDS OTHERS (Philippians 2:1-4)

A. Foundation of Christian Attitudes (v. 1)

1. If there be therefore any consolation in Christ, if any comfort of love, if any fellowship of the Spirit, if any bowels and mercies.

In verse 1 Paul is referring to various aspects which serve as the foundation for proper Christian attitudes. "If" does not mean the statements are only potential. Rather, Paul is assuming they are true in making his statements in verse 1. It is true that there is "consolation in Christ," "comfort of love," "fellowship of the Spirit," and "bowels and mercies." All of these serve as part of the foundation for effective Christian attitudes.

"Consolation" comes from the Greek word *paraklasis*. It is formed from two Greek words, *para* and *kaleo*. The first means "alongside" and the second means "to call." Elsewhere the word is translated "comfort." The word emphasizes the strongest and most assuring kind of comfort, consolation from the presence of someone at your side. It is the comfort of having someone present who can care for you. Christ is the ever-present One for the Christian. He promised that He would never leave nor forsake the believer (Hebrews 13:5)

"Comfort" comes from a Greek word that only appears here in the New Testament. The word means "encouragement" or even "enticement." It speaks of the benefits of love which alleviate the cares of life. It emphasizes the care of love which drew the believer to accept that love.

"Fellowship of the Spirit" emphasizes the oneness of relationship the believer experiences with God in the Spirit. "Fellowship" highlights unity and oneness.

"Bowels and mercies" are two words referring to the emotional part of persons. "Bowels" comes from a Greek word emphasizing "tender affection." "Mercies" comes from a Greek word emphasizing "compassion and pity." Paul is stressing the existence of the inner part of persons which feels strong emotions in behalf of others.

The four parts which form the foundation for Christian attitudes are the comforting presence of Christ, the benefits of God's love, the oneness of the Christian with the Spirit, and the ability within each believer to strongly care for one another. Upon this foundation Paul will appeal to the believers to dwell together in unity.

B. Attitude of Unity (vv. 2-4)

2. Fulfil ye my joy, that ye be likeminded, having the same love, being of one accord, of one mind.

3. Let nothing be done through strife or vainglory; but in lowliness of mind let each esteem other better than themselves.

4. Look not every man on his own things, but every man also on the things of others.

Paul exhorts the believers of Philippi to be united so that his joy may be fulfilled. Paul is very involved with the Philippians. Perhaps more than in any other Epistle he writes, with the exception of the Epistles to Timothy and Titus, does Paul speak so personally to the reader.

In verses 2-5 the key action Paul exhorts them to do is to "think" on certain things. "Think" occurs twice in verse 2 and forms the center of Paul's exhortation to unity in verses 2-4. "Think" also appears in verse 5 and is the primary exhortation the believers were to fulfill regarding Christ.

"Think" comes from a Greek word meaning "to apply thought and judgment in a certain direction and in a certain way." The word focuses not upon the process of thinking, but the object or person upon which the thought is directed. Further, the word does not merely mean mentality. It referred to attitudes, opinions, and judgments. The word indicates that someone "set their mind" to something. Whenever the word occurs in the New Testament and other literature, the object to which thought is directed is very important.

"Likeminded" in the Greek text appears as two words meaning "think same." Paul is asking them to think in the same direction upon the same thing. The object of their thinking was to eventually be

Christ. At verse 2 the object of their thinking is unity.

Corresponding with this unity of thought was to be a unity of love. They were to have "the same love." Also, corresponding with their unity of thought, they were to be "of one accord." "One accord" literally means to be of "one soul." The word refers to harmony among persons which dwells deep within them. It refers to a genuine spiritual unity. Paul repeats his exhortation given at the beginning of verse 2. "Likeminded" and "mind" come from the same word in Greek. Paul repeats the term to emphasize its importance.

Verse 3 continues to describe the manner in which they were to be "likeminded" or think the same. Nothing was to be done through "strife or vainglory." "Strife" comes from a Greek word, which, in ancient literature, simply means a "day laborer." Gradually, the image of someone working for himself took on a bad connotation. Finally, by the time of the New Testament, the word referred to someone who only worked for himself. He was a person of selfish ambition whose only aims were profit and power (*Linguistic Key of the Greek New Testament* by Rienecker and Rogers, p. 549).

"Vainglory" comes from a Greek word which means "empty or ineffective glory." It is glory with no useful purpose. It is only selfish glory that benefits only one person or a select few.

Both terms, "strife" and "vainglory" are preceded by the word "through." The particular word used in the Greek text has the character of "domination." An amplified translation of the first part of verse 3 would be, "Let nothing be dominated by selfish ambition or fruitless praise."

Contrary to the attributes of strife and vainglory, the believer is exhorted to "esteem" others better than themselves. This was to be done in the spirit of a "lowliness of mind." "Lowliness of mind" comes from a single Greek word which meant to give preference to someone else. It was a distinctly Christian concept. The word did not appear in other literature until after it was used in the New Testament (*Philippians, Triumph in Christ*, by Walvoord, p. 51). Someone with "lowliness of mind" practiced the virtue of esteeming the excellence of others before asserting themselves.

Verse 4 is a summary description of what should accompany those who are thinking upon the same thing (v. 2). They will not emphasize their own things and concerns to the exclusion of the needs of others. Rather, they will be attentive to the concerns of others and jointly think with them in a spirit of unity.

What are some foundations for the proper Christian attitudes Paul refers to in verse 1? What kind of comfort is indicated by the word "consolation" in verse 1? What is Paul's primary exhortation in verse 2? What conditions should accompany thinking on the same thing? What is the background of the word "strife" in verse 3?

II. THE MIND OF CHRIST (Philippians 2:5-11)

A. The Example of Christ (v. 5)

5. Let this mind be in you, which was also in Christ Jesus.

The phrase, "let this mind," comes from the same Greek word used earlier in verse 2 where Paul exhorted the believers to think upon the same thing. In verse 5 their thinking and attitudes were to be directed toward that which was in Christ Jesus. In verses 5-11 Paul presents the direction Jesus' attitudes and judgments took. Christ displayed a radical humility that is to be followed by all believers. Christ humbled Himself, accounting others with esteem and gave Himself in obedient sacrifice.

B. Humility of Christ (vv. 6-8)

6. Who, being in the form of God, thought it not robbery to be equal with God.

This verse describes the existence of Christ before He came to earth as Jesus of Nazareth. The description states Christ's existence as God and then gives Christ's

attitude regarding His divinity. "Being" in the Greek text is literally "was continually being." It refers to Christ's eternal existence as God. He was continually God in eternity, even before time was created.

The casual reader might judge the word *form* to indicate an illusion or shadow, something less than God Himself. On the contrary, the word *form* indicates that character and nature of someone is genuinely revealed in the "form." There are other Greek words that might have been used here to indicate false form.

The particular word used here in the Greek text for "form" means an outward expression proceeding from an inner nature. In this verse, it means, "That expression of being which is identified with the essential nature and character of God, and which reveals it" (*The Epistle to the Philippians and to Philemon* by M. R. Vincent, pp. 57, 58).

Though Christ was truly God, He did not think it "robbery to be equal with God." The latter phrase of verse 6 indicates that Christ did not feel that being God was something to be selfishly grasped. "Robbery" comes from a Greek word meaning "something to be grasped, a prize." Christ did not use divinity to attain selfish prizes. Neither did He feel that being God was something to be horded and flaunted.

7. But made himself of no reputation, and took upon him the form of a servant, and was made in the likeness of man.

Verse 7 describes Christ's action in the Incarnation. There are three essential descriptions. The first is that Christ "made himself of no reputation." It was something that Christ did Himself. It was an act coming from within His love and desire to redeem and reconcile the lost. "No reputation" comes from a Greek word which literally means "to empty." This does not mean that Christ emptied Himself of His deity. Rather, this was His refusal to use what He had to His own advantage. It was part of another aspect of the Incarnation, taking on the "form of a servant."

The second description of Christ's action

in the Incarnation was His taking on the "form of a servant." "Form" again indicates something that was an extension of Christ's divine nature. Christ's act in taking on the "form" of a servant expressed the divine service of God. God's love was extended toward man as Christ took on the form of a servant.

The third description of Christ's action in the Incarnation was that He was "made in the likeness of men." This phrase indicates the new state into which Christ entered. It describes the human side of Christ's incarnation. He was willing to become like men.

"Likeness" comes from a Greek word which means "concrete resemblance." This means that Christ became fully like man, yet without sin. Further, He retained His deity. This part of the Incarnation affirms that Christ actually became like actual men. It reflects His willingness to humble Himself to make salvation possible.

8. And being found in fashion as a man, he humbled himself, and became obedient unto death, even the death of the cross.

This verse describes the work of Christ. His work demonstrates His humility and obedience. Further, it exhibits His willingness to sacrifice Himself in behalf of others. The first part of the description of Christ's work notes that He was "found in fashion as a man." "Fashion" comes from a Greek word which emphasizes the outward appearance of Christ. Christ appeared as fully human to others around Him. He was fully God at the same time. His followers eventually confessed that He was God. However, He did appear to those around Him as a man.

Appearing as a man, Christ "humbled himself." This act corresponds directly to the earlier exhortation by Paul in verse 3 to have "lowliness of mind" (a humble attitude). This phrase and the word *humbled* in verse 8 share a common root in the Greek text. They convey the same basic idea. The Christian is to follow Christ's example of humbling Himself. How did Christ humble Himself? That question is answered in His obedience.

Christ humbled Himself by being obedient unto death. Christ was obedient to the Father. Similarly, the Christian's motivation for humbling himself is obedience to God. God has called the Christian to humble himself and esteem others better than himself (v. 3). The humility of Christ was rooted in His obedience. Humility, more than a virtue, is a command from God.

The depth of Christ's obedience is reflected in the climactic end of verse 8. Christ's obedience reached all the way to the point of death, even death on the Cross. His obedience involved all of His life on earth and endured even in the midst of His death. The Cross was a shameful, agonizing death. But Christ endured the shame and agony in an obedient act of humility for the benefit of others.

The Christian is called to have this same humility. God challenges the Christian to have the same depth of commitment to others. Humility is not an option for the Christian. Humility is a command given and exemplified by God in Christ.

C. Exaltation of Christ (vv. 9-11)

9. Wherefore God also hath highly exalted him, and given him a name which is above every name:

10. That at the name of Jesus every knee should bow, of things in heaven, and things in earth, and things under the earth;

11. And that every tongue should confess that Jesus Christ is Lord, to the glory of God the Father.

The word *wherefore* is very important for a proper understanding of the implications and power of humility and the humility of Christ. "Wherefore" is from a Greek word which indicates the strongest sense of inference. It means that primarily based upon Christ's humility, God has exalted Christ. His exaltation was not dependent upon His humility, for Christ has always been God, but the strong conclusion of His humility was exaltation.

"Highly exalted" comes from a single word in Greek. It does not mean that Christ was exalted above a previous state He was in. Rather, it means that He is superior to other powers and authorities. The extent of superiority is that His name is "above every name."

Verses 10 and 11 primarily describe the extent in heaven, in earth, and under the earth of the honor due Christ. The words "every" and "all" leave no doubt about the total superiority of Christ. Bowing of the knees and the confession of the tongue were typical ways of describing not only homage but worship.

What does the word "form" imply in verse 6? What did verse 6 mean when it said that Christ "thought it not robbery to be equal with God?" In what ways is the incarnation of Christ described in verse 7? Is humility an option for the Christian? Is humility just a virtue for the Christian? To what extent was Christ obedient? What was the conclusion of Christ's humility?

III. GOD'S WORK IN US (Philippians 2:12-16)

A. God's Work in the Believer (vv. 12, 13)

12. Wherefore, my beloved, as ye have always obeyed, not as in my presence only, but now much more in my absence, work out your own salvation with fear and trembling.

The word *wherefore* in this verse refers to the obedience of Christ described in verse 8. Paul says, "As ye have always obeyed," emphasizing the importance of obedience. Their obedience was to God. Christ's obedience affirmed His exaltation and lordship. The believer's obedience to God affirms his salvation. This is why Paul exhorts them to be obedient, thereby "working out their own salvation."

"Working out" does not imply that the believer creates his own salvation. It comes from a Greek word which means "to accomplish, work on to the finish." Salvation is the result of God's grace, not the works of man. Paul is stressing here that because of salvation the believer must work that salvation on to the finish of his life.

"Own" stresses the responsibility placed upon each individual for their obedience

to God. "Fear" refers to "godly fear, growing out of recognition of weakness and of the power of temptation" (*The Epistles to the Philippians and to Philemon* by M. R. Vincent, p. 65). "Fear and trembling" emphasize the devout humility of the believer before God required for total obedience.

13. For it is God which worketh in you both to will and to do of his good pleasure.

This verse gives the reason for the admonition of verse 12. The reason is God and the work of God within the believer. "Worketh" comes from a Greek word which emphasizes "effective and productive work." It is work which gives the energy and ability necessary to accomplish a goal.

Paul is emphasizing the necessity of obedience to God. God is the One who is making possible His good pleasure within the believer. Therefore, God is to be honored, feared, and obeyed. Disobedience and the corresponding failure to humble oneself reflects a lack of proper honor, fear, and worship of God. Disobedience and failure in humility also reflect a person's unwillingness to allow the power of God to work His good pleasure within them.

B. Shining in the World (vv. 14, 15)

14. Do all things without murmurings and disputings:

15. That ye may be blameless and harmless, the sons of God, without rebuke, in the midst of a crooked and perverse nation, among whom ye shine as lights in the world.

In these verses Paul specifies the way in which the believer is to be obedient in humility. The scope of this obedience is extensive, "all things." Without exception the believer is to do things without "murmurings and disputings."

"Murmurings" comes from a Greek word which is used in John 7:12 in reference to a secret debate, and Acts 6:1 in reference to a secret displeasure. The opposite of murmurings is to do something "with a cheerful and willing mind" (*Greek-English Lexicon of the New Testament* by Thayer, p. 120).

"Disputings" comes from a Greek word meaning "inward questions and skepticisms." The word reflects rebellion toward others and toward God. This action reflects a lack of obedience to the exhortation in verse 12 to be obedient to God.

The reason for doing everything without murmuring or disputing is not in the benefits of refusing to murmur or dispute. Refusing to murmur or dispute is beneficial. Yet, the motivation for not murmuring or disputing is the believer's relationship with God. This relationship is described in two ways in verse 15. These descriptions serve as reasons why the believer should do all things without murmuring or disputing.

The first reason is that the believer may be "blameless and harmless." "Blameless" refers to relationships before God and man. "Harmless" comes from a Greek word literally meaning "unmixed or pure." The word was used in ancient times to describe unalloyed metal.

The second reason for not disputing or murmuring complements the first reason. The second reason is that the believer is to be a son of God without rebuke. This emphasizes the close relationship between the believer and God the Father. Sonship indicates that the believer is vitally united with the Father. Unity in the body of Christ reflects the close relationship of the believer with the Father.

The result of not murmuring or disputing is a witness before the world. Unity is directly related to witness. This is the emphasis in the words, "Among whom ye shine as lights in the world." Unity among believers is not just for the edification of one another. More importantly, it is an act of obedience to God. Further, unity is a witness to those outside of the body of Christ.

C. Labour That Is Not in Vain (v. 16)

16. Holding forth the word of life; that I may rejoice in the day of Christ, that I have not run in vain, neither laboured in vain.

This verse complements verse 2. In verse 2, Paul gave the Philippians the initial exhortation to fulfill his joy by being unified. He appeals to them in verse 16 to obey his exhortation in order that he may rejoice. He has been exhorting the believers to have a unified attitude. Paul realized that if they failed in unity, the work that had been accomplished in them would be in vain and nullified.

Unity reflects the believer's spiritual condition and value. Without unity, the believer is disobedient to God. Further, the lack of unity nullifies what may have been accomplished in their spiritual life thus far. Unity is nurtured by obedient humility. Unity provides the light to shine before a wicked world. Perhaps, the value of unity may be ignored when someone murmurs or disputes with another believer. However, the value of unity can never be diminished. It marks the spiritual value of the Christian.

REVIEW QUESTIONS

1. What are some of the foundations for Christian attitudes?

2. How does Paul describe the attitude of unity in verses 2-4?

3. In what ways did Christ display humility? Is humility merely a virtue?

4. Why is it important not to murmur or dispute in the body of Christ?

5. What would fulfill the joy of Paul according to verses 2 and 16?

6. How valuable is unity in the body of Christ to the spiritual life of the believer?

GOLDEN TEXT HOMILY

"CHRIST ALSO SUFFERED FOR US, LEAVING US AN EXAMPLE, THAT YE SHOULD FOLLOW HIS STEPS" (1 Peter 2:21)

The world has plenty of examples. Men do not go wrong for want of patterns. The worst man knows more of goodness than the best man does. Models make us neither willing nor able to copy them. What is the use of a headline in a copy, be it ever so beautifully written, if the scholar has no will to imitate it, has a lame hand, and a bad pen with no ink in it? We want something more than examples if we whose disease is that we know the good and choose the evil are ever to be better. So all types of Christianity which merely take Christ as an Example fail to get His example imitated. We must begin with "Christ suffered for us" if we are to live like Christ. Only when I look to His Cross as the great act of His love, by which He gave Himself wholly for me and bore the burden of my sin, do I receive the power to follow Him and live as He lived. That death, if I look to it with faith, opens the deepest springs of love in my heart, which make obedience to and imitation of Him necessary and delightful. It joins me to Him in a union so close that in Him I am crucified to the world, and a new life, the life of Christ himself, is implanted within me. It brings me to a new power of holiness in the Spirit which He gives. Unless the sufferings of Christ are to us the propitiation for our sins, they will never be to us the pattern for our lives. Unless they are the pattern for our lives, it is vain to fancy that they are the propitiation for our sins. What God has joined together let not man put asunder. "Christ has suffered for us"—there is the whole gospel; "leaving us an example"—there is the whole Law. —**Excerpts from** *The Pulpit Commentary*, **Vol. 22**

SENTENCE SERMONS

JESUS CHRIST IS the believer's example in both word and deed.

—**Selected**

A LIFE PATTERNED after Christ's example brings glory to God.

—**Selected**

THEY THAT KNOW GOD will be humble; they that know themselves cannot be proud.

—**John Flavel**

AFTER CROSSES and losses, men grow humbler and wiser.

—**Benjamin Franklin**

EVANGELISTIC APPLICATION

THE MEASURE OF GOD'S DESIRE FOR SINNERS TO BE SAVED IS THE GIFT OF HIS SON ON THE CROSS.

God desires that no one be lost in sin and darkness. God's grace is available to everyone who repents and serves Christ as Lord and Savior. This is without exception. Every person, regardless of their station in life, may receive God's salvation if they accept Christ as Lord and Savior.

The measure of God's desire is the gift of His Son on the Cross. Some may doubt the sincerity or reality of God's desire to save the sinner. However, God gave His Son because of His deep love for man. And, not only did He give His Son, God demonstrated His love by sending His Son to the Cross. That gift and that sacrifice upon the Cross give a measurement that is eternal. It demonstrates how vast God's love is for man. It shows that God is sacrificially willing to save the lost sinner.

Sinners can be assured of God's love for them and desire that they be reconciled to Him. This love never changes. God's desire to redeem those in darkness and sin cannot be changed by time or circumstance. No matter how great the weight of guilt and sin upon a life, God still desires to save that individual. The assurance of God's desire is in the fact that He gave His only Son to die in behalf of the sins of all people.

DAILY BIBLE READINGS

M. Humility Rewarded. 2 Chronicles 33: 10-13

T. Wise Counsel. Proverbs 1:8-19

W. Wholesome Words. Proverbs 15:1-4

T. Marks of Wisdom. James 3:13-18

F. Spiritual Fellowship. 1 John 1:1-4

S. Growing Spiritually. Jude 20-25

Christ, the Believer's Life

Study Text: Philippians 3:7 through 4:13
Supplemental References: Psalms 19:7-11; 23:1-6; 37:1-9; John 11:20-27; 14:1-7; Hebrews 11:24-27; 1 John 5:11-13
Time: Near the end of Paul's first Roman imprisonment, in early A.D. 63
Place: Roman prison
Golden Text: "I press toward the mark for the prize of the high calling of God in Christ Jesus" (Philippians 3:14).
Central Truth: Christ living in us brings righteousness, hope, and joy.
Evangelistic Emphasis: Eternal life can be obtained only through faith in Christ.

Printed Text

Philippians 3:7. But what things were gain to me, those I counted loss for Christ.

8. Yea doubtless, and I count all things but loss for the excellency of the knowledge of Christ Jesus my Lord: for whom I have suffered the loss of all things, and do count them but dung, that I may win Christ,

9. And be found in him, not having mine own righteousness, which is of the law, but that which is through the faith of Christ, the righteousness which is of God by faith:

10. That I may know him, and the power of his resurrection, and the fellowship of his sufferings, being made conformable unto his death;

11. If by any means I might attain unto the resurrection of the dead.

12. Not as though I had already attained, either were already perfect: but I follow after, if that I may apprehend that for which also I am apprehended of Christ Jesus.

13. Brethren, I count not myself to have apprehended: but this one thing I do, forgetting those things which are behind, and reaching forth unto those things which are before,

14. I press toward the mark for the prize of the high calling of God in Christ Jesus.

20. For our conversation is in heaven; from whence also we look for the Saviour, the Lord Jesus Christ:

21. Who shall change our vile body, that it may be fashioned like unto his glorious body, according to the working whereby he is able even to subdue all things unto himself.

4:4. Rejoice in the Lord alway: and again I say, Rejoice.

5. Let your moderation be known unto all men. The Lord is at hand.

6. Be careful for nothing; but in every thing by prayer and supplication with thanksgiving let your requests be made known unto God.

7. And the peace of God, which passeth all understanding, shall keep your hearts and minds through Christ Jesus.

8. Finally, brethren, whatsoever things

are true, whatsoever things are honest, whatsoever things are just, whatsoever things are pure, whatsoever things are lovely, whatsoever things are of good report; if there by any virtue, and if there be any praise, think on these things.

LESSON OUTLINE

I. CHRIST OUR RIGHTEOUSNESS
   A. Commitment to Christ
   B. Purpose for Commitment
   C. Desire to Know Christ
II. CHRIST OUR HOPE
   A. Perfection in Perspective
   B. Taking Hold of Hope
   C. Warning Against False Brethren
III. CHRIST OUR JOY
   A. Call to Rejoice in Christ
   B. Call to Gentleness
   C. Call to Prayerfulness Rather Than Anxiousness
   D. Call to Certain Considerations and Practices

LESSON EXPOSITION

INTRODUCTION

In the latter part of Philippians 2 Paul has discussed plans for two of his companions, Timothy and Epaphroditus. They were close companions in ministry with Paul. Paul had used them to send personal messages from himself to the Philippians.

Paul deeply loved the Philippians and throughout the Epistle he expresses his personal affection for the Philippian saints. His references are without any great sense of mixed emotions. His love for the Philippian saints was strong and secure without hesitation.

In the passage of this lesson Paul reflects his personal feelings about his walk with Christ. He gives a personal testimony. There are many great doctrinal ideas within this passage, but they come as Paul personally experienced them. They are not theoretical principles for Paul. Life in Christ is a living reality which Paul himself has experienced.

Paul frequently used the word "I," in this lesson's passage. This indicates the personal nature of the things he discusses. In fact, throughout the Epistle to the Philippians Paul uses the word *I*, 120

times. In comparison to Paul's other Epistles, he uses "I" more times in Philippians than in any of his other Epistles (*An Introduction to the New Testament*, Vol. 2, The Pauline Epistles, by D. Edmond Hiebert). In the passage of this lesson, 3:7-4:9, Paul uses direct, personal references such as the words *I* and *me* more than 25 times. The message of today's lesson is not just a series of doctrines to Paul, he has experienced them personally.

I. CHRIST OUR RIGHTEOUSNESS (Philippians 3:7-11)

A. Commitment to Christ (v. 7)

The verses immediately preceding verse 7, deal with the importance of joy and Paul's former life in Judaism. Joy is essential in combating error. Paul's confidence was no longer in Judaism. He was now confident and joyous in Christ. He explains the nature of this confident joy beginning with verse 7.

7. But what things were gain to me, those I counted loss for Christ.

Verse 7 sets the stage for verses 8-11. Paul's primary action is to "count" ("consider" in *NIV*) certain things as loss. He has taken the things that may have been "gain" and "counted" them loss. To "count," according to the Greek word used here, means "to perceive something, take an account of it, and then make a certain determination regarding it." The root concept of the word was probably to "lead." The history of the word indicates it probably referred to someone who may "lead" the way on a path or track. In doing so, this person would have to make certain perceptions and judgments about the nature of the path or course. He would have to "count" or "consider" things along the path.

The things that were "gain" unto Paul, he had determined them to be "loss." "Gain" means profit and advantage. These things were, according to the Greek text, an actual, continual source of profit to

Paul. Paul perceived and determined these to be "loss." The particular Greek word used here for "loss" is used two other times in the New Testament. Both of those occurrences are in Acts 27 and refer to the "loss" of ship and cargo at sea. The word indicates a loss which terminates one's relationship with certain possessions.

The reason for Paul casting aside those things that were gain was Christ. Christ was at the heart of his decision to count those things that were gain as loss. The Greek text indicates that Paul's action involved a decision which had a continuing effect. From the initiation of the decision to his present condition, Christ was the reason for Paul's action.

B. Purpose for Commitment (vv. 8, 9)

8. Yea doubtless, and I count all things loss for the excellence of the knowledge of Christ Jesus my Lord: for whom I have suffered the loss of all things, and do count them but dung, that I may win Christ.

In verses 8-11 Paul expands his initial statement of verse 7. Paul makes three primary statements: "I count all things but loss" (v. 8), "count them as dung" (v. 8), and "that I may know him" (v. 10). Under each of these statements Paul indicates several purposes and reasons. The first two primary statements deal with the things Paul considered loss. The last primary statement concerns Paul's gain in Christ.

The first primary statement by Paul is a direct restatement of verse 7, he considered certain things loss for Christ. Verse 8 expands those things that were "gain" (v. 7) to "all things." Not only the profitable things, but Paul surrendered all things for Christ.

Paul gives the purpose and the result of considering all things loss. They expand the purpose, "for Christ," stated at the end of verse 7. The expanded purpose for considering all things loss is the "excellency of the knowledge of Christ." *Excellency* refers to "possession of something superior." *Knowledge* refers to one's personal knowledge of Christ. Therefore, personal knowledge and relationship with

Christ is an experience in excellence and superiority in comparison to things that might be "gain" (v. 7).

The result for considering all things loss is that Paul "suffered the loss" of all things. "Suffered the loss" comes from one Greek word. It is the same word simply translated earlier in verse 7 as "loss." The emphasis in this last use of "loss" is that the loss came to him and he did not deem or consider things as loss. The loss occurred to him as a result of his faith in Christ. Paul not only affirms the loss he caused, he also affirms the loss which comes as the result of being a believer in Christ.

The second primary statement by Paul is that he counts all things that are lost for Christ as "dung." This statement is an emphatic extension of Paul's counting of all things as loss. They are not only loss, they are "dung." They are to be left because they are unfit for further use.

Paul makes four statements which amplify his emphatic consideration of the things lost for Christ as "dung." The first statement is the purpose for his radical commitment. His purpose is to gain Christ. This gain is the result of his commitment and the grace of God extended to him.

9. And be found in him, not having mine own righteousness, which is of the law, but that which is through the faith of Christ, the righteousness which is of God by faith.

The second statement amplifying Paul's emphatic consideration of the things lost for Christ is that he be "found in Christ." This is another reason for his commitment. The statement refers to Paul's desire for vital relationship with Christ, actually "in" Christ. Paul desired to be surrounded by Christ in all of his living. He desired to live within the living Christ.

The third statement amplifying Paul's emphatic consideration of things lost for Christ was that he be found not having his own righteousness "of the law." Paul recognized that before his conversion he had possessed pseudo-righteousness which was based upon his own works rather than Christ. This pseudo-righteousness had originated in his reliance upon the Mosaic Law alone.

Paul's final statement amplifying his emphatic consideration of things lost for Christ was that his righteousness be thoroughly based on faith in Christ. Paul says this righteousness originates from God and is discovered in faith. Paul considered the things he might have gained as "dung" because of the righteousness he had from God by faith. This reveals the value of faith in Christ in comparison to things a person might gain without Christ.

C. Desire to Know Christ (vv. 10, 11)

10. That I may know him, and the power of his resurrection, and the fellowship of his sufferings, being made conformable unto his death;

11. If by any means I might attain unto the resurrection of the dead.

Paul's desire to "know" Christ is the third and final primary statement which stemmed from his initial statement in verse 7 in which he deemed the things that were gain to him as loss for Christ. The word "know" does not refer to mere information or intellectual perception. It refers to a vital relationship with Christ. The nature of this relationship is discussed in five ways by Paul in verses 10 and 11.

The first description is found in the word *Him*. Paul desired a personal relationship with the Savior. His faith was not first in doctrine or information, although they are vitally important. Paul desired to know the divine person Christ.

The second description is in the phrase, *the power of his resurrection*. "Power" referred to the capability of doing what must be done as a Christian. "Resurrection" referred to the depth of power, power over death. This was not mere power or defeat over death, it was power and victory as found in Christ. It was rooted in Christ's work.

The third description of the relationship Paul desired is in the phrase, *and the fellowship of his sufferings*. "Fellowship" comes from a Greek word which means "to be common with." The word implied joint participation. It was a word used in marriage contracts. Paul desired to be in common relationship with Christ's sufferings. "Sufferings" referred to those things which would come upon someone and cause suffering. Paul was identifying himself with the agony, pain, and ridicule Christ endured at the crucifixion. Rather than feeling exempt from the suffering of Christ, Paul desired to be in fellowship with Christ's suffering.

The fourth description of the relationship Paul desired is in the phrase *being made conformable unto his death*. "Being made conformable" comes from a single Greek word which indicates an action done. The word indicates that this action done (to Paul) was a continual action taking place in his life. The word literally referred to acquiring the same "form." "Form" does not merely refer to external form. The term used here in the Greek text means an external form which is representative of one's inner nature (*The Practical Use of the Greek New Testament* by Wuest, p. 86). Paul wanted Christ's death to penetrate his inner being and so become a part of him that it would be reflected externally.

The "form" Paul desired to be conformed to was the death which Christ experienced. This was the death of merciless crucifixion. Not only did Paul desire to be at one with the suffering of Christ, he desired to be at one with the way in which Christ died. Christ's suffering climaxed in the Crucifixion. Paul was willing to suffer with Christ even to the ultimate conclusion of death on the cross.

The final description of the relationship Paul desired with Christ is found in the phrase, *If I might attain unto the resurrection of the dead*. Just as Paul desired the ultimate conclusion of suffering found in Christ, he also desired the ultimate conclusion of victory over death. Paul's commitment to "know" (v. 10) Christ included all of the work of Christ, His suffering, and His resurrection. The call to know Christ is the same for Christians today. The believer is not exempt from the power of Christ. However, both are part of the Christian life.

Is Paul giving a personal reflection of His commitment to Christ in Philippians 3? What is the primary act of commitment for Paul in verse 7? What is the purpose of Paul's radical commitment to Christ? What fivefold description did Paul give in verses 10 and 11 for his desire to know Christ?

II. CHRIST OUR HOPE (Philippians 3: 12-21)

A. Perfection in Perspective (v. 12)

12. Not as though I had already attained, either were already perfect: but I follow after, if that I may apprehend that for which also I am apprehended of Christ Jesus.

In verses 7-11 Paul talked of the commitment he had to Christ. He also began to discuss the work that Christ had done in him. Paul mentions the blessings obtained in Christ in verse 8. In verse 9 he mentions the righteousness obtained in Christ. In verse 12 Paul highlights the effect of Christ's work in him.

Paul highlights Christ's work in him in verse 12 by referring to a perfecting process Christ was performing in his life. The process was not completed. Paul says he has not yet "attained" and is not "perfect." "Attained" could more simply be translated "received." "Perfect" refers to the goal of moral and spiritual perfection.

Rather than perfect, Paul said he was one who would "follow after" Christ. "Follow after" is better translated "strive." The phrase pictures someone hastening after another person. Paul, though not perfect, was hastening to "apprehend" or take over those purposes for which Christ had overtaken Him. He was trying to capture those fruits of perfection Christ had purposed for his life. Paul felt compelled to strive for perfection in Christ.

B. Taking Hold of Hope (vv. 13-16)

13. Brethren, I count not myself to have apprehended: but this one thing I do, forgetting those things which are behind, and reaching forth unto those things which are before,

14. I press toward the mark for the prize of the high calling of God in Christ Jesus.

(Philippians 3:15, 16 is not included in the printed text.)

Paul restates his desire to press on to the perfection which Christ had purposed for him. However, in verses 13 and 14, Paul reassures the reader that his desire is not without hope. The goal of perfection is attainable in Christ Jesus. Paul presses toward this goal.

Paul begins in verse 13, as he did in verse 12, clarifying that he had not yet overtaken and received the perfection Christ had purposed for him. But, rather than being defeated or discouraged because he had not received his goal, Paul expresses the depth and intensity of his striving for the goal.

Paul says he has forgotten the things which are behind him. These are the things he mentioned in verses 7-9. These were things that might have had a certain gain for him, but he now considered them as unprofitable dung. He has not only recognized this detriment to his life, he has completely forgotten them. In order for the Christian to effectively strive for perfection in Christ, he must recognize that the works of self-righteousness are unprofitable and forget them.

Concerning the profitable things of Christ, Paul determines to "reach forth" toward them. "Reach forth" comes from a Greek word which means to "extend out and to lay hold of something." The word is used to describe a runner who extends himself at the finish line of a race in order to win. Paul has the goals of the Christian life clearly before him and he is stretching himself, in fervent effort to reach those goals.

Verse 14 is a further statement about Paul reaching for the goals of the Christian life. Paul describes the prize he is stretching for. "Mark" is a word referring to the specific goal Paul has fixed his eyes on. It is there to guide him as he presses forward.

"Prize" was a word used in footraces for the award given to the runner at the end of a race. "High" indicates that the calling he was striving toward was a heavenly calling, not of this world. The purposes for which the Christian is called by God in Christ are not earthly, but heavenly. They are eternal purposes issued directly from God.

In verses 15 and 16 Paul continues to exhort believers to grow in perfection in Christ. He exhorts them to have their mind focused upon growth in perfection. Verses 15 and 16 serve as a summary for verses 13 and 14. Paul strongly exhorts the believers of Philippi to stretch forward to perfection as he had.

C. Warning Against False Brethren (vv. 3:17-4:1)

(Philippians 3:17-19; 4:1 are not included in the printed text.)

Paul discusses in verses 15 and 16 those who had failed to strive toward growth in perfection. They were false brethren and Paul points out that they would eventually be destroyed. In contrast to the false brethren, Paul exhorts the believers to follow his example of striving to grow in perfection.

III. CHRIST OUR JOY (Ephesians 4:4-9)

In verses 2 and 3 of chapter 4 Paul exhorts specific Christians and the believers in general to strive for unity in Christ. These specific references highlight the personal nature of Philippians. Paul's ministry was not just addressed to the masses, he was concerned enough to address himself to individuals as well.

A. Call to Rejoice in Christ (v. 4)

4. Rejoice in the Lord alway: and again I say, Rejoice.

In chapter 4, Paul continues and summarizes his description of his personal walk in Christ. At the heart of Paul's experience was joy. His faith was filled with joy. His righteousness was filled with joy. His hope was filled with joy. His growth in perfection was filled with joy.

"Rejoice" is an important word in Philippians. It occurs 14 times in Philippians. There are three words in the Greek text of the New Testament which are translated "joy." One word, *agaliaomai*, emphasizes the outward demonstration of joy. Another word, *euphraino*, emphasizes the personal feeling a person experienced while joyous. The third word, *chairo*, which is the word used in Philippians 4, emphasizes "well-being experienced in response to someone or something."

Paul uses the third word for joy, *chairo*, because he is speaking of joy experienced in response to Christ. It is not joy centered around outward demonstrations or personal experience. Those qualities may be evident. However, the center of the joy Paul refers to is Jesus Christ. This is why Paul adds the phrase "in the Lord." Paul's exhortation is not merely to "joy" alone but joy "in the Lord."

B. Call to Gentleness (v. 5)

5. Let your moderation be known to all men. The Lord is at hand.

In addition to an exhortation to rejoice, Paul exhorts the Philippians regarding their "moderation." "Moderation" refers to persons who are fair and equitable. The word in Greek as it appears here means "a humble, patient steadfastness, which is able to submit to injustice, disgrace, and maltreatment without hatred and malice, trusting God in spite of all of it" (*Liguistic Key to the New Testament* by Rienecker, p. 560).

Paul stresses the scope of their moderation in two ways. First, the knowledge of their moderation was to be known by all persons they encountered. This defines the scope of the application of their fairness and equity. Second, the coming of the Lord was a primary motivation for their moderation. Christ was the reason why they should live in humble and patient steadfastness.

C. Call to Prayerfulness Rather Than Anxiousness (vv. 6, 7)

6. Be careful for nothing; but in everything by prayer and supplication with thanksgiving let your requests be made known unto God.

7. And the peace of God, which passeth all understanding, shall keep your hearts and minds through Christ Jesus.

In these two verses Paul explains the value of prayer to the believer. He gives them two exhortations, "be careful for nothing" and "let your requests be made known unto God." Besides these exhortations, Paul indicates the benefit of obeying them, the peace of God would keep their hearts. These exhortations and consequent blessings provide a strong motivation for Christians. Prayer should be important to the Christian, not only because of the answers received, but also because of the personal benefits acquired.

The first exhortation is to "be careful for nothing." The Greek word used here for this phrase is the same word translated "take no thought" in Matthew 6:25. The concept speaks of not becoming overly anxious or fretful about anything. Fretfulness is the condition which develops when the Christian fails to foster fellowship with God in prayer.

In contrast to fretting, Paul exhorts the believers to let their "requests be made known unto God." In contrast to fretting over *nothing,* the Christian in *everything* is to make his requests known to God.

Paul indicates a twofold means by which to make requests known to God. The first is prayer. The second is supplication or "petition." This petitioning should grow out of a sense of lack or need on the part of the petitioner. These actions were to be done in the midst of thanksgiving. Rather than fretting, the Christian must prayerfully recognize his need and be thankful as he makes his requests known to God.

The result of letting one's request be made known unto God is a "keeping" of the heart and mind. The heart and mind are the areas affected most by a fretful lifestyle. Emotional, mental, and spiritual anguish naturally occur when a wholesome prayer life is not developed.

"Keep" comes from a Greek word which indicates "watching over something." The word is a military term which refers to guards who watch over a city gate or something needing protection. In the same manner, the peace of God, which comes to one's heart and mind, watches over and secures the safety and rest of an individual. God's protection in a life is made possible by a rich prayer life.

God's protection in a life is hindered by a fretful lifestyle.

D. Call to Certain Considerations and Practices (vv. 8, 9)

8. Finally, brethren, whatsoever things are true, whatsoever things are honest, whatsoever things are just, whatsoever things are pure, whatsoever things are lovely, whatsoever things are of good report; if there by any virtue, and if there be any praise, think on these things.

(Philippians 4:9 is not included in the printed text.)

Paul brings this section of Philippians to a close by exhorting the reader to "think" on certain things. "Think" is from a Greek word which in this verse means to "consider" or "ponder." It emphasizes dwelling upon something rather than casual reflection or mere logical inquiry.

Paul exhorts the believer to continually consider certain things. Each exhortation in this text is prefaced with the phrase, "whatsoever things." This phrase is used to indicate that the number or amount of things to be considered is great. The only limitation on the things to be considered is stated later in the verse. Paul says, "If there be any virtue, and if there be any praise, think on these things." If they meet this condition, they need to be continually considered.

The things to be considered are those things which are "true," "honest," "just," "pure," "lovely," and "of good report." "True" comes from a Greek word which essentially means things which are "not hidden." They are not hidden and concealed, but open and honest. "Honest" comes from a Greek word which means "grave, venerable, or reverent." The word refers to someone or something which commands a high degree of respect.

"Just" comes from a Greek word which refers to things established by judicial process. They are things that are established and found to be right. The word in this verse emphasizes those things which have been established to be right under the justice of God. "Pure" comes from a Greek word referring to moral purity. It emphasizes things that are free from fault or defilement morally.

"Lovely" comes from a Greek word referring to things which would "attract or draw acceptance and love." "Good report" comes from a Greek word indicating things which are "well spoken of and praise worthy."

Whatever things that pertained to the above virtues were to be considered by the believer if they met two criteria. First, they had to be of "virtue." "Virtue" comes from a Greek word meaning "to be of moral excellence." Second, they had to be of "praise." This indicated their worthiness before God. In summary, the things to be considered by Christians were to be of moral excellence before other persons and of praiseworthiness before God.

Verse 9 summarizes Paul's exhortations to the believers by referring to himself in a humble appeal. Paul then challenges the believers to follow his example. He is confident of the example he has set before them. The life he has exhorted them to is not merely theoretical, it is one which he has personally practiced. His confidence in the testimony of the life he has lived is not in himself. His confidence is in Christ's work which has been done in Him.

REVEIW QUESTIONS

1. How important is rejoicing to the life of the Christian?

2. What does the word "moderation" mean in verse 5?

3. What are the results of an undeveloped prayer life?

4. What is the remedy for anxiety and fretfulness?

5. What are some of the things Paul calls the believer to continually consider and do?

GOLDEN TEXT HOMILY

"I PRESS TOWARD THE MARK FOR THE PRIZE OF THE HIGH CALLING OF GOD IN CHRIST JESUS" (Philippians 3:14).

The Apostle Paul used the Grecian games, a popular sporting event in New Testament times, to convey spiritual truths to the Philippian believers. He compared the rigors in the contest of the foot race and that of the Christian race.

He described himself as a runner straining every nerve to reach the goal and wasting not a moment in looking backward. In a human race the runner does not look back or compare his position to others on the track. His eyes are fixed on the goal and his mind is on the prize.

The Apostle says, "I press toward the mark" as "I pursue along the line." This has reference to the white lines that marked the ground in the stadium, from the starting place to the goal. The runner must not go beyond those lines or he would be disqualified.

In the Christian race the prize is not just to one, but unto all that love Christ's appearing and kingdom. The child of God is always running goal-ward, for in the spiritual race that goal is Christ, "And ye are complete in him, which is the head of all principality and power" (Colossians 2:10).

The prize suggests the crown (1 Corinthians 9:24) and "the high calling," is literally the "upward" calling (2 Timothy 4:8). This calling is of God in Christ Jesus, who will say to the faithful at the end of the Christian race, "Well done, good and faithful servant." The prize is "promised" when the call is issued, and given when the call is fulfilled.—**Kenneth R. Looney, Director of Evangelism and Home Missions, Eastern North Carolina**

SENTENCE SERMONS

CHRIST LIVING IN US brings righteousness, hope, and joy.

—Selected

CHRISTIAN EXAMPLES win more souls to Christ than mere words.

—Billy Graham

THIS WORLD IS but a vestibule of eternity. Every good thought or deed touches a chord that vibrates in heaven.

—Anonymous

EVERY AGE HAS its conflicts between those who advocate pure straightforward faith in Christ and those who would bog it down with other concerns and interests.

—**Charles W. Conn**

EVANGELISTIC APPLICATION

ETERNAL LIFE CAN BE OBTAINED ONLY THROUGH FAITH IN CHRIST.

The Apostle Paul had lived a very sound and upright life before he became a believer in Christ. However, he came to the realization that his own works were worthless. As "good" as he had lived his life, he was still unable to receive eternal life without Christ.

Paul came to realize that faith in Christ was the only means by which he could obtain eternal life. He considered his former life and realized how futile it had been. Paul accepted Christ and gained eternal life by doing so.

Moral excellence in life is extremely important. However, by itself, a virtuous life cannot save a sinner. Faith in Christ is required to receive the gift of eternal life. The benefits of the Christian life are many—the assurance of eternal life, hope in the midst of despair, fellowship with God, and many other blessings. All of these may be obtained by only one means, faith in Christ.

ILLUMINATING THE LESSON

It seems hard to imagine that a son of a slave would be offered a job at one hundred thousand dollars a year.

And it seems incredible that the same man would turn the offer down. But that is what happened to George Washington Carver. The offer was made by the famous inventor, Thomas Edison. And Henry Ford tried to persuade Carver to become a scientist for the Ford Motor Company. But Carver, unimpressed with the offers of money and prestige, chose to live in the South, living in relative poverty, wearing the same suit for forty years. He had already given up a promising position at Iowa State University to work with Booker T. Washington and his struggling Tuskegee Institute. When friends chided him for turning down the big salaries, Carver always had an answer for them. They argued that he could help his people if he had all that money. Carver invariably replied, "If I had all that money I might forget about my people."

And on his tombstone were carved fitting words: "He could have added fortune to fame, but caring for neither, he found happiness and honor in being helpful to the world."

—**Selected**

DAILY BIBLE READINGS

M. Principles of Success. Joshua 1:6-9
T. Prayer That Pleases God. 1 Kings 3:5-13
W. A Believer's Integrity. Job 2:3-10
T. The Living Bread. John 6:48-51
F. Living Water. John 7:37-39
S. The Living Christ. Revelation 1:17, 18

May 1, 1988

A Fruitful Life

Study Text: Colossians 1:1-29
Supplemental References: Genesis 1:28-31; 49:22-26; Psalm 1:1-3; John 15:1-16; 2 Corinthians 8:7-9; Philippians 4:15-20
Time: Probably in the summer of A.D. 62
Place: From a prison, probably in Rome
Golden Text: "Walk worthy of the Lord . . . being fruitful in every good work, and increasing in the knowledge of God" (Colossians 1:10).
Central Truth: God wants every believer to be fruitful in the work of the kingdom.
Evangelistic Emphasis: Spiritual fruitfulness in the believer's life bears witness to the saving power of Christ.

Printed Text

Colossians 1:9. For this cause we also, since the day we heard it, do not cease to pray for you, and to desire that ye might be filled with the knowledge of his will in all wisdom and spiritual understanding;

10. That ye might walk worthy of the Lord unto all pleasing, being fruitful in every good work, and increasing in the knowledge of God;

11. Strengthened with all might, according to his glorious power, unto all patience and longsuffering with joyfulness;

12. Giving thanks unto the Father, which hath made us meet to be partakers of the inheritance of the saints in light:

13. Who hath delivered us from the power of darkness, and hath translated us into the kingdom of his dear Son:

14. In whom we have redemption through his blood, even the forgiveness of sins:

20. And, having made peace through the blood of his cross, by him to reconcile all things unto himself; by him, I say, whether they be things in earth, or things in heaven.

21. And you, that were sometime alienated and enemies in your mind by wicked works, yet now hath he reconciled

22. In the body of his flesh through death, to present you holy and unblameable and unreproveable in his sight:

23. If ye continue in the faith grounded and settled, and be not moved away from the hope of the gospel, which ye have heard, and which was preached to every creature which is under heaven; whereof I Paul am made a minister;

24. Who now rejoice in my sufferings for you, and fill up that which is behind of the afflictions of Christ in my flesh for his body's sake, which is the church:

25. Whereof I am made a minister, according to the dispensation of God which is given to me for you, to fulfil the word of God;

26. Even the mystery which hath been hid from ages and from generations, but now is made manifest to his saints:

27. To whom God would make known what is the riches of the glory of this mystery among the Gentiles; which is Christ in you, the hope of glory:

LESSON OUTLINE

I. WALK WORTHY OF CHRIST
  A. Being Filled With the Knowledge of Christ's Will
  B. Purpose of Being Filled
II. REDEEMED BY CHRIST
  A. Deliverance by the Father
  B. Redemption Through Christ
  C. Preeminence of Christ
  D. Reconciliation by Christ
III. INDWELT BY CHRIST
  A. Reconciliation of the Believer
  B. Paul's Ministry
  C. The Indwelling of Christ

LESSON EXPOSITION

INTRODUCTION

The next three lessons concern the Epistle written by Paul to the church which was at Colossae. The city of Colossae had an interesting background. The city was situated in the mountainous region east of Ephesus. It was on the southern bank of the river Lycus, a tributary of the river Meander (the winding river from which the term *meander* originated).

Colossae lay on the main road from Ephesus to the Euphrates River. It was in a critical mountain pass ten miles long and two miles wide. To the south of the city was Mount Cadmus which was about 8000 feet in elevation. In ancient times before Roman occupation, the city was very large and wealthy. The wealth came from the highway and the wool trade of the city. The region was very fertile and many sheep were raised there supplying the vast wool trade. The wool was dyed into a dark red color.

By the time Paul wrote Colossians, the city was on the decline. It was no more than a "town" by some historical accounts. Colossae had been overshadowed by two other cities in the same valley, Laodicea and Hierapolis.

The church at Colossae was probably composed primarily of converted Gentiles. There were probably converted Jews in the congregation. Some members of the congregation mentioned in the New Testament were Philemon (Philemon 1),

Archippus (Philemon 2; Colossians 4:17), and Onesimus (Philemon 10; Colossians 4:9).

The congregation was probably not converted directly under Paul's ministry. The leader of the congregation was Epaphras. His evangelistic fervor had been responsible for churches in all three cities in the region (Colossians 1:7, 8; 4:12, 13). He came to visit Paul in prison with news of the congregations' faithfulness and to ask his help in dealing with false teachers.

Paul's letter to the Colossians is written to affirm their faith and to combat the teachings of false teachers in their midst. The false teachers were presenting a philosophy based on traditions. Paul does not attack philosophy or tradition. He attacks philosophy and tradition that is not based upon Christ.

I. WALK WORTHY OF CHRIST (Colossians 1:9-12)

A. Being Filled With the Knowledge of Christ's Will (v. 9)

9. For this cause we also, since the day we heard it, do not cease to pray for you, and to desire that ye might be filled with the knowledge of his will in all wisdom and spiritual understanding.

Epaphras had come to Paul in prison with encouraging news about the "love in the Spirit" (v. 8) of the Colossians. Paul responds, "for this cause," with prayer and a desire. These were without ceasing since the day that Paul heard of it.

The purpose of Paul's prayer and desire in their behalf was that they "might be filled with the knowledge of his [Christ's] will." The idea of God's fullness is mentioned often in Colossians. It may have been that the false teachers were claiming to present a "fuller" idea or teaching about God than Epaphras had presented.

Paul defined what he meant by the knowledge of Christ's will when he added, "In all wisdom and spiritual understanding." These were the areas where the wisdom of Christ and spiritual understanding (rooted in Christ) were essential. The foundation of true wisdom and true spiritual understanding was the knowledge of Christ's will. This was in opposition to the ideas of the false teachers.

B. Purpose of Being Filled (vv. 10-12)

10. That ye might walk worthy of the Lord unto all pleasing, being fruitful in every good work, and increasing in the knowledge of God;

11. Strengthened with all might, according to his glorious power, unto all patience and longsuffering with joyfulness.

In these verses Paul presents the purpose for being filled with Christ's will as the basis for wisdom and spiritual understanding. The purpose is that they "might walk worthy of the Lord." "Walk" was a common term used by Paul to describe a person's life and behavior.

They were to walk in a "worthy" manner. "Worthy" indicated that something was of value. This value was set by Christ. The extent to which they were to be led by Christ was "unto all pleasing." The Greek term used for "pleasing" indicates someone exhibiting a high degree of faithfulness and desire for someone else. The word was used at times to describe someone "clinging" to another person.

There are four things that accompany the walk that is worthy of the Lord—(1) fruitful works, (2) increasing knowledge of God, (3) being strengthened, and (4) thankfulness to the Father. All four of these attributes, according to the Greek text, are to be continual traits in the life of the growing Christian.

The first characteristic of the walk that is worthy of the Lord is "being fruitful in every good work." This was to be a continual action. The image of fruit bearing began in verses 5 and 6 where the word of the truth of the gospel had been planted in their heart. This being seed, they were to produce the fruit of the gospel. These were good works. The works resulted from the gospel.

The second characteristic of the walk worthy of the Lord is "increasing in the knowledge of God." The idea of progress is evident in this phrase. The Colossians are admonished to be obedi-

ent to God. This obedience was to grow out of their present knowledge of God. As they were obedient to the knowledge they already had, their knowledge of God would be progressively increased. Increased knowledge is linked with doing good works out of obedience. It is not merely a matter of intellectual progress. It is knowledge received through obedience.

The third characteristic of the walk that is worthy of the Lord is "being strengthened with all might." "Strengthened" comes from a Greek word which refers to "enabling power." This characteristic describes what enables the believer to be able to walk worthy of the Lord. The enablement is the power of the Lord. It is impossible for a person to walk worthy of the Lord except by God's power.

The enabling power of God is described in three ways . First, it is an enablement "with all might." It is entirely sufficient. Second, it is "according to his glorious power." The measurement of the power is God's "glorious power." The Greek word used here for "power" emphasizes the power that is inherent in God. It is God's power which enables the believer.

The third description of God's enablement of the believer is that it is "unto all patience and longsuffering." "Patience" comes from a Greek word which emphasizes "endurance in the face of attack." It refers to fortitude which does not come from mere bravery. It is endurance made possible by God's power. "Longsuffering" comes from a Greek word which emphasizes "gracious reaction to persecution and wrongdoing." It is the ability to not react hastily out of anger or revenge. It is being able to react with the patience that God gives.

12. Giving thanks unto the Father, which hath made us meet to be partakers of the inheritance of the saints in light.

The fourth and final thing that accompanies the walk that is worthy is "giving thanks unto the Father." The first three things were mentioned earlier in conjunction with verses 10 and 11. Thankfulness unto the Father was to be done in association with "joyfulness." "Joyfulness" is at the end of verse 11 and should go with thankfulness in verse 12. The object of thankfulness is God the Father. Paul describes important blessings the Father has given to the believer in verses 12 and 13. These blessings are motivations to increase the believer's thankfulness.

The first blessing is that the Father has "made us meet to be partakers of the inheritance of the saints in light." The primary idea of this blessing is that the Father has made the believer "meet." "Meet" comes from a Greek word which means, "to make sufficient, to qualify, or to authorize."

God has qualified and authorized the believer to be a partaker and inheritor of those things reserved for His saints. "Saints" refers to all believers. Each individual believer has been qualified by God to receive the great reward and inheritance He has reserved for all His people. The second and third blessings for which the believer should give thanks are in verse 13.

What is the purpose of Paul's prayer and desire in behalf of the Colossians? What is the foundation of true wisdom and spiritual understanding? What is the purpose for being filled with Christ's will? What are the four things that accompany the walk that is worthy of the Lord? What does "strengthened" mean in verse 11? What motivation for being thankful does Paul give in verse 12?

II. REDEEMED BY CHRIST (Colossians 1:13-20)

A. Deliverance by the Father (v. 13)

13. Who hath delivered us from the power of darkness, and hath translated us into the kingdom of his dear Son.

This verse gives the other two blessings for which the believer should be thankful unto the Father (v. 12). The first blessing is the fact that God has made the believer "meet" to receive the inheritance of the saints (v. 12). The second blessing is that God has "delivered us from the power of darkness."

"Delivered" emphasizes the manner in which God rescues the believer. The Colossians had previously been dominated by a life of darkness and sin. The redeemed have been rescued from the "power of darkness."

One ancient writer translated "power" in this passage as "tyranny." God has rescued the believer from a tyranny "where evil powers rule (Luke 22:53) and where Satan's authority is exercised (Acts 26:18), transferring them to the kingdom in which his beloved Son held sway" (*Colossians, Philemon* by Peter T. O'Brien, p. 28).

"Translated" comes from a Greek word which means "to remove from one place and transfer to another." The word was commonly used to describe the transport of a person from one country to another. God has not only delivered the believer from a land dominated by the darkness of sin, He has also transferred him to the "kingdom of his dear Son."

B. Redemption Through Christ (v. 14)

14. In whom we have redemption through his blood, even the forgiveness of sins.

After referring to the kingdom of God's "dear Son," Paul writes concerning Christ and His work in verses 14-23. In verse 14 the redemption of the believer is stressed. In verses 15-20 the preeminence of Christ over all things is emphasized. In verses 21-23 the reconciliation of the believer is highlighted.

The central idea of verse 14 is the redemption of the believer. This redemption is accomplished in Christ. "Redemption" comes from a Greek word which stresses the "release from" something. The word is used of releases that were based upon a certain release payment or price. The believer's release price is Christ's blood.

Along with redemption, the believer has "the forgiveness of sins." This stresses the release from the guilt and penalty of sin. The full price of the penalty as well as the imprisonment of sin is paid through Christ's blood. Both redemption and forgiveness, according to the Greek text in this verse, are present possessions of the believer.

C. Preeminence of Christ (vv. 15-19)

(Colossians 1:15-19 is not included in the printed text.)

Verses 15-19 stress Christ's superior position over all creation. These verses emphasize Christ's deity. Christ is the creator and sustainer of all things. All authorities—thrones, dominions, principalities, or powers—are under the authority of Christ. These include things visible and invisible. Christ is God himself who is exalted above all creation.

D. Reconciliation by Christ (v. 20)

20. And, having made peace through the blood of his cross, by him to reconcile all things unto himself; by him, I say, whether they be things in earth, or things in heaven.

Christ has reconciled all things unto Himself. The word Paul used here in the Greek for "reconcile" is not a common word. Some scholars feel it may have been a special expression by Paul. It is only used here, in verse 21, and in Ephesians 2:16. The emphasis of the word is upon exchanging hostility for friendship.

The distinctive of this verse is that Christ reconciles "all things." The concept of reconciliation is usually in reference to God and the believer. "All things" was a major idea of verses 15-19. The phrase refers to all of creation and all of the powers of earth and heaven. Christ's blood on the cross affirmed that all of creation is under Him. No doubt the false teachers in Colossae had been teaching that some things were not subject to Christ. However, the work of Christ included the reconciliation of all things unto Himself and His dominion.

What does the term *delivered* in verse 13 mean? What does the term *translated* in that verse mean? How is the redemption and forgiveness of the believer accomplished? What is the theme of verses 15-19? How extensive is the work of reconciliation in Christ's blood according to verse 20?

III. INDWELT BY CHRIST (Colossians 1:21-29)

A. Reconciliation of the Believer (vv. 21-23)

21. And you, that were sometime alienated and enemies in your mind by wicked works, yet now hath he reconciled

22. In the body of his flesh through death, to present you holy and unblameable and unreproveable in his sight.

Verse 21 describes the condition of the Colossians prior to being reconciled in Christ. In relationship to God they were "alienated" and "enemies." "Alienated" comes from a Greek word meaning "to be shut out from fellowship and intimacy." The word is used in some ancient literature to describe evil estrangement and separation between a married couple. "Enemies" could be translated "hostile ones." The term denotes a conscious antagonism.

Prior to faith in Christ, the believer was alien and hostile to God in his "mind" and because of "wicked works." "Mind" in verse 21 comes from a Greek word which refers to the heart, emotions, and even spiritual nature, as well as the mind. In this verse it includes mentality, as well as the other aspects mentioned.

The inclusion of "works" reveals that alienation and hostility toward God before conversion is not only internal but external as well. Inward hostility toward God reveals itself in external works of evil.

In contrast to this wicked condition whereby a person is separated from God, Christ reconciles this person to Himself. "Reconciled" emphasizes the transformation of hostility into a close, vital relationship. This is accomplished through the body of Christ's flesh and His death. The references to "body" and "flesh" emphasize the humanity and suffering of Christ. The crucifixion was a real historical event. Perhaps this may have been questioned by false teachers at Colossae.

The purpose of Christ's reconciliation was to present the believer "holy and unblameable and unreproveable in his [God's] sight." Two types of "presenting" are given here. The first is a sacrificial presentation. The second is a legal presentation.

The sacrificial presentation is based upon the words "holy and unblameable." These words were used in the Old Testament to describe the required condition of sacrificial animals. The believer is presented for acceptance before God. In Christ, the believer is examined by God and found acceptable.

The legal idea of "presenting" is based upon the term "unreproveable." It was a legal term used in courts. It referred to a person being declared without accusation or simply free from charges. No legal claims could then be made against that person. In Christ, the believer is brought before God, the Judge, and no charges of sin are brought against him.

23. If ye continue in the faith grounded and settled, and be not moved away from the hope of the gospel, which ye have heard, and which was preached to every creature which is under heaven; whereof I Paul am made a minister.

The condition required to be those holy, unblemished, and unreproachable believers is stated in verse 23. This is not the condition which creates their redeemed state. However, it is the condition for the continuance of that redemptive condition, lest they fall from it.

The condition includes a positive continuing "in the faith." Paul assumes that the Colossians had been faithful and would continue to be. "Continue" comes from a Greek word which stresses not just remaining but "remaining at a certain position." This position is the life of faith.

"Grounded and settled" describe the manner in which they were to continue in the faith. They were words typically used in reference to the construction of a building. "Grounded" refers to a properly laid foundation. "Settled" refers to the firmness of a structure. They were to remain at the place of faith, properly housing themselves there.

The condition of verse 23 also included the command to "be not moved from the hope of the gospel." "Moved" comes from a Greek word which means to "move from one association to another." The believer is not to shift from the hope of

the gospel to another hope. The gospel had been heard by the Colossians. It had been declared unto all creation. It was the gospel which Paul preached. They were not to associate with another gospel.

B. Paul's Ministry (vv. 24, 25)

24. Who now rejoice in my sufferings for you, and fill up that which is behind of the afflictions of Christ in my flesh for his body's sake, which is the church:

25. Whereof I am made a minister, according to the dispensation of God which is given to me for you, to fulfill the word of God.

In these verses Paul emphasizes his ministry, especially as it is directed to the church. Paul mentioned in the latter part of verse 23 that he was a "minister" of the gospel. The word for "minister" used here in the Greek is usually translated "servant." The central idea of the word is service. Therefore, Paul is emphasizing the service aspect of his ministry. This is especially evident as he discusses his sacrificial service to the church in Christ's behalf.

Paul mentions the "sufferings" and "afflictions of Christ" he had experienced. His ministry had been one of sacrifice. "Suffering" comes from a Greek word which emphasizes calamity which had come upon him as a result of his ministry.

In his discussion of the afflictions of Christ, Paul is indicating that he must not shrink from the sufferings that these afflictions call him toward. Christ's afflictions had made certain blessings available to Paul. The reception of those blessings meant that Paul had to repay Christ by suffering as Christ did. Paul felt he had to "fill up" with these sufferings because he was "behind" in what he owed Christ.

The sufferings and afflictions did not create Paul's ministry. He already had a ministry. His ministry was in behalf of the church. His sufferings were in response to Christ and part of the purpose of his ministry to the church. The Christian should not be surprised if his service in the church calls him to suffer and sacrifice.

Love for others in Christ often calls the Christian beyond personal comfort.

In verse 25 Paul explains that this ministry, which included suffering, was "according to the dispensation of God" and in fulfillment of "the word of God." Dispensation" comes from a Greek word meaning "stewardship or administration." Paul's ministry had not been guided, dominated, and planned by just anyone or any power. Paul's ministry was administered by God himself. Likewise, the Christian's ministry should be controlled and guided by the will and Word of God rather than principles of the world.

C. The Indwelling Christ (vv. 26-29)

26. Even the mystery which hath been hid from ages and from generations, but now is made manifest to his saints:

27. To whom God would make known what is the riches of the glory of this mystery among the Gentiles; which is Christ in you, the hope of glory.

(Colossians 1:28, 29 is not included in the printed text.)

Paul continues to describe the nature of his ministry by highlighting the "mystery" of the gospel. This mystery was "hid from ages and from generations." By its very nature as a mystery, it was impossible for this mystery to be known. It was hidden and unavailable except through God.

The mystery was finally revealed to a select group. The mystery has been made known unto the "saints" of God. The believer has access to this mystery. To those who are not in Christ, the mystery will remain hidden.

The mystery has been made known by God. The mystery cannot be made known by any other means. It is impossible for the mystery to be known except through God. Further, the mystery is characterized by the riches of the "glory" of God. It is not a simplistic revelation. It holds the glory of God and the riches of His blessings.

The mystery that has been revealed is preached by Paul among the Gentiles. It is not an exclusive mystery, only made known to a select group such as the Jews. The only criterion for knowing the mystery is trusting Christ as Lord and Savior.

The mystery revealed is the fact of "Christ in you." The mystery is that Christ would indwell all that would come to Him in believing faith. Knowing the mystery is not a matter merely of knowledge. It is experiencing the indwelling Christ. Proclaiming that Christ dwells within those who trust Him as Lord and Savior was Paul's ministry. Verses 28 and 29 continue to describe Paul's proclamation of this mystery.

The message of Christ indwelling the believer is the climax of Paul's message in this chapter. Paul has emphasized the glory and position of Christ. However, the gospel is not only the proclamation of who Christ is, but the message that Christ will dwell within those who serve Him. The Christian can rejoice in the fact of Christ's glory. And, much more, the Christian can rejoice that this same Christ has chosen to dwell within anyone who will believe and serve Him as Lord and Savior.

REVEIW QUESTIONS

1. What was the purpose of Paul's prayer and desire in behalf of the Colossians?

2. How is the redemption and forgiveness of the believer accomplished?

3. What was the condition of the believer prior to reconciliation to Christ?

4. What is the condition described in verse 23 required to remain in reconciliation with Christ?

5. Why did Paul endure suffering and hardship in his ministry?

GOLDEN TEXT HOMILY

"WALK WORTHY OF THE LORD . . . BEING FRUITFUL IN EVERY GOOD WORK, AND INCREASING IN THE KNOWLEDGE OF GOD" (Colossians 1:10).

It is reported that a British coal miner prayed a very strange prayer many years ago in a prayer meeting. He solemnly and earnestly prayed: "Lord, aw've yer'd there's two kinds of Christians—Duck-footed Christians, and Hen-footed Christians. Lord, mak' me a Hen-footed Christian!" The petition seemed humorous, yet the congregation dared not laugh since it was offered so seriously. This old saint had observed the uneven gait of the duck as it tried to walk, first one side and then another, while the hen moved along splendidly. Thus he prayed that the Lord might keep him from an unbalanced life.

As Christians we must confess that the wobbling malady is too much with us in contemporary times. There are many reasons for this—doubt concerning our relationship to Christ, ignorance of our privileges in Christ, and neglect of daily fellowship with Christ.

However, as Paul's prayer is answered in our lives, it is our privilege to know we are saved, forgiven, and justified. We will know we are saved from sin's power and guilt. We can have the assurance that His grace is adequate on a daily basis.

Then we can thank God that . . .

In the dailiness of living His love attends us. In our weakness His Strength defends; when we falter, stumble, fall or fail, His mercy commends us.—**E. C. Christenbury, Ed.D., Professor of Education, Lee College, Cleveland, Tennessee**

SENTENCE SERMONS

GOD WANTS EVERY BELIEVER to be fruitful in the work of the Kingdom.

—**Selected**

WHEN WE FIND the comfort of God, we also find the Commission of God.

—**"Notes and Quotes"**

THE TRUE DISCIPLE is a witness to the fact that the Lord gives us His presence.

—**"Speaker's Sourcebook"**

WE DO NOT STAND in the world bearing witness to Christ, but stand in Christ and bear witness to the world.

—**Gordon**

EVANGELISTIC APPLICATION

SPIRITUAL FRUITFULNESS IN THE BELIEVER'S LIFE BEARS WITNESS TO THE SAVING POWER OF CHRIST.

One of the most powerful witnesses of Christ's power is the spiritual fruitfulness of a Christian life. Other external witnesses may testify of Christ's power. Physical manifestations are witnesses of Christ's dominion and power. Supernatural events testify of the power of God. However, spiritual fruitfulness in the believer's life testifies of the indwelling presence of Christ.

When Christ saves a person, He comes to dwell within that individual. The indwelling presence of Christ is at the heart of the message of the gospel. It is the revelation of the mystery of the gospel according to Paul in Colossians 1:27. Other people will see Christ when they see Him displayed through spiritual fruitfulness in the believer's life. Spiritual fruitfulness reveals the presence of Christ within the believer.

Christ can change a life dramatically. Christ can transform a person from a servant of sin and transgression into a new creature in Christ. This transformation within a life is one of the best witnesses of Christ's saving power. By allowing this transformation to be revealed to others, the Christian witnesses in one of the most effective ways possible. It reveals the mystery of the gospel, Christ in the believer, the hope of glory.

DAILY BIBLE READINGS

M. Blessedness. Psalm 1:1-6
T. Righteousness. Psalm 37:18-31
W. Virtue. Proverbs 31:10-31
T. Godliness. Luke 2:36-38
F. Goodness. Acts 11:22-24
S. Holiness. 1 Peter 3:1-6

Spiritual Riches in Christ

Study Text: Colossians 2:1-23

Supplemental References: Psalm 40:1-10; John 4:10-14; Galatians 3:8-14; Ephesians 3:7-12

Time: Probably in the summer of A.D. 62

Place: From a prison, probably in Rome

Golden Text: "We have redemption through his blood, the forgiveness of sins, according to the riches of his grace" (Ephesians 1:7).

Central Truth: Only through faith can a person partake of the eternal riches in Christ.

Evangelistic Emphasis: Through the new birth a person becomes an heir to the unsearchable riches of Christ.

Printed Text

Colossians 2:1. For I would that ye knew what great conflict I have for you, and for them at Laodicea, and for as many as have not seen my face in the flesh;

2. That their hearts might be comforted, being knit together in love, and unto all riches of the full assurance of understanding, to the acknowledgement of the mystery of God, and of the Father, and of Christ;

3. In whom are hid all the treasures of wisdom and knowledge.

4. And this I say, lest any man should beguile you with enticing words.

5. For though I be absent in the flesh, yet am I with you in the spirit, joying and beholding your order, and the stedfastness of your faith in Christ.

6. As ye have therefore received Christ Jesus the Lord, so walk ye in him:

7. Rooted and built up in him, and stablished in the faith, as ye have been taught, abounding therein with thanksgiving.

8. Beware lest any man spoil you through philosophy and vain deceit, after the tradition of men, after the rudiments of the world, and not after Christ.

9. For in him dwelleth all the fulness of the Godhead bodily.

10. And ye are complete in him, which is the head of all principality and power:

16. Let no man therefore judge you in meat, or in drink, or in respect of an holyday, or of the new moon, or of the sabbath days:

17. Which are a shadow of things to come; but the body is of Christ.

18. Let no man beguile you of your reward in a voluntary humility and worshipping of angels, intruding into those things which he hath not seen, vainly puffed up by his fleshly mind,

19. And not holding the Head, from which all the body by joints and bands having nourishment ministered, and knit together, increaseth with the increase of God.

20. Wherefore if ye be dead with Christ

from the rudiments of the world, why, as though living in the world, are ye subject to ordinances,

21. (Touch not; taste not; handle not;

22. Which all are to perish with the using;) after the commandments and doctrines of men?

23. Which things have indeed a shew of wisdom in will worship, and humility, and neglecting of the body; not in any honour to the satisfying of the flesh.

LESSON OUTLINE

I. TREASURES IN CHRIST
  A. Expression of Paul's "Conflict" for the Colossians
  B. Description of Value of Christ
  C. Warning Against Enticing Words
II. COMPLETENESS IN CHRIST
  A. Admonition to Continue in Christ
  B. Warning Against Vain Teachers
  C. The Believer's Position in Christ
III. FREEDOM IN CHRIST
  A. Christ's "Quickening" of the Believer
  B. Warning Against Morality Without Christ as the Source
  C. Warning Against Worship Without Christ as the "Head"
  D. Summary of Vain Worship and Morality

LESSON EXPOSITION

INTRODUCTION

Among the many burdens which daily pressed upon the heart of Paul was one which he described as "concern for all the churches" (2 Corinthians 11:28, *New International Version*). This vital concern and care extended not only to the churches he had founded but also to those established by the effort and influence of his messengers and friends. Such was the case with those of the Lycos Valley, in the cities of Laodicea and Hierapolis and Colossae.

Although he had not met many of the persons face to face, he wanted them to know of his watchcare for their spiritual growth. Indeed, one can sense the earnest appeal of a loving leader as he points to the spiritual riches believers are to enjoy by being faithful to Christ in their daily walk.

This lesson is rich in its application for today. False teachings and erring philosophies were not confined to the first century A.D. They are still confronting men and women of the twentieth century. The admonitions of Paul also speak to our times.

I. TREASURES IN CHRIST (Colossians 2:1-5)

A. Expression of Paul's "Conflict" for the Colossians (vv. 1, 2)

1. For I would that ye knew what great conflict I have for you, and for them at Laodicea, and for as many as have not seen my face in the flesh.

"For" refers to the last verse preceding this one (1:29). In that verse Paul emphasizes his "labour" and "striving" which has been made possible through the work of Christ. Paul explains the focus and nature of his "striving" and "labour" in 2:1. There he refers to the "great conflict" which he has for those to whom he is writing. This "great conflict" is the focus and nature of his striving and laboring.

The word "conflict" is *agon* in New Testament Greek. The English word "agony" comes from this word. The Greek word means "fight," "struggle," or to "engage in a 'contest.'" The contest could be an athletic one or the struggle could be a military one involving the use of weapons. The word reflects the agony displayed in intense athletic competition or military battle. It reflects the intensity of the inner struggle Paul experienced in behalf of the persons he ministered with.

Paul's conflict was in behalf of the readers, those in Laodicea, and those who "have not seen my face in the flesh." This latter expression implies those persons who may have had a knowledge of Paul but not a personal, face-to-face, knowledge of him (T. K. Abbott, *A Criti-*

cal and Exegetical Commentary on the Epistles to the Ephesians and Colossians).

2. That their hearts might be comforted, being knit together in love, and unto all riches of the full assurance of understanding, to the acknowledgement of the mystery of God, and of the Father, and of Christ.

In this verse Paul gives the purpose for the conflict mentioned in verse 1. The word that indicates what follows is the purpose of the conflict. This purpose is the "comfort" of those mentioned in verse 1. The word comfort in Greek means "to call to one's side." It refers to comfort which comes from the presence of another. It is comfort based in personal relationships.

Paul refers to a circumstance he desires to accompany their comfort. This circumstance is based in relationships. It is that they be "knit together in love." The grammar of this phrase in Greek emphasizes a definite action that would take place among them. Further, Paul desires that this unity be within the sphere of love.

The extent to which Paul intends comfort to be applied to them is reflected in the phrase, "Unto all riches of the full assurance of understanding." The word riches expresses the extent or degree of comfort Paul desires for them. "Full assurance of understanding" expresses the kind of riches he desires for them. The comfort is one which is rich in the full assurance of understanding.

"Full assurance" is one word in Greek meaning "to bear something fully." The indication is of bearing something with "conviction." The understanding desired here is to be borne with fullness of conviction. This word provides insight into the kind of comfort that Paul agonizes for them to have. It is a comfort which is accompanied by love for one another to the extent that understanding is borne with full conviction.

How important is it for Christian leaders to bear a burden and "agonize" in behalf of those they are responsible for? What kind of comfort did Paul desire for the Colossians? Why accompanying circumstance?

The area in which this comfort occurs is especially important. Paul desired that it occur in their "hearts." "Heart" is employed in its customary Old Testament sense denoting the inner life of the person, the center of his personality, understood as the source of will, emotion, thoughts, and affections" (Peter T. O'Brien, Colossians, Philemon, Word Biblical Commentary, Vol. 44, p. 93). This was the area, namely their deep inner life, where Paul desired comfort to occur.

The final phrase of verse 2 indicates the ultimate extent and object to which Paul desires this comfort of the heart to reach. The comfort extends unto "the acknowledgement of the mystery of God, and of the Father, and of Christ." "Acknowledgement" stresses knowledge which comes by experience. The readers will acknowledge the mystery of God by experiencing it.

"Mystery" is "that which is hidden and undiscoverable by human means, that which has been revealed by God" (Linguistic Key to the Greek New Testament, p. 570). The mystery which has been revealed pertains to God. The phrase as evidenced in Greek manuscripts emphasizes Christ as the content of the mystery that has been revealed.

B. Description of the Value of Christ (v. 3)

3. In whom are hid all the treasures of wisdom and knowledge.

In this verse Paul expands the theme of the mystery of God revealed in Christ. "Whom" indicates that the mystery revealed is a person. The location of the "hid" treasures of wisdom and knowledge is the Person, Christ. "All" signifies the completeness of that which is hid in Christ.

"Hid" indicates something that is removed and concealed. This is the manner in which the treasure exists. It is not something that is open and obvious. The treasure is only accessible through Christ since it is "hid" or "deposited" in Christ. Christ makes them available to the believer. However, belief in Christ is required to receive these treasures.

"Treasures of wisdom and knowledge" was an expression used in Jewish literature. The literature presented the Law as the place where these treasures were found. This similarity to Judaism indicates that the opposition Paul is facing includes Jewish elements. Paul substitutes Christ for the law as the place where all the treasures of wisdom and knowledge have been placed.

C. Warning Against Enticing Words (vv. 4, 5)

4. And this I say, lest any man should beguile you with enticing words.

5. For though I be absent in the flesh, yet am I with you in the spirit, joying and beholding your order, and the stedfastness of your faith in Christ.

Verse 4 is the warning given by Paul. He indicates that he communicated verse 3 because there were persons who would try to convince them that all the treasures of wisdom and knowledge are not placed in Christ. "Beguile" refers to making statements or conclusions which add to, and thereby distort, the truth. These persons take the truth of the gospel, add to it, and teach erroneous conclusions.

"Enticing words" is a single word in Greek meaning "speech based merely on persuasion." The word is used to describe argumentation based on probabilities and mere persuasion rather than demonstration of actual evidence. "The terminology used here is practically equivalent to our English expression, 'talk someone into something'" (*Linguistic Key to the Greek New Testament*, p. 572).

The reason for the warning of verse 4 is presented in verse 5. Paul recognizes his physical absence from the readers. However, he recognizes the unity of the spirit he has with them. Out of this unity of spirit he is warning them to beware of the false persuaders. Out of this unity of spirit with them he affirms their "order" and "stedfastness of faith." He is warning them to preserve these.

"Order" emphasizes the orderliness, strength, and cohesiveness of the Christians to whom he is writing. Their fellowship had not been set in disarray because of the "persuaders." "Stedfastness of faith" refers to their continued strength in Christ.

They had remained in Christ and not been moved by the false persuaders.

What does "beguile" mean? What does "enticing words" mean? Do people beguile others with enticing words in the world today?

II. COMPLETENESS IN CHRIST (Colossians 2:6-12)

A. Admonition to Continue in Christ (vv. 6, 7)

6. As ye have therefore received Christ Jesus the Lord, so walk ye in him:

7. Rooted and built up in him, and stablished in the faith, as ye have been taught, abounding therein with thanksgiving.

Paul, in verse 6, commands the readers to walk in Christ. His command is that they walk as they "received" Christ. "Walk" emphasizes their manner of life. Their living was to be "in Christ."

Verse 7 describes the conditions which were to be reflected in their living as they "walked in Christ." "Rooted" by virtue of the meaning of the word and the grammar in which it is presented emphasizes a fixed state. They were to be firm and complete, continually rooted in Christ.

"Build up" comes from a Greek word which directly refers to the building of a house. Having been and continuing to be rooted in the foundation of Christ, the readers are to be built up in Christ. "In him" stresses the location of the building. The Christian grows while in Christ. Outside of Christ there is no growth in God for the Christian. The indication in this verse is that this growth is to continuously take place in the Christian's life.

Besides being rooted and built up as they walked in Christ, Paul desired that the readers be "stablished in the faith." This phrase indicates the readers were to continually receive the confirming and establishing results of faith. Their strength was to be related and made possible through faith. Paul desires in verses 6 and 7 that they walk in Christ with the accompanying condition of, first, being rooted in Christ; second, being built up in Christ, and, third, being strengthened ("stablished") in faith.

In the latter part of verse 7 Paul offers a comparison so they may know the manner in which they are to be rooted, built up, and stablished. This comparison relates to that which they had been "taught." The things of faith which they had been taught before by Paul and other teachers of the true gospel were to be the manner of comparison by which they would know they were walking in Christ rightly. This highlights the importance of teaching for properly walking in Christ.

In the last phrase of verse 7 Paul gives the condition which should accompany and underlie one's walk in Christ. The condition is a continual "abounding in thanksgiving." This phrase emphasizes that in thanksgiving a person is to be "outstanding, prominent, excelling" (*Greek-English Lexicon of the New Testament* by W. F. Arndt and F. W. Gingrich, p. 656) as they walk in Christ.

3. Warning Against Vain Teachers (v. 8)

8. Beware lest any man spoil you through philosophy and vain deceit, after the tradition of men, after the rudiments of the world, and not after Christ.

Verse 8 provides a warning. Paul has been expressing his desire that the readers grow in Christ. He has already warned about enticing words. He intensifies his warning with a second admonition to "beware" or "look out" for those who would detrack them from the gospel. The Greek grammar in this opening warning indicates a very serious threat is present.

The warning concerns persons who would "spoil" them. "Spoil" is a severe word in Greek and is used only here in the New Testament. Its use here indicates Paul's deep concern for a critical threat. The word *spoil* means to strip persons of things and to carry them off captive. Paul not only fears the defeat but also the capture of the readers.

The spoil is conducted through "philosophy and vain deceit." These are the means by which the spoil is accomplished. The grammar of the Greek in this phrase indicates Paul is not speaking of philosophy in general but that which is vain and deceitful. "Vain" refers to that which is fruitless, empty, ineffective, without purpose, and failing to reach its goal. "Deceit" is used elsewhere in the New Testament to describe wicked deceit in general (2 Thessalonians 2:10), the deceitfulness of sin (Hebrews 3:13), and deceitful desires (Ephesians 4:22) (O'Brien, p.110).

The end result of this vain deceit is dominated by the measure of two things and the absence of a third. The two things which dominate the end result of the vain deceit are the "tradition of men" and the "rudiments of the world." The seduction of these false teachers was compounded by the measurement of their own traditions. The Greek grammar at this point indicates that it is not tradition itself that is at fault, but tradition which finds its source in these false deceivers.

Besides erroneous traditions the deceit of the false teachers was further compounded by the measurement of the "rudiments of the world." The error is not in the word *rudiments*. It merely means fundamentals or principles. The error is that the "world" and not "Christ" is the basis of these false teachers and their teachings. Their fundamentals (rudiments) are based in the world and not "after Christ."

The heart of the error Paul is combating is the exclusion of Christ. In verses 9-15 Paul expands what it means to have Christ as the center of one's life, "rudiments," "tradition," and "philosophy." Truth and error are determined by Christ. The exclusion of Christ makes any philosophy, tradition, or fundamental way of life erroneous. Verses 16-23 will address the way persons exclude Christ in this manner.

What is Paul's warning to the readers? What does the word *spoil* indicate? How is the spoil conducted? When do philosophy, tradition, and the fundamentals of life become vain?

C. The Believer's Position in Christ (vv. 9-12)

9. For in him dwelleth all the fulness of the Godhead bodily.

10. And ye are complete in him, which is the head of all principality and power.

(Colossians 2:11, 12 is not included in the printed text.)

Verses 9-12 describe the believer's position in Christ as being dependent upon Christ. The believer's relationship to authority, circumcision, and death are discussed in these verses. Each of these areas are transformed and given new meaning and power for the believer because of Christ.

Verse 9 conveys the reason for Paul's warning against the "beguilers" in verse 8. Their "enticing words" removed the focus from Christ. Paul comes back to Christ, the focus of the believer's position. In Christ "dwells" or continually resides the "fulness of the Godhead bodily," the believer's relationship to authority, circumcision, and death is changed.

The "fulness of the Godhead bodily" is the reason for the believer's position. This phrase means that the full essence and nature of God is in Christ. The grammar of the word "dwells" indicates that Christ was and is God throughout eternity. "Bodily" stresses the fact of the Incarnation. The fullness of God became Incarnate. This does not deny the trinitarian reality of the coexistence of the Father and the Holy Spirit. But, it does emphasize the full deity of Christ.

"Complete" is actually "have been made full." The word stresses the fullness and wholeness the believer receives by being in Christ. There are no missing or confused parts for the believer in Christ. The sum total of the believer's life is "complete" and whole.

The reality of this completeness is reflected by Paul in verses 10-12 in the areas of power (authority), circumcision, and death. The believer is not overpowered because Christ is the "head" (superior and source) of all power. The believer is not subject to circumcision because

Christ is the circumciser. The believer is not defeated in death because Christ has defeated death in the Resurrection.

III. FREEDOM IN CHRIST (Colossians 2:13-23)

A. Christ's "Quickening" of the Believer (vv. 13-15)

(Colossians 2:13-15 is not included in the printed text.)

In this section Paul continues to explain the result of the believer being complete in Christ. The heart of this explanation is the word *quickened.* The word in Greek is constructed of three other words combined. The word literally means "to make alive with." In this passage, the word means that the believer is made alive with Christ. Christ is the means by which the believer is made alive. The believer is not simply energized. The believer is brought from a lifeless state to life. This is indicated from the context and the meaning of the word itself.

Verses 14 and 15 give circumstances which accompany this "quickened" state. Verse 14 stresses that the "quickened" believer has the "ordinances" written against him blotted out. "Handwriting of ordinances" was a Greek phrase indicating legal obligations and debts. These represent the former debt of sin.

Verse 15 stresses that evil powers threatening the "quickened" believer are defeated. Three words are used to describe this defeat. The first word is "spoiled." The word in Greek means "stripped" and was used many times to describe a person of authority being "stripped" of their power and dignity. The second word is "shew." The word here emphasizes the public humiliation of a power having been "stripped" and now displayed in public. The third word is "triumph." The word in Greek was frequently used to describe the celebration occurring after a battle had been won. Often, the "triumph" included a parade in which the victor led the conquered enemy before the people to display the "triumph." These words describe the defeat of evil powers by Christ.

B. Warning Against Morality Without Christ as the Source (vv. 16, 17)

16. Let no man therefore judge you in meat, or in drink, or in respect of an holyday, or of the new moon, or of the sabbath days:

17. Which are a shadow of things to come; but the body is of Christ.

Based upon the climactic triumph of the "quickened" believer (see verses 13-15), Paul warns the believers not to let any person judge them by a standard which is not based in Christ. The grammar of the Greek word translated "judge" indicates that persons were currently judging them and perhaps making it a habit. The error was the criterion the judgment was based upon. Persons were judging them by standards which were not first based upon Christ.

The standards used in these judgments were of two basic types, (1) diet ("meat" and "drink") and (2) religious days ("holyday," "new moon," and "sabbath"). In verse 16 Paul said these were mere "shadows" of Christ. The substance of any moral or religious standard by which a Christian should be evaluated is Christ first.

How did Paul describe the reality of the believer being complete in Christ? What does the word "quicken" mean? What are the implications of the believer being "quickened" with and by Christ?

C. Warning Against Worship Without Christ as the "Head" (vv. 18, 19)

18. Let no man beguile you of your reward in a voluntary humility and worshipping of angels, intruding into those things which he hath not seen, vainly puffed up by his fleshly mind,

19. And not holding the Head, from which all the body by joints and bands having nourishment ministered, and knit together, increaseth with the increase of God.

Paul issues a third warning in verse 18. The first warning was in verse 8, "beware lest any man spoil you." The second was in verse 16, "let no man

there judge you." "Beguile" here in verse 18 is not the same word used in verse 4 for "beguile." In verse 18 the word means to "judge against." The root word was used in law courts and athletic events. It meant to make a ruling or umpire an event. It was a decisive judgment carrying the weight of the court or deciding the outcome of the athletic event. The "beguilers" warned against in verse 18 were claiming more authority over the believer than they should have. Their error was in claiming themselves as the primary authority rather than Christ.

Paul describes these "beguilers." They were committing three errors. The first is in the phrase "in a voluntary humility and worshipping of angels." The Greek rendering of this phrase is closer to this, "delighting in humility and worship of angels." This delighting was the first error. "Humility," according to the way the term is used in this chapter and elsewhere in the New Testament, refers to fasting and restrictions on their living. In themselves, these practices are not corrupt. However, these persons were placing their "delight" exclusively and primarily upon these practices rather than upon Christ first. Their "delight" was misplaced. Further, their purpose was to worship angels. This led to their second error, vanity resulting from "high" and "mysterious" worship.

The second error centered around the "intruding" of the beguilers. They had claimed to have "intruded" or "entered" certain levels of "spirituality." This supposedly made them superior. This alleged superiority made them "vainly puffed up." "Vain" means "without purpose" and "puffed up" refers to an inflation and swelling. These beguilers had inflated their importance without legitimate purpose. The reason they had become this way is given by Paul. It was the result of their "fleshly mind." This was a mindset and way of living that was based upon the flesh rather than Christ first. They looked religious with their practices and claims, but they were "fleshly" and not Christ-centered.

The third error is clearly stated by Paul. The beguilers were "not holding the Head," Christ, at the center of all their activity and living. This is the fundamental description of their error. Paul enumerates the benefits which result from having Christ as the Head, (1) "nourishment" and (2) "unity" resulting in (3) "increase." "Nourishment" in Greek is a powerfully descriptive word. It indicates lavish and abundant supply. Both "nourishment" and "unity" are actually accompanying benefits of the primary benefit, "increase." This increase is true growth because it is "with the increase of God."

The beguilers had claimed growth but were only puffed up in the flesh. They claimed to know the mysteries of God but failed to recognize the mystery of God revealed in Christ. In verse 19 Paul focuses upon the central problem of these beguilers. They had constructed a system of morality and worship that did not have Christ as its Head.

D. Summary of Vain Worship and Morality (vv. 20-23)

20. Wherefore if ye be dead with Christ from the rudiments of the world, why, as though living in the world are ye subject to ordinances,

21. (Touch not; taste not; handle not;

22. Which all are to perish with the using;) after the commandments and doctrines of men?

23. Which things have indeed a shew of wisdom in will worship, and humility, and neglecting of the body; not in any honour to the satisfying of the flesh.

In these three verses Paul summarizes the points he has been establishing since 2:1. The basis of the summary is the message of verse 19, that Christ is the proper Head of the body. The connection with verse 19 is clearly indicated by the word *therefore*. It indicates that a summary will follow.

The theme of this summary is verse 20. Paul asks why they are subject now to ordinances. They should not have been because they had departed from the "rudiments of the world." Whereas their lives once originated in the princi-

ple things of the world, as Christians they should have been dead to those. They were acting, "living," conducting their lives, and being "subject" to ordinances instead of Christ. "Subject" is actually "subject oneself." It referred to placing oneself under the authority of another. The authority for them had become the world rather than Christ.

Paul gives a quick summary of the ordinances which had come to replace Christ as the authority in their lives. They were "touch not; taste not; handle not." Given earlier reference in this chapter, dietary restrictions are the topic of these ordinances.

In verses 22 and 23, Paul gives an assessment of these ordinances. He cites three things. First, these ordinances will perish. Second, these ordinances are "after," that is *dominated,* by the commandments and doctrines of men. The error was not in commandments and doctrines themselves. The error was in allowing them to become man centered rather than Christ centered.

The third assessment of these ordinances was that they gave visibility—but not profitability. The visibility is indicated by the word *shew* in verse 23. Their failure to give true satisfaction for the flesh is indicated by Paul in the last part of verse 23. Though these ordinances and claims to spiritual authority looked appealing, they were not based in Christ. Therefore, they failed to give genuine satisfaction to the people of God.

REVIEW QUESTIONS

1. Where was the Apostle Paul when he wrote to the Colossians?

2. What is meant by the term "beguile" as used in verse 4?

3. Are there false biblical teachings circulating in our day? How can the church combat false teachings?

4. What practical applications do you draw from this lesson?

GOLDEN TEXT HOMILY

"WE HAVE REDEMPTION THROUGH HIS BLOOD, THE FORGIVENESS OF SINS

ACCORDING TO THE RICHES OF HIS GRACE" (Ephesians 1:7).

The treasures of Christ are packaged up in the word *redemption*. In the New Testament, redemption always implies deliverance from sin and its effects. The concept of God's saving work among men as deliverance from possession or control by an alien power is one of the fundamental concepts of the Bible. Seeing Himself as humanity's servant, Jesus declared, "Even the Son of Man did not come to be served, but to serve, and to give His life a ransom for many" (Mark 10:45, *New King James Version*).

Look at the golden text. *"In Him" is the source of redemption.* Without Jesus and His coming, we would be hopelessly lost. The new song the saints sang to Christ in Revelation 5 began, "You are worthy . . . For You were slain, And have redeemed us to God by Your blood" (v. 9, *NKJV*).

"Through the blood" is the nature of redemption.

"What can wash away my sins?
    What can make me whole again?
    Nothing but the blood of Jesus."

"The forgiveness of sins" is the nature of redemption. Sinful man cannot be justified without being forgiven. No human effort can erase the guilt of sin. No amount of working can wash it away. No sum of money can buy God's love. Paul makes "the forgiveness of sins" synonymous with redemption.

"God's grace" is the ground of redemption. "For by grace you have been saved through faith, and that not of yourselves; it is the gift of God, not of works, lest anyone should boast. For we are His workmanship, created in Christ Jesus for good works" (Ephesians 2:8-10, *NKJV*).
—**Marcus V. Hand, Editor, *Lighted Pathway,* Church of God Publishing House, Cleveland, Tennessee**

SENTENCE SERMONS

ONLY THROUGH FAITH can a person partake of the eternal riches in Christ.
—**Selected**

NO MAN CAN TELL whether he is rich or poor by turning to his ledgers. It is the heart that makes a man rich. He is rich according to what he is, not according to what he has.
—**Henry Ward Beecher**

WITHOUT CHRIST life is as the twilight with dark night ahead; with Christ it is the dawn of morning with the light and warmth of the full day ahead.
—**Philip Schaff**

EVANGELISTIC APPLICATION

THROUGH THE NEW BIRTH A PERSON BECOMES AN HEIR TO THE UNSEARCHABLE RICHES OF CHRIST.

The riches of God are available to everyone through Jesus Christ. The work of Christ which makes the riches of God available is applied through the new birth. A person is born into the riches of God only by accepting Jesus Christ as their Lord. It is only through Christ Jesus that these riches become available.

God's riches are truly precious. They are unmatched in all of the world. They are riches which come from God himself. They are riches which cannot be analyzed or measured by the world's standards. Even their value is beyond mankind's comprehension. They are riches which can never be earned or deserved by the mere action of humanity. The availability of these riches must come through a divine source.

Claiming that the riches of God come through any person or action other than the person and work of Christ is a major error. The riches are completely available but only through Christ. Therefore, it is imperative for the Christian to always cherish Christ, through whom the riches of God are available. It is also imperative for the sinner to receive Christ in order to receive any of God's riches.

ILLUMINATING THE LESSON

D. L. Moody told of a rich man who lay dying. His little daughter was greatly puzzled over what was happening. Her father loved to have her with him, and she had often sat on his bed wondering why her big, strong father was lying helplessly there. One day the heads of his business came to pay their last call. There the rich man lay looking at his little girl when h—she said, "Father, are you going away?"

Yes, dear, and I am afraid you won't see me again."

Then the little one said, "Have you got a nice house and lots of friends there?"

The successful man of the world lay silent for a while, and then said: "What a fool I have been? I have built a great business here, but I shall be a pauper there."

—**Lionel Fletcher, in** *Life of Faith*

DAILY BIBLE READINGS

M. Blessings of Obedience. Deuteronomy 7:12-15

T. Love That Binds. Ruth 1:16-18

W. Resisting the Enemy. 2 Samuel 23:8-12

T. Rest for the Weary. Matthew 11:28-30

F. Power for the Weak. Acts 1:4-8

S. Rich Through Christ. 2 Corinthians 8:8, 9

Seeking Spiritual Values

Study Text: Colossians 3:1-25

Supplemental References: Ezra 7:10; Psalm 27:4-14; Matthew 6:25-33; John 1:35-39; Romans 14:17, 18; Hebrews 11:8-16

Time: Probably summer A.D. 62

Place: From a prison, probably in Rome

Golden Text: "If ye then be risen with Christ, seek those things which are above, where Christ sitteth on the right hand of God" (Colossians 3:1).

Central Truth: A Christian's values should be based on the Word of God.

Evangelistic Emphasis: God's great desire is to share His eternal wealth with those who seek Him.

Printed Text

Colossians 3:1. If ye then be risen with Christ, seek those things which are above, where Christ sitteth on the right hand of God.

2. Set your affection on things above, not on things on the earth.

3. For ye are dead, and your life is hid with Christ in God.

4. When Christ, who is our life, shall appear, then shall ye also appear with him in glory.

5. Mortify therefore your members which are upon the earth; fornication, uncleanness, inordinate affection, evil concupiscence, and covetousness, which is idolatry:

6. For which things' sake the wrath of God cometh on the children of disobedience:

7. In the which ye also walked some time, when ye lived in them.

8. But now ye also put off all these; anger, wrath, malice, blasphemy, filthy communication out of your mouth.

9. Lie not one to another, seeing that ye have put off the old man with his deeds;

10. And have put on the new man, which is renewed in knowledge after the image of him that created him:

11. Where there is neither Greek nor Jew, circumcision nor uncircumcision, Barbarian, Scythian, bond nor free: but Christ is all, and in all.

12. Put on therefore, as the elect of God, holy and beloved, bowels of mercies, kindness, humbleness of mind, meekness, longsuffering;

13. Forbearing one another, and forgiving one another, if any man have a quarrel against any: even as Christ forgave you, so also do ye.

14. And above all these things put on charity, which is the bond of perfectness.

15. And let the peace of God rule in your hearts, to the which also ye are called in one body; and be ye thankful.

16. Let the word of Christ dwell in you richly in all wisdom; teaching and admonishing one another in psalms and hymns and spiritual songs, singing with grace in your hearts to the Lord.

17. And whatsoever ye do in word or deed, do all in the name of the Lord Jesus, giving thanks to God and the Father by him.

LESSON OUTLINE

I. SEEK ETERNAL THINGS
  A. Seek Eternal Things
  B. Reason for the Command
  C. Future Glory in Christ

II. REJECT CARNAL IMPULSES
  A. Mortify Earthly Things
  B. Put Off Evil Things
  C. Lie Not Among Yourselves

III. LIVE IN HARMONY
  A. Put On the Things of Christ
  B. Let Christ Dwell in You Richly

LESSON EXPOSITION

INTRODUCTION

In the Book of Colossians Paul has had several emphases. In 1:1-14 he greeted the Colossians and gave them a prayer and thanksgiving. In 1:15-23 he presented doctrinal information regarding Christ. From 1:24-2:7 he affirmed his apostleship. In the section preceding today's passage he argues against false teachers and presents the true faith.

In Colossians 3 Paul presents practical teachings of the Christian life. This chapter emphasizes the necessity to translate Christianity into practical living. The previous sections of Colossians were important. Correct doctrine and refuting false doctrines is vital to Christian faith. In addition, Christianity must include practical living applying the principles of faith in Christ.

Discussing the practical implications of Christianity was a common practice of Paul in his Epistles. Paul confronted very specific problems and he answered them with very specific answers. He was not merely philosophical. He put his faith into specific practice. He instructed the believers to act in specific ways in response to the gospel. Christian practice is just as important as Christian doctrine.

I. SEEK ETERNAL THINGS (Colossians 3:1-4)

A. Seek Eternal Things (vv. 1, 2)
1. If ye then be risen with Christ,
seek those things which are above, where Christ sitteth on the right hand of God.

In verse 1 Paul declares the primary condition upon which practical Christian living is based. The condition is the fact that the Christian has been "risen with Christ." In 2:20 Paul emphasized that the believer is "dead with Christ." Now, emphasizing the present life the Christian is to live, Paul says that the believer is indeed risen with Christ and must live in newness of life.

The believer is risen "with" Christ. This concept means that the believer's life is not his own. It is a life "co-lived" with Christ. It is not a life the believer accepts as a carefree option. It is Christ living in the believer. This idea of "co-living" should affect all of the Christian's life.

The result of being raised with Christ is that the Christian is to "seek those things which are above." "Seek" comes from a Greek word which emphasizes the exercising of the will. The Christian needs to make a solid determination to live according to the standards God has called him to.

"Things which are above" emphasizes the heavenly origin of the Christian's practical life. It is not a life guided by earthly standards. The standards of the practical Christian life should come from heaven. To emphasize the authority of Christ in directing the Christian's life, Paul adds, "where Christ sitteth on the right hand of God."

2. Set your affection on things above, not on things on the earth.

Paul again issues the exhortation he gave in the middle of verse 1 to live in newness of life. The command in verse 2 amplifies "seek" in verse 1 to "set your affection." "Affection" comes from a Greek word emphasizing the inner disposition of a person. It refers to a person's thinking. However, it does not merely imply intellect. It considered the moral goals and perceptions of a person. The way a person sets his "affections" has a great effect upon his living.

The Christian is not to set his affections on things of the "earth." This corresponds to the "rudiments of the world" mentioned in 2:20. They are things of the old life before trusting in Christ.

B. Reason for the Command (v. 3)

3. For ye are dead, and your life is hid with Christ in God.

Paul gives two reasons in this verse why the Christian is to set his affections on things above. First, the Christian is "dead." The grammar of the word in the Greek emphasizes that they have indeed already died to things of sin. The Christian's death to sin is the first reason why he should set his affections on things above.

The second reason is that the Christian's life is "hid with Christ in God." This completes the first reason. The Christian is not only dead to sin but alive to God as well. "Hid" implies the privacy where the believer's life is nurtured by God. There the believer is safe from spiritual harm. It also is a place where the believer can affirm his identity with God in Christ; being "hid" is another motivation to set affections on things above.

C. Future Glory in Christ (v. 4)

4. When Christ, who is our life, shall appear, then shall ye also appear with him in glory.

Paul continues his description of the believer's relationship with God in Christ. Paul has alluded to the heavenly implications of the Christian life. In this verse Paul extends his emphasis upon heavenly things by speaking of the eternal outcome of the saints. The Christian life is not controlled by earthly circumstances. The believer is destined to spend eternity with Christ. This is a further motivation for setting one's affections on things which are eternal.

"With him in glory" indicates the unity of the believer with Christ in eternity. Christ will reign in glory in the ages to come. The believer will be present with Christ then, in vital relationship and union with Him. This eternal perspective should motivate believers to live setting their affections on things above. The anticipation of eternal relationship with Christ, sharing in his heavenly glory should bring hope in the midst of the struggle to live the Christian life upon earth.

What exhortation did Paul give the Colossians in verse 1? What implication is laid upon the Christian since he is risen with Christ? What does the word *affection* in verse 2 imply? Why should the believer set his affection on things above? What does the term "hid" emphasize in verse 3? How does the fact of appearing with Christ in His future glory affect the life of the Christian?

II. REJECT CARNAL IMPULSES (Colossians 3:5-11)

A. Mortify Earthly Things (vv. 5-7)

5. Mortify therefore your members which are upon the earth; fornication, uncleanness, inordinate affection, evil concupiscence, and covetousness, which is idolatry.

In verse 5 Paul gives a general command and then lists certain vices coming under that command. The command itself is to "mortify therefore your members which are upon the earth." "Mortify" comes from a Greek word which literally means "to put to death." The grammar of the Greek text indicates an emphasis upon definite action. This is a negative command which is essential for positive Christian living. Being alive in Christ is dependent upon the earthly life being put to death.

"Therefore" indicates that the basis for being able to mortify the earthly life is the glorious victory described in verses 3 and 4. "Members which are upon the earth" was a description which may well have come out of Paul's rabbinic background. Some rabbinical instruction called for each member of the body having a corresponding law to keep its evil desires and actions under subjection. The believer should likewise inventory his earthly existence and be sure that each part is under subjection to Christ.

In the rest of verse 5 Paul lists various

habits and vices which exhibit earthly, unrighteous living. "Fornication" comes from the Greek word *porneia*. It is the basis for the modern English word *pornography*. The word literally means "having a harlot quality." The emphasis of the term may have been upon "selling one's virtue for ungodly and immoral gain." It referred, in ancient times, to prostitution, unchastity, fornication, premarital intercourse, adultery, and basically every kind of unlawful and unnatural sexual activity. It is always forbidden in the New Testament. Surrender to this way of life indicates a lack of fellowship with God. The term was often in connection with idolatrous worship.

The next term used by Paul is "uncleanness." It comes from a Greek term which means "without purity." The term emphasizes a lack of worthiness in the sight of God. Purity is not judged in relationship to an abstract virtue. It is judged according to the judgment of God.

The next area referred to by Paul was "inordinate affection." The phrase comes from the single Greek word *pathos*. It refers to human passions and is the basis for the modern English word *pathological*. In ancient Greek society the Stoics used the word to refer to someone who allowed themselves to be governed by emotions and therefore could not attain peaceful living. The term referred to shameful passions which often lead to sexual excesses. The term pictures a drive or force that does not rest until satisfied.

The term is especially appropriate to identify the attempt by earthly music and art to release emotions into an uncontrollable state. Releasing emotions properly is a natural, human experience. In fact, it is essential at times of grief and difficulty. However, *pathos* refers to inordinate, sinful, immoral passions and emotions.

The next vice mentioned by Paul is "evil concupiscence." This phrase, according to the Greek terms used here, refers to desires and lusts which reach fuller scope and drive than does "inordinate affection." "Concupiscence" comes from a Greek word which literally means to

"rush along." The term aptly describes the drive of lust in emotions given over to sinful pleasure.

The next term used by Paul is "covetousness." It comes from a Greek word which emphasizes an insatiable selfishness and greed. This term, in Greek text, is indicated as the primary vice from which the others find their source. They result from a basic selfish attitude and spirit.

The selfishness described by Paul is not in comparison to other persons as much as to God. Rather than serving God, this person is controlled by these habits selfishlessly (covetously) serving himself. This is why Paul adds the phrase "which is idolatry." The root of these habits is not necessarily in their practice. These practices are wrong, but the initial and primary problem is selfish idolatry. Sin finds much of its source in selfishness. Worship of God is purity and selfless love for God.

6. For which things' sake the wrath of God cometh on the children of disobedience:

7. In the which ye also walked some time, when ye lived in them.

In verse 6 Paul describes the consequences of the vices listed in verse 5. The "wrath of God" refers to the punishment and holy anger of God upon those who give in to these sins. These sins are not optional behaviors or lifestyles, chosen with no consequence. They are violations of God's will for man.

The persons who live the sinful life are described as "children of disobedience." "Children" emphasizes that they are the offspring and followers of disobedience. "Disobedience" stresses the basic sin they commit. They are, first of all, disobedient. A major reason making their actions sinful is that they are disobeying God's Word and commands. A life pleasing to God is one that is essentially obedient unto Him.

B. Put Off Evil Things (v. 8)

8. But now ye also put off all these; anger, wrath, malice, blasphemy, filthy communication out of your mouth.

In strong comparison to the life the Colossians once lived before knowing Christ, Paul admonishes them to "now" put off evil things. In this emphatic exhortation Paul looks at the implications of Christ upon their present Christian experience. The call to shun evil is a constant reality for the Christian.

The essential command of Paul is to "put off" certain things. The context and grammar of this command in the Greek text stresses a definite action. It also highlights the need for personal involvement. Each individual is responsible to do these things for themselves. The phrase "put off" pictures taking off or removing something a person has on them or with them.

The five things listed by Paul in verse 8 emphasize the life of Christians with each other. Whereas the emphasis of the vices listed in verse 5 were sins against God, idolatry; the sins in verse 8 stress violations against God as they occur between Christian brothers and sisters.

The first item listed by Paul is "anger." It focuses upon anger that remains in a life. It is a continual feeling within a person against someone else.

The second item mentioned is "wrath." It comes from a Greek word which means "to rush along." It refers to a burning anger which flares up and burns with great intensity as a roaring fire.

The third item listed is "malice." This term refers to deliberate actions done with the intention of doing harm of some kind to another person. The term is typically used to refer to harm done through speech. Paul will focus upon sins of speech from here through verse 11.

The fourth item mentioned is "blasphemy." The common usage of the word means "an action against God." However, insight into the essential root meaning of the word is beneficial. The primary, literal meaning of the term means "lazy speech." It refers to an action, speech especially, which is careless and dishonorable. It belittles God and others. It is speech which attempts to cause God or others to fall into disgrace or to receive a bad reputation.

The final term listed by Paul is "filthy communication." The phrase comes from a single Greek word which means "shameful or vulgar speech." The phrase "out of your mouth" indicates an emphatic climax for the entire list. Paul is centering upon sins committed in one's speech. In fact, he moves from the command to "put off" (v. 8) to the command to "lie not" (v. 9).

C. Lie Not Among Themselves (vv. 9-11)

9. Lie not one to another, seeing that ye have put off the old man with his deeds;

10. And have put on the new man, which is renewed in knowledge after the image of him that created him:

11. Where there is neither Greek nor Jew, circumcision nor uncircumcision, Barbarian, Scythian, bond nor free: but Christ is all, and in all.

Paul submits a command highlighting a primary need of the Colossians, "lie not one to another." The term here indicates that this had become a continual habit. For some in the church at Colossae, lying had become a manner of life. The tragedy is that it had persisted within a body of believers.

The reason for the command is given in the remainder of verse 9 as well as verses 10 and 11. The reason was twofold. First, they had "put off" the old man of sin with his deeds. Second, they had "put on" the new man in Christ.

Paul gives an extensive description of the new man in Christ. This new man is continually being "renewed in knowledge after the image of him that created him." "Renewed" refers to a process by which the Christian is given a new life, different from that which previously existed. "Knowledge" in this verse comes from a Greek word which emphasizes experiential knowledge. It was not mere intellect, but knowledge from being in relationship with Christ. The Christian's relationship with Christ conforms him to the image of Christ.

Lying and falsehood among the body of believers denies the reality of the Christian's separation from sin and denies the reality of Christ's transformation of the believer into His image. Unity and truth are primary goals for the church. Immorality is often identified with sexual sins and carnal vices. However, there is nothing more immoral than lying and falsehood between Christian believers according to this passage. This is why the theme of verses 12-17 is unity and harmony among believers.

What command does Paul give in verse 5? What vices does Paul list in verse 5 and what does each of them signify? What primary problem does Paul refer to at the end of verse 5? What command does Paul give in verse 8? What things does he list? What tragic sin among believers does Paul emphasize in this section?

III. LIVE IN HARMONY (Colossians 3:12-17)

12. Put on therefore, as the elect of God, holy and beloved, bowels of mercies, kindness, humbleness of mind, meekness, longsuffering;

13. Forbearing one another, and forgiving one another, if any man have a quarrel against any: even as Christ forgave you, so also do ye.

In contrast to the commands in verses 5-9 to "mortify," "put off," and "lie not," Paul now commands the believer to "put on" certain things. They were to put these things on and thereby demonstrate lives befitting the "elect of God, holy and beloved." Their lives were to reflect God's love for them.

In verse 12 Paul lists five characteristics which reflect the image of Christ in the Christian. "Bowels of mercies" refers to inward compassion one has towards other people. "Kindness" refers to a kindness that is expressed in actions and attitudes. "It is the friendly and helpful spirit which seeks to meet the needs of others through kind deeds" (*Linguistic Key to the Greek New Testament* by Rienecker and Rogers, p. 580).

"Humbleness of mind" comes from a single Greek word which means "humility which gives proper esteem to others and

God." It does not refer to mere intellect. "Meekness" comes from a term used frequently to describe the Christian's submissive relationship with God. That relationship results in a gentle and enduring attitude among others.

"Longsuffering" comes from a Greek concept which emphasizes holding out for a long time without giving out heated, passionate responses in difficult circumstances. The word is used particularly to describe patient long-suffering in the face of injustices. It refers to a person reacting without revenge or retaliation, but with hope for eventual betterment. "It denotes that 'longsuffering' which endures wrong and puts up with the exasperating conduct of others rather than flying into a rage or desiring vengeance" (*Colossians, Philemon* by Peter T. O'Brien, p. 201).

Verse 13 gives the manner in which the Christian is to exhibit the five graces listed in verse 12. This essentially is in "forbearing" and "forgiving" one another. "Forbearing" means to bear with and put up with someone. "Forgiving" emphasizes the extending of grace and forgiveness to one another as Christ has extended such to each believer.

The emphasis of the condition presented in the latter portion of verse 13 is Christ's example. The standard of forgiveness is Christ's forgiveness. "Forbearing" and "forgiving" are necessary qualities which facilitate the other graces described in verse 12.

14. And above all these things put on charity, which is the bond of perfectness.

Verse 14 summarizes, completes, and climaxes the other actions and attitudes mentioned in verses 12 and 13. The other actions all center around relationships between people, especially within the church. The summary term for human relationships is "love." As Christ said in John 13:35, "By this shall all men know that ye are my disciples, if ye have love one to another."

The phrase describing love, "bond of perfectness," stresses the unity love creates between Christians. Further, love is the means by which perfection in the body of Christ is attained. Perfection in the body can never be achieved individually. It is only accomplished by loving one another.

In looking at Christian virtues and graces, Paul deals with relationships within the body of Christ. Christianity is not an individual experience which excludes other Christians. Rather, by its very nature, a Christian's experience is maintained by loving others in Christ.

B. Let Christ Dwell in You Richly (vv. 15-17)

15. And let the peace of God rule in your hearts, to the which also ye are called in one body; and be ye thankful.

The emphasis of this verse is upon peaceful relationships between persons, especially believers, being maintained through Christ. The context has been relationships within the church and it continues into this verse. "Peace" refers to peaceful relationships within the body of Christ.

"Rule" comes from a Greek word used only here in the New Testament. The word means "to umpire or judge." The term refers to an umpire at ancient athletic events maintaining the restrictions of athletic events, making judgments about crucial decisions, and presenting rewards at the end of the contest. In the same way Christ can maintain peace among believers.

Paul ends the verse by referring directly to relationships between believers when he describes them as being of "one body." They were to be thankful to each other and to Christ, the One who made their peace with each other possible.

16. Let the word of Christ dwell in you richly in all wisdom; teaching and admonishing one another in psalms and hymns and spiritual songs, singing with grace in your hearts to the Lord.

17. And whatsoever ye do in word or deed, do all in the name of the Lord Jesus, giving thanks to God and the Father by him.

In these verses Paul highlights the centrality of Christ in relationships between believers. The living, revealed Word of God in Christ is to dwell in the believer richly. The songs and activities within the body of Christ are to be "to the Lord." Everything that is said and done is to be done "in the name of the Lord Jesus."

Thanks unto God is to be given in Christ. Christ is absolutely essential to everything that constitutes the life of the believers in the church. The church should be centered around Christ. The resources of a church should begin with Christ.

Christ is to penetrate each individual believer. Just as the peace of God is to be in the heart of every believer (v. 15), the word of Christ is to dwell richly within each Christian. Though the responsibility for unity is upon the entire body of believers, Christ must be allowed to penetrate each individual's heart. Harmony in the body of Christ is accomplished one member at a time. Christ must dwell richly in each individual heart in order to accomplish oneness in the body.

REVIEW QUESTIONS

1. What exhortation did Paul give the Colossians in verse 1?

2. What vices of the sinful life does Paul list in verse 5?

3. What positive Christian graces does Paul list in verse 12? What does each emphasize?

4. What is the overall emphasis of verses 12-14?

5. What does the word "rule" in verse 15 indicate?

6. Who is the essential source of unity within the church as described in verses 16 and 17?

GOLDEN TEXT HOMILY

"IF YE THEN BE RISEN WITH CHRIST, SEEK THOSE THINGS WHICH ARE ABOVE, WHERE CHRIST SITTETH ON THE RIGHT HAND OF GOD" (Colossians 3:1).

Paul uses water baptism to illustrate the new life which the Christian has in Jesus Christ. In baptism the Christian dies and rises again. As the waters close over him, it is as if he was buried in death. As he emerges from the waters, it is like being resurrected unto a new life.

The Christian is a different person, for his thoughts are now set on the things which are above. Trivial things of earth no longer dominate his life.

The North Star, also known as Polaris, is in the Little Dipper portion of the constellation Ursa Minor. Because it is less than one degree from the North Celestial Pole, it has been a very important aid to navigation. It always marks due north from an observer.

Even though modern advances in technology have lessened the dependency upon the stars, mariners have for centuries needed the stars to guide them to their destination.

The new man in Christ also needs direction for his life, and with the complexities of modern life his need for guidance has intensified. In this verse Paul says that Jesus Christ provides a fixed reference point for the Christian, just as the North Star does for the mariner.

The Christian will continue to sail upon the sea of life. He must go on with the work of this world and maintain all the normal relationships. But there is this difference—from now on he will get his directions, not from the uncertain beacons of this world, but from the eternal light of Christ Jesus sitting at the right hand of the Father.—**Christopher Moree, Editor of Missions Publications, Church of God World Missions, Cleveland, Tennessee**

SENTENCE SERMONS

A CHRISTIAN'S VALUES should be based on the Word of God.
—Selected

HE WHO PROVIDES for this life, but takes no care for eternity, is wise for a moment, but a fool forever.
—Tillotson

SINCE WE WILL some day be judged by the Word of God, we should live by it now.
—"Notes and Quotes"

TREASURES IN HEAVEN are laid up only as treasures on earth are laid down.
—"Speaker's Sourcebook"

EVANGELISTIC APPLICATION

GOD'S GREAT DESIRE IS TO SHARE HIS ETERNAL WEALTH WITH THOSE WHO SEEK HIM.

God has never changed in His great desire to share His eternal wealth with those who seek Him. Even though eternal punishment and separation from God await those who refuse to serve Him, God still desires that all persons receive His blessings. The eternal blessings of God will be withheld only because of man's refusal to serve God, not because of a lack of love on God's part.

There are eternal blessings that await anyone who will confess Christ as Lord and Savior, because this is God's great desire. Heaven and eternal relationship with God in heaven await the believer in Christ. The riches of eternity with God and all that God has provided for His own await anyone who will serve Christ. All of these riches are guaranteed by the grace and love of God.

If someone does not receive the eternal wealth God has for the believer, it will be in spite of God's love. God sent His Son to die on the Cross. The Crucifixion displayed the depth of God's desire that no one be lost, but that all receive from His eternal riches.

ILLUMINATING THE LESSON

Over the triple doorway of the Cathedral of Milan there are three inscriptions spanning the splendid arches. Over one is carved a beautiful wreath of roses, and underneath is the legend, "All that pleases is but for a moment."

Over the other is sculptured a cross, and these are the words beneath: "All that troubles is but for a moment." But underneath the great central entrance in the main aisle is the inscription, "That only is important which is eternal."

DAILY BIBLE READINGS

M. Divine Promise. 2 Samuel 7:4-13
T. Divine Provision. 2 Kings 4:1-7
W. Divine Message. 2 Chronicles 20:14-24
T. Seeing Invisible Things. 2 Corinthians 4:16-18
F. Faithful Unto Death. 2 Timothy 4:1-8
S. Anticipating Christ's Return. 2 Peter 3:10-14

With Signs Following

(Pentecost Sunday)

Study Text: Acts 2:1-47

Supplemental References: Isaiah 32:14-17; Joel 2:28-34; Mark 16:17, 18; Luke 24:44-49; John 7:37-39

Time: Probably written in A.D. 63, recording events of A.D. 30.

Place: Scholars differ on the place of writing, but strong evidence gives the place as Jerusalem.

Golden Text: "The promise is unto you, and to your children, and to all that are afar off, even as many as the Lord our God shall call" (Acts 2:39).

Central Truth: The Holy Spirit empowers believers for service.

Evangelistic Emphasis: The Holy Spirit convicts sinners and leads them to Christ the Savior.

Printed Text

Acts 2:14. But Peter, standing up with the eleven, lifted up his voice, and said unto them, Ye men of Judaea, and all ye that dwell at Jerusalem, be this known unto you, and hearken to my words:

15. For these are not drunken, as ye suppose, seeing it is but the third hour of the day.

16. But this is that which was spoken by the prophet Joel;

17. And it shall come to pass in the last days, saith God, I will pour out of my Spirit upon all flesh: and your sons and your daughters shall prophesy, and your young men shall see visions, and your old men shall dream dreams:

18. And on my servants and on my handmaidens I will pour out in those days of my Spirit; and they shall prophesy:

19. And I will shew wonders in heaven above, and signs in the earth beneath; blood, and fire, and vapour of smoke:

20. The sun shall be turned into darkness, and the moon into blood, before that great and notable day of the Lord come:

21. And it shall come to pass, that whosoever shall call on the name of the Lord shall be saved.

22. Ye men of Israel, hear these words; Jesus of Nazareth, a man approved of God among you by miracles and wonders and signs, which God did by him in the midst of you, as ye yourselves also know:

23. Him being delivered by the determinate counsel and foreknowledge of God, ye have taken, and by wicked hands have crucified and slain:

24. Whom God hath raised up, having loosed the pains of death: because it was not possible that he should be holden of it.

37. Now when they heard this, they were pricked in their heart, and said unto Peter and to the rest of the

apostles, Men and brethren, what shall we do?

38. Then Peter said unto them, Repent, and be baptized every one of you in the name of Jesus Christ for the remission of sins, and ye shall receive the gift of the Holy Ghost.

39. For the promise is unto you, and to your children, and to all that are afar off, even as many as the Lord our God shall call.

40. And with many other words did he testify and exhort, saying, Save yourselves from this untoward generation.

LESSON OUTLINE

I. PROPHECY OF PENTECOST
   A. Declaration of Peter
   B. Clarification of Spirit's Move
   C. Fulfillment of Prophecy Contrasted With False Interpretation
II. CHRIST EXALTED
   A. Approved by God
   B. Predetermination of God
   C. Exaltation Prophesied
III. A GROWING CHURCH
   A. Response to Christ
   B. Call to Salvation
   C. Description of the Growing Church

LESSON EXPOSITION

INTRODUCTION

The text of this lesson provides a very important look at the apostle Peter's sermon on the Day of Pentecost. Peter delivered the sermon just after the coming of the Spirit in the Upper Room. It is the first sermon of the early church. It is the first sermon and explanation regarding the coming of the Spirit after Christ's ascension. Peter interprets the Spirit's infilling of the believers for the crowd gathered that day and for readers in the centuries which would follow.

Pentecost would have been incomplete without the proclamation of Peter. If the event in the Upper Room had occurred without a proclamation explaining and declaring the meaning of the event, it would have been another miraculous phenomenon along with the other unusual happenings that have occurred. However, Peter's declaration of God's Word made it clear that the infilling of the believers in the Upper Room fulfilled prophecies foretold in the Old Testament.

For those who heard Peter's sermon and those who have continued to read its message since then, Pentecost has become the event which gave birth to the presence of Christ in the early church. Peter explains that what happened to the Christians was not an unusual phenomenon but part of God's eternal plan as prophesied in Scripture.

Peter's sermon followed a pattern used by most of the apostles in the preaching found in Acts. The pattern had four parts: (1) the proclamation that the age of fulfillment had arrived (2:16-21); (2) a review of the ministry, death, and triumph of Jesus (2:22-24); (3) references to Old Testament scriptures (2:25-36); and (4) a call to repentance (2:38-39) (*The Book of Acts* by F. F. Bruce, p. 69).

Luke's description of the Upper Room event is given in four verses. Nine verses describe the reaction of the crowd. However, for the setting, sermon, and results of Peter's message regarding the coming of the Spirit, Luke used 31 verses. The comparative quantities of verses do not necessarily mean that one section is more important than the other. However, it does confirm that Peter's sermon was a very important event.

I. PROPHECY OF PENTECOST (Acts 2:14-21)

A. Declaration of Peter (v. 14)

14. But Peter, standing up with the eleven, lifted up his voice, and said unto them, ye men of Judaea, and all ye that dwell at Jerusalem, be this known unto you, and hearken to my words.

The crowd which gathered in Jerusalem on the Day of Pentecost was skeptical of the believers who had been in the Upper Room. Verses 5-13 make it clear that the crowd did not understand what had happened to the believers. Verses 12 and 13 use the words "amazed," "doubt," and "mocking" to describe the reaction of the crowd. They were very troubled and even made fun of those who had been in the Upper Room.

In spite of the mocking crowd, Peter stands up to declare the message of the coming of the Spirit. The words, "but Peter," ring with contrast in comparison to the mocking crowd. The crowd was making light and ridiculing the manifestations of the infilling of the Spirit in the life of the believers, but Peter stood up with the other disciples to declare the Word of God regarding the infilling of the Spirit.

B. Clarification of Spirit's Move (v. 15)

15. For these are not drunken, as ye suppose, seeing it is but the third hour of the day.

Peter immediately addresses the false interpretations and accusations of the crowd. He does not ignore them. He clarifies them. Peter introduces clear evidence that these Spirit-filled believers could not be drunk. He refers to the time of the day. The "third hour of the day" was not the time when persons usually became inebriated. It was usually a time of religious sacrifice.

It is significant that Peter takes time to address the concerns and questions of the crowd. Peter clearly focuses upon the Word of God in his sermon. However, he begins by seizing the opportunity to address the concerns of the crowd. He refutes their false assumptions. Then he clarifies what has happened. He then proceeds to answer their question in verse 12, "What meaneth this?"

C. Fulfillment of Prophecy Contrasted With False Interpretation (vv. 16-21)

16. But this is that which was spoken by the prophet Joel;

17. And it shall come to pass in the last days, saith God, I will pour out of my Spirit upon all flesh: and your sons and your daughters shall prophesy, and your young men shall see visions, and your old men shall dream dreams.

In contrast to the false interpretations and accusations of the crowd, Peter

declares the interpretation of God's Word regarding the pouring out of the Spirit. He cites the prophecy recorded in Joel 12:28-32. Joel was a familiar prophet to the Israelites and proselytes gathered that day. Prophecy concerning the last days should have been especially important to them. They were under Roman occupation and they awaited the Messiah and the establishment of God's kingdom on earth.

Rather than wine, the source of the experience in the Upper Room was God. This is the climactic claim in Luke's earlier description of the Upper Room experience. They spoke with other tongues "as the Spirit gave them utterance." The experience of Pentecost is directly from God. This is the first declaration Peter makes regarding the Pentecost experience.

"Pour out" emphasizes the abundance of the Spirit of God. "All flesh" stresses the availability of the Spirit of God to all persons. Both phrases describe the essential feature of God's activity in the Pentecost event and experience. God pours out His Spirit upon all flesh at Pentecost.

Joel's prophecy lists the different kinds of people that would receive the Spirit and be able to prophesy, have visions, and dream dreams. This is in contrast to the expectations of the Hebrews. They felt God would give His Spirit exclusively to the Israelites. Further, prophecy, visions, and dreams, according to the Hebrews, were to be reserved for only special, chosen persons. Joel's prophecy indicates these things were to be given to several groups of people.

The timing of the fulfillment was important. Peter was declaring that the fulfillment was occurring on the Day of Pentecost. The "last days" mentioned in the prophecy and the "day of the Lord" mentioned in verse 20 were now coming to pass.

The Hebrews divided all time into two ages, the present age and the age to come. The age to come was when God would ultimately establish His kingdom. The age to come would first be precluded by the "day of the Lord." This was the time when God would begin to prepare the world for the ultimate age to come. The "day of the Lord" had finally come with the outpouring of the Spirit on Pentecost.

18. And on my servants and on my handmaidens I will pour out in those days of my Spirit; and they shall prophesy:

19. And I will shew wonders in heaven above, and signs in the earth beneath; blood, and fire, and vapour of smoke.

Verse 18 is a restatement of who will prophesy. Verse 17 said "your sons and your daughters" will prophesy. The reference in verse 17 emphasizes the earthly heritage of these sons and daughters. The availability of the work of the Spirit is stressed. In verse 18 "your" is changed to "my" and the heavenly heritage of those who prophesy is stressed. They are God's own servants and handmaidens as well as the sons and daughters of earthly parents.

In verse 18 there is also a restatement of the central event of Pentecost, God pouring out His Spirit. In verse 17 God's Spirit is poured out upon "all flesh." Earthly heritage is stressed. However, in verse 18 God's Spirit is poured out upon God's own servants and handmaidens. Godly heritage is being stressed. This highlights the prerequisite for service unto God. "All flesh" in verse 17 does not indicate an arbitrary and careless selection of who is to receive the Spirit. Verse 18 clarifies that God pours out His Spirit upon all those who would become His servants.

The outpouring of God's Spirit is accompanied by supernatural manifestations on earth. The primary action of God in verse 19 is to "shew" certain things. A primary purpose of God's activity in the last days is to reveal Himself through signs and wonders. This is part of the age of the Spirit. Signs and wonders reveal God's activity. No attempt is made here to specifically explain each miraculous event. What is indicated is that they originate from God and reveal the evidence of His action in the world.

20. The sun shall be turned into darkness, and the moon into blood,

before that great and notable day of the Lord come:

21. And it shall come to pass, that whosoever shall call on the name of the Lord shall be saved.

The description of the things God "shews" forth continues in verse 20. These are signs in the sky, concerning the sun and the moon. The timing is "before that great and notable day of the Lord come." This phrase refers to the final conclusion of the "day of the Lord." This is the time just before the "age to come" mentioned earlier in verse 17.

Peter said earlier that the prophecy of Joel concerned the outpouring of the Spirit at Pentecost. The signs and wonders will be concluded when the day of the Lord is completely fulfilled. This will be just before the final age.

Verse 21 summarizes the prophecy of the theme of repentance. This was the context for the original message of the prophecy. Repentance is the concluding theme of the prophecy itself. Repentance is the eventual theme of Peter's sermon on the Day of Pentecost. Salvation is the eternal theme of God's activity toward men, calling all persons to repentance. God desires that all men everywhere repent and serve Him. This same desire is still present in the midst of the outpouring of the Spirit.

What opinion did the crowd have of the persons who had been filled with the Spirit in the Upper Room? How did Peter respond to the crowd? How did Peter treat their questioning? How important was the Word of God in Peter's response and sermon? What is the central message in the prophecy of Joel? What differences are there between verse 17 and verses 18 and 19? What role does repentance play in Pentecost?

II. CHRIST EXALTED (Acts 2:22-36)

A. Approved by God (v. 22)

22. Ye men of Israel, hear these words; Jesus of Nazareth, a man approved of God among you by miracles and wonders and signs, which

God did by him in the midst of you, as ye yourselves also know.

This description of Christ appeals to the earthly witnesses and events that were well-known to the hearers. Peter assumes they knew of the works and ministry of Christ. It must have been obvious to the crowd that Christ's ministry was of supernatural origin. "Israel" and "Nazareth" are regional descriptions used by Peter to deliberately appeal to the historical fact of Jesus' life and ministry.

The center of the description of Christ is the phrase "a man approved of God." "Man" is another affirmation of the earthly existence of Christ. "Approved" is from a Greek word which emphasizes approval by visual demonstration. Elsewhere it is translated "exhibited." "Of God" declares the source of the visual demonstration and approval of Christ. It comes from God. God himself demonstrates and provides the approval of Christ's ministry.

"Miracles" stressed the divine origin of Christ's work. "Wonders" highlighted the fascination and awe stirred by His work. "Signs" indicated the religious significance of Christ's work. His work came from God and was done in the midst of those gathered. "As ye yourselves know" indicates that the work of Christ was already well-known. Further, it was well-known that His work testified of God's activity and approval.

B. Predetermination of God (vv. 23, 24)

23. Him, being delivered by the determinate counsel and foreknowledge of God, ye have taken, and by wicked hands have crucified and slain:

24. Whom God hath raised up, having loosed the pains of death: because it was not possible that he should be holden of it.

Verse 22 highlighted the work of God in Christ and man's knowledge of that work. Verses 23 and 24 highlight God's action through Christ, man's sinful response to Christ, and God's exaltation of Christ.

Christ was "delivered" by God unto men who crucified Him. This was not an accident. The Crucifixion did not occur as an accident of God's will. God inten-

tionally gave Christ over to men who crucified Him. Christ was delivered "by the determinate counsel and foreknowledge of God." "Determinate" comes from a Greek word which means "to mark off boundaries." God's counsel and foreknowledge set the boundaries for Christ's death on the Cross. Sinners are not saved by an accidental murder. They are saved by a death that was foreseen and under the foreknowledge of God.

When Christ was received by men, they crucified and slew Him. The death of the cross was a brutal death. No doubt, it was still fresh on the minds of the ones Peter preached to at Pentecost. Christ was crucified and slain "by wicked hands." "Wicked" is from a Greek word meaning "lawless." The Greek text emphasizes the word "slain." It can be translated "killed." This was man's response to the One sent from God.

In contrast to man's attempt to eliminate Christ and in contrast to the brutal and lawless treatment given the One sent from God, God himself raised Christ from the dead. The pains of death were real for Christ. He endured the agony of the Cross. Christ was not exempt from the travail of death, even the brutal death of crucifixion. However, when God raised Christ He released Him from the pains of death.

Peter indicates the purpose of the Resurrection. It was not possible that Christ should be held by death. The foreknowledge and counsel of God had also determined that Christ should be exalted as Savior. Christ's sacrificial death had satisfied the justice of God and there was no further reason for death to hold Him. Further, the resurrection of Christ was the demonstration of God's approval of Christ's sacrificial death in behalf of sinners. Scripture also was to be fulfilled. Peter turns to Christ's fulfillment of Scripture next.

C. Exaltation Prophesized (vv. 25-36)

(Acts 2:25-36 is not included in the printed text.)

The resurrection and exaltation of Christ

was foretold in the Old Testament. Peter quotes from a prophecy in Psalm 16:8-11. He then explains that this prophecy did not concern David's death but Christ's. This prophecy was fulfilled in the same Jesus who was crucified. It was "this Jesus" (v. 32) who was raised by God in fulfillment of the prophecy by David. Paul also refers to this same prophecy in Acts 13:35-36.

Peter continues in verse 33 to explain what was occurring on the Day of Pentecost. The events and experiences of the outpouring of the Spirit come from the exalted Christ. The same Christ that fulfilled Old Testament prophecy was now shedding forth what was occurring on the Day of Pentecost. It is important to realize the significance of the continuing ministry of Christ on earth through the Spirit. The theme of Peter and the early church is that Christ is alive and operating through the Spirit.

What does the word *approved* in verse 22 mean? In what ways did Peter contrast the action of God and the treatment of men concerning Christ? Were those who heard Peter's sermons that day aware of the ministry of Christ? What Old Testament prophecy did Peter use in citing the resurrection of Christ? How important is the continuing ministry of Christ through the Spirit?

III. A GROWING CHURCH (Acts 2:37-47)

A. Response to Christ (v. 37)

37. Now when they heard this, they were pricked in their heart, and said unto Peter and to the rest of the apostles, Men and brethren, what shall we do?

Three things occur in the crowd as a result of Peter's declaration on the Day of Pentecost. First, the crowd "heard" the message. Second, they were "pricked in their heart." Third, they inquired as to what they were to do. All three actions prepared the crowd to effectively hear the call to repentance made in verses 38-40.

The hearing of the gospel was the result of the proclamation of Peter. Had the Spirit come upon the believers and filled them without someone to declare the meaning of the event, the gospel would not have been effectively proclaimed. It would have just been an unusual event fascinating the crowd that day.

"Pricked" comes from a Greek word meaning "to pierce or sting sharply." The word was used in ancient literature to signify painful, piercing emotions felt deep within. This was the effect of the message Peter delivered. The pain was applied by the Holy Spirit through Peter's proclamation of the Word of God.

The pain was so strong within them that they were moved to speak. They requested direction. This was primarily a response to the Word of God. They did not specifically mention repentance. They still needed the call to repentance even though they were convinced of God's approval of Christ's work.

B. Call to Salvation (vv. 38-40)

38. Then Peter said unto them, Repent, and be baptized every one of you in the name of Jesus Christ for the remission of sins, and ye shall receive the gift of the Holy Ghost.

39. For the promise is unto you, and to your children, and to all that are afar off, even as many as the Lord our God shall call.

Upon the questioning of the crowd Peter responded in a twofold manner. First, Peter called them to "repent." "Repent" comes from a Greek word which essentially calls for a change in one's thinking. However, this "thinking" is not merely intellectual. This Greek word refers to the "sum total of the whole mental and moral state of being" (*A Greek-English Lexicon of the New Testament* by Bauer, Arndt, and Gingrich, p. 546). Further, repentance refers to a change in the spiritual relationship a person has with God.

The call to repentance was a critical command to the crowd. Previously, they had rejected Christ and killed Him. Now, they were to accept Him as the Messiah and repent of their wickedness.

As a symbol of this inward change of heart, Peter calls the crowd to a second action, baptism. Baptism is the result of repentance. Baptism is neither a substitute nor equivalent to repentance. It is a separate work which gives evidence of the prior act of repentance.

Peter calls them to be baptized "in the name of Jesus Christ." This phrase, according to the Greek text, indicates the baptism in which they would partake is in relationship to Jesus Christ and not another baptism. It is an affirmation of their faith in Christ. It is not a substitute of that faith.

They were to be baptized "for the remission of sins." This phrase does not indicate they were to receive remission of their sins through their baptism. That would exclude the necessity of the prior act of repentance mentioned first. Water baptism was a testimony of the fact of repentance and forgiveness that had already been established inwardly. Because of the Greek word translated "for" and the context of the verse, an expanded translation of the phrase is helpful. "For the remission of sins" would be expanded to, "This baptismal testimony being in relation to the fact that your sins have been put away" (*The New Testament, An Expanded Translation,* by Kenneth S. Wuest, p. 276).

Peter also indicated that the crowd would receive the "gift of the Holy Ghost." "Gift" refers to the Holy Spirit himself. It does not refer to the "gifts" of the Spirit referred to elsewhere in Scripture. Pentecost for Christianity meant the ushering in of the Holy Spirit into the church. The outpouring of God's Spirit was a gift which God was giving man.

The outpouring of the Spirit was promised not only to the crowd that day, but to their posterity as well. Further, the Spirit was promised to as many "as the Lord our God shall call." God has called whomsoever will call upon Him, confess their sins, and accept Jesus Christ as Lord and Savior.

The work of the Spirit in repentance and baptism is emphasized here. This does not indicate that these are the only experiences in which the Holy Spirit ministers. The Spirit's work is evident in sanctification and the baptism of the Holy Ghost. The various ways in which the Spirit ministers are emphasized elsewhere in Scripture. In this particular passage the emphasis is upon the work of repentance and baptism.

40. And with many other words did he testify and exhort, saying, Save yourselves from this untoward generation.

This verse emphasizes the necessity of salvation. Further, it affirms that the emphasis of this passage is upon the salvation of the lost. Peter indicates that salvation is offered by God. However, the sinner is responsible for his own repentance. Without action by the individual sinner, responding to the prompting of the Spirit of God, he will be lost.

C. Description of the Growing Church (vv. 41-47)

(Acts 2:41-47 is not included in the printed text.)

The remainder of Acts 2 is taken up with a description of the early church in the days and weeks following Pentecost. The description gives evidence that many accepted this salvation. The church continued in fellowship, with a strong emphasis upon supporting and caring for another. The description ends with a summary of the praise the church had for God and the favor they had with "all the people." The final sentence of the last verse is careful to give the honor for the growth and prosperity of the church to the Lord.

REVIEW QUESTIONS

1. What was the reaction of the crowd to those baptized with the Holy Spirit in the Upper Room?

2. What was Peter's initial response to the crowd?

3. How important is proclamation to the Pentecost event?

4. How did the crowd respond after hearing Peter's sermon?

5. What two calls did Peter give the audience in response to their questioning in the latter part of the chapter?

GOLDEN TEXT HOMILY

"THE PROMISE IS UNTO YOU, AND TO YOUR CHILDREN, AND TO ALL THAT ARE AFAR OFF, EVEN AS MANY AS THE LORD OUR GOD SHALL CALL" (Acts 2:39).

It is unlikely that the writer of this scripture had a full conception of just how far the scope of his statements would extend. He may have visualized "to all that are afar off" in the terms of the area of the Middle East or even of the then-known world. But there is no way that he could have fully grasped the vast sweep of the promise of this scripture.

Many times we are too small in our thinking when it comes to the promises of God. Even while we are thinking of the infinite possibilities of what God can accomplish, we are probably underestimating Him.

There is an old saying that "what the human mind can conceive, it can achieve." But God can achieve those things that the human mind can never conceive or comprehend. It is impossible to cast the promises of God in such cosmic terms that they fully explore the range of His power.

Dedication to the cause of Christ and surrender to Him will result in signs following the believer. We have that assurance from God. We only need to take hold of that promise and live for Him whether or not the signs are always visible to us ourselves.
—**Excerpts from** The Pulpit Commentary, **vol. 18**

SENTENCE SERMONS

THE HOLY SPIRIT empowers believers for service.

—Selected

PENTECOST WAS only a few drops of the coming shower.

—"Speaker's Sourcebook"

GOD'S CHILDREN are to be aided and assisted through the power of God's Spirit every day.

—Selected

EVANGELISTIC APPLICATION

THE HOLY SPIRIT CONVICTS SINNERS AND LEADS THEM TO CHRIST THE SAVIOR.

The crowd that heard Peter preach at Pentecost was at first confused, and mocked Peter and the other believers. However, by the end of Peter's message the crowd was ready to receive the call to repentance. All that Luke records between the two responses of the crowd is Peter's sermon. There was nothing to coerce or force them to believe.

What led the crowd to repent was the work of the Holy Spirit applying the message Peter proclaimed. The message was applied to their hearts by the Holy Spirit. The Holy Spirit is the One who convicts men of their sins and need for salvation. As persons preach and proclaim the good news, they become instruments in the hands of God. However, the One who leads persons to conviction and repentance of the heart is the Holy Spirit.

Since the work of leading the lost to the Savior is the divine work of the Holy Spirit, it is effective. If the sinner allows the Holy Spirit to truly work in convicting him of sin, and will not resist the work of the Spirit, that sinner will be led to repentance by the Spirit. If left to the ability of man, conviction might be abused and ineffective. However, the Holy Spirit leads persons directly to Christ the Savior. Salvation is of divine origin and so is the work of conviction of the sinner and his being led to Christ.

DAILY BIBLE READINGS

M. Called Witness. Jeremiah 7:1-7
T. Commissioned Witness. Isaiah 6:1-10
W. Dauntless Witness. 2 Timothy 1:1-14
T. Powerful Witness. Acts 4:31-33
F. Dedicated Witness. 1 Corinthians 9: 16-27
S. Exemplary Witness. 1 Timothy 4:6-16

The Blessed Hope

Study Text: 1 Thessalonians 4:13 through 5:10

Supplemental References: Job 14:7-14; Psalms 39:1-7; 78:1-7; Romans 5:1-9; 8:14-25; 1 Corinthians 15:12-20; Titus 1:1-3; 1 Peter 3:15

Time: Probably late in A.D. 51 or early A.D. 52

Place: Corinth

Golden Text: "Looking for that blessed hope, and the glorious appearing of the great God and our Saviour Jesus Christ" (Titus 2:13).

Central Truth: The resurrection of Christ is God's assurance to believers of their future resurrection.

Evangelistic Emphasis: The promise of Christ's return should motivate people to prepare for His coming.

Printed Text

1 Thessalonians 4:13. But I would not have you to be ignorant, brethren, concerning them which are asleep, that ye sorrow not, even as others which have no hope.

14. For if we believe that Jesus died and rose again, even so them also which sleep in Jesus will God bring with him.

15. For this we say unto you by the word of the Lord, that we which are alive and remain unto the coming of the Lord shall not prevent them which are asleep.

16. For the Lord himself shall descend from heaven with a shout, with the voice of the archangel, and with the trump of God: and the dead in Christ shall rise first:

17. Then we which are alive and remain shall be caught up together with them in the clouds, to meet the Lord in the air: and so shall we ever be with the Lord.

18. Wherefore comfort one another with these words.

5:1. But of the times and the seasons, brethren, ye have no need that I write unto you.

2. For yourselves know perfectly that the day of the Lord so cometh as a thief in the night.

3. For when they shall say, Peace and safety; then sudden destruction cometh upon them, as travail upon a woman with child; and they shall not escape.

4. But ye, brethren, are not in darkness, that that day should overtake you as a thief.

5. Ye are all the children of light, and the children of the day: we are not of the night, nor of darkness.

6. Therefore let us not sleep, as do others; but let us watch and be sober.

7. For they that sleep sleep in the night; and they that be drunken are drunken in the night.

8. But let us, who are of the day, be sober, putting on the breastplate of faith and love; and for an helmet, the hope of salvation.

9. For God hath not appointed us to wrath, but to obtain salvation by our Lord Jesus Christ.

10. Who died for us, that, whether we wake or sleep, we should live together with him.

LESSON OUTLINE

I. THE RAPTURE
   A. Call to Knowledge and Hope Regarding the Resurrection
   B. Those to Be Taken in the Resurrection
   C. The Order of the Resurrection
   D. Call to Comfort One Another Regarding the Resurrection

II. SUDDEN DESTRUCTION
   A. The Time of Christ's Coming
   B. The Result of Christ's Coming Upon Unbelievers

III. SPIRITUAL ALERTNESS
   A. Call to Spiritual Alertness
   B. Reason For Spiritual Alertness

LESSON EXPOSITION

INTRODUCTION

The background for Paul's first letter to the Thessalonians contains several vital points. The city of Thessalonica was a very large commercial and political center. Though part of the Roman Empire, it remained predominantly Greek in character. This meant it was able to function with a good deal of autonomy.

The religious character of the church at Thessalonica had several aspects. The church was started by Paul on his second missionary journey. The city already contained a very important synagogue. Paul ministered at the synagogue when he first arrived. His converts were primarily Gentiles who had previously been converted to Judaism from heathenism.

Paul's success was so great, jealous Jews organized severe opposition against him. They charged him, before the city officials, of proclaiming a king, Jesus, which challenged Caesar. This was a serious charge and the Jews convinced the officials that Paul was a threat to the city. Paul had to escape to Athens.

While at Athens, and later Corinth, Paul was concerned about the church at Thessalonica. He sent Timothy to minister and assist those at the young Thessalonian Church. Timothy eventually returned to Paul and gave him a report about the condition of the Thessalonian Church. First Thessalonians was written by Paul as a response to Timothy's report.

Paul's response to Timothy's report contained several elements. He commended the Thessalonians for maintaining their Christian testimony under the tests of persecution. The criticism of Paul in Thessalonica by the Jews and others continued. Therefore, Paul spent time in his letter vindicating his ministry. Paul admonished and instructed the Thessalonians in three particular areas—moral purity, respect for leaders, and the resurrection of the saints. This lesson will focus upon Paul's call and instruction to the Thessalonians regarding the resurrection of the dead and the living at the second coming of Christ.

The first three chapters of 1 Thessalonians deal primarily with Paul's relationship to the Thessalonians. He offers thanks for them in chapter 1. He discusses the circumstances surrounding his first visit in the first part of chapter 2. In the rest of chapter 2 and chapter 3 Paul discusses circumstances that have arisen since he had departed. In the first part of chapter 4 Paul admonishes the Thessalonians regarding Christian conduct. In the text of this lesson, 4:13-5:10, Paul turns his attention to the resurrection and the return of Christ (for more background on 1 Thessalonians consult *An Introduction to the New Testament, Volume Two, The Pauline Epistles* by Edmond Hiebert).

I. THE RAPTURE (1 Thessalonians 4:13-18)

A. Call to Knowledge and Hope Regarding the Resurrection (v. 13)

13. But I would not have you to be ignorant, brethren, concerning them which are asleep, that ye sorrow not, even as others which have no hope.

"But" does not serve to highlight any strong contrast between verse 13 and verse 12. It does highlight the material of verse 13 and might better be translated "now." Paul is wanting to introduce instruction on the Resurrection. This had obviously been an area of controversy among the Thessalonians.

Paul has a strong desire relating to the Thessalonians and the Resurrection at the coming of the Lord. Paul's desire is that they not be ignorant. "Ignorant" literally means "without knowledge." He does not want them to be without knowledge "concerning them which are asleep." The issue that had arisen in Thessalonica concerned the resurrection of Christians who were now dead. Some had thought those living at the return of the Lord would hinder those who were dead.

Paul's purpose in desiring knowledge for them about the believers who had died was their comfort. He did not want them to "sorrow" as if they had no hope. Paul had confidence that the knowledge he was going to provide regarding the resurrection of the Christians who had died would bring encouragement to the Thessalonians. Knowledge of the resurrection of the saints can bring renewed hope into the life of the believer.

"Sorrow," as used in the Greek of this verse, refers to a continuing action. It means "to become sad or sorrowful." This verse does not argue against grieving. It simply argues against Christians, regarding the Resurrection, acting as those who have no hope in the Resurrection. Grief may occur in human experience at times of great loss. However, the hope of Christians is secure from any despair regarding the Resurrection.

B. Those to Be Taken in the Resurrection (vv. 14, 15)

14. For if we believe that Jesus died and rose again, even so them also which sleep in Jesus will God bring with him.

15. For this we say unto you by the word of the Lord, that we which are alive and remain unto the coming of the Lord shall not prevent them which are asleep.

In these verses Paul expands upon the hope Christians have in the Resurrection. Specifically, Paul addresses hope for the resurrection of Christians who have already died. Paul reasons that if one believes in the resurrection of Christ, his faith should include the resurrection of "sleeping" saints as well.

The word "if" in the Greek text indicates a condition which is true. By saying "if we believe," Paul is in no way questioning the resurrection of Christ. He is in fact assuming the truth of the Resurrection. "Even so" indicates that what follows is true as well. The verse stresses the resurrection of the dead in Christ being just as true as the resurrection of Christ.

He further stresses the certainity of the resurrection of the dead in Christ. He continues in verse 15 with the phrase, "By the word of the Lord." By this phrase he appeals to the authority of Christ himself. It is a doctrine from Christ himself guaranteeing that persons who "are alive and remain unto the coming of the Lord shall not prevent them which are asleep."

The latter portion of verse 15 represents the heart of the controversy Paul was addressing. Some of the Thessalonians had become persuaded that the dead in Christ would be at a disadvantage at the Resurrection because of those who were alive when Christ returned. They thought those who were alive would "hinder" those who were dead.

"Hindered" is from a Greek word meaning "precede." The emphasis of the word is upon "priority" (*The Vocabulary of the Greek New Testament* by Moulton and Milligan, p. 667). By "preceding" the dead, those who are alive would be given a greater priority. Paul clarified in verse 15 that those who are alive would not be given a greater priority than the dead in Christ at the return of Christ.

C. The Order of the Resurrection (vv. 16, 17)

16. For the Lord himself shall descend from heaven with a shout, with the voice of the archangel, and with the trump of God: and the dead in Christ shall rise first:

17. Then we which are alive and remain shall be caught up together

with them in the clouds, to meet the Lord in the air: and so shall we ever be with the Lord.

Paul continues to inform the Thessalonians about the Resurrection. In verses 16 and 17 he indicates the events which will occur at the Resurrection and return of the Lord highlighting the order in which the dead and the living who are in Christ will rise.

Paul stresses that his doctrine in verse 15 was by the "word of the Lord." He is stressing the direct involvement of Christ in this doctrine. He continues to stress the direct involvement of Christ when he discusses the Resurrection itself. Paul says the Lord himself will be involved in the resurrection and rapture of the saints.

Christ's primary action at the Rapture will be to "descend." "Descend" comes from a Greek word which means "to come down." This is the central feature of the initial events of the Rapture. The other features mentioned by Paul at the initiation of the Rapture will be the "shout," the "voice of the archangel," and the "trump of God." These will be important. However, the center of these initial circumstances will be the "coming down" of the Lord.

Accompaning the coming down of the Lord will first of all be a "shout." "Shout" comes from a Greek word which means "signal or command." The word was used in the military for a battle cry; it was used on ships to give orders to oarsmen; and it was used by charioteers to signal their horses. In most cases it was an authoritative cry in the midst of great excitement (*Linguistic Key to the Greek New Testament* by Rienecker and Rogers).

Also accompanying the coming down of the Lord will be "the voice of the archangel." This phrase refers to a voice of utmost authority and rank. The final element accompanying the coming down of the Lord will be "the trump of God." Throughout the Old Testament the trumpet was used to signal feast days. The trumpet also accompanied glorious appearances by God. The trumpet served as an instrument of proclamation, announcement, and praise.

The rest of verse 16 and the first part of verse 17 give the order in which the dead and living in Christ will rise at the Rapture. The dead will be taken up first (v. 16). Those who are alive will follow.

They will both be "caught up together . . . in the clouds" (v. 17). "Caught up" comes from a Greek word whose fuller meaning was "to be caused to be snatched up in such a way that no resistance is offered." The word was often used in ancient literature by persons describing how their possessions had been snatched in a robbery. The resurrection and rapture of the saints will be in this quick "snatching" fashion. The Greek text indicates this is a definite occurrence that will take place. The dead and the living will meet together "in the clouds." They will then meet the Lord in the air to be with Him forever.

The order of the resurrection will therefore be as follows: the Lord will come down, a "signal," archangel's voice, and the trump of God will accompany Him; the dead in Christ will rise, the living in Christ will be snatched up to meet the resurrected ones in the clouds; finally, they both will then meet the Lord "in the air" to be with Him forever. This is the essential information regarding the Resurrection Paul desired the Thessalonians not to be "ignorant" (v. 13) about.

In verse 13 Paul did not want the Thessalonians to "sorrow" as if they did not have any hope. Paul returns to this theme of comfort in verse 14.

D. Call to Comfort One Another Regarding the Resurrection (v. 18)

18. Wherefore comfort one another with these words.

Paul's ultimate purpose in conveying certain principles about the doctrine of the Resurrection is comfort. Their comfort for one another was to come by means of the words he had just conveyed about the Resurrection. In this passage, comfort is the purpose behind the message of the Resurrection. Comfort is a vital purpose. Paul indicated in verse 13 that it is possible, by being ignorant or unaware of the proper doctrine of the Rapture and the Resurrection, to be in sorrow and despair without hope.

"Comfort" comes from a Greek word which literally means "to call someone to your side." The word emphasizes comfort which resulted from the presence of another. It refers to a comfort which is derived from relationships with others. Paul was encouraging the Thessalonians to compassionately exhort one another regarding the return of the Lord. Christ's return can be a source of meaningful comfort for the Christian.

What was Paul's desire for the Thessalonians regarding the Resurrection? What role did hope and comfort play in the doctrine of the Resurrection? Who will be taken in the Resurrection? Will the living have priority over the dead in the Resurrection? What will be the order of events in the Resurrection?

II. SUDDEN DESTRUCTION (1 Thessalonians 5:1-3)

A. The Time of Christ's Coming (vv. 1, 2)

1. But of the times and the seasons, brethren, ye have no need that I write unto you.

2. For yourselves know perfectly that the day of the Lord so cometh as a thief in the night.

Paul extends the idea of comfort and hope in chapter 5. He discusses the "hope of salvation" in verse 8. Within this context he emphasizes the need to be ready for the return ("coming down" see 4:16) of the Lord. By being ready for the return of the Lord, the believer maintains his hope and comfort.

"The times and the seasons" refers to the duration and specific events marking the coming of the Lord. Christ had already declared that the times and the seasons were not specifically known by men (Acts 1:7). Paul was reaffirming this fact in verse 1.

In verse 2 Paul reaffirms not only the lack of specific knowledge about the timing of the Lord's return, he also reaffirms the manner in which Christ will return. It will be swiftly. It will be without notice. All that will remain will be the evidence of His coming after it has occurred. It will be similar to robbery. No one may see the robber, but the evidence of his coming remains.

B. The Result of Christ's Coming Upon Unbelievers (v. 3)

3. For when they shall say, Peace and safety; then sudden destruction cometh upon them, as travail upon a woman with child; and they shall not escape.

Paul continues the analogy of a robber which he used in verse 2. "They" refers to those who are not prepared for Christ's return. Just as individuals are unprepared when a robber may come, they will also be unprepared for Christ's return. A robber is able to surprise those who might feel they are safe and secure. A robber may be able to bring violent calamity upon persons who had thought they were completely safe.

The opening phrase of verse 3 indicates when the surprise of the Lord's coming will come upon the unprepared. At the time when they feel the most confident about their "peace and safety," at that very moment, the consequences of the Lord's coming will come down upon them. "Safety" is from a Greek law word which refers to a "bond" or "security." When the unprepared feel a false sense of security, the Lord will come.

Feelings of security and peace (by the unprepared) will not guarantee safety. Destruction will come suddenly in the midst of those who think they are safe. As the "travail" or birth pains come upon a woman about to deliver a child, so will the sudden destruction come upon those who are unprepared at Christ's return. As the pains are inevitable and unescapable at the birth of a child, so will the destruction for not being prepared come upon the unredeemed.

Does anyone know the timing of the Lord's coming? Will the Lord come quickly? To what does Paul compare the quickness of the Lord's coming? What will happen to those unprepared at the Lord's coming even though they think they are safe and secure?

III. SPIRITUAL ALERTNESS (1 Thessalonians 5:4-10)

A. Call to Spiritual Alertness (vv. 4-8)

4. But ye brethren, are not in darkness, that that day should overtake you as a thief.

5. Ye are all the children of light, and the children of the day: we are not of the night, nor of darkness.

In verses 4 and 5 Paul contrasts the Thessalonian believers with those who are unprepared for the Lord's coming. The believer is prepared for the Lord's return for primarily two reasons: who he is and who he is not. The believer is not "in darkness" but a child "of light."

Paul's reference to "darkness," "light," and "day" highlight the Christian's awareness of the Lord's coming. This awareness is not necessarily of the "times or seasons" of Christ's coming. The awareness of the Christian is maintained so that when Christ does come, the Christian will not be surprised. The Christian is not in "darkness" so that he will be taken by surprise as when a thief may come upon an unsuspecting victim.

"Darkness" refers to a condition in which persons are groping in life with no direction. It describes a condition in which the ways of Christ are not visable to an individual, as if they cannot see anything in a dark room.

By contrast, the Christian is in "light." The light reveals the coming of the Lord for the Christian. It is light similar to daylight. The Christian will not be surprised at the coming of the Lord. Rather, the Christian will view and participate in the return of the Lord.

6. Therefore let us not sleep, as do others; but let us watch and be sober.

7. For they that sleep sleep in the night; and they that be drunken are drunken in the night.

8. But let us, who are of the day, be sober, putting on the breastplate of faith and love; and for an helmet, the hope of salvation.

Since the Christian is in the light and has had the awareness of Christ's coming shed upon him, Paul gives a series of admonitions. There are four admonitions—"let us not sleep," "let us watch," and "be sober" (repeated once).

With these admonitions, Paul moves beyond his initial desire for the Thessalonians to not be ignorant regarding the return of Christ and the Resurrection (4:13). Paul moves on to the responses the Christian should have once they become aware of Christ's return.

As one who is in the light of knowledge about Christ's return, the Christian should "not sleep." "Sleep" is similar to "darkness." They both describe a person who is unprepared for Christ's return. "Sleep" refers to a condition of lethargy and slothfulness. A person's perception is dulled and there is no response to things around him. The person will not be aware of the Lord when He returns until after He has left with the redeemed.

Paul admonishes the believer to "watch." "Watch" comes from a Greek word which means to "stay awake." The Greek text indicates a continuing action. Rather than asleep, the Christian should be constantly awake, fully aware that the coming of the Lord is close at hand.

Paul further admonishes the believer twice to "be sober." "Sober" comes from a Greek word which simply means to "not be drunk." Paul admonishes them to not be drunk so they may be alert and aware of the Lord's coming. Paul expands what he means by sober in verse 8.

Before Paul repeats and expands his command to be sober, he explains why the Christian should not "sleep" or be "drunk" concerning the coming of the Lord. Both conditions are done "in the night." This is similar to the theme of "darkness" Paul mentioned in verses 4 and 5. "Night" signifies the spiritual realm in which knowledge of the Lord's coming is hidden. It is the time and condition in which the thief comes (v. 2).

In contrast, Paul admonishes believers to "be sober." Being sober involves "putting on" the breastplate of faith and love and the helmet of the hope of salvation. The action of "putting on" is something that must be done by the Christian. It requires the involvement of the Christian. The

Christian will not be sober and awake at the coming of the Lord if he himself does not take the action. The responsibility is on the Christian.

The latter part of verse 8 is similar to the Christian's armor Paul describes in Ephesians 6. "Breastplate" refers to the piece of armor worn by a soldier to protect his body from his shoulders to his loins. It was either a piece of metal or chain mail. The breastplate Paul describes here is "of faith and love." The breastplate was a defensive piece of armor. Faith and love serve to defend the believer as a breastplate protected a soldier.

Paul uses the themes of faith and love together in Galatians 5:6. There he states that faith "worketh by love." The two virtues are certainly important to the Christian life. They also enhance one another. Paul indicates in 1 Thessalonians 5:8 that they protect the believer and make him aware and alert for the second coming of Christ.

The second piece of armor which is part of being "sober" is a helmet of the "hope of salvation." In ancient Roman times the helmet was a very heavy and decorative piece of armor. Felt or sponge was inside the helmet to make the weight of the metal bearable. "Nothing short of an ax or hammer could pierce a heavy helmet" (*Lingustic Key to the New Testament* by Rienecker and Rogers, p. 542).

The hope of salvation protects the Christian. The emphasis in the Greek text is upon "hope." Salvation is important in this verse, but the hope which salvation gives is Paul's point of emphasis. He does not wish the Thessalonians to be discouraged in the face of the return of the Lord and the events of the resurrection of the dead in Christ. As an encouragement to "be sober," he highlights *hope*. This encouragement is his theme in verse 9.

B. Reason for Spiritual Alertness (v. 9, 10)

9. For God hath not appointed us to wrath, but to obtain salvation by our Lord Jesus Christ.

10. Who died for us, that, whether we wake or sleep, we should live together with him.

Paul began this section of instruction about the events of the Resurrection and the Lord's return by desire that the Thessalonian believers be not ignorant. He wanted them to know the information surrounding these events. Paul ends this section with the message of hope and salvation. This highlights the nature of the knowledge he wanted them to have. It was not just a group of facts but an event to be known by experience. The climax of knowing that experience was the hope and salvation available for the believer.

Paul wanted the believers to "be sober" (v. 8) "for (or because) God hath not appointed us to wrath" (v. 9). The second coming of Christ will not mean the wrath of God for the Christian. It will be a time of severe judgment and destruction for the unbeliever, but it will be a time of hope and salvation for the Christian. "In this hope, with faith and love, the believer is equipped with all necessary protection against the judgment to be unleashed on the Day of the Lord" (*Word Biblical Commentary, 1 & 2 Thessalonians* by F. F. Bruce, p. 112).

Contrary to wrath, at the Lord's return, God has appointed the believer to "obtain salvation." Two aspects of salvation are highlighted by the context of this passage. First, it is a salvation from the wrath of God. Second, it is a salvation to be present with the Lord in newness of life at His return to earth.

The salvation is made possible "by" or through Christ. Paul amplifies the work of Christ by referring to Christ giving His life. Christ's death made the resurrected life of the believer possible. And, not just life but life "together with him." The center of Paul's message in this passage has been twofold and it is climaxed in this verse. First, Christ's death makes newness of life with Him possible. Second, whether dead or alive at His return, all believers in Christ will rise to live together with him forever.

The message of the return of Christ is a message of which Christians must not be ignorant. Further, this message is not one which should be a source of discouragement for Christians. The believer needs to know about Christ's coming, anticipate His return, and use it as a source of hope and comfort.

REVIEW QUESTIONS

1. What terms does Paul use to describe the condition of those who are not prepared for Christ's return?

2. What admonition does Paul give the believer in light of the return of the Lord?

3. In what way does Paul amplify the admonition to be sober?

4. In what way does Paul climax this passage on the return of the Lord?

5. What did Christ do to make newness of life with Him possible?

GOLDEN TEXT HOMILY

"LOOKING FOR THAT BLESSED HOPE, AND THE GLORIOUS APPEARING OF THE GREAT GOD AND OUR SAVIOUR JESUS CHRIST" (Titus 2:13).

Among the words of consolation spoken by Jesus before leaving His disciples, was the promise that He would come again and receive them unto Himself (see John 14:3). Since these words were spoken time has sped noiselessly along; events of vast magnitude have rapidly succeeded each other and left their lessons for the ages to ponder; nations have endured suffering, war and revolution; generation after generation has gone down to the grave; for nearly two thousand years the church of the living God has been strained with intense and anxious expectancy; but still the promise remains unfulfilled.

The promise is unfulfilled; yet the church has not lost confidence in the powerful words of Christ. Faith in the Second Advent of Christ is still firmly held by born-again believers. Long waiting has sharpened the longing, brightened the hope, and clarified the vision. The church is looking for the soon return of the Lord of the church.

Paul the Apostle declares that the return of Christ is the "blessed hope" of the church. He uses the word *hope* not to indicate merely what is wished for but what is assured. This hope which is assured is the glorious appearing of our Lord and Saviour Jesus Christ.

Because we have this "hope" we can say no to ungodliness and worldly passions. We can live self-controlled, upright and godly lives in this present age. We can so live while we are waiting for the appearing of the Son of God.

When He comes, those who are waiting in faith will behold Him. His appearance will be one of glory and power. He will "come in his own glory, and in his Father's, and of the holy angels" (Luke 9:26). He will not only come in divine majesty; He will come to bestow this majesty on those who have believed in Him and who have looked for His return.
—Henry J. Smith, D.Min., Director of Academic Advising, Lee College, Cleveland, Tennessee

SENTENCE SERMONS

THE RESURRECTION OF CHIRST is God's assurance to believers of their future resurrection.
—Selected

THOSE WHO HAVE an eternal hope in Christ are not just whistling in the dark but walking in the light.
—Keith Huttenlocker

HOPE IS not wishful thinking but calm assurance.
—"Notes and Quotes"

OTHER MEN SEE only a hopeless end, but the Christian rejoices in an endless hope.
—Gilbert Beenken

EVANGELISTIC APPLICATION

THE PROMISE OF CHRIST'S RETURN SHOULD MOTIVATE PEOPLE TO PREPARE FOR HIS COMING.

The Bible is clear about the consequences for not being prepared when Christ returns. It will be a time of destruction and judgment. Those who are unprepared will face the wrath of God. The Bible does not argue or debate this point, it is a fact as sure as the second coming of Christ.

The coming of the Lord will be a deceptive time for the unprepared. This deception will not be the result of His coming. Rather, it will be a result of a person's unprepared heart. That person may be very concerned about their peace and safety. They may even be convinced they are safe and secure. However, they have deceived themselves and will miss the return of the Lord.

Preparing for the coming of the Lord's return should have ultimate priority in everyone's life. By believing in Christ's redeeming death and accepting Him as Savior, a person can make preparation for the return of Christ. The return of the Lord is a critical event, but it is not impossible to prepare for it. Making preparation a priority is imperative.

The coming of the Lord will mean blessing for those ready and alert for His coming. It will mean eternal life with Christ. It will mean salvation from destruction and God's wrath. The joys of the return of the Lord as well as the destruction to be avoided, are eternal motivations to be ready for Christ's return.

ILLUMINATING THE LESSON

A soldier lay wounded on the field of battle. When night had settled down, a flickering lantern came his way. He was unable to speak or to turn, but he heard the examining doctor say, "I believe if this fellow lives until sunrise tomorrow he will get well." As he lay with his head to the east, he waited and watched for dawn. After long hours that seemed eternity, the stars went out and the sky began to light up. He would live!

When the Son of God rises in your life, you will live too. In him we have our hope.

—"Notes and Quotes"

DAILY BIBLE READINGS

M. The Blessing of Forgiveness. Psalm 31:1-11

T. God's Strength Provided. Isaiah 40: 27-31

W. Vision of Christ's Glory. Daniel 7:9-14

T. Hope in the Resurrection. 1 Corinthians 15:12-20

F. Hope Anchors the Soul. Hebrews 6: 11-20

S. Faithfulness Rewarded. Revelation 19:6-16

INTRODUCTION
TO SUMMER
QUARTER

The lessons for the summer quarter (June, July, August) are presented under the theme, "The Christian in Today's World." As this theme suggests, the studies focus on matters and relationships the Christian faces in daily living. The studies range from that of sharing the Gospel message to that of personal holiness and selectivity in matters of entertainment.

Few, if any, individual is so isolated as to be void of the pressures of modern society and the realities of evil in the world. On the contrary, Christian persons must deal with many problems while retaining a personal fellowship with the Lord and carrying out effective witness by word and deed.

This series of lessons is certain to cause the conscientious Christian to take inventory of his personal life. They will also challenge the Bible student to a new awareness of the responsibilities the Christian has in society.

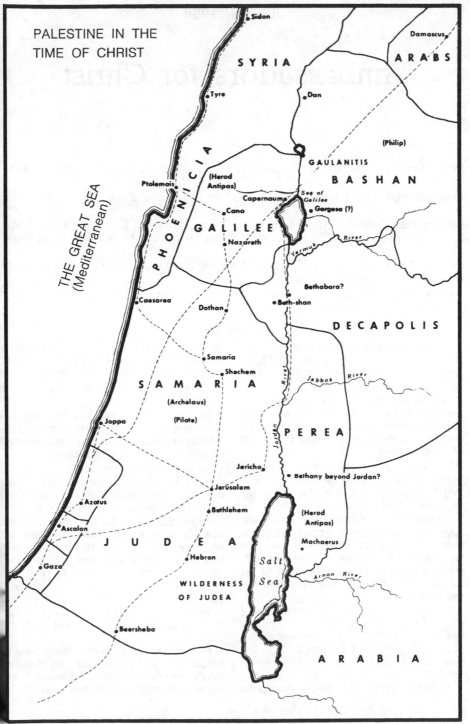

PALESTINE IN THE
TIME OF CHRIST

SYRIA

ARABS

Sidon

Damascus

Tyre

Dan

(Philip)

GAULANITIS

BASHAN

(Herod
Antipas)

Ptolemais

PHOENICIA

Capernaum

Sea of
Galilee

Cana

GALILEE

Gergesa (?)

River

Nazareth

Yarmuk

THE GREAT SEA
(Mediterranean)

Bethabara?

Caesarea

Dothan

Beth-shan

DECAPOLIS

Samaria

Jabbok

River

Shechem

S A M A R I A

River

(Archelaus)

(Pilate)

Jordan

P E R E A

Joppa

Jericho

Bethany beyond Jordan?

Jerusalem

Bethlehem

(Herod
Antipas)

Azotus

Machaerus

Ascalon

J U D E A

Salt

Hebron

Sea

Gaza

Arnon River

WILDERNESS
OF JUDEA

Beersheba

A R A B I A

Ambassadors for Christ

Study Text: John 16:32, 33; 2 Corinthians 5:18-20; Philippians 4:12, 13; Hebrews 12:1, 2; 1 Peter 2:21-24

Supplemental References: Matthew 10:1-8; Philippians 2:5-8; Colossians 3:12, 13

Golden Text: "We are ambassadors for Christ, as though God did beseech you by us: we pray you in Christ's stead, be ye reconciled to God" (2 Corinthians 5:20).

Central Truth: As Christians represent Christ in the world they are assured of His continual presence and strength.

Evangelistic Emphasis: Sin separates people from God, but through Christ sinners can be reconciled to God.

Printed Text

2 Corinthians 5:18. And all things are of God, who hath reconciled us to himself by Jesus Christ, and hath given to us the ministry of reconciliation;

19. To wit, that God was in Christ, reconciling the world unto himself, not imputing their trespasses unto them; and hath committed unto us the word of reconciliation.

20. Now then we are ambassadors for Christ, as though God did beseech you by us: we pray you in Christ's stead, be ye reconciled to God.

Hebrews 12:1. Wherefore seeing we also are compassed about with so great a cloud of witnesses, let us lay aside every weight, and the sin which doth so easily beset us, and let us run with patience the race that is set before us,

2. Looking unto Jesus the author and finisher of our faith; who for the joy that was set before him endured the cross, despising the shame, and is set down at the right hand of the throne of God.

1 Peter 2:21. For even hereunto

were ye called: because Christ also suffered for us, leaving us an example, that ye should follow his steps:

22. Who did no sin, neither was guile found in his mouth:

23. Who, when he was reviled, reviled not again; when he suffered, he threatened not; but committed himself to him that judgeth righteously:

24. Who his own self bare our sins in his own body on the tree, that we, being dead to sins, should live unto righteousness: by whose stripes ye were healed.

John 16:32. Behold, the hour cometh, yea, is now come, that ye shall be scattered, every man to his own, and shall leave me alone: and yet I am not alone, because the Father is with me.

33. These things I have spoken unto you, that in me ye might have peace. In the world ye shall have tribulation: but be of good cheer; I have overcome the world.

Philippians 4:12. I know both how to be abased, and I know how to abound: every where and in all things I am instructed both to be full and to be

hungry, both to abound and to suffer need.

13. I can do all things through Christ which strengtheneth me.

LESSON OUTLINE

I. COMMISSIONED BY CHRIST'S AUTHORITY
  A. The Basis of the Commission
  B. The Purpose of the Commission
  C. The Results of the Commission

II. LIVING BY CHRIST'S EXAMPLE
  A. The Fact of His Example
  B. The Focus of His Example

III. VICTORIOUS THROUGH CHRIST'S EXAMPLE
  A. The Basis for Victory
  B. The Results of Victory

LESSON EXPOSITION

INTRODUCTION

If one should ask what is the chief work of the Christian ministry, the answer is: God has sent us; we are ambassadors for Christ. God has given us our message, and that message is that He has reconciled the world unto Himself; and He sends us to pray and lead every one in the world whom we can reach to be reconciled to Him.

The word *ambassador* comes from a root word meaning "an elder or person of special dignity or rank." So it is with one chosen of God to proclaim the word of reconciliation. The ambassador's task, however, is that of being both a representative and a messenger. He does not speak for himself, but for the country he represents. His authority is derived from those he represents. The messages he communicates are not his own ideas, but those which he has been directed to speak.

I. COMMISSIONED BY CHRIST'S AUTHORITY (2 Corinthians 5:18-20)

A. The Basis of the Commission (v. 18)

18. And all things are of God, who hath reconciled us to himself by Jesus Christ, and hath given to us the ministry of reconciliation.

The basis or the foundation of the Christian's commission is found in the statement "all things are of God." Paul could have no conception of a Christian minister, except as a man who was sent to testify that all things were of God, and that He had, in Jesus Christ, reconciled us to Himself. The Christian must regard himself as receiving his authority and commission from God. No Jew could think that he held any office whatsoever except by God's appointment. If the priest had not been taught to consider himself as chosen and clothed by God for His service at the altar, he would have been the one exceptional man in the whole nation.

Paul continually asserts in his writings that he was an apostle neither of man nor by man. This is evidence of his conviction as far as he was concerned. The apostle never suggests that the difference between the Old and the New Testament is that one was appointed by God and the other was not. He never indicates that those who had the one might call themselves ministers of God, and that those who had the other might call themselves ministers of some society which had chosen them to hold offices on its behalf. What Paul does say is that the ministers of the Old Testament were, to a great extent, ministers of a letter written and carved in stone, and those of the New Testament are ministers of the Spirit. He suggests that the first are ministers of condemnation, and the second of righteousness; that the first are to exhibit the glory of God under a veil, and that the second are to present it openly, as revealed in Jesus Christ.

The Christian who leads another into the experience of reconciliation to God can never take credit for it. He has simply been God's instrument in bringing about this superb transformation. He could no more have done it than a gardener, who plants the seed and tends it, could change a single grain of corn into the perfected plant. God is the Lord of all harvests, spiritual as well as material.

B. The Purpose of the Commission (v. 19)

19. To wit, that God was in Christ, reconciling the world unto himself, not imputing their trespasses unto them; and hath committed unto us the word of reconciliation.

Every Christian is called to be God's agent, God's minister, and is truly, if he is faithful, a minister of the gospel. Although the wonderful change of conversion and regeneration is the work of the Holy Spirit, yet it is also true that in all of this God uses human agents. God uses many methods to effect a change in human nature. He might use a song, a verse read from Scripture, or a sermon. But a human agent must sing the song, read the Scripture, or preach the sermon. All of this is done to let people know that God was in Christ reconciling the world unto Himself. This is the sum of the Good News that Christians are to share throughout the world. It is the message of the Atonement; it is the very heart of Christianity. No one can be a Christian, let alone a Christian worker, without it.

For Paul's message to have meaning, it must be remembered that humanity is in some way separated from God. Man is in a state of estrangement. But the wonderful aspect of the apostle's statement is that God loved the world, even though it was dead in trespasses and sins. However, there is the implication that God's love, if it is to take effect in the highest sense, if it is to secure and accomplish the reconciling of the world, must be expressed and manifested in some form of supernatural interposition.

According to this verse, the preexisting love of God takes a positive form and is made manifest by a divine act. There are two reconciliations referred to by Paul. There is one which is accomplished by God, and there is another to be secured by man. The reconciliation on God's part was accomplished by His doing two things. Paul says, "For he hath made him to be sin for us, who knew no sin" (2 Corinthians 5:21); then, as the result of this, He did not impute to men their transgressions. The one thing became possible because of the other. In this reconciliation and return of God to the world,

a foundation is laid for the return to and reconciliation of man with God.

Christ's death for us and our humble acceptance of this atonement gave God the opportunity to forget our sins. It is this message that Paul insists has been given to the Christian. He emphasizes that God has committed unto the Christian the word of reconciliation. It is really a very practical process. Words must be spoken, the gospel must be presented in some way, and the word—written or spoken—must come from some human being. It is a great responsibility, but also a glorious privilege.

C. The Results of the Commission (v. 20)

20. Now then we are ambassadors for Christ, as though God did beseech you by us: we pray you in Christ's stead, be ye reconciled to God.

An ambassador is an officer of the highest rank in the diplomatic service. He represents the head of a sovereign state at the court or capital of another country. An ambassador is an honorable and responsible statesman.

In the Roman Empire there were two types of provinces. One was under the control of the Senate; the other was under the direct control of the Emperor. The peaceful provinces, not occupied by troops, were under the control of the Senate. Those provinces in which troops were stationed were under the control of the Emperor. The administrator of the province on behalf of the Emperor was called the legate. The Latin word stands for a man under direct commission from a superior. The Apostle Paul regarded his commission as coming direct from Christ. This should be true for every Christian.

As Christ's ambassador, the Christian is given a diplomatic mission. As Christ's representative, he is to seek men in behalf of Christ to be reconciled to God. This is why we are made ambassadors to do what was done by the great Ambassador, Jesus Christ. We are to present to men, not God's command threat, or condemnation, but God's entreaty. The Almighty condescends to beseech His creatures. There is no humility like God's.

It is not God's wish for His enmity to be emphasized, though God must be reconciled to men as well as men to God. But God's love, mercy, and free forgiveness are waiting, eager, and ready. God, in Christ, has come more than halfway. He would gladly go all the way if he could without cheapening the gift. He would gladly force His forgiveness on sinners, if that would do them any good. He has done all He can. The acceptance of the new birth awaits our movement toward God. This is the supreme opportunity which the ambassador must emphasize.

Jesus Christ voluntarily submitted to crucifixion for the personal salvation of every man. The most astonishing and challenging calling that could come to any man is the calling to be an ambassador, a representative of this Christ who gave Himself for us.

II. LIVING BY CHRIST'S EXAMPLE (Hebrews 12:1, 2; 1 Peter 2:21-24)

A. The Fact of the Example (Hebrews 12:1, 2)

1. Wherefore seeing we also are compassed about with so great a cloud of witnesses, let us lay aside every weight, and the sin which doth so easily beset us, and let us run with patience the race that is set before us,

2. Looking unto Jesus the author and finisher of our faith; who for the joy that was set before him endured the cross, despising the shame, and is set down at the right hand of the throne of God.

Many years are spent in preparation before one is able or ready to represent his country as an ambassador. In pursuit of his preparation he will find many role models to follow. This is also true for those who would be ambassadors for Christ.

Looking unto Jesus! How we need to know and to see the One who has gone before us. He is the One who knows the course and can guide and inspire. The goal often seems so distant and obscured by hurdles and obstacles that it is necessary to have an example, a coach with one and in front of one all the time.

Christianity proposes a prize which is worthy of all our efforts, which may well stand at the end of our life-race, and inspire the runners with a holy and boundless ambition. But to make our life a Christian race it is necessary that we run in the right path. In every race there is a prescribed course. It is not left to the runner to develop this for himself. He must keep to the course or he forfeits the very possibility of winning the prize. There are two characteristics by which we may know the Christian's way. The first is faith and the second is loving obedience.

The Christian race must be run in the right manner and spirit. The New Testament tells us that we must *so* run as to obtain (1 Corinthians 9:24). Everything depends on the manner and spirit in which we run—our comfort, progress, and success. We must strip ourselves of every unnecessary encumbrance. We must have concentration of purpose. We must run in a spirit of dependence upon God.

The author of Hebrews suggests that it is a great encouragement that we are running in the view of so many onlookers, all concerned for our progress, and deeply interested in our success. This was one of the inspiring aspects in the great athletic contests of ancient times. The runner was conscious that the eyes of his assembled countrymen were upon him. The nation was present to observe. The consciousness of this could not fail to be the inspiration of all. This widened the glory of victory and deepened the agony of defeat. Is it not the same in the Christian race? The witnesses here are the best and greatest that humanity has produced.

The cloud of witnesses is not the object on which the writer of Hebrews would have us fix our hearts. They testify of faith, and we cherish their memory with gratitude. We walk with a firmer step because of the music of their lives. Our eyes, however, are fixed, not on them, not on many, but on One; not on the army, but the Leader; not on the servants, but the Lord. We see Jesus only. It is from Him that we derive our true strength, even as He is the Light of our life. There are many witnesses, and yet Jesus is the only true and faithful witness. His example is the great motive of our obedience of faith.

As our example, Jesus walked by faith. He, who in the eternal counsel undertook our salvation in obedience to the Father's will, entered by His incarnation, on the path of faith. Herein is the power and efficacy of the obedience of Jesus; that it is the voluntary condescension and obedience of the Son of God; that it is a true and real obedience, submission, dependence, struggle, suffering; that it is the obedience of faith.

Jesus is the Author and Finisher of our faith—the only perfect, complete embodiment of faith. Jesus believed. Since without faith it is impossible to please God, and since Jesus always and perfectly pleased the Father; since faith is the very root and spirit of obedience, and Jesus was the servant of the Lord, who finished the God-given work, Jesus was perfect in faith. The whole realm of faith was traversed by Him. He ascended the whole scale, from the lowest to the highest step; He endured and He conquered all things.

Races are never won by looking back. Jesus is our man of faith, very man of very man. Faith for Him was seeing the end from the beginning and enduring as seeing Him who is invisible. He is our example and life is possible when we look to Jesus.

Looking unto Jesus gives us power to persevere in well-doing as ambassadors. He, unto whom we look, knew all things. He was able to reconcile discrepancies, and to solve mysteries which baffle our finite mind. The perpetuation of these difficulties may be, for the present, a part of our life. This does not matter if we have before us the example of One who, knowing the meaning of what to us is inscrutable, showed us how a Christian ought to work by working even to his own death.

B. Focus of the Example (1 Peter 2:21-24)

21. For even hereunto were ye called: because Christ also suffered for us, leaving us an example, that ye should follow his steps:

22. Who did no sin, neither was guile found in his mouth;

23. Who, when he was reviled, reviled not again; when he suffered, he threatened not; but committed himself to him that judgeth righteously:

24. Who his own self bare our sins in his own body on the tree, that we, being dead to sins, should live unto righteousness: by whose stripes ye were healed.

Peter declares that Christ left us an example of faultlessness. His own sense of this startles us. He never utters one word to God or to man which implies the consciousness of a single defect. Read the lives of the great servants of God in the Bible—Abraham, Moses, Samuel, David, Elijah, Peter, Paul. They all confess sin. They all humble themselves before men. They all ask for the mercy of God. Think of any great person whom you have ever known, or whose life you have read. He has feared God, loved God, worked for God through long years; yet he is aware of the inconsistencies and imperfections pervading his life. He is always ready to acknowledge his weakness and sin.

Jesus Christ reproaches Himself for nothing, confesses nothing, regrets nothing. He is certain of all that He says and does. His own words are: "I do always those things which please him [the Father]" (John 8:29). In this sinlessness He is, although our example, yet beyond our full reach of imitation. We cannot, in our human and broken life, reproduce the complete image of the immaculate Christ. The best of men knows that in his best moments he is bothered by motives, thoughts, inclinations, from which Christ was absolutely free. But this does not destroy—on the contrary, it enhances—the value of His ideal example. In all areas of thought and work the ideal is strictly speaking, by man unattainable. Yet we must never lose sight of the ideal. In the Gospels, ideal human life appears in a form of flesh and blood. It is the ideal, and, therefore, it is beyond us; yet it is not the less important as an example and guide to our efforts at being what God would have us to be.

One of the most important aspects of the example of Jesus is His simplicity. This feature runs through His whole character. In nothing that He says or does can we detect any trace of striving for effect. The number of men of whom anything remotely like this is true is very small. The effort to create an impression is the result sometimes of timidity, sometimes of insecurity, sometimes of pride, but it always impairs moral beauty, whether in speech or action.

Jesus always says what He has to say in the most natural and unpretending words. His sentences unfold themselves without effort just as persons and occasions demand. Every situation offers an opportunity, and He uses it. He attends a wedding; He cures a paralytic; He stoops to write upon the ground; He eats with a Pharisee; He raises a corpse to life; He washes the feet of His disciples, just as it comes, just as it is right from day to day, from hour to hour, from minute to minute. The most important and useful acts follow on with the most trivial and ordinary. There is no effort, no disturbing or pretentious movement. All is as simple as if all were commonplace. It is this absence of anything like an attempt to produce unusual impressions which reveals a soul possessed with a sense of the majesty and the power of truth. Depend upon it, to the degree to which any man becomes really great, he also becomes simple. This is what Christ is looking for in those who would become ambassadors in His work.

III. VICTORIOUS THROUGH CHRIST (John 16:32, 33; Philippians 4:12, 13)

A. The Basis for Victory (John 16:32, 33)

32. Behold, the hour cometh, yea, is now come, that ye shall be scattered, every man to his own, and shall leave me alone: and yet I am not alone, because the Father is with me.

33. These things have I spoken unto you, that in me ye might have peace. In the world ye shall have tribulation: but be of good cheer; I have overcome the world.

Jesus spoke these words to prepare His disciples for the pressure they were about to experience. It was said to humble them. They must realize that they could not depend upon themselves when the hour of Christ's sufferings should come. He used the word "Behold" to get their attention. He told them they would be scattered. Without the Shepherd they would be dispersed abroad. Each of the disciples would provide for his own safety and security. He knew that when the storm broke there would be shelter for all but Himself. The work of atonement would be performed alone, because He alone was qualified to do it.

It was gracious of Christ to say to His disciples, "And yet I am not alone, because the Father is with me." This was intended to comfort their heart. But the consciousness of the Father's presence was the stay of His own heart. It was the prophet Isaiah who said: "For the Lord God will help me; therefore shall I not be confounded; therefore have I set my face like a flint, and I know that I shall be not ashamed" (50:7). His disciples are often scattered from His presence, but He is not alone. He abides in what He is, and the Father is with Him.

After referring to the terrible hour that was approaching, Jesus offers a parting word of encouragement and victory. He was concerned about the disciples and reminds them they have peace in Him. He was thinking more of others than of Himself. Even though the bitter cross was near, He forgets His own grief in the grief of the disciples. He offered them the comfort of His own peace. Of course this peace can only be enjoyed by communion with Him. It is significant that even though He had referred to their forsaking Him; He would never forsake them.

What an assurance of victory is found in the words, "Be of good cheer; I have overcome the world." The world has a lot of influence and power, but it is not all-powerful. It has been in a battle and has been defeated. One greater than the world has conquered it. It has been said that Noah condemned the world, but Christ conquered it.

So Christ says to the ambassador in His work, "Take courage, I have overcome the world." Therefore the storms of trial and persecution that beat fiercely upon the Christian can be used to drive him closer to Christ.

B. The Results of Victory (Philippians 4:12, 13)

12. I know both how to be abased, and I know how to abound: everywhere and in all things I am instructed both to be full and to be hungry, both to abound and to suffer need.

13. I can do all things through Christ which strengtheneth me.

It has been well said that Christian contentment is not a narrowing down of our desires to our poor possessions, but a consciousness of infinite wealth in Christ, in whose hands are all things already working for His servants, moment by moment, to their highest good. The person who has this consciousness is independent of his environment.

It is interesting that for most of us it requires more effort to learn how to be prosperous and not puffed up by it than to be debased and not crushed by it. Paul had learned this and the ambassadors of Christ must also learn this.

Paul makes an assertion of virtual omnipotence when he states, "I can do all things," but he immediately introduces the source of his strength with the words, "through Christ who strengthens me." The apostle is suggesting that he can do whatever lies in the line of duty and necessity. From the inward union with Christ is derived the strength to do all things Paul has to do. It was the power of Christ within him that gave him spiritual contentment.

Paul was assured that all things were possible to him. He felt equal to all the labor and toil which duty could ever involve. He felt equal to all the suffering which could become his as an ambassador for Christ. Not as a Jew, not as a child of Abraham, not as a disciple of Moses, but as a Christian, Paul said, "I can do all things through Christ which strengtheneth me."

The ambassador of Christ has been initiated into the great mystery of contentment. He knows how to reconcile himself to every extreme, how to conduct himself in plenty and in need, in abundance and in hunger. He knows that success comes in cans.

REVIEW QUESTIONS

1. What is said about God's relationship to Christ in the act of reconciliation?

2. Define reconciliation.

3. According to the figure used in Hebrews 12:1 to illustrate the Christian life, where will Christians find their biggest hinderances in living for Christ?

4. In what way does Peter indicate that patient enduring of suffering is an aspect of holy living (2:21)?

5. Relate Philippians 4:13 to 4:19. What lessons do you learn?

GOLDEN TEXT HOMILY

"WE ARE AMBASSADORS FOR CHRIST, AS THOUGH GOD DID BESEECH YOU BY US: WE PRAY YOU IN CHRIST'S STEAD, BE YE RECONCILED TO GOD" (2 Corinthians 5:20).

Weeping seems to be a condition common to those concerned with the spiritual welfare of others.

The psalmist said, "He that goeth forth and weepeth . . . shall doubtless come again with rejoicing, bringing his sheaves with him" (126:6). Jeremiah said, in reference to the sin of Israel, "Oh that my head were waters and mine eyes a fountain of tears" (9:1). I can imagine the agony in our Lord's voice as He looked over the Temple City just days before His death and said, "O Jerusalem . . . how often would I have gathered thy children together, even as a hen gathereth her chickens under her wings, and ye would not!" (Matthew 23:37).

When Paul expressed himself to the Corinthians, there is this same unmistakable intensity about eternal matters.

Notice the words "as though God did beseech you by us" and "we pray you in Christ's stead." These are phrases that reveal the tremendous personal investment Paul felt in the conversion and discipling of these people. What for some may have been the business of religion was for Paul a passion of eternal proportion. And its effect depended on his witness.

That must be why he chose to illustrate his position with the word *ambassador*. This is is one who is fully aware of the issues involved, intimately acquainted with the one he represents, and invested with the authority to complete a contract.

So we, too, are called to invest ourselves completely in interceding with souls who need to enter into fellowship with God. And we may find ourselves weeping.
—**Calvin L. Eastham, Chaplain, First Calvary Division, Killeen, Texas**

SENTENCE SERMONS

AS CHRISTIANS represent Christ in the world they are assured of His continual presence and strength.
—**Selected**

THE CHURCH is a workshop, not a dormitory; and every Christian man and woman is bound to help in the common cause.
—**Alexander MacLaren**

IT IS NOT the possession of extraordinary gifts that makes extraordinary usefulness, but the dedication of what we have to the service of God.
—**Fredrick W. Robertson**

IF YOU WISH to be a leader you will be frustrated, for few people wish to be led. If you aim to be a servant you will never be frustrated.
—**Frank W. Warren**

EVANGELISTIC APPLICATION

SIN SEPARATES PEOPLE FROM GOD, BUT THROUGH CHRIST SINNERS CAN BE RECONCILED TO GOD.

An ambassador for a civil government has to be prepared to serve his country in a variety of ways to accomplish the overall goal of representing that country. The goal of the Christian ambassador is to represent his Christ. This too must be done in a variety of ways. The simple, lovely prayer of Francis of Assisi illustrates this so well:

Lord, make me an instrument of Thy peace:

Where there is hatred, let me sow love.

Where there is injury, let me sow pardon.

Where there is doubt, let me sow faith.

Where there is despair, let me sow hope.

Where there is darkness, let me sow light.

Where there is sadness, let me sow joy.

ILLUMINATING THE LESSON

An ambassador of a country often has to deal with some very difficult people in the pursuit of his responsibilities. So does the ambassador of Christ. So did the Apostle Paul. The secret of his ability to do this was his unfailing love for people. The victory of love in Paul can become the victory of love in us. With the love of unfailing goodwill, we can love that difficult person. We can love that hard-to-love person.

The story is told of a young man from a wealthy family who became a Christian. The rest of the family, bitterly opposed to Christianity, said, "We will take away your share in the inheritance." Completely unembittered, he let them do it. But soon they were quarreling among themselves over his share. Finally, in order to break the deadlock, they ask him to step in as mediator, since he was the only one that all of them could trust. There he sat, arbitrating the distribution of property, stolen from him. Most of us would have said, "I can't, and I won't." Not he. With a heart saturated with Calvary-love he said, "I can"—and he did.

DAILY BIBLE READINGS

M. Confidence in God. Psalm 27:1-14

T. Called by God. Isaiah 6:1-8

W. Proclaiming God's Message. Ezekiel 33:7-16

T. Christ's Witnesses. Luke 24:36-48

F. Fruitful Believers. John 15:1-8

S. Song of Victory. Revelation 15:2-4

Honoring God in the Home

Study Text: Deuteronomy 31:11-13; Joshua 24:14, 15; Psalm 91:9-12; Proverbs 3:32, 33; Acts 10:1-4; 2 Timothy 3:14, 15

Supplemental References: Job 1:1-5; Luke 1:5, 6, 57-64; Acts 16:32-34

Golden Text: "As for me and my house, we will serve the Lord" (Joshua 24:15).

Central Truth: God's blessing and protection are promised to the home where He is honored.

Evangelistic Emphasis: Families who honor the Lord give a strong witness to their community.

Printed Text

Joshua 24:14. Now therefore fear the Lord, and serve him in sincerity and in truth: and put away the gods which your fathers served on the other side of the flood, and in Egypt; and serve ye the Lord.

15. And if it seem evil unto you to serve the Lord, choose you this day whom ye will serve; whether the gods which your fathers served that were on the other side of the flood, or the gods of the Amorites, in whose land ye dwell: but as for me and my house, we will serve the Lord.

Deuteronomy 31:11. When all Israel is come to appear before the Lord thy God in the place which he shall choose, thou shalt read this law before all Israel in their hearing.

12. Gather the people together, men, and women, and children, and thy stranger that is within thy gates, that they may hear, and that they may learn, and fear the Lord your God, and observe to do all the words of this law:

13. And that their children, which have not known any thing, may hear, and learn to fear the Lord your God, as long as ye live in the land whither ye go over Jordan to possess it.

2 Timothy 3:14. But continue thou in the things which thou hast learned and hast been assured of, knowing of whom thou hast learned them;

15. And that from a child thou hast known the holy scriptures, which are able to make thee wise unto salvation through faith which is in Christ Jesus.

Psalm 91:9. Because thou hast made the Lord, which is my refuge, even the most High, thy habitation;

10. There shall no evil befall thee, neither shall any plague come nigh thy dwelling.

11. For he shall give his angels charge over thee, to keep thee in all thy ways.

12. They shall bear thee up in their hands, lest thou dash thy foot against a stone.

Proverbs 3:32. For the froward is abomination to the Lord: but his secret is with the righteous.

33. The curse of the Lord is in the house of the wicked: but he blesseth the habitation of the just.

LESSON OUTLINE

I. COMMITTED TO THE LORD
   A. A Noble Appeal
   B. A Noble Example
II. GUIDED BY THE WORD
   A. The Importance of the Word
   B. The Power of the Word
III. ASSURED OF GOD'S CARE
   A. The Attending Angels
   B. The Security of Wisdom

LESSON EXPOSITION

INTRODUCTION

No human interaction has greater impact on our life than our family experience. Early family experience determines our adult character structure. It influences the perception we have of ourselves, how we see others and feel about them. It has a great bearing on our concept of right and wrong. Our capacity to establish the close, warm, sustained relationships necessary to have a family of our own is derived to a great extent from the family. Our attitude toward authority and toward the Ultimate Authority in our life, and the way we attempt to make sense out of our existence comes basically from the family.

Many social scientists have been warning for years that the family is disintegrating and they are predicting that it will not survive this century. Some writers have criticized the family and stated that this process of disintegration ought to be encouraged. One British physician suggested doing away with the family because it is a primary conditioning device for Western, imperialistic world views. An American writer states that the family must go because it oppresses and enslaves women. This idea is reflected in women's liberation literature.

Will the American family cease to exist? Most Christians do not seem to think so. A larger percentage of Americans marry today, have children, and commit themselves to living in a family household than ever before. But Christians do, however, have serious cause for concern— not that the family will disappear, but that certain trends prevalent in today's society will incapacitate the family, destroy its integrity, and cause its members to suffer crippling emotional conflicts in such a way that they will become an intolerable burden to society.

I. COMMITTED TO THE LORD (Joshua 24:14, 15; Acts 10:1-4)

A. A Nobel Appeal (Joshua 24:14, 15)

14. Now therefore fear the Lord, and serve him in sincerity and in truth: and put away the gods which your fathers served on the other side of the flood, and in Egypt; and serve ye the Lord.

15. And if it seem evil unto you to serve the Lord, choose you this day whom ye will serve; whether the gods which your fathers served that were on the other side of the flood, or the gods of the Amorites, in whose land ye dwell: but as for me and my house, we will serve the Lord.

The most important decision that any person can ever make is to become a servant of the Lord. Such a commitment cannot be dissolved even by death. It is entered into for eternity. However, there are times when it is necessary for us to think about the commitment and to renew our loyalty and fidelity to Jehovah. Joshua provides us with an example of the earnestness with which we should do this.

Once more Joshua reminds the people of their true character as the chosen people of God. He is now able to present facts as evidence of the truth which had once been matters of faith. He is able now to point to what God has done. He can now call the people themselves to verify that all the promises of God have come to pass. The evidence is there that not one good thing that God has promised has failed.

This man in his old age found nothing to retract of what he had believed or said concerning God and the people, and the relation of the one to the other.

Joshua implores the people to guard against backsliding. He tells them to go on as they had begun and God will bless them. But if they turn back from serving the Lord, shame, misery, and damnation will be the result. The great leader is declaring that, in case of the Israelites going back from their exalted position as the people of God, God would punish them as severely as He had in the past blessed them bounteously. The possession of the land had been the reward of obedience; the loss of the land would be the punishment for disobedience.

Note the brave and faithful words of Joshua: "As for me and my house, we will serve the Lord." This is the appeal of a brave and faithful man. These words express a great and high purpose. But they also remind us of an important fact—the home is infinitely important. They tell us that serving God as a family is important. They reveal to us the family as what in truth it is and what God designed it should be—the home and citadel of religious faith in the heart of the nation.

God has always had His great work for individuals to do. He brought Moses upon the mount to take the Law down. He sent Paul out to preach the gospel. He called Augustine to defend it, Luther to reform it, and Wesley to revive it. But more important than all this, deeper than all this, though more hidden than all this, is the task God has committed to every believing household upon earth. It is the task of taking the seed that these great sowers of the Word have sown and cherishing it beneath the tender, gracious, and mighty influence of home. Such is God's will and God's purpose for the preservation of His Word. The family is the safe hiding place and the true nursery for God's Word. It should be guarded so that none can invade or desecrate.

B. A Noble Example (Acts 10:1-4)

1. There was a certain man in Caesarea called Cornelius, a centurion of the band called the Italian band,

2. A devout man, and one that feared God with all his house, which gave much alms to the people, and prayed to God alway.

3. He saw in a vision evidently about the ninth hour of the day an angel of God coming in to him, and saying unto him, Cornelius.

4. And when he looked on him, he was afraid, and said, What is it, Lord? And he said unto him, Thy prayers and thine alms are come up for a memorial before God.

Cornelius was a familiar and honorable name in Latin. It was the name of a distinguished Roman family. A centurion was, strictly speaking, the commander of a hundred men; but the title was applied, with some degree of latitude, to those who led the subdivisions of a legion. It was called an Italian band because it was probably composed of Romans.

Luke describes the character and previous religious history of Cornelius in verse two. He was a devout man. This means he was pious and reverent, not merely in the heathen sense, but as the fruit of divine grace. He feared God. This indicates the one true God, as opposed to the many gods of heathenism. He involved his whole household in the service of God. He was the teacher and example of all those dependent on him. He gave much alms. This suggests that he practiced many charities, not merely to the poor in general, but to the people of God, among whom he lived and from whom he had learned the true religion. His religion included praying to God. He asked of God, or looked to Jehovah, or the God of Israel, and not to idols, for the supply of his necessities in general, and for spiritual guidance in particular.

This is not the description of a proselyte, in any technical or formal sense, but of a Gentile whom divine grace had prepared for the immediate reception of the gospel, without passing through the intermediate state of Judaism, although long familiar with it, and indebted to it for such knowledge of the Word of God as he possessed.

This is a remarkable picture of a little household governed by a godly man outside of Hebraism. It is a remarkable testimony for a man to have. He prayed to God, worshiped God, honored and respected God with all his household. He kept his children in line, so that when the time came to honor God, they took part in the worship.

God had taken note of the sincerity of

Cornelius, and the way he prayed. He had taken note of the way in which he (Cornelius) gave to the poor. Now God was ready to reward his devoutness, piety, and acts of charity. There were other things waiting for Cornelius and his family. A larger life was opening its doors to him.

What a contrast between Cornelius in the Book of Acts and Eli in the Old Testament. Cornelius showed concern for his family and took the time to worship with them. Eli was preoccupied with his profession and apparently paid little attention to the needs of his family. Eli was too busy being a priest and a judge to do anything significant to meet many of his family's most important needs. Where was he in his sons' formative years? Why wasn't he there to see their cynicism when it arose? A child reveals his heart by his actions and by his words. The parents who have sensitive, open eyes will witness signs of defiance in their children very early and will begin to deal with it then. But even though Eli was sensitive enough to know when God was speaking to Samuel, he failed to pick up on the rebellion of his own children against the things of God. He was preoccupied with his work, and his family paid the price for it.

II. GUIDED BY THE WORD (Deuteronomy 31:11-13; 2 Timothy 3:14, 15)

A. The Importance of the Word (Deuteronomy 31:11-13)

11. When all Israel is come to appear before the Lord thy God in the place which he shall choose, thou shalt read this law before all Israel in their hearing.

12. Gather the people together, men, and women, and children, and thy stranger that is within thy gates, that they may hear, and that they may learn, and fear the Lord your God, and observe to do all the words of this law:

13. And that their children, which have not known any thing, may hear, and learn to fear the Lord your God, as long as ye live in the land whither ye go over Jordan to possess it.

Moses felt the Word of God was impor-

tant in the life of Israel. This is evidenced by the fact that he entrusted it to a special group, the priests, and placed it in the ark of the covenant for security reasons. But just having God's redemptive law was not sufficient, he required that it be read publicly to Israel periodically. By this method the people could be reminded with a fresh new force of the things of God. This could help them gain a greater understanding and appreciation for the Word of God.

It is important to note that God's Word was to be brought to all the people. It is especially significant that He included the children. As He has abundantly provided for their physical and mental needs during the long period of dependence upon adults, so He provides for their spiritual and moral needs through His Word.

The importance of the Bible can be seen for what it is. It is a divine revelation from God to man; a revelation of the fatherly heart of the eternal God himself, a revelation of man—his fall and recovery through the Lord Jesus Christ. It is a revelation of the highest ideals possible in life. It calls for the highest ethical conduct. The Bible is the greatest and most complete code of laws ever published. It is the book of wisdom, making the foolish wise; the book of divinity unexcelled; the greatest book of biography ever published; the best covenant ever executed, and the best testament ever signed. It is the youth's best instructor and companion. It is the learned man's masterpiece, the ignorant man's dictionary.

One could hardly conceive of a spiritual awakening without a Bible. Certainly we could not conceive of a Christian country without a Bible. If we would become Christian and remain Christian, we must have the Word of God. The Bible has been back of all civilizing and reviving movements and it is the only thing that can sustain them.

An unknown writer has paid this tribute to the Bible: This Book contains the mind of God, the state of man, the way of salvation, the reward of saints, and the doom of sinners. Its histories are true, its doctrines holy, and its precepts binding. It contains light to direct you, food to support you, and comfort to cheer you. It is the traveler's map, the pilgrim's staff, the pilot's compass, the soldier's sword, and the Christian's charter. It is a river of pleasure, a mine of wealth, and a paradise of glory. It is given you in life, will be open at the judgment, and will be remembered forever. Read it to be wise, believe it to be safe, and practice it to be holy. It is the book of culture, the book of ethics, the book of the philosophy of the plan of God, especially in redemption and the way of salvation. It is the Book eternal.

B. The Power of the Word (2 Timothy 3:14, 15)

14. But continue thou in the things which thou hast learned and hast been assured of, knowing of whom thou hast learned them;

15. And that from a child thou hast know the holy scriptures, which are able to make thee wise unto salvation through faith which is in Christ Jesus.

Paul has been talking about deceivers in the church. Now he turns directly to Timothy with a personal word and appeal. The words "but . . . thou" sets Timothy apart from the deceivers. The apostle suggests that Timothy will find the power to stand true to God through his experience with the Scriptures. It will help Timothy to remember Paul's heroic sufferings. It will undergird Timothy's endurance to realize that suffering is the lot of all believers. But the ultimate source of his power to stand firm must be found in the Word of God. Paul reminds him of his past experience with the Word and also the nature and function of that Word.

It is Paul's firm conviction that the continual degradation of the self-willed deceivers, referred to earlier, makes it imperative that Timothy adhere firmly to the divine truths which he has accepted. The words of the apostle are: "Abide thou in the things which thou hast learned and hast been assured of." This abiding must be constant. He must remain in these things and not turn away from them like the false teachers.

The apostle does not intend to prohibit young Timothy's moral, spiritual, or intellectual progress. But all true progress must be within, not away from, the divine fundamentals of the Christian gospel.

Timothy had learned and been assured of the sacred truths to which the apostle referred. Greek scholars say that the phrase "hast been assured of" means "has been firmly persuaded of" and points to that inner conviction concerning the truth and reality of the truth which has come to him. This kind of assurance produces stability. Moral steadfastness is never fostered by doubts and uncertainties concerning the Word of God.

Paul reminds Timothy of the teachers from whom he had learned Christian truth. He had been a most fortunate young man. He not only had Paul to share with him gospel truths, but his esteemed mother and grandmother shared the truth with him. His knowledge of the truth had not come from unknown or suspicious sources. His sources were reliable and dependable. Teaching content is very important, but so also is the character of the teacher. The reliability of the things he has learned is assured by his personal knowledge of the teachers.

The knowledge of divine things which Timothy possessed was not derived merely from human sources, however esteemed and trustworthy. He had the great advantage of a consistent training in the Scriptures from early childhood. The words "from a babe" point to the very early age at which his instruction in the Scriptures began. In Jewish families, children were taught to memorize passages from the Old Testament as soon as they could speak.

The Word of God was the ultimate source and authority for Timothy's religious faith. The phrase "hast known" suggests continuous action. The idea is that his knowledge, begun in early childhood, continues to the time that Paul was addressing him. In fact, Timothy could probably not remember a time in his life when he did not know the sacred writings, and he had continued to know them better and better.

Paul meant the recognized Hebrew Scriptures when he used the term "sacred writings." He was not referring merely to religious literature in general. The word "sacred" emphasizes the esteem and veneration in which the Hebrew Scriptures were held by the Jews and the early Christian Church. This was the source from which Timothy had received his knowledge of divine truth.

According to Paul, there is value in knowing the holy scriptures. They can do what no secular writings can do, namely, "make thee wise unto salvation." The phrase "which are able" emphasizes the continuous and abiding power resident in these writings. What they did for Timothy they continue to do today. They enlighten and instruct those instructed therein. The Word of God has an abiding power on the human heart.

Paul does not mean to suggest that there is a magical power in the Scriptures which guarantees salvation to those knowing their contents. He means that the truths of Scripture present to the human mind the true objects of faith. They are the medium through which the Holy Spirit performs His renewing, saving function. This process requires that there be a personal appropriation through faith on the part of the believer. This is indicated by Paul's words "through faith which is in Christ Jesus." The Scriptures reveal that saving faith centers in and rests upon faith in Christ. The means through which salvation as found in the Word of God is grasped is faith. This faith in Christ is the bridge which spans the gulf of sin and unites the Old and New Testaments. All the Scriptures must be studied in the light of the revelation which was made in Jesus Christ.

III. ASSURED OF GOD'S CARE (Psalm 91:9-12; Proverbs 3:32, 33)

A. The Attending Angels (Psalm 91:9-12)

9. Because thou has made the Lord, which is my refuge, even the most High, thy habitation;

10. There shall no evil befall thee, neither shall any plague come nigh thy dwelling.

11. For he shall give his angels charge over thee, to keep thee in all thy ways.

12. They shall bear thee up in their hands, lest thou dash thy foot against a stone.

The fact of the existence of angels is well established as shown by the teaching of the Old Testament which is unquestionable and clear. It is also substantiated by the teaching of the New Testament. So much is said in the Scriptures of good and evil angels, and such important functions are ascribed to the good angels, both in the providence of God over the world, and especially in the experience of His people and of His church, that what the Bible says concerning them should not be overlooked.

In this psalm the writer refers to angels as attending God's people. In the first section of this psalm, "He that dwelleth" is viewed objectively in some instances in the third person, in others in the second person as though God were speaking. In this portion of the Psalm, God is addressed in the second person when the psalmist regards himself as one who dwells. He addresses God in the third person when he speaks to a fellow believer.

The writer of the psalm declares that he is not alone. He can call God "my refuge," and at the same time know that to his friend this same God is "thy habitation." Now he testifies to his friend what he learned directly from God. He, too, can have security in God though evil and affliction assail him. God is so concerned that He sends angels to protect His own.

"He shall give his angels charge." In these words the restful spirit of absolute trust in God rises to its loftiest height. It is a glorious statement of what God does for His own. It reveals how close God is to the soul that trusts in Him.

The psalmist refers to angels as "his angels." This shows a close, happy, exalted relation to God. It indicates a relationship of nearness, love, and service.

The mighty power of angels are willingly and obediently exercised in ministering to the welfare of God's children. Their power is inconceivably great. One angel was able to destroy Sodom and the other guilty cities. The same angel gently, though firmly, led Lot out. One angel smote the firstborn in Egypt. One angel delivered Peter from prison.

The implication of the psalmist is minute as well as mighty. One false step may be fatal; but "he shall give his angels charge over thee." We are to recognize in the writer's words our Father's care. "He shall give his angels charge." All their power, wisdom, care, and love flow from God as their Source. His care and love are over each one of His children every moment, dispatched through angels. "Over thee to keep thee." What care, comfort, and consolation.

B. The Security That Wisdom Brings (Proverbs 3:32, 33)

32. For the froward is abomination to the Lord: but his secret is with the righteous.

33. The curse of the Lord is in the house of the wicked: but he blesseth the habitation of the just.

The wise man in these verses contrasts the way of the man of violence, the perverse, the house of the wicked with the way of the Lord, which is the way of the upright, the righteous, and the lowly. The curse of Jehovah is upon those who refuse the way of the Lord, but those who walk in His way experience His friendship. The word "friendship" here comes from a Hebrew word which means "council, intimate circle of friends, intimacy, and familiar conversation." Those who accept God's friendship receive His blessing and His grace. Those who choose against the Lord only heighten their shame. While those who choose the way of the Lord shall inherit His glory.

What greater joy can there be than to enjoy the friendship of discerning minds? But to live on such terms with God is the privilege of the true soul. This is indescribable.

REVIEW QUESTIONS

1. What conclusions can you draw about Joshua from verse 15?

2. How would you describe the character of Cornelius?

3. What specific charge was given to the priests and elders in Deuteronomy 31:11-13?

4. What was the importance of reading the law to the people at periodical intervals?

5. According to 2 Timothy 3:14, 15 what will the Scriptures do for us?

GOLDEN TEXT HOMILY

"AS FOR ME AND MY HOUSE, WE WILL SERVE THE LORD" (Joshua 24:15).

Instability, insecurity, and low morals secretly plague millions of Christian and non-Christian homes in today's world. In every generation since the beginning, the devil has sought to weaken and destroy the home. If he can destroy the home, he can deceive the next generation into dishonoring God. "As the whirlwind passeth, so is the wicked no more: but the righteous is an everlasting foundation" (Proverbs 10:25). "The fear of the Lord prolongeth days: but the years of the wicked shall be shortened" (Proverbs 10:27). So is the strength of any family, community or nation. When there is a loss of power within the church, it can always be traced back to the neglect of honoring God in the homes of those who are the leaders of that church.

Joshua knew that if the leaders in these homes did not make this commitment as individuals that Israel would be only a short-lived nation in the land of Canaan. He knew that no power can depend on past victories, relationships, charms, or forms to give victory today. We can brag and boast about past leaders and their contributions to the cause of Christ but what will count in this world today will be those who are willing to accept the responsibility TODAY to choose as Joshua did.

As Joshua set the example for the Israelites, Christ has set the supreme example for us. The Christian in today's world is faced with a greater challenge to follow this example more than ever before.

If we are to remain a Christian nation we must proclaim as Joshua did: "As for me and my house, we will serve the Lord" (Joshua 24:15).—**Aaron D. Mize, Clinical Chaplain, Alcohol and Drug Treatment Center, Parchman, Mississippi**

SENTENCE SERMONS

GOD'S BLESSING and protection are promised to the home where He is honored.

—**Selected**

THE DUTIES of home are discipline for the ministries of heaven.

—**Anonymous**

THE BEAUTY of the home is order;
The blessing of the home is contentment;
The glory of the home is hospitality;
The crown of the home is godliness.

—**Fireplace motto**

THE HOME is a lighthouse which has the lamp of God on the table and the light of Christ in the window, to give guidance to those who walk in darkness.

—**Henry Rische**

EVANGELISTIC APPLICATION

FAMILIES WHO HONOR THE LORD GIVE A STRONG WITNESS TO THEIR COMMUNITY.

More than any other influence, the family determines the lifelong direction in which a person is going to develop. Although the most dramatic evidence of this influence is discernible in childhood, the family places its mark on every sphere of a person's experience. Like the watermark on stationary, every page of one's personal story is written against the background of his family. The Christian home has a strong influence on leading children to receive Christ as Savior.

Obviously before parents can provide Christian training for their children, they must know the Lord themselves. Win children to the Lord and you may or may not lead parents to Him. But lead parents to Christ and they will automatically become concerned about the salvation of their children.

ILLUMINATING THE LESSON

The Christian family needs to constantly review its internal strengths and resources so that each member can function with his or her full potential. Every one of us have hurts, fears, and anxieties. A Christian family should help each other over these valley experiences with encouragement and tools at hand. The very presence of one's family speaks louder than many words.

The family can be a stabilizing and strengthening factor in each of our lives. When we help one another over the rough spots we form a circle around and across which God's love flows. The schedules we keep, the tomorrows we plan, and the successes we achieve happen because of, not in spite, our family circle. In such a group every person counts, from the newborn infants to the great-grandparents. Each is special in the sight of God and each should minister to others in the family.

DAILY BIBLE READINGS

M. Teaching God's Law. Deuteronomy 6:1-9

T. Choosing to Serve God. Ruth 1:6-18

W. Security of the Godly. Psalm 112:1-10

T. God's Providence. Matthew 6:25-34

F. Welcoming Christ in the Home. Luke 10:38-42

S. Obeying the Word. James 1:19-25

Confronting Evil

Study Text: Ephesians 6:11-13; 1 Timothy 4:1, 2; 2 Timothy 3:1-8; 1 Peter 1:3-9; 5:8, 9; Jude 24, 25

Supplemental References: Daniel 12:10; 2 Timothy 4:3, 4; 2 Peter 3:3-9

Golden Text: "Take unto you the whole armour of God, that ye may be able to withstand in the evil day" (Ephesians 6:13).

Central Truth: Believers must be alert to spiritual danger while trusting the Lord to keep them by His power.

Evangelistic Emphasis: Christ can save us from sin and give us victory over evil.

Printed Text

2 Timothy 3:1. This know also, that in the last days perilous times shall come.

2. For men shall be lovers of their own selves, covetous, boasters, proud, blasphemers, disobedient to parents, unthankful, unholy,

3. Without natural affection, trucebreakers, false accusers, incontinent, fierce, despisers of those that are good,

4. Traitors, heady, highminded, lovers of pleasures more than lovers of God;

5. Having a form of godliness, but denying the power thereof: from such turn away.

Ephesians 6:11. Put on the whole armour of God, that ye may be able to stand against the wiles of the devil.

12. For we wrestle not against flesh and blood, but against principalities, against powers, against the rulers of the darkness of this world, against spiritual wickedness in high places.

13. Wherefore take unto you the whole armour of God, that ye may be able to withstand in the evil day, and having done all, to stand.

1 Peter 1:3. Blessed be the God and Father of our Lord Jesus Christ, which according to his abundant mercy hath begotten us again unto a lively hope by the resurrection of Jesus Christ from the dead,

4. To an inheritance incorruptible, and undefiled, and that fadeth not away, reserved in heaven for you,

5. Who are kept by the power of God through faith unto salvation ready to be revealed in the last time.

6. Wherein ye greatly rejoice, though now for a season, if need be, ye are in heaviness through manifold temptations:

7. That the trial of your faith, being much more precious than of gold that perisheth, though it be tried with fire, might be found unto praise and honour and glory at the appearing of Jesus Christ:

8. Whom having not seen, ye love; in whom, though now ye see him not, yet believing, ye rejoice with joy unspeakable and full of glory:

9. Receiving the end of your faith, even the salvation of your souls.

LESSON OUTLINE

I. FOREWARNED BY THE SPIRIT
   A. Impending Danger
   B. Characteristics of the Danger
II. RESISTING THE DEVIL
   A. The Fight
   B. The Adversary
III. KEPT BY GOD'S POWER
   A. The Hope
   B. The Presentation

LESSON EXPOSITION

INTRODUCTION

The Christian is in battle. He is in a battle with evil. It is a battle we win, but we win not by escape. There is no escape. The struggle will never cease this side of heaven. It is here now, as we all know, and we must accept this struggle to the very end. In the world we shall have tribulation. While we are in the world there is absolutely no way of averting or avoiding the conflict. This may be discouraging to some, but Jesus said "be of good cheer; I have overcome the world" (John 16:33). We, too, in Him, and by following His instruction, may also overcome.

We are to be strong in the Lord. We are to be mighty in Jesus Christ. We are to be powerful in God. There is victory for us against every opposing force and foe. It is worth our serious consideration to know how, and only how, we may be made strong for the most strenuous struggle that has ever been known.

Equipment is provided. The Bible introduces us to the Divine Armory. The Lord displays the most wonderful protection for the complete person. He demonstrates to us how we may become invincible, unconquerable. It is all in Jesus Christ.

God is offering the protection of heaven to His followers. If we will only accept what God puts at our disposal, we are assured of triumph in all circumstances and in every situation along the way. We are assured of being able to stand against the wiles of the devil and not only to stand, but also to withstand. What a thrill to know that we can live in the world against the greatest odds, in a world filled with the most fearful foes and yet be more than conquerors.

I. FOREWARNED BY THE SPIRIT (1 Timothy 4:1, 2; 2 Timothy 3:1-8)

A. Impending Danger (1 Timothy 4:1, 2)

1. Now the Spirit speaketh expressly, that in the latter times some shall depart from the faith, giving heed to seducing spirits, and doctrines of devils;

2. Speaking lies in hypocrisy; having their conscience seared with a hot iron.

The Apostle Paul, in the beginning of this chapter, is introducing a contrast between the mystery of redemption that he has been dealing with (which is the basis of the Christian faith) and the falling away from the faith which the Spirit said was coming.

Paul wanted Timothy to be aware that he would have to fulfill his ministry with this grim prospect in view. He issues a warning concerning the anticipated apostasy. He indicates that Timothy must receive the strength to face this through his faithfulness and behavior as a minister of the gospel.

There is a warning in these verses of which the minister must be aware as he preaches. There will be those who will believe and receive the faith he proclaims and at the same time there will be those who will fall away from this very same faith. This is vitally significant today. Christians simply cannot afford to be ignorant about this apostasy. It is important enough that the Spirit revealed it to the apostle.

The author of the prediction which the apostle refers to is the Spirit of prophecy, the Holy Spirit himself. The Spirit was clear and explicit in His prediction. The apostle used the word "expressly." Christ had predicted this would occur, but the reference here is to a special revelation made by the Spirit.

Paul does not indicate to whom the Spirit revealed this message. It could have been himself or some other New Testament personality. The apostle does, in his letter to the Thessalonian Christians, give a fuller revelation of this apostasy. Greek scholars suggest that the word "faith" indicates the message was being given more than once. But the emphasis is on the message—not on personalities.

According to Paul, the time of this prediction would be "in the latter times." This means some time in the future to the speaker. No precise date is mentioned, but it would seem that the apostle felt it would begin in the near future. However, the full effects of the apostasy would not be felt until the end of the age.

The basic idea in the message is that "some shall fall away from the faith." The term "faith" refers to the basic doctrines of the Christian faith. The term "fall away" suggests a deliberate turning away from the faith once professed. It was not an accident. An apostate is one who forsakes the truth of the Christian faith; not one who simply gives up his profession of being a Christian.

The statement "giving heed to seducing spirits, and doctrines of devils" reveals how this apostasy was to be brought about. Paul emphasizes that it will have its origin in the devil. There are those who are the tools of Satan. These are seducing spirits. Their goal is to lead believers away from the truth. They are hostile to the things of Christ and they give rise to doctrines that will destroy the soul. This is the source from which apostates are to draw their inspiration and their teachings.

It is important that Christians realize they cannot live in a state of neutrality. We are either for Christ or against Him. We are either influenced by the Holy Spirit or the wrong spirit. If we do not give heed to the doctrine of God, we leave ourselves open to other doctrines from the wrong source.

Paul indicates the instrumentality of the apostasy when he says, "Speaking lies in hypocrisy; having their conscience seared with a hot iron." He is stating that heretical teachers will be motivated by evil spirits to lead innocent souls astray from the truth of the gospel. Those who neglect the teachings of Scripture and

the leading of the Holy Spirit leave themselves open to any and every thing the devil has to offer. They can become instruments in the hands of Satan.

Those who lead Christians astray are described as speakers of lies. They present evil as the truth. They are like people wearing masks. They profess to be very pure and right, but this is just a mask to conceal their evil nature. They have allowed their conscience to be branded as criminals were branded. They were branded where the marks of their evil could not be concealed from themselves.

B. Characteristics of the Danger (2 Timothy 3:1-8)

1. This know also, that in the last days perilous times shall come.

2. For men shall be lovers of their own selves, covetous, boasters, proud, blasphemers, disobedient to parents, unthankful, unholy,

3. Without natural affection, trucebreakers, false accusers, incontinent, fierce, despisers of those that are good,

4. Traitors, heady, highminded, lovers of pleasures more than lovers of God;

5. Having a form of godliness, but denying the power thereof: from such turn away.

6. For of this sort are they which creep into houses, and lead captive silly women laden with sins, led away with divers lusts,

7. Ever learning, and never able to come to the knowledge of the truth.

8. Now as Jannes and Jambres withstood Moses, so do these also resist the truth: men of corrupt minds, reprobate concerning the faith.

There are two things which Paul wants Timothy to do, according to these verses. First, he must constantly realize that troublesome days will come; and second, he must turn away from the kind of people who will make these days so troublesome. Note the characteristics these people will have. They will be:

self-loving: Eminently selfish and probably under the garb of religion. Self becomes the main reason for living and tramples on all who would interfere with that. He does not consider the rights and comfort of others.

covetous: Lovers of money. They will do anything to get a buck, regardless of what it does to themselves or to other people. They will manipulate and scheme to get what they want.

boasters: This originally meant "wandering." The idea is one who is an empty pretender, talking constantly about his accomplishments. He is the kind of person who if you could buy him for what he is worth and sell him for what he thinks he is worth you would never have to work again.

proud: Haughty. The word means "to show above." This is one who thinks he is above other people. This type of individual thinks he is God's special gift to all mankind.

blasphemers: When they speak, they hurt or injure. They use scornful language, insulting God and man.

disobedient to their parents: This constitutes a foundation for their disregard of all authority. If children do not learn to obey their parents, whom God has set over them, it is not likely they will be obedient to other authority, whether human or divine. This is a frightening characteristic of our time.

unthankful: These persons are unappreciative of all the benefits which they have received from their parents. This unthankfulness naturally extends itself in their response to other human benefactors, and to God himself. Ingratitude has always been regarded as one of the worst of sins. It is said here that it would characterize that wicked age of which Paul has been speaking, and its prevalence would, as it always does, indicate a decline in religion. Religion makes us grateful to every benefactor—to God, and to man.

unholy: Impious, respecting and revering nothing as sacred. The word describes one's disregard of their duties toward God. They do not reverence the established sanctities. This implies that they are unfeeling, or unsympathetic, heartless, lacking even in natural affection such as

parents have for their children, and children for their parents.

without natural affection: They are destitute of love toward those for whom nature herself claims it. By their indifference to and utter disregard for the welfare of those with whom they are connected by natural ties they sink lower than the beasts.

irreconcilable: They refuse to enter into a truce to terminate a state of hostilities. Their feuds never end.

slanderers: They are false accusers.

without self-control: They have never learned to exercise a restraint upon their lusts and passions.

fierce: They are harsh, severe, and cruel.

not lovers of good: They have no love for virtue, no love for that which is good or helpful to others.

traitors: They betray confidences and any trust placed in them.

headstrong: They are rash and reckless. They plunge ahead without forethought in their impetuous deeds.

puffed up: They are blinded by pride and conceit. No one can tell them anything, for they know it all.

lovers of pleasure more than lovers of God: They love their own pleaures and are completely controlled by them. They do not love God at all.

having a form of godliness without power: They have a mere semblance or appearance of piety, but deny its power. They lack spiritual dynamite.

The people to whom the apostle refers are not open and above board in their dealings with people. They attempt to spread their views by ingratiating themselves first with women, and through them to influence men.

Paul advises that Christians refrain from having anything to do with such people.

II. RESISTING THE DEVIL (Ephesians 6:11-13; 1 Peter 5:8, 9)

A. The Fight (Ephesians 6:11-13)

11. Put on the whole armour of God, that ye may be able to stand against the wiles of the devil.

12. For we wrestle not against flesh

and blood, but against principalities, against powers, against the rulers of the darkness of this world, against spiritual wickedness in high places.

13. Wherefore take unto you the whole armour of God, that ye may be able to withstand in the evil day, and having done all, to stand.

It must be clear to all believers that the Christian life is one of constant conflict. It is a strenuous struggle from start to finish. The Bible indicates clearly that we must struggle every foot of the way. But the Bible also says that we are to be conquerors. We are always to face the encounter with Christ, and thus we can win. The words "in Christ" are the vantage point for the Christian conflict. We must never lose sight of the fact that we are to face the foe always in Christ. We must always be in Christ as we press the battle; otherwise it is dangerous and defeat is certain.

Paul says that we are to "Put on the whole armour. . . . for." Because of the powerful forces arrayed against us, we need divine provision and protection. The fight is not only against human powers, but in a much larger way against superhuman powers.

Believers need to recognize how mighty these powers are. They are not myths. We are not playing with foolish and fickle children. It is a terrible conflict, and we all need the ingenuity of the Holy Spirit to see us through. Divine wisdom, divine energy, and divine astuteness alone can combat these perilous powers. Only as we are walking in complete harmony with God can we expect to be a match for the enemy of our soul.

The apostle identifies our enemies as principalities, powers, rulers of the darkness, and spiritual wickedness in high places.

The word "principalities" is sometimes translated "rule." At first it meant the origin or beginning of things. It then came to mean the first person, a leader, the originator, or the first thing in a series of things. Later again it came to mean the first power in a series of powers or the principal power. The principal power

is the government and in that sense the word is sometimes rendered "governments." Evidently there is a combination of evil powers headed up by a giant leader. This power is set in motion to undertake the destruction of the people of God.

The original word for powers meant "lawful." It was sometimes translated "authority." Some say it might mean the power that comes from authority. It is clear that the established government of evil headed by one outstanding personality delegates authority and power to a host of the workers of iniquity. In addition to the devil and his established government of evil, he has, in his employ, a tremendous host of helpers who have indescribable and almost unbreakable power as they go forth in a determined effort to destroy the followers of God.

The term "rulers of the darkness" comes from two words meaning "world" and to "have strength." The term means "a ruler of this world"—the one who has power or strength over the world. In the Gospel of John, Jesus refers to this outstanding personality of evil. In each case He calls him "the prince of this world." (See John 12:31; 14:30; 16:11.) There is evidently a powerful personality who has a special sphere of activity in the world since he was cast out of heaven, and as long as we are in the world we are going to be exposed to his influence. But as we allow the Spirit of God to control our life, the less influence the god of this world has on us.

Spiritual wickedness in high places probably refers to the host or forces of wickedness. The word "wickedness" means "depravity or iniquity." So we are talking about spiritual forces whose essential nature is wickedness.

The conflict is fierce, but the victory is assured to us if we put on the armor God has provided.

B. The Adversary (1 Peter 5:8, 9)

8. Be sober, be vigilant; because your adversary the devil, as a roaring lion, walketh about, seeking whom he may devour:

9. Whom resist steadfast in the faith, knowing that the same afflictions are accomplished in your brethren that are in the world.

As the Apostle Peter penned these words he may well have remembered the appeal of Jesus to him and his companions in the garden of Gethsemane, "Could ye not watch with me one hour?" (Matthew 26:40). His failure on that occasion to exercise his privilege to watch and pray, connected as it was with the approach of Jesus, may have deepened in him the importance of the Christian virtue which he in this passage pressed upon his readers.

Peter urges his readers to watchfulness. This should not be surprising. We need to be watchful because of the uncertainty of the future. No one can plan upon events succeeding one another with regularity. Therefore, no one can make provision for time to come, and abandon himself to ease with assurance that all things will continue as from the beginning. In the teachings of Jesus we find frequent warnings of changes and catastrophes, accompanied by exhortations to vigilance.

Peter cites the adversary as the reason for watchfulness. Behind the forces antagonistic to the church, Peter sees another—the master foe, the one great force, "your adversary the devil."

Three ways are listed by which we may resist Satan. We are to be *sober*. Sobriety is the opposite of intoxication. Anything that intoxicates strengthens the baser forces in our nature, deadening the conscience and reason. We can become intoxicated not only on drugs or alcohol, but also on money, power, work, worldly status, applause, and many other things in life.

We are to be *vigilant* or *watchful*. Victory is sure in no other way. Sometimes Satan so takes us by surprise that we hardly know we are doing wrong until we have sinned. Take heed that he does not catch you off guard.

The apostle also urges his readers to resist the devil with *steadfastness in the faith*. Faith in God is the fort from which

the adversary would dislodge us. Driven from that, all is lost, unless God in His mercy brings us back. Satan can do us no harm as long as we are shut up in the stronghold of faith in God.

III. KEPT BY GOD'S POWER (1 Peter 1:3-9; Jude 24, 25)

A. The Hope (1 Peter 1:3-9)

3. Blessed be the God and Father of our Lord Jesus Christ, which according to his abundant mercy hath begotten us again unto a lively hope by the resurrection of Jesus Christ from the dead,

4. To an inheritance incorruptible, and undefiled, and that fadeth not away, reserved in heaven for you,

5. Who are kept by the power of God through faith unto salvation ready to be revealed in the last time.

6. Wherein ye greatly rejoice, though now for a season, if need be, ye are in heaviness through manifold temptations:

7. That the trial of your faith, being much more precious than of gold that perisheth, though it be tried with fire, might be found unto praise and honour and glory at the appearing of Jesus Christ:

8. Whom having not seen, ye love; in whom, though now ye see him not, yet believing, ye rejoice with joy unspeakable and full of glory:

9. Receiving the end of your faith, even the salvation of your souls.

The Christians to whom Peter wrote were entering a period of severe trial. The apostle wanted to send them encouragement and support. So in these verses he bursts forth with praise. The reason for such gratitude is the believer's hope. The importance of this Epistle may be summed up in one word: hope. Paul was preeminently the apostle of faith; John the apostle of love; Peter the apostle of hope.

What is there about this lively hope that caused Peter to rejoice and bless God? He says "God . . . hath begotten us again unto a lively hope." God has made us His children by regeneration and heirs to an incorruptible inheritance in heaven.

The apostle declares the inheritance to be permanent. "Incorruptible, undefiled, and that fadeth not away." All three of these words imply permanence, but they treat it in different ways. "Incorruptible" means "spiritual, not material." The blessedness of that state will not depend on anything that can decay. The blessedness of heaven will be in the development of our spiritual nature. "Undefiled" means "untainted, unblemished by earthly defects and human infirmities." The phrase "that fadeth not away" means all this is to be everlasting.

The inheritance promised to believers is certain. Peter assures us it is "reserved in heaven for you, who are kept by the power of God." No earthly heritage is sure, but this is. The phrase "reserved in heaven for you" means it is safe. And who "are kept by the power of God" means we are safe in God's love.

The resurrection of Jesus Christ makes our inheritance sure. Jesus Christ, our brother, representative, and Lord, identified Himself with us in life and death, and made us one with Himself in resurrection, which is God's seal and "amen" to all Jesus said and did.

In Peter's words we see also reflected the dark shadows which were gathering over the scattered saints. He suggests that manifold trials were part of the believer's lot. To suffer as a Christian sometimes meant the loss of business, reputation, and home; desertion by parents, children, and friends; misrepresentation, hatred, and even death.

For ourselves, trials generally come from three sources: those brought on us by others; those caused by our own sins, mistakes, and indiscretions; and those allowed as tests from God, our Father. Beneath this pressure, it is no wonder that, at times, the heart is bowed down.

According to Peter, the saints' joy can grow out of manifold trials—joy and sorrow at the same time. The believer ought to always be rejoicing. This is confusing to many. But there is a difference between always rejoicing and only rejoicing. The idea that a believer ought only to rejoice is as foolish as it is false. But it is possible always to rejoice; "as sorrowful, yet always rejoicing." In Peter's words we have some of the grounds of joy. They are faith, hope, and love.

In the words of the apostle we experience salvation in heaviness. "Ye rejoice . . . receiving the . . . salvation." Our salvation is a mystery to be fully revealed in heaven. But the unfolding of this mystery begins in divine joy on earth. It is possible to anticipate heaven, to receive now the salvation of our soul, despite the heaviness of manifold temptations.

B. The Presentation (Jude 24, 25)

24. Now unto him that is able to keep you from falling, and to present you faultless before the presence of his glory with exceeding joy,

25. To the only wise God our Saviour, be glory and majesty, dominion and power, both now and ever. Amen.

Jude ends his letter with words of assurance for God's people. Shall we be able to keep ourselves in the love of God? Can we avoid contamination in our contacts with the ungodly? Is it possible for us to walk uprightly in the land of the living? The answer is given crystal clear. We can so live, because the One who loved us and gave Himself for us is also able to keep us from falling.

Jude's message of triumph for the Christian is that he is kept by the power of God. It is God himself who will bring us into the presence of His glory, without fault and with exceeding joy.

REVIEW QUESTIONS

1. How does the apostle state the warning concerning apostasy came?

2. Identify the characteristics of the apostasy.

3. Compare what Paul says about apostasy with the present age.

4. What does Ephesians 6 teach about preparation for spiritual battles?

5. What was Peter's attitude toward the enemy of God's people?

GOLDEN TEXT HOMILY

"TAKE UNTO YOU THE WHOLE ARMOUR OF GOD, THAT YE MAY BE ABLE TO WITHSTAND IN THE EVIL DAY" (Ephesians 6:13).

The individual Christian must be armed to meet temptation and to win a triumph. Many a sanguine young Christian soldier has fallen shamefully through rushing rashly into the fray without due preparation.

We cannot forge our own armour. Our own resolutions, like home-made weapons, will be sure to betray some weakness and clumsiness. A steel breastplate is no protection against a poision-cup. The character of our defences must be spiritual and holy, like the character of God, in order that we may be able to withstand great spiritual foes.

It is necessary to secure a complete suit of armour. "The whole armour." We are assailable in every part of our nature. It is useless to be only half-armed, for the subtle tempter is sure to aim his dart at the most vulnerable spot. We are all inclined to make much of favourite graces and to fortify ourselves against certain selected sins. Where we think ourselves most secure we are likely to be most open to attack. It will not be sufficient to be sound on all points but one. Achilles was said to be vulnerable only on the heel. But that was enough. His one weak place was fatal to him. God knows both the variety of foes we have to face and the different susceptibilities of our own constitution, and has provided complete armour accordingly.—**Excerpts from** *Pulpit Commentary*, **vol. 20.**

SENTENCE SERMONS

BELIEVERS MUST be alert to spiritual danger while trusting the Lord to keep them by His power.

—Selected

TEMPTATIONS THAT find us dwelling in God are to our faith like winds that more firmly root the tree.

—"The Encyclopedia of Religious Quotations"

THE DEVIL is no idle spirit, but a vagrant, runagate walker, that never rests in one place. The motive, cause, and main intention of his walking is to ruin man.

—Thomas Adams

The great need of the world today is the spiritual power necessary for the overthrow of evil, for the establishment of righteousness, and for the ushering in of the era of perpetual peace; and that spiritual power begins in the surrender of the individual to God. It commences with obedience to the first commandment.

—William Jennings Bryan

EVANGELISTIC APPLICATION

CHRIST CAN SAVE US FROM SIN AND GIVE US VICTORY OVER EVIL.

During an earthquake the inhabitants of a small village were very much alarmed, but at the same time they were surprised at the calmness and apparent joy of an old lady whom they all knew. At last, one of them, addressing the old lady, said, "Mother, are you not afraid?" "No," said the mother in Israel, "I rejoice to know that I have a God who can shake the world."

ILLUMINATING THE LESSON

The informed Christian has no excuse for stopping short of attaining all God has provided for maturity and stability. The passions and pitfalls leading to bondage and blindness cannot enslave the informed Christian who has learned to rely on God's grace and to counter the enemies of his soul with the true knowledge of Christ.

DAILY BIBLE READINGS

M. Godliness in Evil Times. Genesis 6: 1-9

T. God's Greatness. 1 Chronicles 29:9-13

W. God's Sovereignty. Daniel 2:19-23

T. Kept From Evil. John 17:6-15

F. A Blameless Life. 2 Peter 3:10-18

S. Faithfulness Rewarded. Revelation 3: 7-10

Facing Personal Conflicts

Study Text: Matthew 10:16-22; Hebrews 11:32-40; Revelation 2:26-28; 21:1-7

Supplemental References: Daniel 3:16-26; John 15:18-21; Acts 4:19-33; 8:1-4; Romans 8:31-39

Golden Text: "Let them that suffer according to the will of God commit the keeping of their souls to him in well doing, as unto a faithful Creator" (1 Peter 4:19).

Central Truth: Christians can expect opposition from the world, but will be rewarded by God for staying true to Him.

Evangelistic Emphasis: By accepting Christ, the individual receives a new source of wisdom and power to face personal conflicts.

Printed Text

Matthew 10:16. Behold, I send you forth as sheep in the midst of wolves: be ye therefore wise as serpents, and harmless as doves.

17. But beware of men: for they will deliver you up to the councils, and they will scourge you in their synagogues;

18. And ye shall be brought before governors and kings for my sake, for a testimony against them and the Gentiles.

19. But when they deliver you up, take no thought how or what ye shall speak: for it shall be given you in that same hour what ye shall speak.

20. For it is not ye that speak, but the Spirit of your Father which speaketh in you.

Hebrews 11:32. And what shall I more say? for the time would fail me to tell of Gedeon, and of Barak, and of Samson, and of Jephthae; of David also, and Samuel, and of the prophets:

33. Who through faith subdued kingdoms, wrought righteousness, obtained promises, stopped the mouths of lions,

34. Quenched the violence of fire, escaped the edge of the sword, out of weakness were made strong, waxed valiant in fight, turned to flight the armies of the aliens.

35. Women received their dead raised to life again: and others were tortured, not accepting deliverance; that they might obtain a better resurrection:

36. And others had trial of cruel mockings and scourgings, yea, moreover of bonds and imprisonment:

37. They were stoned, they were sawn asunder, were tempted, were slain with the sword: they wandered about in sheepskins and goatskins; being destitute, afflicted, tormented;

38. (Of whom the world was not worthy:) they wandered in deserts, and in mountains, and in dens and caves of the earth.

39. And these all, having obtained a good report through faith, received not the promise:

40. God having provided some better thing for us, that they without us should not be made perfect.

Revelation 2:26. And he that overcometh, and keepeth my works unto the end, to him will I give power over the nations:

27. And he shall rule them with a rod of iron; as the vessels of a potter shall they be broken to shivers: even as I received of my Father.

LESSON OUTLINE

I. EXPERIENCING OPPOSITION
   A. Religious
   B. Civil
   C. Family
   D. Community

II. FAITHFUL WHEN TESTED
   A. Endurance of Faith
   B. Perfection Through Promise

III. REWARDED AS OVERCOMERS
   A. The Invitation and Promise
   B. God's Plan for the Future

LESSON EXPOSITION

INTRODUCTION

Christianity is never a completed thing. It is a process, a constant action. When you become a Christian, the real stress has started. This Christian conflict is never concluded. We cannot lay down our arms at the end of a battle. Rather, there must be a new taking of them up in readiness for more of the wiles of the enemy. We finish one experience only to go on into another.

There is always something more ahead for the child of God, always more situations to conquer, always more to endure; more service; more struggle; more suffering. This side of heaven, we shall never fully attain; but we strive after it. One lesson is concluded and another has begun. It must always be so in Christ. There can be nothing final in spiritual contemplation and achievement. There are lulls in the conflict but never the end. It often appears as if the end has come and at the time it is very difficult and serious, but still the end does not come. The situation of the moment may bring an awful wound and it may look like we cannot recover, but we soon discover that the end is not here. We must all stand before the judgment seat of Christ. We must so live that we shall not be ashamed when that time comes.

I. EXPERIENCING OPPOSITION (Matthew 10:16-22)

A. Religious (vv. 16, 17)

16. Behold I send you forth as sheep in the midst of wolves: be ye therefore wise as serpents, and harmless as doves.

17. But beware of men: for they will deliver you up to the councils, and they will scourge you in their synagogues.

Jesus warned His disciples of the dangers their mission would bring to them before He sent them out. He wanted them to be aware of some things before they departed. He looked forward to their future work and prepared them for the dangers of their office. He reminded them of the dignity of their calling and of the source from which their commission came.

Their mission came from Christ. "I send you," He declared. This statement would remind them of their apostleship, its dignities, and its duties. They were sent by Christ! What consolation! But they were sent into the midst of dangers. They would be like sheep—harmless and helpless—in the midst of wolves. In human terms, their task seemed hopeless. They were but a few weak men sent out to grapple with the whole wicked world. Their case seemed desperate and success seemed impossible. But it was the Lord who sent them and it was He who was their hope and strength.

The disciples were told by Jesus what He expected of them in relation to their conduct. He suggested they not seek martyrdom but be wise, discreet, and careful not to give unnecessary offense. Their lives were important and they were to preserve them by all lawful means. To accomplish preservation they would have to be as wary as a serpent (though they were not to have a serpent's guile). On the other hand, they would have to be as harmless as doves. They had to be genuine, truthful, and free from selfish motives.

Jesus told His followers they should be prepared for rejection by religious people. Sometimes this would be by formal and ceremonious judgments before the councils, and at other times by tumults in the synagogues. This disclosure was designed to eliminate any false enthusiasm with which they might begin their work.

B. Civil (vv. 18-20)

18. And ye shall be brought before governors and kings for my sake, for a testimony against them and the Gentiles.

19. But when they deliver you up, take no thought how or what ye shall speak: for it shall be given you in that same hour what ye shall speak.

20. For it is not ye that speak, but the Spirit of your Father which speaketh in you.

The disciples of Jesus could never accuse Him of trying to deceive them in order to get them into His work. He told them in no uncertain terms about the sufferings that awaited them. Not only would they be scourged by Jews but they would be brought before Gentile courts and kings. They would be persecuted.

The suffering of the followers of Jesus was to be a testimony to Jews and Gentiles. It would be a testimony to the depth and reality of their faith as well as to the power of God who strengthened them.

According to Jesus, His disciples were to trust Him and not be afraid when they were brought before the rulers in political settings. They were not to be anxious about their defense when placed before those to whom they had to give account for their behavior. They were not to think about these things. He meant they were not to be anxious about them. They were not to allow their mind to be distracted from their work by worrying about defending themselves, for they were in the hands of God and His peace would sustain them.

Jesus promised the assistance of the Holy Spirit to the disciples. He would strengthen them in the hour of danger.

He would teach them what to speak, and He would be their peace in the midst of turmoil.

C. Family (v. 21)

21. And the brother shall deliver up the brother to death, and the father the child: and the children shall rise up against their parents, and cause them to be put to death.

The preaching of the gospel not only would bring good news but also would introduce a new division into the world. Households would be divided. Natural affection would be overpowered by fanaticism. Christians would become the object of persecution in their own home.

D. Community (v. 22)

22. And ye shall be hated of all men for my name's sake: but he that endureth to the end shall be saved.

Jesus indicates that the struggle with evil men is unavoidable. The conquest is not one we have to create. It is a conquest already created for us. It is a struggle already in existence in which every true believer must engage to be true to his calling. The battle is not ours but God's, and our being God's possession, we have entered into the conflict as part of the inheritance that has come to us in Christ. If we are His children, living by His Spirit, then the warfare is inevitable. Because we are here in a world that is hostile to God, being children of God, the world's hostility and hatred will be heaped upon us. There can be no escaping it until we are removed by our Captain to the ranks above.

There was a promise of a reward for those who remained faithful—"He that endureth to the end shall be saved." He shall be saved who remains faithful in spite of hatred, who flinches not in danger, agony, or fear of death. If he is faithful, he will be saved from sin, from everlasting death, and from hell. The faithful will be brought safely through trials, persecution, sufferings, and difficulties into the promised land of God. This was the hope of the early followers of Jesus. It is our hope today.

II. FAITHFUL WHEN TESTED (Hebrews 11:32-40)

A. Endurance of Faith (vv. 32-38)

32. And what shall I more say? for the time would fail me to tell of Gedeon, and of Barak, and of Samson, and of Jephthae; of David also, and Samuel, and of the prophets:

33. Who through faith subdued kingdoms, wrought righteousness, obtained promises, stopped the mouths of lions,

34. Quenched the violence of fire, escaped the edge of the sword, out of weakness were made strong, waxed valiant in fight, turned to flight the armies of the aliens.

35. Women received their dead raised to life again: and others were tortured, not accepting deliverance; that they might obtain a better resurrection:

36. And others had trial of cruel mockings and scourgings, yea, moreover of bonds and imprisonment:

37. They were stoned, they were sawn asunder, were tempted, were slain with the sword: they wandered about in sheepskins and goatskins; being destitute, afflicted, tormented;

38. (Of whom the world was not worthy) they wandered in deserts, and in mountains, and in dens and caves of the earth.

The author of Hebrews finds in the history of Israel too many examples of overcoming and enduring faith to continue his description of them in detail. The list is altogether too long for him to give an account of the great evidence of faith in their lives. All of them needed and deserved to be considered and his readers would know them. He has exercised great brevity in what he has thus far said about the ancients of the faith. Now he must abbreviate still more.

In his continuing record he lists a few more notable names to which the readers may add more. He supplies only a few names from the Book of Judges and from the Books of Samuel.

The names are listed in pairs, but the order is reversed, the second in history becomes the first in the list. Among the judges Gedeon is mentioned first even though he came after Barak. This is probably because he was considered the most famous hero, as well as being more remarkable in history for faith and heroism. Israel's life under the judges is represented by Gedeon and Barak, Samson and Jephthae; under the monarchy by David, the greatest of Israel's kings, and under the prophetic order by Samuel.

The deeds listed in verses 33 and 34 need not be assigned exclusively to particular heroes, but may rather be taken as generally illustrating the kind of exploits by which faith was evidenced throughout the history of Israel.

The nine items have been divided into groups of three by some Bible scholars. This has been called the "sledgehammer style." Each item is presented by itself. As one succeeds the other, the effect increases. Chronology is not followed. It seems that only content counts. The tenses of the words express historical facts. The reader is left on his own to locate the facts in their proper place in history. The emphasis is that each achievement was accomplished by means of faith.

Note the list:

Subdued kingdoms—This is a general phrase which could be applied to several of the judges. The action is similar to that of an athlete who wrestles down his antagonist.

Worked righteousness—This applies to the righteous rule of any of the judges.

Obtained promises—This can perhaps mean either "who came into possession of the blessings which God had promised them," or "who had received words of promise from God."

Stopped the mouths of lions—This may refer to Samson, David, and Daniel.

Quenched the violence of fire—This is probably in reference to the three companions of Daniel—Shadrach, Meshach, and Abednego.

Escaped the edge of the sword—This may apply to any escape in battle but also to Elijah's escape from the sword of Jezebel and perhaps also to the escape of Elisha.

Out of weakness were made strong— This could refer to Samson, perhaps also to the courage inspired by David's victory over Goliath which enabled Israel to triumph.

Waxed valiant in fight and turned to flight the armies of the aliens—Both of these can be interpreted in the same manner. They could refer to the campaigns of Joshua, the judges, and David.

The thought turns to what faith can endure in verses 35-38, the emphasis being on the sufferings of the people. Faith enables as well as equips, and through faith people can suffer and be strong.

F. B. Meyer has a beautiful statement of how faith can master insuperable difficulties:

"It is difficult to be singular; but faith enabled Abel to offer a more excellent sacrifice than Cain. It is difficult to walk constantly with God, when wickedness is great on the earth, and all flesh has corrupted its way; but it is not impossible— for Enoch walked with God on the very margin of the flood, and obtained the testimony that he pleased Him. It is difficult to lead a pilgrim life, and such difficulties would be probably as keenly felt by the patriarchs; but what faith did for them it will do for others. It is difficult, amid the cares of business or public office, to keep hearts fresh, devout, and young; but it is not impossible to faith, which maintained the spirit of patriotism and devotion in the heart of Joseph, though sorely tempted to sink into an Egyptian grandee. It is difficult to face the loss of all things, and the displeasure of the great; but Moses did both, under the spell of faith in the unseen.

"There are many difficulties before us all. Stormy seas forbid our passage; frowning fortifications bar our progress; mighty kingdoms defy our power; lions roar against us; fire lights its flaming barricade in our path; the sword, the armies of the alien, mockings, scourgings, bonds, and imprisonment—all these menace our peace, darken our horizon, and try on us their power; but faith has conquered all these before, and it shall do as much again.

We will laugh at impossibility; we will tread the shores of the seas, certain they must make us a way; we will enter the dens of wild beasts and the furnaces of flame, sure that they are impotent to injure us; we will escape the edge of the sword, out of weakness become strong, turn to flight armies of the aliens, and set at nought all the power of the enemy: and all because we believe in God. Reckon on God's faithfulness. Look not at the winds and waves, but at his character and will. Get alone with him, steeping your heart and mind in his precious and exceeding great promises. Be obedient to the uttermost limit of your light. Walk in the Spirit, one of whose fruits is faith. So shall you be deemed worthy to join his band, whose names and exploits run over from this page into the chronicles of eternity, and to share their glorious heritage" (*The Way Into the Holiest,* Zondervan).

B. Perfection Through Promise (vv. 39, 40)

39. And these all, having obtained a good report through faith, received not the promise:

40. God having provided some better thing for us, that they without us should not be made perfect.

These verses are a summary statement about all these worthies whose faith was acknowledged, though they did not obtain what God had promised. One writer said the reason for this was that God's time had not come. He did not intend them to be placed by themselves. They had to wait for us, and now, through Christ, the Old Testament saints have been put in a better position and are able to share in the spiritual blessings provided by Christ. The entire Epistle is occupied with this thought of the inferiority of spiritual privileges under the Old Covenant compared with those which are our portion now. Thus, in the old days, sin was set aside, while now it is sent away; in the old days, sins were constantly remembered, now they are completely removed. Christ, as portrayed in the completeness and glory of His work, has actually provided the "better things," which God all along had fore-seen for them and for us. When it is said that "they without us should not be made perfect" we have again the thought of "perfection," so characteristic of this Epistle, referring to the mature and ripe experi-ence which was only possible when Christ the Son of God and our High Priest accomplished His work on our behalf.

III. REWARDED AS OVERCOMERS (Rev-elation 2:26-28; 21:1-7)

A. The Invitation and Promise (vv. 26-28)

26. And he that overcometh, and keepeth my works unto the end, to him will I give power over the nations:

27. And he shall rule them with a rod of iron; as the vessels of a potter shall be broken to shivers: even as I received of my Father.

28. And I will give him the morning star.

Although no explicit call to repentance is given to the church at Thyatira, it is implicit. The church is tolerating Jezebel. They are permitting her to occupy a place in their midst. If they are to inherit the blessing of the coming kingdom they must act now. The Lord reminds them that he sees into the very hearts and minds of men; he knows not only their thoughts, but also the intents of their heart.

Christ's reward on that day will be just. His reward will not be based upon out-ward appearances. Each will be rewarded according to his works.

Jesus says to those who had been faithful, "I will put upon you none other burden. But that which ye have already hold fast till I come" (2:24, 25). To those who overcome the temptations of Jeze-bel and keep performing good works until Christ returns, will be given power by Christ and they will participate with him in the overthrow of the forces of evil.

The Pulpit Commentary has some inter-esting comments on the statement "I will give them power over the nations."

"Those who hold fast with an unrelaxing grasp all the good they had, triumphed over evil, and held on loyally to the end, shall receive power over the nations.

What power? Moral power—power over the minds and hearts of nations. He only is the true sovereign who governs minds and hearts. All other sovereignties are shams. The morally right has in it the highest elements of might. Right is might, and there is none other. He shall rule them with a rod of iron. Right is a rod of iron unbreakable and all-crushing, dash-ing to pieces, shriveling into atoms all the kingdoms of evil and wrong. He is the greatest king of his age who has the most truth and goodness on his side and in his soul; hence the saints will one day judge the world."

The believer is promised an inheri-tance of the highest possession in the words, "I will give him the morning star." The "morning star" is none other than Jesus himself. He is the bright and morn-ing star. This is the title He gives himself: "I Jesus am the Root and Offspring of David, and the bright and morning star" (Revelation 22:16). The good man shall have Christ, and possessing Him, shall have more than the universe itself.

Those who repent are to receive into their hearts Jesus himself. But there is special significance in the name "morning star." The times were out of joint. The days were dark. Bitter persecution was, for many, putting out the sun. But they who received Jesus received light. They received that light that was the prophecy and promise of the dawning of a new day. He was the one sure hope for a better tomorrow for the Christians of Thyatira, as he is for us. They, receiving the Light, were to give light to others. They were to be heralds of hope for a despairing world.

B. God's Plan for the Future (vv. 1-7)

1. And I saw a new heaven and a new earth: for the first heaven and the first earth were passed away; and there was no more sea.

2. And I John saw the holy city, new Jerusalem, coming down from God out of heaven, prepared as a bride adorned for her husband.

3. And I heard a great voice out of heaven saying, Behold the tabernacle of God is with men, and he will dwell

with them, and they shall be his people, and God himself shall be with them, and be their God.

4. And God shall wipe away all tears from their eyes; and there shall be no more death, neither sorrow, nor crying, neither shall there be any more pain: for the former things are passed away.

5. And he that sat upon the throne said, Behold, I make all things new. And he said unto me, Write: for these words are true and faithful.

6. And he said unto me, It is done. I am Alpha and Omega, the beginning and the end. I will give unto him that is athirst of the fountain of the water of life freely.

7. He that overcometh shall inherit all things; and I will be his God, and he shall be my son.

The apostle indicates that everything that has been defiled by sin and Satan will be purified and made new. The earth was defiled by sin; it will be destroyed. The atmospheric heavens, being the present domain of the prince of the power of the air, will also be purified.

John does not explain how the process of making things new is to be accomplished, but Peter, in his Second Epistle, has some interesting ideas on this. He gives us what some believe to be the most thorough description of how the Lord is going to create the new heavens and the new earth. He gives us one of the most advanced and scientific statements of the composition of the earth and its final destruction found anywhere in Scripture. "But the heavens and the earth, which are now, by the same word are kept in store, reserved unto fire against the day of judgment and perdition of ungodly men" (2 Peter 3:7).

Scientists of our day say that the earth is stored with fire, Peter knew this 1900 years ago. God has always known it, for He made the earth.

Within the new heaven and on the new earth there is the holy city. It is called New Jerusalem. Before the apostle became a prisoner under Domitian, the Jerusalem of old had fallen. Many devout Jews were heartbroken when they thought that the sacred places existed no more. With a great touch of tenderness, John looks far ahead to a new Jerusalem, in which all that was important in the past shall be reproduced and exceeded—a Jerusalem which would indeed be holy, which would be free from the alien's footprints, and which would endure forever.

John states that there will be no more sea. It is important to remember that to the ancient Jews, the sea was an object of almost unmixed terror. Most of the allusions to it in the Bible tell of its destructive power and of its peril. The Jews were never a seafaring people. They dreaded it. They associated it with their old bondage. They remembered its terribleness in connection with the Flood, the Exodus, and Jonah. They referred to it as being troubled, raging, and roaring. So it is no wonder that John, in telling of the new and blessed home of the future, would say, "And there is no more sea."

According to John, much that we have known here we shall not know there, for they will be no longer. There will be no more tears, death, sorrow, crying, and pain. All these have passed away. That will be heaven in itself. But there is more.

John is told that God will be present with men in the new earth and in the New Jerusalem. Frequently in the Bible the presence of God connotes fellowship and blessing. This will certainly be true in the new home of the believers. The inhabitants of the New Jerusalem will be the people of God and God will not only be with them but will also be their God. There will be no more remorse on the part of the inhabitants of the city because the presence of God assures comfort.

REVIEW QUESTIONS

1. What does Jesus advise believers to do when faced with opposition?

2. What are the sources of opposition for believers?

3. What does the writer of Hebrews say about the endurance of faith?

4. List some of the exploits of the faithful from Hebrews 11:32-40.

5. What does John say will be absent in the New Jerusalem?

GOLDEN TEXT HOMILY

"LET THEM THAT SUFFER ACCORDING TO THE WILL OF GOD COMMIT THE KEEPING OF THEIR SOULS TO HIM IN WELL DOING, AS UNTO A FAITHFUL CREATOR" (1 Peter 4:19).

This first epistle of Peter is written to the believers, who are scattered throughout Asia Minor as a result of increasing persecution from the Roman rulers. The purpose of this epistle is to encourage the Christians to remain faithful to God during these difficult times. He tells them that they should not think it strange when they have to suffer for Him. "All that will live godly in Christ Jesus shall suffer persecution" (2 Timothy 3:12). Even Christ was willing to patiently endure His suffering and to die upon Calvary's Cross, to redeem the lost.

Peter also says that not all suffering merits a reward. Some suffering is of evil deeds. Other suffering is simply a result of natural consequences. The suffering that brings an eternal reward is that which comes to us due to our living for Christ and being committed to Him. This assurance is found in 2 Timothy 2:12, "If we suffer, we shall also reign with him."

The suffering that one receives may be physical abuse, emotional stress, rejection from family, verbal abuse, or even death. Yet when we recognize and accept our suffering as the will of God for our lives and that it holds for us an eternal reward, it becomes easier to bear. We can even rejoice that we are counted worthy to suffer with Him.

After accepting suffering as God's will, we as Christians must then commit the keeping of our souls to God, with full assurance that He will not allow us to have more put on us than we can bear. We should then continue working for God, putting our hearts into our labor for Him and totally committing ourselves to Christ, as He was totally committed to doing the will of his heavenly Father.

—David Simpson, M.Div., Chaplain/ Therapist, Lifesprings Mental Health Services, Scottsburg, Indiana

SENTENCE SERMONS

CHRISTIANS CAN EXPECT opposition from the world, but will be rewarded for staying true to God.

—Selected

HARDSHIP AND OPPOSITION are the native soil of manhood and self-reliance.

—"Speaker's Sourcebook"

WHEN FAITHFULNESS is most difficult, it is most necessary.

—"Speaker's Sourcebook"

THE GROUND is pure white after a snowfall. The grass is greener after a heavy rain. How are you after a stormy trial?

—"Notes & Quotes"

EVANGELISTIC APPLICATION

BY ACCEPTING CHRIST, THE INDIVIDUAL RECEIVES A NEW SOURCE OF WISDOM AND POWER TO FACE PERSONAL CONFLICTS.

Some of the Old Testament heroes of faith "obtained promises," but none of them received *the* promise in the sense of witnessing its fulfillment. But now the promise has been fulfilled; the age of the New Covenant has dawned; the Christ to whose day they looked has come. By His death on Calvary He procured for the Old Testament saints—and for us—peace with God and an eternal home in heaven.

DAILY BIBLE READINGS

M. Trusting God's Power. 1 Samuel 14: 1-7

T. God Our Helper. 2 Chronicles 32:1-8

W. God Our Strength. Nehemiah 6:1-9

T. Steadfast in Trials. Acts 20:16-24

F. Spiritual Weapons. 2 Corinthians 6: 1-10

S. Courageous in Suffering. Philippians 1:21-30

The Intellectual Battlefield

Study Text: Romans 8:5-8; 12:1, 2; 1 Corinthians 2:9-16; 2 Timothy 4:3, 4; 2 Peter 3:1-4

Supplemental References: Genesis 3:1-5; Jeremiah 17:5; Ephesians 4:17-23

Golden Text: "To be carnally minded is death; but to be spiritually minded is life and peace" (Romans 8:6).

Central Truth: When the Holy Spirit controls the believer's mind, he will not conform to the world's thinking and reasoning.

Evangelistic Emphasis: Through Christ we can escape the world's philosophy which leads to eternal destruction.

Printed Text

2 Timothy 4:3. For the time will come when they will not endure sound doctrine; but after their own lusts shall they heap to themselves teachers, having itching ears;

4. And they shall turn away their ears from the truth, and shall be turned unto fables.

2 Peter 3:1. This second epistle, beloved, I now write unto you; in both which I stir up your pure minds by way of remembrance:

2. That ye may be mindful of the words which were spoken before by the holy prophets, and of the commandment of us the apostles of the Lord and Saviour:

3. Knowing this first, that there shall come in the last days scoffers, walking after their own lusts,

4. And saying, Where is the promise of his coming? for since the fathers fell asleep, all things continue as they were from the beginning of the creation.

Romans 8:5. For they that are after the flesh do mind the things of the flesh; but they that are after the Spirit the things of the Spirit.

6. For to be carnally minded is death; but to be spiritually minded is life and peace.

7. Because the carnal mind is enmity against God: for it is not subject to the law of God, neither indeed can be.

8. So then they that are in the flesh cannot please God.

12:1. I beseech you therefore, brethren, by the mercies of God, that ye present your bodies a living sacrifice, holy, acceptable unto God, which is your reasonable service.

2. And be not conformed to this world: but be ye transformed by the renewing of your mind, that ye may prove what is that good, and acceptable, and perfect, will of God.

1 Corinthians 2:12. Now we have received, not the spirit of the world, but the spirit which is of God; that we might know the things that are freely given to us of God.

13. Which things also we speak, not in the words which man's wisdom teacheth, but which the Holy Ghost teacheth; comparing spiritual things with spiritual.

14. But the natural man receiveth not

the things of the Spirit of God: for they are foolishness unto him: neither can he know them, because they are spiritually discerned.

LESSON OUTLINE

I. SKEPTICISM AND UNBELIEF
   A. Rejecting the Truth
   B. Denying the Truth
II. SECULAR HUMANISM
   A. The Comparison
   B. The War
III. THE SPIRIT-CONTROLLED MIND
   A. The Dedication
   B. The Instruction

LESSON EXPOSITION

INTRODUCTION

An expert on the human brain and computers has said that if we could invent a computer that would duplicate the capabilites of the human brain, it would take a structure the size of the Empire State Building just to house it. The human brain is the most complex mechanism in the world. It is the most influential organ in the human body. It is responsible for the ability to think, remember, love, hate, feel, reason, imagine, and analyze.

Weighing about three pounds, the average human brain contains 12 billion cells, each of which is connected to 10,000 other brain cells, totaling about 120 trillion brain connections. This is what makes scientists say the human brain is the most complex arrangement of matter in the universe.

The brain supervises all human activities. This includes everything from the involuntary beat of the heart to the conscious decisions that are made. It controls hearing, sight, smell, speech, appetite, learning, and every aspect of human behavior.

Individual traits, temperament, physical growth, and all the other characteristics inherited at birth are controlled by the brain.

The mind or the intellect is a major part of the brain. It is also influenced by inherited temperament. The mind is the principal place of memory. This is where we make deductions, judgments, and decisions. It has been said that it is the mind that makes the body rich. This is true because it is through the mind that we become aware of God, His Word, and His plan of salvation through Jesus Christ. The mind is where the battle rages for the human soul. This is why Satan tries so hard to control the human intellect. This is why the Holy Spirit is ever wooing and encouraging us.

I. SKEPTICISM AND UNBELIEF (2 Timothy 4:3, 4; 2 Peter 3:1-4)

A. Rejecting the Truth (2 Timothy 4:3, 4)

3. For the time will come when they will not endure sound doctrine; but after their own lusts shall they heap to themselves teachers, having itching ears;

4. And they shall turn away their ears from the truth, and shall be turned unto fables.

In chapter 3:1-8 Paul reminded Timothy of the great apostasy which was to be expected in the church. He said this would be characterized by danger, persecution, and trial. He is probably referring to this same period when he says "the time will come." Now he adds some additional characteristics of this period.

It will be a period when people will not endure sound doctrine. The Greek word here means "healthful" doctrine. Healthful doctrine is that which contributes to the health of the soul, or to salvation. But the apostle says people will be more interested in the kind of instruction that will conform to their wishes and feelings.

Why will people not seek sound doctrine? According to Paul it is because they are following their own lusts. They seek the kind of preaching that will not condemn their carnal desires; or such as will excuse their evil desires, and deal gently with their sins. It was Isaiah the prophet who referred to people who said,

"Speak unto us smooth things; prophesy deceits" (Isaiah 30:10).

Because the people of whom Paul is speaking have itching ears, they will heap to themselves teachers. By turning away from Timothy and sound doctrine, they will not abandon all religious teachers, but will rather multiply them. The word *heap* does not occur anywhere else in the New Testament. It means to "heap up upon, to accumulate;" and here it means "to multiply." The word *itching* also occurs only in this place in the New Testament. It means "to rub, to scratch; and then to tickle," and in this case, it means "to feel an itching for something pleasing or gratifying." This image comes from the desire we have, when there is an itching sensation, to have it rubbed or scratched. Simply stated, these people wanted someone to satisfy their restless and uneasy desires and to gratify their religious whims.

Those to whom Paul referred might have felt at home in our contemporary society with the current attitude that many have toward the ministry. It is reported that a dear old Scottish lady referred to a young man of her acquaintance as obviously fitted for the ministry because he was "a right harmless laddie." One bishop has described some preachers as "mild-mannered men standing before a mild-mannered congregation, asking them to become more mild." Someone else has referred to "bland leaders of the bland."

Ministers are cynically said to be too busy looking for the lost coin to be out looking for the lost sheep. Undoubtedly, many ministers do fit the popular image of the man of God as a smiling, congenial, asexual, religious mascot whose handshake is always soft and whose head is always bobbing in the perpetual yes of universal acquiescence.

It is a fact that when the virile, prophetic emphasis goes out of preaching and teaching; when the sermon never goes deeper than the emotional moralism of a religious columnist; when the minister becomes a mechanic tinkering incessantly with ecclesiastical machinery, then the congregation becomes a fellowship of mediocrity whose religious insights and understanding remain on the level of the kindergarten.

The apostle tells us that those with no more serious intentions than to satisfy their own desires will not only lack sufficient discernment to distinguish between truth and fables, but will, in fact, turn away their ears from the truth. This suggests a deliberate refusal to hear it. The reason appears to be their fascination with fables. The idea seems to be that there is a deviation from the true course, and a wandering into counterfeits, with no awareness that truth has been left behind.

B. Denying the Truth (2 Peter 3:1-4)

1. This second epistle, beloved, I now write unto you; in both which I stir up your pure minds by way of remembrance:

2. That ye may be mindful of the words which were spoken before by the holy prophets, and of the commandment of us the apostles of the Lord and Saviour:

3. Knowing this first, that there shall come in the last days scoffers, walking after their own lusts,

4. And saying, Where is the promise of his coming? for since the fathers fell asleep, all things continue as they were from the beginning of the creation.

The spiritual welfare of the Christians of Asia Minor was of deep concern to Peter. He felt a great affection for them. He called them "beloved" four times in this chapter. We do not know if he had seen them face-to-face. It is believed by some that Silas told him about their circumstances, dangers, and temptations. So he wrote to them. In his first letter, Peter comforted them in the midst of persecution. In the second one, he warned them about the seductions of false teachers.

Peter says that he wrote to stir up their pure minds (v. 1). Their minds were pure. They were single-minded Christians. Their commitment to Christ was genuine. Nevertheless, it was appropriate to stir them up. We all need to be aroused from time to time. If not, we may live in the same way day after day. Our daily life may become too routine. There is always the danger of becoming lukewarm, formal, and acting from habit rather than from a conscious desire to please God. Thus the need for exhortation. We ought to continually ask God to stir up the wills of His faithful people. It is only He who, by the power of His Spirit, can really arouse us. But He uses His servants as instruments. He used Peter as His agent to stir up the mind of the Christians in Asia Minor.

The Apostle Peter also wrote to remind the Christians of the words of the prophets and apostles. He urged the study of prophecy in the first chapter of this letter. He dwelt upon the subject of prophetic inspiration in both letters. Christians ought to study the Prophets and give heed to the Word of prophecy. We should always be mindful of the Lord's commandments given through His apostles. The writings of the prophets and apostles have a message for us. It is important that we recognize this message. To neglect it shows a lack of reverence and gratitude to Him from whom the message comes. The commandments delivered to us by the apostles are, in truth, the commandments of our Lord and Savior.

Peter warned his readers that scoffers would come. It has always been so. There have always been men who mocked those who trusted in God. It was so with Lot in Sodom, with Isaac the heir of promise, with the psalmist, and with the Lord Jesus himself. Those mockers of whom Peter spoke were men of sensual habits, walking after their own lusts. There is such a thing as honest doubt, such as that of Thomas. But in all ages many of those who profess skepticism are using that to cover up an ungodly life—men who reject the faith because they are unwilling to believe. The pure morality of the gospel offends their self-judgment. It is a reproach to them. The teaching of Scripture concerning judgment is repulsive to them, therefore they try to keep such thoughts from their mind. Besides this, sin hardens their heart. A sensual life blinds the eyes of the soul, and makes men incapable of appreciating spiritual truth.

The apostle said that men will come with mockery, saying, "Where is the promise of his coming?" The fathers have fallen asleep; generation after generation has passed away. Christians have lived in expectation of the Lord's coming, but still He has not come. Are we to spend our life waiting for an advent which seems to be continually delayed? Yes, we are to wait for and expect the Lord to come. The mockers are wrong. The Lord will come again just as He promised.

The mocking inquiry, "Where is the promise of his coming?" is characteristic of this evil age. Jesus said that many would do this very thing. Therefore, we should not be astonished by this, but rather confirmed in the faith.

II. SECULAR HUMANISM (Romans 8:5-8)

A. The Comparison (vv. 5, 6)

5. For they that are after the flesh do mind the things of the flesh; but they that are after the Spirit the things of the Spirit.

6. For to be carnally minded is death; but to be spiritually minded is life and peace.

A nationally known American said early in 1980, "The major political confrontation in the 1980s will not be between the liberals and the conservatives or between the socialists and the anti-socialists, but between Christianity and humanism."

It will be a war to the death, and everything will be done to disguise from the Christians the reality of the battle, so that at the time when it really matters, they (the Christians) will hesitate, uncertain, between the two opinions.

The lines of battle have been drawn. Humanism has crept into a position of virtual prominence in this country. It is subtle and deceptive, like the devil himself.

Christians must really know what they believe as Christians in order to strengthen our convictions based on the Word of God. Christians must also become well aware of the strategy of the devil.

What is humanism? It is a man-centered philosophy that attempts to solve the problems of man and world independently of God.

Humanism rejects God. It can find no reason for Him. They (humanists) believe that no test proves His existence, and they therefore deduce He does not exist. They are not really atheists, but nontheists; even if God does exist, they don't care.

The humanist believes that morality depends on what seems right to him at the moment, or whether it feels good, and not on any biblical or theological standards. They hold ethics to be autonomous and situational—what seems right to them at the time. They strive for the good life here and now and are dependent only on their own reasoning and intelligence.

Humanism looks to world law and order. They look to the development of a system of world law and order, based upon transnational, federal government. They believe that a commitment to mankind is the highest commitment of which we are capable. This transcends the narrow allegiances that an individual might hold for the church, state, party, or race.

Anyone can be a humanist. In fact everyone is, to some extent. Christians are not immune. All that is required is to place the needs of man (self) ahead of the lordship of Jesus Christ.

A humanistic society promotes self-gratification. This has always been the theme of Satan's work. It can be seen as Eve took the bait of humanism in the Garden of Eden. She wanted to be as God, to be in control, to turn away from the expressed instructions of God, to do what was right in her own eyes, to use her own natural wisdom to decide, instead of spiritual leading.

Contemporary society is headed in the same direction that past societies have taken. For example, in Greek and Roman societies the State was on the throne, with an emperor—a dictator—as its leader. The basic question still is, "Who will be Lord? Who will be in control? Whose kingdom is sovereign in the government? in the church? in the family? in the heart?"

What is the end of humanism? Well, Paul says to be carnally minded is death. Paul's description of a carnally minded individual vividly portrays the guilt and frustration of a society intent on serving itself, pleasing itself, expressing itself, and killing itself.

What is the answer or antidote to humanism and carnality? The same apostle gives us the answer when he says "to be spiritually minded is peace and life."

Paul gives us the answer to humanism when he describes the state of the believer as being "in Christ." This phrase is peculiar to the New Testament. It expresses clearly the condition into which the Christian, as soon as he believes, is brought into Christ.

Paul was referring to the character of the believer in verse one. It was Jesus who said, "The tree is known by its fruit" (Matthew 12:33). The believer does not walk "after the flesh, but after the Spirit." In writing to the Galatians the apostle declares, "For the flesh lusteth against the Spirit, and the Spirit against the flesh; and these are contrary the one to the other" (Galatians 5:17). And so the believer does not walk after the flesh, nor "obey it in the lusts thereof" (Romans 6:12). In this respect he is different from the unbeliever. The unbeliever is concerned with time and sense. The believer is concerned with eternity.

The Christian walks after the Spirit. He possesses a new, heavenly principle, under the influence of which he lives day by day. His citizenship is in heaven where Christ sits at the right hand of God. He is not tuned into anything that does not advance the glory of God. He is not interested in anything that does not honor the Christ who bought him with His blood.

Paul described the twofold nature of the believer's new liberation. First, it is a liberation from "the law of sin and death" —from the dominating principles of sin which issues in death. Second, it is a liberation unto the "law of the Spirit of life in Christ Jesus."

Paul gave us a very meaningful statement when he said that the Holy Spirit's power liberates the Christian from the dominion of sin, thus making the daily diet of the child of God the fruit of spiritual life rather than the fruit of spiritual death. Many try to dodge this truth. However, the apostle categorically declared that it is possible for a Christian, by the abiding presence of the Holy Spirit, to live day by day with constant victory over sin.

In talking about the spiritually minded, Paul does not equate "no condemnation" with "no mistakes" or "no failures" or even "no sins." Believers fail; they make mistakes; they sin. It is difficult to admit that Abraham lied about his wife (Genesis 20:1-18); David committed adultery (2 Samuel 11:4); Peter tried to kill a man with his sword (John 18:10) and lied about knowing Jesus (Matthew 26:69-75). To be sure, these persons suffered the consequences of their sins. They did not suffer the condemnation of their sins, however, because they repented. They failed, but they did not allow their sins to remain unconfessed and hinder their walk with God.

B. The War (vv. 7, 8)

7. Because the carnal mind is enmity against God: for it is not subject to the law of God, neither indeed can be.

8. So then they that are in the flesh cannot please God.

A new and spiritual principle is infused into us by the Holy Spirit when we believe in Christ. And when that principle exists, it, of necessity, manifests itself by its appropriate operations. Therefore, our carnal nature and our spiritual nature are clearly distinguished. The carnal nature follows after carnal things. Whatever our feelings or our pursuits, we are influenced by that principle which we have in common with all men. We seek nothing beyond the things of time and sense. Pleasure, riches, and honor are the source of our happiness. They alone are considered worthy of our attention.

It must seem strange, to those who do not know what is in the heart of man, that persons who appear to be alike in outward behavior should be judged by God as belonging to different worlds. But in the most imperfect of the regenerate, there is a predominant principle of love to God whereas in the heart of the best unregenerate men there is a rooted enmity against God. This alone makes their character different.

The apostle had been talking about the goals to which a carnal mind and a spiritual mind would lead. Because it may have seemed strange that the one

should terminate in death and the other in life, he stated the reason for this. The carnal mind, in fact, is enmity against God, and a person under its influence is incapable of giving God acceptable service. This is the disposition that rules in the heart of every man who has not accepted Christ as Savior.

III. THE SPIRIT-CONTROLLED MIND
(Romans 12:1, 2; 1 Corinthians 2:9-16)

A. The Dedication (Romans 12:1, 2)

1. I beseech you therefore, brethren, by the mercies of God, that ye present your bodies a living sacrifice, holy, acceptable unto God, which is your reasonable service.

2. And be not conformed to this world: but be ye transformed by the renewing of your mind, that ye may prove what is that good, and acceptable, and perfect, will of God.

In verse one the apostle alludes to the sacrifices that were offered under the Law. The victims were brought to the door of the tabernacle of the congregation and were there slain. The bodies were then disposed of according to the particular directions given in the Law.

In reference to these Old Testament sacrifices, we are to present our bodies as a living sacrifice unto the Lord. The term *body* is used here to represent our total personality or self. No part of us should be under the dominion of any other lord. As we have in the past yielded ourselves instruments of sin, we must now yield ourselves completely to God. Every sin, of whatever kind, must be mortified; and every grace, however difficult and self-denying, must be put into the service of God.

God calls us to holiness. He says, "Be ye holy; for I am holy" (1 Peter 1:16). The sacrifices in the Old Testament were to be without spot or blemish; and so must we. We are to present ourselves a living sacrifice, holy. It is true that we cannot be holy until we are renewed by the Holy Spirit; but it is equally true, that, when we come to Christ in faith, He will give us that which we need to be clean and holy.

A holy sacrifice will be acceptable to God. Absolutely nothing so pleases God as a broken and contrite heart (Psalm

51:17). As for all the legal sacrifices, He had no delight in them except as they pointed to the Lord Jesus Christ, and were offered with reference to Him. A heart filled with gratitude to Him, devoted to His service, is worth more than all the Old Testament sacrifices. Every act of obedience proceeding from faith and love, is, in God's sight, the most acceptable tribute that man can possibly offer to Him.

It is only as we surrender to God that His power can take over and give us the willpower and the "won't power" that we need to be victorious Christians.

B. The Instruction (1 Corinthians 2:9-16)

9. But as it is written, Eye hath not seen, nor ear heard, neither have entered into the heart of man, the things which God hath prepared for them that love him.

10. But God hath revealed them unto us by his Spirit: for the Spirit searcheth all things, yea, the deep things of God.

11. For what man knoweth the things of a man, save the spirit of man which is in him? even so the things of God knoweth no man, but the Spirit of God.

12. Now we have received, not the spirit of the world, but the spirit which is of God; that we might know the things that are freely given to us of God.

13. Which things also we speak, not in the words which man's wisdom teacheth, but which the Holy Ghost teacheth; comparing spiritual things with spiritual.

14. But the natural man receiveth not the things of the Spirit of God: for they are foolishness unto him: neither can he know them, because they are spiritually discerned.

15. But he that is spiritual judgeth all things, yet he himself is judged of no man.

16. For who hath known the mind of the Lord, that he may instruct him? But we have the mind of Christ.

Ours is a day of skepticism, irrationality, and unbelief. A mood of restlessness and despair characterizes our world. Men seek help but do not know why. Broken hearts lie beneath veneers of prosperity and achievement. Many are confused about their place in a depersonalized and harsh world. So this is the time we need to allow the Holy Spirit to really control our life.

Sometimes we have a tendency to think of ourselves as worthless, as failures, as never being able to accomplish anything for God. We are too quick to admit defeat. But it is God who has placed us where we are and has made us useful to Himself. We all have certain abilities, and we should seek to let the Holy Spirit use them to their fullest.

We must face the future unafraid. We rely on more than a set of religious precepts, for we are related to the living God.

The Holy Spirit is at work within us. He even prays for us at times. Our daily problems are no longer ours alone. He is with us all the time. We must allow Him to control our life.

What a full and rich life we can now live because the Holy Spirit controls our life. The darkness is passed and the true light now shines. God himself is now revealed to us. The mysterious plan of redemption is now opened to us. The happiness of God's people is now a part of our living. We can see the eternal purpose of His grace and His personal dealings with mankind.

As Teacher, the Holy Spirit reveals these things to us. As Instructor, He reveals them in us. As our Leader, He brings us into subjection to them. As Witness, He testifies of our conformity to them.

REVIEW QUESTIONS

1. Identify the way we may reject the truth.

2. Define secular humanism.

3. List the approaches secular humanism uses to control our life.

4. Compare the carnal and the spiritual man.

5. How may we permit the Holy Spirit to control our life?

GOLDEN TEXT HOMILY

"TO BE CARNALLY MINDED IS DEATH;

"BUT TO BE SPIRITUALLY MINDED IS LIFE AND PEACE" (Romans 8:6).

Day after day Christians are confronted with the world's claims of answers to all our problems: "This is the right toothpaste to prevent cavities, this is the best car for you, this person can bring about world peace" and on and on it goes. Sometimes it all sounds good. But we still get toothaches, the car still breaks down, and certainly the world is further away from peace than ever before.

We call ourself "Christian" because we have chosen to accept the promise of eternal life by accepting the gift of salvation through Jesus Christ. But who or what leads us through this earthly life? Do we always choose the way of life? Paul warns us that we have a choice of two spheres of influence upon our life; that of the world, and that of the Spirit.

The world certainly can put its promises in pretty, attractive packaging; a sharp contrast to the starkness of the Cross. At times even the church attempts to present the gospel message blended with ideas which will appeal to our contemporary society.

Paul warns us that these two different mind-sets cannot be mixed; for the way of the world always leads to death, while the way of God leads to life. As Christians we must always be cautious of the voice we are following—the voice of the world or the voice of the Spirit of our Savior.

A mind set on the world will lead us to death, bring a hostility and insubordination toward God into our life, and cause us to live a life that is unacceptable to our Lord. But a mind controlled by the Spirit of Christ will lead us to life and peace.

As we live with a single heart for Jesus, let us live with a single mind for Him too.—**Dr. Hector A. Chiesa, Chaplain, Woodbourne Correctional Facility, Woodbourne, New York**

SENTENCE SERMONS

WHEN THE HOLY SPIRIT controls the believer's mind, he will not conform to the world's thinking and reasoning.
—**Selected**

ON HIS DEATHBED, Thomas Paine expressed the wish that all copies of his most famous work, *Age of Reason*, had been thrown into the fire, for "if ever the devil has ever had any agency in any work, he has had it in writing that book."
—**"Quotable Quotes"**

THE INTELLIGENT PERSON is one who has learned how to choose wisely and therefore has a sense of value, a purpose in life and a sense of direction.
—**J. Martin Klotsche**

EVANGELISTIC APPLICATION

THROUGH CHRIST WE CAN ESCAPE THE WORLD'S PHILOSOPHY WHICH LEADS TO ETERNAL DESTRUCTION.

The infidel finished giving an argument against Christianity and salvation. He challenged anyone who cared to argue the point to come to the platform. A gray-haired Christian slowly walked up and sat down on the platform bench. "What is the argument?" asked the infidel.

The elderly man took an orange from his pocket, pealed it, and began to eat the fruit, much to the wonder of everyone. When he finished eating the orange, he asked, "How did the orange taste which I ate?"

"I do not know; I did not taste it," replied the puzzled skeptic.

"Just so with salvation," replied the believer. "You are talking against something you have not tasted or experienced. But I have tasted and seen that the Lord is good, and I advise you to do the same."

DAILY BIBLE READINGS

M. Enlightened Understanding. Psalm 73:12-55

T. Remembering God. Ecclesiastes 12: 1-4

W. Trusting God. Jeremiah 17:5-8

T. Spiritual Knowledge. Matthew 13:10-17

F. Freedom Through the Truth. John 8: 31-36

S. Taught by the Spirit. 1 John 2:20-27

Everyday Relationships

Study Text: Romans 13:1-10; Philippians 2:14-16; Colossians 3:22 through 4:1; 1 Peter 2:13-17

Supplemental References: Leviticus 19:9-13; Proverbs 14:15-22; Matthew 22:17-21

Golden Text: "Owe no man any thing, but to love one another: for he that loveth another hath fulfilled the law" (Romans 13:8).

Central Truth: The Christian is called to honesty, responsibility, and love in his everyday relationships.

Evangelistic Emphasis: The way a Christian treats others can be a help or hindrance to his witness for Christ.

Printed Text

Colossians 3:22. Servants, obey in all things your masters according to the flesh; not with eyeservice, as menpleasers; but in singleness of heart, fearing God:

23. And whatsoever ye do, do it heartily, as to the Lord, and not unto men;

24. Knowing that of the Lord ye shall receive the reward of the inheritance: for ye serve the Lord Christ.

25. But he that doeth wrong shall receive for the wrong which he hath done: and there is no respect of persons.

4:1. Masters, give unto your servants that which is just and equal; knowing that ye also have a Master in heaven.

Romans 13:1. Let every soul be subject unto the higher powers. For there is no power but of God: the powers that be are ordained of God.

2. Whosoever therefore resisteth the power, resisteth the ordinance of God: and they that resist shall receive to themselves damnation.

3. For rulers are not a terror to good works, but to the evil. Wilt thou then not be afraid of the power? do that which is good, and thou shalt have praise of the same:

4. For he is the minister of God to thee for good. But if thou do that which is evil, be afraid; for he beareth not the sword in vain: for he is the minister of God, a revenger to execute wrath upon him that doeth evil.

5. Wherefore ye must needs be subject, not only for wrath, but also for conscience sake.

6. For for this cause pay ye tribute also: for they are God's ministers, attending continually upon this very thing.

7. Render therefore to all their dues: tribute to whom tribute is due; custom to whom custom; fear to whom fear; honour to whom honour.

8. Owe no man any thing, but to love one another: for he that loveth another hath fulfilled the law.

9. For this, Thou shalt not commit adultery, Thou shalt not kill, Thou shalt not steal, Thou shalt not bear false witness, Thou shalt not covet; and if there be any other commandment, it is briefly comprehended in this saying, namely, Thou shalt love thy neighbour as thyself.

10. Love worketh no ill to his neighbour: therefore love is the fulfilling of the law.

LESSON OUTLINE

I. RELATIONSHIPS ON THE JOB
  A. Responsibilities of Employees
  B. Responsibilities of Employers
II. RELATIONSHIPS TO GOVERNMENT
  A. Reasons for Submission
  B. Attitudes in Submission
III. RELATIONSHIPS IN THE COMMU-
  NITY
  A. Love and Law
  B. Positive Examples

LESSON EXPOSITION

INTRODUCTION

The mature Christian is one who has sought the will of God and is attempting to carry this out to the best of his ability. He not only has sought for and found the general will of God for his life, but daily he seeks the will of God for specific tasks. He quietly says each day, "God give me the leadership of thy Spirit for today, and make me adequate to carry out that will as You shall lead." But at the same time he tests carefully the impressions he receives to determine whether they are in line with basic teachings and principles of the New Testament.

When one is a Christian and follows the spiritual leadership that is inherent in the Christian relation, he, through experience, gains growth and development toward maturity. He finds his life becoming more and more free from qualities of selfishness and hate. He finds that his relation is bringing into his life love and compassion to replace the negative attitudes he has felt. He discovers new ways of living. He finds life possesses challenges and zest of which he had never dreamed. He finds that he can assume responsibility that he had thought impossible. He finds himself becoming more secure and self-reliant. He is better able to face up to the difficult situations in life with a quiet, moral constancy in line with the teachings of Jesus. He finds that to be in line with the teachings of Jesus is more and more a natural response. He finds a quiet, inner peace that will stand almost any kind of trial or testing. He gains an inner strength that can accept grief and hardship without wavering. He finds himself capable of judging situations without being swept away by group pressure, mob actions, or crowd hysteria. He becomes the kind of individual who can maintain the right kind of relationships in the most difficult of circumstances. These circumstances can be on the job, in the community, or even in government.

I. RELATIONSHIPS ON THE JOB (Colossians 3:22-4:1)

A. Responsibilities of Employees (vv. 22-25)

22. Servants, obey in all things your masters according to the flesh; not with eyeservice, as menpleasers; but in singleness of heart, fearing God:

23. And whatsoever ye do, do it heartily, as unto the Lord, and not unto men;

24. Knowing that of the Lord ye shall receive the reward of the inheritance: for ye serve the Lord Christ.

25. But he that doeth wrong shall receive for the wrong which he hath done: and there is no respect of persons.

In Paul's day, slavery was an established institution. It is estimated that at least half of the people were slaves. Many of these people were the best educated in the country. Many of them carried great responsibilities in the homes of the wealthy and the leaders of the community.

We do not have slaves as such in our society. But the principles given by Paul can be applied to any type of honest employment. Christians should be the best employees on the job.

Many years ago a newspaper want ad revealed the attitude of non-Christians toward Christian employees: "Wanted a cook; a Christian will do if she can cook."

Christians should never think they should be granted special favors and given leniencies. Christians should not only compete with non-Christian employees, but they should do a better job and turn out more work. They should be able to hold a job without pull.

In one study of the attitudes of employees, the question "Should I turn out as much work as I can every day?" was asked. Two thirds of the office workers questioned answered, "Yes." The percentage of "yes" answers among skilled factory workers was slightly lower, and barely half of the unskilled laborers believed in giving a good day's work for their pay.

Abraham Lincoln reportedly said, "My father taught me to work, but he never taught me to love it." However, Lincoln knew few limits at the hard work of splitting rails or solving national distress. It is not what you know—but what you get done—that the world remembers.

All people have trouble with "alibiitis." Some common symptoms are: "I need a better job." "I don't know how." "I'm doing too much already." "No one appreciates it, so why bother?" "They expect too much of me." "They just make it hard on Christians." All of these alibis keep people from doing a good job.

Ralph Waldo Emerson had some interesting ideas about work. He said, "If you have an ungrateful master, serve him all the more. The longer the payment is withholden, the better for you; for compound interest on compound interest is the rate of this exchequer." This not only applies to what the Apostle Paul says in Colossians, but it is also in keeping with the wise man Solomon in the Old Testament. "Seest thou a man diligent in his business? he shall stand before kings" (Proverbs 22:29).

Too many Christian employees are like the zoo elephant who, for years, walked in a circle around a peg to which he was chained. When his chain was broken, he continued to walk in the same circle. Don't be held back by a chain that refuses to let you go the extra mile.

The history of retail sales records an interesting story about William Lever. He was an enthusiastic soap salesman. He finished his rounds early one afternoon. Glancing at his watch, he decided he could either go home or could call in a new town he had not yet touched. In the new town he made five calls and three of them resulted in orders being placed. The boss did not want the expanded business, but young Lever kept on going the extra mile. Soon he was placed in charge of the branch office that had to be opened in the new territory. Lever kept on going the extra mile until the branch office outgrew the home headquarters. By one extra mile after another William Lever developed the Lever Brothers' Company which expanded into more than 40 different countries.

Health experts say that it is the extra pull on muscles that develops strength. It is the extra miles that develop Christian employees into Christian employers.

B. Responsibilities of Employers (v. 1)

1. Masters, give unto your servants that which is just and equal; knowing that ye also have a Master in heaven.

Paul explains the responsibility of the master toward his slave in terms of dealing justly and equitably with him. Another way of saying it is that he (the master) is to do what is right and fair. It must be remembered that in the Roman Empire slaves were not thought of as people and thus had no rights. They were looked upon as being only animated tools. But in this verse, Paul teaches that responsibility is not all on the side of the slave. Masters themselves have responsibilities.

This verse can also be applied to Christian employers. It gives a reason for employers to provide for employees that which is just and equitable: "knowing that ye also have a Master in heaven." Christian employers are reminded, in other words, that they are accountable to God for their treatment of their employees. Both they and their employees bow before one Master, and with Him there is no respect of persons. The plush office of the employer does not attract His eye, and it is not averted from the deplorable treatment of the employee.

Christian employers and employees will be Christian in their treatment of each other if they are filled with the Spirit and the Word. The heart of every problem is the problem of the heart, and only the Spirit of God and the Word of God can change and control the heart of man.

II. RELATIONSHIPS TO GOVERNMENT (Romans 13:1-7; 1 Peter 2:13-17)
A. Submission to Authority (1 Peter 2:13-17)
13. Submit yourselves to every ordi-

nance of man for the Lord's sake: whether it be to the king, as supreme;

14. Or unto governors, as unto them that are sent by him for the punishment of evildoers, and for the praise of them that do well.

15. For so is the will of God, that with well doing ye may put to silence the ignorance of foolish men.

Christianity, in New Testament times, was revolutionary in character. But it was spiritual, and not social or political. This is perhaps why Peter gave the advice to "Submit yourselves to every ordinance of man."

We might be disposed to hesitate in our submission to every ordinance of man. But the command continues, "Submit . . . for the Lord's sake." Why should we go on in patient well doing amid the detraction of ignorant opposition of foolish men? Why? "For so is the will of God, that with well doing ye may put to silence the ignorance of foolish men." Though we are free, we must not use our liberty as a veil for evil living. We are the servants of God.

We are to submit, not through the fear of punishment, but to follow Christ's example, to carry out Christ's will, and for the best interests of Christ's church.

It is no secret that the world, from the beginning, hated the principles for which Jesus died. The world professed to suspect His followers as being an evil threat. A favorite charge against the early Christians was that they were plotting the overthrow of the Roman Empire, and the dethronement of Caesar, in favor of Jesus. The private worship services of early Christians were said to be held for unlawful purposes. Therefore, it was important to eliminate from the thinking of men the idea that Christians were subversive and were intent on destroying the established government and social order.

16. As free, and not using your liberty for a cloak of maliciousness, but as the servants of God.

Both Paul and Peter especially exhorted early Christians to conform, as far as they could, to the just demands of government. They were to render to Cae-

sar the things that were Caesar's. Accepting the order, safety, and privileges of civil and national life, they were to bear their share of its cost, and submit to the government, agreeing to modify or alter it only by orderly and peaceful methods.

Christians were therefore called upon to render to all their dues, tribute to whom tribute, custom to whom custom, fear to whom fear, honor to whom honor. Their goal was to lead a quiet and peaceable life, submitting to laws, and doing well. Thus, in time, would they disarm prejudice and conciliate their foes.

Roman history records how literally these precepts were obeyed. Tertullian contrasted the early Christians with the heathen. He said the heathen delighted in the bloody gladiatorial games of the amphitheater, whereas Christians were excommunicated if they went to the games. When pagans deserted their nearest relatives in the plague, Christians ministered to their sick. When unbelievers left their wounded on the field of battle, and cast them into the streets, the Christians hastened to relieve their sufferings. Thus they muzzled the ignorance of sinful men. The tide began to turn. The more microscopic the inspection of the world became, the more evident it was that a new and blameless character was found in the followers of Christ.

17. Honour all men. Love the brotherhood. Fear God. Honour the king.

There are four commands for Christians in verse 17. First, "Honour all men." Perhaps "value" or "esteem" would be a more appropriate translation for "honor." Christians should manifest a genuine interest in all men.

But what if the men are not honorable? Actually every man, however wicked or degraded, has been created in the image of God. That image may be sadly defaced, but it is still to be honored. God had taught Peter this in a wonderful way on a housetop in Joppa when He said, "Do not call any man common or unclean" (Acts 10:15, paraphrase). Peter had not forgotten his lesson.

Christians are to recognize the worth of all men. There is some worth in the

your enemies, bless them that curse you, do good to them that hate you, and pray for them which despitefully use you, and persecute you" (Matthew 5:44).

The mature Christian has learned how to accept others. He is not always demanding something from others, but is ever eager to give compassionate service. A mature person has a kind of love that meets hatred expressed in others, not by expressing hatred in return, but by expressing love in return.

Mature love is enduring, even under adverse circumstances. It is free from pride and self-glory. It is full of righteousness and truth. It is a quality of seeing the good in others, rather than always seeing the detrimental and the bad.

Love is the key to a mature Christian life. It is the basis of true Christian service. Love is the essential quality of Christian expression. Love is so vital to Christian living that Paul once wrote that if he possessed every quality of goodness, power, and superiority, and he failed to have love he would be worthless (1 Corinthians 13:1, 2).

B. A Positive Example (Philippians 2:14-16)

14. Do all things without murmurings and disputings:

15. That ye may be blameless and harmless, the sons of God, without rebuke, in the midst of a crooked and perverse nation, among whom ye shine as lights in the world;

16. Holding forth the word of life; that I may rejoice in the day of Christ, that I have not run in vain, neither laboured in vain.

Paul is exhorting the Philippians to a quality of life possible only through surrender to God. God alone can provide the strength of purpose and strength of performance to produce the kind of goodwill referred to here. There should be an absence of murmurings in the life of a believer. This condition exists when the believer allows selfishness to get the upper hand in his life. This is certainly contrary to the example of Jesus as cited by Paul.

When Paul refers to "disputings" he may be referring to disagreements or dissensions among believers. He may mean that some of the Philippian believers had gone into the courts of law with their problems. This had been the case in Corinth (1 Corinthians 6).

The reason for this suggestion is given in verse 15. Paul wanted them to be "blameless" and "harmless" and without rebuke (or above reproach). These terms refer to both the inward and outward condition of the believer. Outwardly, his conduct should be above reproach. Inwardly, his condition should be literally unmixed, unadulterated, and pure. The term used here refers to wine or metals unmixed with impurities.

Paul wanted the Philippians to possess reputations that would reflect positively their relationship with Christ. He wanted them to be untarnished, above reproach, blameless, and harmless.

Verse 16 indicates that if the Philippians lived according to Paul's suggestions they could be the right kind of Christian example in the midst of a messed up world.

REVIEW QUESTION

1. How does Paul describe working relationships?

2. What reasons does Paul give for submission to authority?

3. Compare Paul's statements concerning submission with those of Peter.

4. What does Paul say about love in Romans 13:8-10?

5. What kind of example should the Christian be in his community?

GOLDEN TEXT HOMILY

"OWE NO MAN ANY THING, BUT TO LOVE ONE ANOTHER: FOR HE THAT LOVETH ANOTHER HATH FULFILLED THE LAW" (Romans 13:8).

Paul in Romans 13:7 states that the Christian has an obligation to render taxes, tribute, fear and honor to whom it is due. By so doing he will "owe no man any thing." These debts will come due periodically; they are to be paid when due.

But there is one debt that the Christian will continue to owe. This debt will never be liquidated, and that is the debt "to love one another." One can satisfy earthly or civil claims, but love's claims can never be fulfilled. The more one pays this debt of love, the deeper one seems to be in debt. The practice of love makes the principle of love deeper and more active.

The emphasis of verse 8 concerns our relationships in the community. The word *another* has reference to one's neighbor. The whole law can be summed up in loving God and loving one's neighbor. Paul is saying if one honestly seeks to discharge this debt of love, he will automatically keep the commandments. The law defines the meaning of love. Love is expressed by law keeping. Love fulfills the law and is not to be substituted for it.

"We are bidden to honour all men; to respect their rights, their feelings; to reverence in all men, however humble and ignorant, the image of God; to remember that all are precious in the sight of God; ransomed with His life, redeemed with His precious blood and that love, that respect, should be like the feeling with which we regard ourselves—real, true, sincere" (*Pulpit Commentary*).

God is love, and in proportion as we are loving we are like Christ and the Father above.—**Leon Percy Dennis, Chaplain, Draper Correctional Center, Elmore, Alabama**

SENTENCE SERMONS

THE CHRISTIAN is called to honesty, responsibility, and love in his everyday relationships.

—Selected

WHEN A MAN gets in the straight way he finds there is no room for crooked dealings.

—"The Presbyterian"

IF YOU ASPIRE to the assignment of big jobs, be faithful in the performance of little ones.

—"Speaker's Sourcebook"

THE ONLY WAY to do much for God is to ask much of God.

—"Speaker's Sourcebook"

EVANGELISTIC APPLICATION

THE WAY A CHRISTIAN TREATS OTHERS CAN BE A HELP OR HINDRANCE TO HIS WITNESS FOR CHRIST.

Not only *can* Christians succeed, they *must* succeed. It is their obligation to the kingdom. A very well-to-do doctor was showing a friend through his new house.

"Here," he said pointing to a large window in one of the bedrooms, "is where I kneel to pray every night. I ask God to help me in my work and to make me the best doctor I can possibly be. I preach the same idea to my boy. The kids at school are watching him. As a Christian, he can't afford to be any less than the best he can be. His grades ought to be the best he is capable of making. He wants to be a doctor too, and I tell him he should set out to be best doctor in town. As Christians, we have an obligation to God to develop the ability within us. We fail the kingdom if we fall short of this."

DAILY BIBLE READINGS

M. Treat Others Fairly. Leviticus 19:9-13

T. Wise Counsel. Proverbs 11:9-14

W. Contrasting Relationships. Proverbs 14:15-22

T. Duty to Government. Matthew 22:17-21

F. Live an Honest Life. 1 Thessalonians 4:9-12

S. Rich in Good Works. 1 Timothy 6:17-19

Ministering to Human Needs

Study Text: Isaiah 58:6, 7; Luke 10:25-37; Romans 15:1, 2; 1 Corinthians 10:23-33; Galatians 6:9, 10

Supplemental References: Zechariah 7:8-10; Matthew 11:28-30; Acts 4:32-35; James 1:27

Golden Text: "As we have therefore opportunity, let us do good unto all men, especially unto them who are of the household of faith" (Galatians 6:10).

Central Truth: Today's world presents many opportunities for the Christian to minister to the needs of others.

Evangelistic Emphasis: Ministering to the human needs of the unsaved helps prepare them to receive the gospel.

Printed Text

Isaiah 58:6. Is not this the fast that I have chosen? to loose the bands of wickedness, to undo the heavy burdens, and to let the oppressed go free, and that ye break every yoke?

7. Is it not to deal thy bread to the hungry, and that thou bring the poor that are cast out to thy house? when thou seest the naked, that thou cover him; and that thou hide not thyself from thine own flesh?

Luke 10:33. But a certain Samaritan, as he journeyed, came where he was: and when he saw him, he had compassion on him,

34. And went to him, and bound up his wounds, pouring in oil and wine, and set him on his own beast, and brought him to an inn, and took care of him.

1 Corinthians 10:23. All things are lawful for me, but all things are not expedient: all things are lawful for me, but all things edify not.

24. Let no man seek his own, but every man another's wealth.

27. If any of them that believe not bid you to a feast, and ye be disposed to go; whatsoever is set before you, eat, asking no question for conscience sake.

28. But if any man say unto you, This is offered in sacrifice unto idols, eat not for his sake that shewed it, and for conscience sake: for the earth is the Lord's, and the fulness thereof:

29. Conscience, I say, not thine own, but of the other: for why is my liberty judged of another man's conscience?

30. For if I by grace be a partaker, why am I evil spoken of for that which I give thanks?

31. Whether therefore ye eat, or drink, or whatsoever ye do, do all to the glory of God.

32. Give none offence, neither to the Jews, nor to the Gentiles, nor to the church of God:

33. Even as I please all men in all things, not seeking mine own profit, but the profit of many, that they may be saved.

Romans 15:1. We then that are strong ought to bear the infirmities of the weak, and not to please ourselves.

2. Let every one of us please his neighbour for his good to edification.

LESSON OUTLINE

I. COMPASSION FOR OTHERS
   A. The Substance of Compassion
   B. The Example of Compassion
II. CONSIDERATION FOR OTHERS
   A. Balancing Freedom and Responsibility
   B. Respect Without Sharing
III. SERVICE TO OTHERS
   A. Christian Self-denial
   B. Christian Helpfulness

LESSON EXPOSITION

INTRODUCTION

Sinners become Christians through union with the resurrected Christ. This experience brings them into the family of God. The more they mature in their understanding of God and His way in their life and in the world, the more they realize the Christian life is as broad and as deep as life itself. There is enough in the Christian life to challenge one to the end of life's journey.

This continuing challenge is based on the fact that the God we worship and serve is the sovereign God of the universe. As sovereign, He is interested in and concerned about the totality of the life of the individual and of the world. He has a unique concern for all aspects of life and cannot be restricted to any one segment of life.

The more Christians become thoroughly acquainted with the basic teachings of the Scriptures, the more they will see that God expects His children to be like Him. This means, among other things, that His children are to be interested in the totality of life. In turn, this means that no individual, regardless of class, color, creed, or culture, should be outside of the believer's genuine concern. It also means that there will be concern for not only souls, but for whole persons.

I. COMPASSION FOR OTHERS (Isaiah 58:6, 7; Luke 10:25-37)

A. The Substance of Compassion (Isaiah 58:6, 7)

6. Is not this the fast that I have chosen? to loose the bands of wicked- **ness, to undo the heavy burdens, and to let the oppressed go free, and that ye break every yoke?**

7. Is it not to deal thy bread to the hungry, and that thou bring the poor that are cast out to thy house? when thou seest the naked, that thou cover him; and that thou hide not thyself from thine own flesh?

Although the Old Testament is primarily concerned with Israel's relationship to God, it also abounds with condemnations of social injustice and with exhortations to be concerned about those in less fortunate circumstances.

The Bible not only condemns personal sin, it also condemns social evils. Speaking through His prophet Amos, the Lord declared: "For three transgressions of Israel, and for four, I will not turn away the punishment thereof; because they sold . . . the poor for a pair of shoes; That pant after the dust of the earth on the head of the poor, and turn aside the way of the meek: and a man and his father will go in unto the same maid, to profane my holy name" (Amos 2:6, 7). Biblical scholars believe that some kind of legal fiction underlies the phrase "sold . . . the poor for a pair of shoes." This mistreatment of the poor was legal. In one breath God condemns both sexual sins and legalized oppression of the poor.

Through His prophet Isaiah, God said essentially the same thing: "Woe unto them that join house to house, that lay field to field, till there be no place, that they may be placed alone in the midst of the earth! In mine ears said the Lord of hosts, Of a truth many houses shall be desolate, even great and fair, without inhabitant. . . . Woe unto them that rise up early in the morning, that they may follow strong drink; that continue until night, till wine inflame them!" (Isaiah 5:8-11). God condemns the wealthy who amass large land-holdings, doubtless at the poor's expense, and the drunken.

In Amos 5:10-15 God reveals His displeasure at evil institutions. Israel's court sessions were held at the city gate. Amos says, "They hate him who rebuketh in the gate [in the court]. . . . I know your manifold transgressions and your mighty sins . . . take a bribe, and they turn aside the poor in the gate. . . . Hate the evil, and love the good, and establish judgment in the gate." In other words, get rid of the corrupt legal system that allows the wealthy to buy their way out of trouble and does not give legal satisfaction to the poor.

If one is a member of a privileged class that profits from social evil and if one does nothing to try to change things, one stands guilty before God. Social evil is just as sinful as personal evil. Over and over again, God declared through His prophets that He would destroy the nation of Israel because of its idolatry and because of its mistreatment of the poor.

B. The Example of Compassion (Luke 10:25-37)

25. And, behold, a certain lawyer stood up, and tempted him, saying, Master, what shall I do to inherit eternal life?

Christ was evidently seated, in the posture of a teacher, with the crowd around Him, listening, asking questions, and responding to His questioners. The fame of Jesus as a teacher had reached "a certain lawyer," and he wanted to see for himself if Jesus was really the teacher others claimed Him to be. The question of the lawyer was not meant to badger, but to test or prove or verify Jesus' wisdom and learning. In this situation, Jesus respected the inquiry and submitted to investigation.

The lawyer asked, "What shall I do to inherit eternal life?" The tense of the verb *do* implies that by a single performance of some one thing "eternal life" could be secured. "What heroic act must be performed? What great sacrifice made?" he inquired.

We have to keep in mind that this man was a legalist. He was a man who conceived of eternal life as an inheritance— something to be received at some future time, as the appropriate reward for being good. He never conceived of eternal life as God's free and immediate gift to the morally bankrupt.

26. He said unto him, What is written in the law? how readest thou?

The very business of the man questioning Jesus was to know the Law. He should have been able to answer his own question. To the Law, which the lawyer honored, studied, and taught, Jesus turned his attention: "What is written in the law? how readest thou?" (v. 26).

27. And he answering said, Thou shalt love the Lord thy God with all thy heart, and with all thy soul, and with all thy strength, and with all thy mind; and thy neighbour as thyself.

The lawyer answered by quoting from Deuteronomy 6:5 and 10:12. No words were more familiar to the Jews. They were part of the *Shema,* or "Hear," so called from its opening word in Hebrew. The *Shema* was repeated twice a day by every devout Jew, and written on the parchment enclosed in the phylacteries (little boxes worn on the sleeve).

The heart signified the affections. The soul signified the spiritual essence or personality. The strength signified the physical nature. And the mind signified the mental capacity. We are to love God with body, mind, soul, and not merely with emotion. This is the great meaning of this statement.

The lawyer also quoted Leviticus 19:18, "Thy neighbour as thyself." This was the answer to a similar question by the great Hillel. Love of one's neighbor summarizes morality just as love of God summarizes religion. The two together constitute the highest wisdom.

28. And he said unto him, Thou hast answered right: this do, and thou shalt live.

Jesus was always ready to praise where He could, giving even to His critics and His foes all possible commendation. It was true that perfect love to God and man would constitute godly living. It was also true that love would manifest itself in good deeds. The verb here translated *do,* because of its form in the original language, should be understood as "continually do, be doing, or make a habit of doing."

29. But he, willing to justify himself,

said unto Jesus, And who is my neighbour?

At once the lawyer saw that he had convicted himself by asking a question to which he really knew the answer. In his embarrassment he asked another question to show that he really did have a point—"Who is my neighbour?" The Jews split hairs over this question, and used the term *neighbor* conveniently. By definition a neighbor was a "nigh dweller," but the Jews made racial exceptions.

The lawyer had no trouble accepting the reality of God and the necessity of loving Him with heart, soul, strength, and mind. What troubled him was his neighbor. As a lawyer, he belonged to a class of teachers who taught that no Gentile was a neighbor. For him, as a Jew, neighborliness was limited to the Jewish nation.

The lawyer asked the question to justify himself, not with the crowd around him, but with his own conscience. In his own mind there lurked the suspicion that the rejection of a Gentile, simply because he was a Gentile, was not right. Dodging the issue, he tried to throw the responsibility on Jesus, who answered the lawyer with the parable of the Good Samaritan. It was far more important the lawyer know how to be a neighbor than to identify his neighbor.

30. And Jesus answering said, A certain man went down from Jerusalem to Jericho, and fell among thieves, which stripped him of his raiment, and wounded him, and departed, leaving him half dead.

Jesus identified two geographical boundaries in His parable: Jerusalem and Jericho. Jerusalem, meaning "the vision of peace," was the seat of blessing, of history, of religion, of privilege. This was the city where God had chosen to place His name, the center of worship and communion with Himself. Jericho was the city of curse (see Joshua 6:26), yet a scenic city, where priests lived when not fulfilling their tasks in Jerusalem.

Jesus said that a man going from Jerusalem to Jericho was attacked by thieves who robbed him, beat him, left him half-dead, and departed. This was

an exceptional act of violence and brutality.

31. And by chance there came down a certain priest that way: and when he saw him, he passed by on the other side.

"By chance" a priest was going from Jerusalem to Jericho at this particular time. The word used here for *chance* is "coincidence." It has been described as the occurrence of one event with another, which often seems chance to us, but is indeed the working of a Higher Power. The priest could not avoid meeting the man who needed help. He, however, did not look upon the event as a happy coincidence, a God-planned opportunity to help a needy soul. He saw the beaten, bleeding traveler, but passed by on the other side.

32. And likewise a Levite, when he was at the place, came and looked on him, and passed by on the other side.

The Levites were of the same tribe as the Pharisee, but they came from one of the inferior branches. They were appointed to assist the priests, but were not themselves, like Aaron and his sons, to approach the most holy things.

The priest may have known that the Levite was behind him, and may have thought the care of the wounded man was more in keeping with his duties; the Levite, in turn, may have excused himself on the ground that he was only following the example of the priest. The Levite, moved more by curiosity than by humanity, came and looked at the bleeding form, but that was all. He passed by on the other side.

33. But a certain Samaritan, as he journeyed, came where he was: and when he saw him, he had compassion on him,

34. And went to him, and bound up his wounds, pouring in oil and wine, and set him on his own beast, and brought him to an inn, and took care of him.

35. And on the morrow when he departed, he took out two pence, and gave them to the host, and said unto him, Take care of him; and whatsoever

thou spendest more, when I come again, I will repay thee.

The Samaritans were a mixed race, descendants of idolatrous Israelites and Assyrian captives. They occupied the central position of Palestine between Galilee and Judea. The Jews hated the Samaritans because of their mixed race and their imperfect adhesion to Judaism. They would have nothing to do with them. Indeed, it was considered an act of pollution for a Jew to pass through the country of the Samaritans, and the feeling was mutual. The Samaritans had just recently refused to receive Christ and His disciples because they were on their way to Jerusalem (Luke 9:53).

The lawyer must have been surprised when Jesus introduced a Samaritan as the only one on the lonely, dangerous Jericho Road willing to assist a helpless Jew. The very man from whom no needy Jew could expect the least relief was the one who gave it.

The Samaritan could have excused himself on the grounds that the road from Jerusalem to Jericho led through Jewish territory, and that cases of distress ought to be cared for by the Jews. But he did nothing of the sort. He saw a man in need. He asked no questions. He thought of no difficulites. He at once gave the appropriate assistance.

36. Which now of these three, thinkest thou, was neighbour unto him that fell among the thieves?

37. And he said, He that shewed mercy on him. Then said Jesus unto him, Go, and do thou likewise.

Jesus returned to the original question— the definition of neighbor. He asked, "Which now of these three, thinkest thou, was neighbour unto him that fell among the thieves?"

It is interesting that the lawyer avoided using the hated name Samaritan. His answer was simply, "He that shewed mercy on him."

The words of Jesus to the lawyer were: "Go, and do thou likewise."

The meaning is plain: Christian kindness is more than words. It reveals itself in deed and in truth.

II. CONSIDERATION FOR OTHERS (1 Corinthians 10:23-33)

A. Balancing Freedom and Responsibility (vv. 23-27)

23. All things are lawful for me, but all things are not expedient: all things are lawful for me, but all things edify not.

To exercise Christian forbearance is no small accomplishment. There is a continual need of it in the Christian world. Some things are neutral, which we may accept or reject. Others are quite pointed, and we have to accept them as they are. The problem is that we do not see things in the same manner as do others. But Paul showed that although we may differ to a degree in our concepts and conduct, we must conduct our life in an acceptable manner to God. He based his assertion on the idea that Christians should act from a conscientious desire to please God.

Some things may be morally indifferent to us, but before we act on them we should ask ourselves how such action will affect others, and the peace of the church. We get our word *edifice* from the verb *edify*, which means "to build up" or "to make strong." Anything that tends to weaken or destroy the high ideals of the Christian faith, or the undivided earnestness and sincerity of any fellow Christian, is sin. Each of us is either building up or tearing down the lives of other Christians.

24. Let no man seek his own, but every man another's wealth.

Judging from the world's view of behavior, we may think little is required of us in Christian conduct. But not so. God's requirement of us is different. We must judge our concerns and actions not on the basis of our tolerance, but on the basis of the infallible standard of God's Word.

One thing we are required to do is to renounce self. Self is the idol of the unregenerate world. Unbelievers study only to please and exalt self in every area of their life. But we who are Christians live to please God and to glorify His name through service to others.

25. Whatsoever is sold in the shambles, that eat, asking no question for conscience sake:

26. For the earth is the Lord's, and the fulness thereof.

27. If any of them that believe not bid you to a feast, and ye be disposed to go; whatsoever is set before you, eat, asking no question for conscience sake.

Paul believed that few things were unclean in themselves. He spoke as one who was in the Spirit and who saw things from Christ's perspective. In other words, most material objects do not have in themselves qualities which make them unclean.

The problem is the way in which we regard them and use them. He also appealed to the fact that individual conscience, however misguided, must never be violated. To follow conscience, in itself, is no security that we are doing what is right; but to violate conscience, which is our personal persuasion of right and wrong, is always wrong.

Vital Christianity consists in the turning of the heart to the observance of God's laws. This is the great promise of the gospel. It is also the certain effect of it.

B. Respect Without Sharing (vv. 28-33)

28. But if any man say unto you, This is offered in sacrifice unto idols, eat not for his sake that shewed it, and for conscience sake: for the earth is the Lord's and the fulness thereof:

29. Conscience, I say, not thine own, but of the other: for why is my liberty judged of another man's conscience?

30. For if I by grace be a partaker, why am I evil spoken of for that which I give thanks?

31. Whether therefore ye eat, or drink, or whatsoever ye do, do all to the glory of God.

32. Give none offence, neither to the Jews, nor to the Gentiles, nor to the church of God:

33. Even as I please all men in all things, not seeking mine own profit, but the profit of many, that they may be saved.

A remarkable contrast exists between spiritual judgment and carnal judgment. Carnal persons judge from the standpoint of personal opinion. Spiritual persons judge from the standpoint of God's love and God's mind. The first is self-centered, dogmatic, ignorant, and often unjust. The second is compassionate, unselfish, wise, and always merciful.

Paul warned against people becoming stumbling blocks to other Christians. Stumbling block, from which our word *scandal* comes, indicates "a trap or snare—something placed in the way of another, causing one to fall." In Corinth, the danger was that the opinions and acts of the stronger Christians would provide occasion for weaker ones to fall, through sin or unbelief.

It was Paul who told the Romans, "If your brother is distressed because of what you eat, you are no longer acting in love" (Romans 14:15, *New International Version*). That is, if a weak brother suffers because of something the strong Christian does, the latter is acting contrary to love. A strong Christian may be able to do a certain thing without any rebuke of conscience, knowing that he is not offending the Lord; yet a weaker brother may suffer in observing him, because to him it is sin.

If Christ is our pattern, any sacrifice of tastes and liberties for our brother's sake is plain duty.

It was also Paul who told the Romans, "Let not your good be evil spoken of" (Romans 14:16). Christian liberty, the freedom of conscience which has been won by Christ, will inevitably get a bad name if it is exercised in an unloving fashion.

III. SERVICE TO OTHERS (Romans 15:1, 2; Galatians 6:9, 10)

A. Christian Self-denial (Romans 15:1, 2)

1. We then that are strong ought to bear the infirmities of the weak, and not to please ourselves.

2. Let every one of us please his neighbour for his good to edification.

Paul's philosophy of life was that both strong and weak are to pursue the things that make for peace and mutual edification. We must live not merely so as to avoid irritation, but, much more, so as to do no harm to the work of God's grace already begun in another person's heart. No one must destroy the work of God's grace for the satisfaction of a mere personal whim.

Paul states a worthy goal when he says we ought to please our neighbor. By pleasing him we have access to him "for his good to edification." Though we think he is leaning too much in the direction of needless restrictions or superstitions, we should still act toward him with tenderness and forbearance. If he is offended or grieved at our liberty, we should cheerfully condescend to his infirmity in a way of conciliation and concession. To win his soul should be reward enough for the kindness we can manifest and the self-denial we can exercise. This was the kind of behavior Paul both suggested and practiced. However, Paul never suggested giving in to whims or unreasonable requirements of those who are not sincerely following the Lord, or who are merely trying to mature through religious fanaticism.

B. Christian Helpfulness (Galatians 6:9, 10)

9. And let us not be weary in well doing: for in due season we shall reap, if we faint not.

10. As we have therefore opportunity, let us do good unto all men, especially unto them who are of the household of faith.

These verses are an encouragement to persevere in well-doing. Paul indicates that well-doing is the duty, the dignity, and the destiny of believers. Paul told the Ephesians, "We are his workmanship, created in Christ Jesus unto good works" (2:10). It is good and profitable that we, who are Christians, maintain good works. Should not we follow His example "who went about doing good" (Acts 10: 38)? "For so is the will of God, that with well-doing ye may put to silence the ignorance of foolish men" (1 Peter 2:15).

Every believer who attempts to live a straightforward Christian life knows what it is to grow weary in doing what he knows is right. It is a constant battle. There are the enemies of the flesh we live in; of the world about us, its habits, customs, and low ideals; and of Satan himself.

Every one must know what it is to be weary of the load, to have lost heart; every one must have felt—perhaps only for a moment—a dislike for circumstances, tired of his particular load. It was Martin Luther who said, "It is an easy matter for one to do good once or twice, but to continue and not be discouraged through the ingratitude and perverseness of those to whom he has done good, that is very hard."

Weariness passes in the physical realm when we change our environment or our work, when we take a few days off. Likewise, in the spiritual realm, when we take our minds off ourselves, and think of what Christ has done for us, weariness passes.

The church on earth is frequently designated as the house or family of God. The apostle began chapter 6 by calling fellow believers "brethren," a word assuming a relationship of love. He now concludes by speaking of the brethren as members of a household, a word likewise indicative of love. Love always desires the good of others. Notice the phrase, "as we have opportunity." Opportunities do not tarry long. An opportunity lost may never be regained. An opportunity to do good for a person may soon be lost by that person's death or removal from our midst. "Do it now" is the watchword.

REVIEW QUESTIONS

1. How may one balance freedom and responsibility in the Christian life?

2. How did Paul handle weak Christians?

3. How important did Paul feel one's conscience to be?

4. How does one determine if he is a strong or weak Christian?

5. What does Paul say about Christian reaping?

GOLDEN TEXT HOMILY

"AS WE HAVE THEREFORE OPPORTUNITY, LET US DO GOOD UNTO ALL MEN, ESPECIALLY UNTO THEM WHO ARE OF THE HOUSEHOLD OF FAITH" (Galatians 6:10).

These words of the Apostle Paul reflect the teaching of Jesus regarding our obligation to love others. Jesus taught that we should love all people—the good and the bad, neighbors and enemies. Love for all dictates that we shall do good to all as we have the opportunity.

Notice, however, the special emphasis which the Apostle Paul placed upon our duty to do good to fellow Christians. Paul knew all too well that some professing Christians were not good to other Christians, much less to neighbors or enemies. We need only to read the Epistles of First and Second Corinthians to know that Paul had been mistreated and exploited by his fellow Christians.

Why is it so important that we do good, "especially unto them who are of the household of faith"? Because Jesus not only commanded us to love neighbors and enemies, He also commanded that Christians love one another. And He said, "By this shall all men know that ye are my disciples, if ye have love one to another" (John 13:35). Simply put, the world will not believe we are Christians if we fail to love and do good to fellow Christians.

Is there anything more obnoxious than one Christian disrespecting, mistreating, or exploiting another Christian? Courtesy, respect, hospitality, consideration, and mutual care should abound between Christians. Truth is, it is most unlikely we will do good to all people or love our enemies if we have not learned to love and do good to our brothers and sisters in Christ.—**Daniel L. Black, Th.D., Editor, Adult Sunday School Literature, Pathway Press, Cleveland, Tennessee.**

SENTENCE SERMONS

TODAY'S WORLD presents many opportunities for the Christian to minister to the needs of others.

—Selected

COMPASSION is your pain in my heart.

—"Quotable Quotations"

DON'T LET the brightness of your idealism blind your compassion.

—Gary Gulbranson

OBEDIENCE TO our heavenly Father starts with our loving service to a needy brother.

—William A. Ward

EVANGELISTIC APPLICATION

MINISTERING TO THE HUMAN NEEDS OF THE UNSAVED HELPS PREPARE THEM TO RECEIVE THE GOSPEL.

Like the Jews of Jesus' time, we are in danger of limiting the concept: "Who is my neighbor?" We do this in our thought, in our feeling, and in our practice. Whom do we feel bound to love and help? our relatives? our fellow citizens from whom we want the interchange of fellowship? our countrymen? Do we draw the line there? If so, we "have not the faith of our Lord Jesus Christ" in this matter; we are falling out of rank as His disciples. There is nothing especially Christian about the affection we feel or the kindness we show to these. Going this far, we are no better than pagans (Luke 6:32). We must transcend this if we are to be worthy of Him whose name we bear. We must see our neighbor everywhere and in everyone, but more especially in the man who has need for us.

ILLUMINATING THE LESSON

Our society is becoming increasingly selfish and individualistic. We give heartily to charitable purposes, but most of the time our giving is mechanical. The spirit of neighborliness is disappearing. The advances of technology have made it possible for us to be more independent, while at the same time we become dependent on others. While our vast welfare system may be necessary, there is no love in it. We allow government to mechanically and officially bear burdens of others while we, more and more, look out for ourselves. But someone has aptly said, we cannot lift another's burden without bearing it ourself.

DAILY BIBLE READINGS

M. Generous Hospitality. Genesis 18:1-8

T. Example of Compassion. 1 Samuel 30:11-15

W. Call for Compassion. Zechariah 7:4-10

T. Refuge for the Weary. Matthew 11: 28-30

F. Sharing With Others. Acts 4:32-35

S. Pure Religion. James 1:22-27

Growing Spiritually

Study Text: Matthew 21:21, 22; Romans 4:13, 19-21; Philippians 4:6, 7; 1 Timothy 1:3-11; 4:8, 12; 2 Peter 1:5-8

Supplemental References: Genesis 17:15-21; Proverbs 3:1-12; Hebrews 5:11-14; 1 John 2:13-17

Golden Text: "Let no man despise thy youth; but be thou an example of the believers, in word, in conversation, in charity, in spirit, in faith, in purity" (1 Timothy 4:12).

Central Truth: The Christian grows spiritually by exercising his faith, praying effectively, and living a godly life in this present world.

Evangelistic Emphasis: A Christian's witness is enhanced by his demonstration of spiritual maturity.

Printed Text

1 Timothy 1:3. As I besought thee to abide still at Ephesus, when I went into Macedonia, that thou mightest charge some that they teach no other doctrine,

4. Neither give heed to fables and endless genealogies, which minister questions, rather than godly edifying which is in faith: so do.

Matthew 21:21. Jesus answered and said unto them, Verily I say unto you, If ye have faith, and doubt not, ye shall not only do this which is done to the fig tree, but also if ye shall say unto this mountain, Be thou removed, and be thou cast into the sea; it shall be done.

22. And all things, whatsoever ye shall ask in prayer, believing, ye shall receive.

Romans 4:13. For the promise, that he should be the heir of the world, was not to Abraham, or to his seed, through the law, but through the righteousness of faith.

19. And being not weak in faith, he considered not his own body now dead, when he was about an hundred years old, neither yet the deadness of Sarah's womb:

20. He staggered not at the promise of God through unbelief; but was strong in faith, giving glory to God;

21. And being fully persuaded that, what he had promised, he was able also to perform.

1 Timothy 4:8. For bodily exercise profiteth little: but godliness is profitable unto all things, having promise of the life that now is, and of that which is to come.

12. Let no man despise thy youth; but be thou an example of the believers, in word, in conversation, in charity, in spirit, in faith, in purity.

DICTIONARY

Ephesus (EFF-uh-sus)—1 Timothy 1:3—A city on the western coast of Asia Minor in an area of what is now Turkey. It was situated on the main trade route between Greece and Asia Minor.

Macedonia (mass-eh-DOH-ni-ah)—1 Timothy 1:3— A country lying to the north of Greece and formerly under Greek yule, but afterwards enlarged and formed into a Roman province. It is to the latter that the term applies in the New Testament.

LESSON OUTLINE

I. SOUND DOCTRINE
  A. The Charge
  B. A Further Explanation
II. STRONG FAITH
  A. The Possibilities of Faith
  B. The Promises of Faith
III. EFFECTIVE PRAYER
  A. The Possibilities of Prayer
  B. Right Praying
IV. GODLY LIVING
  A. An Example
  B. Diligence

LESSON EXPOSITION

INTRODUCTION

Spiritual immaturity affects a rather sizable group in most churches. The people in this group are of constant concern to the spiritual leadership of the church. This is because a great many of the problems that plague the church stem from their having not grown up spiritually. They have not been able to assume responsibility for their life. They react as little children. They lack poise and confidence. They are filled with fears and uncertainties. They are plagued with a sense of inferiority. They are afraid to launch out into a full courageous life of faith, because they are afraid of failure. No matter how hard they try they seem to be incapable of confident, forceful action.

The Apostle Paul believed that Christian believers should work for spiritual maturity. He believed this so strongly that he rebuked the Corinthians for not being mature people. He so stated it by admonishing, "Brethren, be not children in [mind] understanding . . . yet in malice be ye children, but in understanding be men" (1 Corinthians 14:20). He again rebuked the Corinthians by saying, "And I, brethren, could not speak unto you as unto spiritual, but as unto carnal, even as unto babes in Christ. I have fed you with milk, and not with meat: for hitherto ye were not able to bear it, neither yet now are ye able" (1 Corinthians 3:1, 2). He was saying that they were still acting like little children when they should have been acting like grown men. He was urging them to work at the task of growing up.

The church is hampered today by a lack of maturity on the part of many of its members. These people are those who have merely accepted a creed, or a faith, or an initial emotional experience, and then have been satisfied to simply rest on their oars. They have not learned the experience of daily fellowship with God. They have not found the deep privilege of prayer. They have never tried to be creative in the area of the spiritual. They are stagnated people, infantile and childish in their reactions to the work of the church and of the Kingdom. Nor does it stop there, for generally their whole personality reacts in much the same manner to all responsibilities of life. They have never applied the principles of the Bible, which, if applied properly, would bring insight, spiritual understanding, and growth.

I. SOUND DOCTRINE (1 Timothy 1:3-11)

A. The Charge (vv. 3-7)

3. As I besought thee to abide still at Ephesus, when I went into Macedonia, that thou mightest charge some that they teach no other doctrine,

4. Neither give heed to fables and endless genealogies, which minister questions, rather than godly edifying which is in faith: so do.

Paul does not hesitate to give the purpose of his writing this Epistle. He urges Timothy to implement the command given to him at Ephesus when Paul left for Macedonia. Timothy's first task was to deal with the false teachers who were perverting the gospel.

Paul gives the details of the charge given to Timothy in verses 3 and 4. Here we have the historical setting and occasion for the letter. In identifying the nature of the charge the apostle cites the circumstances for its impartation as well as its contents.

The first part of verse 3 clearly implies that Paul and Timothy had been together in Ephesus and that when Paul left for Macedonia, Timothy was urged to remain to carry out the task assigned to him. This was one of the most important of the Asiatic churches, both strategically and culturally. Timothy's somewhat timid nature may well have rebelled from so difficult a task.

The words "As I exhorted thee" remind Timothy of a previous exhortation given him. The implication is that they had discussed the matter and that the charge had been given orally. Now it is given in writing and could be used as evidence to those who might object to the stand taken by Timothy.

Timothy is now reminded that he is himself a man of authority. He has a definite commission to hold the false teachers in check. It seems evident that Timothy was to take a hard line with them. This is based on the term "charge." It is a military term which means literally to pass commands from one to the other. It implies authority. As Paul's representative, Timothy is to use that authority in dealing with the certain men to whom Paul refers.

The words "*that they teach no other doctrine*" suggest that there was already in existence a recognized standard of Christian doctrine. They also imply that these men were already teaching other doctrine but that they must stop.

The apostle next characterizes the false teaching as fables and endless genealogies. The fables referred to were probably the idle superstitions of many of the Jewish rabbis. The word translated *fable* means properly "speech or discourse," and then "fable or fiction," or a "mystic discourse." Such things abounded in the Greek and Jewish culture. Paul is probably referring to Jewish lore here. This was composed of frivolous and unfounded stories, which they regarded as of great

importance, and which some seemed to have wanted to incorporate into the teachings of Christianity.

The term "endless genealogies" also refers to Jewish teaching. It is known that from early times the rabbis would spin their yarns—and endless yarns they were. On the basis of what they considered some suggestion supplied by the Old Testament, they would take a name from a list of pedigrees and expand it into a story. These became part of what was considered the inspired record and were used in the synagogues. They were subsequently to become that part of the Talmud which is known as Haggadah.

Paul suggests that it was a waste of time to engage in such behavior and it resulted in diverting the attention from the truth.

5. Now the end of the commandment is charity out of a pure heart, and of a good conscience, and of faith unfeigned:

6. From which some having swerved have turned aside unto vain jangling;

7. Desiring to be teachers of the law; understanding neither what they say, nor whereof they affirm.

Timothy had been urged to deliver a charge to the church at Ephesus. He had been asked to pass along a message which had special reference to certain men. This charge was not limited to negative injunctions concerning false teaching. It also implied that they were to bear witness to the sound gospel and to exercise living faith in Jesus Christ. This faith operates by means of love.

Paul suggests in verses 6 and 7 that the failure of the false teachers was due to the departure involved in their life and the impure motive behind their teaching.

B. A Further Explanation (vv. 8-11)

8. But we know that the law is good, if a man use it lawfully;

9. Knowing this, that the law is not made for a righteous man, but for the lawless and disobedient, for the ungodly and for sinners, for unholy and profane, for murderers of fathers and murderers of mothers, for manslayers,

10. For whoremongers, for them that

defile themselves with mankind, for menstealers, for liars, for perjured persons, and if there be any other thing that is contrary to sound doctrine;

11. According to the glorious gospel of the blessed God, which was committed to my trust.

The apostle wishes to impress upon Timothy and through Timothy upon the Ephesians, particularly upon those who were promoting false teachings, that the proposition, "Constant law study is an excellent thing," is not new. The apostle indicates that this is a widely recognized principle and something we all know very well.

Paul does not mean to imply that any and all use of the law is admirable. It is only of practical value when one makes a lawful use of it. If it is buried under a pile of traditions it is nullified. If it is used as a take-off point for orators about ancestors, it loses its power. If it is used as an excuse to become puffed up, arrogant, boastful, haughty, self-righteous, or in any other way sinful it is being misused.

In characteristically Pauline fashion the apostle gives a list of sinners. The list may be viewed as falling into two groups. First, sinners as arrayed against God. They are named in three pairs, apparently all condemned by the first table of the law. Second, sinners as arrayed against society. The first three pairs represented states of minds; what follows are examples of violations of specific commands.

Paul ends his list of sinners by saying, "if there be any other thing that is contrary to sound doctrine." By this we are to understand that there are other forms and shapes of unrighteousness. Only overt acts, and those the worst examples of which the law can recognize, are listed; hence the tenth commandment, which deals with the inner desire, is not given.

II. STRONG FAITH (Matthew 21:21; Romans 4:13, 19-21)

A. The Possibilities of Faith (Matthew 21:21)

21. Jesus answered and said unto them, Verily I say unto you, If ye have faith, and doubt not, ye shall not only do this which is done to the fig tree, but also if ye shall say unto this mountain, Be thou removed, and be thou cast into the sea; it shall be done.

In this verse Jesus gives us a formula for power in living. He said, "If ye have faith." Mark records it as, "Have faith in God." We all like to feel a sense of mastery over the circumstances of our life. No one wants to feel weak and defeated. But when we face up to the circumstances that confront us we often feel powerless and almost hopeless. Yet, Jesus tells us how to change that. He says, "Have faith in God." Confidence in God's power and will to help every believer in Christ, and in the truth of every word that God has spoken, is the great secret to success and prosperity in following Christ and living for Him. It is, in fact, the saving element in Christianity. "By it the elders obtained a good report . . . .he that cometh to God must believe that he is, and that he is a rewarder of them that diligently seek him" (Hebrews 11:2,6).

Do we wish to grow in grace, and in the knowledge of Christ? Do we wish to make progress in our walk with the Lord, and become strong Christians? Then let us daily exercise faith in God.

Faith is an indispensable condition of prevailing prayer. There is such a thing as offering benevolent desires, which are acceptable to God as such, but do not include the exercise of faith in regard to the actual reception of those blessings. Such expression of our desires to God cannot be called prevailing prayer, although God in His loving kindness may see fit to grant the things desired. But true faith insures the things it seeks. When we pray, we are to believe that we shall receive, not something, or anything; but the particular thing for which we pray.

B. The Promises of Faith (Romans 4:13, 19-21)

13. For the promise, that he should be the heir of the world, was not to Abraham, or to his seed, through the law, but through the righteousness of faith.

Paul expressed the promise of Abraham in terms that showed he would inherit the world or be heir of the world. That which concerned the apostle, however, was not so much the content of God's promise to Abraham as the question of who were to be included in the promise and under what condition it was fulfilled.

Who were to be the heirs of the promise—the people of the Law or the people of faith? If it were to be the people of the Law, faith was vain. Besides that, the promise itself would have been without validity; for in the very fact of the promise Paul saw reference to faith. The Law had no part in faith. To speak of the Law, in connection with the promise, was to introduce an alien element that robbed the promise of its meaning.

The promise that was given to Abraham said that he should be the father of many nations. The immediate meaning of that promise was that in the physical sense he should be the father of many persons. But the promise found a much greater and more glorious fulfillment. Abraham indeed became the father of many nations, the father of all who believe. He is today not only the father of the circumcision, his physical progeny, but also of those who follow him in his footsteps of faith.

The promise to Abraham was fulfilled in its deepest meaning in Paul's own day. Later, the Gentiles would come to believe in Christ and thus become the children of the faithful Abraham. Paul stated in Galatians "The scripture, foreseeing that God would justify the heathen through faith, preached before the gospel unto Abraham, saying, In thee shall all nations be blessed" (3:8).

19. And being not weak in faith, he considered not his own body now dead, when he was about an hundred years old, neither yet the deadness of Sarah's womb:

20. He staggered not at the promise of God through unbelief; but was strong in faith, giving glory to God;

21. And being fully persuaded that, what he had promised, he was able also to perform.

Notice the triumphant expression of faith in verses 19-21. "Being not weak in faith . . . he staggered not . . . was strong in faith . . . giving glory to God . . . fully persuaded . . . he was able also to perform." With Abraham there was complete absence of hesitation and indecision. There had been a time when his faith had swerved and he had questioned the possibility of God's fulfillment of His promise. He therefore had provided his own method of fulfillment. But God strengthened his faith and led him to rest once more on the divine Word. Abraham's trust rose again, and he was able to go forward in hope and joy. He rested everything on God's promise. He continued believing until he became strong in faith, giving glory to God.

III. EFFECTIVE PRAYER (Matthew 21:22; Philippians 4:6, 7)

A. The Possibilities of Prayer (Matthew 21:22)

22. And all things, whatsoever ye shall ask in prayer, believing, ye shall receive.

In this verse Jesus gives His disciples instructions concerning praying in faith. Faith is the source of prayer. The measure of faith is the measure of our success in prayer. Prayer is the interpreter of faith; it nourishes, increases, preserves, and makes it fruitful in good works. Many people pray, but few proportion the fervency, humility, and perseverance of their prayers to the greatness of the blessings for which they pray.

The Bible teaches the efficacy of believing prayer. "If ye abide in me, and my words abide in you, ye shall ask what ye will, and it shall be done unto you" (John 15:7). "That whatsoever ye shall ask of the Father in my name, he may give it you" (John 15:16). "This is the confidence that we have in him, that, if we ask any thing according to his will, he heareth us" (1 John 5:14). "Ask, and it shall be given you; seek, and ye shall find; knock, and it shall be opened unto you" (Matthew 7:7). "The effectual fervent prayer of a righteous man availeth much" (James 5:16). By such prayer, to use the language of Scripture, we take hold upon the strength of Omnipotence.

B. Right Praying (Philippians 4:6, 7)

6. Be careful for nothing; but in every thing by prayer and supplication with thanksgiving let your requests be made known unto God.

Paul seems to be suggesting that we can turn every care into a prayer. If we take Paul's advice, we can pray about the smallest thing and about the greatest thing. We do not have to set boundaries with respect to God's care. It is a wide open concern. Nothing is too little for Him to notice.

"Be careful for nothing," or "Be anxious about nothing." Anxiety is an idle thing. It is an enfeebling thing. It eats the very life out of the energies. It leaves the individual, not only where he was, but less capable and less vigorous than at the beginning. It is an irritating thing. It ruffles the temper. It upsets the balance of personality. It is the source of moodiness, sharpness, petulance, and anger. It puts a man at war with himself, with his neighbor and with God. Anxiety is a sign of mistrust. It is a sign of feeble faith, of flagging energy, and languid obedience.

In Christ's presence, in His compassionate heart, we may lay aside our anxieties. We may rest from our burdens. We may take refuge from our fears and from our sins.

"In everything." He is not a man of little faith who puts little things into his prayers. That very attitude shows him to be a man of great faith. Prayer in secret is a pouring out of the soul before God. If it is not a pouring, it is not prayer. Anything left behind, cherished in you but concealed from God, invalidates all.

"By prayer and supplication with thanksgiving." Prayer is the soul's believing and reverential approach to God. Supplication means the needs which demand supply or the asking which springs from a sense of emptiness.

7. And the peace of God, which passeth all understanding, shall keep your hearts and minds through Christ Jesus.

The word translated *peace* can also be translated tranquility, harmony, concord, security, safety, prosperity, and felicity. Negative attitudes cannot survive in this kind of atmosphere. Just as negative thoughts and worry divide the mind, so peace unites the mind. It fastens it upon worthwhile goals and stimulates it with worthwhile motives and actions. The peace that Paul refers to is the genuine peace begotten of God. It is based upon fact. It is not a self-manufactured illusion designed to color the facts. This is a peace based upon the fact that God is all-sufficient. It is based upon His willingness to accept us when we cast ourselves in self-confessed helplessness upon Him. When we do this He lives through us His own life, bringing harmony, purpose, meaning, and poise to our life.

This peace passes all understanding. We cannot grasp the full meaning of it with our limited concepts. It is deeper, broader, and more satisfying than we can explain. But we enjoy what we cannot understand.

This peace "shall keep your hearts and minds through Christ Jesus." This means it is indestructible. The word translated "shall keep" is a military word which means "kept with a garrison." Paul brings together the two concepts of peace and war. This peace of God takes upon itself military-like functions. It garrisons the heart and mind.

By heart and mind are meant the emotional and intellectual faculties of man. It includes the emotions and purposes as well as the affections and thoughts. The peace of God garrisons and guards the whole man in the full scope of his manifold operations. This divine peace can be enjoyed in the midst of warfare. It is an indestructible peace that guards and garrisons against all care, anxiety, change, suffering, and conflict. It gives unalterable rest in God.

IV. GODLY LIVING (1 Timothy 4:8, 12; 2 Peter 1:5-8)

A. An Example (Timothy 4:8, 12)

8. For bodily exercise profiteth little: but godliness is profitable unto all things, having promise of the life that now is, and of that which is to come.

In this Epistle Paul has been giving Timothy advice concerning spiritual advancement and the methods appropriate for this. He now says, "Train yourself for godly living." He indicates that while physical training is of some benefit, this godly living is of benefit in every way.

Athletics was one of Paul's favorite resources for illustrations of spiritual truths. On this occasion he refers to the popular Greek gymnasium. It consisted of facilities for running, wrestling, and many other sports. It was a place where young men would attempt to promote the grace and vigor of their bodies through physical training. If they wanted to be successful in athletics they were told to gymnasticize.

Paul applies this same principle to the Christian life. He tells Timothy to gymnasticize. He is told to train himself with a view to godliness or godly living. The exercise which he is urged to participate in is to be of a spiritual nature.

The apostle probably had several ideas in mind concerning Timothy's training. He probably meant that just as a Greek youth in the gymnasium exerts himself to the best of his ability, so Timothy, too, by God's grace and power, must spare no effort to attain his goal in the spiritual realm. He was also suggesting that just as every youth striving for athletic success must discard everything that would be a handicap or burden in the training process, so Timothy should divest himself of all that would be encumbering to his spiritual progress.

12. Let no man despise thy youth; but be thou an example of the believers, in word, in conversation, in charity, in spirit, in faith, in purity.

It is guessed that Timothy was between thirty and forty years old at this time. Many of the elders with whom he would be working would have been much older than he. Compared to Paul, he would have been young for the kind of responsibility he had. Paul did not think him too young for the task. According to Paul, he is not to let them push him around because of his youth.

The positive injunction "but be thou an example of the believers" balances the previous negative statement. His life is to be one that will silence every adverse reaction about his youth.

Paul lists five things in which Timothy is to be an example: in speech, that is, in personal conversation; in conduct, that is, in customs, habits, and ways of dealing with people; in love, that is, in deep personal affection with his fellow Christians; in faith, that is, in the exercise of that gift of God from which love springs; in purity, that is, in complete conformity with God's moral law.

B. Diligence (2 Peter 1:5-8)

5. And beside this, giving all diligence, add to your faith virtue; and to virtue knowledge.

Faith is the first gift of God for Christian living. This is the precious faith of which Peter spoke so warmly throughout his first letter. Faith, the first gift of God, cannot remain alone; it must work and out of its active energies issue virtue.

Virtue is strength. It is the holy courage which enables Christians to act with boldness in the service of Christ.

With virtue comes knowledge. Courage and firmness may do damage unless they are directed by knowledge. Christian virtue leads to knowledge.

6. And to knowledge temperance; and to temperance patience; and to patience godliness.

The next grace of Peter's list is temperance. This is another word for self-control. Without self-control there is no unity of purpose. Self-control enables a man to govern his appetites, and to keep them under the control of a Christian conscience.

Side by side with self-control comes patient endurance. He who controls his appetites will learn to endure hardness.

Godliness is the next grace mentioned. Godliness is the spirit of reverence, the holy fear of God. The godly man sets God always before him; the thought of God controls his life.

7. And to godliness brotherly kindness; and to brotherly kindness charity.

Brotherly kindness naturally follows godliness. Out of godliness must flow the love of the brethren. God's people are knit together in one family and fellowship.

Charity is the last grace on Peter's list. Christian love must not be confined within the limits of the body of believers. It is especially due to those, but it cannot stop there. Love comes from God, who is love, and whose love is without limits.

8. For if these things be in you, and abound, they make you that ye shall neither be barren nor unfruitful in the knowledge of our Lord Jesus Christ.

Peter says that if we give all diligence, we must succeed, for the divine power is with us. When we make these graces our own through the Holy Spirit we will not be unfruitful. Love, the crown of all the graces of Christian character, is spiritual energy. It will not allow the Christian to be idle; it must work, and in its working it will bring us nearer to full knowledge of Christ.

REVIEW QUESTIONS

1. Define sound doctrine.

2. What was Timothy to avoid in Ephesus? Why?

3. What does Jesus say the basis of answered prayer is?

4. How did Abraham interpret the promise of faith?

5. According to Jesus, what are the possibilities of prayer?

GOLDEN TEXT HOMILY

"BE THOU AN EXAMPLE OF THE BELIEVERS, IN WORD, IN CONVERSATION, IN CHARITY, IN SPIRIT, IN FAITH, IN PURITY" (1 TIMOTHY 4:12).

The Apostle Paul was cognizant of Timothy's relative youthfulness with regard to his responsible position in the Church. Paul did not believe lack of chronological age was necessarily a hindrance to effective Christian service. He exhorted his younger protege to excel in those qualities in which youth are prone to be deficient, thereby to serve as an example to the believers.

Timothy was to be an example in word; that is, in language or manner of speaking.

The speech of unbelievers often contains profanity, filth, gossip, and malice. Unfortunately, Christians may acquire some of the speech patterns of the society in which they live. It is well to remember the teaching of our Lord, "Let your communication be Yea, yea; Nay, nay: for whatsoever is more than these cometh of evil" (Matthew 5:37).

The word translated *conversation* in this verse means much more than our modern English word. It means "manner of life, behavior, or conduct." Not only should the Christian be an example in speech but in actions.

Charity is a translation of the word *agape*, which means "affection, goodwill, love, or benevolence." In this context it refers to that love of believer toward believer as a result of their relationship to Christ.

The Christian is to be an example in faith; believing in God who is the creator and ruler of the universe, the bestower of salvation and other blessings promised in the Scriptures. It may also mean "faithfulness or fidelity," of which the believer should also be a model.

Finally, the Christian's conduct is to flow from a life of purity that is undefiled by this world. If a believer is to be an effective witness for Christ, he must be a Christlike example.—**Richard Y. Bershon, Chief, Chaplain Service, VA Medical Center, Tomah, Wisconsin**

SENTENCE SERMONS

THE CHRISTIAN GROWS spiritually by exercising his faith, praying effectively, and living a godly life in this present world.

—Selected

HE WHO WOULD leave footprints on the sands of time must wear work shoes.

—"Notes and Quotes"

THE GOLDEN RULE is not to measure others, but to measure self—your own love and service.

—Selected

GROWING IN faith and love helps keep us steadfast in the Lord.

—Selected

EVANGELISTIC APPLICATION

A CHRISTIAN'S WITNESS IS EN-
HANCED BY HIS DEMONSTRATION OF
SPIRITUAL MATURITY.

The story is told of two Irishmen, Pat
and Mike, who had narrowly escaped
death on a sinking ship. They were
floundering around in icy waters on a
couple of planks. Pat was addicted to
the grossest profanity and he bethought
himself that he would repent of it and the
Lord would come to his rescue. Mike
thought his theology sound. Pat assumed
the countenance of a horrified Pharisee
and began to pray. Just before arriving
at the main thesis of his repentant prayer,
Mike spotted a ship coming toward them.
As delighted as Columbus when he first
sighted land, Mike yelled, "Hold it, Pat.
Don't commit yourself. Here's a ship."
Pat immediately stopped praying. Isn't
that the way many of us are? The only
time we consider spiritual growth is when
we are in a jam. As soon as things
improve we forget God.

ILLUMINATING THE LESSON

The secret to spiritual growth is to be
surrendered to the presence of the living
Christ. As Grant said to Buckner in Fort
Donelson during the Civil War, "No terms
but unconditional surrender can be
accepted." So it is in the Christian life.

No terms but unconditional surrender can
bring about spiritual reality in the Christian
life that will foster spiritual growth. The
individual must give himself wholeheartedly
to the Christian way of life. Growth comes
about as a natural process. This growth
takes place when one through a surrendered life gains greater wisdom, keener
judgment, better organized direction,
greater constancy of moral actions, greater
courage, and deeper convictions.

The process of surrender is a constant
one. It is one in which the individual
learns to apply the principles of the
Kingdom to a greater area of his life. The
way to spiritual growth, then, may be
summed up in this way: to discover the
will of God and to do it consistently
without fear or hesitancy.

DAILY BIBLE READINGS

M. Prayer That Prevails. 1 Kings 17:19-
24

T. Guide for Godliness. Psalm 119:9-16

W. Demonstration of Faith. Daniel 3:16-
26

T. Growing in Knowledge. 1 Corinthians
13:9-12

F. Growing in the Word. Hebrews 5:11-
14

S. Overcoming the Evil One. 1 John
2:13-17

The Christian's Place in the Church

Study Text: 1 Corinthians 12:4-31; 1 Timothy 5:17, 18; Hebrews 13:17

Supplemental References: Ezra 3:10-13; Psalm 24:1-10; Matthew 16:13-18; Ephesians 2:18-22

Golden Text: "Ye are the body of Christ, and members in particular" (1 Corinthians 12:27).

Central Truth: As members of the body of Christ, believers should edify one another and support spiritual leaders.

Evangelistic Emphasis: Christians who consistently congregate with other believers are strengthened and challenged to reach out to the lost.

Printed Text

1 Corinthians 12:4. Now there are diversities of gifts, but the same Spirit.

5. And there are differences of administrations, but the same Lord.

6. And there are diversities of operations, but it is the same God which worketh all in all.

7. But the manifestation of the Spirit is given to every man to profit withal.

8. For to one is given by the Spirit the word of wisdom; to another the word of knowledge by the same Spirit;

9. To another faith by the same Spirit; to another the gifts of healing by the same Spirit;

10. To another the working of miracles; to another prophecy; to another discerning of spirits; to another divers kinds of tongues; to another the interpretation of tongues:

11. But all these worketh that one and the selfsame Spirit, dividing to every man severally as he will.

12. For as the body is one, and hath many members, and all the members of that one body, being many, are one body: so also is Christ.

13. For by one Spirit are we all baptized into one body, whether we be Jews or Gentiles, whether we be bond or free, and have been all made to drink into one Spirit.

14. For the body is not one member, but many.

15. If the foot shall say, Because I am not the hand, I am not of the body; is it therefore not of the body?

16. And if the ear shall say, Because I am not the eye, I am not of the body; is it therefore not of the body?

17. If the whole body were an eye, where were the hearing? If the whole were hearing, where were the smelling?

18. But now hath God set the members every one of them in the body, as it hath pleased him.

27. Now ye are the body of Christ, and members in particular.

28. And God hath set some in the church, first apostles, secondarily prophets, thirdly teachers, after that miracles, then gifts of healings, helps, governments, diversities of tongues.

1 Timothy 5:17. Let the elders that rule well be counted worthy of double

413

honour, especially they who labour in the word and doctrine.

18. For the scripture saith, Thou shalt not muzzle the ox that treadeth out the corn. And, The labourer is worthy of his reward.

LESSON OUTLINE

I. MEMBERS OF ONE BODY
   A. Unity
   B. Diversity

II. MANIFESTING SPIRITUAL GIFTS
   A. The Origin of Gifts
   B. The Bestowal of Gifts

III. SUPPORTING LEADERSHIP
   A. The Fact of Leadership
   B. The Responsibility of Leaders
   C. The Responsibility of Followers

LESSON EXPOSITION

INTRODUCTION

Paul portrays the church as the body of Christ in the twelfth chapter of First Corinthians. His Division has arisen and he is pleading for unity. He compares the church to the human body. "For as the body is one, and hath many members, and all the members of that one body, being many, are one body: so also is Christ" (v. 12). Suppose the members of the body—the foot, the ear, the eye, and so on—should begin to quarrel among themselves. What would be the result? The whole body would suffer. Each member of the human body is dependent upon every other member, and the health and well-being of the whole body is dependent upon the proper functioning of each separate part.

Therefore, it follows, "that there should be no schism in the body; but that the members should have the same care one for another" (v. 25). "Now ye," Paul declares addressing the members of the church at Corinth, "are the body of Christ, and members in particular" (v. 27). Some members have one function, some another; some have one gift, some another; but all are fellow members of the body of Christ, and if one member fails, the whole body becomes crippled.

I. MEMBERS OF ONE BODY (1 Corinthians 12:12-26)

A. Unity (vv. 12, 13)

12. For as the body is one, and hath many members, and all the members of that one body, being many, are one body: so also is Christ.

Many images are used in discussing the church in the New Testament. It is called a family, an army, a temple, a bride, and a body. Each of these images has important lessons to teach us. In three of his letters Paul uses the image of the body to emphasize the church. In each of these letters, he pointed out the same important truths: unity, diversity, and maturity.

The comparison of the church with a living body is not one that we find in the teachings of Christ himself; but He used essentially the same image when He said to His disciples, "I am the vine, ye are the branches" (John 15:5). Whether we take the image of the body or of the tree, basically the same ideas are presented. There is in each case an organization animated by a mysterious principle of life. And the hidden life is the cause of the organization, determines it, shapes it after its kind. The life is the formative principle. The growth of the body or of the tree is not by addition from without, but by development from within. The materials that nourish and build it up lie without, but it is the life that appropriates them, assimilates them, transforms them into its own substance, turns them into its proper use (Pulpit Commentary).

The Christian church is the result of the work of the Holy Spirit in the minds, consciences, and hearts of men. Its beliefs, its worship, its fellowship, its work, all have real worth in them just so far as they are the expression of the Spirit that dwells within, and no further.

13. For by one Spirit are we all baptized into one body, whether we be Jews or Gentiles, whether we be bond or free; and have been all made to drink into one Spirit.

This moral change by which believers

are united to Christ, and constituted living branches in the True Vine, includes in it a death to sin, a burial of the old man, and a resurrection from spiritual death to a new life of holy obedience. "Therefore we are buried with him by baptism into death"; that is, as Christ was buried in the grave, so we, by the baptism with the Spirit, are brought into this state of death to sin, "that like as Christ was raised up from the dead by the glory of the Father, even so we also should walk in newness of life."

B. Diversity (vv. 14-26)

14. For the body is not one member, but many.

Each individual member must be recognized as something in itself, as having an autonomy, as created for a distinct purpose and designed to do its own special work. In no other way could the body be worthy of its place as head of the physical world and represent the mind of man.

Someone has likened this wonderful organism, the body, to a community. Every cell is an independent activity, a citizen with rights of its own and entitled to protection against all hostile influence.

Paul gives prominence to the idea of each organ as performing its functions and as essential to the whole. If this unity is brought about from within, then it is reasonable to believe that every member must share the same life-giving principle.

15. If the foot shall say, Because I am not the hand, I am not of the body; is it therefore not of the body?

16. And if the ear shall say, Because I am not the eye, I am not of the body; is it therefore not the body?

17. If the whole body were an eye, where were the hearing? If the whole were hearing, where were the smelling?

18. But now hath God set the members every one of them in the body, as it hath pleased him.

(1 Corinthians 12:19-26 is not included in the printed text.)

The human body needs different functions if it is to live and grow. So does the church. Members should never compare or contrast themselves with other members, because each one is different and each one is important. The eye cannot hear, the ear cannot walk, the nose cannot see, yet each organ has an important ministry to perform. Diversity does not suggest inferiority. Unity without diversity would produce uniformity, and uniformity tends to produce death. Life is a balance between unity and diversity.

Paul liked to emphasize the law of order in the human body. He does this in other Epistles also—for example, Romans 12:4, 5; Ephesians 4:16; 5:30; and Colossians 2:19. To the apostle the human body presents a very striking illustration of diversity of gifts, each member having its own special endowment and use; unity amidst diversity, since each member shares the same common life; and mutual dependence, as each member is efficient for its particular use only with the support of all the others.

Paul believed that unity, not unvarying uniformity, is the law of God in the area of grace as in the natural world. As the many members of the body compose an organic whole, and none can be dispensed with as needless, so those variously gifted by the Holy Spirit compose a spiritual organic whole, the body of Christ, into which all are baptized by the one Spirit.

The apostle emphasizes that harmony is the key word. This is true as long as each part and portion does its own particular work efficiently and well. Schism in the body is disease, common helplessness, and the beginnings of death. Therefore, the apostle urges that there be constant empathy and rapport among the various members.

II. MANIFESTING SPIRITUAL GIFTS (1 Corinthians 12:4-11)

A. The Origin of Gifts (vv. 4-7)

4. Now there are diversities of gifts, but the same Spirit.

5. And there are differences of administrations, but the same Lord.

6. And there are diversities of operations, but it is the same God which worketh all in all.

7. But the manifestation of the Spirit is given to every man to profit withal.

Paul directed the attention of the Corinthians to the origin and use of spiritual gifts. He does this to counteract and correct the abuses of these gifts in the church. The apostle declared that the gifts were imparted by the Spirit according to His own sovereign will, without any reference to the merits or attainments of the people themselves. Spiritual gifts had been bestowed not for the promotion of favored individuals, but for the benefit of the church, in worship and service.

Paul talked about the administration of the gifts before he identified specific gifts. He said the Holy Spirit not only baptizes believers into the body of Christ, He also endues them with power to become functioning members.

The apostle uses the term "speaking by the Spirit" in verse 3. This refers to inspiration by the Holy Spirit working within a human spirit submitted to God. It also refers to inspiration resulting in the writing of the sacred Scriptures in 2 Timothy 3:16.

Spiritual gifts are numerous and varied but they are all given by the same Spirit which is the Holy Spirit (v. 4). It is the Holy Spirit who apportions them as He wills. Gifts are given not for personal, competitive rivalry, but for the church's corporate advantage. Gifts are many, but the Spirit is one. Gifts vary but the Spirit is unchangeable as the source of the gifts.

Paul uses the word *manifestation* in verse 7 to refer to the operation of the Holy Spirit through His gifts. This makes evident His presence in the church. Spiritual gifts, in fact, are necessary avenues of revelation, and necessary vehicles of adoration. No meeting for divine worship can be complete without the Holy Spirit. Spiritual gifts are also necessary instruments of power for service.

B. The Bestowal of Gifts (vv. 8-11)

8. For to one is given by the Spirit the word of wisdom; to another the word of knowledge by the same Spirit.

In his list of gifts the apostle identified three in relation to understanding—wisdom, knowledge, and discernment. The gift of wisdom is the ability of spiritually endowed persons in the church to judge rightly and to follow sound courses of action. Wisdom also includes the idea of the development and use of manual skills, as in the case of Hiram, who was "filled with wisdom" in the craft of metallurgy (1 Kings 7:13, 14).

As a spiritual gift, wisdom is the miraculous enlightenment of the spiritual mind by the Holy Spirit. Paul identified this gift in 1 Corinthians 12:8 as "the word of wisdom." One translation describes it as "the utterance of wisdom," while another gives it as "the gift of speech."

Whether manifesting itself in mental enlightenment or in supernatural utterance, wisdom is an essential component in a spiritual experience. This is not to say that all Spirit-filled persons are especially blessed with the gift of wisdom, but that the Spirit indeed endows whom He will, in His own time, for manifestations of wisdom.

Paul identifies the "word of knowledge" as a second gift of understanding. Knowledge is spoken of here not as a natural grace, but as a gift of the Holy Spirit. Consequently, the gift of knowledge includes in its function the supernatural and the miraculous. Knowledge, in the sense of a spiritual gift, is the declaration of some aspect of divine omniscience through Spirit-filled human beings in the church to implement a sovereign purpose in the mind of God.

Omniscience—or all knowledge—belongs to God. Only He knows all things. And although there is some knowledge God chooses to keep to Himself, there are times when He imparts some of His knowledge to us. At such times, the gift of knowledge is a manifestation of a gift in which the Holy Spirit for a specific purpose on a particular occasion imparts to us information known only to Him. He imparts this knowledge to assist the church in its ministry.

9. To another faith by the same Spirit; to another the gifts of healing by the same Spirit.

Someone has said that the gift of faith is faith carried to its extreme. It is faith that impregnates godly desires with divine power, whether they be in spoken words or in acts of obedience.

Though the gift of faith produces results that transcend natural law, it is not identical with the gift of miracles. The gift of miracles operates with immediacy in overt action as a public testimony to the greatness of God. It has an objective effect. In contrast, the gift of faith has its effect primarily inwardly upon the Spirit-filled person. Its essential functions are to afford divine protection, to provide for physical needs, and to aid in one's work. Unlike the gift of miracles, its outcome may be deferred—a circumstance doubtlessly intended to increase our reliance upon God.

Another gift of the Spirit is identified by Paul as "gifts of healing." Divine healing is a basic fundamental Christian belief. It has its foundation in the Holy Scriptures. That healing is divine means it proceeds from God. We receive healing, therefore, directly from God. The word *healing* means the restoring of a sick person to health by divine means.

Harold Horton in discussing the gifts of healing states:

"First, we must notice the important plurality in its title. It is not the gift of healing. It is the gifts of healing. Three times in this twelfth chapter it is mentioned (vv. 9, 28, 30), and each time in the original the two nouns are in the plural."

These gifts are for the supernatural healing of diseases and infirmities without natural means of any sort. They are the miraculous manifestation of the Spirit for the banishment of human ills—whether organic, functional, nervous, acute, or chronic.

10. To another the working of miracles; to another prophecy; to another discerning of spirits; to another divers kinds of tongues; to another the interpretation of tongues.

A miracle has been defined as a supernatural intervention in the ordinary course of nature, a temporary suspension of the accustomed order, an interruption of the system of nature as we know it.

Harold Horton is of the opinion that the gift of the working of miracles operates by the energy or dynamic force of the Spirit in reversals or suspensions of natural laws. A miracle is a sovereign act of the Spirit of God irrespective of laws or systems. Horton further believes that a miracle does not, as some cynical unbelievers say, demand the existence of an undiscovered law to explain it. A miracle has no explanation other than the sovereign power of the Lord.

There are many illustrations of miracles in the Bible. The parted waters of the Red Sea, the constant provision of manna in the wilderness, and the crumbling walls of Jericho serve as examples of miracles wrought during the Old Testament era. In the New Testament one only has to trace the ministry of Jesus and then the ministry of His disciples to observe the fact of miracles.

It has been observed that in most instances miracles were the result of the faith of Spirit-filled men. On occasion, however, God worked mighty acts without any help from man. Daniel was delivered by a sovereign act of God. Elijah was fed by ravens according to a uniquely executed plan of God. Paul and Silas were delivered from prison by an earthquake that could have been only the direct intervention of God. The point is that it is God who performs miracles.

In its simplest form, prophecy is divinely inspired utterance. It is entirely supernatural. As speaking with tongues is supernatural utterance in an unknown tongue, so prophecy is supernatural utterance in the prophet's own tongue. But it is a manifestation of the Spirit of God, and not one of the human mind. It has no more to do with human powers of thought and reasoning than walking on water has to do with powers of equilibrium. Prophecy is a miracle straight from heaven.

Prophecy may be "predictive" or "proclamative"—it may speak of things to come, or of things that are. Most prophetic utterance is proclamative. For example, when Simon Peter preached on the Day of Pentecost he interpreted certain Old Testament passages in the new way of Pentecost. The Holy Spirit manifested Himself in prophetic speaking through Peter's preaching.

The word *discerning* means "judging through." Robinson defines it as "a distinguishing, a discerning clearly." The basic idea seems to be that discernment is "a piercing of all that is merley outward, a seeing right through, then forming a judgment based on that insight."

Harold Horton defines *discerning of spirits* as "that which gives supernatural insight into the secret realm of spirits." Discernment reveals the kind of spirit motivating a person who is manifesting supernatural knowledge or power. The gift supernaturally conveys information that could not be obtained apart from this gift. Horton further states that by the operation of discernment we may know the true source and nature of any supernatural manifestation, whether divine or satanic, and the character of such spiritual manifestation can only be determined by the use of this gift. It is not discernment of everything in general, but of spirits.

Tongues may be defined as "supernatural speaking in a language unfamiliar to the speaker and his hearers." Speaking in tongues has nothing to do with linguistic ability or with the human mind or intellect. It is a manifestation of the Holy Ghost employing human speech.

Although one who speaks in tongues never loses control of himself, his mind, his intellect, and his understanding become quiescent. The linguistic skill of man is no more employed in speaking in tongues than the surgical skill of man was employed when at Peter's words, "Rise up and walk," the lame man instantly arose, leaped, and walked. Speaking in tongues— either "other" tongues or the "unknown" tongue—is an act of the Holy Spirit.

The interpretation of tongues as a manifestation of the Holy Spirit is vastly superior to human thought and volition. This gift may be defined as an inspired explanation in commonly understood language of an inspired utterance in a tongue or tongues unknown to the speaker or hearers. Interpretation of tongues makes possible and meaningful the use of tongues in the meeting for worship and edification.

Donald Gee is of the opinion that the gift of interpretation comes directly from the Holy Spirit, and does not imply the slightest natural knowledge by the interpreter of the language spoken in tongues. Therefore, it logically follows that the interpretation is received, not so much by close attention to the words of the one speaking in tongues, as by a close concentration in spirit upon the Lord—who alone gives the interpretation. The words are given by revelation and follow the rules of prophecy and all inspired utterances, coming either by vision, by burden, or by suggestion, whichever the Lord may choose.

The gift is one of interpretation, not translation. It means to explain thoroughly, and as such it can be descriptive or literal. Translation seeks to duplicate in another language every word spoken. Interpretation seeks to give meaning to utterances not understood.

11. But all these worketh that one and the selfsame Spirit, dividing to every man severally as he will.

Verse 11 indicates the sovereignty of the Holy Spirit in the distribution of spiritual gifts. Why does He bestow gifts at all? Or why does He bestow them upon the people whom He does? The answer is because it pleases Him to do so. "[He] worketh all things after the counsel of his own will" (Ephesians 1:11).

III. SUPPORTING LEADERSHIP (1 Corinthians 12:27-31; 1 Timothy 5:17, 18; Hebrews 13:17)

A. The Fact of Leadership (1 Corinthians 12:27-31)

27. Now ye are the body of Christ, and members in particular.

28. And God hath set some in the church, first apostles, secondarily prophets, thirdly teachers, after that miracles, then gifts of healings, helps, governments, diversities of tongues.

(1 Corinthians 12:29-31 is not included in the printed text.)

On these verses *Pulpit Commentary* says: "Each Christian has his several functions to discharge in the Church and for the Lord. There are diversities of gifts and consequent diversities of ministries; and this diversity is itself a witness to the individual, the personal nature of the membership of every one in him who is the Source of all true blessing and power. All cooperate for the same end. That this is so is evident; and how can it be so, except as a result of such common subjection to the one Head as secures the mutual harmony and coordination of all the members? Each is selected for his own part and qualified for his own position."

B. The Responsibility of Leaders (1 Timothy 5:17, 18)

17. Let the elders that rule well be counted worthy of double honour, especially they who labour in the word and doctrine.

18. For the scripture saith, Thou shalt not muzzle the ox that treadeth out the corn. And, The labourer is worthy of his reward.

The apostle focuses his attention on the officials in the church with special attention concerning their pay. He suggests that ample provision should be given them on the basis of their having done their work well. It would seem that their leadership responsibilities not only included ruling well, but also excelling in preaching and teaching the Word and doctrine.

Paul sets forth the duty of supporting the elders by quoting from the Old Testament: "Thou shalt not muzzle the ox that treadeth out the corn" (see Deuteronomy 25:4). He connects this statement with a statement from Jesus: "And, the labourer is worthy of his hire" (see Luke 10:7).

It would seem that Paul wanted Timothy to understand that a divine sanction underlies the principle of fair support for those who serve the church.

C. The Responsibility of Followers (Hebrews 13:17)

(Hebrews 13:17 is not included in the printed text.)

The writer has given an appeal in verse 7 to recall past teachers. He now gives another appeal to obey those who at present have the responsibility for guidance and control. The picture is that of an ideal ministry, "they watch for your souls, as they that must give account."

Happy is the congregation which has such a pastor, and happy is the pastor who fulfills this requirement. The result will be joy and not grief to the pastor, and unspeakable profit to the congregation.

REVIEW QUESTIONS

1. According to 1 Corinthians chapter 12, how can there be unity in diversity?

2. How does Paul compare and contrast the members of the body in 1 Corinthians 12:12-26?

3. Why does God bestow various gifts?

4. Does Paul imply that each Christian ordinarily has one gift instead of several?

5. Does Paul intend to establish a rating of the gifts in 1 Corinthians 12:8-10?

GOLDEN TEXT HOMILY

"YE ARE THE BODY OF CHRIST, AND MEMBERS IN PARTICULAR" (1 Corinthians 12:27)

We have here in general terms the summation and application of the foregoing illustration of the human body as a picture of Christ's body. Paul concludes that members of the body are "members in particular."

"Now are ye the body of Christ." That which is set in the body is set in the interest of the whole body. The eye is the servant of the whole body, and so with all members. Using the human body Paul exerts great effort to show the need of different parts to make the whole. The ear, foot, hand are not the body. They are parts of the body. While not the body, each is necessary in making up the body. The body has many parts, but the many parts make up one body when they are all put together. Not one of the members is everything, but every member is something!

Christ is the Head of the whole church. He presides over all and individual members sustain to each other the relation of fellow-members in the same body. All are subject to the same head.

Collectively, each of you in all your diversity make up the body of Christ. But your individuality and uniqueness is not lost in the union. Unlike a drop of water falling in a river loosing its identity as it becomes part of the river, you are "members in particular."

Individual members do not get lost in the union—eyes remain eyes, ears remain ears, hands remain hands. Different gifts and functions continue to operate making the body of Christ what it is—mutually interdependent on each other. Isolated from each other neither is complete without the others.

To belong to Christ's body means not only to belong to Him, but to help each other, honor one another, and be sensitive to one another.—**Joel Harris, M.Div., Registrar and Coordinator of Public Relations, School of Theology, Cleveland, Tennessee**

SENTENCE SERMONS

AS MEMBERS of the body of Christ, believers should edify one another and support spiritual leaders.

—Selected

THE MEASURE of your responsibilities to the body of Christ is the measure of your opportunities.

—Bob Jones, Sr.

THE QUICKEST WAY to get a church on its feet is for its members to get on their knees.

—William Ward Ayer

FELLOWSHIP WITH the holy God promotes holiness among men.

—"Speaker's Sourcebook"

EVANGELISTIC APPLICATION

CHRISTIANS WHO CONSISTENTLY CONGREGATE WITH OTHER BELIEVERS ARE STRENGTHENED AND CHALLENGED TO REACH OUT TO THE LOST.

A young man in the Civil War went with a group of friends to enlist in the army. While the others were signing, he stood around with hesitancy. Finally he went forward and signed the necessary papers for enlistment. Someone asked him, "Why did you keep hesitating?" He answered, "Because when I signed the papers, I was signing my life away."

This is what the individual does when he surrenders to Jesus Christ. He signs his life away to receive a greater one. He writes off a life full of insecurity, helplessness, inadequateness, and selfishness to receive in return a life full of joy, hope, peace, certainty, and security.

ILLUMINATING THE LESSON

One of the greatest needs of the church today is for authoritative, spiritual, and sacrificial leadership. Authoritative, because people love to be led by one who knows where he is going and who inspires their confidence. Spiritual, because a leadership which is carnal and explainable in terms of the natural, be it ever so competent, can result only in sterility and spiritual bankruptcy. Sacrificial, because it is modeled on the life of the One who gave Himself a sacrifice for the whole world, and who stated that the path to leadership was by the lonely road of sacrificial service.

DAILY BIBLE READINGS

M. God's Glory Fills the Temple. 1 Kings 8:5-11

T. God's People Worship. Ezra 3:10-13

W. The King of Glory. Psalm 24:1-10

T. Christ's Promise. Matthew 16:13-18

F. Growth of the Church. Acts 2:37-47

S. The Household of God. Ephesians 2: 18-22

Reaching Out to the Lost

Study Text: Isaiah 53:6; Luke 24:46-49; John 1:35-45; 4:7-26; Acts 1:6-8; 8:26-40; Romans 3:23; 6:20-23

Supplemental References: Isaiah 53:1-12; 55:1-13; Matthew 22:1-9; 28:16-20; Acts 1:1-8

Golden Text: "All we like sheep have gone astray; we have turned every one to his own way; and the Lord hath laid on him the iniquity of us all" (Isaiah 53:6).

Central Truth: Every believer has the privilege and responsibility to share the message of salvation with the lost.

Evangelistic Emphasis: Every believer can experience the joy of leading people to salvation through faith in Christ.

Printed Text

Romans 6:20. For when ye were the servants of sin, ye were free from righteousness.

21. What fruit had ye then in those things whereof ye are now ashamed? for the end of those things is death.

22. But now being made free from sin, and become servants to God, ye have your fruit unto holiness, and the end everlasting life.

23. For the wages of sin is death; but the gift of God is eternal life through Jesus Christ our Lord.

Luke 24:46. And said unto them, Thus it is written, and thus it behoved Christ to suffer, and to rise from the dead the third day:

47. And that repentance and remission of sins should be preached in his name among all nations, beginning at Jerusalem.

48. And ye are witnesses of these things.

49. And, behold, I send the promise of my Father upon you: but tarry ye in the city of Jerusalem, until ye be endued with power from on high.

John 1:40. One of the two which heard John speak, and followed him, was Andrew, Simon Peter's brother.

41. He first findeth his own brother Simon, and saith unto him, We have found the Messias, which is, being interpreted, the Christ.

42. And he brought him to Jesus. And when Jesus beheld him, he said, Thou art Simon the son of Jona: thou shalt be called Cephas, which is by interpretation, A stone.

Acts 8:29. Then the Spirit said unto Philip, Go near, and join thyself to this chariot.

30. And Philip ran thither to him, and heard him read the prophet Esaias, and said, Understandest thou what thou readest?

31. And he said, How can I, except some man should guide me? And he desired Philip that he would come up and sit with him.

32. The place of the scripture which he read was this, He was led as a sheep to the slaughter; and like a lamb dumb before his shearer, so opened he not his mouth:

33. In his humiliation his judgment was taken away: and who shall declare his generation? for his life is taken from the earth.

34. And the eunuch answered Philip, and said, I pray thee, of whom speaketh

the prophet this? of himself, or of some other man?

35. Then Philip opened his mouth, and began at the same scripture, and preached unto him Jesus.

LESSON OUTLINE

I. MAN'S LOSTNESS
   A. Man's Iniquity
   B. Sinners by Birth
   C. The Control
II. GOD'S CALL TO WITNESS
   A. The Charge to Christians
   B. The Source of Witness
III. PATTERN FOR OUR WITNESS
   A. The Individual in Witnessing
   B. The Word in Witnessing

LESSON EXPOSITION

INTRODUCTION

The unanimous testimony of the New Testament is that all men outside of Jesus Christ are lost. Those who accept the Scriptures as authoritative and valid in matters of human belief and conduct cannot deny this tragic fact. According to the Bible there are really only two kinds of people, the saved and the lost. Every human being is in one of these two classes. There is no middle ground. There is no halfway place.

It is difficult for the natural man to accept this. He recoils from considering his lost condition. He realizes he is not perfect, but he can hardly accept the idea that his situation amounts to lostness. He feels that there must be something in him, or something he can do, which will commend him to God and gain some favor in God's sight.

The natural man thinks that surely God is not so unmerciful as to cast him out altogether. Persons living according to average high moral standards find great difficulty in accepting the scriptural portrait of themselves, at least until the Holy Spirit does convicting work in their lives.

The only reliable source of knowledge we have on this point is the Bible. Philosophy, science, ethics, and nonbiblical

religions are not revelational, and therefore tend to commend man instead of condemn him. Human thought and reason are altogether untrustworthy, for man as a sinful creature has a depraved heart and a darkened mind. He cannot form correct judgments about himself apart from divine revelation.

The biblical plan of redemption rests upon the truthfulness and factuality of the utter lostness of mankind. We must accept the Bible's teachings here or else reject them all along the line.

I. MAN'S LOSTNESS (Isaiah 53:6; Romans 3:23; 6:20-23)

A. Man's Iniquity (Isaiah 53:6)

It is generally accepted that Isaiah meant both his nation Israel and the race of mankind when he said, "all we like sheep have gone astray." Either would have been true. Israel had gone astray repeatedly. The New Testament points out that all have sinned and come short of the glory of God.

Man has turned away from God and has gone his own selfish way. This is what the prophet means by the statement, "We have turned every one to his own way." The way of the natural man is not the way of God. It is the way by which man is lost. It is a way that is filled with sorrow, disappointment, death, and eternal separation from God.

"And the Lord hath laid on him the iniquity of us all." Someone has suggested that if God has laid my iniquities on Christ, then they are no longer on me. This is what the prophet meant by these words. This is also what John the Baptist meant when he said, "Behold the Lamb of God which taketh away the sin of the world" (John 1:29). When a sinner believes in Jesus Christ, receives Him as his Savior, he is no longer under the condemnation of sin. Sin is no longer on him, that is, the guilt, the condemnation, the penalty of sin, is no longer upon him. Why? Because the guilt, condemnation, and penalty of our sins were transferred to our Substitute.

B. Sinners by Birth (Romans 3:23)

A study of the New Testament indicates that there may be wide variation in degrees of human sinfulness, but no variation in the fact of sinfulness and separation from God. Some are worse sinners than others, but all are sinners. Sinners are completely lost. They are lost now unless they repent and believe in Jesus Christ. They do not have to wait until their works are investigated and weighed before the judgment bar of God to know their status and destiny. These are determined here and now by their attitude and relationship to Jesus Christ.

Until the teachings of the Bible concerning the lost sink deeply into their hearts, Christians will never experience a compassionate concern for their salvation. Christians must know the desperate condition of men before they will attempt to try to win them to Christ.

The three most revealing passages in the Bible concerning the lost are Romans 3:9-23, Ephesians 2, and John 3. In these passages, listing the items separately, can be found at least a hundred ways in which the New Testament describes the lost condition of humanity. Many of the items are mentioned in the Psalms, one of the most loved books in the Old Testament. Every condition and sin named is true of every unsaved person, either actually or potentially.

C. The Control (Romans 6:20-23)

20. For when ye were the servants of sin, ye were free from righteousness.

All men are the servants of sin until they experience the saving grace of God. All are not slaves to the same sin. Some are led captive by their lusts and passions. Others are drawn away by the pleasures and vanities of the world. Many are under the power of pride and self-righteousness. But all, without exception, are alienated from the life of God. All are possessed with unbelief and self-sufficiency.

The Bible asserts this humiliating and indisputable truth throughout its pages. History confirms it in the lives of the most eminent saints. They confess it to have been the case in their lives. Personal experience proves it with respect to our own life. The very excuse which men use to justify their life when they say "I cannot live as God requires" establishes this truth.

21. What fruit had ye then in those things whereof ye are now ashamed? for the end of those things is death.

Paul entreats every one to consult the records of his own conscience and answer the question, "What does sin provide?" He implies that the unprofitableness of sin can easily be seen through experience. Whether men have drunk deep of the pleasure of sin, or have followed their selfish desires with more measured steps, the question still is, "What does sin provide?"

Sin, previous to engaging in it, promises much. But what real satisfaction has it given us? Suppose a man to have had all the means of gratification that Solomon possessed, and, like him, to have withheld his heart from no joy; still, the question could be asked, Was your pleasure lasting? Was it without consequences? Is not what Solomon said true, "Even in laughter the heart is sorrowful; and the end of that mirth is heaviness"? (Proverbs 14:13).

What about the man who has sought his happiness in less dramatic ways, but has wasted in mere earthly pursuits the time that was given him to prepare for eternity? If he could recall his misspent years, would he not rather that they had been spent in seeking those things belonging to eternity and that make for peace of mind? Although he may not look with envy on a pious individual who has given himself in surrender to God, does he not secretly respect that man, and wish that his last days could be like his?

The apostle suggests that there will be no pleasure in our dying hour to reflect on the fact that we have, on such and such an occasion, gratified our sinful desires by revelling in excessive pleasures. Nor will having simply lived a life of external decency provide any comfort, when we remember how we have neglected God and our own soul. Shall we not wish in that hour that we had lived with Christ as our Savior and the Holy Spirit as our guide?

22. But now being made free from sin, and become servants to God, ye have your fruit unto holiness, and the end everlasting life.

The Christian is a slave who has changed masters. This is the way Paul describes the Christian's situation. He was formerly a slave of sin; now he is set free from sin, but bound in the service of righteousness. The apostle is declaring that the Christian in his entirety is a bondslave to righteousness. He illustrates this absolute subjection by reference to the former status under sin, for that, too, was a total bondage.

Paul knows that this parallel has only a limited validity and that the comparison falls short in some respects. To begin with, the difference between the two forms of bond service spoken of is as wide as the heavens. The service of sin is an actual bondage, and the service of righteousness and of God is an actual freedom. Christians live their life on the border between two worlds. They live "in Christ"; but have not thereby ceased to share the fate of the children of Adam. They live "in the spirit"; but they still feel the drag of the flesh. Because of the weakness of the flesh, there is need for such advice that Paul gives.

23. For the wages of sin is death; but the gift of God is eternal life through Jesus Christ our Lord.

In this one tremendous sentence, Paul sums up the Bible, the need of man, the provision of God. But what is this thing we call sin? The average man's conception of sin is usually hazy and inadequate. We need to see sin in all its heinous reality to properly deal with it, and to realize the extent of the plan of redemption from sin which we have in Jesus Christ.

Men have suggested numerous definitions of sin. Some of the leading ones are: sin is finiteness as opposed to freedom; sin is a necessity of the good;

sin is the frustration of order; sin is a moral defect; sin is part of man's primitive animalism, which he is gradually overcoming. These conceptions of sin are totally inadequate. There is some truth in some of them, but if we combine what is true in all of them, we are still without a proper understanding of sin.

According to Christian theology, sin is: lack of conformity to the moral law of God either in act, disposition, or state; sin is selfishness; sin is pride; sin is unbelief; sin is sensuality; sin is rebellion against God.

The New Testament gives some illuminating statements as to the nature of sin: sin is transgression of the law of God, 1 John 3:4; sin is unrighteousness, 1 John 5:17; sin is omission of the good, James 4:17; sin is unbelief, or lack of faith in God, Romans 14:23; sin is state, or nature, Romans 7:14.

The scriptural diagnosis of sin is surprisingly exact, thorough, and complete. This is what we would expect. No other book brings such self-consciousness as does the Bible. It is really God's mirror to reveal to man his sinfulness.

Paul said that the wages of sin is death. The ages have proved the truth of Paul's words. It was death when Adam and Eve were driven from Eden and the mark of mortality was placed on their foreheads. It was death when the flood waters of God's wrath deluged the earth, destroying every living, breathing thing outside the ark. It was death. It is death. It shall continue to be death until Christ, the Conqueror, vanquishes that last dread enemy.

The wages of sin is death in our time. It is physical death, mental death, moral death, spiritual death, the second death. It is death to character, to personality, to ambition, to reputation, to love, to influence, to life, to homes, to businesses, to schools, to churches. It is universal death, it is inescapable death, and it is eternal death.

Paul declares the wages of sin is death, but the gift of God is eternal life through Jesus Christ our Lord. That means there is a way of escape from the curse, from the condemnation, from the doom, from the damnation of sin. It is a God-promised, a Jesus-provided, a Holy Spirit-proffered way. It is the Bible way, the gospel way, the way of the cross, the way of the blood, the way of Calvary. It cost God all that He was and all that He had, but He offers it freely to all men.

The apostle emphasizes that salvation from sin is through Jesus Christ. In Christ there is absolute, total, eternal, effective salvation for every soul to the ends of the earth. This is based on the biblical facts that Jesus came to save; He died to save; and He lives to save.

II. GOD'S CALL TO WITNESS (Luke 24:46-49; Acts 1:6-8)

A. The Charge to Christians (Luke 24:46-49)

46. And said unto them, Thus it is written, and thus it behoved Christ to suffer, and to rise from the dead the third day.

On this verse *Pulpit Commentary* had this to say: "The message which the Church is to deliver: the Christ whom God has sent, and the world needs—the historical Christ, incarnate, suffering, risen; and this Christ presented as the fulfillment of all Scripture, the consummation of Divine thought and purpose, 'the Lamb slain from the foundation of the world,' the Prophet, Priest, and King, by whom man is redeemed, in whom the nature and want, the hope and desire, of all nations are interpreted. The Church is called to teach that 'thus it behoved Christ to suffer, and to rise from the dead the third day.' Wide is the realm of truth, and the Church must cover this realm in its vision; but this is the center of all the circle" (*Pulpit Commentary*).

The fifty-third chapter of Isaiah is one of the great chapters in the Old Testament predicting the suffering of Christ. It is very significant that almost every passage in the Old Testament referring to "the third day" has in it the idea of renewal of life, deliverance, or resurrection.

47. And that repentance and remission of sins should be preached in his name among all nations, beginning at Jerusalem.

This is Luke's account of the Great Commission of Christ to evangelize the world. (Compare this with Matthew 28:18-20; Mark 16:15-18; Acts 1:8.)

According to G. Campbell Morgan, repentance is the desire in man for renewal and reconstruction. Apart from it, no man is ever regenerated or renewed. Remission of sins is the answer of God to that repentance. Where there is no repentance, there can be no remission. Genuine repentance based on faith and expressing itself in faith is always answered by remission of sins.

Following His declaration that all the holy writings of the previous ages had pointed to Himself, Christ now announces that all the redemptive work to be accomplished in the ages to come must arise through the proclamation of repentance and remission of sins in His own name. By His death on the cross, He had made the remission or cancellation of our sins possible.

The writer of the Book of Hebrews states that without the shedding of blood, there is no remission of sins (9:22). Unless this is preached, the gospel has not been preached. In fact, the central theme of New Testament preaching is repentance and remission of sins. If this does not occur, there is no true carrying out of the Lord's Great Commission. Unless this is the basis of our preaching, preaching is in vain.

48. And ye are witnesses of these things.

A New Testament witness is one who is convinced of a basic truth, who has surrendered his life to that truth, who is transformed by that truth, and who spends his time proclaiming that truth. It was A. B. Bruce who said that it does not take a great man to be a good witness, and to be witnesses of Christian truth was the main business of the apostles.

49. And, behold, I send the promise of my Father upon you: but tarry ye in the city of Jerusalem, until ye be endued with power from on high.

If Christians are to undertake witnessing concerning Jesus Christ, they shall need power for service; power in their lives and power in their work. The truth will never be proclaimed with conviction to the hearts of sinners, nor will they ever be born again, unless it is by the supernatural power of the Holy Spirit.

Dr. Andrew Murray said: "We may know all that the Gospels record and all that Scripture further teaches of the person and work of Jesus; we may even speak from past experience of what we once knew of the power of Jesus. But this is not the witness of power that is promised here and that will have effect in the world. We can truly witness to just as much of Jesus as the Holy Spirit is witnessing to us in life and truth. Unconditional submission to the power in our inner life is the one condition of our being clothed with it."

B. The Source of Witness (Acts 1:6-8)

(Acts 1:6-8 is not included in the printed text.

It is believed that the reference here (v. 6) is to either the meeting of the Eleven with the risen Lord in Jerusalem, or to the conference on the Mount of Olives to which Christ led them from the Upper Room.

The question of the disciples indicates that, even after all that Christ had taught regarding the spiritual nature of His kingdom, the disciples still clung to the idea of its political character. They believed it must involve the freedom of the Jews from Roman bondage, and the restoration of the glories of David's kingdom.

The interest of the disciples in the setting up of the kingdom of God here upon earth and the restoring of the kingdom of Israel according to the promises was not an unnatural interest, nor was it an unscriptural interest. Jesus did not rebuke them for that. He simply replied, "It is not for you to know the times or the seasons, which the Father hath put in his own power" (v. 7).

Jesus directed the attention of the disciples away from the restoration of a kingdom to Israel to personal power for witnessing. Power means effectiveness. We will be made effectual. We will be so blessed of God that our witnessing will have an effect upon people. We shall be able to witness with power.

Jesus gave a sweeping view of the complete program of the church, as well as an outline of the Book of Acts: "In Jerusalem"—at home; "in all Judea"—in your family; "in Samaria"—among your neighbors; "and unto the uttermost part of the earth" (Acts 1:8). Someone has said it is as if you dropped a stone into a pool of water, and the waves would go out from the point of impact to the shore on all sides. So it is with the gospel. The gospel will fall into your own heart, radiating into your home, then into the circle of your friends and relatives, then to your neighbors, and then to the uttermost part of the earth.

III. PATTERN FOR OUR WITNESS (John 1:40-42; Acts 8:26-40)

A. The Individual in Witnessing (John 1:40-42)

40. One of the two which heard John speak, and followed him, was Andrew, Simon Peter's brother.

41. He first findeth his own brother Simon, and saith unto him, We have found the Messias, which is, being interpreted, the Christ.

42. And he brought him to Jesus. And when Jesus beheld him, he said, Thou art Simon the son of Jona: thou shalt be called Cephas, which is by interpretation, A stone.

Andrew was among the first disciples to come to Jesus. He also had the distinction of bringing the first convert to Jesus. He brought Simon Peter, his own brother.

It is interesting that the first convert was won to Christ through the use of personal experience. Andrew told Peter that he and John had found the Messiah. For him it was the ultimate, the greatest, the highest—"the Christ."

Andrew would make an ideal Christian layman if he were living today. An ideal layman is not one who gives the most money, or makes the best speeches in board meetings, or organizes effective committees, important as these are to the church. An ideal layman is one who engages in reproduction—making disciples. Bringing people to Jesus Christ is the greatest work that we can do and the highest honor that we can achieve.

The biblical record does not indicate that Andrew became a great preacher like Peter, nor a writer like Paul. He won recognition by bringing his brother to Christ.

B. The Word in Witnessing (Acts 8:26-40)

26. And the angel of the Lord spake unto Philip, saying, Arise, and go toward the south unto the way that goeth down from Jerusalem unto Gaza, which is desert.

27. And he arose and went: and, behold, a man of Ethiopia, an eunuch of great authority under Candace queen of the Ethiopians, who had the charge of all her treasure, and had come to Jerusalem for to worship.

Philip simply took the angel of the Lord at his word and went. There was no argument, no asking for an explanation. He simply obeyed.

The eunuch would be comparable to our "Secretary of the Treasury." He was the comptroller of the realm. He was a Jewish proselyte who believed in the Jewish teaching and had come to Jerusalem to worship.

28. Was returning, and sitting in his chariot read the prophet.

The eunuch was probably reading the Greek version, the Septuagint or Translation of the Seventy, made in Alexandria, Egypt, by 70 scholars.

29. Then the Spirit said unto Philip, Go near, and join thyself to this chariot.

30. And Philip ran thither to him, and heard him read the prophet Esaias, and said, Understandest thou what thou readest?

Listening to the Spirit, Philip ran. He was ready, quick to obey. He initiated the conversation by asking if the passage was understood by the reader.

31. And he said, How can I, except some man should guide me? And he desired Philip that he would come and sit with him.

32. The place of the scripture which he read was this, He was led as a

sheep to the slaughter; and like a lamb dumb before his shearer, so opened he not his mouth:

33. In his humiliation his judgment was taken away: and who shall declare his generation? for his life is taken from the earth.

34. And the eunuch answered Philip, and said, I pray thee, of whom speaketh the prophet this? of himself, or of some other man?

The eunuch was reading from the fifty-third chapter of Isaiah which deals with the death of Jesus. He did not understand the passage and asked Philip what it meant.

35. Then Philip opened his mouth, and began at the same scripture, and preached unto him Jesus.

All Scripture has to be related to Jesus Christ. Start with any scripture, and lead the listener to see the Lord Jesus. That is the most important thing any witness can do.

36. And as they went on their way, they came unto a certain water: and the eunuch said, See, here is water; what doth hinder me to be baptized?

37. And Philip said, If thou believest with all thine heart, thou mayest. And he answered and said, I believe that Jesus Christ is the Son of God.

38. And he commanded the chariot to stand still: and they went down both into the water, both Philip and the eunuch; and he baptized him.

The eunuch was asking Philip, when he asked about baptism, if there was any reason he could not be a Christian. The ceremony of baptism was an outward act, performed by people who made a profession of their faith. The eunuch knew this and asked why he could not be baptized.

Notice Philip's answer. "If thou believest with all thine heart, thou mayest" (v. 37). Philip was not just saying, "If you understand all the reasons why, or if you are sure that you believe all the things we say." The believing that Philip was talking about involved committing one's self to God. It meant entering into a personal relationship with Jesus Christ. It meant receiving Him as a Savior.

Upon the confession of faith of the eunuch, Philip baptized him.

39. And when they were come up out of the water, the Spirit of the Lord caught away Philip, that the eunuch saw him no more: and he went on his way rejoicing.

40. But Philip was found at Azotus: and passing through he preached in all the cities, till he came to Caesarea.

Observe the work of the Holy Spirit in the situation described in verses 39 and 40. He led Philip to the eunuch after He had prepared the way through the use of the Word of God. He then led Philip away to others who needed the work of a witness; but He stayed with the eunuch.

The eunuch went his way rejoicing. He was not rejoicing because Philip was gone. He was rejoicing because the Lord was with him.

REVIEW QUESTIONS

1. What does it mean to be a witness for Christ?

2. What is the charge given to Christians by Jesus?

3. What are the areas of responsibility included in the witnessing described in Acts 1:6-8?

4. What was Andrew's approach to witnessing for Christ?

5. Describe Philip's experience in witnessing to the eunuch.

GOLDEN TEXT HOMILY

"ALL WE LIKE SHEEP HAVE GONE ASTRAY; WE HAVE TURNED EVERY ONE TO HIS OWN WAY; AND THE LORD HATH LAID ON HIM THE INIQUITY OF US ALL" (Isaiah 53:6).

Today the gift of God is still eternal life through Jesus Christ to everyone who believes. Yet people choose to go their own directions in life like sheep that have gone astray. It is not by chance that God calls us sheep. We often behave just like sheep. And we need a shepherd.

Scripture points out that most of us are a stiff-necked and stubborn lot. We prefer to follow our own fancies and turn to our own ways as our text points out. This we do deliberately, repeatedly, even to our own disadvantage. There is something almost terrifying about the destructive self-determination of a human being. It is interlocked with personal pride and self-assertion. We insist we know what is best for us even though the disastrous results may be self-evident. We humans cling to the same habits that we have seen ruin other lives.

God laid on His Son the iniquity of our sins and stubborn self-will. He was wounded for our transgressions and bruised for our iniquities as the ultimate sacrifice. Our response must be acceptance and obedience.

It is the Word of God that comes swiftly to our hearts with surprising suddenness to correct and reprove us when we go astray. It is the Spirit of the Living God, using the living Word, that convicts our conscience. In this way we are kept under control by Christ who wants us to walk in the ways of righteousness.

There is always, however, a percentage of people who refuse to allow God to lead them. They too must be reached for Christ since they insist on running their own lives and following the dictates of their own wills. They insist they can be masters of their own destinies even if ultimately such destinies are destructive. They don't want to be directed by the Spirit of God—they don't want to be led by Him—they want to walk in their own ways.

As believers we can experience joy as we fulfill our responsibility of leading these people to salvation through faith in Christ.
—Robert D. McCall, Youth Missions Coordinator, Church of God General Department of Youth and Christian Education, Cleveland, Tennessee

SENTENCE SERMONS

EVERY BELIEVER has the privilege and responsibility to share the message of salvation with the lost.

—Selected

THE TRUE DISCIPLE is a witness to

the fact that the Lord gives us His presence.

—Selected

THE CHURCH would be a lot stronger if it had fewer "I" beams and more "sunbeams."

—Keith Huttenlocker

YOU CAN'T STOP a runaway world by keeping still.

—Sam Shoemaker

EVANGELISTIC APPLICATION

EVERY BELIEVER CAN EXPERIENCE THE JOY OF LEADING PEOPLE TO SALVATION THROUGH FAITH IN CHRIST.

One minister said that he never knew what it meant to be lost until a little girl was lost in the town where he was a pastor. This little girl and her brother went into the woods to look for the cows, but they did not find them. When nightfall overtook them, they got into an argument as to which way their home was. Neither one would give in. Each went his way.

When the little boy arrived home after dark, the mother frantically asked, "Son, where is your sister?"

"She said I was lost and would not come home with me. She went the other way."

The parents knew the beasts would devour the child. News went out for miles around and neighbors gathered to help in the search.

The next morning about daylight the little girl was found unharmed. That day there was much rejoicing in the community.

The minister said it was then that he thought, "We spent all night searching for this little girl and justly so and are now rejoicing because she is found. Yet there are hundreds of lost souls in our community—lost to Christ. We have spent no sleepless nights in prayer or in search for them."

ILLUMINATING THE LESSON

If we could see our loved ones and neighbors through the eyes of Jesus—see them as they really are—we would be moved with a compassion and a passion for their souls. But how did Christ see people in the multitudes that thronged Him? He saw them departed from God, depraved in sin, destined for hell, and in despair without a shepherd.

It is as we see the lost in this way that we will be moved to reach out in love to them.

DAILY BIBLE READINGS

M. Wounded for Our Transgressions. Isaiah 53:1-5

T. Justified Through Christ. Isaiah 53:7-12

W. Invited to Partake. Isaiah 55:1-7

T. Share the Message. Matthew 22:1-10

F. Command to Witness. Matthew 28:16-20

S. Called to Witness. Acts 1:1-8

August 14, 1988

Personal Holiness

Study Text: Romans 14:1-12; 1 Thessalonians 4:1-7; 1 Peter 1:13-16
Supplemental References: Deuteronomy 28:1-9; Isaiah 35:1-10; Romans 6:15-23; Hebrews 12:12-17
Golden Text: "Be ye holy; for I am holy" (1 Peter 1:16).
Central Truth: God calls the believer to holy living and provides the strength to obey.
Evangelistic Emphasis: Holy living is a powerful testimony in persuading people to accept Christ as Savior.

Printed Text

1 Peter 1:13. Wherefore gird up the loins of your mind, be sober, and hope to the end for the grace that is to be brought unto you at the revelation of Jesus Christ;

14. As obedient children, not fashioning yourselves according to the former lusts in your ignorance:

15. But as he which hath called you is holy, so be ye holy in all manner of conversation;

16. Because it is written, Be ye holy; for I am holy.

1 Thessalonians 4:1. Furthermore then we beseech you, brethren, and exhort you by the Lord Jesus, that as ye have received of us how ye ought to walk and to please God, so ye would abound more and more.

2. For ye know what commandments we gave you by the Lord Jesus.

3. For this is the will of God, even your sanctification, that ye should abstain from fornication:

4. That every one of you should know how to possess his vessel in sanctification and honour;

5. Not in the lust of concupiscence, even as the Gentiles which know not God:

6. That no man go beyond and defraud his brother in any matter: because that the Lord is the avenger of all such, as we also have forewarned you and testified.

7. For God hath not called us unto uncleanness, but unto holiness.

Romans 14:1. Him that is weak in the faith receive ye, but not to doubtful disputations.

2. For one believeth that he may eat all things: another, who is weak, eateth herbs.

3. Let not him that eateth despise him that eateth not; and let not him which eateth not judge him that eateth: for God hath received him.

4. Who art thou that judgest another man's servant? to his own master he standeth or falleth. Yea, he shall be holden up: for God is able to make him stand.

LESSON OUTLINE
I. CALLED TO HOLINESS

A. The Motive for Holiness
B. The Model for Holiness

II. WALKING IN HOLINESS
   A. Exhortation to Purity
   B. Maintaining Purity
III. RESPECTING OTHERS
   A. Individual Understanding
   B. Individual Responsibility

LESSON EXPOSITION

INTRODUCTION

Holiness is grounded in the nature of God. It coexisted with God and graced the inner chambers of eternity. Holiness is older than the fall of man or the sin of angels. Our God is a holy God. It is a holy God who requires holiness in His people.

Holiness is given a place of supreme importance in the Bible. In the words of an unknown author: "It breathes in the prophecy, thunders in the Law, whispers in the promises, supplicates in the prayers, resounds in the songs, sparkles in the poetry, shines in the types, glows in the imagery, and burns in the spirit of the whole scheme from its alpha to its omega— its beginning to its end. Holiness! Holiness needed, holiness required, holiness offered, holiness attainable, holiness a present duty, a present privilege, is the progress and completeness of its wonderful theme. It is the truth glowing all over and voicing all through revelation; singing and shouting in all its history, and biography, and poetry, and prophecy, and precept, and promise, and prayer— the great central theme of the system."

I. CALLED TO HOLINESS (1 Peter 1:13-16)
A. The Motive for Holiness (vv. 13, 14)

13. Wherefore gird up the loins of your mind, be sober, and hope to the end for the grace that is to be brought unto you at the revelation of Jesus Christ.

Peter refers to Eastern clothing when he uses the term "gird up the loins." The hot climate dictated the wearing of long, loose, flowing robes. That was fine as long as the movement of the body could be deliberate. But if there had to be movement in a hurry, then the clothing could be hampering. Therefore, they must gather up their garments so as not to impede their progress. When the Israelites were expecting the summons to leave Egypt, they stood around the tables on which the paschal lamb was smoking. They were ready for the journey with their loins girded. Elijah, the prophet of fire, girded himself for the swift courier run before Ahab's chariot, from Carmel to Jezreel (1 Kings 18:46).

The Apostle is admonishing the Christian to guard his tastes, appetites, affections, and inclinations. He uses the term "gird up the loins of your mind" because sin begins in the thought life. Here the idea is entertained before it becomes part of a behavior pattern. We must not let our thoughts stream as they will; we do so at our peril.

As one of the ancient preachers said, "We must 'gird up' the habits of our souls, and trim ourselves, so as to pass as quickly and easily as possible through the thorny jungle of the world."

F. B. Meyer put it this way: "Hold your spirit in a tight hand. Put a curb on appetite. Say no to luxurious pleasure seeking. Curtail your expenditure on yourself. Do not spread yourself too widely. Watch eye and lip, thought and wish, lest any break from the containing cords of self-control. Keep thy heart with all diligence. Give Vanity Fair as little chance as possible, by passing swiftly and unostentatiously through" (*Tried by Fire*).

The Apostle urged his readers to "be sober." *Sobriety* is an interesting word in the New Testament. Elders, deacons, women, aged men, young men, and maidens are constantly exhorted to be sober. The word means "temperance, self-control, and having a balanced estimate of oneself in the world."

Some counterfeit sobriety by assuming a superior spiritual posture. They assume an austere and forbidding attitude. They denounce everything that is innocent and natural. They treat severely those who do not accept and yield to their scruples.

The genuinely sober individual moves freely through the world. He enjoys the beautiful and innocent pleasures God has given. He uses them without abuse. He rejoices in all the good things God has blessed him with, but he never allows any of them to control him. His affections and his will are fully surrendered to God. This is why he can enjoy the life God has given him.

Peter urges believers to hope to the end. Hope motivates the believer onward. It helps him through the discomforts of the journey. It provides an inward joy that keeps things bright within his heart.

Grace is the object of the believer's hope. Grace comes from God. It is His favor. He gave the first gift of grace. It is never deserved by any merits of men. Someone has very aptly said that grace is glory begun and glory is grace completed. So it is for the one who surrenders to Jesus Christ.

14. As obedient children, not fashioning yourselves according to the former lusts in your ignorance.

The hope of salvation will motivate the believer to follow after holiness. "Every man that hath this hope in him purifieth himself" (1 John 3:3). Holiness is complete separation from all that defiles. Believers must, as obedient children, forsake the lusts of the world, the flesh and the devil.

Lust is natural inclination run wild, overthrowing all restraint and asserting its own arrogant will. Those in darkness, unillumined by grace, allow their lusts to fashion their lives. They become molded or fashioned, as clay by the potter's hand. Being ignorant of the abominableness of sin, of its disastrous results and its insidious growth, unbelievers yield to it until it becomes a tyrant and eventually ruins their lives.

Peter suggests that the obedient believer will not allow lust to dominate his life. Obedience is not holiness. Holiness is absolute surrender to God; it is the possession of the soul by God. But holiness always leads to obedience. The obedient soul is the holy soul.

B. The Model for Holiness (vv. 15, 16)

15. But as he which hath called you is holy, so be ye holy in all manner of conversation;

16. Because it is written, Be ye holy; for I am holy.

Peter states that the model for holiness is the all-holy God himself. One of the early theologians said that the essence of religion consists in the "imitation of Him we worship."

Pulpit Commentary makes some interesting statements on these two verses. "The heathen gods were represented as actuated by human passions and stained with hateful sins; their character must have reacted upon their ignorant worshipers; their worship was degrading. Our God is the most holy One, awful in holiness. He has not called us unto uncleanness, but unto holiness; He has set us apart for Himself, that we should be holy to Him. Holiness unto the Lord was written upon the miter of the high priest; it should be written in the hearts of Christians who are a holy priesthood, dedicated to the service of God. Holiness lies in the imitation of God. 'Be ye followers of God as dear children,' says Paul. The word *followers* literally means 'imitators' " (*Pulpit Commentary*).

Obviously believers cannot be perfect imitators of God in holiness because holiness in God is inherent; in believers it is acquired. In God, holiness is infinite and unchangeable; it admits no increase, no diminution; it is an immutable attribute of the divine nature. Holiness in believers admits of degrees and can only be maintained by perpetual increase. Saints on earth and saints in heaven will become more intelligently holy, beautiful in worship, and exact in obedience as the ages roll on.

Holiness in men is conditional, and may be lost, at least while probation continues; in God it is integral and substantive, and can no more be lost than God can cease to be. In God, holiness is commensurate with infinite capacity; in man, it is measured by infinite and fallen capabilities—capabilities limited and weak.

II. WALKING IN HOLINESS (1 Thessalonians 4:1-7)

A. Exhortation to Purity (vv. 1-3)

1. Furthermore then we beseech you, brethren, and exhort you by the Lord Jesus, that as ye have received of us

how ye ought to walk and to please God, so ye would abound more and more.

By using the phrase "furthermore then," Paul is indicating that all that remains for him to do is to offer the exhortations which follow. It suggests that he has reached the end of his argument or discourse.

The phrase "we beseech you" means "we ask you" or "we request you." It is not as strong as the word *exhort* which follows. The word translated "exhort" in this verse is used to mean "earnest exhortation." All of this is to emphasize the importance of the subject being dealt with.

Paul reminds the Thessalonians that what he is saying is in the name and by the authority of the Lord Jesus.

The Apostle had given them many instructions concerning how to live the Christian life, and he hopes they are following those instructions more fully.

2. For ye know what commandments we gave you by the Lord Jesus.

Undoubtedly the Thessalonians would remember what Paul had taught them since it had been but a short time ago. Again the Apostle reminds them that what he had shared with them had been from the Lord.

3. For this is the will of God, even your sanctification, that ye should abstain from fornication.

God's will for every believer is sanctification. B. C. Caffin has some interesting thoughts on this verse. "He willeth that all men should be saved; but salvation is possible only through sanctification; for without holiness no man shall see the Lord. Sanctification is the separation from all that is evil, the entire consecration of the whole man to the service of God, the gradual conforming of the human will to the blessed will of God. Christ is our sanctification. He of God is made unto us wisdom, and righteousness, and sanctification. Faith brings us near to Him, and He becomes our righteousness; then the work of sanctification begins. The more the believer grows in the knowledge of the Lord Jesus Christ, the

more does that blessed knowledge exert its hallowing power. The beauty of holiness, the sweetness of fellowship with God, the glories of His coming kingdom are more and more deeply felt. Then, when the affections are set upon things above and the heart's love is centered upon God, the soul reacheth forth after Christ, longing above all things to be like Him, yearning for holiness with a strong, intense desire, eagerly striving to purge itself from the defilement of sin, and to advance ever onwards in the work of sanctification; and that because the Lord Jesus Christ dwelleth there Himself, and the pulses of His love beat in the converted heart. He is our sanctification" (*Pulpit Commentary).*

Paul warned his readers to "abstain from fornication." He comes at once to particulars in his fight against impurity in these words. Though adultery and incest were crimes among the heathen, fornication was not looked upon as a sin at all. This makes it clear why this sin was emphasized in the letter sent to the Gentile churches from the Jerusalem Council (Acts 15:20-29). The Gentiles "walked after the flesh in the lust of uncleanness."

B. Maintaining Purity (vv. 4-7)

4. That every one of you should know how to possess his vessel in sanctification and honour.

Paul uses the word *vessel* here to refer to the human body. It is the duty of males and females as well as married and unmarried to maintain pure bodies. The human body should not be debased or polluted. It should be honored as a noble work of God. It should always be used for pure purposes.

5. Not in the lust of concupiscence, even as the Gentiles which know not God.

The Gentiles were known for their extremes in sensual desires and activities. Paul warns those who have been converted to Christ and are still surrounded by unbelievers to be on guard. They were especially to guard against letting their normal sexual desires become sensual passions. What was to be accounted for in the Gentiles by their ignorance of God was not to be excused in those who had been blessed with the knowledge of God.

6. That no man go beyond and defraud his brother in any matter: because that the Lord is the avenger of all such, as we also have forewarned you and testified.

Impurity is a sin against man. Impure desires assume the form of love. Uncleanness usurps and degrades the sacred name of love. *Pulpit Commentary* states: "The sensual man ruins in body and soul those whom he professes to love. He uses words of tenderness. He is the most cruel, the deadliest enemy in his wicked selfishness. He cares not for the nearest and holiest ties. He sins against the sanctity of marriage. He brings misery upon families. Seeking only the gratification of his own wicked lusts, he transgresses and wrongs his brethren. But his sin will bring swift punishment upon him. The Lord is the avenger in all such things."

7. For God hath not called us unto uncleanness, but unto holiness.

What is holiness? One way of explaining it is to say that it consists of theory, experience, and practice. Theory is to be believed by the intellect; experience is to be enjoyed by the sensibilities; and practice is to be lived by the will. Theoretical holiness has to do with a man's head; experimental holiness has to do with a man's heart; and practical holiness has to do with a man's hand. Therefore, we have the head sound in doctrine, the heart pure in love, and the hand clean in life.

Theory has to do with doctrine. Doctrine is the mainspring of our spiritual activities, the foundation of our spiritual building. Doctrine has to do with what we believe. Some would tell us it does not matter what we believe, just so we are sincere in it. That may sound well, but it has more sound than sense. Salvation does not depend on sincere thinking; it depends on right thinking. Theory is important, for you can't get an experience without it. Everybody goes into religion headfirst. The intellect must first be convinced before the heart can be converted. You must know about God before you can know God.

Creed is important, but experience is imperative. It is not enough to know about God; we must know God. The experience is an epochal experience, a conscious experience, a perfective experience, an emancipative experience, and it is an emotional experience. The modern trend is for an experience without emotion. A religion without emotion is a religion without God; for God is love, and how could you have love and not have emotion? A religion without emotion is too dry to kindle a fire, to say nothing of saving a sin-captured, devil-enslaved world.

Holiness is ethical as well as doctrinal. You could be doctrinally straight and at the same time ethically crooked. The Christian church is strong enough in doctrine to save the world, but weak enough in practice to become its laughingstock.

Peter had the ethics of holiness in mind when he said, "Be ye holy in all manner of [life]"—holy in your business life, public life, domestic life, and secret life. To be holy in all manner of life is more than a mere profession of holiness. If we give each aspect of holiness a proper emphasis, we will produce Christians that will be an asset to any church. If we unduly stress theory, just preach doctrine, we will produce formalists. If we unduly stress experience and say but little about doctrine, we will produce fanatics. If we unduly stress practice, we will turn out Pharisees.

III. RESPECTING OTHERS (Romans 14:1-12)

A. Individual Understanding (vv. 1-6)

1. Him that is weak in the faith receive ye, but not to doubtful disputations.

Acceptance is needed by those who are weak in faith concerning Christian liberty. They need to be welcomed into Christian fellowship. Those who are strong in the faith are not to sit in judgment of the weak, but to show a spirit of love and understanding. It is perhaps wise not to discuss certain issues with them. We know it is Christian not to pass judgment but to welcome them lovingly into the church fellowship.

"Weak in the faith," as mentioned here, refers not to any essential or inherent defect in character, but to a lack of spiritual maturity. Faith in Christ saves us from sin, but it does not make us spiritually mature at the same time. This requires growth, which takes time.

2. For one believeth that he may eat all things: another, who is weak, eateth herbs.

It is interesting that Paul does not give the reason why the group in the church refrained from eating certain things. He apparently assumes that the issue was so well known to the congregation that he does not need to stop to describe it. It is generally accepted that it was not a group of Jewish Christians who wanted to force Jewish ways on the church. This assumption is based on the fact that there was no commandment in Judaism not to eat meat or drink wine. Paul was always against efforts to bind the Christian believers with Jewish shackles. In Galatians he wrote, "To whom [them] we did not yield submission even for an hour" (2:5; New King James Version). He was inflexible when the issue was the Christian's freedom from the law.

There have been some who advocated that the abstention of "the weak" was related to a widespread religious vegetarianism in antiquity, rooted in the dualism of the Hellenistic view of existence. But such a view would be so basically at variance with the Christian view that it is hardly possible that Paul would have exercised the patience that he now shows to the weak.

It is very probable that the weak abstained from meat and wine that they might not be contaminated by things that were unclean because they had been offered to idols.

3. Let not him that eateth despise him that eateth not; and let not him which eateth not judge him that eateth: for God hath received him.

What should be the attitude of the church toward the weak in faith? What should be the attitude of the church toward those who create a disturbance in the church? The answer of Paul is this: "As for the man who is weak in faith, welcome him." Do not reject or despise

him. Receive him as a brother, for he too is a genuine member of the church.

Paul had instructed the strong to welcome the weak, but he adds, in verse 1, that this should not be for disputes over opinions. It would be easy for us to think that the strong ought to accept the weak with the view in mind that they will make them strong. But Paul would not agree to that approach. His attitude was that fellowship among Christians is not to be based on arguing and trying to convert others to a particular point of view so that it is accepted as the norm for Christian behavior. Sameness is not a Christian ideal, and acceptance should not be based on such secondary considerations. Christians are not all alike, nor should they be.

4. Who art thou that judgest another man's servant? to his own master he standeth or falleth. Yea, he shall be holden up: for God is able to make him stand.

5. One man esteemeth one day above another: another esteemeth every day alike. Let every man be fully persuaded in his own mind.

6. He that regardeth the day, regardeth it unto the Lord; and he that regardeth not the day, to the Lord he doth not regard it. He that eateth, eateth to the Lord, for he giveth God thanks; and he that eateth not, to the Lord he eateth not, and giveth God thanks.

Along with the question of diet came the question of holy days. Under the law, Israel was required to observe certain holy days, such as the Sabbath which was divinely instituted and binding.

The New Testament does not enjoin any kind of legal observance of the Old Testament Sabbath. There is mention only of the Lord's Day. Paul was very open-minded concerning this. He said, "Let every man be fully persuaded in his own mind." It is good and proper for us to esteem Sunday as a day of worship, but we should regard every day as holy unto the Lord.

Probably the true attitude toward days and foods is found in the words "unto the Lord." Everything we do is to be done or left undone as "unto the Lord."

B. Individual Responsibility (vv. 7-12)

7. For none of us liveth to himself, and no man dieth to himself.

8. For whether we live, we live unto the Lord; and whether we die, we die unto the Lord: whether we live therefore, or die, we are the Lord's.

9. For to this end Christ both died, and rose, and revived, that he might be Lord both of the dead and living.

The vital thing in the Christian faith is that one belongs to the Lord through faith. It is really not important that one eats or refrains from eating. Faith is the thing that is true of all Christians. It is the fact that unites them, whether they are strong or weak in the faith.

Paul states that a Christian no longer lives to himself; he lives for his Lord, and Christ lives in him. In life and in death he belongs to the Lord. That was the reason for Christ's death and resurrection, that we should become His and He become our Lord.

10. But why dost thou judge thy brother? or why dost thou set at nought thy brother? for we shall all stand before the judgment seat of Christ.

11. For it is written, As I live, saith the Lord, every knee shall bow to me, and every tongue shall confess to God.

12. So then every one of us shall give account of himself to God.

On these verses C. H. Irwin states: "Where we differ from our fellow-Christians in details of doctrine, worship, or practice, we are very prone to be uncharitable in our judgments. We are inclined to doubt their Christianity because they do not see just as we do in such matters. One great fact the Apostle would have us remember when we are tempted to condemn our brethren. It is the fact of the judgment to come. . . . It is not we who are to be the judges of our fellow-Christians, but God. We would not like it if they were our judges; then why should we judge them? The thought that we must stand before a higher judgment seat, where all our sins and secret thoughts and unchristian motives shall be known,

should make us more cautious in our condemnation of others" (*Pulpit Commentary*).

REVIEW QUESTIONS

1. How does Peter describe the life of holiness?

2. Compare Peter's approach to holiness with that of Paul.

3. How does Paul suggest that one should maintain a life of holiness?

4. Describe a person who is "weak in the faith."

5. Describe a person who is "strong in the faith."

GOLDEN TEXT HOMILY

"BE YE HOLY; FOR I AM HOLY" (1 Peter 1:16).

According to the best manuscripts this verse is literally saying "Ye shall be holy for I am holy." Holiness is the very nature of God. When we accept Jesus as Savior, we take on the very nature of God. Our holiness, like God's, is spontaneous. It is not learned or cultured, but it is a natural outflow of the new nature because of the New Birth.

One does not possess holiness because of a self-disciplined or self-restrained life. If this were true, holiness could be learned. An athlete could be holy since his is a self-disciplined and self-restrained life. He does not smoke or drink because he knows this will impair his ability to perform. Just because a person possesses these characteristics does not make him holy. Many people today do discipline themselves to live a good moral life, but neither their nature nor their thoughts has changed. They may look and act changed on the outside, but on the inside they still have that old nature unyielded to the Lord. Christ said these are "like unto whited sepulchres . . . but are within full of dead men's bones" (Matthew 23:27).

A duck is a duck because his mother is a duck. He was born a duck and has the very nature of a duck. He does not learn to be a duck. He does not even learn to swim because it is his very nature to take to the water. When we take on the nature of God we take on His holiness also. Holy living is as second nature to us as swimming is to the duck.

As we look at children we think of their innocence, but innocence does not make a person holy. That child does not behave himself because of innocence or holiness but because the parents have instructed, disciplined, and, at times, forced that child to abstain from evil by imposing a penalty upon him if he does not. It is not even a child's nature to be holy. In Proverbs 22:15 we read, "Foolishness is bound in the heart of a child but the rod of correction shall drive it far from him."

How then can we be holy? We cannot be holy except it be our nature through Christ Jesus. "Ye *shall* be holy because I am holy"; it will be an automatic and spontaneous change of nature. Holiness is of the heart, and we fashion ourselves after the desire and lusts of our heart.
—**Gene A. Robinson, Pastor, Chicago, Illinois**

SENTENCE SERMON

HOLINESS VANISHES when you talk about it but becomes gloriously conspicuous when you live it.
                        —**"Speaker's Sourcebook"**

EVANGELISTIC APPLICATION

HOLY LIVING IS A POWERFUL TESTIMONY IN PERSUADING PEOPLE TO ACCEPT CHRIST AS SAVIOR.

A man who had been converted on Sunday from a life of drink was dreading going to work on Monday morning. He feared that, being in the atmosphere of other sinful men, he would not be able to hold out. As he went to work on the first morning of the new week, he was praying for the Lord to help him not to drink. He decided the best way to do it was to live this new life one hour at a time. If he could make it for one hour, he could make it for two, and so on.

Later that week a man came into his office, and while sitting and talking noticed a lot of straight marks on the calendar on the wall. He inquired about this. The saved man said, "I was converted last Sunday night. I have prayed every hour on the hour for the Lord not to let me fall. Every hour I make it, I put a mark on the calendar for that day." There on the wall was the evidence that he had been kept, hour after hour.

ILLUMINATING THE LESSON

A great artist stood viewing a beautiful scene as the crowds rushed by. Occasionally some would stop and comment as they looked also, catching a glimpse of the beauty here or there in the scene which the artist pointed out to them, before they hurried away.

The artist was a very busy man, but he always returned to this scene. It was his constant inspiration in all his work, and he made it his task to reveal to others as much of its loveliness as possible whenever possible.

Finally, though, he set up his easel and painted the picture. All the highlights were clearly brought out against a vivid background, so that everyone who stopped to study the picture might see all the wonders that had been revealed to the artist through the years.

Looking at the picture, then at the scene, people comment, "I see it now; strange I never saw it before," as they point out one highlight after another.

Having completed his masterpiece, the artist continued his busy life for only a short time before he folded his easel, laid down his brushes, put aside his colors, folded his smock, and went to meet the Creator of the beautiful scene and to thank Him for the revelation and the opportunity to reveal it to others.

The great artist? The surrendered life.

The picture? Holiness triumphant.

DAILY BIBLE READINGS

M. Holy People. Deuteronomy 28:1-9
T. Worship in Holiness. Psalm 29:1-11
W. Way of Holiness. Isaiah 35:1-10
T. Serve in Holiness. Luke 1:68-75
F. Holiness Needed. Hebrews 12:12-17
S. Live a Holy Life. Romans 6:15-23

The Christian and Entertainment

Study Text: Romans 14:13-23; 1 Corinthians 8:4-13; 9:24-27; 1 Timothy 6:11-16

Supplemental References: Nehemiah 9:6-8; Psalm 12:1-8; Galatians 5:16-26; 1 John 5:15-17

Golden Text: "Love not the world, neither the things that are in the world. If any man love the world, the love of the Father is not in him" (1 John 2:15).

Central Truth: The believer's choice of entertainment must be consistent with biblical principles.

Evangelistic Emphasis: The believer's selection of entertainment activities can affect his testimony to the unsaved.

Printed Text

Romans 14:13. Let us not therefore judge one another any more: but judge this rather, that no man put a stumbling-block or an occasion to fall in his brother's way.

14. I know, and am persuaded by the Lord Jesus, that there is nothing unclean of itself: but to him that esteemeth any thing to be unclean, to him it is unclean.

15. But if thy brother be grieved with thy meat, now walkest thou not charitably. Destroy not him with thy meat, for whom Christ died.

16. Let not then your good be evil spoken of.

1 Corinthians 8:7. Howbeit there is not in every man that knowledge: for some with conscience of the idol unto this hour eat it as a thing offered unto an idol; and their conscience being weak is defiled.

8. But meat commendeth us not to God: for neither, if we eat, are we the better; neither, if we eat not, are we the worse.

9. But take heed lest by any means this liberty of your's become a stumbling-block to them that are weak.

10. For if any man see thee which hast knowledge sit at meat in the idol's temple, shall not the conscience of him which is weak be emboldened to eat those things which are offered to idols;

11. And through thy knowledge shall the weak brother perish, for whom Christ died?

12. But when ye sin so against the brethren, and wound their weak conscience, ye sin against Christ.

9:24. Know ye not that they which run in a race run all, but one receiveth the prize? So run, that ye may obtain.

25. And every man that striveth for the mastery is temperate in all things. Now they do it to obtain a corruptible crown; but we an incorruptible.

26. I therefore so run, not as uncertainly; so fight I, not as one that beateth the air:

27. But I keep under my body, and bring it into subjection: lest that by any means, when I have preached to others, I myself should be a castaway.

1 Timothy 6:11. But thou, O man of God, flee these things; and follow after righteousness, godliness, faith, love, patience, meekness.

12. Fight the good fight of faith, lay hold on eternal life, whereunto thou art also called, and hast professed a good profession before many witnesses.

LESSON OUTLINE

I. CAREFUL IN SELECTION
   A. Affecting Others
   B. Developing Priorities
   C. Assisting Others
II. CONSISTENT IN EXAMPLE
   A. Knowledge
   B. Considerateness
III. TEMPERATE IN ALL THINGS
IV. FAITHFUL IN SPIRITUAL THINGS
   A. Conduct
   B. Incentives

LESSON EXPOSITION

INTRODUCTION

The right is not always so attractive as the wrong, and duty is seldom as appealing as pleasure.

Many years ago an army general, in referring to some West Point students who violated their code of honor, made the following interesting and thought-provoking observation:

"They have fallen into evil ways. They have not, in the words of the Cadet Prayer, 'preferred the harder right, instead of the easier wrong,' and in their failure have brought sorrow upon themselves and upon the military academy."

The choice of the "easier wrong" is as old as Adam. In fact, he started it. He set the example. He chose what he wanted in preference to what he knew was right. This is the essence of sin.

Someone has very aptly said that character is built only as one chooses the right even when it is not so attractive. A Christian does not do right only when it pleases, or when it is expedient, or when it promises to pay off. He does right any time and all the time because it is right. Any benefit is a by-product, not an incentive.

This principle is as applicable to entertainment, amusement, or leisure time activity as to any other aspect of human behavior.

I. CAREFUL IN SELECTION (Romans 14: 13-23)

A. Affecting Others (vv. 13-15)

13. Let us not therefore judge one another any more: but judge this rather, that no man put a stumblingblock or an occasion to fall in his brother's way.

Christian forbearance is very difficult to exercise; however, it is very important in the life of a Christian. Some things, including many amusements, are quite neutral. We may accept or reject them. Other things, including amusements, are very definite and we have to deal with them as they are. The problem is that all Christians do not have the same understanding. But Paul explained that although we may not agree in many things, we must live in a way that is acceptable to God. His attitude is based on the fact that Christian behavior must come from a sincere desire to please God.

The Apostle warned against Christians becoming stumbling blocks to other Christians. Stumbling block, from which comes our word *scandal* suggests "a trap or snare—something placed in the way of others, causing them to fall."

14. I know, and am persuaded by the Lord Jesus, that there is nothing unclean of itself: but to him that esteemeth any thing to be unclean, to him it is unclean.

To Paul, few things were unclean in themselves. He believed that material objects do not have qualities in themselves which make them unclean. The problem is our attitude and use of them.

Paul appealed to the individual's conscience. He felt that however misguided, it should never be violated. He does not mean to suggest that to follow conscience is absolute proof that what we are doing is right; but to violate conscience, which is our personal persuasion of right and wrong, is always wrong.

15. But if thy brother be grieved

with thy meat, now walkest thou not charitably. Destroy not him with thy meat, for whom Christ died.

If a weak Christian suffers because of something the strong Christian does, the latter is not acting in love. A strong Christian may be able to engage in certain types of entertainment, amusement, or leisure time activity without any rebuke of conscience, knowing that he is not offending the Lord; yet a weaker Christian may suffer in observing him, because to him it is sin.

Paul's position is that if Christ is our pattern, any sacrifice of tastes and liberties for our brother's sake is plain Christian duty.

B. Developing Priorities (vv. 16-18)

16. Let not then your good be evil spoken of.

Christian liberty, the freedom of conscience which has been won by Christ, will invariably get a bad name if it is exercised in a loveless fashion.

Freedom to follow convictions must be balanced by our love for other Christians and by personal responsibility to do what is best for them.

It really is not a question of, "Can I feel free to do certain things?" but "Can I, by doing or not doing certain things, fulfill my Christian responsibility to help others live and grow in the Christian life?"

How can this principle be applied today? We do not disagree over eating meat, especially the kind offered to idols. But we do disagree over many things classified as entertainment. Unfortunately, there is little general agreement over such things as sports, movies, music, reading materials, and others.

There is, however, a basic principle that is applicable: the principle that Paul suggests to the Romans—the principle of love. Let us not do anything that would hurt or demean someone for whom Christ died. We do have a responsibility to act in love toward our fellow Christians.

17. For the kingdom of God is not meat and drink; but righteousness, and peace, and joy in the Holy Ghost.

18. For he that in these things serveth Christ is acceptable to God, and approved of men.

Some Christians either are not willing or not able to distinguish between the essentials and the nonessentials of Christianity. Perhaps there is in every person the desire to force his ideas upon others, at least at times. But real Christianity calls for mutual regard and forbearance in relation to things not essential to salvation in order to promote peace and harmony in the body of Christ.

C. Assisting Others (vv. 19-23)

19. Let us therefore follow after the things which make for peace, and things wherewith one may edify another.

Many things may be morally neutral to us, but before we engage in them we should ask ourselves how such action affects others and the peace of the church. Our word *edifice* comes from the verb *edify*, which means "to build up" or "to make strong." Therefore, anything which tends to weaken or destroy the fellowship of Christians or to reflect on Christ should be avoided.

20. For meat destroy not the work of God. All things indeed are pure; but it is evil for that man who eateth with offence.

Christians must live so as not to do harm to the work of grace already begun in another person's heart. We must not destroy the work of God's grace for mere personal satisfaction.

21. It is good neither to eat flesh, nor to drink wine, nor any thing whereby thy brother stumbleth, or is offended, or is made weak.

Christians should not eat, drink, or do anything that will cause a fellow Christian to stumble or fall. Even the most insignificant things should be avoided for the sake of a weak Christian.

22. Hast thou faith? have it to thyself before God. Happy is he that condemneth not himself in that thing which he alloweth.

23. And he that doubteth is damned if he eat, because he eateth not of faith: for whatsoever is not of faith is sin.

Christian liberty should never be paraded in public. It should never call attention to itself. Those who think they have it should be careful that they do not deceive themselves and override their conscience. *Restraint* is the key word for believers.

Christians who have difficulty in deciding concerning right and wrong should also exercise restraint—restraint in making hasty decisions in regard to their own behavior and restraint in judging others.

All Christians when in doubt should give Christ the benefit of the doubt.

II. CONSISTENT IN EXAMPLE (1 Corinthians 8:4-13)

A. Knowledge (vv. 4-6)

4. As concerning therefore the eating of those things that are offered in sacrifice unto idols, we know that an idol is nothing in the world, and that there is none other God but one.

Paul knew that what some people called a god was nothing more than a piece of stone, wood, or metal. Calling it a god certainly did not make it one. He knew that an idol was simply a figment of an active imagination. It was an empty unreality and sacrificing an animal does not change the meat in any respect. The meat would be the same as it was before the ceremony. He also knew that the great central affirmation of both Judaism and Christianity was that there is but one God.

5. For though there be that are called gods, whether in heaven or in earth, (as there be gods many, and lords many,)

6. But to us there is but one God, the Father, of whom are all things, and we in him; and one Lord Jesus Christ, by whom are all things, and we by him.

The Apostle means the sun, moon, planets, and stars as worshiped by the heathen when he refers to the gods of heaven. The gods of the earth would include the idols and other objects such as sacred trees, rivers, mountains, and animals that were worshiped by the heathen. The number of things called gods and worshiped as lords in the heathen religions were really innumerable.

Paul knew that the one God was the Father of all beings, the Source of all power, and the Creator of all things. He believed that whatever is came from God and that He is Self-existent. He is Jehovah, the I Am of the Old Testament, and the heavenly Father of the New Testament.

The Apostle believed that men should live for God, who made them for Himself that He might enjoy them, love them, be companions with them, receive from them the worship and praise which are His due.

Paul declares there is one Lord, Jesus Christ. It was the great Bible scholar of many years ago, Horatius Bonar, who stated: "Some want a Christ who is not God; others, a Christ who is not a sacrifice; a Christ without a cross, and without blood; a Christ who will teach but not expiate sin; a Christ whose life and death are an example of self-surrender to the utmost, but not to atonement; a Christ who is not a judge, nor a lawgiver, nor a priest, and only a prophet in the sense of teacher. Thus in the present day there are many Christs. It has been so all along; only the Apostle John calls them not Christs but Antichrists—'many Antichrists.' To us there is but one Christ, He who proclaimed Himself as come to seek the lost."

Jesus is God the Son, the eternal Word or Reason of the Father. He is the Agent by whom God works in the creation, preservation, redemption, and regeneration of all things.

B. Considerateness (vv.7-13)

7. Howbeit there is not in every man that knowledge: for some with conscience of the idol unto this hour eat it as a thing offered unto an idol; and their conscience being weak is defiled.

The Apostle has identified the principle of Christian liberty based on Christian knowledge. He recognized that an idol was nothing, and that knowledge left him free to eat meat that had been offered to idols. He had no compunctions of conscience concerning this. But Paul recognizes another principle which modifies and restricts his personal liberty. It is this principle which he declares beginning with verse 7.

Paul explains that some have not matured enough to recognize that idols and all that belongs to idol worship means nothing. Idolatry still means something to them. They have been engaged in idol worship so long that idolatry is almost instinctive with them. Their reason denies it but their emotional makeup is still attached to it. They know that meat offered to idols is no different from other meat, but they cannot get over the feeling that it is different.

The important point is that their conscience is weak in that it is not controlled by reason, by revelation, by religious teaching, by the judgment of the church, but by their emotions. Thus eating sacrificial meat would remind them of all the old superstition, fear, passion, and lust which had led them into the heathen orgies, and they would be overcome by their former defilement.

8. But meat commendeth us not to God: for neither, if we eat, are we the better; neither, if we eat not, are we the worse.

The point is that there is no moral quality either in eating or in refraining from eating. God is a Spirit, and commends the spiritual in us. It is not what we eat, but how we eat.

9. But take heed lest by any means this liberty of your's become a stumblingblock to them that are weak.

Paul uses the word *liberty* here to mean "lawful power or right." It refers to the freedom that every Christian has from ceremonial law as he walks in the grace through which Christ has made him free.

"Stumblingblock" refers to an obstacle thrown in the way of the weak and over which they may stumble or fall in the moral sense. This would be because they do not have the strength either to overcome their scruples or to disregard an example contrary to their conscience.

10. For if any man see thee which hast knowledge sit at meat in the idol's temple, shall not the conscience of him which is weak be emboldened to eat those things which are offered to idols.

Paul illustrates his point by describing a situation in which a weak brother, who still thinks eating meat offered to idols is wrong, sees one in whom he has great confidence engaging in such practices. He is led to eat meat himself, though his conscience tells him that he is doing wrong. If the weak brother does a thing that is right for someone else, while his conscience tells him it is wrong for him, then to him it is wrong.

11. And through thy knowledge shall the weak brother perish, for whom Christ died?

The Apostle suggests that the weak brother is still a Christian brother. Therefore, he should be tenderly cared for by the strong Christian. Christ died for the weak brother, and the strong Christian should certainly live for him. Strong Christians certainly do not want to cause weak brothers to perish eternally.

The great Alexander Maclaren made some striking comments on this verse: "There is no greater sin than to tempt weak or ignorant Christians to thoughts or acts which their ignorance or weakness cannot entertain or do without damage to their religion. There is much need for laying that truth to heart in these days. Both in the field of speculation and of conduct, Christians, who think that they know so much better than ignorant believers, need to be reminded of it."

12. But when ye sin so against the brethren, and wound their weak conscience, ye sin against Christ.

Jesus identified Himself with the weak believer over and over again during His earthly ministry. He was especially concerned with the beginner in the Christian life. It was Jesus who declared that "whoso shall offend one of these little ones which believe in me, it were better for him that a millstone were hanged about his neck, and that he were drowned in the depth of the sea" (Matthew 18:6).

Charles Hodge, the theologian, says of this verse: "It is a manifestation of want of love to Christ, an insult and injury to Him to injure His people, and moreover, He and they are so united that, whatever of good or evil is done to them is done also to Him."

13. Wherefore, if meat make my brother to offend, I will eat no flesh while the world standeth, lest I make my brother to offend.

For his weak brother's sake, Paul was ready to go the limit in denying himself. Of this verse, Alfred Plummer states: "The declaration is conditional. If the Apostle knows of definite cases in which his eating food will lead to others' being encouraged to violate the dictates of conscience, then certainly he will never eat meat so long as there is real danger of this (1 Corinthians 10:28, 29). But if he knows of no such danger, he will use his Christian freedom and eat without scruple (1 Corinthians 10:25-27). He does not mean, of course, that the whole practice of Christians is to be regulated with a view to the possible scrupulousness of the narrow-minded. That would be to sacrifice our divinely given liberty (2 Corinthians 3:17) to the ignorant prejudices of bigots."

It was Marcus Dods who declared: "As an Arctic voyager who has been frozen up all winter does not seize the first opportunity to escape, but waits until his weaker companions gain strength enough to accompany him, so must the Christian accommodate himself to the weakness of others, lest by using his liberty he should injure him for whom Christ died."

III. TEMPERATE IN ALL THINGS (1 Corinthians 9:24-27)

24. Know ye not that they which run in a race run all, but one receiveth the prize? So run, that ye may obtain.

25. And every man that striveth for the mastery is temperate in all things.

Now they do it to obtain a corruptible crown; but we an incorruptible.

26. I therefore so run, not as uncertainly; so fight I, not as one that beateth the air:

27. But I keep under my body, and bring it into subjection: lest that by any means, when I have preached to others, I myself should be a castaway.

The subject is still Christian liberty. In these verses Paul identifies some principles which are applicable to the question of eating meat offered to idols. The real Christian must do more than merely abstain from things that are evil. To win the race, he must sternly discipline himself.

By using the word *race*, Paul is probably referring to the Isthmian games. They were given this name because of the isthmus on which Corinth stood. These contests were really a great national and religious festival. Every second year they drew eager throngs to the city of Corinth.

According to Charles R. Erdman, only freemen could participate in these games. The contestants must give proof that for 10 months they had undergone the necessary preliminary training. For 30 days before the contests, all candidates were required to attend exercises at the gymnasium, and only when they had properly fulfilled all such conditions were they permitted to contend in view of the assembled crowds.

The Apostle contends that the true believer should view the Christian life in a similar manner, striving to win the prize. However, he points out two differences between the Christian race and an earthly contest. In the earthly race, only one wins the prize; in the Christian life all may win. In the earthly contest, the prize is a corruptible crown; in the Christian life it is an incorruptible one.

Paul identified some similarities between the athlete and the Christian. The athlete is temperate in all things. He abstains from any practice which might prevent him from winning the race, even though these things may be harmless in themselves. The athlete has a purpose in mind, and he is always working toward that purpose. He therefore keeps his body and its natural desires under control. Paul says the Christian must do the same. He did not want to be the means of starting others on the Christian race and then himself become a "castaway"—"disapproved"—that is disqualified.

IV. FAITHFUL IN SPIRITUAL THINGS (1 Timothy 6:11-16)

A. Conduct (vv. 11-14)

11. But thou, O man of God, flee these things; and follow after righteousness, godliness, faith, love, patience, meekness.

Paul uses a title given to prophets in the Old Testament when he refers to Timothy as a man of God. A man of God is one who has given his life to God. He is one in whom God works out His purposes and who lives a surrendered life for the glory of God.

Timothy is told to flee the things that Paul has been warning Christians about in the preceding verses. Then Timothy is told to follow after some positive things. Righteousness and godliness refer to our relationship to God. Faith and love are the outstanding virtues of a Christian man—faith toward God and love toward our fellowmen. Patience and meekness refer to one's behavior during days of difficulty and trouble.

12. Fight the good fight of faith, lay hold on eternal life, whereunto thou art also called, and hast professed a good profession before many witnesses.

We might paraphrase Paul's first statement by using Jude's words "earnestly contend for the faith" (v. 3). The Apostle is saying to Timothy, "Do not weaken or retreat in the great battle into which your life of faith in God will lead you." Paul is encouraging Timothy like a good friend to renewed energy. He is also reminding him of his confession of faith and where and under what conditions it was made.

13. I give thee charge in the sight of God, who quickeneth all things, and before Christ Jesus, who before Pontius Pilate witnessed a good confession.

Jesus made such a confession all during His ministry; but it was when His life was on the line and depending on the decision of Pilate that His trust in the protective love of His Father was most tried.

14. That thou keep this commandment without spot, unrebukeable, until the appearing of our Lord Jesus Christ.

The word *commandment* here refers to all behavior becoming to a Christian, the law of love, the things that a Christian should always be doing. The fact of Christ's coming, when taken seriously, is always an encouragement to holy living.

B. Incentives (vv. 15, 16)

15. Which in his times he shall shew, who is the blessed and only Potentate, the King of kings, and Lord of lords;

16. Who only hath immortality, dwelling in the light which no man can approach unto; whom no man hath seen, nor can see: to whom be honour and power everlasting. Amen.

Paul lists five things about God in these verses: He is the blessed One, the solitary Ruler of the universe, the only possessor of immortality, the Being who is infinitely remote from human scrutiny as dwelling not in accessible light, and the invisible, at least to the eye, whether of sense or of natural intellect. What an incentive to be faithful and to stay in the Word!

REVIEW QUESTIONS

1. How does a Christian's behavior affect others?

2. What does Paul say concerning developing priorities?

3. How can a Christian show considerateness to others in reference to entertainment?

4. Describe Paul's attitude concerning being temperate.

5. What is Paul's advice to Timothy concerning spiritual things?

GOLDEN TEXT HOMILY

"LOVE NOT THE WORLD, NEITHER THE THINGS THAT ARE IN THE WORLD. IF ANY MAN LOVE THE WORLD, THE LOVE OF THE FATHER IS NOT IN HIM" (1 John 2:15)

Love in this passage is the enticement by evil desire or base appetite that is forbidden. This is brought out in the following verse where it says, "For everything in the world—the cravings of sinful man, the lust of the eyes and the boasting of what he has and does—comes not from the Father but from the world" (v. 16, *New International Version*).

Craving for sensual gratification and greedy longings of the mind comes from a satanic (worldly) system of evil dominion (1 John 5:19). It is Satan's ability to entice the believer, to pull him away from the love of the Father.

The word for "world" (*kosmos*) is used six times in verses 15-17 and means something completely different here than in John 3:16. There the Father's love of the world is based on His will to create that which was good, righteous, and holy for His honor and glory.

Secular entertainment is our own interest being captivated by sensual gratification. It is diverting our thought from the will of God for ourselves. Just as Satan beguiled Eve, he charms people into the indulgence of our carnal nature thereby transferring our love and affection from our Creator. What captivates our attention and is hard to pull ourselves away from—prayer or TV; a sports activity or reading God's Word; and so forth?

Sin is a monster of such awful men,

That to be hated needs but to be seen,

But seen too oft, familiar with face,

We first endure,

Then pity,

Then embrace.—Alexander Pope
—Joseph L. Stephens, Pastor, Stockton, California

SENTENCE SERMONS

THE BELIEVER'S CHOICE of entertainment must be consistent with biblical principles.

—Selected

SOME PEOPLE are so busy with entertainment and incidentals that they have no time for fundamentals.

—Selected

YOU SIMPLY CAN'T be spiritually minded and worldly minded at the same time.

—"Notes and Quotes"

FOOLS ARE NEVER uneasy. Stupidity is without anxiety.

—Goethe

EVANGELISTIC APPLICATION

THE BELIEVER'S SELECTION OF ENTERTAINMENT ACTIVITIES CAN AFFECT HIS TESTIMONY TO THE UNSAVED.

Some years ago a great bridge spanning the unharnessable Mississippi River was wrenched from its strong foundations and smashed into the turbulent, muddy currents of the wild waters. A few moments later, a man rushed down the highway in his automobile and into the river before he could see the great bridge disaster. Being a good swimmer, he made for the shore; dripping wet, he climbed upon the highway, took out his handkerchief, and proceeded to warn approaching motorists. Several cars came speeding down the highway, and the man faithfully waved his kerchief for them to stop. Not one regarded the signal but plunged headlong into the violent waters. At last, a passenger coach came and stopped for his warning.

The man did all that was in his power for the wrecked as well as for the saved. Should not the church, as a duty to humanity, be faithful to this generation by offering a kind warning to all of disaster? Then, surely, some will heed the signal, slow down, and be saved from the raging torrents of much that is called entertainment.

ILLUMINATING THE LESSON

A sick conscience is the result of sin. Guilt is caused by it. Sin is the willful violation of God's known law.

In order to save our consciences we seek alibis for our actions. We try to excuse ourselves in various ways. The most common of these is by hiding behind the conduct of others. Because they indulge in certain activities, we take license to do the same, even though our consciences rebel.

Whenever the behavior of others becomes a moral measuring rod for my life, I am in danger. Here are some of the perils.

First, whose conduct shall I select as my guide? Why do I make such a choice and turn down the conduct of others? What is my criterion? Right or desire? If desire, then I am voting for what I want rather than what I know. If right, then I am again back to my conscience.

Second, if another's conduct is my guide, how do I know but what that person is transgressing his conscience, and thus if I follow him I will be doing wrong, as he is?

Conscience is my monitor, my guide, my imperative. If I follow it, I follow my better self. If I disregard it, I betray my highest self.

DAILY BIBLE READINGS

M. Choose Wisely. Proverbs 1:8-15

T. Be Faithful. Nehemiah 9:6-8

W. Put God First. Psalm 1:1-6

T. Walk in the Spirit. Galatians 5:16-25

F. Be an Example. 1 Thessalonians 1: 1-8

S. Be an Overcomer. 1 John 5:1-5

Freedom From Fear

Study Text: Psalms 46:1-11; 91:1-16; Isaiah 26:1-4; John 14:27

Supplemental References: Job 28:23-28; Psalm 23:1-6; Ephesians 5:14-21; 1 John 4:7-21

Golden Text: "He that dwelleth in the secret place of the most High shall abide under the shadow of the Almighty" (Psalm 91:1)

Central Truth: Because the believer lives continuously under God's protection there is no need to fear.

Evangelistic Emphasis: An individual is delivered from fear of judgment when he accepts Christ as Savior.

Printed Text

Psalms 46:1. God is our refuge and strength, a very present help in trouble.

2. Therefore will not we fear, though the earth be removed, and though the mountains be carried into the midst of the sea;

3. Though the waters thereof roar and be troubled, though the mountains shake with the swelling thereof. Selah.

4. There is a river, the streams whereof shall make glad the city of God, the holy place of the tabernacles of the most High.

5. God is in the midst of her; she shall not be moved: God shall help her, and that right early.

6. The heathen raged, the kingdoms were moved: he uttered his voice, the earth melted.

7. The Lord of hosts is with us; the God of Jacob is our refuge. Selah.

91:1. He that dwelleth in the secret place of the most High shall abide under the shadow of the Almighty.

2. I will say of the Lord, He is my refuge and my fortress: my God; in him will I trust.

3. Surely he shall deliver thee from the snare of the fowler, and from the noisome pestilence.

4. He shall cover thee with his feathers, and under his wings shalt thou trust: his truth shall be thy shield and buckler.

5. Thou shalt not be afraid for the terror by night; nor for the arrow that flieth by day;

6. Nor for the pestilence that walketh in darkness; nor for the destruction that wasteth at noonday.

Isaiah 26:3. Thou wilt keep him in perfect peace, whose mind is stayed on thee: because he trusteth in thee.

4. Trust ye in the Lord for ever: for in the Lord Jehovah is everlasting strength.

John 14:27. Peace I leave with you, my peace I give unto you: not as the world giveth, give I unto you. Let not your heart be troubled, neither let it be afraid.

LESSON OUTLINE

I. COPING WITH WORLD CONDITIONS

A. Confidence in God

B. Confidence Vindicated

II. COPING WITH PERSONAL PROB-
LEMS
  A. Sense of Belonging
  B. Sense of Security
III. POSSESSING GOD'S PEACE
  A. Trust
  B. Assurance

LESSON EXPOSITION

INTRODUCTION

Fear is one of man's worst enemies. Some doctors estimate that neurotic conflicts, which in some way always go back to fear, play a part in over 50 percent of all ailments brought to them.

Fear can unbalance minds. It can sap one's vitality, retard one's work, hinder careers, and destroy personal relationships.

But the most ironic thing about fear is that in most instances its cause is imaginary. We cross bridges that we never have to meet. We worry about things that never come to pass. We fear that we'll have some dreaded disease; we worry about losing our job; we fear an examination in school; we dread going to the dentist; we fear that we'll be killed.

Many things we anticipate we never meet, and most of the things we do meet are less painful than we imagined. We expend much nervous anxiety uselessly.

Life is full of fears, dreads, terrors, frights, anxieties. The glow of loving is paled, the radiance of life is dimmed, the beauty of living is dulled—and because, for the most part, of bridges that don't exist, imaginary ills, remembered tragedies.

I. COPING WITH WORLD CONDITIONS (Psalm 46:1-11)

A. Confidence in God (vv. 1-7)

1. God is our refuge and strength, a very present help in trouble.

It is believed that the routing of Sennacherib's army by the Lord in 701 B.C. was in the mind of the psalmist as he wrote this psalm. The Hebrew people were filled with fear and they were frustrated because they thought their situation was hopeless. But God intervened on their behalf.

It is significant that Israel's boast on this occasion is in Jehovah, the only true and living God. She could not boast in nor depend on her armies or fortresses.

It was Charles Spurgeon who declared: "Others vaunt their impregnable castles placed on inaccessible rocks and secured with gates of iron, but God is a far better refuge from distress than all these: and when the time comes to carry the war into the enemy's territories, the Lord stands His people in better stead than all the valor of legions or the boasted strength of chariot and horses."

We must never forget the fact that God is as much our refuge as He was when the psalmist penned these words. God alone is our all in all. All other refuges will ultimately fail. All other strength is really weakness. Power belongs to God alone. He alone is sufficient. When He is our defense and strength we are equal to all emergencies.

The psalmist declares that God is a very present help in trouble. Adam Clarke says of these words: "A help found to be very powerful and effectual in straits and difficulties. The words are very emphatic. He is found an exceeding, or superlative, help in difficulties. Such we have found in Him, and therefore celebrate His praise."

2. Therefore will not we fear, though the earth be removed, and though the mountains be carried into the midst of the sea;

3. Though the waters thereof roar and be troubled, though the mountains shake with the swelling thereof. Selah.

President Roosevelt once said: "America has nothing to fear but fear itself." What did he mean? He meant that we had sufficient manpower, sufficient resources, sufficient techniques, and that no nation on earth could defeat us. We need not fear that we would be overpowered. But, if we become fearful, fear itself would weaken us and ultimately bring our destruction. We would be defeated from within by our fear aroused by imaginary forces.

The same is true in the life of an individual. Fear can weaken the system, muddy the consciousness, stultify the will, and lead to defeat.

The psalmist declares that with God on our side, fear is irrational. Where He is, all power is, and all love; why therefore should we be afraid?

The message of verses 2 and 3 is this: Let worse come to worst, the child of God should never give way to mistrust; since God remaineth faithful, there can be no danger to His cause or His people. Such confidence is needed desperately in the latter half of this twentieth century.

4. There is a river, the streams whereof shall make glad the city of God, the holy place of the tabernacles of the most High.

5. God is in the midst of her; she shall not be moved: God shall help her, and that right early.

Jerusalem did not have a river. There was what had been called a wadi or Kidron and it had a spring-fed pool called Siloam, but not a river. The term "river" is probably used in a symbolic sense to mean God's grace. The words "city of God" are used to represent God's people.

Since God dwells within His people they have His help and they cannot be defeated. This explains the confidence the believer has in his God.

6. The heathen raged, the kingdoms were moved: he uttered his voice, the earth melted.

7. The Lord of hosts is with us; the God of Jacob is our refuge. Selah.

The writer foresees and announces the destruction of the enemies of God's people. The ground of this assurance is the fact that the Lord of hosts is with His people. He is on the side of believers and He is ready to help.

God is referred to as the "God of Jacob." This is to indicate that He is the covenant God, the One who entered into a covenant with Abraham, Isaac, and Jacob.

B. Confidence Vindicated (vv. 8-11)

8. Come, behold the works of the Lord, what desolations he hath made in the earth.

God effected the deliverance of Israel by desolations or devastations among the nations guilty of subjecting her to bondage. The same application can be made in contemporary times in respect to God's people or to nations that honor God. He will deliver those who believe and trust Him.

9. He maketh wars to cease unto the end of the earth; he breaketh the bow, and cutteth the spear in sunder; he burneth the chariot in the fire.

During the early days of Israel when God delivered her from oppressors, He permitted a period of peace to follow. This would range from 20 to 80 years. This is foreshadowing the final peace when God shall have put down all His enemies and placed the rule of government in the hands of Christ.

Isaiah refers to this as a time when all offensive weapons of war will be destroyed. He says that nothing will hurt or destroy in all of God's holy mountain.

Chariots of war were largely used by the Assyrians. Such chariots formed the main strength of the army of Sennacherib as recorded in the second Book of Kings. But such an army of 185,000 was no match for the angel of the Lord.

10. Be still, and know that I am God: I will be exalted among the heathen, I will be exalted in the earth.

Generally, God requires man to co-operate with Him. As Paul said, "We are workers together with God." But there are some situations in which man must stand aside and watch God work. For the Hebrew people, the invasion of Sennacherib was such a situation. Human effort would have been futile. Only divine intervention would bring deliverance.

In the Old Testament times when a deliverance was obviously miraculous, the God of Israel received special honor among the neighboring heathen nations. They could not deny that a supernatural act had taken place and so God was exalted among them.

11. The Lord of hosts is with us; the God of Jacob is our refuge. Selah.

What assurance is ours when we know the Lord of hosts is with us! It is said that when John Wesley was dying he could only be understood with great difficulty, though he often attempted to speak. At last, with all the strength that he had, he cried out, "The best of all is, God is with us."

II. COPING WITH PERSONAL PROBLEMS (Psalm 91:1-11)

A. Sense of Belonging (vv. 1, 2)

1. He that dwelleth in the secret place of the most High shall abide under the shadow of the Almighty.

Spiritual safety is available only in the secret place, under the shadow. Those are the words of the psalmist. He employs divine names that are both ancient and universal. They were used by the Western Semitic people when they referred to God. It was Melchizedek who first used the term "the Most High." Later it was repeated by Abraham in apposition to the special Hebrew name, *Yahweh* (see Genesis 14:19-22). The name occurs about 30 times in the Old Testament. It is closely associated with the concept of majesty. Abraham used the term "Almighty" as an identification for God. He did so in a covenant theophany in Genesis 17:1. The Hebrew name is *Shaddai*. It basically refers to the idea of power. God is greater than the Evil One, so when we abide in His presence we are safe.

2. I will say of the Lord, He is my refuge and my fortress: my God; in Him will I trust.

The general sentiment expressed by the psalmist in verse 1 is followed by a personal application in verse 2. He is not only aware of the reality of God, he is also willing to acknowledge his dependence upon Him. Too many people are ready to proclaim their doubts, and even to boast of them. So it is refreshing to hear someone speak up for God. Those who believe in and know Him should speak their belief. Such bold declarations not only honor God, they also lead others to seek the same confidence.

The words *refuge* and *fortress* reveal a spiritual truth of experience. The protective mercies of God are truly adequate. His power is sufficient to meet the assaults of any and all attackers. The psalmist was sure that he belonged to God. The Lord is not merely a refuge, but "my refuge." He is not merely a fortress, but "my fortress." And we confess that He is our God.

Charles Spurgeon said of this verse: "Now he can say no more; 'my God' means all, and more than all, that the heart can conceive by way of security. We have trusted in God; let us trust Him still. He has never failed us; why then should we suspect Him? To trust in man is natural to fallen nature; to trust in God should be as natural to regenerated nature."

B. Sense of Security (vv. 3-11)

3. Surely he shall deliver thee from the snare of the fowler, and from the noisome pestilence.

When we accept refuge in God we must not think that He will be passive; that is, we must not assume that He will simply protect us without participating in our struggle. On the contrary, to have God with us is to realize that He is the active deliverer. He is the strong warrior who defeats the enemy of our soul.

The words "the snare of the fowler" suggest a victim stalked by a clever hunter with murder in mind. His weapon would probably be a net or a trap. Applied spiritually it suggests dangers that are vicious and not easily detected. But the writer states that the believer is safe because God is able to deliver him from the enemy.

Some Bible scholars say the term "noisome pestilence" means literally "the spoken word of destruction." In this case it would mean much more than a contagious disease. Some believe the expression to be a technical term for a curse pronounced by a magician. This would be in keeping with the beliefs of many of the people in the Near East. There were few things that frightened them more than a curse. But the words of the psalmist declare that God is able to nullify the effects of a curse or any kind of real danger.

4. He shall cover thee with his feathers, and under his wings shalt thou trust: his truth shall be thy shield and buckler.

It is interesting that the writer draws on a scene from nature to picture the protecting care of God. He refers to the tender concern of a mother hen for her chicks as she carefully gathers them under her wings or pinions. He does not refer to the outspread wings of the cherubim, which overshadowed the ark of the covenant. Nor does he refer to the mighty wings of the eagle, whose home was on the lofty crag, and her path through the sunlit sky. But in keeping with the condescension of God, he uses a homely scene.

Shields and bucklers were developed for fierce combat. They were made strong and tough for protection. For the believer, God's truth is like a shield and buckler. His true promise and His faithfulness to that promise shall be the protection of those who believe in God. His truth will quench the fiery darts, blunt the swords, and be effective as a coat of armor. What more protection do we need?

5. Thou shalt not be afraid for the terror by night; nor for the arrow that flieth by day;

6. Nor for the pestilence that walketh in darkness; nor for the destruction that wasteth at noonday.

The psalmist knew how crippling fear can be. He was quite contemporary in his insight. Fear is basic in human nature. Fear is innate in human nature. Even though the infant is not discriminate in his fear reactions he shows definite fear response quite early in life.

The psychophysical basis of fear, real or imaginary, is this: Fear pulls the trigger of the nervous system and an adrenal secretion is shot into the bloodstream. The result is flight or fight. Respiration is quickened, the heart gallops, and the sweat glands overwork. Too much adrenaline can upset the whole system, resulting in all sorts of functional disturbances, finally causing organic disorders.

God can deliver from fear. He can enable us to face life confidently, courageously, victoriously. In the end, faith, not fear, will win.

Charles Spurgeon said of the statement, "Nor for the arrow that flieth by day"; "When Satan's quiver shall be empty,

thou shalt remain uninjured by his craft and cruelty; yea, his broken darts shall be to thee as trophies of the truth and power of the Lord, thy God."

Some Bible scholars believe that the word *pestilence* in verse 6 should be understood as evil omens or curses rather than as a disease. It was commonly believed by pagans that demons walked under the cover of darkness and engaged in such activities.

It is interesting that God's death angel carried out its mission at night, both in the tenth plague and in the destruction of the Assyrian army before Jerusalem in 701 B.C.

The psalmist felt sure that those "under his wings" would be secure and safe when God's judgments strike.

The word *destruction* in verse 6 is taken by many to refer to sunstroke. The noonday sun was particularly dangerous in Palestine during the hot summer months. Many who lived in Eastern countries personified this danger and named it Qetev. It was supposed to be a demon which was singularly ugly and evil.

7. A thousand shall fall at thy side, and ten thousand at thy right hand; but it shall not come nigh thee.

What comfort for God's people in this verse! The writer says though a thousand or even ten thousand should fall at your side in battle, or through pestilence, or sunstroke, yet, it shall not come near you. The danger, whatever it may be, shall not harm you; you shall be protected from it.

8. Only with thine eyes shalt thou behold and see the reward of the wicked.

The writer declares that the believer, without suffering anything himself, shall look on and see the punishment of the ungodly. This was certainly true for Israel in the land of Goshen. They looked on and saw the calamities of the Egyptians. The basic meaning is that in God believers are completely safe.

9. Because thou hast made the Lord, which is my refuge, even the most High, thy habitation;

10. There shall no evil befall thee,

neither shall any plague come nigh thy dwelling.

Observe that the psalmist addresses God in the second person when he regards himself as one who dwells; and he addresses God in the third person when he speaks to another believer. He knows that he is not alone. He can call God "my refuge," and at the same time tell his friend that this same God is "thy habitation."

One nineteenth-century Bible scholar said of verse 9: "Our safety lies not simply upon this, because God is a refuge, and is an habitation, but because thou hast made the Lord which is my refuge, thy habitation, there shall no evil befall thee. It is therefore the making of God our habitation upon which our safety lies; and this is the way to make God an habitation, thus to pitch and cast ourselves by faith upon His power and providence."

Charles Spurgeon records a personal incident illustrating the power of verses 9 and 10 to soothe the heart, when applied by the Holy Spirit. He states: "In the year 1854, when I had scarcely been in London twelve months, the neighborhood in which I labored was visited by Asiatic cholera, and my congregation suffered from its inroads. Family after family summoned me to the bedside of the smitten, and almost every day I was called to visit the grave.

"I gave myself up with youthful ardor to the visitation of the sick, and was sent for from all corners of the district by persons of all ranks and religions. I became weary in body and sick at heart. My friends seemed to be falling one by one, and I felt or fancied that I was sickening like those around me. A little more work and weeping would have laid me low among the rest; I felt that my burden was heavier than I could bear, and I was ready to sink under it.

"As God would have it, I was returning mournfully home from a funeral, when my curiosity led me to read a paper which was wafered up in a shoemaker's window in the Dover Road. It did not look like a trade announcement, nor was it, for it bore in a good bold handwriting these words: *Because thou hast made the Lord, which is my refuge, even the most High, thy habitation; There shall no evil befall thee, neither shall any plague come nigh thy dwelling.*

"The effect upon my heart was immediate. Faith appropriated the passage as her own. I felt secure, refreshed, girt with immortality. I went on with my visitation of the dying in a calm and peaceful spirit; I felt no fear of evil, and I suffered no harm. The providence which moved the tradesman to place those verses in his window I gratefully acknowledge, and in the remembrance of its marvelous power, I adore the Lord, my God."

It has been said that dependence on Christ is not the cause of His hiding us, but it is the qualification of the person that shall be hid.

11. For he shall give his angels charge over thee, to keep thee in all thy ways.

The psalmist had learned what God was willing to do for His people. He knew that God had provided security and safety even though evil and affliction assail him. He knew that God is so concerned that He sends angels to watch over His own.

One English Bible scholar of the last century declared of this verse: "Not one guardian angel, as some fondly dream, but all the angels are here alluded to. They are the bodyguard of the princes of the blood imperial of heaven, and they have received commission from their Lord and ours to watch carefully over all the interests of the faithful."

It should be noted that the promise in verses 11 and 12 was quoted by Satan to Jesus on the Mount of Temptation. But Jesus answered by letting Satan know that God's promises were given because of His mercy toward sinful and needy man. He did not and does not give them so they may be used against Him as weapons.

It is a comfort to know that God's faithful are under the constant care of angels who guide them and direct them perpetually.

III. POSSESSING GOD'S PEACE (Isaiah 26:3, 4; John 14:27)

A. Trust (vv. 3, 4)

3. Thou wilt keep him in perfect peace, whose mind is stayed on thee: because he trusteth in thee.

The word *peace* comes from a root word which can also mean "tranquillity, harmony, concord, security, safety, and prosperity." Peace is uniting the mind. It is fastening the mind upon worthwhile goals and stimulating it with worthwhile motives.

The prophet is referring to peace in the superlative. He means the greatest or perfect peace. It includes inward peace, outward peace, peace with God, peace of conscience, peace at all times, under all circumstances, God's own peace, the peace which God's own Son knew and left as a gift to His disciples.

God gives His own peace to those who trust Him. This peace of God takes upon itself military-like functions. It garrisons the heart and mind.

4. Trust ye in the Lord for ever: for in the Lord Jehovah is everlasting strength.

The prophet issues a call for continuous trust. The words "for ever" in the prophetical books are a figure for "always, continuously, under all conditions"; even in times when trust seems to have no foundations we may keep on trusting because our trust really is in God. We can trust in God because He is what He was; He will be what He is and has ever been. He is an everlasting Rock. He has been abundantly proved. Secure and blessed always are they who put their trust in Him.

B. Assurance (v. 27)

27. Peace I leave with you, my peace I give unto you: not as the world giveth, give I unto you. Let not your heart be troubled, neither let it be afraid.

This is the divine benediction of Jesus upon His disciples. He is blessing them with conditions and protections that will surround them in His absence. It is His legacy. He is bestowing His own treasure

upon His heirs. It is the gift of an untroubled heart which is priceless to its possessor.

The specific gift bequeathed by Jesus is peace. It is the peace of reconciliation to God, of eternal life and salvation, of forgiveness with all the debt of sin paid and all the stain of sin removed, of fellowship with God, and of security against life's changing conditions.

The gift of Jesus was a peace which the world could not give. The world could give treasure, pleasure, honor and fame, but not peace. What we get from the world is temporary. What we get from Jesus is permanent peace and prosperity with true and unfailing joy.

REVIEW QUESTIONS

1. Define confidence in God according to Psalm 46.

2. How was the psalmist's confidence vindicated in Psalm 46:8-11?

3. List some of the negative aspects of fear.

4. Can fear ever be positive? Explain.

5. How would you define assurance according to John 14:27?

GOLDEN TEXT HOMILY

"HE THAT DWELLETH IN THE SECRET PLACE OF THE MOST HIGH SHALL ABIDE UNDER THE SHADOW OF THE ALMIGHTY" (Psalm 91:1).

A great truth is laid down in this verse. Those who live a life of communion with God are constantly safe under His protection, and may, therefore, preserve a holy serenity and security of mind at all times. He that by faith chooses God for his guardian shall find all that he needs or desires.

It is the character of a true believer that he "dwells in the secret place of the most High." The believer is at home in God, returns to God, and is able to repose in God as his rest. He makes heart-work of the service of God, worships within the veil, and loves to be alone with God to converse with Him in solitude.

The reward of those who are determined to dwell "in the secret place of the most

High" is that they "shall abide under the shadow of the Almighty." That is, God shelters them and comes between them and everything that would annoy or detract from the sunshine of their life. They shall not only have an admittance, but a residence under God's protection.

God is faithful to those who put their trust in Him. Never has a believer been forsaken by the great God of the universe who sees all things from beginning to end.—**Excerpts from** *Matthew Henry's Commentary*, **Vol. III.**

SENTENCE SERMONS

BECAUSE THE BELIEVER lives continuously under God's protection, there is no need to fear.

—Selected

FEAR IS UNBELIEF parading in disguise.

—"Speaker's Sourcebook"

PEACE IS that state of contentment that comes to a heart surrendered to God.

—"Notes and Quotes"

I COULD NOT live in peace if I put the shadow of a wilful sin between myself and God.

—"I Quote"

EVANGELISTIC APPLICATION

AN INDIVIDUAL IS DELIVERED FROM FEAR OF JUDGMENT WHEN HE ACCEPTS CHRIST AS SAVIOR.

It is not difficult to have faith in God if you have faith in yourself. It is hard to believe in yourself if you know you are not worthy of faith—if you are insincere, untruthful, dishonest, hypocritical, and corrupt. Most schools of psychiatry agree that behind every anxiety neurosis is a sense of guilt. When guilt is removed, most anxieties disappear. Then one can have faith in himself, can believe in others,

and can have faith in the goodness, justice, and power of God. One can then say with the psalmist, "I will fear no evil: for thou art with me" (23:4). One will be able to say with Isaiah, "Say to them that are of a fearful heart, Be strong, fear not: behold, your God will come with vengeance. . . . he will . . . save you" (35:4).

ILLUMINATING THE LESSON

There is a place for fear in religion. Jesus advised men to fear that power in the world that could destroy the souls of men. Men without hope for the future have every right to fear for the future. Men without hope for the future based on a deep and significant faith will invariably be men of fear. Close study of the lives of men who have no faith principle with which to meet everyday problems of life will show that many of their actions are based on fear reactions. Fear is typical of those without a dynamic religious faith. A man without faith is a man of fear. A man of fear is an individual without a foundation on which to build an enduring life. When Jesus spoke of a man building a house on sand, He was stating a practical principle of everyday living. Even though an individual without a foundation refuses to recognize his fear; even though he bluffs his way along pretending a kind of self-sufficiency, the results are the same. The denying of fear in the area of awareness and the repressing of it back into the deep recesses of the mind does not remove but only intensifies its effect.

DAILY BIBLE READINGS

M. Fear and Wisdom. Job 28:23-28

T. Fear No Evil. Psalm 23:1-6

W. Fear and Knowledge. Proverbs 1:1-7

T. Fear Not. Luke 12:22-34

F. Fear of God. Ephesians 5:14-21

S. Fear Cast Out. 1 John 4:7-21